A History of France, 1460–1560
The Emergence of a Nation State

A History of France, 1460–1560

The Emergence of a Nation State

DAVID POTTER

St. Martin's Press   New York

First published in the United States of America in 1995

Printed in Malaysia

ISBN 0–312–12479–1 (cloth)
ISBN 0–312–12480–5 (pbk.)

Library of Congress Cataloging-in-Publication Data
Potter, David, 1948–
A history of France, 1460–1560 : the emergence of a nation state /
David Potter.
    p.   cm.
Includes bibliographical references and index.
ISBN 0–312–12479–1 (cloth) — ISBN 0–312–12480–5 (pbk.)
1. France—History—15th century.   2. France—History—16th
century.   3. Louis XI, King of France, 1423–1483—Influence.
4. France—History—House of Valois, 1328–1589—Historiography.
5. Monarchy—France—History.   6. National state.   I. Title.
DC95.6.P68   1995
944' .02—dc20   94–32239
                                                      CIP

Contents

Preface

An explanation is perhaps necessary for the title of this book. It is not to be asserted that a 'nation state' in the modern sense came into being in France during the Renaissance. In fact, the political system of France was a profoundly dynastic one, an *état royal* as French historians express it, in which kingship played a central role in the ideology of the nascent state. It was not, essentially, a 'proprietorial' one although an element of dynasticism remained. It was rather a country in which the growing elements of the idea of the *nation-France* (a term employed by Colette Beaune and Pierre Nora) were already in place and centred on monarchy, religion, aristocratic honour and clientage. It was thus a very distinctive, *sui generis* form of nationhood organised around loyalty to some very traditional principles that were conscripted into the formation of a much more effective state. That state was characterised by the idea of reform (in finance and provincial administration, for instance), as was the church in the same period. The result was a period of relatively harmonious order and rule that was eventually broken after 1560 by the hypertrophy of one of its vital constituent elements: the waging of 'wars of magnificence'.

The century of French history before the outbreak of the Wars of Religion has seldom been surveyed as a coherent whole. Beginning with the accession, in Louis XI, of one of the most formidable rulers in French history it closes with the death of Henri II, whose reign was one of the most innovative. It was in that century that the patterns of later French public, social and political life were established. Yet the custom of viewing the later years of the fifteenth century as either the 'twilight' of the medieval era or as its culmination has become deeply rooted in general assumptions. In some senses this goes back to the idea that the impact of the Italian Renaissance in France after 1494 and particularly during the reign of Francis I, 'restorer of letters', worked a profound transformation in French culture. In some ways, the idea of a revival of letters at that time goes back to the conscious views of humanists themselves; Joachim du Bellay announced that Francis I had 'first restored all the good arts and sciences to their ancient dignity: and our language, which before was harsh and ill-polished, he has thus rendered elegant'. So, *tenebrae* are dispelled by *lux* and Rabelais, in the much quoted letter of Gargantua to Pantagruel, declared: 'The time was then in shadows because of the calamity of the Goths, who had destroyed all good literature. But by the grace of God, light and dignity have been restored to letters in my time.' The idea was to lead directly to the concept of the Renaissance as prelude to the Enlightenment and in turn this did much to shape the historiographical framework built by Burckhardt and Voigt.[1] The subsequent revival of interest in French medieval learning and the debate over its autonomous tradition have tended to obscure the issue. It is clear enough from the work of Franco Simone that humanism had a powerful impact in France at the time of Petrarch, that the chaos of the earlier fifteenth century did much to interrupt this but that French humanism, of a distinctive kind shaped by the configurations of the French learned world, was in existence well before the Italian wars. Humanists and rhetoricians in the University of Paris like Robert Gaguin and Guillaume Fichet were already thinking of the previous age as one of 'barbarism' in the 1470s.[2]

The same framework customary in cultural history, that of a reawakening, has slipped imperceptibly into the commonly accepted views of French society in general and of its political structures. In a survey of the historiography of the state in France, Bernard Guenée has argued against the artificial barriers which have concealed the unity of the three centuries from the mid-thirteenth to the mid-sixteenth centuries. The institutions of the era of Francis I, he pointed out, were rooted in the Middle Ages.[3] One of the main reasons for the continuation of these barriers remains the tendency of historians to specialise as 'medievalists' or 'modernists', despite the primacy given by historians of the *Annales* tradition to the *longue durée* in historical experience. In part, this stems from the fact that the sources for social history – estate records, tax lists, population evidence – become more varied and voluminous after the beginning of the sixteenth century and generate new sets of problems. The emergence of the great religious fissure that was to explode in the form of a lengthy civil war also itself raises some new problems and generates new forms of criticism and speculation.

It is not the intention of this book to engage in the stale argument between the Middle Ages and the Renaissance but rather to stress the fundamental proposition that the society, politics and

culture of France in the first phase of 'absolute' power and of the
French Renaissance were shaped by a continuous process of
change and adaptation within existing institutions begun in the
fifteenth century; that the institutions, social configurations and
assumptions were conditioned by deeply laid substructures and
also by remarkable innovations from the late fifteenth century
onwards. The century between 1460 and 1560 can be called 'the
fair sixteenth century' in that it constituted a relatively unusual
century of growth and, despite periodic natural calamities and
rebellions, favourable conditions for the mass of the people. This
was the underlying foundation of the relative quiescence of
French society between the Hundred Years War and the Wars of
Religion that was to prove crucial in the development of a stable
polity, a focus of loyalty and a set of attitudes that allowed the survival of the idea of France as a nation through first the disorders
and then the dire economic conditions that followed until the
eighteenth century.

The idea that the later fifteenth century witnessed major
changes is, of course, not a new one and is clearly present also in
the political history of the period, especially in the notion of the
'new monarchies' of Louis XI and his contemporaries. However,
the significance of all this is now no longer so clear as it once was.
It would be a foolhardy student who repeated the old ideas about
a Louis XI or Ferdinand of Aragon forging alliances with the
urban bourgeoisie against the 'relics' of feudalism in order to
establish Absolutism.[4] That such rulers found essential supporters
among town oligarchies and merchant capital is evidently the case
and a confrontation with networks of aristocratic opposition certainly took place. It should be remembered, though, that such
alliances and confrontations were characteristic of Ancien Regime
polities down to the end of the seventeenth century at least and,
taken in the longer term, look more like endemic conflicts built
into the system. There is, in addition, a danger of slipping into
the view, characteristic of Roland Mousnier, that the French
monarchy represented the only guarantee in a vulnerable and
diverse society against 'civil war, dislocation and dismemberment
by neighbouring powers'. It is too readily assumed that such a
society needs a strong state in order to exist.[5] Monarchical
Absolutism was a polity which concentrated legitimate authority
in the sacralised figure of the king, who then delegated his powers

to officers and bishops, in effect his own appointees. It generated
a kind of politics that diverged from that of the city states and
republics of the era in largely failing to take advantage of the most
dynamic economic movements of the sixteenth century and
instead offered war, taxation, repression and revolt. Far from
being intrinsically a stable order, it was at times highly precarious.
Maulde-la Clavière, one of the most learned nineteenth-century
scholars of the age of Louis XII, painted a moving picture of the
harmony of the French society in the age of the 'père du peuple'
but thought that his age and even more so that of Francis I saw
the fundamental deformation of the French political system by
the annexation of inordinate power over the church by the
crown.[6] In fact, as will be shown in chapters 1 and 7, such power
was deep rooted.

Recently, the work of J.-P. Genet under the aegis of a thematic
study programme of the Centre Nationale des Recherches
Scientifiques has drawn attention to the problem of the genesis of
the modern state in the late medieval and early modern periods.
Perry Anderson argued forcefully, from a Marxist standpoint, that
Absolute Monarchy was a development of European feudalism,
that its bureaucratic and military structures, making it a machine
built for the battlefield, had roots in long-established social and
mental structures.[7] Genet and his colleagues have advanced the
subject from a more empirical point of view, arguing that the
developments of the twelfth to the fourteenth centuries in
western Europe generally were crucial in the formation of the
state. It was in the twelfth century that the extension of royal
justice began to give a spatial identity to the state, in the fourteenth and fifteenth that monarchs put in place new systems for
raising revenue for defence (including the convocation of assemblies of estates), that political ideologies and nascent national
identities formed for their justification and that the great economic and social crisis beginning with the Black Death churned
up the channels of command characteristic of classical feudalism.
Finally, the sixteenth century gave a cultural dimension to the
state, articulated through classical vocabulary around the hero-
prince. In this society, domination remained in the hands of the
professional military class, which had originally assured the
defence and economic expansion of western Europe in the early
middle ages but was increasingly admixed with a wider

technocratic and literate stratum of society. War therefore remained central, providing the raison d'être for the ruling class and the social cement for a society of '*fidélités*'.[8]

However, Genet and his colleagues would readily acknowledge that this genesis of modern state structures led into many different channels (limited monarchy, absolutism, republicanism, etc.) The experience of France in the century from 1350 to 1450 was one of massive economic crisis, semi-permanent war and the severe contraction of the power of the crown (manifested, for instance, in the stagnation of its financial resources). However, the view that the fifteenth century saw some fundamental shifts in direction is a persuasive one. Roland Mousnier juxtaposed 'the feudal France up until the middle of the fifteenth century' with 'the France of *fidélités*' which succeeded it (see chapter 6).[9] Ladurie has characterised the period from 1450 to 1789 as that of the 'monarchie classique'. In this view, the political system in place from about 1460 rests on a new buoyant social and demographic phase, subject to crisis certainly but never again traumatised in the form of a gigantic catastrophe.[10]

Around 1460, as Ladurie has argued, France still remained poised in some sense between unitary and decentralised models of the state, sharing characteristics both of England and of the Empire, with a royal government at the centre and the continuation of important appanages.[11] But the massive military conflicts of the fifteenth century had generated the power of a transformed political elite dominated by the middle ranking nobility and the 'peuple gras' who have been called by Mikhail Harsgor 'les maîtres du royaume' (see chapters 3 and 4). With the transformation of the army and of the role of the nobility in it, the ways in which power was manipulated and the links between those holding power began to change. The form of state regeneration which developed in France was one leading to what is sometimes called the 'second absolutism' of the seventeenth century. At any rate, the French monarchy and its servants increasingly stressed an already existing Absolutist ideology (see here chapter 1). In a kingdom where the weakness of the crown in the crucial fourteenth–fifteenth century period left it unable to establish the right to tax the nobility, the latter aimed increasingly to participate in the fruits of power rather than to limit it.[12] From the 1460s, Ladurie has argued, the French monarchy was increasingly 'administrative et taxatrice', that is, capable of moving beyond the judicial functions of the *état de justice*.[13] Though still relatively lightly governed, the administrative cadre of France was proportionately the largest of the comparable kingdoms.

There is a contrast but also continuity between the political institutions strengthened under Louis XI, and suffused by his energy, and the state which reached its apogée in the period of the Renaissance. Without the victories of Louis XI the splendour of the age of Francis I is scarcely imaginable. Louis's methods remained a model for his successors. Louis's critic, Thomas Basin, reported that just after his accession, and faced with demands for tax reductions, he declared that 'he was king and he could do as he liked'. Francis I's reported comment to the Emperor Charles V that his revenues could amount to as much as he wished seems a curious echo. Francis is supposed also to have remarked that, though Louis XI was 'a little too cruel and bloodthirsty' yet 'he was the one who got the kings of France out of leading strings'. The poet Ronsard addressed Henri II optimistically in 1555 by pointing up the changes: 'You are not like a king Louis XI ... who had his seditious relatives and brothers.'[14] The style of the two reigns is startlingly different, both in the manner of the rulers, their courts and also in policies. Louis XI, a practical ruler unimpressed by status and show, toyed with the idea of rendering nobility fully compatible with commerce and thus encouraging the development of trade. This came to nothing and Gaston Zeller spoke of it as a 'great lost opportunity'.[15] The contrast between Louis and Francis I, 'first gentleman of the kingdom', whose reign saw great changes and yet who would never have considered tampering with the social order, reveals the innovativeness of his fifteenth-century predecessor. The apogée of the monarchy in the Renaissance is unthinkable without the transformations that had been going on since the middle of the fifteenth century.

Professor Knecht in his important work on the reign of Francis I has stressed the authoritarian temperament of that monarch and argued that his style of rule represented the furthest possible extent of Absolute monarchy in the sixteenth century.[16] The kingdom of France in the first half of the century had productive land, people and tax resources in abundance. Yet, in comparison with the reign of Louis XIV, the steps were tentative, the machinery of control and order ramshackle and society profoundly influenced by concepts of clientage and fidelity which were a direct continuation of the feudal age. Moreover, in comparison with other states of the sixteenth century, Venice being the outstanding example, and despite the fourteenth-century idea of France as the best governed of all kingdoms, French public life and administration were chaotic.[17]

In France the leading characteristic of public power from 1450 onwards was perhaps that of the royal *office*, a form of bureaucracy that was to be characteristic of the Ancien Regime.[18] Stemming originally from the view of the monarchy as an *état de justice* (which France remained despite the rapid progress towards the *état de finance* under Louis XI) the office was created by *lettres de provision* which permitted its holder to exercise a jurisdiction under the crown, often conveying personal nobility and implicitly the possibility of hereditary ennoblement. It was extremely difficult for an *officier* to be removed and the rapid development of venality in this period stabilised the proprietary nature of the institution. The regime of *offices* was an intrinsically limited one which transmitted some of the characteristics of feudal society into the modern state in France.[19] As Jean Jacquart has pointed out, hereditary office-holding was established in contradiction to the Absolutist tendency of the crown.[20]

But to this was added in the course of the Renaissance the network of government by royal *commissaires* (especially from the 1550s onwards), thus creating one of the principal tensions of the Ancien Regime. The power to appoint royal commissioners was present in the Middle Ages, but it seems that the precursors of the *intendants de justice* can first be seen in the 1550s.[21] Whatever form it took, however, the penchant of Ancien Regime administration was for collective decision-making, government *par bon conseil* (see chapter 3) rather than individual administrative fiat, which remained in evidence down to the eighteenth century.[22]

Most general studies have tended to concentrate either on the fifteenth century, in the case of P.S. Lewis and, recently, A. Demurger[23] or on the sixteenth century in the case of J. H. Salmon, H. Lloyd and, most recently, E. Le Roy Ladurie's survey of the state from Louis XI to Henri IV.[24] Among works that cover part of the period of this book, that of Henri Lemonnier in the old Lavisse history is still a very serviceable narrative but covers

only the period 1494 to 1547. Another, older history, Bridge's
history from 1483 to 1515 is still of extraordinary value. More
recently Janine Garrisson's brief survey of the period 1483 to 1559
has the merit of attributing sufficient importance to the court and
to personalities as well as the continuing diversity of the
kingdom.[25] In addition, there are now some excellent studies of
the reigns of the period: notably by Yvonne Labande-Mailfert on
Charles VIII, Bernard Quilliet on Louis XII, Robert Knecht and
Jean Jacquart on Francis I and Ivan Cloulas and F.J. Baumgartner
on Henri II.[26] Representative institutions during the sixteenth
century have been exhaustively studied by John Russell Major and
it is not intended to cover the same ground here.[27] The work that
follows is essentially one of analysis and synthesis of recent
research made possible largely by the explosion of historical work
over the last generation that has some bearing on the period,
either by contributing important insights in the course of the
study of social structures and attitudes, or as a result of the
significant work of French, English and American scholars on the
institutions, politics and religion of France in the period. In addition some chapters are based rather more on original sources
where secondary works are still lacking. There is certainly room
for an attempt to make some preliminary sense of it all. Ultimately,
though, this book is the product of what interests one particular
writer.

    In a work such as this, my principal debt is to the many histor-
ians whose work has provided an inspiration and a guide. In addition, specific thanks are due to Maurice Keen for valuable advice
on structure, to Peter Roberts, for suggestions on chapter 2 and,
above all, to Robert Knecht, who generously read the whole text
and enabled me to avoid some egregious errors.

List of Maps

Note on Money and Measures

French coinage in circulation was defined in terms of a notional 'money of account', the *livre tournois* (*lt.*), sometimes called the *franc* in the reign of Louis XI. This was divided into 20 *sols* and 240 *deniers* like the old pound sterling, though the latter was worth roughly nine times its value (much as the modern pound and *franc*). Money of account had the advantage of providing a standardised accounting mechanism but the disadvantage that it was an artificial value created by the crown's power to define the intrinsic value of the coinage it issued and, inevitably, to manipulate it. The publicly declared value of the coinage reflected both the supply of precious metals and the crown's needs to maximise the value of the coin it was receiving in taxation. It therefore sometimes varied from the market value of the coinage. The most widely used gold coin from the late fifteenth century was the *écu d'or soleil*, fixed at 36s.3d. in 1498 (it was then worth 4s.6d. sterling). It moved to 40s. (i.e. 2 *livres*) in 1516, 45s. in 1533, 50s. in 1551 and 60s. in 1574. All prices expressed in money of account need to be adjusted for this decline in its value against real currency. The most widely used silver coin, the *teston*, was fixed at 10s. in 1498, 10s.6d. in 1541 and 12s. in 1561. Another money of account, the *livre parisis*, was used less in the sixteenth century. It was a larger unit (1 *sol tournois* = 15 *deniers parisis*).

Every region, and indeed locality, of France had its own units of measurement for dry goods and wine. Under Henri II the crown encouraged the adoption of the Paris measure but with very limited success. In Paris, the *sétier* for grain was equal to 156 litres. Twelve *sétiers* made one *muid*.

Introduction: French Society and its Identity

In the late fifteenth century, France remained a highly region-alised and diverse society, its identity shaped by a long period of war and socio-economic catastrophes. We need to understand both the social consequences of that period and the nature of inherited social attitudes in order to judge the country's view of itself. When Louis XI became king in 1461 large areas of the kingdom lay in ruins. The previous decade had seen the fruition of an exhausting effort to reverse the disastrous consequences of a century of English military intervention in French civil conflicts. In the 1460s, the conflict turned inward as the great princes, allied with Burgundy, struggled in the War of the Public Weal (1465) to place limits on the king's power. Louis himself, profiting from the success of his policy in England during 1470, relaunched the attack on Burgundy that was to culminate in 1477 and rumble on amidst the troubles of Charles VIII's minor-ity until 1493. Epidemic, economic depression and chaotic government had compounded these problems. 'Grievous oppressions, mutilation of men, rape of women and girls, arson, robbery and ransom' were the lot of the people according to a royal letter of remission of the reign of Charles VII. Towards the end of the next century, Jean du Port could write that: 'France was then so ruined and depopulated that it seemed more like a desert than a flourishing kingdom, for there was no one in the fields, the country folk had fled to the churches and strong-holds, not daring to emerge for fear of the gendarmerie which was usually in the countryside. It had become fallow, full of thickets and woods by the continuous wars under three kings and more like the haunt of beasts than of men.'[1]

Like similar descriptions of England after the Wars of the Roses there is a degree of exaggeration in all this, compounded by letters of remission and the petitions to the Pope by devas-tated religious houses. There is more justification when we consider heavily fought over areas like Normandy, Picardy, Champagne and Ile-de-France, some western areas and Agenais-Quercy. Even here, though, there has been a tendency to .

1

minimise the restoration already in hand before 1450. The famous example of Magny-les-Hameaux south of Paris, completed deserted of people between 1431 and 1455, has been repeatedly quoted. The villages of the Orléanais have produced similar evidence.[2] Chroniclers added to the picture: Thomas Basin wrote that Louis XI, on his return to his kingdom from Flanders, was confronted by a veritable desert around his capital, the peasants 'so thin and tattered that they looked as though they had just come out of prison'. It was shortly after this time, on a journey to Paris, that Sir John Fortescue formed his view of the French peasantry as a pitiful lot. However, these commentators were over-impressed by the devastation north of Paris. Philippe de Commynes, in describing the landscape around Montlhéry in 1465, described 'fields full of wheat and other good grains, for the land was good there'.[3]

Signs of demographic and economic recovery are visible before the end of the Hundred Years War, with the restoration of village life in the most favoured areas well established by the 1450s. For the country around Paris, Guy Fourquin has pointed to the victory of Pontoise (1441) and the consequent freeing of economic movement on the river Oise, as the turning point.[4] But the accession of Louis XI and perhaps the conclusion of the War of the Public Weal in 1465 really did coincide with a reversal of the trend of demographic and political collapse which had dominated the history of France for a century. It is essential not to underestimate the significance of that period in the transformation of French society. In politics, it saw the last major fling of princely independence but also the definite affirmation of royal power in binding the country together.

Louis sought economic independence and was thus keen to stimulate textiles, mining, armaments and silk-weaving, all conducive to the peaceful recovery of production.[5] The three generations that followed, which might almost have been encompassed by the life of one man, saw a remarkable recovery and expansion. The early sixteenth-century writer Claude de Seyssel could write, in a much quoted passage of his eulogy of Louis XII, 'many places and wide spaces that used to be fallow are now cultivated and scattered with houses and villages so that a third part of the kingdom as a whole has come under the plough in the last thirty years.'[6]

Ideas on Society

Along with its economic background, France inherited a deeply conservative social ideology, that of the three orders of the clergy, the nobility and the third estate. As Philippe de Poitiers put it in the Estates General of 1484: 'the Church should pray for others, give counsel and exhortation; the nobility should protect others by the exercise of arms and the people should nourish and support them by paying taxes and tilling the soil.'[8] This powerful and directive myth was widely articulated but represented no more than an ideology of public power. It did not necessarily correspond to reality and, indeed, the frequency of its repetition gives some cautious reason for viewing it as 'propaganda' in the modern meaning of the word.

It hardly needs to be stressed that French society was at once more complicated and more diffuse than the classical definition of the three orders would suggest. As Bernard Guenée put it, there was not so much a 'church' as clerics of different kinds; not so much a 'nobility' as nobles of different fortunes; not a Third Estate, rather rich merchants, artisans and peasants.[9] Indeed, Philippe de Mézières in the *Songe du Vieil Pèlerin* of c.1390 suggested in the idea of 'quatre gérarchies, chacun triple, des troys estaz du royaume de Gaule' four categories of dignity: church, nobility, Third Estate and the people, each divided into upper, middle and lower levels; this envisaged a sort of social grid that would integrate a division of society into 'orders' and putative social 'classes' based on wealth.[10] In the early sixteenth century, Claude de Seyssel clearly found it impossible to manage with a simple framework of society in three orders when he introduced the concept from the Italian of the 'peuple gras' (*popolo grasso*) between the nobility and the common people, while setting the clergy in a parallel hierarchy.[11] The idea is expressed in the story of Louis XI's ennoblement of a merchant of Tours (Jean Briçonnet). On his first appearance thereafter, Louis is supposed to have said to him: 'Good day, sir gentleman. When I seated you at my table I regarded you as the first of your condition. But now you are the last, I would do an injury to the others if I showed you the same favour.'[12] Louis himself seems to have taken a sceptical view. If the *Rosier des guerres* did reflect his thinking we find the idea that 'since one man is a knight, another a merchant and another a farmer and the gain of one is the loss of another, so wars and hatred grow'. Elsewhere, though, he likens the 'conditions of this world' to a game of chess: 'each person is in the place and degree suitable to his estate while the game lasts, but when it is finished, all the pieces go back into the bag without any distinction made.'[13]

The question of whether France should be viewed as a society of orders or of social classes is a well-worn one. R. Mousnier argued that the 'society of orders' based on the thinking, among others, of Charles Loyseau in the early seventeenth century, should be accepted as the principal mode of social classification in the early modern period.[14] It is a view seriously questioned by historians who wish to incorporate a degree of class conflict into their understanding of the period. They deny Mousnier's view that early modern society must be categorised in terms which it would have recognised itself, in a sense equating 'the ideational with reality'. Mousnier's approach, they add, based ultimately on a certain sociological theory which has been called 'normative' or mechanistic, gives too little room for the explanation of social change and innovation. The overall result is to stress social harmony, relegating the disharmonious impulses to a minority critique of the social order. One of Mousnier's most cogent critics has argued for a balanced view of early modern social relationships which stresses the interdependence of at least the nobility and bourgeoisie.[15] There is a striking contrast between such a view and H. Heller's placing of social conflict at the heart of sixteenth-century French society.

Regional Diversity

It we look at France in basic practical terms, we see an extraordinarily diverse kingdom of 425,000 km^2 at the start of Louis XI's reign (rising to 460,000 at the end – modern France is 551,000).[16] Guenée has pointed out that the demands of distance and space meant that the impact of political power would vary roughly in proportion to the distance from the locus of the main royal institutions in Paris, the Parlement and financial courts. The royal household, which remained peripatetic in the sixteenth century, actually served to counteract this tendency to some extent but the deep traditional variations between provinces and especially between the territories north and south of the Loire meant that monarchical 'centralisation', in so far as it existed, tended to have its impact first of all in northern France. Recruitment into the cadres of the royal administration and army among the petty nobility could vary widely, for instance between the Auvergne and Picardy, while extremely disparate social structures underpinned these regions.

The diversity is reflected in the varieties of customary law that were being codified gradually between the mid-fifteenth and mid-sixteenth centuries and which testify to ancient 'fault lines' across the kingdom. The *ordonnance* of Montils-lès-Tours of 1454, prescribing the redaction of written customs, marked an important divide between the oral and written culture of France and the slow work was pursued over the next century. It also incidentally introduced a degree of coherence in actually defining areas of custom within the *ressort* of the *bailliages* or for great provinces like Normandy and Brittany that had representative estates. However, it could not go beyond that. In fact, the idea of publishing a single code of French law discussed at the Assembly of Notables in 1517 ran up against the profound divergences within the law itself.

Much has been made of the differences between the territory of 'written' law and 'customary' law and it is certainly the case that the customs of the Midi stemmed in origin from the tenets of Roman law. However, the sixteenth century 'redactions' of customs turned even the 'customary' areas into ones where a fixed legal code prevailed. Jean Yver has shown that the real divisions, dating from the very formation of customs in the thirteenth century, were between those areas in which the customs prescribed strict equality in the division of property between heirs and those where the testator could 'advantage' one heir in particular.[17] Broadly, the whole of the Midi took, to a greater or lesser extent, from the code of Justinian the principle that a father, though he could not leave all his property to one son, could significantly advantage him. For this reason, the drawing up of a will was widespread in that area and the existence of *cadastres* allowed, for much of the region, the levy of direct tax as *taille réelle* rather than *personelle*. In France, Brittany, Normandy, Orléanais and Champagne the principle of equal division prevailed, with certain variations, connected with a weakening of the *lignage* in face of the nuclear family unit. The customs drawn up in the early sixteenth century, especially in eastern France and the southern Low Countries (like Artois), tended to see a spread of the 'unequal' principle.[18] One great exception to these rules, however, stemmed from the fact that the nobility generally benefited from the privilege of *droit d'ainesse* (a right to at least two-thirds of property for the eldest son) and that, in certain areas of customary law, the device of 'advantaging' by marriage settlement could be used to keep an inheritance together by wealthy commoners.[19]

These profound customary divergences were reinforced by the continuing linguistic diversity of a kingdom of five languages: French, *occitan* (Provençal, Auvergnat, Gascon, etc.), Basque, Breton and Flemish. There is no doubt that French became increasingly identified with the 'nation' of France from the fourteenth century but the process was slow and unplanned until Francis I. Clément Marot recalled in 'L'Enfer' of 1542 that in coming to 'France' from Quercy at age of 10, 'I forgot my maternal tongue and crudely learned the paternal French language, so esteemed at court'.[20] The provision in the *ordonnance* of Villers-Cotterêts of 1539 was only one step in the process by which the dominance of French in law and administration gradually recruited the social elites of the Midi to the French language. In Limousin, the consuls of Limoges introduced French into their records in 1488, the *notaires* in 1518 and the canons of the cathedral in 1542. The first private diary in French started in 1558. At Toulouse, the last time a poem in *occitan* won a prize in the annual Floral Games was in 1513. Thereafter, although individuals could read poems in their own language, only verses, increasingly *chants royaux*, in French could triumph. It was at Toulouse that Etienne Dolet mockingly ascribed the king's early departure in August 1533 ('he came, he saw, he departed') to the barbarous language of the city.[21] In terms of its relationship to Latin, however, the law of 1539 stands at the end of a long process that had an important role in the shaping of a French identity. Its appeal to a French 'langue maternelle' and Joachim du Bellay's 'defence' and celebration of French can only be understood in the context of a long development of the vernacular. The jurists of the chancellery and high courts had worked essentially in French from the fourteenth century and this opened the way for the triumph of French as the literary language.[22]

General Social and Economic Trends

All these disparities in institutions and culture were accompanied by widely divergent social patterns that mean there can be little certainty in exact estimates of the most basic phenomenon, the overall population. That the century from 1460 to 1560 was one of long-term demographic movement into boom and over-population cannot be doubted, however. The period began and ended with significantly different economic crises. That of 1458–62 was short-term and France was at the start of a period of boom conditions in the long term.[23] The crisis of 1557–62 was an ominous prelude to civil war and collapse.

How, though, can we attain a reasonable estimate of population? Not before the 1539 *ordonnance* of Villers-Cotterêts did the crown enact the requirement for the parish clergy to keep records of births and deaths for the purposes of proving wills and even after that the implementation of the process was patchy. There is virtually no sign of the implementation of the requirement to deposit registers at the local *bailliage* courts. On the other hand, individual bishops had long required their clergy to maintain such registers. In 1406 the bishop of Nantes ordered the keeping of baptismal registers, having heard that too many uncanonical marriages were being contracted for lack of knowledge about parents and godparents. As a result isolated registers do survive from before 1500, though they are difficult to use statistically.[24] Only general figures emerge from very rare state surveys conducted for tax purposes. It has been usual to rely on the *Etat des paroisses et des feux* of 1328 as our point of departure. After that, there is no absolutely reliable general survey until the 1690s. Between those two certainties, we can only piece together the picture from regional studies based mainly on tax records. One reasons for this was the intense hostility of the communities of the realm to general surveys. Jean Juvenal had advised Charles VII, on biblical precedent, not to 'number' his people. The scheme proposed in 1491 by the estates of Normandy for a new *recherche générale des feux* foundered on the suspicions of other provinces that their taxes would be consequently increased.[25]

What, then can be said about overall trends in population during the undocumented centuries from the 1320s to the 1690s? It began with the catastrophic collapse of the French population between 1350 and 1450. After that came a patchy revival which swung into a population boom in the first half of the sixteenth century, hesitated again in the later sixteenth century and achieved a certain stability, still punctuated by severe mortalities, in the seventeenth.

It is possible to use the 1328 survey because Lot showed that it was a survey of the whole kingdom, not just of the royal domain, as had sometimes been supposed, and that the hearth (*feu*) surveyed was a real one rather than a fiscal unit.[26] There are still some severe problems since not all the *bailliages* sent in returns and, of course, the land area of the kingdom in 1328 was different from that of the early modern period. Lot calculated, with 24,500 parishes (using a coefficient of 5 per rural hearth) that the population of the then kingdom was just over 16 million, with that within the present boundaries of France 21.5 million. These figures, yielding a density of 7.87 hearths per sq km, have been thought impossibly high but in fact France at the start of the fourteenth century was exceptionally densely populated, although that density varied enormously. The greatest densities were to be found in the north: Normandy, Picardy, Ile-de-France. In an area of 3500 km^2 around Paris, the average density attained 14 hearths per km^2.[27]

After 1328, we embark on uncertain waters, charted only by occasional regional or anecdotal evidence. The late fifteenth century was a time when everyone was aware of rapid population growth that went unreflected in the tax rolls. This is clear enough from Claude de Seyssel's impression.[28] Mousnier, extrapolating from 1328 and suggesting that most of the intervening losses had been made good by 1515, produced for that year the figure of 18 million and a density of 40 people per km^2 in a kingdom now of 460,000 km^2. He did this by just adding the 1700 parishes and 175,611 hearths acquired by the kingdom since 1328 (e.g. Dauphiné and Provence). Pierre Chaunu has suggested 16 million for 1500 and Ladurie 20 million for c.1560.[29] Needless to say this procedure is at best rough and ready.

There were several unofficial estimates of population in the later sixteenth century. At the Estates-General of Blois of 1576, absurd figures like 600,000 towns and villages and 20 million hearths were bandied about, although a more sober figure of 3 million hearths is recorded in Nevers' journal in 1577. Among the most serious attempts to estimate population was the *Secret des finances de France* (1581) by 'Nicolas Froumenteau' (probably Jean Frotté), a work designed to calculate the extent of losses during the civil wars and comparing tax levels under Louis XII and Henri III. By using tax records, he calculated 38,651 parishes and 4.5 million hearths. Such figures are only a rough guide. By the time of the Vauban survey at the end of the seventeenth century, we find for a kingdom of 541,869 sq km a population of 18.7 million in which the density is concentrated in much the same regions of the north as in 1328.[30] This had been 12–14 hearths per km^2 (roughly 50–60 inhabitants); in 1469 northern France had a density of nearer 30 per km^2 and can be usefully compared with the densely populated parts of the Netherlands at 66–78 per km^2.[31] France remained a predominantly rural society despite the extensive move of labour from country to town as a result of pressure on the land in the sixteenth century; as an urban society it remained somewhat under-developed in the sixteenth century. The urban population remained at between 6 and 10 per cent of the total: 'much birth in the country, much death in the town.'[32]

A degree of exactitude can only be found in local surveys. Historians tend to agree that the second half of the fifteenth century was a period of population recovery 'surprising in its rapidity and extent' and that the period 1450–1560 in western Europe generally was 'marked by strong growth in the rural population'.[33] In France, the signs of this are evident in the high number of marriages in Artois in 1460–5 or in the large families apparent in rental agreements in Quercy, where the restoration of cultivation that began around 1440 was followed by a generation of very rapid growth. It can be seen, too, in the expansion in the numbers of families in Ile-de-France from around 1450, especially the high birth rate around 1540, and the demographic explosion in eastern Normandy after 1460.[34] The principal explanations seem to have been the shifting to an earlier general age of marriage as a result of economic expansion and the decline in mortality, particularly infant mortality, in the period 1460–1520 (roughly at 30–31 per cent). The scourge of leprosy died out during the first half of the sixteenth century, to be replaced by that of syphilis. There were certainly continuing outbreaks of 'la peste', but what this was can only be guessed; typhus may well have been one of the diseases observed from the late fifteenth century.

However, the overall trend, despite severe outbreaks in 1518–19 and 1530, was for the scourge of epidemics to recede. All this permitted the expansion of families.[35]

There was also urban growth and immigration: Lyon grew from 20,000 in 1450 to 40,000 in 1500 and 70,000 in 1550; over the same period Rouen grew decisively from 20,000 to a population of 60,000–70,000 by 1560 (it had been only 40,000 before the plague); Bordeaux from 20,000 to 60,000; Paris attained 300,000 by around 1560, indeed prompting what Jean Jacquart has called the 'anaemia' of the smaller towns in a sphere of 100–200 km around it. The country around Paris attained a density of settlement (often between 30 and 40 hearths per km^2 by the early sixteenth century, that compelled an exodus of population to the capital itself. This was largely a result of concentration of population on the better soils, leading quickly to the subdivision of tenures, rather than the 'invasion' of the countryside by a bourgeoisie which concentrated its acquisitions in the plain of France nearest the city. Generally, this process was accompanied by migration of population from less advantaged to richer regions, the revival of villages, even emigration (for instance from France to Spain). Richard Gascon's work on the inmates of the hospital at Lyon after 1529 shows a high proportion (40 per cent) of immigrants, mostly local peasants but some from the north.[36]

Thus, much of the population loss of the fourteenth–fifteenth centuries had been made good by 1560 but regional studies reveal differences in rhythm of the general population boom from around 1480 to 1560–70. In Provence, for instance, the number of households roughly tripled between 1470 and 1540, with the main growth coming after 1500, although it seems this was near the epicentre of an exceptional boom which was spreading from east to west from Liguria to Catalonia.[37]

In Languedoc, the boom started slightly later, 1500–10, with roughly a doubling of taxpayers over two or three generations, c.1500–60 (11.5 per cent average growth 1500–60). This was all fuelled by a decline in disease. Evidence of the growth may be observed in the settlement of marginal land and particularly in deforestation after 1520, while recourse to 'intensive' cultivation in the form of the establishment of olive production and vineyards alongside grain is another sign. On the other had, there was no doubling of grain production, as revealed by tithe records, and

though there was an increase, it seems to have reached its peak
around 1520–30. The plain fact was that, in view of the intractable
nature of much of the land available, grain production in
Languedoc was outstripped by population increase around
1530–40.[38] Still in southern France, fragmentary records of house-
holders contained in seigneurial *terriers* for Auvergne indicate that
the main boom there came earlier, in the 60 years before 1478 (a
rise of population of 225 per cent) and that, though growth continued into the sixteenth century it was much slower (33 per cent
in the years 1478–1544) and declined again after the middle of
the century, especially between 1580 and 1600. There too, grain
production as revealed in seigneurial *dîmes* indicates a faltering in
yield after roughly 1520.[39]

In northern France there are some significant contrasts. The
number of households per parish in Picardy had fallen from an
average of 100 in 1328 to around 30 in 1469 but probably
regained the losses by around 1560. A detailed study of figures for
the neighbouring province of Artois indicates that the most
savage years had been the 1430s and 1440s, that recovery started
after 1460, though limited by the outbreak of the Burgundian
wars in the 1470s.[40] In another area where the Burgundian wars
proved destructive, Bar-sur-Seine, while there were only 5 or 6
people per km[2] in 1478, there were 10 times as many in 1544.[41] In
Cambrésis, population recovery started a little earlier, in the
1450s, collapsed after 1477 because of the fighting but started to
grow again in the 1480s. Relatively slow growth in the earlier sixteenth century brought the population back to its 1365 level by
1540, helped, as in Languedoc, by a decline of plague after 1516.
Here, too, growth in grain production from the last quarter of the
fifteenth century came to a standstill around 1550, probably
because of the inability of the productive system either to inno-
vate or exploit traditional methods fully.[42]

The pattern was not uniform and it seems likely that growth was
more rapid and complete in southern than in northern France,
since in eastern Normandy the population was still only 75 per
cent of its 1314 level by 1550.[43] The revival of population growth
in the Nantes region of Brittany seems to have started in the last
decade of the fifteenth century, both in the countryside and the
towns, but to have faltered around 1560. Where comparisons are
possible, in four out of ten rural parishes in the region there was a

50 per cent increase in the number of baptisms, and in two others 30 per cent, during the period 1500–60.[44]

In parts of Ile-de-France, restoration, begun tentatively in the 1440s after the battle of Pontoise in areas near to Paris or with good soils, did not begin elsewhere in the region until 1470. The famous case of Magny-les-Hameaux continues to tell its story: 14 habitations in the early fourteenth century, 27 in 1521. But in the south-east of Hurepoix, it is true, villages like Antony tripled in numbers between 1467 and 1503; Bures, with one survivor in 1467, had grown to 260 in 1527. Chevreuse, in the more marginal west, dropped from 1500 in the early fourteenth century to less than 200 in 1467, to grow to around 1200 by the mid-sixteenth century.[45] Jean Jacquart has argued that the summit of population growth came in the Ile-de-France in the period 1560–80 at levels around 10 per cent higher than they were to be in the early eighteenth century. The population of the Paris basin would, then, have stood at around 1.5 million (or 52–55 per km^2) around 1560.[46]

If we turn to the effects of all this growth on social relations, we find that in much of northern France the pattern of reconstruction took the form of remarkable restoration – Guy Fourquin called it a 'profoundly conservative convalescence' – of the pattern of settlement and system of tenures associated with the concession of *censives* to peasant cultivators by landlords. By 1550, there may have been a slight increase in seigneurial *granges* since the fourteenth century but this was marginal. By the early sixteenth century, peasant *censives* covered two-thirds of the poorer soils, much more in the richer ones. One obvious consequence was the smallness of peasant holdings. In the seven seigneuries of the Hurepoix studied by Jacquart, the average hearth in the mid-sixteenth century had only 1.3 hectares of land. In the vineyards of the Bordelais around 1460, landowners failed completely to reimpose dues, recall serfs or introduce a sharecropping (*métayage*) system. As Marc Bloch made clear, the countryside was re-established very much 'according to the old principles' and there was no great move towards the direct exploitation of estates by landlords despite the incentive posed by the steady fall in the value of money of account in this period.[47]

Allied to this was the final collapse of serfdom linked to tenure as landlords competed for labour in the late fifteenth century and the notion of manumission as a pious and useful act was pressed by both the church and the crown. As the crown expressed it in an act of 1544 that abolished *mainmorte* in part of its domain, 'serfdom is a law contrary to nature'. *Mainmorte*, anyway, had become difficult to collect and the concession of freedom produced a useful once-for-all payment for lords or, in sixteenth-century Burgundy, the concession of a plot of land by the enfranchised community.[48] However, dues and rents to lords should not be viewed in isolation. Despite the relative scarcity of *taille* roles for villages, it is clear that from the reign of Louis XI there was a sharp increase in payments to the state. The peasants around Paris in the late fifteenth century probably paid the king in *tailles* and indirect taxes twice what they paid their landlords and their money obligations may have been heavier than they had been at the start of the fifteenth century.[49] The situation could only have been sustained by increased production but was ominous in its implications for the future.

The picture that emerges, then, taking account of considerable regional variations, is that by 1560 the population of France had more or less returned to the levels of the early fourteenth century, with all the implications for the unstable densely-populated world that that has. Analysis of the evidence produced by tithe yields shows, in a number of regions, the rapidity of the rise in production from about 1460 to 1560 and that after around 1540 a growth in production levels in comparison with the early fourteenth century is visible. However, it is also plain that this extra growth was not enough to keep pace with the growth of the population in the middle decades of the sixteenth century.[50]

The most salient consequence of all this was the reversal of the favourable employment conditions that had prevailed for working people in the fifteenth century, both in town and country. A bad sign from the late fifteenth century was a perceptible increase in land rents, the replacement of the *cens* by leases for between 3 and 9 years (for instance around Paris after about 1520) and the inexorable rise in the price of grain, revealed by the *mercuriales* of Paris beginning in 1520 (a steady rise in the price of best wheat from an index of 100 in 1526 to 188 in 1554). At Lyon, where the price of wheat quadrupled between 1475 and 1565 and tripled between 1510 and 1565, the overall cost of living index doubled between 1535 and 1565. Hauser's statistics on the southern

Dauphiné show a tripling of prices since the mid-fifteenth century, with a notable aggravation from the late 1520s marked by the rebellion known as the *Grande Rebeyne* at Lyon (1529) and disturbances in the Cévennes, and a repetition of the crisis in 1539–40.[51] In some areas, notably the centre and south during the reign of Francis I, sharecropping began to spread.

Emmanuel Le Roy Ladurie, in his study of the peasants of Languedoc, argued that a 'crisis in depth' ended the favourable conditions of the Renaissance in the years around 1530. He plotted the decline by examining the real wages of harvesters in some Languedoc villages. At the end of the fifteenth century, they had received every tenth *sétier* they cut, from 1525 every eleventh and from 1546 only every twelfth (a contraction from 10 to 9 per cent and then to 8.3 per cent of the harvest). After 1560, it dropped further to every 18th *sétier* (5.5 per cent) by 1600.[52] It is worth remembering that the price of wheat doubled in Languedoc from 1480 to 1560, while the wages of agricultural employees remained virtually static. Where comparisons in the food rations of labourers are possible between the late fifteenth and the late sixteenth centuries, there had been a definite deterioration in the quality of the diet, bread being substituted for meat and poor wine for good.[53]

The wages of artisans in Languedoc followed a similar pattern. The daily wage of a master stonemason (at the top of the scale of urban workers) at Montpellier purchased 15 kilos of bread at the end of the fifteenth century but only 9 in 1530–50. A vineyard worker in the same period was receiving 6.6 kilos (at a time when 2 kilos a day per person were needed), a disparity reflecting the fact that the wages of agricultural labourers were only ever on a par with unskilled town workers. Broadly speaking, whereas the price of bread sextupled between 1480–1500 and 1585–1600, daily wages of stonemasons, carpenters and farm workers only tripled.[54] Contemporaries were well aware that France in the first half of the sixteenth century was a country of low wages which exported labour, usually temporary, from areas like Languedoc, Provence, Auvergne, Limousin and Gascony to Spain where labour costs, according to Jean Bodin, were triple those in France.[55]

Similar patterns can be seen in other regions. At Cambrai, wages of workers, adjusted for grain prices, started to fall precipitously after 1470, recovered slightly in the 1490s but began a 40-year fall around 1500.[56] At Paris, real wages of building labourers fell from an index of 100 in 1460–9 to one of 24.7 in 1560–9. In the countryside to the south of the capital, the wages of farm labourers, after a peak under Charles VIII, began to fall again. In general, it has been suggested that the purchasing power of wages for workers dropped 40 per cent between the late fifteenth and the late sixteenth century.[57]

The growth of the fear of vagabondage is a sign of insecurity rather than an indicator of poor conditions. Bronisław Geremek has shown that the campaign against marginal people started while wages were rising or stable in the fourteenth–fifteenth centuries. There had been concern about masterless men ever since the middle of the fourteenth century but this became more acute in the disorders of the early fifteenth. In 1450, Dijon made vagabondage a crime and in 1473 the Parlement of Paris issued a decree for the capital which became the basis for further repression. The decree distinguished between individual idlers and organised marauders and also speeded up the action to be taken. Charity was available only to those prepared to work. Around 1500, the *Livre des gueux* encouraged fear of sturdy beggars, vagabonds (*belistres*) and other marginal people. The general fear of incendiaries and *mauvais garçons* evident in the town chronicles of the 1520s is a further sign of disquiet. By then, the growth of vagabondage seems more clearly linked to adverse economic conditions. There were two answers to this problem.[58] In some circumstances, local authorities simply had recourse to the traditional carrot-and-stick approach. At Toulouse, they were prepared to help the destitute old and widows while punishing 'vagabonds' severely. Elsewhere, however, new institutions for the alleviation of the poor were developed, like the *Grande aumône* set up at Lyon and publicised in print in 1531. From mid-May to early July, 250,000 loaves were distributed to 5000 poor. Within a few months, it was reported that 'the poor and sick no longer go begging their bread in the streets as they did before but are fed at home by the *Aumône*'. As Etienne de Médicis, a consul at Le Puy-en-Velay, put it in commenting on these times, 'when God travails his people by famine, the government of the communities is very difficult'. The establishment of a permanent mass of the genuinely destitute provoked a new and innovative solution that was to be imitated all over France in the long run. The sharp drops of real wages at Lyon (for instance in the building trade) in the later 1530s and mid-1540s are examples of a volatility that was to become worse in the second half of the century.[59]

Such a society was increasingly vulnerable to natural calamity; the poor harvests of 1526–8 provoked severe famine in 1528–9 followed by disease and the extension of debt and vagrancy in the countryside. Grain prices soared and, where possible, local notables like the Estates of Languedoc tried to prohibit grain movement out of their province, thus exacerbating shortages in cities like Lyon, sparking off the rebellion of the *Grande Rebeyne* and the measures just outlined. Similar policies were adopted at Nantes during crises of food shortage. Movements of grain out of the region were prohibited by the magistrates in 1525. The rich bourgeois, acting privately, took on the responsibility of feeding the poor and keeping out new beggars in the severe crisis of 1529–31. Alms were regularly distributed on Sundays throughout the crisis.[60] The outbreak of strikes in the printing industries – trades that were, of course, new and not yet organised into ossified guild structures – in Paris and Lyon in 1539 and 1542 were caused by a desire of the journeymen to restrict the number of new apprentices and thus raise wages. This provoked a royal edict that they would:

> give example and occasion to other craft journeymen and servants in our kingdom to do the same on other occasions, which is a real foundation and encouragement of mutinies and seditions that in the end can only be to the detriment of the public weal.

The hostility of the crown to acts of disorder should not be surprising. What is noteworthy is the extent of the organisation of these movements that, after all, invented a word for 'strike' (*tric*).[61] The crown responded to the perceptible growth of vagabondage from the last quarter of the fifteenth century by legislation that criminalised it, though with what effect is as yet uncertain. In 1496, the crown ordered the transfer of the unemployed and vagabonds to the galleys. The bad years around 1530 led to a further change in attitudes both to trade and to the poor, marked by the edict of Compiègne, April 1534, against beggars.[62]

The Idea of France in the Late Middle Ages and Renaissance

Given all this diversity both of cultural, political and of economic development, can we talk of the 'identity of France' or of some kind of 'national' consciousness in this period? The triumph of the French language in government and noble culture in the fourteenth and fifteenth centuries had obvious implications here but in view of the country's diversity, 'loyalties' existed at many different levels and had various meanings in different social groups. In the fourteenth century, 'France' could be made to mean 'free' (i.e. of taxes) or 'valiant'. The 'France' of Ronsard's Virgilian Hymn of 1549 is a literary idea. It would be absurd to posit the idea of national consciousness in the nineteenth and twentieth-century form. The period of Jeanne d'Arc and of the struggle with the English crown tends to prompt the conclusion that the 'Frenchness' was in some ways defined in the course of the Hundred Years War. That conflict, whose role was in the view of Philippe Contamine 'despite everything ... essential in the awakening of French national consciousness' and for P. S. Lewis 'always more than one over inheritance rights', had, in order to be conclusively settled, to generate the resources of entire countries. An interest in the historical foundation for national mythology spread consequently among the learned and then in wider circles.[63] Bernard Guenée has concluded that, despite the differences of language and manners, the French by 1500 had come to believe they were a 'nation' and had probably done so since the fourteenth century. Thomas Basin's description of the people of Normandy in 1450 'calling back their old and natural French sovereignty ... as the source of their natural tranquility' is a further indication. The Languedoc bishop Bernard de Rosier, in his *Miranda de laudibus Franciae* of 1450, was quite explicit: France, a country of two *pays* and two languages (*Gallicana and Occana*, as he called them) was knit into one by its church and the government of the Most Christian King, a government with exceptional virtues and prerogatives.[64]

Colette Beaune, in an important work on the genesis of French national consciousness in the late Middle Ages, has underlined the profoundly religious origins of the idea of France and its roots in a kind of royal religion which had certain messianic and utopian implications. In a sense, this was the inevitable consequence of the fact that the church provided the crown with the most obvious network of communication throughout the kingdom and the clergy were, on the whole, loyal. She has stressed how the identification of the 'Most Christian' kingdom of France with Israel from the early fourteenth century, and the legend of Clovis, as indicative of divine providence, generated the notion of an elect nation. The conflict with Pope Boniface VIII pushed forward the idea of the kingdom as held of God alone and the late fourteenth century saw the *Très chrétien* title applied specifically to one prince, the king of France. From this it was a short step to the idea of France as a peculiarly faithful Christian kingdom so that Claude de Seyssel in the early sixteenth century could write that 'even when they were pagans they were devout in their observance. Coming to the Christian faith, they were among the first Christian nations to receive it.' Such religious faith was held to generate the list of 'privileges' of the king and the kingdom which were finally codified as twenty in a work of Jean Ferrault in 1520 and which contributed to the idea of the Fundamental Laws. The idea of 'la douce France', fair mistress of the faithful chevalier, emerged as early as 1100 in the *Chanson de Roland*, though perhaps more clearly in the Chronicle of du Guesclin. But it was from the early fifteenth century that 'France' started to be visualised in art as a graceful woman and from the mid-century it was commonplace to liken the country to a garden of paradise. A good example is André La Vigne's *Le Verger d'honneur* of the early sixteenth century. The image of the 'tree of France', with its roots set deep in time and its branches displaying allegorically all the qualities of the kingdom and its rulers, runs from Christine de Pisan's *Discours des états et offices* to Charles Figon's *Arbre des Estats et Offices* of 1579.[65]

It has been argued that the duty to sacrifice one's life for one's country was revived in the late Middle Ages as a 'fundamental value' in the name of which temporal powers could make demands. Whereas consciousness of France as a 'patrie' is quite limited until the fifteenth century, the *Chronique de Charles VI* had declared 'it is a natural law to fight for one's country'. During the 'wars of magnificence' in Italy during the reign of Charles VIII, French soldiers began to replace the battle-cry 'Montjoie Saint-Denis' with that of 'France, France'. Around 1480, Pierre

Choisnet in the *Rosier des guerres* praised the merit of defending the common good and claimed 'there is merit in death for the common good and everyone ought to fight for his country (*pais*)'. With the crusading ideal moribund, the military *chants* of the 1520s and 1530s praise men as lowly as valets who were prepared to 'die for France', while the crown explicitly appealed to the sentiment of 'patrie' at the time of the siege of Rouen in 1562. The compulsion to praise the country and compare it favourably with other lands is clear in Commynes's judgement that 'there is no country in the whole universe better situated than France'.[66] However, we must also remember that in the later sixteenth century Brantôme could still question the idea of 'mourir pour la patrie' as an idea invented by 'legislators, kings, communities and republics to preserve themselves'. Fine words, he says 'but to observe it so strictly as to abandon all other duties and obligations is a stupid abuse'.[67] In the learned world, Etienne Dolet's celebrated diatribe, as orator of the French 'nation' at the university of Toulouse in 1533, against the local magistrates, suggesting that his compatriots were beleaguered by 'barbarians', was a piece of literary effrontery as offensive to Gascons and Provençaux as it was to Germans and Spaniards.[68]

Every country of western Europe seems to have derived its national consciousness to some extent from historical myth, as G. R. Elton has pointed out.[69] Central to such mythology was the question of origins, whether among the descendants of Trojans or of biblical figures. Ancestors were held in some sense to encapsulate the destiny of a people, while the glorious deeds of founders, where impossible to document from 'historical' sources, could always be narrated in what would now be called a 'mythical' form in which it was normal to seek the origins of the reigning dynasty in extremely remote times and an earlier civilisation.[70] That historical foundation was crystallised in later fifteenth-century France, after the establishment of printing, in the form of the *Annales et Chroniques* of Nicolle Gilles (1492) and the *Compendium de origine et gestis Francorum* by Robert Gaguin (1495), which enjoyed enormous popularity among the literate. The formulation of French history they represented, exploring national origins in the distant Gauls and the Frankish conquest, and conceiving history largely in terms of the succession of kings from the mythical Pharamond, reinforced the idea of the crown as the centre of French identity and loyalty to that crown as its prime quality. Gilles posed the basic question: 'whence comes the *lignage* of the most noble kings of France?'[71] There was already, however, a tension in their interpretation of the past which raised uncertainties about the true origins of the French nation: whether sought amongst the Gauls or the Franks.[72] The problem of the Germanic origin of the Franks remained unsettled, for whereas Gaguin tentatively accepted it, he nevertheless saw the Gauls as central to the nature of the French people. Moreover, arguments which sought the origins of the French kingdom either in Trojans or in Germans could hardly be satisfactory in terms of national identity.[73]

Gaguin claimed to be producing a new history but in fact his innovations were largely stylistic rather than of substance, since he based his material on the tradition of the *Grandes Chroniques,* though in his writings other than the *Compendium* he was prepared to go beyond this and explore classical sources.[74] As late as 1527, Jean Bouchet's *Epitaphes des Roys de France* deployed the Trojan myth in its entirety. The problem was, as many recognised, that the ancient writers had paid relatively little attention to the glorious conquests of the ancient Gauls. As Joachim du Bellay put it in the *Deffence et illustration de la langue françoyse* (1549), the Romans had a multitude of writers to record their deeds; the Gauls 'before they fell into the power of the French, and the actions of the French themselves since they gave their name to the Gauls, have been so ill-collected, that we have almost lost not only the glory of them, but even the memory of them'. This did not prevent Ronsard in his *Franciade* from laboriously constructing his eagerly awaited but disappointing story of the kings from Francus son of Hector, published in 1572 and dragged out only as far as Pepin the Short.[75]

The chroniclers and poets just discussed made scarcely any distinction between myth and history in their search for the honourable and glorious traditions of the Gauls and Franks but they were at least trying to write history on a learned level. Such mythological stories, based as usual on the story of the Trojan origins of the Franks, medieval in origin, and the antiquity of Gallic civilisation, came to fruition in the *Illustrations de Gaule* of Jean Lemaire de Belges, produced between 1509 and 1549 and reprinted six times. Lemaire exploited fully the largely forged 'discoveries' of

Annius of Viterbo's 'Berosus' (published 1498 and at Paris in 1510) that were to add such detail to the Trojan myth. For Lemaire, Trojan origins were the common patrimony of all Christian princes and in particular of the houses of France and Austria. Nationality for Lemaire was a unitary force in Christendom. The purpose was to stress the unity of all Christian princes against the Turks and he viewed the French and Germans as fraternal nations. 'The Gallic and French nation', that had conserved in its purest form the blood of Hercules and was 'the most noble nation of the world' would lead a crusade. But 'while Trojan origins united all Christian princes, they also united the French nation, both Gallic and French.'[76]

To seek for the added dimension of 'popular' historical consciousness, we must look at the vast progeny of mediocre 'histories' based on the Trojan myth which, though fairly crude, represent a good idea of the effects of royal and national propaganda. One such example was the anonymous *Arbre de France* published in 1542 to celebrate the antiquity of the royal line and refute the claims of Spain and the Emperor Charles V, against whom war had just been declared. After the recitation of the succession of the kings of Gaul, some of them Trojans, with stories of Lugdus and Paris, then the familiar story of the Trojan origins of the Franks and assertion of the *concorde* between the two nations, the culmination is reached with Francis I, worthy successor of Charlemagne and Saint Louis, heads of the 'illustrious house of France' which was the true 'defender of the Catholic faith'.[77]

The succession of the kings of France was a predominant theme in the writing of history and was generally seen as a proof of the antiquity of the kingdom, although occasionally a writer like Claude de Seyssel could step out of line. Seyssel's main point in the *Louanges de Louys XII* was to assert the greatness of his king and to do this he did not scruple to rake up as many disreputable stories about his predecessors as would serve the purpose of favourable comparison. This was hardly the case of the first complete humanist history, Paolo Emilio's *De rebus gestis Francorum*, published between 1517 and 1539 and translated into French. To some extent, this did for France what Polydore Vergil did for England and Emilio was influential in the importance he attached to Clovis as the miraculous founder of the French state. However, Emilio was more concerned with elegance of style than substance or criticism.[78] Gaguin raised doubts at the end of the fifteenth century. With the publication of the *Rerum germanicarum* of Beatus Rhenanus in 1531, and of the *Apologie* of the Italian Marius Equila in 1550 in which he asserted it was 'not less puerile than worthy of mockery', the scholarly world could no longer sustain the Trojan myth. After 1560 the literary world was much less disposed to accept it either.[79] This may explain the failure of Ronsard's *Franciade*.

It was to be the work of legal experts like Estienne Pasquier in his *Recherches de France* (1560), that set French history on the road to critical scholarship. He set out to free it from the straitjacket of the Trojan myth in order to visualise the history of a people, the people of Gaul, rather than to narrate a succession of kings and their deeds and to explore institutions. In Pasquier's time, the duality of the Gallic and Frankish origins of France was naturally still debated among writers. There was a degree of celtomania in the 1550s that led a writer like Jean Picard in his *De prisca celtopaedia* (1556) to argue that the Gauls had taught the arts of civilisation to the Greeks. The crisis in relations with the Papacy in the mid-sixteenth century produced what is sometimes called a 'Gallican' view of history that sought to make the ancient Celts the civilisers of Rome. Some chose to explain the problem in terms of the original identity of the Franks and Gauls. Thus, the civil lawyer François Connan argued that French law was neither Roman nor Germanic but Gallic. The Franks, he argued, were an offshoot of the ancient Gauls themselves and this view was later accepted by Bodin in his *Methodus*.

The 'Gaulish' view was in part a reaction against the spread of 'pangermanist' notions built on editions of the *Germania* of Tacitus from the late fifteenth century onwards. Essentially, these argued that French institutions stemmed from the conquest of Gaul by the Franks. Charles Dumoulin – the Gallican feudal lawyer whose controversialist work at the time of the crisis with the Papacy in 1551, *Les petites dates*, and his treatise on *L'Origine* ... *du royaume et monarchie des françois* (1551, published 1561) led him to formulate a new and distinctive view of French history – argued that the major institutions of France and especially its liberties, were derived from 'Germanic' traditions. Dumoulin is important for the rigorous legal basis that he built into an historical understanding of French identity (incidentally conceiving of France as a 'mixed monarchy'). Curiously, though, even the acute Dumoulin affected to believe in the historical existence of Francus, seeing in his existence the guarantee of the all-important longevity of the French monarchy. Others by the early seventeenth century chose to take the course of seeing in the Franks the originators of the nobility and in the Gauls the progenitors of the common people.[80] Against all this Pasquier could only raise the banner of scepticism. Noting the various views of the nations that sought their origins in the Trojans, he said 'As for me, I do not dare completely to contravene this view or completely agree with it. However, it seems to me that to dispute the ancient origins of nations is a delicate matter because when they began they were so insignificant that the ancient authors were not bothered to explore them.' Whatever the conclusion, the late fifteenth and early sixteenth centuries had laid out the agenda for the discussion of history as the shaper of the identity of France. Charles Dumoulin claimed to write history 'in order to adorn the commonwealth of France' and for 'the good and honour of the French people'.[81]

If all the evidence points to the centrality of the monarchy to French identity, one aspect of the genesis of a sense of national community that has perhaps been neglected is the active role of the crown in propaganda. The work of Colette Beaune and Bernard Guenée has made clear that the national loyalties that already existed in the fourteenth and fifteenth centuries were profoundly monarchical in theme. The concept that all French were *subjects* of the king rather than his *vassals* of various kinds, that the king was 'emperor in his kingdom' and that the church in France should be autonomous under the king encouraged royal jurists to think in universal terms about the scope of royal legislation. The preambles to the *brevets de tailles* sent to the *élections* and provincial estates often provided in effect public manifestos of royal policies. From the reign of Louis XII the king's advisers began to take advantage of printing to disseminate letters and edicts meant for public consumption with preambles that appealed to the unity of the kingdom and to the king's role of supreme giver of justice. Henri II's proclamation in 1554, concerning manumissions of serfs in Burgundy, that:

we desire our kingdom to grow and increase with men who may be free in fact as well as in name, considering that, having received from us all the blessings of freedom, which is the greatest that men can desire after life itself, they can do us all the offices that free and well born men can do to their prince and natural lord.[82]

The high-blown rhetoric may have concealed the aim to make a profit but nevertheless indicates the sentiments to which it was thought appropriate to appeal. Throughout the period from Louis XI to Henri II it became customary for the crown to maintain close and frequent contacts with the *bonnes villes* in order to make them *au courant* with great events such as victories, defeats, births and deaths in the royal family, for which intercessory processions or bonfires were desirable. By the 1550s, the public *Te Deum* had become the ceremony par excellence that carried out this function.[83]

Essential to the formation of that French identity was also the definition of the territory of the kingdom. Though it was once thought impossible to define medieval frontiers exactly, it is now thought that many of them were of great antiquity, while the main difference between older and early modern conceptions of frontiers lay in the greater complexity of the former. By the fifteenth century, the classic definition in terms of the Pyrenees and the rivers Rhône, Saône, Meuse and Escaut, defining the *mouvance* of the kingdom, inherited at a distance from the 843 treaty of Verdun, was no longer particularly useful, although it retained its rhetorical influence into the sixteenth century. The popular histories of Gaguin and Gilles actually stressed the rivers as frontiers, although in technical fact the two had never corresponded exactly.[84] The early modern period, in any case, was one which saw the co-existence of the two concepts of *limite* and *frontière*; the terms still sometimes overlapped in popular usage in the sixteenth century. Their significance is that the *limites* of the kingdom or of any territory within it were produced essentially by the feudal age; they were indifferent to geographical facts and naturally accommodated enclaves and anomalies. The *frontière* was essentially a concept of military defence, of the desire to *faire front* to the enemy and, by adaptation in the sixteenth century, a line of fortifications that might halt enemy armies near the frontier. The contribution of historical scholarship to this is revealed in the writings of Sebastian Munzer in the 1540s and his discussion of the so-called Gallic frontiers of France.[85]

As Peter Sahlins has pointed out, in the sixteenth century the state was still 'something less than a territorial one', basing itself on sovereignty over subjects rather than over defined territory.[86] Royal jurists were still using the concept of *mouvance* to define what we should call the quasi-territorial rights of the crown. Hence the lengthy legal disputes in the region of the Argonne on the Meuse as to whether territories dependent on the duchy of Bar should be considered part of France. This had enabled the inhabitants to play off the French and imperial authorities against each other for generations.[87] Up to 1525, Artois and Flanders were regarded as within the *mouvance* of the kingdom and both crown and Parlement still attempted to exercise jurisdiction there from time to time. In effect, however, the Habsburg government successfully resisted this and from the treaties of Madrid and Cambrai these territories were removed from the kingdom for the first time since 843.[88]

It is significant that such disputes should concern the northern and eastern frontiers of the kingdom, where the overlap between the ideas of *mouvance* and territory was at its greatest. Already under Louis XI, a distinction was drawn in military administration among those mercenaries 'of the French language, Savoyards, Gascons, Lorrainers and others who are not of the German nation' and other subjects of the Empire, the crown refusing to treat the former as true German formations.[89] The increasing political and military preoccupations of the crown with the security of the eastern frontier and its interests in the Empire were bound, by the middle of the sixteenth century, to generate discussion of the identity of interest between the kingdom and the French-speaking territories of the Empire, as cardinal de Tournon made clear in the 1540s. During talks over the project for electing the dauphin Henri emperor in 1546, Tournon spoke of the wish of Francis I to accept the lordship 'of all the lands of the Empire on this side of the Rhine and of the French language, like Metz, Verdun, Cambrai and others'. This came into sharper focus with Henri II's 'German campaign' of 1552 and the establishment of French outposts on the Meuse and Moselle. The diplomat Jean de Fraisse reported the agreement of the German princes in 1551 to concede that 'Metz, Toul and Verdun and all other towns not of the German tongue would be placed in your name as Vicar of the Empire'. The pretensions of French kings to the Imperial throne were fading in significance but the king could still pose credibly as 'Protector of German liberties';

the establishment of solid territorial claims to the cis-Rhenanian lands of the Empire was in its infancy.[90]

This set of ideas about the nation current by the sixteenth century reflects, in Colette Beaune's words, 'the society that created it ... monarchical, clerical and noble', yet she also insists that there was a degree of penetration of 'national sentiment' among the peasantry, if we only consider the case of Jeanne d'Arc or the fierce resistance of the Norman peasantry in the 1430s–50s; the move of the court to the Loire from Paris may well have expanded the region of instinctive loyalty to the crown.[91] It is important to ask how far this had gone by 1560. It has become usual to draw attention to the effects of polemical writings of the period of the Wars of Religion in generating this consciousness. However, one Russian historian, in an analysis of peasant guerrilla movements mounted to combat Charles V's invasion of Provence in 1536, drew attention to its part in the creation of national consciousness. Although the emperor himself thought the resistance of the peasants stemmed from their fear 'of being punished as were those who favoured the late M. de Bourbon', local writers, in describing the events, underscored the peasants' allegiance to France. The Marseilles bourgeois, Honorat de Valbelle, described the wish of the 'contadins' to 'prove their loyalty to the fatherland'; the occasional Latin verse composed to celebrate the events by members of the provençal bourgeoisie emphasised this even more. Admixed with this was a large dose of hostility towards any marauding soldiery.[92]

Until the late fifteenth century, Fawtier argued, it was impossible to establish a clear visual image of France. Writers were aware of certain general characteristics, of course, as when Commynes observed that France, bordering as it did Flanders and Germany in the north and Italy and Spain in the south, 'part of the country being hot, and part of it cold, our people are of two complexions'. Commynes, indeed, though he was fully aware of the cultural diversity of the France of his time, had no doubt about its institutional unity under the crown.[93] J.-P. Genet has contrasted the men of the tenth century, without the means, or indeed the need, to draw maps, and those of the fifteenth, who evidently did.[94] P. Contamine has argued that the persistence of the absurd but flattering myth that there were 1,700,000 parish churches in France, and a general reluctance to use available statistical information, despite the existence of the 1328 survey in the archives of the *Chambre des comptes*, demonstrates this. Until the fourteenth century, it was usual to proceed by lists, in concord with the view of the kingdom as more a collection of rights than of territories. Indeed, there were customary lists of duchies, counties and cities. The assimilation of the idea of the kingdom in that of a great *seigneurie* was a powerful tool in the hands of medieval administrators.[95]

Traditional empirical estimations made the kingdom 22 days' journey from north to south and 16 from west to east at the widest point while, locally, it was possible to state that Normandy was six days' long and four wide.[96] Louis XII even commissioned a geometrician, Louis Boulenger of Albi, to measure his kingdom and learned from this that the distance from Saint-Jean de Luz to Geneva was 200 leagues, as was that from Boulogne to Marseille, while the circumference of the kingdom was 800 leagues (of 4 million *pas*). The area he estimated at the equivalent of 783,000 km2 and the population at 25 million *feux* and 100 million people. The fact that the *Chambre des comptes* had a good idea of the true number of parishes (around 27,000) and that the machinery for raising the infantry by a levy of one *franc-archer* per parish was expected to produce 16,000 men testifies to empirical knowledge. However, it also shows the unwillingness of those outside administrative circles to accept what would now be thought to be accurate statistics.[97] The organisation by Louis XI in 1464 of an effective royal postal system, with a network of stations and post horses under the *grand écuyer*, which enabled him and his successors to be more quickly and reliably informed of events, presumably gave those at the centre a more precise picture of their world. Louis, for instance, heard of the death of his enemy the duke of Burgundy much earlier than the ducal court. By the first half of the sixteenth century, riders in haste could achieve 70, occasionally 80 km a day and could get to London from Paris in the remarkable time of six days, with the wind favourable.[98] However, this was still an expensive luxury to be used by special envoys and ambassadors only.

Bernard Guenée has to some extent refined Fawtier's original view by pointing out the increasingly sharp awareness of physical space in twelfth- and thirteenth-century Europe. Whether Charles V's portolan, drawn up by Abraham Cresques to illustrate his reconquests from the English, can be classified as a truly geographical enterprise, as Philippe Contamine implies, is open to question.[99]

However, an ability to visualise the territory of France was not a new phenomenon but rather one built up gradually by the accumulation of a 'geographical consciousness' throughout the late Middle Ages, whether it produced maps or not. The measure of this is in the first visual surveys reduced to the form of true maps which were produced by specific commissions of enquiry in the sixteenth century, such as the survey conducted by the estates of Quercy, Périgord and Rouergue for tax purposes from the 1530s or, more directly, the border surveys for the fixing of the northern and eastern frontiers of the kingdom in the 1450s and then in 1559–60 after the treaty of Cateau-Cambrésis.[100] General maps of France only became widespread with the issue of the first poorly printed ones in Germany between 1480 and 1500. In France, it was the work of Orance Fine (d.1555) and the publication of Charles Estienne's *Guide des chemins de France* (1552) that began to disseminate a definite visual image of the kingdom.[101] Then Catherine de Medici commissioned Nicolas de Nicolay to 'reduce and put in volumes the maps and geographical descriptions ... of each province of this kingdom', though in fact he completed only those for Berry, Bourbonnais and Lyonnais (1567). Nevertheless, it is important to remember that, considering the state of preservation of printed sixteenth-century maps and of our knowledge of their print runs, it is impossible to be categorical about how wide their dissemination actually was. Those that have been preserved seem to have been printed in relatively small numbers and, as Daniel Nordman has pointed out, it is not clear who could have found such maps of any practical use in the sixteenth century.[102]

In social and cultural terms, then, the century from 1460 to 1560 was an immensely varied and constructive period, witnessing the prodigious reconstruction of French society, the beginnings of new problems and the crystallisation of national identity around the essentially traditional notion of loyalty to the king. The next chapter will consider in detail the emerging image of royal power in this period.

1. The Monarchy: Ideology, Presentation and Ritual

Bernard Guenée remarked, in the course of a study of the ceremonial of the *joyeuse entrée* in the late Middle Ages, that 'the secret of the state's cohesion should be sought in the minds' of Frenchmen.[1] The purpose of this chapter is to explore the ways – modes of thought, ceremonial, ritual – in which the power of the crown was conceived and visualised in this period. Jacques Krynen has drawn attention to the preoccupation with the growth of public power and the state in late medieval drama (e.g. *Le mistère du siège d'Orléans*), in poetry (Christine de Pisan, Eustache Deschamps and Guillaume de Machault) as well as in the vast literature on law and rights.[2]

The salient works on public power written in France before Jean Bodin, the *Songe du Vergier*, Philippe de Mézières's *Le Songe du Vieil Pélerin* and Seyssel's *Monarchie de France* are apt to be used to illustrate the relative poverty of political thought in late medieval France in comparison with the works of Occam, Fortescue, Marsilius and Machiavelli written over a comparable period. This is not perhaps an unfair judgement but it should not obscure the lively interest in France in the question of legitimate power or the 'corps de policie' explored by P. S. Lewis.[3] We have already seen that the theory of the Trojan origins of the French kings gradually fell out of favour during the Renaissance. However, lawyers and administrators were passionately concerned with the practical issues of a specifically French kind, such as the legitimacy of the English claim to France or the territorial jurisdiction of the king and the power of the crown vis-à-vis the Papacy.[4] Not surprisingly, therefore, an intelligent ruler like Louis XI took a keen interest in the historical legitimacy of his power. The arguments, which still aroused uneasiness among the chroniclers of the late Middle Ages, about the dynastic transfer of power from the Merovingians to the Carolingians and from the latter to the Capetians concerned politicians as well.[5] This was despite the official doctrine of the thirteenth century which viewed the kings from Philip Augustus onwards as true descendants of Charlemagne, the so-called *reditus regni ad stirpem Karoli.*

Louis XI conceived of the Merovingian kings as *prédécesseurs* or *progéniteurs*.[6] In the peace negotiations of 1480, Louis denied female succession to the apanage of Artois in terms which clearly show how aware he was of the importance to his dynasty of the Salic law: 'if we consent that females inherit, I would lose the crown and it would go to the kingdom of Navarre and then to another, that it says in your book the other daughter had, and then to the king of England.'[7] It is tempting here to see a reference to the *Généalogie* of the French kings and a refutation of English claims first printed with a false attribution to Alain Chartier in 1489 (reprinted in 1494 and 1529) but written in the 1420s on the basis of Jean de Montreuil's *Traité contre les Anglais*. Numerous such genealogies appeared in the fifteenth century.[8]

The king of France was first of all a seigneur supported by vassals who in the fourteenth and fifteenth centuries were slowly transformed into 'subjects'. In fact, the king remained 'seigneur naturel' of the French and the relations between government and governed were conceived in the form of a feudal obligation. Feudal law remained a powerful instrument for the demonstration of superiority in the sixteenth century.[9] By the fifteenth century, the king was also 'seigneur souverain' and in this sense the notion of sovereignty had already been worked out by the glossators of the thirteenth century. An *ordonnance* of 1304 had referred to the 'plenitude de la puissance royale'. It was during the fourteenth and fifteenth centuries that the concept of sovereignty was disseminated in the course of speculation about the king's legislative powers and how far the power to initiate legislation extended beyond that of the purely positive law. The sixteenth century saw the idea of the 'marks of sovereignty', which defined the authority of the king, above all in military command and legislative power.[10] Gradually, the concept of the crown as an abstract entity, a *dignitas*, took shape. Crucially, however, French political thought tended strictly to the view that, once raised to the throne, the private person of the king was annihilated or subsumed in the royal. Ernst Kantorowicz, in his influential discussion of the idea of the 'king's two bodies', argued that it was virtually absent from continental political theory. This may be accepted in the strict terms of the distinction between the physical body supposedly within the political body of the king in English theory, but there was no single orthodoxy and much cranky theorising. The royalist Gallican Charles de Grassailles wrote in 1538 that the king of France had 'two guardian angels, one by reason of his private person, the other by reason of his royal dignity'. For the more substantial Charles Dumoulin in the mid-sixteenth century, there were in the king 'two persons': 'the intellectual, which is the majesty and dignity including the Republic', while the 'private person' merely acted as the instrument of this. A. Boureau has pointed out, in a salutary work on the notion of the king's 'sacred body', that the idea of duality must be regarded as effectively an aesthetic 'fiction' which provided an elegant argument but was not in reality widely believed. However, the main point is that the idea of the crown as a *dignitas* was not in France separated from the person of the king.[11]

In another doctrine dating from the early Middle Ages, the 'mystical' body of the king gave rise to the idea of the king on earth as the *Imago deitatis*. Even in the early sixteenth century, the prosecutor in marshal de Gié's trial for treason in 1504, invoked the commentary of Baldus: 'the prince is God incorporate for the subjects of his kingdom. He must be honoured above all earthly matters of the kingdom; for, as God is worshipped in heaven so the prince is worshipped on earth because he is proconsul of God almighty.' Ronsard could write in 1555: 'In short, the king of the French is a great God'; and in the reign of Henri III: 'Alone among humans he assumes the venerable and redoubtable image of God: He is His mirror'. What has been called the *Christomimesis* of medieval kingship, the picturing of the king as a sort of Christ-figure, is thus still a lively idea in the sixteenth century.[12]

All this had taken shape partly through the practical exercise of power, what Boureau calls 'its own economic-political logic'. Thus, by the fifteenth century, the 'crown' is virtually synonymous with what was to be the concept of the 'state'. This is clear enough from Machiavelli's usage 'le cose della corona e stato di Francia'. Commynes and Seyssel in the late fifteenth and early sixteenth centuries were the first French writers to use the word *état* in its modern sense of the governing institution, adapted from the common medieval usage *status regis et regni*. The idea behind the 'state' was present by the fifteenth century but expressed up to that time by the term *respublica* or 'the crown'.[13] This, allied to the idea of public law (the development of the doctrine of *cas royaux* and *cas privilégiés* for instance) and utilisation of canon law, generated the idea of public authority as non-patrimonial. H. H. Rowen's concept of 'proprietary dynasticism' in the early modern period, a view which stressed the continuing function of the king during the Absolute Monarchy as supreme landowner, is thus theoretically questionable.[14] It was in the late fifteenth century, too, that a dictum, ultimately biblical and canonist in origin, 'One God, one faith, one baptism', began to take on a new incarnation. At the duke of Bourbon's trial in 1461, the king's *avocat* declared: 'In this kingdom there is but one king, one crown, one sovereignty'; Louis XI himself notably called for 'une loy, ung poix et une monnoie' and at the start of the sixteenth century a painting of the coronation of Louis XII proclaimed 'Ung Dieu, Ung Roi, Une Foi', a device repeated for the entry of Francis I into Boulogne and regarded as a standard heraldic device in Paris by the mid-sixteenth century. The dualities God/king: faith/law were to become commonplaces of the rhetoric of Absolute Monarchy.[15]

Hand in hand with these developments went changes in the conception of the king of France as emperor in his kingdom. The principle was present in France by the thirteenth century and constantly invoked in the fifteenth and sixteenth. However, it was from the late fifteenth that it became elaborated, alongside the transition from *Rex francorum* to *roi de France*. It was Charles VIII's invasion of Italy and the accompanying propaganda that gave powerful impetus to all this. For the French monarchy, the emperor in Germany was already just another monarch without ecumenical pretensions. In the Calais negotiations of 1521, cardinal Duprat forthrightly rejected Charles V's claims that as emperor, he was in a special position and could be no man's vassal: 'the empire and the kingdom of France have nothing in common and the idea is beyond all reason.'[16] Grandiloquent claims were normal, stemming partly from the legal dictum of the king as emperor in his own kingdom, partly from the propaganda of the period. In the early sixteenth century, Jean Thenaud wrote of the 'most serene king and emperor of the sacred gallic monarchy'; Charles de Grassailles, loyal 'royal Gallicanist', called the king of France vicar of Christ in his kingdom, and for Symphorien Champier, the title of *Rex Gallorum* given by him to the king of France deliberately laid claim to the inheritance of Charlemagne.[17] The prevalent concept of the four Empires posed a succession from Assyria, Persia, Greece to Rome. Others actually claimed that the succession of empires went from Macedonia to Rome, Greece and then France. This *translatio imperii* was meant to complement the voguish idea of *translatio studii*.[18] For one of the greatest protagonists of Gallicanism, Charles Dumoulin, it was the king's role as successor to Charlemagne, himself successor by 'translation' of the Roman emperors, that gave him the plenitude of imperial power and also the right, not only to govern the church and appoint to benefices, but also to reform it. His argument was historical and, as has already been seen, a profoundly national one.[19]

Charles VIII's propagandists had made great use of the idea of the king as successor to the Byzantine emperors through his supposed transaction with the heir of the last emperor, Andreas Palaeologus. As late as 1532, a French diplomat claimed that an expedition to the east was planned as his master was rightfully emperor of Constantinople. However, the conventional wisdom was perhaps best summed up by Jean du Tillet; although the 1566 presentation copy to Charles IX of his great work showed Charles VIII with the imperial crown which had become embedded in royal imagery by that time, of the imperial title itself he could write: 'it is not more eminent than that of king, which sounds better and sweeter'. In this sense he was at one with Dumoulin's conviction that French traditions stemmed from Charlemagne as king of the French rather than as Roman Emperor and that the contemporary Empire of Charles V was a lesser and later creation than the kingdom of the Franks. Henri II, who consistently stressed his imperial pretensions in public imagery from 1550, took on the position of 'defender of German liberties' in 1551.[20]

Jacques Krynen has shown how the doctrine of the *rex christianissimus* weakened the right of resistance, emphasised the imperial status of the king and gave him authority over the Gallican church. This was despite the presence of subversive concepts like *quod omnes tangit* and the practical will of jurists, especially of the Parlement, to exercise a degree of surveillance over the exercise of royal power.[21] All this leads to the conclusion that the French monarchy was already Absolutist in doctrine by the fifteenth century.

It would, however, be a mistake to suppose that there was ever a monolithic doctrine of political power in early modern France.

There was much scope for differences of emphasis on the nature of the king's absolute power, the 'regime of the king's good pleasure' associated with the period from the reign of Louis XI. Philippe Pot's argument in the Estates-General of 1484 that, in the event of a royal minority, sovereign power reverted to the people and 'by the people I mean all the subjects of the crown of whatever rank', although it sounds radical is in fact grounded on a well-established Roman law-based theory of ascending sovereignty. It also had the practical political effect of challenging the pretensions of the princes of the blood.[22] Within the Parlement of Paris, for instance, the lawyers in 1491 could entertain the idea of an *avocat* that the king's power 'is not subject to opinions', while in 1489 it had claimed the role of a senate like that of ancient Rome 'of which the emperor was a member and the head'.[23] This idea had been in circulation among the Parisian lawyers by the early fifteenth century.

Claude de Seyssel in the *Monarchie de France* of 1515–19 wrote specifically of the limits to absolute power, noting that the Parlements had been created 'to the end of restraining the absolute power which kings would use'.[24] Seyssel, as is well known, categorised the limits on power in terms of the three types of law: divine law, the rules of natural justice and the accumulated legislation of the kingdom (religion, justice and police). However, contemporaries selected these ideal qualities of restraint according to their taste. Francis I in a speech to the Parlement in 1515 declared: 'the government of a kingdom consists of three things: firstly in force, secondly in the matters of finance and thirdly in justice.' President Charles Guillart in the famous *lit de justice* of July 1527 could use the same concepts in a very different way. He underlined religion, justice and force, making it clear that, without force there could be no justice and therefore no 'tranquility of peoples'. However, since the force had to be paid for by the people's taxes, it was the duty of the king to guard them from the oppression of those for whom they paid. The words echo almost exactly the 1498 declaration of president of the Parlement Courthardi that it was 'strange that the said men-at-arms, who are supported by money paid by the people to defend them' nevertheless oppress them.[25]

An 'official' view of the purposes of legitimate rule may be found in a lengthy and extraordinary preamble to an *ordonnance*

issued in September 1523 for the suppression of military disorder:
'between the kings of France and their subjects', it declared,
'there has always been the greatest linking and conjunction of
true love of any other Christian monarchy.' The king recalled that
he had been called by God:

> in the flower of our age, as one of his principal ministers, to
> the rule, government and administration of this noble and
> worthy kingdom and crown of France, divinely and miracu-
> lously instituted ... for the moderation, direction, guidance and
> protection of all the estates of the same and especially for the
> preservation, support and defence of the common and popular
> estate, which is the weakest, humblest, lowest and least knowl-
> edgeable of all the other estates and consequently the easiest to
> oppress.

What was the purpose of this calling? The maintenance of the
love for their prince of a people ever marked by a humble and
gracious obsequiousness by the assurance of justice and peace:
justice, fairly and evenly administered, allowed the 'bon homme'
to live in security and had been assured by 'fine ordonnances';
peace had been secured through treaties and marriage alliances
with Christian princes. All this, however, had excited the enmity
and malice of other rulers, who had waged war against the king
and from which all evils flowed.[26] This florid and even oily language conveys the full flowering of a paternalism that was already
part of the repertory of monarchical rhetoric in the fifteenth
century. Pierre Choisnet's semi-official *Rosier des guerres* of 1481–2
had claimed that the obedience of the subjects was earned by
kings who reigned in justice and that the pillars of government
were 'justice, the respect of the people and the mutual love
between the king and his subjects'. Chancellor Duprat in his
speech to the 1517 Assembly had declared that 'the *police* and
good administration of the public weal consists in ensuring the
tranquility, peace and wealth of the subjects'.[27]

   Some scholars of political thought in the period insist on the
reinforcement of the 'Absolutist' tendencies of the French monarchy under Francis I, based on both Roman and canon law, and
note 'an irreversible evolution towards an authoritarian exercise
of power'. The key works are usually regarded as Guillaume

Budé's *De Asse* of 1515, which became a celebration of the new reign, and his *Institution du prince* of 1519, with its appeal to the Platonic ideal of the philosopher ruler transmitted through Erasmian humanism. The researches of humanist philologists also brought to the fore new interpretations of key texts such as that by Lefèvre d'Etaples of Romans XIII (1512): 'the powers that be are ordained of God.' In 1517, Erasmus declared in his *Paraphrase* of Romans: 'order is the foundation of the state.'[28] From this perspective, Claude de Seyssel's ideas can be made to seem obsolete, with their insistence that it was impossible to envisage a monarchy both absolute and limited at the same time. Such ideas were not at the end of their life, however. A century later, Charles Loyseau, in a period when 'mixed monarchy' was still under discussion, could still envisage a form of 'limited absolutism'. We must distinguish between Absolutism as a political theory, as a *de jure* political system and as a *de facto* practice.[29] Roland Mousnier long ago sought to show that Absolutism was indeed a constitutional system to be differentiated from despotism.

Chancellor Duprat's remark to the Parlement in 1518, therefore, that 'we owe obedience to the king and it is not for us to question his commands' should be seen as part of an extended debate on the nature of power rather than a statement of fact.[30] J. L. Bourgeon has recently drawn attention to what he calls the continuing guerrilla war between the Parlement of Paris and the crown during the sixteenth century, one indeed that was not settled by Francis I's authoritarian pronouncements in 1527. The opposition of the Parlement to the policies of the first ten years of Francis I was generated primarily by the determination of the magistrates, who were in essence the king's councillors, to retain their role at the centre of the judicial system, not by any desire to impose 'bridles' on the crown. They were profoundly shaped by the idea of the king as first and foremost a dispenser of justice. As a deputy to the Estates-General at Orléans in 1560 declared: 'Justice alone distinguishes kings from tyrants, for both of them have the same power.' The *Parlementaires* were led, therefore, to view the problems of power as essentially moral ones that stemmed from corruption and abuses. The idea of government as a machine susceptible to checks and balances was at this stage quite alien.[31]

It is in this context that Nicholas Henshall's assertion that Absolutism was a 'myth' should be viewed. It is apparent that the existence of the concept of 'absolute power' and the king's acting through his 'full powers and personal action' ('pleine pouvoir et propre mouvement' to use the chancellery executive formula attacked by Estienne Pasquier[32]) was widely understood. Such action indisputably covered the conduct of foreign policy, the command of the army and the rendering of public justice for the common good. In areas where the king exercised authority that impinged on his subjects' private rights, however, there was rather more readiness to argue that a degree of consent had to be sought (greater or lesser in different areas). We may link this to the idea of the king's 'retained' and 'delegated' jurisdiction. Not even Bodin advocated royal power to tax without the consent of the subject, being more concerned with the definition of sovereignty and the clear separation of subject and sovereign. Even the councillors of the Paris Parlement held quite contradictory views on the nature of Absolute power. In the Remonstrances the Parlement made to the Regent Louise of Savoy in April 1525 it suggested that, for the king, 'it is not necessary that he often use his absolute power, which is reserved for great and urgent affairs, not for the profit of private persons'. Yet, two years later, in a speech often viewed as challenging many of the king's policies, president Charles Guillart declared the very different emphasis that absolute rule in itself was 'in itself more like brute nature than reason'. Nothing could stop the king using it, but he ought not: 'it is better to use it little or not at all.'[33] There in essence, in the opinion of contemporaries, lies the divergent and paradoxical nature of definitions of Absolutism that have so puzzled historians.

The customary constitution of France was made up of a series of 'fundamental laws'. This term, common only from the sixteenth century, described an extremely fluid yet powerful concept, in effect a supple constitution under which Loyseau in the early seventeenth century could envisage Absolute power limited by divine and natural law as well as the fundamental laws of the state. Ralph Giesey demonstrated how the fundamental laws as understood in the sixteenth century, an amalgam of Roman, canon, feudal and customary law, came into being in a haphazard way by the association of annointed kings with a specific *lignée* in early Capetian times. They then developed during the crisis over the succession in the early fourteenth century. The famous Salic law, *de alodis*, was not widely commented on until the fifteenth century but its principle was enacted through the remarkably smooth transmission of the crown from one branch of the royal house to another in 1498 and 1515. In 1483, Louis d'Orléans had been declared 'second person of this kingdom'. François d'Angoulême received the same title in 1507 as did Charles d'Alençon, the heir presumptive in 1515. The writings of Seyssel, Charles Dumoulin's *Coutumes de Paris* of 1539 and the work of Jean Bodin brought to fruition a style of thinking on the constitution which underlined the need for legitimacy and the title of a particular blood line to the throne. A major stage was reached during the disputes at the time of Henri II's coronation over the status of 'princes of the blood' and their claim to pre-eminence, hitherto not formally recognised, over peers of the realm. The implication here was that membership of the royal *lignée* should override all other considerations. The arguments then advanced by the duke of Montpensier elevated the dynastic principle at a time when there had been a marked contraction in the number of male Capetian princes from at least 23 in 1450 to only 10 in 1550. However, not until 1576 was the issue finally settled in favour of the princes of the blood.[34]

The early modern state needed both finance and legitimacy. Without money it was hamstrung but without legitimacy it could not sustain its ideological supremacy. Such legitimacy could be sought in other realms by acceptance of the *quod omnes tangit* principle and the interaction with representative assemblies or it could be generated by the appeal to Roman law principles, the 'fundamental law' of legitimate kingship and the cultivation of the public imagery of supremacy in ceremonial. On balance, the French monarchy took the latter road, and also relied on symbolic messages in order to reinforce its legitimacy. It was P.E. Schramm, in a major study of monarchy, who showed that to understand it, we have to look at both the 'symbols of power' like crowns, sceptres and vestments as well as 'gestures' by which rulers communicated what they thought themselves to be and what their subjects expected of them. Much of the royal regalia, like the hand of justice, the sceptre of Charles V and the original coronation crown (last used in 1574), remained in use for centuries. (It is worth noting that an orb, with its ecumenical claims, was never part of the royal regalia in France, though sometimes used by artists and extensively in Henri II's visual propaganda.) Among the most striking changes in monarchical imagery were the imperial salutations given to Charles VIII in Lucca, Siena and Florence in 1494 and the adoption by some artists of the closed or arched crown in portraits of him. Such a crown had been adopted by the English monarchy in the late fourteenth century and by the kings of Bohemia and Hungary much earlier. France, in contrast, retained until 1774 its veneration for the lily-ornamented open diadem with a high crimson bonnet. However, it could not stand aside as the *reges simplices*, as they were known, upgraded their regalia. The imperial crown quickly established itself in the formal imagery of the monarchy firstly at the entry of Louis XII into Paris, then for the first time on a public monument with the tomb commissioned by Louis XII for his predecessor, and finally under Francis I. It triumphed when the new personal crown made for Henri II's coronation in 1547 was of the arched imperial type and the new royal seal represented this. Most coronation ornaments were held by the abbey of Saint-Denis or the cathedral of Rheims but in 1530 Francis I created the nucleus of the 'crown jewels' of France as an inalienable collection to be passed on to his successors.[35]

Ceremonial and ritual were an area of public life characterised by such an acute historian as Gaston Zeller in 1948 as 'only of picturesque and anecdotal interest'.[36] Much of the most stimulating research of the last generation on this period has been done, under the influence of the American historian Ralph Giesey and his followers, on precisely this field of public ritual and its message. The original impetus was Kantorowicz's idea of the 'king's two bodies' which, though absent in theory from France, seemed to Giesey to suffuse ceremonies like the royal funeral. Collectively, their work amounts to a significant shift in focus on the theory of the monarchy in France, particularly for the period of the Renaissance, from systematic legal discussion to the interaction between rulers and their subjects. However, this 'ceremonialist' argument should not encourage the view that the whole justification of French monarchy converged exclusively on ritual. Rather, ritual should be seen as an important adjunct to the manipulation of power.

Certain rituals, like the *sacre*, were of great antiquity, of course. The latter was the supreme act of inauguration down to the end of the legitimist monarchy in 1830 and contained within it both the sacred act of anointing – always the central feature of the French coronation ceremony – and the oath, with its constitutional implications.[37] The latter were much diminished with the fifteenth century development of the idea of the kingship as a *dignitas*. There is no reason to suppose that monarchs like Francis I regarded their authority as stemming in any real sense from their coronation, but rather from the feudal dictum, 'le mort saisit le vif'. As Jean Bodin put it, 'the king is no less a king without crowning or consecration'. However, the printed coronation order of 1515 presented the king as no longer a pure layman by his anointing, priestly vestments and access to the chalice. This accords with the tendency to replace the *sacre*'s constitutional significance with the idea that it conveyed God's blessing on the dynasty. There was some 'invention of tradition' even in the fifteenth and sixteenth centuries. The kings of the Renaissance period always proceeded rapidly to their coronation but remained in the background of public events until it had been accomplished.[38] The ceremony of the royal pardon and releasing of doves was a late sixteenth- and early seventeenth-century invention, while the *sacre* itself had not entirely lost its constitutional significance (as was the case perhaps from the seventeenth century) and could also be invested with a rich seam of ritual befitting a monarchy increasingly preoccupied by public grandeur and grandiloquent claims. The coronation oath by the end of the fifteenth century included two separate promises: to maintain the privileges of the church and the oath 'to the kingdom' to maintain peace and justice and root out heresy.

The composition of an *ordo* for Henri II in 1547 from earlier texts led to the embedding of the archaic elective idea by the introduction of the *acclamatio* between the two oaths, a device fraught with implications when the elective principle came back into debate in the second half of the century. The inalienability of the kingdom, much discussed in the fifteenth century, was underlined by Louis XII's coronation oath in 1498, a point stressed by a specific royal *ordonnance* of 1517 that revoked alienations of the domain (in the kingdom as a whole rather than the narrower royal domain).[39]

Henri II's coronation was innovative in a number of other ways. One was the bestowal of the ring, announced in Godefroy's description as symbolic of the marriage of the king and the kingdom, an image first invoked for the second coronation of Anne of Brittany in 1504, dwelt on in a speech by the president at the *Lit de justice* of December 1527 and theoretically developed by Charles de Grassailles in 1538. The marriage of the king and the kingdom, an old idea originally ecclesiatical in origin, took on a new charge in the sixteenth century. It reinforced the ideas of kingship as a *dignitas* and the inalienability of the royal domain. In 1523, a Parlement lawyer had put it thus: the domain, 'because it is the dowry that the commonwealth brings to the king her spouse *in matrimonio politico*', can belong to the king alone. Robert Descimon has even suggested that it performed the same function in France as the idea of the 'king's two bodies' in England.[40] Another innovation of 1547 was the distribution of gold and silver 'jetons' to the people after the crowning, a gesture of largesse evidently of Byzantine origin, creating a further link to imperial traditions. Again, this had already been used for the coronation of queen Claude under Francis I. Finally, there was the institution of the *offrande* by the king.[41] After the *sacre* the king proceeded by long tradition to inaugurate his mystical powers to heal scrofula at a special ceremony at the shrine of Saint-Marcoul at Corbeny, a rite which retained its full vitality throughout the sixteenth century.[42]

The liveliness of traditions is particularly the case in the development from 1422 of the royal funeral ceremony, with its complex panoply of the 'living' effigy of the dead king, first used for the funeral of Charles VI in 1422. As Giesey has so clearly shown, the culmination of all this was the funeral of Francis I in 1547, with the elaboration of the service offered to the king's funeral effigy in his chamber and the subsequent magnificent if sombre procession through Paris to Saint-Denis. Yet the reasons for this development are not easy to discern. In 1547, there were practical advantages in spinning out the old king's funeral in order to effect sweeping changes in the political elite behind the scenes and checkmate the leading figures of the old court. Alain Boureau has provided a major reinterpretation of this ritual that stresses the political context and also the inventiveness of those who planned the ceremonies. The custom of the new king remaining in retirement during the funeral is a case in point. Giesey argues that the reason for this was the unease still felt in the early sixteenth century as a memory of the times when there had been an extended interval between the death of one king and the coronation of a new one. The interval was thus acted out despite the doctrine of 'le mort saisit le vif'. Giesey has argued that in the fifteenth century the new monarch was in some sense inaugurated when, at the burial of his predecessor, the latter's officers cast their staffs of office into the grave and the title of the new king, hitherto unmentioned, was proclaimed. Yet this very 'ritual' was relatively new. It was generated by the special circumstances which had prevented Charles VII, Louis XI and Charles VIII from attending and the political problems which encouraged Louis XII to keep away. By the reign of Francis I this had come to seem an immemorial custom. The immense expense and complexity of the 1498 funeral ceremony, which came to be viewed as the model, was provoked by the political determination of *grand écuyer* Pierre d'Urfé to demonstrate the solidarity of the old king's household and an unspoken warning to Louis XII not to repeat the mistake made by Louis XI in 1461 of dismissing too many of his predecessor's servants.[43]

By 1547, the passion for ceremony and its proper organisation began to take over and accept all this as immemorial custom. Behind the ceremonial, Giesey argues, lay the powerful if unspoken concept of the 'king's two bodies' and the idea that, though the physical body of the king may die, yet kingship is eternal. It was in the early sixteenth century that the proclamation: 'Le roi est mort, vive le roi!' became part of the royal funeral ceremony.[44] It is certainly the case that the masters of ceremonies of the Renaissance courts were more interested in acting out ideas than their predecessors or successors. The ancient coronation ceremony had incorporated an element of the initiation into knighthood by a vigil and the raising of the monarch from his bed on the morning of the *sacre*. Charles VIII, Francis I and Henri II were all greeted in this way. But not until the *sacre* of Charles IX in 1561 was the curious device of the summoning of the 'sleeping king' before his coronation used to demonstrate the distinction between the physical and the mystical body of the king and also to stress the fact that the king was 'God given' even before his coronation. In 1610, the ceremony was further elaborated for Louis XIII.[45]

The concrete symbol of a royal 'religion', if it can be so called, was the new mortuary chapel of the Valois kings at Saint-Denis with its sumptuous monuments which far outstripped those of the kings down to the late fifteenth century, in terms of architectural grandeur as well as decorative significance. The royal necropolis had first been organised in the middle of the thirteenth century as a symbol of the claims of the Capetians to be the true heirs of Charlemagne. Only Philip I, Louis VII and Louis XI (who was devoted to Notre-Dame de Cléry and generally indifferent to traditions) were not interred there. Charles VIII's tomb, by Guido Mazzoni of Modena, displayed a *priant* figure of the king in life prominently set facing the high altar, the first royal tomb at Saint-Denis to do so, although Louis XI was shown as a *priant* figure before the Virgin at Cléry. However, it was the tomb commissioned by Francis I for Louis XII and finished in 1531 that for the first time displayed the juxtaposition of the *transi* in death agony with the *priant* figure (the monarch in full state). Moreover, despite a certain doubt over their secular or religious meaning, there is no doubt that the reliefs on the royal tombs from Louis XII to Henri II showed the kings as victorious *imperatores* in the Italian wars. Catherine de Medici commissioned the domed chapel by Primaticcio to be built out of the north transept of the abbey in 1559, though it was not ready to receive the tombs until 1594. The neglect of the Bourbon dynasty to complete it and its demolition in 1719 are a telling commentary on changing attitudes to the royal funeral in the seventeenth century.[46]

Largely secular occasions, such as the entry ceremonial, when the king first formally visited one of his great cities, saw a remarkable evolution from the late fifteenth century. The essence of such ceremonies had, until that time, served the purpose of an oath by the citizenry in exchange for the king's formal promise to observe their privileges. The visual imagery tended to stress the local and the particular. Even in the early sixteenth century, such events gave an opportunity to the *bourgeois* to explain, in complex circumlocutions of course, what they expected of a king, while allowing them to glory in their own traditions. Even in the mid-sixteenth century, for a proud and independently-minded city like Toulouse somewhat distanced from the centre of power, the accent was still upon the history and traditions of the city rather than providing a theatre for the glory of the king. When the *bourgeois* of Le Puy learned in 1533 that the king and his court were planning to visit their shrine, the chronicler Etienne de Médicis recorded an earlier visit, no less than that of Julius Caesar to the temple of Apollo at Polignac, and spelled out the region's claims to fame: the resistance to Julius Caesar of the Arverni. Médicis then recorded how the town fell to in setting up the necessary tableaux. The speech by the judge in the *bailliage*, welcoming the 'sovereign prince, king and Emperor, of whom the sun in its course since the creation never saw the equal' could nevertheless note the town's 'peu de possibilité' and hoped its loyalty would excuse its inability in other ways.[47] The opportunity to profit from the occasion of the king's oath to the privileges, in order to request concessions, was great. This, however, required considerable investment in the splendour of the occasion, that was also a matter of competition between the regional towns. The council of Nîmes voted 10,000 *lt.*, nearly three times its annual budget, to pay for the event.[48]

In the north, the change to ceremonial centred on the king came rather earlier but in fifteenth-century Paris it was still popularly believed that an important aspect of the ceremony was the king's oath 'that he would do loyally and well all that a king should'. A rhymed account of Charles VIII's entry had him swearing to sustain all estates and maintain justice. Louis XII promised in 1498 'that he would maintain the nobles, also the farmers, as well as the merchants in their good laws and old customs, that he would do justice to the least as well as to the great and would protect his peoples from their enemies.'[49]

From the fifteenth century it is clear that city councils and private persons were anxious to keep records of these great occasions and copied their programmes out in detail. From the entry of Charles VIII into Rouen in 1485 and that of Anne of Brittany into Paris in 1492, the events were printed in the form of relations. The earliest illustrated relations were manuscripts but from 1533 the printed versions also began to have illustrations. (Oddly enough, France failed until the later sixteenth century to see the development of separate illustrated news sheets of the sort that developed in Germany, Italy and the Netherlands.[50]) The emotional and visual charge of these ceremonies quickly emerges from a reading of them. Francis I's arrival at Le Puy in 1533 was, for that little town, an event of great significance for the collective life of the community, from the opening speeches of welcome through the procession of the population before the king's *séjour d'honneur* to the presentation of the keys and the king's formal ride through the town. After this, he inspected its buildings and fortifications, his route marked at intervals by edifying texts from the Psalms, then by a scaffold with seven liberal arts proclaiming the king as learned prince. The whole day testified to a remarkable effort of imagination and skill.[51]

If we consider Francis I's entries into Lyon in 1515 and Rouen in 1517 and Henri II's entries into Lyon in 1548, Paris in 1549 and Rouen in 1550 we see the gradual infiltration of classical themes. At Lyon, both biblical and classical themes appeared to proclaim both the city's loyalty and the king's rights to Milan.[52] The 1517 entry into Rouen, staged at a moment of expansionism and optimism, utilised associations with the myth of the Golden Age and in particular linked the king to the 'marvellous boy' of Virgil's fourth *Eclogue*, whose birth was to usher in the Golden Age under the aegis of Astraea. The fourth and culminating *tableau* staged for the city proclaimed 'Iam nova progenies celo demittur alto' ('And now a new life comes down from high heaven').[53] This imagery played on the Christian and imperial implications usually read into the story. Curiously, medieval entry tableaux at Paris had also portrayed the king as a child, possibly associating him with the infant Jesus, possibly also stressing the need for him to take counsel.[54] By the sixteenth century, such imagery, anchored in the idea of mutual obligations, was being submerged. When Henri II entered Rouen in 1550, though the figure of the Golden Age reappeared atop a triumphal arch, the emphasis was different. Now the king's martial exploits in Scotland and Boulogne were central, the principal motifs conveyed by a Roman triumph in three elaborate chariots, each with a message. The third held a lifesize statue of the enthroned king and, above his head, the figure of Fortune holding an imperial crown 'to declare that the sovereign majesty of the kings of France is held only of God'.[55] The Rouen festivities were perhaps most notable for the 50 Brazilian Indians, Topinambous and Tabagerres, brought by local merchants from the New World, who were displayed in a 'native' village specially erected and encouraged to embark on a 'tribal' war. It may be suspected that this appealed much more than the classical conceits which would have been fully comprehensible to only a tiny minority. We know, for instance, that at Rouen in 1550 the imperial ambassador was utterly bemused and got most of the meaning wrong. Much of the detail would probably have been lost on the king himself.[56]

The biblical and historical tableaux on temporary stages displayed at certain points in royal *entrées* took a central place in the acting out of political and social messages. Down to the 1530s, there remained a religious element in that the analogy between the king's coming and Christ's epiphany was implicit in the cries of 'Noël!' that greeted him. Generally, though, except in great ceremonies like the *sacre* and the funeral, after 1500 the emphasis on the Bible withers in favour of new motifs drawn from pagan classical sources: the king as Gallic Hercules, for instance. In sharp contrast to the entry of Charles VIII into Paris in 1483, of the seven *tableaux* mounted for the entry of Louis XII in 1498, only one had a biblical theme. A new visual vocabulary was also employed to depict the king and, through him, the state. The medieval stages gave away increasingly to triumphal arches, the *tableaux vivants* to sculptures. In these sumptuous ceremonies, the *joyeuse entrée* of the Middle Ages had been transformed into a quasi-imperial *adventus*, the *entrée royale*, which stressed also the divine origins of monarchy and God's design.[57] This was part of a process by which the inherited rituals of medieval monarchy were transformed into what can loosely be called pageantry designed to emphasise the grandeur of the state. Thus, the lavish entry of Henri II into Paris shifted the emphasis from popular participation to royal grandeur and freely employed classical motifs in triumphal arches to do so.[58] An important aspect of this change was that, from the fifteenth century, entry ceremonial started to be performed according to a written or rhetorical script, while the more playful aspects of the *tableaux* along the streets were brought under control. For Mary Tudor's entry into Paris as queen in 1514, the entire event was scripted by one man, the poet Pierre Gringore, with the objective of stressing the benefits of Louis XII's foreign policy and the virtues of peace.[59] Previously, they had conveyed their meaning of mutual relations between king and people entirely by unscripted gesture. This was perhaps the main reason for the development of printed programmes or descriptions spelling out the script and its message in lavish detail for a wide audience.

At Paris, there was a traditional processional route from the reception before the Saint-Denis gate, down the rue Saint-Denis to the Châtelet and across the river to the cathedral. There the king was received by the clergy along the lines of a traditional clerical *joyeuse entrée* and swore to maintain their privileges. The day usually ended with a quite separate banquet in the great hall of the *palais*. Louis XI, in refusing to renew his father's officers on his accession, deprived the Parlement and civic officials of a formal place at his entry. Subsequent monarchs chose not to do this and the magistrates of Paris always played a significant role thereafter in the ceremonies designed to remind the king of his duty to preserve justice and their privileges.[60] Earlier tradition had the great sword of state, assumed by the king at the *sacre*, borne before the king, who would be dressed in a lily-strewn blue mantle. From the late fifteenth century, the king assumed a more martial aspect, riding in armour and with a lily-crowned helmet borne before him to symbolise imperial authority. Though Henri II chose to cultivate a startling effect at Lyon in 1550 by appearing in black velvet edged with silver and jewels, at Paris in 1549 he had entered the city in extraordinarily lavish armour which gave him the appearance of a conquering Roman emperor. Charles VIII and Louis XII abandoned the sword of state for their entries, although Francis I reintroduced it in 1515, and always the great seal, symbolising the king as fount of justice, was borne in a casket on a horse immediately before the king. Finally, the canopy beneath which the king processed was a special attribute that drew attention specifically to the sacred character of the monarch, since it resembled the canopy of the sacrament.[61]

As the late fifteenth and sixteenth centuries saw such a fertile period of elaboration in state ritual, it should not be too surprising that one of the most characteristic state ceremonies of the Ancien Regime monarchy in its Absolutist phase, the *lit de justice*, with the king enthroned as supreme justiciar, came to fruition at that time. It is here above all that ritual, ceremony and constitutional thinking intertwine. The child king Charles VIII resumed in 1484 the practice, in abeyance since 1413, of holding formal sessions of the Parlement of Paris. In the fourteenth century such sessions had seen the king 'in his royal majesty' or 'magnificence' as the registers put it, seated on a raised canopied dais, the *lit de justice*[62] at the apex of the diamond shaped *grand-chambre*, lay and ecclesiastical peers at his side. This presaged the vigorous revival of the practice of royal sessions in the subsequent generation, at a time when the original meaning of the term *lit de justice* had been lost and commentators began to imagine that was the name of the session itself. The *lit* had come to symbolise judicial monarchy but the revival of the royal session (5 under Charles VIII, 7 under Louis XII, 6 under Francis I) did not immediately see a return to the use of the term *lit de justice* to describe the state throne. Suitably, the *grand-chambre* of the Parlement was sumptuously redecorated and gilded under Louis XII in a way that minimised the decorative distinction between the chamber itself and the canopied throne.

Whether, as Sarah Hanley has argued, the *lit de justice* had always been understood by the clerks of the Parlement to apply only to the 'imperial throne' (to use Christine de Pisan's term) on which the king sat and that the two meetings held by Francis in July and December 1527 amounted to a new kind of constitutional assembly is at best debatable. She argues that these meetings should strictly be marked off from the revived practice of royal sessions and that at this stage the *lit* should not be regarded as a weapon of Absolutist power since it was convoked solely for great matters of constitutional importance connected with the conflict between the king of France and the emperor. The meeting of July 1527, with the king 'holding his *lit de justice* in the parquet of the Parlement' was, in Hanley's view, convoked for the posthumous trial of the constable of Bourbon for treason and concerned the inalienability of the royal domain. The king held other meetings of this type in December 1527 to annul the treaty of Madrid and in January 1537 to declare Charles V deprived of Artois and Flanders. The common aspect of all these meetings was that they concerned major aspects of the public law of the monarchy and thus had a great deal to do with the final stage by which the fundamental laws took shape. Hanley argues that the crown was consciously creating a new ritual by likening these meetings to a consultative assembly quite different from the normal judicial business of royal *séances*.[63] However, as Robert Knecht has now made clear, the main thrust of the meeting of July 1527 was to deal with the accumulating jurisdictional quarrels between his council and the Parlement, while the meeting of December 1527 is better described as an Assembly of Notables.

Constitutional terminology throughout this period is notoriously imprecise and it is highly likely that some of the royal sessions of the fourteenth and fifteenth centuries were regarded as especially important and called by some *lits de justice*. Moreover, Hanley's argument that there were no such meetings again until the early seventeenth century is no longer secure.[64]

In Hanley's complex discussion of the inevitably conflicting interpretations of these events, it becomes apparent that the definition of certain kinds of royal session became a weapon in the battle between the crown and Parlement over the definition of the latter's political independence, a battle discussed cogently by J. Bourgeon. Both sides wished to use the history of the Parlement for their own ends. Naturally, in view of the four-teenth-century usage, it was possible to construct different histories. Henri II, who held a number of royal sessions but no *lits de justice*, held a splendid *séance* in July 1549 in which chancellor Olivier adumbrated in a lengthy speech a controversial view of the Parlement's function as purely judicial, except when constituted as a court of peers.[65] By this stage, the clerks of the Parlement wanted to view the *lit de justice* as the revival of practice going back to the fourteenth century. Eventually these views coalesced in a reinterpretation of the constitutional history of France by *greffier* Jean du Tillet in the middle of the sixteenth century and first published posthumously in 1577.[66] This in turn fuelled a lively debate on the nature of the constitution.

The use made of the image of the *lit de justice* as a visual symbol for royal justice as a whole draws attention to the importance of visual imagery in the presentation of political and social concepts. The king's appearance in majesty in the Parlement or, very rarely, above the choir at Rheims during the *sacre*, were highly theatrical occasions. The state, as embodied by the monarch, had to appear in a definite context. As will be shown in chapter 2, the king who was 'emperor in his kingdom' lived in relatively simple terms within his own household, open to access by all and sundry, living in the midst of a growing crowd of people. Despite a certain move towards privacy under Francis I, with the private staircase giving access to the park or garden, and the innovation of the royal *antichambre* under Henri II, the royal apartments were effectively public rooms. It was only on special occasions of the kind already discussed that the full 'majesty' of the sovereign was fully displayed but the monarchy in this period lacked impressive stages. One of the most well-known occasions of this kind was the *salle de fête* set up in the courtyard of the Bastille in December 1518 for the reception of an English embassy and celebration of the recent treaty with England for the return of Tournai. Here a temporary *salle* beneath an azure cloth scattered with stars and signs of the zodiac had the king and his sister seated on a high dais at the culmination of a great theatrical space. The king himself appeared in an extraordinary brilliant white satin robe covered with devices of clocks and compasses that were probably meant to convey his wisdom but also to intrigue his guests.[67] The great royal *salles* of the Renaissance built at the Louvre at the end of Francis I's reign or at Fontainebleau under Henri II were, however, noticeably smaller than the great halls of medieval ducal castles like Montargis, Bourges and Coucy. On the occasion of royal entry ceremonial such as that at Rouen in 1550, a special royal *loge* was constructed where the king could appear before and above his subjects to witness their presentations.[68]

The contrast between the physically unimposing kings of the senior branches of the Valois house from Charles VII to Louis XII and the vigorous stature of Francis I has often been made. The first king of the Angoulême branch seemed made for the visual imagery with which he was endowed from the striking of the 1512 commemorative medal *Maximus Franciscus Francorum Dux*, showing him in profile crowned with a laurel wreath. The contrast with traditional royal French iconography, showing the king in full face with all the usual attributes of judicial power, could not have been greater. In fact, in the absence of a developed school of engravers in France, medals and *jetons* proved powerful instruments. The latter, either issued by the council and sovereign courts each year from Francis I's reign in fairly large numbers, or used as largesse at the time of the *sacre*, bore allegorical devices.[69] As for medals, they were destined for a more select audience. Already in the 1460s, Louis XI had a medal struck *à l'italienne* with the message *Concordia et Augusta*, Charles VIII had another in 1495 (*Victoria et Pax*), and Louis XII with *Cominus et eminus* (in close or distant combat), the motto of the Orléans chivalric order of the porcupine, adopted by Louis as his personal badge on the order's disbandment in 1498. Henri II's motto *Donec totum impleat orbem* ('until it fill the whole world') conveyed the idea of ever expanding French power. Devices, used for subtle messages on royal policies, in this way grew out of the late medieval aristocratic penchant for mottoes and the climax of the passion for orders of chivalry in the decades around 1400.[70] Such personal devices could, like Louis XII's porcupine, be gradually introduced on the reverse of new coinage, or, as in the entry ceremony of 1498, displayed in conjunction with the French *cerf volant* and the Visconti serpents, to announce the king's claims to Milan. The portrait medal, increasingly in vogue from the late fifteenth century, gradually prepared the way for the large-scale dissemination of the individual king's likeness, rather than the image of the king 'type'. Louis XII was the first king of France whose profile regularly appeared on the silver coinage, the teston, in imitation of developments a little earlier in Italy; Louis issued such coins as lord of Asti and duke of Milan but this did not happen in France itself until 1514.[71]

Francis I's device of the Salamander, like Louis XII's porcupine the 'house beast' of his family, and motto *Nutrisco et extingo* was deliberately ambiguous, interpreted subsequently as 'I maintain the good and destroy evil'. Yet properly translated it means something like 'I feed from the good fire and put out the evil', behind which lies complex neo-platonic discourse; public imagery was meant in some sense to be an enigmatic 'veil' which would stimulate thought and wonder.[72] The public image of the Renaissance king was in some sense 'invented' by the circle of theologian-*rhétoriqueurs* such as François Desmoulins, Jean Thenaud and André de La Vigne, assembled by Louise of Savoy before Francis I's accession, men high in the confidence of the house of Angoulême and originating from its sphere of influence in the west. Their role was partly to act as prompters of conscience and reflection in the form of a dialogue with the ruling family. Louise of Savoy, Anne of Brittany and queen Claude all had a special devotion to the cult of the Franciscan François de Paule, whose influence had grown in princely circles since his stay in Touraine (1482–1507), and through them a certain mysticism entered into the royal circle. Francis I replaced the collar of shells of the Order of Saint Michael with a gold double *cordelière*, the symbol of Saint Francis and a device already used for Anne of Brittany. The *rhétoriqueurs* also sought to filter and present a form of occult neo-platonism to their patrons which stressed by signs the theme of divine election for the future king Francis I. The ill-fortune of

Louis XII in being unable to father a male heir, the accidents of death which carried off other princes who may have stood in the way, confirmed the predestined succession of the young duke of Valois, whose qualities and hopes were woven into complex allegorical works.[73]

The curious significance of the first day of the first week of the first month (January 1515) was lost neither on Louise of Savoy in her private calendar nor on contemporaries; the theme of new beginnings is echoed in the speech made to the king by a member of the University of Paris just after his accession, explaining the jubilation of that body:

> first because you have come to the crown through right line of succession, secondly, because you have come to the said crown as a young prince of 21 years, a fair prince and the first of your name; thirdly you succeed as a valiant and prudent prince experienced in war; fourthly because you succeed at a time of peace with no danger of sedition or civil war and have begun your reign with mercy and benignity; fifthly because of the great hope of every one to live in peace by means of the great prudence by which your noble person is adorned.[74]

Symbolism was a highly potent form of state propaganda. The *rhétoriqueurs* wove endless verses dissecting the significance of Francis I's name (on the argument that all kings of a new name had been great figures). Some visual symbolism, for instance the great seal showing the king frontally, enthroned with the sceptre and the hand of justice, remained fixed. Other such symbols were constructed for conveying messages at many levels; at various times the phoenix, the Gallic cock and the winged stag (*cerf volant*), a royal image dating from Charles VI, were invoked in the early sixteenth century. The frontispiece attached to the early editions of Robert Gaguin's *Compendium*, for instance, was an extraordinarily compressed pictorial description of the monarchy as it stood around 1500, conveying the ideas of faith and justice, imperial jurisdiction and the status of the peers.[75] Perhaps the most powerful visual symbol was that of the sun, the *Sol Iustitiae*. At the fête of the Bastille in 1518, the sun was placed in the canopy above the king's position. Since the fourteenth century, the monarchy had invoked the image of the sun but only as the symbol of God and Justice. The 1497 portrait of Charles VIII with the imperial crown (BN fr.2228 fo.1) was surmounted by a rayonnant sun. In 1514, however, the programme by the poet Pierre Gringore for the entry of Mary Tudor into Paris used the device of the moon, standing for France, receiving its light from the sun, signifying the king. A speech in the Parlement of Paris in 1527, and then Charles de Grassailles in 1538 (*et dicitur [rex Franciae] secundus sol in orbe terrarum*), developed a serviceable image of royal power as the sun which was taken up by royal propagandists from Henri III to Louis XIV 'but given its real impetus from Charles IX's appearance at a carnival in 1571 dressed as the sun.[76]

Many of the works involved were, of course, highly private (particularly the illustrated presentation copies of manuscripts). The programme of decoration for the gallery of Francis I at Fontainebleau rested in some senses upon a complex game of interpretation open to very few. However, works devised for public consumption, like the programmes for royal entries or fêtes and royal mottoes and coinage, symbols and devices for public buildings, contained highly charged messages. One further form should be borne in mind when considering the reception of ideas on power and the state by the people. Much of what has already been discussed can be situated in the social and intellectual context of an elite. The power and majesty of the monarchy, though, could be communicated and absorbed in more simple and direct ways. The royal symbol of the fleur de lys, with its mystical and religious charge, was attached, of course, to royal castles and palaces. But it could also be used to demonstrate powerfully the identification of sacred and secular power. At the cathedral of Auch under bishop François de Clermont-Lodève, a great window of 1510 placed a huge fleur de lys above the crucifixion. At the cathedral of Albi, redecorated under the aegis of the two bishops Louis I and II d'Amboise between 1474 and 1513, the triumphal procession of Old and New Testament figures applied to the vaults was accompanied by a proliferation of fleurs de lys, stressing the legitimacy conferred by God on the temporal power and the close identification between the church and the state. Moreover, the frescoes of the Last Judgement commissioned at Albi between 1475 and 1480 and those between 1509 and 1513 depicting the coronation of the Virgin, can be read as, for the first, exalting the role of the king as supreme judge on earth and as mirror of the judge of all things, and for the second, as an amalgamation of religious mysticism and the mystic marriage between the king and the kingdom already discussed. The overall glorification of the church as sole means to salvation implicitly glorified the monarchy by which the church was now effectively controlled. The invasion of the fleur de lys image emphasised this.[77]

Even the poetic and artistic competitions of confraternities devoted to the cult of the Virgin played their part in providing a response to or collaborating with royal imagery. In the early sixteenth century, the confraternity of the *Puy Notre-Dame* at Amiens was particularly vibrant, commissioning devotional paintings of the Virgin in the context of the hierarchy of secular rulers and clergy (also in effect collective portraits of the confraternity itself) for the yearly competition in February. This called for poetry based on an annual motto, or *palinod*, in honour of the Virgin, usually a fairly banal line from the Song of Songs. The poem was a *chant royal*, a form ultimately derived from the *trouvère* tradition which ended in an address to the Prince but was actually a prayer to God. Some of the finest paintings (from the years 1518–22) have survived. A strong connection with the monarchy was established by the end of the fifteenth century, for the painting of 1501 on the *palinod*, 'Sacrée ampoule à l'onction royale', was accompanied by two altar pieces, now in the Cluny Museum, showing the coronations of David and of Louis XII. It was the latter which notably proclaimed the dictum: 'Ung Dieu, Ung Roi, Une Foi' (one God, one King, one Faith) already mentioned.

When the court visited Amiens in 1517, Louise of Savoy saw the collection of paintings and her interest stimulated the confraternity to commission a manuscript copy of the entire collection which showed Louise on the presentation page in the same aspect as the mother of Christ in the following paintings. This, too, was the year each *chant royal* was to conclude: 'mère humble et franche au grant espoir de France' ('a mother humble and pure, to the great hope of France'). The identification between the Regent and the Virgin was complete. There was precedent in the portrayal of queen Anne of Brittany on a medal in 1494 with her newborn son, the dauphin Charles-Orlando, as the Virgin and child. In addition, the Amiens confraternity decided to magnify the king's role in the paintings of the following years. In that of

1519, the *maître* of the confraternity, also *procureur du roi* at Amiens, asked for the king to be given the leading role in a redemptive allegory of the Virgin, relegating the Pope and the emperor among secular rulers to a more obscure role, this in the year in which Francis I challenged Charles of Habsburg for the imperial crown.[78]

All this was discourse shaped essentially by the *presentation* of works of art and of entry *tableaux* to the king (which his subjects would naturally view). It is easy to see in them flattery on the one hand and propaganda on the other. However, it is important to remember that the conventions of the sermon and of flattery could be combined and that, in the context of extravagant praise, it was possible to convey to the monarch what was expected of him in terms of sparing his subjects or bringing peace. The underlying messages of these diverse symbols and works of art were, in the view of Anne-Marie Lecoq, the assertion of special links between the king and the kingdom of France, Heaven and ancient Rome with its inheritance. In the course of this exchange, two main images of the king were generated for public consumption: that of the *roi Très chrestien*, the title current from the fourteenth century, placed under the special protection of Heaven. To this, the entourage of Louise of Savoy added the specific theme that Francis I himself was by providence under the special protection of God, as manifested by numerous occult signs. The other image is that of the king as direct inheritor of the powers of the Roman Caesars, portrayed as a triumphant *imperator*, even though the kings of France did not physically take part in such Roman-style triumphs.[79]

The ideological justifications and buttresses of royal power in the late fifteenth and sixteenth centuries emerge, then, as an amalgam of systematic theory derived from diverse interpretations of Roman and feudal law and a living tradition of ritual, gesture and symbol which would eventually be transformed into pure ceremony or pageantry but as yet remained within the world of symbolic discourse. This was a world in which it was still considered valuable to 'invent' ritual in order to embody or underscore an important and immutable truth. Within this was an idea of the relations between rulers and subjects which was to some extent anchored in imagery and may best be regarded as metaphor. The warnings of some historians against supposing that such fictions were necessarily believed literally should be taken seriously. But they also took a more concrete form than systematic political theory that was more accessible to a wide audience and in some ways interacted with it. The living representation of power responded actively to the demands of power and politics; it was not fixed and provided a flexible vehicle for inculcating the idea of loyalty to the state embodied in the person of the king.

2. The Court of France: from Louis XI to Henri II

The Royal Affinity

The extensive anti-courtier literature of the sixteenth century and the opinions of respected historians such as Pierre de Vaissière have created the impression that the Valois court remained until the Wars of Religion a fairly modest institution by later standards. It has been assumed that it was kept at arm's length by the mass of the nobility, who were apt to believe court life synonymous with corruption and servitude. The true picture is far from being so straightforward and is in many ways quite different; the repetition of clichés by poets, *rhétoriqueurs* or memoir-writers is testimony enough to the attractive power of the court and, indeed, its political and social significance. Francis Decrue long ago argued that it was in the sixteenth century that the French nobility ceased to be territorial and became a court nobility. Although this itself is also an exaggeration, studies of the court as an institution and a political centre made over the last generation quite plainly require a reassessment of its place in public life during the Renaissance.[1]

Blaise de Monluc, writing in retrospect of his long career, remarked that 'if I could return to my younger days, I would not take pains to enter the service of the king and queen, but rather those who have credit with their Majesties ... their honour is to have servants they call creatures. If the king gave of his bounty only by his own volition, he would clip their wings. But he who wants reward, who wants to be known, must commit himself to monsieur or madame, for the king gives everything to them and only knows of others by their report.'[2] This formulation should be viewed carefully from the perspective of the civil wars and the difficulties of royal patronage at the time. Monluc had started his career as a *fidèle* of François de Vivonne, sr. de La Chataigneraie, *échanson* and *gentilhomme de la chambre* in 1547, and then of a number of increasingly important figures until he attached himself to the duke of Guise and, finally, to the king during the Italian campaigns. As a principal royal *fidèle* he was made responsible for the re-establishment of order in the south-west during the 1560s.

During the period from 1460 to 1560, the crown had proved remarkably successful in drawing into its circle of *fidèles* like Monluc a wide range of princes, great aristocrats, military men and administrators which constituted a royal 'affinity'. The devices used were pensions, the court, the army and the administration. As Jean du Tillet wrote later in the century: 'In the first household account of Francis I, we see officers from great families and that others of old and rich nobility held themselves advanced and honoured to serve the king for a small salary, so that in peace his court was magnificent and in war his entourage very strong ... in the offices for the nobility, there have always been poorer gentlemen, brought up by honest affections and childhood rearing with the princes, just reward or occasion. Such favour has not put off the rich or men of greater house. The richer nobility, who used to hold them in high regard, now disdains them.'[3] Du Tillet's argument was that a royal household employing nobles of standing for little reward was to have been a sort of moral example to the kingdom as a whole.

A few examples will illustrate the nature of this royal affinity. The Gouffier family, for instance, was long in royal service. Guillaume, sieur de Boisy, servant of Charles VII, restored to favour after the Public Weal, was made *sénéchal* of Saintonge (1467) and governor of Touraine under Charles VIII, dying in 1495. Allied with similar families of the royal affinity, the Amboise and Montmorency, his sons Artus and Guillaume became leading figures of the court of Francis I in its early years and in the next generation were provincial governors.[4] Ymbert de Batarnay, sr. de Bouchage, one of Louis XI's most trusted and well-rewarded confidants, remained in royal service in the council and household as well as being captain of Mont-Saint-Michel from 1461 to his death in 1523. Among the many councillors who survived into the regency in 1483, he leapt into Louis XII's favour in 1498 by bringing him the good news of his predecessor's death. Governor to Charles VIII's son Charles-Orlando, he ended his career as governor to Francis I's children. Originally a modest squire from the Dauphiné, in 1518 he arranged for his grandson and heir René, later *enfant d'honneur* at court, to marry Ysabeau, daughter of the bâtard de Savoie, cousin to Francis I's mother and sister-in-law of Anne de Montmorency (see p. 377). René went on to become a gentleman of the chamber and governor of Berry in 1529 and count of Bouchage in 1540.[5] One of the most successful lineages of this type was the house of Chabannes, which rose to prominence in the mid-fifteenth century with Antoine, count of Dammartin (d.1488), *grand maître* under Louis XI and one of that king's most confidential advisers as well as an able general. His great-nephew, Jacques II, marshal de La Palisse, was one of the most famous commanders of his day and was killed at Pavia. His son was in turn killed at Metz in 1552.[6]

On a somewhat less exalted level, the Poitevin Saint-Gelais family, some of whom served in the household of Louis XI, were principally devoted to the service of the counts of Angoulême at Cognac in the fifteenth century and, through the patronage of Louise of Savoy, rose high in royal service during the early sixteenth. The family was called by Maulde-la-Clavière 'the archetypal successful court *lignage*'. Alexandre (d.1522) started as *chambellan* to Jean d'Albret, king of Navarre, and passed to the service of Louis XII and Francis I, of whom he was a confidant and ambassador. Mellin, count of San Severino, was *premier maître d'hotel* to Francis I until 1525. Other brothers included Jean, the historiographer of Louis XII, a favourite of Louise of Savoy at Cognac; Jean, bishop of Uzès; Octovien, the poet high in the favour of Louise, was the father of Mellin, court poet to Henri II, keeper of the royal library and enemy of Ronsard. Alexandre's son Louis, sieur de Lansac, was one of the leading diplomats of Henri II's reign.[7]

At a more modest level was the family of the court poet Ronsard; his grandfather Olivier, gentleman of the Vendômois, despite a brief flirtation with the Public Weal, was an *échanson* to Louis XI and, forgiven by him, entered his military household. His father Loys was a follower of Louis of Orléans on the expedition of 1494, gentleman of his military household after his accession and related by marriage to other servants of the crown such as Rabodange and Batarnay. Both Loys and his cousin Antoine de Thibivilliers erected celebrated chimneypieces, often the most extravagantly decorated feature of modest manor houses, that proclaimed symbolically their devotion to royal service. When Loys took his son Pierre, the poet, to court at Lyon in 1536 to join the army for Italy, he was entered as a page in the dauphin's household just before his sudden death, passing thence to the service of the king's younger son Charles. Ending his service as page in 1539, he entered the *écurie du roi*. The long tradition of service to the royal family is unmistakable.[8]

This does not mean, however, that the crown always acted directly as a fount of patronage. Clearly in a complex and varied society this was not a practical proposition. There were always channels of access to royal favour, those men whom the king chose to trust. Under Louis XI, these had been a mixed group of middle rank nobles and commoners who were either his own servants, like Jean Bourré, or attracted from the *clientèle* of other princes, like Commynes or Esquerdes. Under the Beaujeu regency, though there was continuity with the regime of Louis XI, power became a matter for competition between a number of princes, like Jean II of Bourbon and his brother Pierre de Beaujeu, who sought to place their *fidèles* in the royal council and important offices.[9] Success at the summit depended on flexibility and a willingness to slide from the service of a great patron either to that of the king or to the group holding and representing royal power like Pierre and Anne de Beaujeu.

Similarly, under Francis I advancement depended on preferment firstly by those who had the confidence of the king: his mother, his uncle the bastard of Savoy, admiral Bonnivet and, increasingly after 1525, the twin poles of interest Anne de Montmorency and Philippe Chabot. The latter two sought to increase their influence and importance by placing individuals in posts at court or in the provinces and it is significant that the struggle between them became increasingly bitter in the early 1530s.[10] From the time when Anne de Montmorency's correspondence starts in 1522, it is clear that he is active in fostering the careers of men like the later marshal, Oudart du Biez, who could write to him that he was 'after the king, my principal lord'. The dominance in government of Montmorency from 1536 to 1541 posed problems in that it generated deep resentments which were revealed at the time of his fall from grace in 1541 and also raised problems for his clients, many of whom had to adjust to the new circumstances or go under. Du Biez was able to survive but it should be remembered that, despite the patronage of Montmorency, the marshal should be regarded principally as a royal *fidèle* who owed all he had to royal service.[11] The king's immediate household was a rich field for the exercise of patronage and the assembly of a body of royal *fidèles* and we must now consider it in detail.

La maison du roi

Francis Decrue argued that the use of the word *cour* to describe the phenomenon of the royal entourage was relatively new in the sixteenth century; what had been called the court in the Middle Ages was no more than an assembly of vassals. The duke of Burgundy's entourage, he added, had often outshone the king's. This is a view often expressed by modern writers: J.-F. Solnon, a modern authority on the subject, begins his massive study with the words: 'In the Middle Ages, the kings of France had no court.' Ellery Schalk has called it *'simply* the enlarged household of the king. It lacked a sense of permanence'.[12] The word *cour* had, of course, been established for a long time in usage but the increasing institutionalisation of the court and the centrality of its core, the king's household, in social and political life had been taking shape long before the end of the fifteenth century. The complexity of household administration and struggles over the entourage of John II in the mid-fourteenth century make this quite clear.[13] Until the reign of Henri III, however, there were few systematic regulations issued for the 'reform' of the court, since the procedures of the royal household were to some extent governed by immemorial usage – the 'old *ordonnances*' – though there were, of course, special orders for specific aspects of court life. Much of our knowledge of the institution, therefore, in the first half of the sixteenth century stems from the reports of ambassadors coupled with the bare statistics provided by the incomplete series of original accounts and the compilations of copies and abstracts made by seventeenth- and eighteenth-century administrators. To this may be added the writings of late sixteenth- and seventeenth-century theorists such as du Tillet and Loyseau, who were not always accurate. Fundamental problems like the structure of the court's personnel, the modes of appointment, the kinds of patronage involved, have simply not been studied and, in some cases, it may be that precise solutions are impossible in view of the incomplete nature of the evidence.

There is as yet no systematic study of the organisation of the court in the century or so before the reign of Henri III, though certain aspects of its political weight, organisation and cultural influence have been addressed by historians such as Robert Knecht.[14] In particular, the degree of structural continuity of the court from the reign of Louis XI into the Renaissance has not been measured. In the main, the royal household was conservative in its traditions of organisation. Knecht has pointed out that, though the royal household was so personal that it was deemed to be disbanded on the king's death, in fact many servants were retained from reign to reign; in addition, any perusal of the administrative documents of the household contradicts the notion that the royal household was an impermanent personal arrangement for each monarch, even in the fifteenth century. Clearly some functions of court life were to a degree bureaucratised. On the other hand, the expanding numbers and its political role during the sixteenth century profoundly modified its nature.

The 'court of France' was made up of several interlocking *maisons*, principally the king's, of course, but also those of the other members of the immediate royal family, his queen, the royal children. *La maison du roi* (the king's household in particular) was made up traditionally of several *services de l'Hôtel du roi* dating from the thirteenth century: *paneterie, échansonnerie, fruiterie, cuisine, fourrière* for the king's table service (these were accounted for separately as a department for the *bouche*, the king's table service, and the *commun*, that of the king's entourage). In addition to these, however, by the fifteenth century the *chambre, chapelle, vénerie, écurie and fauconnerie* had begun to take on an independent existence for the social and spiritual needs of the king and the *argenterie* for financial payments. Financial control of the *hôtel* through the budget was assured by the *chambre aux deniers*, headed by its *maître*.

The services of the medieval household were subject to frequent change and adaptation, sometimes autonomous, sometimes dependent on a more important *caisse*, the accounts frequently held cumulatively by the same officials. The original competence of the *premier chambellan*, the *chambre*, had been absorbed partly by the *argentier* and partly by the *maître de la chambre aux deniers* in the early fourteenth century. By the late fifteenth century, many of the king's victualling needs were handled by the *argenterie*. This operated a dual account: the *ordinaire* for garments, linen and related necessities; the *extraordinaire* for the costs of festivities and state occasions like funerals.[15] The inevitable fraud and waste were periodically combated by special orders. In July 1550 new rules were issued for the purchase of equipment by the *maître de la garderobe* La Bourdaisière and in December 1550 Henri II ordered in the *conseil privé* that the 24,000 *lt.* *(livres tournois)* spent by the *argenterie* be confined to his own needs in 'table linen, knives, purchase of pewter and silver vessels, wardrobes, coffers and the wages of 18 children of the kitchen'. All else was to be specially authorised by Saint-André as first gentleman of the chamber and president Bertrand of the *conseil privé*. Expenditure for masques, tournaments and other celebrations was to be authorised separately.[16]

Louis XI at the start of his reign detached an important part of the *maître de la chambre aux deniers'* competence to create a separate service of the *chambre* to administer his intimate expenses, gifts, pensions, wages and diplomatic messengers. The surviving account for 1469–70 shows an expenditure of 58,000 *lt.*, one of the most important of the household, administered by the *commis* who also paid the *officiers domestiques*. In 1470, however, Louis detached pensions and assigned them on public accounts. The *chambre* was finally absorbed by the *maître de la chambre aux deniers* again in 1483, when there emerged a new department, that of the *menus plaisirs du roi*, which was to remain a permanent feature of the household until the end of the monarchy.[17]

Until the 1520s, the domestic officers were paid by a *commis* who was often also *maître de la chambre aux deniers*. By the 1520s, this department was a separate one under Jean Carré and interestingly in 1526–7 Guillaume Tertreau carried out payments both as *commis* for the *officiers domestiques* and *trésorier de l'hostel* with responsibility for coordinating the budget of the whole household.[18] Later in Francis I's reign Jacques Bochetel emerges as *trésorier de la maison*, followed in 1547 by Anne de Montmorency's secretary, Nicolas Berthereau.[19] The posts of financial importance in the household were held by a group of closely related families who were also powerful in the finance of the state. Until the 1520s, most of the accounting officials had been office-holders and also *notaires et secretaires du roi*, though there were also several *commis* whose functions were temporary. Office-holders were not, however, entirely secure. François Doulcet, *maître de la chambre aux deniers* and *commis* for the *officiers domestiques* shortly after the accession of Louis XII in 1502–3, was dismissed from office in 1505 and replaced by François Briçonnet (d.1515).[20] Nevertheless, there is a distinct sense in which the accounting officialdom of the royal household was overlapped by the Tours financial oligarchy that largely controlled the *généralités*. Families like the Berthelot, Bohier, Briçonnet, Morelet du Museau figure largely. The Berthelots, father and son, ran the *chambre aux deniers* from 1471 to 1499, though the son was among those condemned for peculation in 1528.[21] It seems probable that condemnations heaped on these families in 1527–8 speeded the changes visible in the account for the whole household in 1526–7, the *trésorerie de la maison*, and the emergence in the management of court finance of men who were closely linked to either the secretarial families (Bourdin, Bochetel) or to Montmorency.

The list, or *état*, of the officers of the household was drawn up every year, without any regularity of date, signed by the king and countersigned by a *secrétaire des commandements*, usually Jean Breton in the 1530s, Gilbert Bayard up to 1547 and Cosme Clause thereafter. Not infrequently, individuals would be accidentally omitted and had to receive their pay for the year by special warrant.[22] At any rate, the administration of the court was managed through a series of separate accounting bodies: *maître de la chambre aux deniers, trésorier de la maison, argentier, receveur de l'écurie, trésorier, receveur et payeur de la vénerie et fauconnerie*. It is the accounts of each of these offices, surviving in broken series, which provide the bulk of the information on court administration.[23] An annual budget of the court was drawn up by the king in consultation with the *gens des finances*, as part of the crown's yearly *état par estimation* (roughly, budget) establishing the necessary expenditure for each of these departments. Until the early 1520s, each department received an assignation on one or more of the provincial *généralités*. From the 1520s, along with other spending departments, the individual treasurers received cash firstly on allocation by the *Épargne*.

Certain great aristocrats held court offices with grandiloquent titles: the first duke of Guise was *Grand Veneur de France* and Charles de Cossé, marshal of France, was *Grand Fauconnier de France*.[24] But by the beginning of the sixteenth century it was the *grand maître de l'Hôtel*, or *grand maître de France* (later classed among the great officers of state), who was in charge of the entire administration of the court for the services of the *Hôtel*. Under Francis I, the *grand maître* was a political figure of the first order in the king's confidence such as Boisy and René de Savoie. From 1526 Anne de Montmorency made the post the lynchpin of his political influence, combining it with that of *premier gentilhomme de la chambre* (1526–42), which gave him control also of the administration of the inner household of the chamber. He was the official whose approval was needed for any hope of preferment in the household down to the lowest level and Montmorency's correspondence is replete with requests for position. In 1528, for instance, Clause Gouffier de Boisy, a *gentilhomme de la chambre*, asked Montmorency 'for love of me' to confirm his appointment, at the request of the cardinal of Lorraine, of the son of a *sommelier* of the hôtel as *ayde de sommelier* and recommended him to the *grand maître*: 'the boy is very careful of the king's service... you will be acting according to our master's will.'[25] In the same period, the *grand maître*'s brother, La Rochepot, asked him for a post in the household of the queen or the *dauphine* for a man who was cousin of one of Louise of Savoy's secretaries, was known to *gens de bien* and 'has always been brought up at court'.[26] Montmorency placed in the household as many individuals who were obliged to him as possible. What is more, his post involved the function of overseeing the yearly *état* (or list) of active members of the household to receive their *gages* (emoluments). Thus, when in January 1531 it was known that he was drawing up the *état* for the next year, Marguerite of Navarre passed on through Jean du Bellay the hope that her secretary, the vicomte Adrien, should be restored to his pay of 240 *lt.* as *valet de chambre du roi*.[27] The exercise of patronage was particularly significant in the context of court faction.

The numbers employed in the king's household are usually seen as showing an inexorable rise from the relatively modest numbers under Louis XI to 366 officers in 1495–6 (with 343 in the queen's household) and then to just over 600 later in the reign of Francis I. A greater increase came during the brief reign of Francis II, when large numbers were pushed into the household by the Guise faction.[28] The significance of the increase between 1463[29] and 1484 is clear and it seems reasonable that the inflation of numbers to 1049 in 1560 was the result of pressures on a weak regime. However, as the detailed figures in Table 1 show, the inflation of numbers of courtiers during the reign of Francis I was not straightforward. That reign saw substantial additions in the form of *aumôniers*, bishops holding honorific unpaid positions, and of the *gentilshommes de la chambre*, who grew in

Table 1 Numbers of members of the royal household[a]

year end. Oct.	1463	1484	1498	1499	1505	1512	1516	1546	1547	1548	1551	1555	1557–9	1560
Chambre/service de table														
chambellan	15	–	–	6	3	2	–	–	–	–	–	–	–	–
gentilhomme	–	–	–	–	–	–	21	55	64	67	80	96	99	113
maître d'hôtel	7	9	33	13	13	15	16	24	27	29	27	22	23	
écuyer d'écurie	7	9	10	10	12	11	13	21	19	26	29	23	20	
valet tranchant	1	8	7	7	8	6	14	9	17	17	12	9	4	
écuyer d'honn.	1	–	–	–	–	–	–	–	–					
enfant d'honn.	34	10	27	9	20	39	30	–	–					
panetier	–	9	8	7	7	7	16	28	38	43	57	77	75	
échanson	–	8	9	8	7	7	16	17	28	32	34	39	35	
valet de chambre	12	10	6	24	22	19	21	28	52	52	52	52	67	79
secr. chambre				2		2	2	5	11	26	19	24	22	33
librarian		1	1				1	2						
huissier, chamb.		2	2				4	5						
chantre, chamb.								7						
peintre, métier		4	4					17						

Table 1 *cont'd*

year end. Oct.	1463	1484	1498	1499	1505	1512	1516	1546	1547	1548	1551	1555	1557–9	1560
Chapelle														
aumônier		2	2	3	2		17	57						
chapelain		3	2				7	5						
somm. chapelle		2	11	12	11	10	6	6						
Garderobe														
maître	—	1	1				1	1						
valet	—	4	8	13			23	8						
sommelier	—	—	—			10	—	—						
porte-manteau	—	—	—	—	—		—	8						
Medical service														
médecin	1	2	7	6	5	4	6	11						
apothicaire	1	1	1	1	1	1	1	1						
barbier	—	1	3	2	2	2	3	4						
chirugien	—	2	7	6	5	4	6	10						
astrologue	1	—	—	—	—	—	—	—						

Table 1   *cont'd*

year end. Oct.	1463	1484	1498	1499	1505	1512	1516	1546	1547	1548	1551	1555	1557–9	1560
Administration, gardes														
capitaine, porte		1	1	1	1	1	1	1						
portier	–	5	12	14		17	?	17						
mar. de logis	–	2	4	4		2	4	4						
sergent d'armes		2	2	–	–	–	–	–						
huissier d'armes	3	2	3	3		2	–	–						
clerc d'offices		5	6	5		3	8	4						
huissier, salle	–	5	7	4	4	4	7	–						
fourrier		17	16	?		?	?	19						
Cuisine de bouche et communs														
Paneterie, bouche		5	7	4		6	11	7						
Paneterie, commun		6	16	10	?	10	19	13						
Echansonnerie, bouche		6	10	5		9	10	10						
Echansonnerie, commun		12	14	20		15	17	17						
Cuisine, bouche		12	18	19		27	21	28						
Cuisine, commun		42	58	61		70	90	68						

Table 1 *cont'd*

year end. Oct.	1463	1484	1498	1499	1505	1512	1516	1546	1547	1548	1551	1555	1557–9	1560
Autres														
tapissier	3	7	5			4	6	8						
lavandières	5	3	3			5	4	4						
Musique														
tabourin				2			3	3						
fiffre							5	1						
cornette							3	2						
joueur d'instruments							–	2						

aDocumentation: apart from the isolated original accounts for separate departments of the household surviving from the later fifteenth century (see note 23), we have to rely on copies. The original series of accounts dispersed in the seventeenth and eighteenth centuries would have included those for the *payeur des officiers domestiques* from the reign of Francis I, while in the fifteenth century the names of the chamber staff were listed in the yearly accounts of the *commis* for the *chambre du roi* and the *maîtres d'hôtel* and those of the *chambre aux deniers*. Fortunately, the copies made in the late seventeenth century enable us to establish general trends. There has been discussion as to their accuracy. The copies in BN fr. 7853–56 list the officers by department for each reign and are obviously attempts to tabulate in which there may be some inaccuracies. However, it should be stressed that the record-keeping for the household was fragmented and complex even in the fifteenth century and contradictions frequently occur even in the original accounts. For the reign of Francis I, the copies in BN fr. 21449–50 are of the *états* of the *officiers domestiques* for each year of the reign in so far as they survive. These continue to 1549. For 1550–1, we have the original *états* in BN Clair.813 and fr. 3132. The original account for 1557 is now in AD Calvados F.4177.

numbers throughout the reign, but on the other hand the posts of *chambellan* and *enfant d'honneur* disappeared as a result, it has been suggested, of some attempts at retrenchment after 1523.[30] There were certain discontinuities between the households of Louis XII and Francis I (rather more so than between Francis I and Henri II), yet even in the earlier changeover, the careers of certain individuals indicate the role of *fidèles*. So, Louis de Poysieu-Capdorat, *écuier d'écurie* to Louis XII 1498–1512, then *maître d'hôtel* 1512–14 was succeeded by Michel de Poysieu-Capdorat in the household of Francis I, as *gentilhomme de la chambre*, 1516–21. The Italian Pier-Francesco Nosseto, count of Pontremoli, *écuier d'écurie* to Louis XII in 1510, emerged as *gentilhomme* to Francis I but only in 1524.[31]

The greatest numerical increases came, however, in the kitchen staff, the two departments of the *cuisine de bouche* and *commun*, rather than of socially or politically important individuals and it is clear that table expenditure was one of the main reasons causing the cost of the court to rise. An example of an attempt to get things under control was Francis I's order (c.1520–3) to divide each section of the chamber service (except the *gentilshommes*) into service by quarters and to supervise the expenditure of 'extraordinaires' to be authorised by the *maître d'hôtel* in service, paid by the *maître de la chambre aux deniers* but then repaid to that department 'without further charge on ordinary expenditure'. It aimed as well to cut down on those taking meals at the tables of the *grand maître*, *amiral* and La Trémoille without proper authorisation.[32] Table expenditure was controlled by daily accounts called *dépenses de bouche* submitted for audit, some of which survive. The table expenses for the court on one day, 23 February 1554, when the king himself was not present, were 182 *lt*.[33]

To the *maison du roi* proper, must be added the various other households of the immediate royal family (though not, perhaps, that of Louise of Savoy in the first half of Francis I's reign as this was not defrayed formally from the royal budget). That of the king's sons in 1535 included 85 officers of the chamber, table and hunt, 34 chaplains, secretaries and medical men, 52 wardrobe, ushers and administration, 37 *sommeliers* for table service, 62 kitchen staff, 16 lodging staff, 34 stable staff, 18 craftsmen and musicians, 6 washing staff, 11 pensioners and the treasurer, Jean du Val, who as usual was paid one of the highest salaries, 1400 *lt*.[34]

The total salary bill was 64,444 *lt.* when the entire expenses of all the royal children and their household had been only 60,000 *lt.* in 1523.[35] The correspondence between Francis I and his children's governor in their early years, Ymbert de Batarnay, shows that, until 1523 at least, the king was determined to keep the expenses under control, limiting them to 25,000 *lt.*, but the children were growing up and demands were on the increase.[36] The *maison* of the royal sons under Francis I provided an opportunity to place the sons of courtiers influential in the king's house and thus perpetuate their influence into the next reign. From the early 1530s, the Coligny brothers had offices in it, while the governor, Jean d'Humières, found places for two of his sons. All of them were to find important places in the household of Henri II after 1547. After 1538, the king's two surviving sons set up their own separate households, to some extent constituting rival networks of *clientèle.*[37] The household of the queen also served the purpose of providing places for the sons of courtiers for young noblemen anxious to make their way. Queen Léonore's household included Sarcus and Castillon, respectively the king's *maître d'hôtel* and *gentilhomme de la chambre*, as *maîtres d'hôtel* as well as relatives of the king's mistress, Mme d'Étampes, later placed in the king's chamber.[38] An English observer in 1540 actually thought a rift had occurred between the dauphin and Montmorency over the latter's wish 'at the tyme of makyng of the Dolfyns estate of hys house' to put in three names 'which he utterly refused',[39] testimony enough to competition for such places. The clerical lawyer and diplomat, Charles de Marillac, acquired 'entire authority' over the '*mesnage*' of the dauphin's household 'even when the cardinal of Lorraine came to deal with it'.[40] This was a role like that of his close friend Michel de l'Hospital in Marguerite of Navarre's household. Marillac's brother and his cousin, Jean des Formes, became royal messengers in the mid-1540s and by 1557 the latter was a *valet de chambre.*[41]

In the king's own household, with notable exceptions like those of the *gentilshommes de la chambre* and the court doctors, and the *premier maître d'hôtel*, the deputy to the *grand maître* in the household, salaries remained fixed between 1484 and 1550. Only the kitchen menials in fact received pay rises to offset inflation (Table 2). This would tend to explain du Tillet's contention that the nobility held it an honour to serve at court for

Table 2   Salaries of courtiers (in *livres tournois*)

	1484	1499	1516	1546
trésorier	2000	1800	?	2500
aumônier	1200	–	–	
chapelain	120	180/240	200	240
sommelier, chapelle	180	120/180	180	180
prem. maître d'hôt.	800	800	800	1200
maître d'hôtel	700	600	600	600
chambellan		400	–	–
gentilhomme, chambre	–	–	400	600/1200
premier panetier	800	800	800	800
panetier	400	400	400	400
premier échanson	–	600	600	600
échanson	400	400	400	400
prem. valet tranchant	800	600	600	600
valet tranchans	400	400	400	400
premier éc. d'écurie	–	600	600	600
écuyer d'ecurie	400	400	400	400
enfant d'honneur	240	240	240	–
huissier d'armes	240	240	–	–
huissier de chambre	180	–	240	240
premier valet, chambre	1200	600	–	–
valet de chambre	3/400	3/400	240	240
maître de garderobe	240	?	400	–
valet de garderobe	240	–	180	200/240
premier mar. de logis	?	800	1200	–
maréchal de logis	?	600	800	800
médecin	500	600	800	800
apothicaire	1000	800	800	800
chirurgien	240	180	120/200	240
barbier	180	180	210/300	240
libraire	180	?	240	240/400
clerc d'offices	180	180	240	240
écuyer, cuisine	180	180	200/240	220/240
queux, bouche	240	240	240	240
queux, cuisine	120	various	220	180
potager/boulanger	120	90/120	180	160/180
galopins	26	24	80	?

small recompense. There was also the real incentive of privileges conferred on court officers, which often included exemption from taxes, forced loans, military *logement* and civic guard duty.[42] This is why it was worth seeking a court post even if it was listed 'sans gages'. (Henri III had 216 in this category in 1584.) Similarly the *gens de métier*, merchants and artists attached to the court (growing from about 100 in 1500 to 160 in 1547 and 500 in 1600), enjoyed exemptions from tolls and guild regulations.[43] However, in the very important case of the most highly paid official of the court, the *trésorier*, the keeper of the accounts, the salary rose from 2000 *lt.* during the reign of Charles VIII to 2500 at the end of Francis I's (it was only 1800 *lt.* under Louis XII).

The steady increase in numbers of the chamber staff necessarily inflated costs. An account by the payer of officers of the *hôtel du roi*, Jean Carré, for 1524 gives a total of 85,703 *lt.* paid in salaries, while that for 1527 specifies 149,055 *lt.*[44] Of the latter, 82,780 were salaries of chamber and table staff. It seems, therefore, that a significant increase in the latter took place on the king's return from captivity. Salaries of officials were only a small proportion, although the largest single item, of the total budget for the court. This had stood at 85,615 *lt.* in 1490 but had soared to 500,175 in 1495 during the Italian campaign.[45] This remained the level over the next generation. The court budget of 1523, for the king's and the queen's household, hunting establishment included, stands at 543,800 *lt.* with salaries at 90,000. The budget for 1532 for the entire court, by extrapolating from the *état par estimation* of the *Epargne* for the first quarter was 834,243 *lt.* (see Table 3).[46] The increase is explained by a further rise in wage costs in the households of the king and queen but also by the emergence of the households of the royal children. These had cost but 60,000 in 1523 but now cost 206,608 *lt.* A foreign report of the *état* drawn up by Henri II in 1547, for the household with *chasse* and *fauconnerie* was 400,000 *lt.*, with another 200,000 *lt.* for Catherine de Medici's household, which, if correct, may represent an attempt at economy as the costs of the royal children were not included. However, by 1549 the *état par estimation* for the court budget gave the king 616,298 *lt.* and the dauphin 100,000 (though the queen's budget is unknown). Thus, taking account of inflation, only a quite modest increase had occurred in the generation since the Italian wars began.[47]

Table 3   The court budgets 1523–49 (in *livres tournois*)

	1523[a]	1532[b]	1549[c]
Chambre aux deniers (table, food, etc.)	50,000	60,000	72,000
Gaiges des officiers	90,000	194,725	303,183[d]
receiver of *écurie*	36,000		
To same for harness	3,000		
Total *écurie*	39,000	69,694	131,406
To *argentier* for wardrobe, etc.	30,000	24,000	24,000
vénerie et fauconnerie	36,000	40,024	58,450
For *plaisirs du roi*	24,000	24,000	–
For *menus affaires* of the chamber	4,000	5,000	6,000
For *chantres* and *chapelle ord.*	14,500		11,880
violons	–	–	1,979
Aumônes ordinaires du roi		6,000	7,400
TOTAL: King's household	287,500	423,443	616,298
Queen's *Chambre aux deniers*		65,000	
Queen's *menus affaires/apothicaries*		6,000	
Queen's *officiers*		73,402	
Queen's *menus plaisirs*		12,000	
Ecurie de la reine		36,000	
Queen's *argenterie*		12,000	
TOTAL: Queen's household	165,000	204,400	?[e]
Royal sons, *chambre aux deniers*		40,000	
Same, *écurie*		14,000	
Same, *gages des officiers*		45,420	
Same, *argenterie*		14,000	
Same, *menus affaires, chambre, plaisirs*, etc.		5,000	
Royal daughters, *chambre aux deniers*		42,300	
Same, *écuries*		11,578	
Same, *gages des officiers*		27,310	
Same, *argenterie*		6,000	
Same, *apothicaries*		1,000	
TOTAL: Household of the royal children	60,000	206,608	100,000[f]
Passe of the same	8,300	–	
Etat of Mme Renée de France	24,000	–	
'Maison de Madame'			80,000
TOTAL	543,800	834,451	

Table 3   *cont'd*

	1523[a]	1532[b]	1549[c]
Guards:[g]			
200 *gent. de l'hôtel*	100,400	84,400	63,650
400 *archers de la garde*	135,062	122,044	128,996
Cent Suisses de la garde	16,600	16,600	16,300
Prévôté de l'Hôtel	8,560	8,600	11,920

[a] R. Doucet (ed.), *Etat des finances de 1523*, pp. 87–8

[b] *Estat de la recepte et despence de l'espargne*, quarter of Jan.–Mar. 1532 (figures for the equivalent heads of 1523 multiplied by four to give an equivalent).

[c] *État par estimation*, signed 2 Jan. 1548/9, BN fr. 3127 fo. 91–3.

[d] For an intermediate figure, see *Rôle des officiers domestiques*, signed by Francis I, 9 June 1527, BN fr. 3898 fo. 109–26: *Lt.* 149,055.

[e] No figure given for the queen's household but not included in the figures for the king's. The overall budget of this *état* was over 3 million in deficit.

[f] The figure for the dauphin's household only. No figures for the other royal children.

[g] Doucet, pp. 77–80. Slight fall in 1532 (BN fr. 20502 fo. 108–10) probably explained by the absence of the costs of officers in the latter.

The scale of 'salaires' or expense accounts established in 1554 for royal servants while on duty away from home reveals something of the hierarchy of importance. First came *maîtres d'hôtel* and captains of the guard, equivalents of presidents of the sovereign courts and *trésoriers de France* (60s. a day). Next came *prévôts de l'hôtel, pannetiers, valets trachans*, equivalent to counsellors in the sovereign courts (100s.), *valets de chambre*, royal secretaries, equivalent to lieutenants of the *bailliages* (80s.).[48] Another gauge of importance is the provision made for clothing by the *argenterie* of the court. In 1549, there were two categories of royal servant for provision of headgear for *jeudi absolut*. The first (84 in all) received highest quality cloth and included the royal family, constable, princes, grand almoner, 10 chapel staff, 4 masters of requests, 25 gentlemen of the chamber, 6 captains of the guards of the gate, *prévôt de l'hôtel* and four *secrétaires des finances*, president Bertrand, the *trésorier de l'Epargne*, controller of the household and the *argenterie* and the *maître de la chambre aux deniers*. The rest (109 in all) received slightly inferior cloth.[49]

The Courtier's Career

Francis I is usually considered a king who did little by new regulations to alter the structure of the household, but he did introduce a major innovation in the form of the corps of *gentilshommes de la chambre*. These were charged with important representative functions and consisted of a body of the king's most trusted nobles who profoundly modified the social and political influence of the royal household.[50] Their origins have not been well understood. Some historians have repeated Jean du Tillet's guess that they originated in the growing distaste of the king's intimate servants in the late fifteenth century for a title such as *valet de chambre*, by then associated with lesser domestics. It had, he said, 'formerly been a title signifying nobility but was now considered very low'.[51] In fact, some *valets de chambre* under Louis XI and Charles VIII (e.g. Olivier le Daim) were royal intimates, others no more than lesser servants, while du Tillet himself elsewhere makes clear that he thought the inception of the *gentilshommes de la chambre* was designed to replace the small number of traditional royal *chambellans*: 'Francis I, who favoured the nobility, at his accession instituted the gentlemen of the chamber, which allowed commoners to come in as valets, which they had not been before except *valets de garderobe* and the *chambellans* in small numbers converted into gentlemen of the chamber in unbridled numbers.'[52] Brantôme was later to remark that in the time of Francis I, 'kings and great princes of the blood used gentlemen as *valets de chambre*, as I have heard from many old people'.[53]

These opinions indicate that the reasons for such evolutions in the royal household were no longer understood by the end of the sixteenth century. The *chambre*, as a distinct section of the *hostel du roi*, was established before the reign of Louis XI and indeed, as has been seen, accounted for the most substantial expenditure of all the old departments according to the one surviving account of 1469–70. Not only were a great number of personal servants paid but the department accounted for a large proportion of the king's expenses in secret messages and negotiations of the kind defrayed by the *Epargne* from the 1520s.[54] The number of servants of the chamber at any one time could not have been as large as the list of 1469, however. Up to the reign of Louis XII, the number of *chambellans* of the household had steeply declined; there were only two in 1512. The corps of *valets de chambre* was numerous (between 19 and 26) but only a few of them were, like Jacques Galiot and François de Crussol, men of substance and these were the only two to find places as *gentils-hommes* under Francis I.[55] During the reign of Francis I the title of *valet de chambre*, though still sometimes held by diplomats, was becoming increasingly honorific, conferred on artists and crafts-men for royal service, and conferring the sorts of privileges already mentioned. Some, however, remained confidential royal servants, like Jean de La Barre, in 1515 *valet de chambre* and *maître de la garderobe*, responsible for the king's *menus plaisirs*[56] and later *premier gentilhomme de la chambre*, and Guillaume Féau, sr. d'Yzernay. La Barre was ambassador in Florence, 1517, and Rome, 1521. Yzernay went to Venice in 1529 and Flanders in 1530. Another, Bordry, was called in 1543 'a man for his degre well estemed, and noted wise and sobre'.[57] At the higher levels of diplomacy, one *valet de chambre*, Christophe Richer, was an influential ambassador to Scandinavia and Germany, while another, Octavian Bosso, was a frequent royal messenger and also military *commissaire* under Henri II.[58] Among the lesser valets, we find, for instance, Jean le Prebstre, barber to Henri II, who received the confiscation of an executed adventurer.[59]

There was clearly a call for men of political or social weight who had found no place in the traditional structure of the court. Firstly, Commynes had already referred, when describing Charles VIII's funeral, to 'his intimates, like *chambellans* and ten or twelve young gentlemen who were of his chamber'. On his accession Francis I chose to continue the employment of *gentilshommes de la chambre* who had been a feature of his household as duke of Angoulême.[60] The start of his reign therefore marked something of a change in the inner personnel of the royal household. Although a few family names crop up in later lists of the household that testify to long-term traditions of royal service (for instance Créquy, Laval, Vatan, Rochechouart, Galiot, Cossé, Poysieu) there was some discontinu-ity. Some of Francis I's *gentilshommes* before his accession, like Philippe Chabot and Anne de Montmorency, found places as *gentilshommes de la chambre* in the new reign. Others were given posts such as *échanson* and *maître d'hotel*. Francis I's *gentilshommes* after 1515 were of the illustrious sort previously appointed *chambellan* or *enfant d'honneur* (and their pay was at first similar). Secondly, such a household structure was common among the great princes in the late fifteenth century. Finally, it had been the conservatism of the royal household, its reluctance to adapt to new titles and functions, which had delayed the emergence of such a category of royal servant before that. Thus, there had been a long contraction in the number of active royal *chambellans* in the late fifteenth century, probably because the title seemed to have little meaning when that of *conseiller et chambellan* was so widely distributed.[61] For a while, their place seemed to be taken by the corps of *enfants d'honneur* but this also contracted. A royal *ordonnance* of 1534 described them as 'young gentlemen who have hitherto been brought up at court', and specified that they should now first serve in the gendarmerie, although they remained numerous in the household of the royal sons.[62] By the end of the reign they had disappeared from the king's house. The lists of the royal household in the late fifteenth and early sixteenth century testify to changing needs and a consequent uncertainty in nomenclature.

The *gentilshommes de la chambre* were paid 600 *lt.* up to 1524 and 1200 after the king's return in 1526, though there was a supplementary list of 'other gentlemen' who were paid 600 *lt.*[63] Some of these eventually found places on the full *gages*. In the household account of 1527, they were for the first time placed immediately after the chapel, a sign of their pre-eminence, whereas before they had followed all the other officers of the chamber and table. The 1528 order of precedence for processions placed them after the ambassadors and the Parlement. In 1516 there were 21 of them, with Guillaume Gouffier-Bonnivet as first and five others who had also been members of Francis's household as duke of Angoulême. Bonnivet was succeeded as first gentleman by René de Puyguyon in 1518, Anne de Montmorency in 1520, Jean de La Barre in 1523 and Montmorency again from 1524 until he was replaced by Claude d'Annebault in 1543 or 1544. Francis I also briefly revived the office of *Grand chambrier de France*, presumably the equivalent of the *grand maître* for the chamber, and appointed his younger sons to the position. Under Henri II, the concentration of authority over the household enjoyed by Montmorency from 1526 to 1543 was not repeated. The king's friend Jacques d'Albon, sr. de Saint-André (son of a *gentilhomme de la chambre*), took the post of *premier*. The *premiers gentilshommes* were also responsible for the payment of the pages, for which they received 1800 lt. in 1524, though from 1540 Sourdis was responsible for them, and by 1550 Saint-André defrayed the cost of 15 'pages of the chamber, their straw, palleasses, wood, candles, expenses of three men serving them'.[64] The numbers of gentlemen increased constantly throughout the reigns of Francis I and Henri II, though there was a marked acceleration in the 1540s. A remark of Henri II in 1557 that 'they are simple retainers that the king for his own reasons accords to personages who are recommended to him for their services and merits, etc., who are not all included in the pay list of the household nor paid salaries, but only enjoy the title' should be borne in mind for the later part of the period. There were, for instance, 39 *gentilshommes* on the household list for 1550 but the list of those actually paid in 1551 includes only 30 names.[65]

It is possible to establish numbers precisely from the *rôles* of household officers. In those surviving between 1516 and 1551, there were 203 *gentilshommes de la chambre*. Of these, there was one prince of the blood (Condé), one duke (Etampes), 2 marquesses, 19 counts, 1 viscount, 5 barons and one *vidame*. The rest were members of the middle nobility. Some families supplied several members of the chamber: the most prominent in this respect, all with four members, were Montmorency, Chabot and Gouffier, then come Rohan, Humières, and Savoie-Villars, all with three, followed by the La Loue, Tiercelin, Silly, du Prat, Hangest-Genlis, Annebault, Escars, Saint-Jullien, Strozzi and La Marck, all with two. Besides the power in the council of cardinal Jean du Bellay, three members of the du Bellay family, Guillaume, Martin and François, comte de Tonnerre, were *gentilshommes de la chambre* and two others, Jacques, count of Tonnerre, and Louis 'dit le Millort pannetier', were *panetiers ordinaires* in 1550.[66] Although it is fairly clear that there were some appointments made to gratify useful foreign military commanders (such as count of Pontremoli, Jean-Paul de Cere d'Orsini, the house of Savoie-Villars, the earl of Arran, the lansquenet commanders Fontenoy and the Rhingrave) there was a core of royal *fidèles*. Some were exceptionally long-serving. Montmorency and Chabot de Brion (both 1516–43) were among the longest, while Jacques Galiot de Genouillac, *grand maître de l'artillerie*, Adrien Tiercelin and Pecalvary all served for the entire reign of Francis I. The record went to Charles du

Solier, sr. de Morette, courtier and diplomat, superbly painted by Holbein, who served without interruption from 1516 to 1550.[67] Of the 128 *gentilshommes* who served in the court of Francis I, there was a nucleus of around 70 individuals who were significant in central and provincial administration. Between them they shared the positions of 33 *baillies* or *sénéchaux*, 27 provincial governors and 28 ambassadors (mainly extraordinary but some residents). Of the 66 persons assigned pensions of 1200 *lt.* and above in the list for 1532, 18 were *gentilshommes de la chambre*.[68] What we see here very clearly is a powerful political elite deliberately assembled by the crown in the context of the court.

Certain *gentilshommes de la chambre* were employed repeatedly as military agents, or for important missions as special envoys. Examples of external missions include: Antoine de Lettes, sr. de Montpezat (in the chamber 1520–44) was ambassador in England in November 1519, summer 1521 and resident 1532–3; Guillaume du Bellay (1524–42) was one of the major diplomatic representatives of France in Germany during the 1530s as well as governor of Piedmont for a while;[69] Charles de Cossé-Brissac (1537–47), was given missions to the governor of Piedmont in May 1537, to the emperor in Spain in October 1538 and again to the emperor in the summer of 1538 and over the winter of 1539–40. In the next reign, Brissac, eventually marshal of France, was to carry out the same function as envoy to the emperor in 1547.[70] Charles de Coucys, sr. de Burie, *écuyer d'écurie* and then gentlemen of the chamber in 1531, was envoy to Switzerland in July 1526 and lieut. governor at Turin in 1537, of Guyenne in 1541, and Languedoc in 1546.

Members of the king's household carried a wide range of routine missions of a more or less confidential nature. One of the most significant under Francis I was Pierre de Warty, *écuyer d'écurie* from 1518, gentleman of the chamber from 1521 to 1550, *grand maître des eaux et forêts*, whose name is ubiquitous in the instructions for confidential and public missions of all kinds. Not a politician of the first rank, he was a man without whom the court could not have functioned.[71] Antoine de Lettes, already discussed above as an ambassador, was attached as a youth to the service of Francis I before his accession, when he became an *écuyer tranchant*. Son of a Languedoc seigneur and nephew of the bishop of Montauban, he was gentleman of the chamber from 1520, appointed *châtelain* of Montluçon in 1523 and by the 1530s was governor of the duchy of Châtellerault (a post he resigned to his son Melchior, also *gentilhomme de la chambre*, in 1536). Later he was *sénéchal* of Poitou, governor of Fossano and from 1540–4 Montmorency's replacement as governor of Languedoc, succeeding Robert Stuart as marshal in 1544.[72] Examples of fairly routine missions are the despatch of Sansac, as gentleman of the chamber, to convey the king's opinions to Montmorency on what was to be done about the Guyenne disturbances in 1548, or to join with others negotiating with the lansquenet colonel, margrave Albert of Brandenburg in 1552.[73] Louis d'Humières was sent on mission to Picardy in 1552 and Diego de Mandosse was deputed to negotiate with lansquenet colonels in 1558–9.[74]

Louis de Perreau, sr. de Castillon, *valet de chambre* in 1524 and *panetier* in 1528, *gentilhomme de la chambre* from about 1537 to 1544, became ambassador to England in 1537 and was restored to the post of *gentilhomme* in 1547, evidently as a Montmorency client. Jean Pot, sr. de Chémault, *premier valet tranchant* with the accession of Henri II in 1547, was special envoy to Rome in 1547–8 sent to arrange the marriage of Anne d'Este, resident ambassador to England in 1550–1, special envoy to the emperor, 1549, 1551–2, and special royal representative in Touraine to oversee pacification in 1561 and 1563.[75] François, baron de Fumel, killed by the Protestants in 1562, who had been captain of the gate under Francis I, seems to have been a gentleman of the chamber under Henri II (though not on the household list). He was sent on mission to Venice and Constantinople in 1547 and to the governor of Champagne in 1552.[76]

At the level of routine missions, it was the other officers of the household like the *maîtres d'hôtel* who were particularly prominent. Fewer in number than the *gentilshommes* (there were 90 appointed between 1516 and 1551), they seem to have carried out a more practical range of services for the king and their attendance for their quarter was strictly required. Appointed by *lettres de retenue* to the *maître de la chambre aux deniers*, the *maîtres d'hôtel* were listed each year at the head of the accounts. In 1479 there were 17 of them, a figure which did not increase notably in the sixteenth century.[77] There was more continuity at the change of reign in 1515, four of Francis I's initial *maîtres d'hôtel* having served Louis XII in the same capacity, while another was the son of one of

Louis's *chambellans,* Loys Picart.[78] Of the 78 who served Francis I, only 9 were *baillis* or *sénéchaux* and only one a provincial governor during his tenure (Jacques de Barres, Saluzzo, 1540). On the other hand there were 13 ambassadors, including La Pommeraye, Passano, Morlelet du Museau,[79] Boisrigault, Livio Crotto and Boisdaulphin residents in sensitive posts like England, Flanders and Switzerland and with the German princes. As diplomats with special skills they did not so frequently transfer to the king's chamber, the only exceptions in the period 1515–51 being Nicolas de Bossut-Longueval, Guigo Guiffrey and Dom Diego de Mandosse. The longest-serving example, 1528–55, installed through the patronage of Montmorency, is François de Rasse, sr. de La Hargerie. A Picard landowner with expertise in military administration (he began his career at court under Louis XII in the company of 100 gentlemen of the *Hôtel*), he served his quarter regularly in the household (involving royal service in person, overseeing funerals and festivities) while carrying out countless missions in his own province, visits to Brussels, transmitting news of the frontier, acting as military victualling commissioner and diplomatic negotiator with the local Netherlands representatives, considered for appointment as resident ambassador in England in 1530. Routine functions for the *maîtres d'hôtel* included, within the household, dealing with extraordinary expenditure on receptions and festivities and, in administration, the witness of supply contracts for army victualiers. One such, in August 1549, was witnessed by three of them.[80]

Within the hierarchy of the household, it was usual to progress as in a kind of *cursus honorum.* Young gentlemen by the reign of Francis I began their lives at court as pages in one of the royal households. Then, *mis hors de page,* they could move on to the *écurie du roi,* where as Brantôme put it there were 'brought up more than a hundred pages of the chamber, of the great and lesser stables, the hunt and falconry, all gentlemen of good breeding'.[81] This also constituted both a nursery of military talent and a pool from which young men could be selected for attachment to embassies abroad, as when Ronsard joined Lazar de Baif's mission in 1540. From the *écurie* they could hope for the post of *pannetier, échanson* or *valet tranchant* and afterwards one of the higher paid posts of *maître d'hôtel* or *gentilhomme de la chambre.*[82] Philippe de Longueval-Haraucourt, a military administrator, began as a page of the chamber in 1524 to become *maître d'hôtel* in 1544.[83] Marin de Montchenu began as *échanson* in 1516 and became *premier maître d'hôtel* from 1526 until the end of Francis I's reign. Such figures constituted a group who owed their advancement from obscure status to service at court. Such was the du Plessis de Richelieu family; Louis du Plessis was an *échanson ordinaire* in the late reign of Francis I, his son going on to become *Grand Prévôt* under Henri III.[84]

The King's Routine

The court of France was renowned for its openness and access to the royal apartments, for respectable people, throughout the early modern period. Even the anti-court poet Jean Bouchet, in building up his ideal picture of the rural French nobility, admitted that the French nobles (as did, he thought, their English and Scottish fellows) lived with their kings on a footing of 'liberty and priviness without ceremony'.[85] One feature of this was that, until the reign of Henri III, the layout of the royal apartments at Fontainebleau, for instance, was relatively simple, with the *salle* leading on to the king's *chambre*, essentially his state bedroom where much public business was conducted, and a private *cabinet*. Francis I was particularly proud of his work at Fontainebleau and chose frequently to show it off to foreign envoys; the Englishman Cheyney justly called it 'to me a thing incredible, onles I had sene it myself'. John Wallop, Cheyney and Lord Lisle were all shown it in the 1540s and reported to England. Cheyney in summer 1546, having attended the king's morning dinner in his *salle* was taken with a select few into Francis I's *chambre* or what he called the 'Privey Chambre, which was so cold and freshe as could be devised, considering the tyme of the yere; which is a gloriouse chambre, and so is thother without, where he dyned'. He was then given the tour of the gallery, 'very gallant and costly', and the bath suite beneath.[86] Francis I was relatively well provided for at Fontainebleau, with his new galleries, and in Pierre Lescot's new wing of the Louvre, begun in 1546, with several cabinets. As early as 1530, with the old Louvre, Neufville's report on the reorganisation of the castle indicates that the king had, leading from his *salle*, three cabinets, all richly and differently coffered, one with a

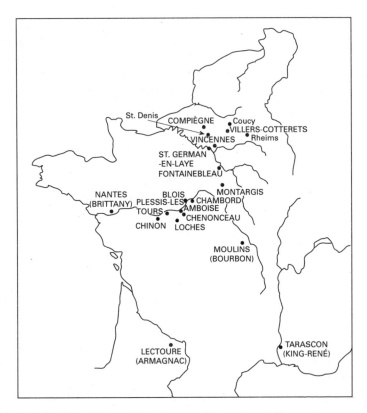

Map 1   Royal and Princely Residences, Fifteenth and Sixteenth Centuries

spiral stair to the bridge and other access to the queen's apartments above. From the king's *salle* there was now a gallery to the tennis gallery. Recent work on the royal apartments at Saint-Germain-en-Laye, based on a buildings account of 1549–50, confirms, however, that there were relatively few private rooms reserved for the king himself, though usually these had some form of private egress from them to a park or courtyard, via the apartments of Diane de Poitiers, that avoided the *salle*. What is apparent is that the private space available to the monarch was small. At Saint-Germain, the *chambre* was 120 m², while the *cabinet* was only 4.2 m across.[87] Although Henri II attempted to institute an *antichambre* between the *salle* and the *chambre* (possibly to accommodate meetings of the *conseil des affaires*), the 1552 *argenterie* account still refers repeatedly to furnishings for 'the king's two rooms'.[88]

At Saint-Germain, in fact, the limit of the king's privacy was the door of his *chambre*. Beyond that lay the *salle* which, in principle, anyone of respectability could enter and which the king would cross diagonally through the throng to reach the grand staircase and the council chamber. The Tudor monarchs of England lived in formality and privacy; their private rooms led from a privy chamber, itself isolated from the public presence and watching chamber by a closet and passage. In contrast, the kings of France led an intensely public life.[89] No serious attempt was made to alter this state of affairs or the general press and hurly-burly until the reforms of Henri III after 1578.[90]

The ordering of the royal day in the first half of the sixteenth century is discussed in a celebrated letter, in which Catherine de Medici fully described for one of her sons the court arrangements that had prevailed under Francis I and Henri II. Her intention was to praise the arrangements which had applied during those reigns and to advise that they be reinstated. However, it is her description of the king's daily routine that is most important, for in it we can see how rigid the king's daily programme had become and how significant access to the monarch was thought to be:

> I would wish you to fix a certain time for your *lever*, and to satisfy your nobility, as did your late father; for when he took his shirt and the raiment came in, all the princes, lords, captains, knights of the order, gentlemen of the chamber, *maîtres d'hôtel* and gentlemen servants being there, he spoke to, saw and contented them. That done, he went to his business and everyone left except the four secretaries.[91]

Venetian envoys tell us that the king rose at dawn in summer and in candlelight during the winter. Mass at ten was followed by dinner at eleven and the rest of the day was supposed to run by the clock. While the king only occasionally attended the *conseil privé* after dinner, under Henri II there was a public royal audience two days a week, followed by an hour or so with the queen, added Catherine, 'so that the style of the court be known, which is a thing that pleases the French greatly, their having been accustomed to it'. This was the famous 'circle' of courtiers, both male and female, in which good conversation was supposed to reign. This period in public should be followed by time in the study and then, at three, exercises of an *honneste* (gentlemanly) kind. A supper *en famille* was followed twice a week by dancing in the *salle de bal*, 'for I have heard the king your grandfather say that two things were necessary to live in peace with the French so that they love their king: to give them mirth and exercise'. The increased refinement of life at court in the late Middle Ages gave rise to a comportment that favoured games and sport. Sharing in the pleasures of the king was a significant honour. Princes played games and passed their time only with their equals or their trusted servants. The fact that Francis I played *boules* or the *jeu de paume* with Montmorency or Chabot was an undoubted sign of their intimacy.[92]

Dining in public was a well-established custom. In the reign of Louis XI, the royal table service was a relatively simple affair, to judge by the king's regulations,[93] though there is little doubt that the scale of public ceremonial increased in the sixteenth century. Informality extended to behaviour. Until the reign of Louis XII, gentlemen could remain covered in the king's presence, except when speaking to him or during his meals; some even claimed that to take off your cap in the royal chamber was an act of vanity. This was a fashion that so scandalised the Italians during Louis's expeditions that he had to ask his French lords to take off their caps in the royal chamber when they saw an Italian present. Custom thus began to change and Francis I ordered that only ambassadors should remain covered in his presence. Although in 1551 Henri II ordered the death penalty for anyone remaining covered in his presence, it was a major step when Henri III at the start of his reign instituted a barrier between himself and the court when he was dining.[94]

The Keeping of Order

Catherine de Medici, in her description of the Renaissance court, gave the rather favourable impression that under Francis I and Henri II, the 'police' of the court was effective in guarding its good order. Then, 'no man was so bold as to dare injure another in their court, for if it had been heard of, he would have been

brought before the *prévôt de l'hôtel.*' Her picture of the halls and
staircases of the court patrolled by archers of the guard, to
prevent the disorders and blaspheming by the pages and lackeys,
was an ideal one.[95] Growing numbers alone would have made this
difficult. Francis I had issued an edict in 1530 prescribing the
noose for larceny within the court, caused by the 'great flood of
people gathering daily in our residence' and committed by
'people who, in the guise of being well dressed and accoutred, are
allowed to enter everywhere'. He issued a declaration in October
1546 against 'secretaries and servants of princes, prelates, lords
and gentlemen and others of whatever quality ... that henceforth
they should cease to follow, reside or be at our court', ostensibly
to cut down on the press of suitors but more likely to limit the
activities of foreign agents, who were also forbidden at this time to
use ciphers in their messages.[96] Security and decorum seem to
have been an increasing problem. The *conseil privé* in March 1549
issued detailed regulations for the behaviour of archers of the
royal guards: they were to be properly armed at all times, accom-
pany the king in all his public appearances, such as going to mass,
in formal ranks and not as a crowd, and maintain constant vig-
ilance in the courtyard. The order was to be repeated in
December 1559. The problem of crowding was still apparent in
March 1560, when the government of Francis II issued a detailed
edict on the police of the court which sought to establish exactly
who was in residence by, prescribing the registration of all
members of the royal family's households as well as those of the
great princes and lords. Petitioners were told to see to their business and depart as quickly as possible. Much attention was also
paid to decorum, avoiding fights over lodgings and victualling at
fair prices. Judging by a *règlement* of the following year, the 'police'
of the court was still chaotic.[97]

The household remained an unruly and sometimes violent place.
In 1552, the *conseil privé* issued an order against 'giving the lie',
challenging to a duel, at court and declaring that the shame of
being reputed a coward should be borne by the challenger, who
would have to pay a fine 'because none should be unaware that the
king's house is a *lieu de franchise* and it is forbidden to seek revenge'.
It was also forbidden to 'beat, tap, snub, stab, draw a sword against
anyone in the king's house' on pain of hanging. Cutting off of the
hand was to be the penalty for effacing the marks placed on houses

by the lodging officers of the court.[98] Usually, cognisance of such cases came before the *prévôt de l'hôtel*, the responsible judicial officer for the area within the verge of the court. The *prévôt*'s jurisdiction was defined in an edict of 1522 that removed the right of appeal from his sentences in criminal cases, provided they were approved by trained lawyers, either *maîtres des requêtes* or members of the *Grand conseil*. The reason given then was that 'because our court and the jurisdiction of the *prévôt* of our household are itinerant', delinquents had been managing to delay the reckoning by appeals until they had a chance to escape.[99] In addition, until 1551 there had been disputes between the *prévôt* and the heads of the various departments of the household who wanted to judge the faults of those in their charge. The king in council ordered a compromise in December 1551, giving cognisance of all domestic officers to the *prévôt* in cases involving fines or corporal punishment and all lesser cases to the heads of departments.[100]

Conclusion

Manners and behaviour remained rough and ready, though the court in general was becoming more institutionalised in its routine as well as a highly significant centre for the dissemination of civility and culture. Until the late fifteenth century, the households of great princes like Jean II duke of Bourbon and his successor Pierre de Beaujeu at Moulins rivalled that of the king's household as poles of cultural patronage. The power of the court as a cultural centre, quite consciously cultivating polite manners and elegant literature, stemmed evidently from the interests of the Renaissance kings and pre-eminently of Francis I, as Robert Knecht has emphasised. Although Henri II was not, perhaps, so cultivated, there is no doubt that the court in the mid-sixteenth century, the age of Ronsard as court poet, continued to accumulate a cultural pre-eminence in French society as a whole.[101] Ellery Schalk has argued that, until the reign of Henri IV, the cultural role of the court remained to some extent that of a beleaguered island, failing to transform significantly the military self-image of the nobility. In fact, far from being the emasculating agent that it was later thought to be, it was not until the very end of the sixteenth century that the court and the mass of the nobility began to share common values. This may to some extent explain the continued popularity of the clichés about court corruption throughout the period of the Renaissance.[102]

Conventional strictures against court life should not conceal the fact that the royal household was plainly the centre of power by the first half of the sixteenth century and arguably before that. The play of politics, though it took place at court, was generated not so much by the institutions of the household as by the practical fact that power and patronage stemmed from proximity to the monarch. Competition for influence with him, increasingly virulent by the mid-sixteenth century, naturally formed part of this.

It was partly this competition and partly the desire of monarchs to use their entourage for wider political contacts that shaped the evolution of the royal household from the relatively modest numbers under Louis XI to the large and growing household of the mid-sixteenth century. The basic institutions were well established and in many cases survived through the sixteenth century but the purpose of the court, both political and cultural, was substantially overhauled. The inception of new posts and the use of existing ones for both confidential and routine political functions placed the court at the centre of political and social life. The ever-increasing cultural primacy of the court of France gave it an undoubted magnetic quality; the culture of the court became a yardstick by which cultural life in general came to be judged. Great aristocratic households remained and indeed flourished in the sixteenth century but could no longer compete with the brilliance of the court of France. The deliberate display of magnificence was built up relentlessly as an overt demonstration of the king's role as supreme patron in the arts and of political power. Even during the chaos of the civil wars after 1560, the court continued to flourish as a cultural influence down to the collapse of Henri III's power in 1588.

3. The King, his Council and the Secretariat

The French monarchy was invested with the *plena potestas* of Roman law as well as with supreme judicial authority at the apex of the feudal hierarchy. In practical terms this authority was limited by the physical and technological constraints placed upon the exercise of power in the medieval centuries, constraints which could engender physical insecurity for the monarch or his domination by those in control of armed force. Nevertheless, the legal basis of Absolute Monarchy, the capacity of the crown to recover from repeated shocks and the benefits available to men of energy and ability in its service, proved decisive.

Thus a powerful identity of interest existed well before the fifteenth century between the king and the array of officials which staffed the high organs of administration. The Absolute monarchy was in this sense the vehicle in which a substantial political elite rode in order to control the machinery of order, power, patronage and private interest. It is fatal to regard the crown as in any sense divorced from the complex structure of the French political society. It should also be remembered that, as Michel Antoine has pointed out, the most powerful shaping principle of French government in the Ancien Regime was collective decision-making.[1]

The supreme example of this fact is demonstrated by the highest organ of public power in the fifteenth and sixteenth centuries, the *conseil du roi*. The vast number of individuals calling themselves *conseillers du roi* has been called by Michel Harsgor, in a major prosopographical study of the royal councillors from 1480 to 1515, 'the homage rendered by society to the supreme institution of the monarchy'. All counsellors bore the title *conseiller et chambellan* and received *lettres de retenue* like those drawn up for Ymbert de Batarnay in 1468,[2] but the title was also held by scores of others in every province who gravitated around the court to a greater or lesser extent, described by Harsgor as 'a gigantic mystical council comprising all the loyal men of substance (*gens de bien*) in the kingdom'.[3] The essential point is that, by the reign of Louis XI, loyalty (*fidélité*) was the main determinant for regular participation in the council. The princes and dukes might participate, sometimes frequently, but the royal summons must come first. The council was also made up of a spectrum of individuals whose influence differed from province to province. Under Louis XI, for instance, there was a contingent of Picard lords such as Piennes and Esquerdes, through whom the towns of the north could make representations. Other provinces lobbied through other councillors: La Rochelle through chancellor Doriolle and Jean Bureau, Poitiers through Louis de Crussol. Later on Rouen relied on Georges d'Amboise.[4]

The idea of collectivity in decision-making within the Absolute monarchy was profoundly related to that of government by 'good counsel', in other words government that was not arbitrary but, rather, considered and consistent. Collectivity of action remained a fundamental principle until the end of the Ancien Regime, all acts of the crown emanating from one council or another, rather than from individual ministers.[5] Thus, in the fifteenth and sixteenth centuries, the many royal letters-patent *de par le roi en son conseil* ('By the king in council') were in effect orders of the council issued collectively. In addition, many of the acts issued *De par le Roi* ('By the king') were commanded by informal gatherings of councillors.[6] As for 'good counsel', the widely read Symphorien Champier argued that 'God does not help those who act without counsel and only by their own understanding'. No one prince was so capable that he could rule alone. 'Without counsel all is disordered', in the words of a verse once attributed to Jeanne de France, Louis XI's daughter. Robert de Balsac in 1502 declared that 'the Prince only has the same mental capacity as others, which through weakness or carelessness can fail to understand'.[7] As Commynes clearly understood, there was a profound practical difference between a ruler who could control the agenda of his councils and one who could be led by the nose by his advisers.

Of course, the composition and organisation of the council could, and did, change considerably, especially in this period, but there was no ideological diversity about the very foundation of monarchical power, widely regarded as the apex of a society bound together by divine and human laws of which the king was the guardian. This is the sense in which Roland Mousnier argued that Absolutism was the direct opposite of despotism.

The Theory of Government by Good Counsel

With the theory of Absolutism well established by the start of the sixteenth century, the real question was: how should the supreme authority of the prince be exercised? Here there was considerable disagreement, since obviously the nature of 'good counsel' was open to different interpretations. Those who were to proffer advice to the prince might have widely different programmes of action. The theory of government by good counsel was well established in the writings of Philippe de Mézières and Christine de Pisan in the fourteenth century, the latter clearly understanding that 'the good prince should take advice from different men according to the different problems' he faced.[8] Both display the compatibility of Absolutist theory with the ideas of good counsel. While urging councillors to advise their prince effectively, François Hallé was clear that 'it is impossible in a monarchy (for the king) to have a peer or colleague'.[9] It was presupposed that 'nowhere in his kingdom was the king as absolute as in the body of his council'.[10] For Commynes, many councillors are needed since 'the wisest often err' through partisanship or mood and 'things done after dinner should not be taken for counsel'. Jean d'Auton in the reign of Louis XII argued that the council was there to give mature judgements to acts of state according to realities, not to act itself. Claude de Seyssel in 1516, writing that 'it is not possible that one man alone, or even a small number of men however accomplished, should be able to understand and manage the affairs of such a great Monarchy' did not mean this as an argument against Absolutism but as a definition of how it functioned effectively; the monarch should not act through 'unconsidered or sudden will'.[11] On the other hand, there was no fixed ideology other than this need to give and take counsel.

By the middle of the fifteenth century, it was already clear that the council was a differentiated body and the reign of Louis XI saw the definite subtraction of judicial cases in favour of a judicial section of the Council, the *Grand Conseil de justice* dealing with *cas privilégiés* evoked from the Parlement and other courts. The registers of this body are preserved from 1483 and at first it remained in the royal entourage, but there was considerable overlap of personnel with the *conseil du roi* and the only fixed personnel were the Chancellor and the *maîtres des requêtes de l'hôtel*. Although, at first, there was no significant conflict with the Parlement, it was clear by the 1480s that recourse to the *Grand Conseil* was an abuse used by those who felt they had a poor case in order to delay judgement. The Parlement became increasingly restive, a portent of the great quarrels that were to build up in the first quarter of the sixteenth century over *évocations* of cases concerning benefices and, ultimately, the implementation of the Concordat of Bologna. The definitive *ordonnances* of 1497 and 1498 that gave it its structure as a sovereign court of 20 *conseillers* (rising to 32 by 1544) presided over by the Chancellor, aimed to fix it in one place. Although it gradually ceased in the later sixteenth century to be closely related to the royal council, there is no reason to suppose that it 'went out of court' until the reign of Henri III. However, the chancellor ceased to preside over it after 1526 and it tended to meet in important towns rather than, like the chancellery, more or less following the king's itinerary.[12]

The true engine of power at the centre had come to be called the *Conseil Etroit* by 1484, a term used to distinguish it from the *Grand Conseil*.[13] It was made up of the inner councillors and princes of the blood, between 15 and 20, drawn from different factions, and remained the nucleus of the effective royal council until the middle of the sixteenth century. It was equivalent to the council of 12 postulated by Seyssel in his biblical analogy and indeed that number was much talked of during the debates in the Estates of 1484. Yet within this council there was to be an inner 'secret' council of three to discuss the most sensitive matters. These terms, *conseil étroit* and *conseil secret* were to be much used throughout the first half of the sixteenth century but unfortunately with little clear definition and sometimes confusion.

The Composition of the Council

In the fifteenth century, Ghillebert de Lannoy made the interesting observation that a council should not exclude the greedy or rapacious, since these would have useful qualities, but that they should not be allowed to lead. This view was held also by Commynes, who thought that, with a range of councillors, individual passions would be cancelled out. Nor should there be any appointments of men under 36. This was a purely practical piece of advice. As a body of men, the *conseil du roi* had no fixed social identity and cannot be equated with the great *corps* of the state.[14]

The exact composition of the council under Louis XI and during the minority of Charles VIII has been a matter of debate. The complicated manoeuvres in the Estates-General of Tours involved calls for the monitoring of the royal council's composition. In the event, this developed into a struggle between two factions, those of the Beaujeus and those of the princes led by the duke of Orléans, for control of the council. The existing structure was blamed for what were regarded as abuses during the reign of Louis XI. In fact, despite these convulsions, the composition of the royal council remained remarkably constant throughout the late fifteenth and early sixteenth centuries.

An essential point to remember about the council is its non-institutionalisation in this period. Unlike the judicial bodies that come to be defined as the 'sovereign courts', the council remains fluid in procedures and composition principally because it has no existence except in conjunction with the exercise of royal power and has no fixed membership list. There was no membership for life, though an individual like Ymbert de Batarnay could seem to be a fixture. A reflection of the informality is the absence of surviving formal records between 1484 and the middle of the sixteenth century. The published records which exist for March 1484 to January 1485 are in fact the register of acts commanded by the *conseil étroit* to two *greffiers*, Jean de Mesme and Etienne Petit, in matters largely excluding finance and war (as well, of course, of justice). Thus, though they were responsible for a *procès-verbal* of sessions, what they in fact did was keep a register of acts which, as *notaires et secrétaires*, they were responsible for drawing up.[15]

Between 1484 and 1546 there are no direct records of the council's activities. The consequence has been to minimise its significance in the political developments of the period. When the next consecutive record appears, it is a rather different sort of document, in fact the transactions of the *conseil privé* from 1546 enregistered by its *greffier*, Guillaume Bochetel, including acts commanded to different secretaries. The development had taken shape in the intervening years but it is largely hidden by absence of adequate sources.

The main fifteenth-century source, used by P.-R. Gaussin and M. Harsgor, for the composition and activities of the council, other than the isolated register of 1484–5, is the presence lists attached as authentication to royal acts promulgated in the council. The requirement for such lists goes back to the early fourteenth century and they continue through the sixteenth. From the early sixteenth century, these have to be supplemented lists of presence at the *jussio*, the command of royal acts pure and simple.[16] A collation of such lists does allow conclusions to be drawn about the functions and composition of the council in the reign of Francis I and especially the proportions of membership.

Under Louis XI, 462 persons held the title *conseiller du roi*, though 51 of these seem never to have participated in business. Of these, 183 (40 per cent) are only recorded as present once, some of them great lords like Albret and Maine. Another 72 (16 per cent) sat twice. This leaves 155 *conseillers* (33 per cent) who were present at least on three occasions but some of these were active only over short periods. In all, 119 (25 per cent) were present over lengthy periods. Although it is true that Louis dismissed nearly all his father's counsellors and introduced a large number of commoners, after the war of the Public Weal these diminished and princes were again the most numerous category among the influential group, though they were eclipsed again in the 1470s. Throughout the reign, the most consistent group were the nobles and military commanders, who constituted between two-fifths and a half. Thus, in a rare list of the entire council in February 1475, of a total of 38, there were 4 princes or counts, 4 bishops, 6 nobles, 24 commoners. A more telling picture emerges from an analysis of attendance at 58 known sessions throughout 1477. Of those who attended more than 10 of these meetings, thus the most influential, 28 per cent were princes, 39 per cent nobles and 33 per cent commoners. For the whole reign, taking the 33 most active counsellors, 21 per cent were princes, 42 per cent nobles and 37 per cent commoners. This represents a slight diminution of princely attendance in comparison with the previous reign, stability in noble participation and a slight rise in commoner presence (particularly noticeable in the last years of the reign). The king, of course, had the ultimate word in choice of counsellors but it is also worth noting that, of the 33 most influential, 42 per cent were in effect *grands commis,* or high specialist civil servants, while 33 per cent can be described as *familiers du roi* (personal followers of the king).[17]

During the last years of Louis XI, the *conseil étroit* included one prince of the blood, one bastard of France, 14 nobles (48.2 per cent), 15 commoners (51.75 per cent) and 2 clergy. On the transition to the reign of Charles VIII, 10 of these were dropped and 19 continued. Political pressures increased the membership to 39, roughly balanced between the Beaujeu adherents and those of the princes, though the indeterminate numbers of lawyers and financiers (usually described as 'others' in the lists) must give rise to caution.[18] However, if all presences in the councils between 1484 and 1515 are computed, 66 per cent of those present during the last years of Louis XI continued into the next reign and in the early 1480s some 69.4 per cent of councillors had experience during the previous reign. The debates in the Estates-General at Tours ultimately made no difference to membership, as Noël Valois surmised. Harsgor confirmed that 90 per cent of the councillors present in January 1484 went on through to August.

The *Guerre Folle* mounted by Louis of Orléans and his partisans entailed the withdrawal of a number of his adherents from the council but the nucleus of seven continued: the sire de Beaujeu, Esquerdes, Pompadour, chancellor Rochefort, Baudot, Commynes and Vesc. Surprisingly enough, the accession of Louis XII brought only limited changes; 59 per cent of his councillors continued from the previous reign and, of the most frequent attenders, only two were new.[19]

The conclusion to be drawn on the period up to 1515 is that an active nucleus dominated the proceedings of the council and maintained continuity; change took place slowly through natural processes of death or retirement. In the final phase of Louis XII's reign, of 34 individuals who attended the council, only 10 attended three or more times and the obvious central group consisted of chancellor Ganay, Ymbert de Batarnay, Etienne Poncher and Florimond Robertet. This hardly changed from the previous period of 1503 to the death of cardinal d'Amboise in 1510: 30 individuals, 8 attending two or more times with the nucleus consisting of the cardinal, Guy de Rochefort, Ganay, Robertet and Poncher.[20]

From the start of Francis I's reign, we are largely in uncharted territory. Decrue's Latin thesis is now rather dated, Noël Valois too general and the brief study by Mlle Postel[21] only scratches the surface. Her survey of 70 *conseillers* during the reign produced the conclusion that 17 per cent were princes, 13 per cent great officers of the crown and, of the rest, 28 per cent were sword nobles, 14 per cent magistrates of the sovereign courts, 12 per cent financiers and 14 per cent ecclesiastics. Of the total, there were 14 clergy. Of the 56 others, 37 were sword nobles. Naturally, such figures tell us little about the weight of influence, except the aristocratic bias. The vast compilation of the *Actes* of Francis I unfortunately omits the witness lists but, by using those documents selected for the printed *Ordonnances* we can establish a basis of evidence (with the provisoes already discussed).

Of those mentioned by the royal secretary Jean Barillon as constituting the inner council of the Regent in 1515, we find in Batarnay and Guillaume de Montmorency well-established members of the council.[22] An intriguing report from court to Jean d'Albert, king of Navarre, in May 1516 gives a list of 'those who attend the council': this includes the king himself 'often' and his mother 'usually', 'My lord is there sometimes' (probably the *grand maître* Artus de Gouffier-Boisy), Jean d'Albret-Orval 'usually', Louis de La Trémoïlle, the new chancellor Duprat, René bâtard de Savoie, the king's uncle, Guillaume de Montmorency, G. de Dinteville-Des Chenetz and J. de Beaune-Semblançay. When finances were discussed Nicolas de Neufville, *secrétaire ordinaire au conseil* was called and Robertet when available.[23] This is what we have already called the council nucleus in previous reigns. In addition, though, this source make it clear that for 'great affairs', Louise de Savoie, Duprat and Gouffier-Boisy meet and sometimes in the latter's absence his brother Bonnivet 'for at present he has great credit'. This is the inner or 'secret' council. Again, there is continuity, since Duprat, La Trémoïlle, Semblançay and Montmorency had attended in the previous reign.

Statistical analysis of presences over 58 acts containing presence lists from January 1515 to January 1519 (the predominance of *grand maître* de Boisy) reveals those with 20 mentions and more: Boisy and chancellor Duprat; those with 9 to 20 mentions: René bâtard de Savoie, Jean d'Albert-Orval, Jacques de Chabannes-La Palisse, the duke of Alençon; those with 6 to 8 mentions: Jean Calveau, bishop of Senlis (*maître des requêtes*), the dukes of Bourbon and Vendôme, Louis de La Trémoïlle, Guillaume Gouffier-Bonnivet and Guillaume de Montmorency. In addition,

Florimond Robertet countersigned 24 times, Robert Gedoyn 13 and Neufville 8, all technical experts from the previous reign.[24]

In the next period from January 1519 to December 1524 (that is before the disaster of Pavia), we have 96 acts, which show the decline in the numbers of those witnessing at the *jussio* (19). Duprat and the bâtard de Savoie are present more than 20 times, Bonnivet for 18 and the rest well below: La Trémoïlle 6, the duke of Vendôme 4 and Châtillon, La Palisse, Poncher at 3 each.

The widely reported transformation that accompanied the disaster of Pavia is reflected in new membership of the council. From 1525 to the end of 1529, with 42 acts, the leaders in terms of presence at the *jussio* were Anne de Montmorency(11), François cardinal de Tournon (9), Duprat (7) and, surprisingly, the first prince of the blood, duke of Vendôme (7). Otherwise, the only notable attendance numbers were admiral Chabot-Brion with 5 and the cardinal of Lorraine, Louis de Brézé, count of Maulevrier and king of Navarre all with 4. These names tally very much with the observations of foreign ambassadors interviewed by the Council. In June 1526, for instance, we find Duprat, Vendôme, Lautrec and Robertet at such a meeting and in February 1528, the *grand maître* Montmorency, now increasingly observed as dominant in business, Tournon, Jean Brinon, chancellor of Alençon (who usually does not figure as witness), and Chabot. The council left at Paris, while the King was at Fontainebleau, to deal with diplomatic negotiations in June 1528 consisted of Duprat, Tournon and first president Jean de Selve.[25] Louise and part of the court stayed at Saint-Germain in mid-July, Selve keeping the *grand maître* informed of diplomatic developments.[26]

For the period January 1530 to December 1536, when the court was roughly balanced and before the emergence of Montmorency's supremacy, from 88 acts containing 25 individual names in presences, chancellor Duprat (19), Montmorency (21) and Chabot-Brion (15) constitute the inner core with some important figures attending less frequently: cardinals of Lorraine (6), Tournon (7) and du Bellay (4). Occasionally attendances came from the duke of Vendôme (3), M. de Longjoue, bishop of Soissons (3) and J. de Laval-Chateaubriand (3). Again ambassadors tend to confirm this impression, the nuncio reporting the council in March 1535 as Duprat, Tournon, Vendôme, Montmorency, Chabot and Longjoue.

In the last period of the reign open to scrutiny at this stage, January 1537 to November 1539, the predominance of Anne de Montmorency is clear: out of 65 acts, 13 presences as opposed to 4 for chancellor Du Bourg, 5 for cardinal du Bellay and 5 for cardinal de Lorraine and 4 for M. de Longjoue, 3 for cardinal de Bourbon and 3 for cardinal de Tournon. This pattern is confirmed by a report of April 1540 that the king has been 'in council' more frequently of late and that, whereas he has been consulting only Montmorency and cardinal de Lorraine, he was now calling cardinals de Tournon, du Bellay and Mâcon and the bishop of Soissons more frequently.[27]

A common feature clear from the composition of the council in so far as it is accessible in this period is, firstly, its overwhelmingly aristocratic composition (provided it be acknowledged that the many acts *Par le Roy en son conseil* have only a countersignature and the 'others' clause obviously conceals judicial and financial officers). Secondly, aristocratic predominance takes the form from the late 1520s of a formidable body of cardinals as active members of the council: not only the chancellor but also Bourbon, Lorraine, Tournon, du Bellay and Mâcon. These were not individuals occasionally convoked but look like regular members.

Relations between the Councils and Order of Business

As already pointed out, the council, consisting of a working core of a dozen or so members to which the *gens des finances* and others could be convoked as necessary, was clearly known as the *Conseil Etroit* by 1484. Within this group, it is also obvious that an inner ring existed in order to shape the agenda and deal with secret matters like high diplomacy. This was why Claude de Seyssel chose a biblical analogy of the 72, the 12 and the 3 to describe his ideal conciliar structure. We have also seen that, in the early years of Francis I, the inner group consisted of Louise de Savoie, *grand maître* de Boisy (latter his brother Bonnivet) and chancellor Duprat. Probably the *bâtard* de Savoie belonged to this group. After 1525, it consisted of Anne de Montmorency, Chabot-Brion and the chancellor. This was the group who met the king early in the morning to discuss high matters of state and, for instance, was the 'secret council' that met cardinal Wolsey in Louise of Savoy's bedchamber at Amiens in August 1527.

Jean du Tillet was later to write that Francis I divided his council into three parts from 1515 to 1525 – matters of state, justice and finance. On his return from captivity in 1526, du Tillet adds, Francis instituted the *conseil des affaires* for secret matters.[28] In this analysis, he showed the influence of the traditional definitions. In reality, membership was still interchangeable. Guillaume de Montmorency reported to his son Anne in 1523: 'The council is working every day to set order in the matter of finance and other affairs and it has pleased the king that I should attend.'[29] As late as 1527, there is clear evidence that the *Conseil Etroit* was the main formally organised council. The edict concerning the jurisdiction of the Parlement of Paris was promulgated by an *arrêt* of the *Conseil Etroit*, at which the king of Navarre, the duke of Vendôme and his brother Saint-Pol, the chancellor, Montmorency, Brézé-Maulevrier, Tournon and Robertet were present. This is a presence very similar to other meetings attested in acts *De par le roy*. A *règlement* of 11 June 1528 actually attests the existence of a register of this council.[30]

In the 1520s and 1530s, an institutional distinction began to appear between the inner council and the administrative body increasingly known as the *conseil privé*.[31] The latter term was at first used interchangeably with that of *conseil étroit* but had supplanted it by the mid-1530s. Thereafter, the old term tended to be used only by foreign observers. At all events, this was the council that dealt with administration and finance.[32]

By February 1542, a *rôle* of those members of the council to deal with finance, with the other members of the *conseil privé* admitted for 'requests', establishes the clear fact that functions within the *conseil privé* were specialised. Tournon, now *lieutenant-général* at Lyon, again governed through a section of the *conseil privé*.[33] From the 1530s, this was the body that was dealing, among other things, with town deputations, military administration and consular affairs.[34] Chief ministers like the Constable and the Chancellor attended it and are known to have clashed there.[35]

Noël Valois drew attention to Etienne Pasquier's recollection that it was the work of chancellor Guillaume Poyet 'who had been brought up from the cradle to shape law cases' that had heavily increased the work of the *conseil du roi* in judicial matters, though he points out elsewhere that the *conseil* had very quickly back-tracked in the fifteenth century on the notion that justice should be dealt with only by the *Grand Conseil*. The movement in business between the two bodies was in both directions: cases evoked to the *conseil du roi* and sent from the latter to the *Grand Conseil*. For instance, in 1548 a case involving the princess of Gavre was sent from the *conseil privé* to the *Grand Conseil* 'because of the great and urgent business with which our said council is daily occupied'.[36]

The first surviving register of business of the *conseil privé*, important in that unlike earlier registers it is not a record of acts commanded to one particular secretary and therefore gives a good idea of the scope, though not a full transcript, of its business, indicates that matters of 'state' and of justice were both part of its remit. By 1560 business was organised in shifts, with the first given over to administration and only then were the *maîtres dès requêtes* admitted for judicial matters.[37] The administrative matters dealt with included a large proportion of military administration: supply and estimates of expenditure for the *extraordinaire des guerres* as well as financial business such as the apportionment of the *taillon* of 1549 (itself allied to military requirements). Henri II wrote to the Constable in 1548 that, having been informed that it was necessary to open the *traites* for grain 'having had on this the advice of my council, I have commanded the requisite despatches'.[38] There was also court expenditure settled. In addition, the *conseil privé* continued the work of the *conseil étroit* in dealing with foreign ambassadors when their business involved what would now be called consular matters. One report of December 1540 has secretary Breton kneeling in council to report on English merchant suits. The ambassador could be summoned before the council and on occasion a *procès-verbal* of the exchanges could be made.[39]

What do these records tell us about membership of the inner group and the *conseil privé* under Henri II? The list drawn up shortly after his accesssion by Henri II for entry to the council divided it in two. For the morning council, to consult on 'matters of state and finance... and advise the king so he can ordain his good pleasure', the list was the king of Navarre, cardinal of Lorraine, duke of Vendôme, the constable, chancellor, François de Guise, Sedan, Humières, Saint-André father and son, president

Betrand and Villeroy with the four secretaries of 'state'. After dinner, four cardinals, three dukes and president Remon were to join them. It is uncertain whether the morning meeting could have been an inner *conseil des affaires* with so many in attendance. The main distinction was envisaged in the security of the meetings: before dinner the council was to meet behind locked doors with the ushers outside. After dinner, the ushers were to be within. After dinner the business was to be 'general affairs' and judicial business presented by *maîtres des requêtes*.[40] Nevertheless, it seems that, in practice, the king's early morning meeting with intimates came to consist of an inner group. As for the main *conseil privé*, royal letters on the *gabelle* in Poitou of September 1549 were issued in council, with the presence listed of the duke of Vendôme, cardinal de Guise, constable de Montmorency, chancellor Olivier, marshal de Saint-André, president Bertrand, André Guillart and Jean de La Chesnaye for finance 'all councillors in the privy council'.[41] Another letter, of 1 March 1552, issued in the king's presence has the same range of witnesses. In other words, the effective *conseil privé* consisted of a variable number of the *conseil des affaires* with around two technical experts (in this period, Guillart and La Chesnaye, *général des finances*).[42] This is clear from one of the commonest administrative acts involving the *conseil privé*, contracts with victualling contractors, when a *maître d'hôtel* often attended as *rapporteur*.[43]

A revealing document of January 1552 makes clearer the relationship between the *conseil privé* and the *conseil des affaires*. This is an *arrêt* of 'the king, being in his morning council, where were *messieurs* the cardinal of Lorraine, dukes of Guise and of Montmorency...the keeper of the seals, the lords of Sedan and Saint-André...present', which institutes d'Urfé as *conseiller au conseil privé* with all prerogatives and salaries attached.[44] This *conseil du matin* is obviously the meeting much described by Venetian ambassadors in the period, in which the king discussed high matters of state while being prepared for the day by his attendants. An order of 1616 assumes a degree of formality for the *conseil des affaires*. Participants were to be seated with the secretaries reading out all the confidential despatches.[45]

Saint-Mauris, the imperial ambassador, when describing Henri II's routine in 1547 wrote that 'according to the importance of the matters, he attends the council after dinner, though this is not often, but, in the morning, he deals every day with his affairs, which is his *conseil estroict'* and added that Henri II would see no one except Saint-André until he was dressed.[46] It seems, then, that the old title *conseil étroit* was by some given to the small inner group. Whatever the terminology, this is the direct continuation of the inner group discussed by the theorists of the fifteenth century and in existence in the early days of Francis I. One of the most quoted descriptions of a council meeting in the period, by Blaise de Monluc in 1544, took place after dinner with the king seated at a table and in the presence of Saint-Pol, Annebault, Galiot de Genouillac, Gouffier-Boisy and the dauphin. While this was a meeting of military men to discuss campaign strategy in Italy, there is at least the possibility that it was a meeting of the *conseil privé* that was being described, since there were others there not named. A clearer description is to be found in the history of events in 1557–8 written by secretary Robertet de Fresne. Fresne, who was in a position to know, tells us how the king held a meeting of the military council at Compiègne attended by Guise, Nevers, Aumale, Francesco d'Este, Piero Strozzi, Termes, Sansac, Bourdillon and Sénarpont. The business was to discuss alternative strategies and Guise, of course, took the lead. But Fresne tells us that 'this council was held in appearance, to distract the world. The king's resolve was otherwise, for the following morning he called to his affairs M. de Sénarpont, whom he had summoned expressly for this purpose, and there the enterprise of Calais was proposed by him.'[47]

The *conseil des affaires/du matin* dealt with the most sensitive diplomatic and governmental despatches and, according to Venetian ambassadors, its *arrêts* were more likely to be obeyed by the Parlement than those of the *conseil privé*. By its nature its deliberations were usually unrecorded except when it was acting as a preparatory meeting for business of the *conseil privé*. In the absence of records, we must use the reports of foreign ambassadors. The Venetian Dandolo noted in March 1541 that since the Constable's disfavour, 'the council, which was usually prepared in the *sala* of the Constable is prepared in the king's *sala* and the Constable shows no resentment'.[48] Another reported that when Jean de Monluc, a messenger from the peace negotiations near Calais in 1546, arrived at Fontainebleau at dawn on 9 May, he found the king in bed and went to Tournon, who then assembled the council. At the king's *lever*, he presented Monluc, who made his report before the king went to mass. During the latter, Monluc returned to the council chamber, where discussions went on until dinner at 11 a.m .[49]

In January 1532, Francis I had spent 'three or four full hours' in council after dinner discussing diplomatic despatches and general matters.[50] In 1544, after an early morning council in his chamber, Francis I gave a long audience to an imperial envoy on the implementation of the peace of Crépy, and then moved to go to mass, when he was met at the chamber door and given a packet from Italy, opening it himself and reading two or three, leaving the others open in the hands of secretaries Bochetel and Bayard.[51] An observer at Compiègne in 1554 followed the Constable from the king's dinner to the *conseil* 'so that I had no means to salute and talk to him, since he was all the time talking angrily to one man or another'. Just afterwards, the same observer noted that the king, having given audiences after dinner, spent two hours with the cardinals of Lorraine, Tournon and Guise, and the duke of Guise 'devising of affairs', while the Constable went off to the Council. [52] In reality, business could not be clearly divided between the two bodies, nor did contemporaries attempt to do so. In June 1541, an ambassador was led to the king's 'privy chamber' by the cardinals Tournon, du Bellay, Lorraine and Ferrara and on the king's withdrawal into his *garderobe* the councillors sat down to deliberate on the business in the 'great chamber'. At the same time it was reported that, in view of the pressure of business, the 'council', consisting of Chabot de Brion, Poyet, Annebault, cardinals de Tournon, Ferrara and du Bellay, were sitting daily from before daylight to six at night. Early in the following month, the *conseil privé* stopped its continual sessions but some of them were at work harder than ever, attending on the king at dinner and dealing with business while the servants withdrew.[53] When the king was away from his advisers, matters had to wait. A jurisdictional conflict which arose with the emperor in 1546, for instance, was first placed before the king when he was hunting north of Fontainebleau without his council 'which at the moment I do not have with me'. The matter was deputed to a technical expert, president Rémon, for report. This, however, actually took place, on the chancellor's orders, at a *conseil du matin* in November.[54] Such evidence is a good indication that, even though faction and conflict were rife in the later years of Francis I, the king had not lost his grip on business.

Whatever the name used or the membership involved, this extremely supple instrument, the *conseil du roi,* acted as the central engine of the machinery of state from the late fifteenth century, became increasingly specialised and diversified and was eventually transmuted into the higher level of the state bureaucracy, the ministers and their *commis* of the eighteenth century, when, as Michel Antoine has shown, acts of government departments were still nominally promulgated by the *conseil du roi* in one of its forms rather than in the name of individual ministers.

The period from about 1480 to 1560 was the one which saw it take shape and embrace the increasingly complex and interventionist government of the monarchy, not as a rigid bureaucratic *corps* but as a supple organism for integrating the demands of society with those of the state.

The Royal Secretariat

The business of the council was recorded by a nucleus of trusted royal secretaries, some of whom would be present at the morning council, though they could not always participate. The first half of the sixteenth century saw the rapid development of the group of administrative experts who would by the middle years be called 'secretaries of state'. They carried out functions which would later develop into those of ministers, although in the sixteenth century they still had the archaic characteristics of office-holders.

The corps from whom the secretaries were recruited was the company of *notaires et secrétaires du roi,* whose privileges were codified in an *ordonnance* of 1482. In number notionally 60 (including the king himself), in fact each post was divided in two for purposes of profits. Their headquarters was at the Celestins monastery, where they had a chapel and they regarded themselves as under the protection of the four evangelists. Their privilege consisted essentially of a monopoly of engrossment or drafting of all the acts of the great royal chancellery, from which they derived profits on a fixed scale. By the sixteenth century, they were full office-holders and there is no doubt that the posts were regarded as a financial investment, transmitted as property and to some extent venal.[55]

It was from this corps of 119 secretaries that an inner group of trusted royal secretaries was drawn who followed the king's person and drew up acts necessary to express his will. From the fourteenth century, there had been a *premier secrétaire du roi* and, though this title seems to have lapsed by 1460, Louis XI undoubtedly employed Jean Bourré in this capacity. In addition, there were a number of other secretaries whom Louis employed extensively to draw up his correspondence, while he deputed men like Batarnay to sign for him or even imitate his writing[56] (see appendix I, ii). Under Louis XII, Florimond Robertet occupied the same position although he was a much more powerful, even ministerial, figure with much scope in foreign policy. At the age of 50 in 1504, he married the 16-year-old daughter of the financier Michel I Gaillard. This brought him not only an enormous dowry but eventually kinship with the royal house, for his brother-in-law Michel II Gaillard married Francis I's natural sister Souveraine d'Angoulême. This and his remarkable ability assured favour in the new reign.

The key to Robertet's position was his commission to 'sign in finances', that is authenticate royal acts emanating from the king's power to ordain expenditure and grants. Such functions had been carried out by *secrétaires des finances* since the fourteenth century; there had originally been a dozen but by Louis XI's reign there were no more than four or five. As time went on, the scope of their activity vastly expanded beyond simple finance and came to cover most acts of state. In addition, Robertet absorbed the functions of the *secrétaires des guerres* appointed from 1472 as well as those of *greffier* of the Council carried out by Mesme and Petit under the regency in 1483–4. Robertet himself kept a register of the acts commanded in the royal council. His staff constituted a training-school for the secretariat of the whole sixteenth century and Robertet was as significant in the genesis of the power of the secretary as was Thomas Cromwell in England.

In 1515, Francis I confirmed Robertet and Robert Gedoyn in their posts and added Nicolas de Neufville. The secretaryship was already turning into a domain for related families. Gedoyn had succeeded his father-in-law Robineau and when Francis returned in 1526, he appointed Robertet's son, François, as his successor with the added provision of 'all letters that shall be commanded to him by us and ordained in our council'. This was a role continued by Nicolas II de Neufville, appointed in 1542. It was customary to attach one or two such secretaries to the commanders of armies on the frontiers in times of crisis to draw up financial orders (e.g. in 1513 and 1522, probably Robertet and Gedoyn).[57] A list of the *secrétaires des finances* of the late 1530s includes Nicolas I de Neufville, Jean Breton, Gilbert Bayard, Philibert Babou, Jean Dorne and Jean Duval, all of whose names are very familiar on the royal acts of the period, though for increasingly specialised areas. Before the end of the reign, Claude de L'Aubespine and Guillaume Bochetel also appeared. Usually, then, there were about six to eight *secrétaires des finances*.

However, well before the end of Francis I's reign, it is clear that certain secretaries had access to the most confidential business and were especially trusted. It may well be that they were already informally designated *secrétaires des commandements* and had access to the inner group of the council. Certainly, by the mid-1540s, this was the role of Gilbert Bayard and Claude de L'Aubespine. It was they who handled the confidential and secret diplomatic affairs, drawing up despatches to ambassadors as well as to provincial governors. Thus it was that the designation of four particular *secrétaires des finances* for the expedition of 'affairs of state' in 1547 was probably only a regularisation of the procedures already existing. Guillaume Bochetel and Claude de L'Aubespine were already there. Jean du Thier and Cosme Clausse were added for their position as secretaries in the trust of the Constable and Henri II before 1547. The new development, as has long been known, was the formal division of business, both internal and external, into areas, though even here there was some precedent in the division of business between Breton and Robertet in the late 1520s, while under Francis I Breton and then Bayard held the post of *secrétaire et contrôleur des guerres*, and this was taken on by Clausse under Henri II.[58] Nicola Sutherland has shown how fluid and theoretical these divisions actually were and any look at the papers of one of these secretaries of the period does indeed show that they took on other business as necessary.[59] Nevertheless, with greater knowledge now available for du Thier's papers in Moscow it is quite clear that his foreign business was largely confined to Italy.[60]

The inner core of the secretaries consisted of a group of men who had been brought up in the confidential service of the crown. Florimond Robertet had trained Gilbert Bayard, Jean

Breton and Guillaume Bochetel 'in affairs of state'; in turn Breton
trained Jean du Thier and Bochetel trained Claude de
L'Aubespine and Jacques Bourdin. Gradually, these men became
linked by ties of marriage, as was natural in such a society, and
passed on their offices to their sons or sons-in-law.[61]

Although the first clear uses of the term *secrétaire d'état* do not
appear until 1558, the term 'affairs of state' was current in the
1530s and that of 'expeditions and despatches of state' was used
in 1547.[62] There is no doubt, however, that by 1543 they sat in the
conseil privé as full councillors and not just as record-keepers. In
1547, the list of the *conseil du matin* specifies that the four secretaries should also be present. Although they continued to be
responsible for a wide range of royal acts under the great seal,
these were handled by their subordinates. The existing *secrétaires
des finances* not deputed for affairs of state, Hurault, Burgensis and
Villeroy, continued to authenticate acts concerned with matters
like taxes and the *don gratuit* and it was not until after 1559 that
their function became clearly more subordinate. The main politi-
cial function of the secretaries of state was the drawing up and
countersignature of acts issued over and authenticated by the
king's signature and secret seal (missives, letters-close, etc.) concerning foreign affairs, the royal household and the army. The
four secretaries seem to have kept jointly the records of the *conseil
privé* from 1547 to 1554, though this task was given to a simple
secrétaire des finances subsequently. They also kept parallel registers,
sometimes original *rôles*, of acts commanded by the king or by the
king-in-council. These have survived from 1546, though there is a
register of such acts kept by Florimond Robertet from an earlier
period. Such records were more important in the sixteenth
century, with the increase in the scope of acts beyond the format
of the sealed documents of the chancellery and the breakdown of
old uniform chancellery practice which authenticated acts ver-
bally commanded by the 'presence' of witnesses.[63]

In addition, the secretaries of state kept the drafts, or *minutes*,
of letters commanded by the king and his principal advisers as
well as the originals of the incoming correspondence. The archive
of Jean du Thier has survived virtually complete in 66 volumes
and 8200 documents for 1547 to 1559. For the period of
Montmorency's supremacy in 1538–40, it is the papers kept by du
Thier, who was then his private secretary, which contain the bulk

of the surviving diplomatic correspondence. Substantial portions of the archives of Claude de L'Aubespine and Jacques Bourdin also survive for the same period.[64]

The intermarried group of royal secretaries of state that had emerged by 1560 and its working procedures are evidence that the administrative developments that took place in the late fifteenth and sixteenth centuries in response to the demands of war were beginning to create a more coherent government machine with a collective memory and archives necessary for the management of a vast enterprise. However, it is essential to see these changes in their proper context. Later institutional historians were apt to see in the four secretaries of state the lineal origins of the ministerial posts of the Ancien Regime. In some ways this is understandable since it was customary for a seventeenth-century minister to purchase the office of a secretary of state. Yet what is most salient about the working methods of the secretaries of the mid-sixteenth century is the way they retained the *collective* working methods of the rest of the governing organs like the councils and finance administration. It is therefore not surprising that both foreign affairs and domestic administration were divided between them in their portfolios. There was no single 'minister of foreign affairs' or of the interior among them.

Directive power was retained by the king in conjunction with his inner group of confidants in the morning council and, for practical purposes, was committed to a small group or an individual like Montmorency from 1547 to 1559, who held the 'maniement des affaires' and had charge of the king's secret seal. If Montmorency, with all his extraordinary pre-eminence at certain times and his tireless labours, appears as a sort of 'prime minister', this was very much a personal role and not an institutionalised one.

4. The Crown, Administration and the Provinces

Expansion of the Royal Domain

The way in which the kingdom was ruled in its different provinces had always varied according to the degree that power had been permanently or temporarily devolved to apanage princes and great nobles or that representative assemblies continued to function. It is therefore axiomatic that there was no 'system of government' in the France of the Renaissance. The question is: was there a tendency for the kingdom to become more centralised? R. Bonney has wisely cautioned against the over-use in French history of the term 'centralisation', a term coined in 1794. The main distinction drawn in the early modern period, as Mousnier made clear, was that between the king's 'delegated' and 'retained' justice, the latter covering all the public affairs of the kingdom in which the crown was supreme and the former the private affairs of his subjects.[1] No one would pretend, however, that a clear line of division was ever established between the two.

If we consider the case of the apanages and great fiefs, for instance, the century from the reign of Louis XI is usually considered definitive in their suppression. In 1480, there were around 80 great fiefs. By 1530 around half of these still existed. The rest were in abeyance or held by members of the royal family. Within the royal house, the apanage of Orléans was reunited to the crown on the accession of Louis XII, although thereafter used periodically for the endowment of the king's younger son, permanently so after the reign of Louis XIV. The complex of territories held by the Bourbon and Bourbon-Montpensier families fell by the treason of the Constable in 1523. Burgundy (and temporarily Artois and Franche-Comté) were taken over in 1477. Among the great fiefs, the county of Comminges was united to the crown on the death of count Mahieu de Foix in 1453, the domains of the Armagnacs (such as the county of Rodez) were confiscated on the destruction of Jean V at Lectoure in 1473. They found their way by the reign of Francis I into the hands of the royal family, through the marriage of Jean V's sister to the count of Alençon. The last Alençon duke,

Charles, married Francis I's sister, Marguerite of Angoulême, and Alençon's sister, Françoise, married duke Charles of Vendôme, grandfather of Henry IV. Brittany was acquired through war and marriage alliance in the 1490s, Provence and the domains of the house of Anjou after the death of king René and then of Charles d'Anjou in 1481. The archives of the *Chambre des comptes* of Anjou for the early 1480s give ample evidence of the king's determination to exploit his new acquisition as soon as possible.[2]

It should not be assumed that the crown pursued a consistent determination to lay hands on all these territories and rule them directly. There was usually a more or less lengthy period of adjustment to a new status. Some apanages and territories taken over by Louis XI were absorbed into the general administration of the rest of the kingdom. This was clearly the case with Burgundy and Picardy-Artois in 1477, both of them in the area under the jurisdiction of the Parlement of Paris. Yet even here, Louis XI had to tread warily in winning over the support of the regional nobility and discontent was apt to break out until the end of the fifteenth century. On Louis's death, for instance, a rising occurred in Picardy at Bertrancourt near Doullens, with cries of 'there is no longer a king in France, long live Burgundy!' The absorption of Artois proved to be an impossible undertaking and had to be renounced in 1493.[3]

Elsewhere, absorption of apanages that were distant from the centre of royal power left affairs locally much as they had been before. The little Pyreneen county of Comminges was governed much as it had been under its counts, with privileges confirmed by Charles VIII in 1496. Only with the work of royal commissioners in the tax-assessing process in the 1540s, the first time an outside power had actively intervened in the affairs of the local nobility, did this begin to change.[4] Auvergne, an apanage raised to a duchy in 1360, was confirmed to the Bourbons in 1425 on condition that their whole domain became an apanage. The duchy was confiscated from the Constable in 1523 but transferred by the king to his mother in 1527 and only absorbed into the royal domain in 1531. Even after that, it formed the dower of Charles IX's queen and then part of the apanage of François d'Anjou, his brother. In the contiguous county of Forez, also confiscated in 1523, little local opposition emerged to the change of regime; although the local *chambre des comptes* was shortly suppressed, most local judicial officials, along with the entire administrative structure, were retained. Except for a few partisans of the Constable, it seems that there was no great upheaval.[5] Louise de Bourbon, the Constable's sister and princess of La Roche-sur-Yon, demanded a share of the inheritance – Forez, Beaujolais and Dombes. Beaujolais and the principality of Dombes eventually went to Louise's son, Montpensier.[6]

The county of Auvergne, enclaved in the duchy, was held by the duke of Albany in his wife's name, and was then inherited from the last of the La Tour d'Auvergne family by Catherine de Medici. Catherine brought it to the crown by her marriage with Henri II in 1533 but she continued to administer it as her own property. She left it to Charles IX's bastard, Charles de Valois, but her daughter Marguerite made good her claim to it in 1606 and it only entered the royal domain definitively when she willed it to Louis XIII.[7]

Map 2   Major Fiefs in the late Fifteenth and early Sixteenth Centuries

After her marriage to Charles VIII in 1491, Brittany was admin-istered as her own property by queen Anne, technically still duchess but in reality sharply circumscribed in her power, until her husband's death restored some of her freedom of action in 1498. Having already established friendly relations with Louis XII when he was still duke of Orléans, she was prepared to accept his offer of marriage after the annulment of his marriage to Louis XI's daughter, Jeanne, had been agreed. The contract which accompanied the marriage in January 1499 tied the duchy to the crown provisionally on condition that it always passed to the second son of the marriage, while in the absence of issue the duchy was to revert to Anne's heirs on her own side.[8] Anne was able to act rather more independently during her marriage to Louis XII though the conditions of the contract were not observed. On her death Brittany was inherited by her elder daughter Claude, wife of Francis I, who transmitted her rights to her son the dauphin. The queen had, however, transferred the government of the duchy to her husband in 1515 and he continued to rule it in the name of his son François on Claude's death, entitling acts as 'légitime administrateur et usufructuaire' of his son's property.[9] When the dauphin's majority in 1532 brought the question of the imminent personal union of the duchy to the kingdom to the foreground, it was arranged for the Breton estates to 'request' full union with France but on terms which guaranteed Breton privileges and maintained the principle that the dauphin would be duke of Brittany. Only in 1536, on the death of the dauphin, was the union with the kingdom complete and no more dukes were crowned at Rennes. What had been done was the annulment of the Breton succession law, which included females, in favour of the French royal succession law.[10] Late in 1539, it was decided that the new dauphin Henri would have the government of Brittany 'to govern as he pleases', though the documents were delayed by the king's illness. A 'Declaration' transferring Brittany to Henri was drawn up in 1540.[11] In practice, the government of the duchy seems not to have been much changed.

The lands of the house of France-Anjou posed a complex problem. René of Anjou, titular king of Jerusalem, Sicily, Aragon and Naples, was count of Provence in his own right, of Maine and Anjou as *apanagiste* and Guise by succession. As early as 1478, Louis was scheming to ensure that king René, who had no surviving son, did not leave his territories of Anjou, Provence and Bar to his grandson, René II of Lorraine, warning the *général* of Languedoc that his region would be 'destroyed' if Provence fell into other hands. On the 'good' king's death in 1480, most of his domains passed to his cousin Charles IV d'Anjou, count of Maine, who died childless in 1481, when Maine and Anjou reverted to the crown, thereafter to be granted out to members of the royal family such as Louise of Savoy. At the same time Provence was acquired by Louis XI by Charles IV's will and the county of Guise was disputed between the houses of Armagnac-Nemours, Lorraine (heirs of René I of Anjou and successors as titular kings of Jerusalem and Sicily) and Pierre de Rohan, marshal de Gié.[12] From 1481, however, the king ruled in Provence as 'count of Provence and Forcalquier'. The lord of Soliès, Palamède de Forbin, who had persuaded Charles d'Anjou to leave the county to the king, was rewarded with the post of governor. The major change came in 1535 with the edicts of Joinville and Is-sur-Tille on the government of Provence, limiting the scope of the old institutions of the Estates and the *Sénéchal* and increasing that of the Parlement of Aix in justice and of the royal governor in administration.[13] Curiously, Francis I was reported as having said that he felt an obligation to 'ceux de Guise', the house of Lorraine in France, since Louis XI had despoiled them of their inheritance of Provence and Anjou.[14]

The major surviving complex of apanage lands by the middle of the sixteenth century was that held by Antoine de Bourbon, now first prince of the blood and next in line to the throne after the immediate royal family, and his wife Jeanne d'Albret. These involved a group of territories held by different tenures. The Albret inheritance brought the titular kingship of Navarre with a small fragment of the ancient kingdom of Navarre north of the Pyrenees that was held in sovereignty. In the counties of Foix, Albret and Béarn, the family held effective sway under only the most distant royal sovereignty, though Louis XI saw fit to pose as the protector of the young François-Phébus in 1472. In 1476, he sought to revise local tariffs against Albret interests and in 1480 attempts to levy a *taille* for the *gendarmerie* there stirred up a rebellion.[15] In western France, the duchy of Vendôme, erected as late as 1515 to detach it from dependence on the duchy of Anjou, was held as an apanage under rather closer royal supervision. In the north, the complex of lands administered from La Fère-sur-Oise and centring the county of Marle was held directly of the king or of the Habsburg ruler of the Netherlands, rendering the family, to some, unreliable.[16] Practical power stemmed from the holding of the governorships of Picardy and of Guyenne by the Bourbons and Henri d'Albret.

Other independent territories persisted, such as the *vicomté* of Turenne, where the *vicomte* (of the La Tour d'Auvergne family) ruled with regalian rights until the eighteenth century, could raise taxes, coin money, make war and render justice as a limited monarch in conjunction with very active local estates.

How far did the acquisitions made by the crown in the century after 1460 actually change the way the provinces were governed? In practically every case, arrangements were made by which the estates of the territories concerned retained the right to vote direct taxes in various forms, while where local supreme courts (like the Parlement of Aix) had developed, these were retained in full force and fulfilled the function of registration, publication and enforcement of law held by the Parlement of Paris. Deputies from Poitiers, La Rochelle and Limoges, in arguing for a provincial Parlement in 1454, had said that 'in view of the greatness and size of this kingdom ... it is unlikely that all the parts of the kingdom should be required to go and seek justice in the city of Paris'. Although Poitiers was unable to make good its repeated claims down to the 1520s, the classic framework of the provincial Parlements was the creation of the second half of the fifteenth century and was extended during the reign of Francis I for territories newly brought under royal control. Each Parlement claimed sovereign jurisdiction in its own territory and not all edicts registered at Paris were registered in the provinces. They thus remained unimplemented. However, only the Parlement of Paris could admit *officiers* or constitute itself as a chamber of peers.[17]

In Gascony after the killing of Jean V d'Armagnac in 1473 there was never again any question of the reconstitution of the major independent fief that had been the dream of its *sires*. Despite their unattractive personalities, the fifteenth-century rulers could count on the loyalty of their people and established close links across the Pyrenees. However, their 'state' had always been limited, to some extent, by the competition of other powers like the Albret and Foix dynasties and the fall of Lectoure in 1473 was

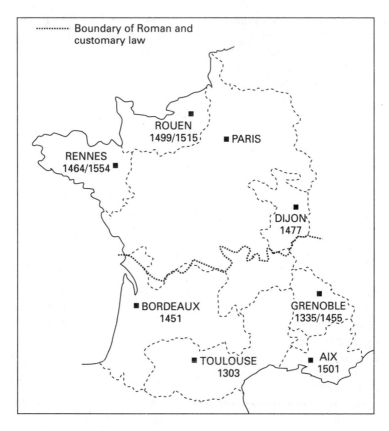

Map 3   Parlements in the Sixteenth Century

a severe blow. The last sire, Charles d'Armagnac, was restored to his title in 1484 but only after a decade in which royal functionaries drawn from the lesser nobility had effectively implanted Louis XI's authority in the region. Charles received only the 'domain utile' not the ancient regalian rights, which were completely suppressed. Charles's death, reputedly the owner of only one shirt, in 1497 saw the installation of a court cleric, Louis d'Amboise, bishop of Albi, as governor with another royal servant, Jacques de Genouillac, as *sénéchal*. The local estates of Bas-Armagnac were still summoned to vote taxes to the king despite the creation of *élections* but were no match for the king's representatives. The

succession to the lands of Armagnac became one of the most celebrated unsettled cases in the Parlement, with thirty claims still
pending in the *Grand Conseil* in 1526. In practice, however, it was
the Alençon family which had the support of the crown and their
rights eventually went to the Bourbons (see p. 378).[18]

In the case of Auvergne, the removal of the level of the great
princes meant that most of the province was in the hands of small
or middle ranking seigneurs with no more than a dozen
seigneuries. Obviously, there was no possibility thereafter of
mobilising power to oppose the crown directly. But at the very
moment that the apanage disappeared, the crown, by creating the
provincial governorship with very extensive powers, opened the
possibility for such power to be mobilised in the future. Such
figures were built up as men who could help the local community
at court; indeed, they were often great lords without close local
connections (Etampes in the 1530s) or great courtiers with some
local landholdings (Albany in the 1520s: Saint-André in the
1550s). The latter particularly managed to hold a sort of vice-regal
position. None are comparable with the low-born Jean de Doyat
appointed by Louis XI in 1480–3 to combat the authority of the
duke of Bourbon. Even in the heyday of the Bourbon dukes of
Auvergne, they had had to obtain the royal permission for the
raising of taxes from their subjects. Doyat 'who was then calling
himself and behaving as governor' of Auvergne had done his best
to impede this and Charles II of Bourbon got royal letters in 1484
allowing the revenue officials to proceed to raise the tax for the
duke.[19]

The Provincial Governors

Any discussion of the impact of the state on the provinces in the
sixteenth century must deal with the role of provincial governors.
They have been viewed in the past alternately as perpetuators of
feudal diversity, instrumental in the growth of chaos after 1560, or
as new though essentially military agents of royal power. They certainly constituted, alongside the Parlements which often con-
tested their powers, the summit of royal authority at the provincial
level but the nature of their powers is notoriously difficult to
define.

'Governors' (under various names) had appeared in France during the fourteenth century but became much more common in the second half of the fifteenth. While it was clear that their competence placed them above the *baillis* and *sénéchaux* in many respects and that the *gouvernement* was a collection of territories hierarchically superior to the *bailliages*, the definition of their power was always difficult. Legal historians preferred to see in the *gouverneur*, who was also the king's lieutenant-general, a purely military commander and adduced the fact that they were appointed primarily in frontier regions. Gaston Zeller largely demolished this view in two major studies which showed that the definition of the governors in military terms emerged from the edict of May 1545 and comments upon it by Parlement jurists like Jean du Tillet. These were anxious to minimise the competence of administrators who were major competitors of the Parlements, particularly in the key function of the *police des villes*. Despite this, the old view has proved tenacious and Zeller himself perpetuated the view that, when not resident in their provinces, the governors were mainly holders of sinecures.[20]

It has been common to see them not as office-holders but rather the supreme holders of revocable royal commissions. Yet it is obvious that this revocability was not a prime characteristic of their power and, indeed, they were appointed by letters of provision verified by the Parlements and were paid fixed emoluments like other office-holders. They therefore shared some of the characteristics of *officiers* and *commissaires* and their hybrid posts are best described in the contemporary term *estat ou charge*.[21]

The essence of the governor's power was to be found in two facts: his role as personal representative of the king (hence his title of *lieutenant-général*) and the fact that his letters of provision gave him authority over a specific *pays*, usually one of the apanage principalities absorbed by the crown in the course of the fifteenth century. As representatives of the king, they could be given specific commissions to act in finance or administration, but their broad function, in the words of their provisions, was the 'guard, *tuition* and defence' of their governments. They stood, therefore, at the centre of the process by which monarchical France was being constructed in that period; no longer did they hold the virtually unlimited powers of fourteenth-century governors but they formed part of the process by which the institutions of provincial *pays* like Burgundy, Provence or Dauphiné were maintained in the interests of stability and effective delegation of power. Thus, as representatives of the king's person in their provinces, they were accorded quasi-regal status in the ceremonies which attended their first entrance into the major cities.[22]

Hesitant at first about appointing governors to the newly reconquered provinces like Normandy or Guyenne, the crown provided even these areas with them from the 1470s and the terms of office were extended. In Champagne, Ile-de-France, Normandy and Guyenne from 1461 to 1472 there were 21 governors appointed

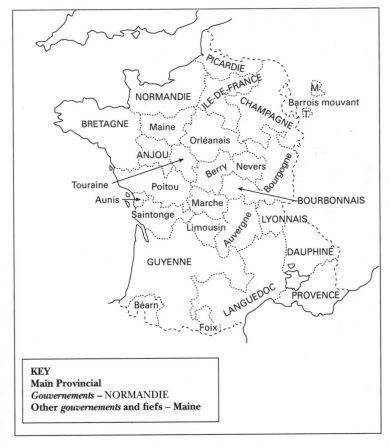

KEY
Main Provincial
***Gouvernements* – NORMANDIE**
Other *gouvernements* and fiefs – Maine

Map 4   Provincial *Gouvernements* by the Mid-sixteenth Century

with an average term of three and a half years; during 1473–83 there were 12 serving on average for five years. As elsewhere throughout the royal administration in this period, the majority of posts were given to middle ranking noblemen dominant in the Council: Charles d'Amboise, Jean de Daillon, Philippe de Crèvecoeur. The reaction after 1483 is clear: of the 44 governors between then and 1520, 23 were princely in origin, including members of the Bourbon and Orléans collateral branches of the royal house. In this period, half the governors seem to have maintained their positions for life; Jean d'Albret-Orval was governor of Champagne from 1487 to 1524. This, too, was the period when the dominance of leading families in particular provinces, so characteristic of the sixteenth century, became established. In Languedoc, the rule of the dukes of Bourbon from 1466 to 1523 was succeeded after 1527 by successive heads of the house of Montmorency.[23]

The generation from 1483 to the 1520s saw the generalisation of the network of governors, based either in newly acquired territories where the king had never exercised supreme jurisdiction, such as Brittany and Provence, or in others where the crown had resumed authority in territories which had been shaped into principalities, like Burgundy. There were thus ten of these by 1498 (Provence, Dauphiné, Languedoc, Guyenne, Champagne, Burgundy, Picardy, Ile-de-France, Normandy and Brittany). Elsewhere, as has been seen, the continuation of apanages of the royal family or other *pays* in the centre was analogous to the provincial government. In all these territories, the model of royal power became similar.

By the reign of Francis I, it seems that the corps of princely provincial governors stood in an ambivalent position. They represented the person of their kinsman the king, they were responsible for the routine settlement of all sorts of disputes, and at the same time the custom had grown up of regarding them as in some sense the protectors of the interests of their provinces vis-à-vis the central administration. From the late fifteenth century, they increasingly received or screened deputations from the *bonnes villes* and thus absorbed part of the petitioning process. The development of the post of deputy governor (*gouverneur en l'absence*), usually drawn from the ranks of the middle nobility, from the late fifteenth century should not be seen as a device of the crown for circumscribing their powers. Princely governors

were as influential at court as in the provinces. Some, like the
Bourbon governors of Picardy, were seldom absent and treated
their deputies as local coadjutors.[24] Others, like Montmorency in
Languedoc, could hardly spend much time in the province but
kept close surveillance on its affairs through the deputy governor,
Clermont. That the crown generally regarded the governors with
suspicion in this period is improbable. It is the case that Louis
XII's 1499 *ordonnance* of Blois sought to limit their powers of
pardon and ennoblement but it confirmed their other powers.
The edict of May 1542, by which Francis I annulled their powers,
has been revealed largely as a device for stripping Anne de
Montmorency and his brother La Rochepot of their governorships of Languedoc and Ile-de-France and Picardy. The *ordonnance* of May 1545 certainly limited the title of lieutenant-general
to the frontier provinces but this did not significantly limit the
very vague range of governors' powers.[25]

By the middle of the sixteenth century, the governors were an
essential feature of the provincial administration. Whether they
are seen, as by Bernard Chevalier, as real agents of growing royal
power or, as by Robert Harding, as an example of the patrimonial
system shot through with clientage, is a matter of taste. For
Harding, the patronage of the gendarmerie companies, household officials and the provincial nobility was essential to the governors' power. That power, however, was inescapable. Harding's
view that the period of the Habsburg–Valois wars saw increasing
challenges to the local authority of governors is debatable. There
is no doubt that, in some provinces, Parlements were at odds with
their governors. It is certainly the case that Parlements as much as
any other provincial institutions represented the trend of 'centralisation' in justice. However, not all governors were faced by self-
confident magistrates and some of them seem to have drawn
extra authority from their military commands during the wars. In
any case, at no time in this period were governors entitled to
manipulate funds on their own account, being confined to spending moneys authorised by the competent military treasurers.

Harding thought that our knowledge of the process of transition from this 'patrimonial' system to that of the intendancy of
the administrative monarchy is 'incomplete and confused'. Since
the work of Michel Antoine and others on the archives of Henri
II's secretary of state du Thier (in Moscow) the picture is much

clearer. It has already been pointed out that governors could be specifically commissioned to carry out particular tasks but in essence held very vaguely defined powers to act for the king 'as we would do ourselves if we were present'. The late fifteenth and early sixteenth century, however, with the expansion of the royal domain that generated the development of the governors, also gave impetus to the device of government through *commissaires* appointed to carry out all manner of fiscal, military or general tasks. Unlike *officiers*, these men were appointed by letters-patent that clearly restricted the area and time of their function.

If the practical scope of the governors' powers was wide and ill-defined, this did not absolve them from the very obligation to govern by good council that their lord the king was under. For this reason, their councils of advisers covered a wide range of problems and were recruited not only from their own civil and military entourages but also from the ranks of trained lawyers. As early as the 1530s, there are signs that the crown was taking an active interest in the composition of governors' councils. Brissac in 1550 was told to have a *maître des requêtes* ready to help him in Piedmont.[26] Henri II, well aware of the weaknesses of provincial control revealed by the 1548 Guyenne uprising, issued a declaration in November of that year, for which the text has not been preserved, substantially increasing the scope of the governors' judicial powers. Although opposition from the Parlements led eventually to a retreat from this in the 1550s, there were consequences. When the king decided to appoint a number of 'super-governors', mainly prelates like the cardinal de Bourbon, to represent him in his absence on the German campaign in 1552, he appointed legal experts, 'presidents' or 'superintendents', to their councils for matters of justice and finance by specific letters-patent of commission. In effect they were ministers appointed to the staffs of the governors. In all his appointments for territories in Italy – Piedmont, Corsica, Siena – during the 1550s, the king continued this device. These appointments were intended as supplements to the governors' authority, not as threats to them. The prince of Melphi in Piedmont actually asked the king through Jean du Bellay to send him a *maître des requêtes* in 1547 since 'he was not as equipped with knowledge as is necessary in the matter of justice' and, in view of an ominous dispute between the governor and the local nobility 'such a person as I have described could be a mediator between my lord and the prince and them'.[27] Henri II envisaged *chevauchées* by *maîtres des requêtes* in an edict of 1553 and gradually they were attached to the 17 *généralités* to inspect local courts. The political crisis of 1560 pushed the process further with the formal appointment of *maîtres des requêtes* to the staff of a number of governors to help deal with the spread of disorder, while the need to enforce Pacification edicts during the Wars of Religion continued it. The device of the appointment of such agents was to be an extremely fertile one; it was certainly one source of the intendancy as developed in the second third of the seventeenth century.[28]

Administrative Personnel: Office-holders

Any analysis of the weight of government during the Renaissance period must start from a consideration of numbers. Roland Mousnier, in a study of the size of the bureaucracy in Ancien Regime France, computed on the basis of Dupont-Ferrier's list in *Gallia Regia* that in 1515 there was a minimum of 4041 executive office-holders under the crown. These included 1455 officers of judicature (e.g. the 197 Parlement officials, the officers of the 93 *bailliages* and *sénéchausses*); 418 ordinary finance officials, 79 domain; 1139 extraordinary finance officials concerned with the direct taxes and the gabelle, etc. (e.g. about 230 *élus*); 603 higher military officers.[29] Pierre Chaunu has extended the enquiry by seeking to quantify the full numerical 'weight' of the state in the sixteenth century by taking into account all sorts of officials in the government service and excluding seigneurial officers and parochial clergy who also carried out public functions. In 1515, there were 1455 officers of justice and 1557 of finance (indicating the survival into the sixteenth century of the monarchy as an *Etat de justice*). Chaunu has suggested that the true figure for *officiers* would have been around 5000 and, with *clercs* and *commis* of the *officiers*, the 'administrative technostructure' would have been somewhere between 7000 and 8000 people. This, at a time when the kingdom covered 460,000 sq km gives one bureaucrat per 57.5 sq km and, in a population of (very roughly guessed) 16 million, one per 2000 people. With their families, the *officiers* themselves constituted 0.15 per cent of the population and the whole bureaucracy with theirs (say 40,000) 0.25 per cent. If we add to this the norm of permanent armed forces of 20,000 men, there were 60,000 people dependent on the state (roughly 0.4 per cent of the population).[30]

Clearly, this is a feeble number when compared even with the bureaucracy of the later seventeenth century. An enumeration of all offices made for Colbert in 1665 gave 46,047 expanding to 80,000 state employees (with their families 400,000 people) and a permanent army of at least 50,000. Chaunu has estimated the total dependent on the state therefore at roughly 3 per cent in place of 0.4 per cent in the early sixteenth century. In fact, in some areas of the administration about half the increase took place during the reigns of Francis I and Henri II, starting with the massive sale of 200 new offices in 1522. In the Parlement of Paris, a new *chambre des enquêtes* was set up in 1522 (with 20 offices) and another 20 new counsellors created in 1543. Henri II's creation of the *Parlement semestre* in 1554, whereby posts were divided in two and shared on a six-monthly basis, brought the total of officers to 165 and the new creations were retained as a new *chambre* when the alternation idea was abolished in 1558. The numbers of the Parlement of Bordeaux rose from 29 to 66 and of Toulouse from 24 to 83 in 1559. In 1515 there were 11 *maîtres des requêtes* and in 1547 there were 18. The number of royal *officiers* at Amiens in 1559 was 123, with 81 lawyers in the royal courts, and 300 municipal officials (out of a population of at most 20,000).[31] The pressure behind this came both from royal financial needs during the wars with the Habsburgs and the embracing of venality of office by a society anxious to use it in order to acquire the trappings of hereditary nobility.

The development of venality of office is one of the most characteristic features of the sixteenth century. There is plenty of evidence that it existed in the fifteenth from the repeated royal *ordonnances* against it and the demands of the Estates-General of 1484 to suppress it. The basic problem was the conception of the office as property and thus, by extension, a source of profit. Private sale of offices in finance was more or less accepted from the reign of Louis XI even though *ordonnances* from 1493 continued through the sixteenth century to prohibit the sale of offices of judicature. It is obvious that this remained a dead letter. Louis XII first formally avowed a sale of office in the *cour des aides* in 1499, although his officials preferred to keep the sales at arm's length by complicated transactions. The demands of war expenditure required that when the *Epargne* was created for the centralisation of revenues in 1522–3, its treasurer was also made the recipient of the *parties casuelles* or irregular revenues, including profits from sales of office. However, the profits were relatively small in the 1520s and probably disappointing and there seems to have been no systematic programme of sales. In general, it seems that the desire to sell offices on the part of the crown was reluctant and a concession to necessity, and it was not very efficiently handled.[32]

Mousnier has shown how all offices, whether of finance or of justice, were for sale with rare exceptions such as that of *premier président* of the Parlement of Paris. The creations of 1512–13 and 1521 in that Parlement were made specifically for sale while some offices were created to reimburse merchants who had lent money to the crown. The Venetian ambassador in 1546 noted that practically all offices were for sale and Henri II's financial needs dictated the creation of many more. All this was fed by the concession (in return for payment) of the right to transmit offices to heirs (thus withdrawing them from the market) and payments for *survivances*. Thus was born (by 1534) the famous 'forty day rule', which nullified resignations *in favorem* in the event of the resigner's death within forty days of the act. This was meant to increase the number of offices on the market, the market sale price for the office being greater than the resignation tax. Even here, the wish of the crown to create new offices for the market was overridden by the social pressure to transmit offices to heirs.[33]

The notion that 'modern' or effective government required monarchs to employ bourgeois or low-born advisers is no more than an enduring myth. Mikhail Harsgor has shown how the administrative elite of late fifteenth- and sixteenth-century France was built up from an alliance of members of the *peuple gras* and of the middle ranking nobility whose common interest was the exercise and control of political power. The close alliance between the middle nobility and the crown, that had been sealed by the creation in 1445 of the new army and the taxes to pay it, symbolised the twin foundations of state power: solid finance and the support of the nobility. By the later fifteenth century, many of the dominant figures remained nobles but their power stemmed from their ability to control the networks of patronage and administration rather than from their noble status. The extent of their authority is conveyed by the fact that, in the period 1483–1515, members of the royal council controlled just over 50 per cent of the provincial *bailliages, sénéchaussees* and *gouvernements,* and those the most important. Of the 109 bishoprics outside Brittany (but including Nantes), there were 44 bishops who were council members, another 88 were members of their families. Thus, well over 70 per cent of episcopal appointments came from the central elite. The latter was held in its loyalty to the crown by offices, pensions, gifts and lands. These in turn enabled its members to constitute *clientèles* of their own.[34]

This scheme of a fluctuating group around a central core whose power rested primarily on the domination of the state rather than on their lands or private wealth, is far more convincing an explanation of the relative stability of the period than the view of Absolutism as underpinned by a single social class. As Christopher Stocker has shown, royal loans to the king in return for the right to sell office could provide patronage for men as diverse as Semblançay and the king of Navarre, Hurault and Lautrec.[35]

The prosperous bourgeois and nobles who staffed the councils, the finance offices and the high courts did not, however, form a homogeneous social group and in fact intermarried little in the sixteenth century. Thus the Briçonnet, Beaune, Poncher and Robertet families remained unrelated to the old families like Montmorency, Gouffier and Pot, but together they formed the nucleus of the state apparatus (See genealogical table IV). Some wealthy bourgeois officer families achieved rank in the sword nobility, but it is interesting that others, like the Briçonnet and Le Gendre, never chose to do so, though they put together formidable fortunes. Pierre Le Gendre, *trésorier de France* (d.1524) was the son of an ennobled merchant who had entered royal financial administration and was himself created a *chevalier,* family marriages allied him to the Ponchers, Briçonnets and Neufvilles. The meteoric rise of the Selve family, Limousin bourgeois of legal background, was the result of the brilliance of Jean de Selve, whose capacities as a lawyer at Toulouse brought him to Louis XII's notice. There followed promotions through the Parlements that led to his emergence in 1520 as one of the most distinguished of the *premiers présidents* of Paris, vice-chancellor of Milan and major diplomat. The promotion of his two sons, Odet as ambassador and Georges as bishop and ambassador, was largely the result of the esteem in which Jean de Selve was held by Francis I. This family, although it bought seigneuries, did not seek to enter the old nobility, although another branch took the long road towards the *épée* in the seventeenth century by a military career.[36]

The road to power for the great families of the *peuple gras* opened up during the period of the fifteenth century when the court was confined to the Loire and Tours was effectively the capital. B. Chevalier has isolated 15 families which benefited from their role in the management of the great *charges* in finance. From Tours itself came the Bérard, Briçonnet, Beaune, Burdelot, Bernard, Berthelot, Fumée, Poncher and Ruzé families. From Blois came the Gaillard, Hurault and Cottereau; from Bourges the Lallemant and Le Roy and from Auvergne the Bohier. Imbart de la Tour argued that in the course of all this merchant capital was in the process of taking over the state.[37] Far from being a 'rise of the bourgeoisie' however, their prosperity represented the triumph of a small group of families which were both bourgeois and noble. One important feature of their success was the *charge* in finance, which seems to have opened up great vistas for the able family. The characteristic success stories were of families like the Beaune of Tours, which rose from petty finance offices rather than from business.[38] The story of the Ruzé family is not uncharacteristic: emerging in Tours at the end of the fourteenth century, state finance office and close links to the ducal family of Orléans seem to have made the fortune of Louis II Ruzé (d.1488). Thereafter, like so many others, the family gradually migrated to Paris and the acquisition of offices in the judicature and municipal administration through specilisation in civil law. The large proportion of the sons of this family who went into the church gave them an added dimension. This confirms a pattern by which families which started in finance could later attain offices in the Parlements, though rarely the other way round.[39] While the attack on Semblançay and the other financiers in the 1520s may have represented an attempt by the nobility to exclude the *peuple gras* from the summit of power, in practice it made little long-term difference. Jean Ruzé (d.1532), though hard hit by the attack on the financiers in the 1520s, move on into a career in royal justice in which his brothers were already well established.[40]

There remained a dominant role in both central and local government for members of the old nobility, as is shown by the career of marshal d'Esquerdes and by the rising fortunes of the Montmorency family in the court, council and provincial government from the late fifteenth century onwards. A scion of a former princely family, cardinal Georges d'Armagnac, offspring of an illegitimate son of the last count, was raised under the wing of Marguerite of Angoulême, became bishop of Rodez and cardinal by her intervention, and administered her domains in the region as well as acting as a major figure in French diplomacy towards Italy.[41] Under Francis I, the growing influence of the house of Lorraine in the church, the royal council and provincial government is self-evident.[42]

Local Administration: Lawyers and Justice

In his important study of the *bailliage* of Senlis in the late Middle Ages and up to 1550, B. Guenée has shown not only the way in which jurisdictions changed and were defined (with great complexity but still intelligible to contemporaries) but also the basic substratum of the judicial system up to the middle of the sixteenth century. France in 1515 consisted of roughly 100 *bailliages* (these are difficult to enumerate exactly because of constant revisions – there had been 89 at the end of the fifteenth century). The bedrock of the system of law and administration was the *châtellenie* or *prévôté* (the latter called in Normandy a *vicomté*), consisting of a castle, dependent lands and rights with, significantly, only one 'custom' prevailing in it. *Bailliages*, as Guenée put it, were not divided into *châtellenies*, they were made up of them. The *châtellenie* was the essential administrative unit, sometimes a royal *châtellenie*, sometimes seigneurial. These were absolutely stable units in the minds of their inhabitants and, though higher circumscriptions might 'float around', they did not change significantly. Thus, the *châtellenie* of Pontoise consisted of 43 parishes in 1403 and exactly the same in 1562.[43]

What, then, were the formal institutions for the maintenance of order? At the level of the network of courts of first instance, *prévôtés* and *châtellenies* and the royal *bailliage* courts, contrary to what we have seen at the level of the *grands corps* of the state

(Parlements) and of the presidial courts created in 1552, the late fifteenth and early sixteenth centuries saw no great increase in the number of judicial officials at work. In the *prévôté* of Paris (the equivalent of a *bailliage*) there were around 800 judicial officers in the mid-fifteenth century and still only about 900 in 1515. It was the reigns of Francis I and Henri II that saw a significant increase there to 1600 by 1559. Guenée in his study of Senlis confirms this trend, while pointing out that there was a noticeable increase in the number of *praticiens* or lawyers at work on such levels. At Compiègne, there were 6 *avocats* in 1494 and 11 in 1539; at Senlis there were 13 *procureurs* in 1506 and 52 in 1539. With this went increasing domination by law graduates.[44] That the milieu of the law embraced a wide variety of incomes and professions is certain, though the common value of service to the king may have created a certain esprit de corps in defined areas like Paris. Only when past the trainee stage and into the charmed circle of offices that led on to higher promotion, could an individual enter the relatively closed and intermarried world of the 'robe', which in the sixteenth century formed such an important part of royal administration. We shall return to this theme in our discussion of the French nobility as a whole (chapter 6).

The Extent of Physical Control

Every individual had his *juge ordinaire*, known clearly and usually determined by the place of residence in village or town. However, the competence of such a judge was circumscribed by the existence of exemptions and privileges (e.g. nobles and clergy). These were the cause of disputes. Judges could hold high, middle or low justice or all three and the categories of appeal from them to higher courts could therefore vary. High justice covered capital crimes and crimes against the person and involved penalties from fines to death. Low justice dealt either with property disputes or small injuries and disturbances of the peace. The concept of middle justice appeared in the fourteenth century as a hybrid, enriching lower justice with some of the competence of high and permitting the exaction of higher fines. *Châtelains* held high, middle and low justice, symbolised by prisons, pillories, and gallows. Usually town councils exercised all forms of justice. This was the case generally in northern France except that in some towns, like Amiens, the crown reserved certain cases to itself (*cas réservés*). In others, like Abbeville, as *villes de loi* they exercised high justice without any qualification and even judged in cases of heresy and blasphemy.[45] Punishments ranged from fines, public penance and banishment to execution.

The only regular force for the maintenance of order, the *prévôts des maréchaux* and their small companies of archers (actually in embryo the origin of the modern *gendarmerie*), were responsible for the policing of the *gens d'armes* of the heavy cavalry. In 1520, Francis I increased the number of *prévôts* to 30 with the aim of establishing better policing of the highways. As delegates of the king, they had the power to convoke four local notables and decree summary sentences on brigands. However, they were regarded with hostility by local courts and there were plainly inadequate numbers.[46] In the absence of a substantial number of royal law-enforcement officials, the execution of royal edicts and the bringing to book of malefactors could not be done exclusively by agents of the state. In countless royal edicts and orders, provincial communities were made responsible for checking their observance and pursuing criminals. What this meant in effect was that landowners had the duty of maintaining basic local order by organising troops of a hundred or so men to round up violent criminals or, as in Dauphiné in 1493, to form squadrons to suppress unruly elements such as unpaid soldiers. The 'nobles and the commune' of Poitou were called out in 1523 to suppress 1500 'mauvais garçons' and took casualties of 600 dead. In the same year, the 'Mille diables', a band of *mauvais garçons* led by an Auvergnat noble called 'le roi Guillot' ransacked the Marche and Limousin and were only stopped by a pitched battle. In the Boulonnais during the 1550s, the nobility and the 'communes' were repeatedly summoned to deal with violence, vagabonds and illegally armed gangsters.[47] Elizabeth Teall has pointed out that, in the well-known case in the Cotentin of Gilles de Gouberville, it was the *sire* who settled local disputes about inheritances, property and theft around the kitchen table of his manor-house before they ever came into a court. This should not be taken too far, though. During the period he kept his diary, Gouberville confronted no great rural uprisings until the disorders of 1562. When outright violence and murder happened, as in the attack on the manor-house of the sire de Cosqueville by his enemies in 1558, Gouberville could only pick up the pieces of a case that would eventually lead to the scaffold in Rouen.[48]

With the exception of Paris, the number of agents available for the implementation of royal justice was, then, extremely small in the sixteenth century. Each province had its *prévôt des maréchaux* with a company of about 12 archers and sergeants. A quarrel involving claims by Galiot de Genouillac (grand master of the artillery) and Robert Stuart d'Aubigny in 1530 caused Jean du Bellay to remark that 'one of them has credit in Berry, the other in Gascony; both having companies of *gens d'armes*, reputations and friends who would, in circumstances where the king took no action, make a disturbance and assembly of men in this kingdom'. He therefore advised great caution in dealing with them.[49] In Auvergne two cases 60 years apart illustrate the same problems. The refusal of a Nemours follower to accept the confiscation of some castles in 1478 led him to take direct action which the king was unable to defeat, even in his own courts.[50] In 1543, the arrest of a noble charged with murder led to severe fighting.[51]

In northern France, the effectiveness of royal power was greater, though even here there were problems. In the whole region of Picardy and Artois, where the duke of Burgundy still held sway until 1477, there was a high level of insecurity and general disorder generated by its position as border country.[52] In 1469, it was naturally still difficult in the region for royal justice to deal with noble malefactors but as late as 1484, an attempt to apprehend the bâtard d'Aveluy for robbery and extortion provoked a full-scale attack on the royal *sergens*.[53] Noble feuds, like those between the Mailly and Cressonsacq families, dragged on for decades into the early sixteenth century and were lost in inconclusive cases before the Parlement.[54] Perhaps more suprisingly, as late as the 1520s royal intervention on behalf of one claimant in a violent succession dispute concerning the Mailly family proved ineffective without armed self-help by the claimant concerned.[55]

The weakness of controls is vividly underlined by Francis I's rough handling of the Parlement of Rouen, created out of the old *Echiquier* in 1515 and notorious for corruption as well as vexatious to the king in its failure to register the *Ordonnance* of Villers-Cotterêts. In 1540, on the advice of chancellor Poyet, the king came to Normandy and suspended it, replacing its jurisdiction by *Grand Jours* at Rouen and Bayeux to root out 'the unruly insolence of the nobility and the connivance of local judges'. Most malefactors went to ground and could only be executed in effigy, while it is curious that most of the magistrates were reinstated in 1541.[56] This is in line with a general pattern for dealing with disturbances in the first half of the sixteenth century: a short descent and application of shock tactics followed by compromise with local officials who were supposed to have been taught a lesson.

Bernard Chevalier has suggested that the internal calm of the *bonnes villes* in the period 1480 to 1520 was deceptive. Crime and vagabondage were, as has been pointed out, on the increase. Towns were increasingly prone to sentence malefactors to long periods of banishment. Robert Muchembled has investigated this for the towns of Artois.[57] Many disturbances and crimes were dealt with by the *bonnes villes* as holders of some variant of high justice. In France, the records of the town of Péronne (Somme) in the early sixteenth century bear witness to the anxiety of the magistrates over disorders. One major incident stemmed from a charivari claimed in 1510 by the 'compaignons' but which part of the city council refused to sanction. The case caused a split aggravated by the determination of some members to profit from royal letters of justice. In 1512 a major riot occurred over grain shortages, when some of the merchants who were responsible for exports to the Low Countries were attacked by a mob in the market place on the incitement of some artisans who 'by their seditious words and tumults provoked the people and stirred them to anger to the scandal and dishonour of justice'. Punishment included banishment for three years or public penance. These were major incidents that took up much of the council's time. Such incidents form part of a pattern that has been drawn by Henry Heller in his analysis of social conflict in sixteenth-century France but they could be said also to be the tip of an iceberg. Crime and personal violence were endemic.[58] The *échevinage* of Péronne entered full records of crime over a short period in its register. Between 1516 and 1521 a stream of judgements involving banishment and death were handed down for larceny, violent affray and murder. This seem to have been the normal stuff of urban justice.[59]

Above all, though, it is in the series of *lettres de rémission* for serious crimes issued by the royal chancellery that the most vivid testament to the state of public order emerges. As N. Z. Davis has pointed out, these documents were issued by the crown for money, not as arbitrary suspensions of justice but as statements of cases which then had to be accepted by the royal courts in the provinces. They make ritual claims of self-defence and blame of the deceased for 'lack of due care'.[60] She has seen in them primarily evidence of story-telling technique but they also provide a body of evidence on attitudes to violence and disorder. Those studied by Robert Muchembled for Artois are comparable with their French equivalents and show that the government of Charles V issued more remissions largely because it was in a more effective position to do so.[61] The picture they reveal of a society profoundly insecure at the village level, widely armed with daggers and more offensive weapons, full of young men ever ready to defend their honour, prone to violence at certain seasons and especially through drunken brawls at night, could be repeated in every other French province. His argument, that violence was more a public expression of virility and a spectacle rather than an expression of marginal and deviant attitudes, seems to be confirmed by the overwhelmingly 'frontal' nature of injuries in murder cases as well as their delayed effect. The vast majority of murderers were country men, neither destitute nor rich, and the same pattern is replicated in the towns of the province. A recent massive study of the letters of remission in France during the fourteenth and fifteenth centuries adds the point that town and country are much the same in this respect. Of crimes dealt with by them 57 per cent were homicides, most committed among neighbours or people who knew each other and seldom at night.[62]

The French royal chancellery records also demonstrate increasing numbers of remissions in the sixteenth century (600–700 a year). The ready recourse to weaponry during quarrels, often after drink, at taverns or over the dinner-table, is one of the most obvious points to emerge from them. In 1523, a butcher of Doullens murdered his wife at dinner because she made a scene after they had quarrelled about how long they had been married and he called her a 'vielle incontinante'. Often, there was some collective violence going on. A murder at Abbeville in 1498 happened on a feast day after the perpetrator had already escaped a tavern brawl with some soldiers, went off to practise archery and was persuaded by some friends to go drinking again. The result was a street fight outside the inn, with the brother of the innkeeper dead.[63] We may add to this the propensity for communities to band together against outsiders in order to secure justice by self-help. At Clermont-Ferrand in 1546, when a local nobleman, the sieur de La Richardière, came to buy silk, he fell to quarrelling with the merchant over the value of the coin he offered and was thrown out. Outraged, he resolved on the advice of his friends to return and teach the man a lesson but, finding only the merchant's wife there, he abused her luridly instead. Shortly afterwards the whole town was in uproar, the tocsin was ringing and Richardière and his friends had to fight their way to safety.[64] As Robert Muchembled has argued, we should see in the expansion in cases of letters of remission both the configurations of a violent society and also the increasing, if often impotent, interest of royal justice and lawyers in dealing with such matters.

Conclusion

The 'weight' of government in terms of its impact on the varied provinces of France undoubtedly increased over this period but remained restrained in comparison with developments of the seventeenth century. The last remains of the greater apanages and fiefs were dismantled imperceptibly, step by step, and often retained some of the forms under which they had been ruled by the great princely or feudal magnates. More and more, though, they were held by princely families closely related to the royal family or those high in favour at court. Independent jurisdictions became rarer. The newer institutions that grew up over them, provincial governments, retained many traditional characteristics and the role of the great nobility within them increased. There is little suggestion that the crown regarded them with suspicion; on the contrary, it fostered them and sought to make them more effective guarantors of the unity of the kingdom, especially in the middle years of the sixteenth century.

However, below the level of the provincial governors and the other main institution of provincial control, the Parlements, France remained a very lightly policed society, in which violence and self-help were habitual. The royal courts could only hope to handle a fraction of this trouble and the most characteristic feature of royal justice in the Parlements was the lawsuit that extended over decades and, as the saying went, 'dribbled from blood to ink'. This was despite the undoubted growth of numbers of lawyers and of the law as a profession in this period. In the maintenance of local peace and order, it was again the nobility that continued to play a central role.

5. The Taxation System and its Burdens

Louis XI declared in 1464 that 'the conduct and police of the common weal of our kingdom ... consists principally in justice'. A characteristic of the Ancien Regime state, in the view of modern historians, is its transformation from predominantly judicial institution (as an *état de justice*) to one primarily ordered for the raising of revenue (the *état de finance*), though both coexisted until 1789. In the course of the century from 1460 to 1560, the crown embarked on vast military operations which demanded the expansion of money resources, customarily called, following Quintus Curtius, 'the sinews of war'.[1] Did this mean the power and financial burden of the crown increased as a result? The function of the monarchy as an administrative system drawing the bulk of its resources from the taxation of a largely monetised society goes back to the decades around 1300, while the principle of extraordinary taxation was virtually established during the wars of the 1350s. This had, however, sustained a severe reverse as a result of the combined economic and political crises from the late fourteenth century onwards.[2] With the recovery of the mid-fifteenth century, the taxation functions of the state revived.

The basic framework of the financial administration was in place by 1400, though it was then still fluid. The main features were the separation of ordinary (domain) and extraordinary (taxation) revenue and of the functions of expenditure and accounting. The geographical specialisation into four main areas, the four *grandes charges* of the *généralités*, dates from the reorganisations of the years 1436–50. To these, the late fifteenth century saw the addition of certain subordinate *charges* like the *généralité* of Picardy after 1470. In effect there were four juxtaposed colleges each containing agents for expenditure and accounting in both the extraordinary and ordinary revenues. These were, for domain revenue, the *trésoriers de France* and *clercs du trésor* who dealt with expenditure (with the *changeur du trésor* for accounting) and, for extraordinary revenue, the *généraux sur le fait des aides* or *des finances* (and the *contrôleurs* for accounting). In all there were 20 high officials and there was no hierarchy among them.[3]

The administration of royal finances was thus collective and there was no conception of the finances of the state as a unity by 1500. The term, *Messieurs des finances*, by which they were increasingly designated from the 1470s, reveals clearly enough that the crown had no wish to create a ministry of finance. Furthermore, the chancellor had held, since the fourteenth century, a pivotal role in the handling of finance and regularly participated in councils on finance. The leading position of first Pierre Briçonnet and then Semblançay from 1518 to 1522 (though without the name of *surintendant*) should not obscure

Map 5   New *Généralités* in the Sixteenth Century

this. The changes which accompanied the creation of the *trésor de l'Epargne* in 1522–3 (essentially devised to assure a more effective war fund) mask the fact that the true significance of the sixteenth-century reforms was to maintain the principle of collegiality in the administration of finance. Certainly, the *trésoriers* and *généraux* were effectively demoted in being required to reside locally in a much larger number of generalities. This was accomplished by a series of changes beginning with the Edict of Cognac (1542), creating sixteen *généralités* and that of Blois (1552), unifying the local control of domain and extraordinary revenue under new *trésoriers-généraux* who were to reside in their districts. These changes went on inexorably between the 1520s and the 1550s. But when the dust had settled it is clear that the administration of finance continued in the hands of collective bodies, the royal council, the *contrôleur général* appointed from 1547 and the *intendants des finances* in operation from 1552. M. Antoine has called the the latter the 'dorsal spine' of the administrative monarchy.[4]

The Financial Community

Besides the twenty or so high officers of finance, *trésoriers de France* and *généraux des finances,* the nature of government led to the multiplication of officials concerned with funds. Those handling state finances, for instance in a provincial *recette,* had to supervise in person the arduous collection of funds necessary for the payments they had to make. Inexorably, each function of crown finance (represented by each chapter of the general budget) acquired its treasurer (*comptable*) to handle both collection and payment, looking after deficits by personal funds, and each employed clerks (*commis*) to assist them. Their qualifications were accounting experience, credit and a capacity for hard work in the inspections (*chevauchées*) they were required to make. Elaborate education was unnecessary but initial funds were vital. The *recette* of Languedoil cost 10,000 *lt.* – roughly the value of 3000 hectares of good land; lower down the post of *payeur* of the Swiss guard cost 500 *lt.* The existing holder of an office had to be paid: thus François Doulcet of Blois charged Jean Cottereau 6000 *lt.* and a quarter of the profits for the post of *maître des comptes.*[5] Moreover, the number of posts was limited and the demand so high that a recommendation in the form of resignation *in favorem* was needed.[6] Wealth was needed so that officers could act as creditors to the king and in effect as depositories of the public debt. Thomas Bohier, as accountant for the king's *menus plaisirs* in 1491, was owed 36,311 *lt.* and required a 6 per cent premium for it.[7] Financial office was one solution for merchants in search of capital. At Toulouse, Jacques Beauvoir, pastel merchant, became a *trésorier de France* in 1480 and Pierre de Chéverny *général des finances* in 1558. Both of them were seeking to make the sorts of profit that publicists complained of by their use of royal patronage, though it seems the profit was never enough for merchants in quest of serious capital.[8]

Given the risks of the investment, the rewards were commensurately high. The salaries of the finance officials were among the highest paid by the crown and far outstripped those of courtiers. Jacques de Beaune as *trésorier* and *receveur général* in 1492 got 2000 *lt.* p.a., a *premier maître d'hôtel* 800 and *chambellans* 400–600. A *général des finances* received 2490 *lt.* plus a 1200 *lt.* pension, almost as much as the chancellor's 5000 *lt.* At court the *commis* for the pay of the royal guards received twice as much as their captain. Such salaries should be regarded as the necessary premium paid to a man having to manage a fund of 30,000 *lt.* or more p.a. Such payments were well below the level of the court aristocracy like the Constable on 24,000 *lt.* or La Trémoïlle as admiral of Guyenne on 3000 *lt.* plus a pension of 13,000 *lt.* But the *général des finances* received in salary 138 times what a manual worker at Tours earned in 1480–1500 and that does not take account of royal gifts and other perquisites.[9]

Such men rarely rose directly from the business world but rather from small finance posts. An exception was Adam Fumée, son of a draper, but he rose through learning, having studied as a physician before rising to be a *maître des requêtes*.[10] Often service in a princely household proved a springboard to greater success. Tradesmen sometimes went on to be receivers in such households, like the tailor Landois at the Breton court. For the financiers of Tours, service in the household of the local dukes of Anjou led, through queen Marie d'Anjou, to posts at court. Jean Cottereau became secretary to the duke of Orléans (later Louis XII) and was privy to his innermost affairs.[11] The advantage in all this lay in the fact that great aristocrats saw an advantage in placing 'their' men in as many royal offices as possible.

The remarkable correspondence between Louis XI and his *général des finances* in Languedoc from 1478 to 1483 reveals the vast scope of the latter's activities and the risks involved. François de Genas, born at Valence in 1430, entered Louis's service while he was still dauphin but was not promoted to the *présidence* of the Dauphiné *Chambre des Comptes* until the king's visit in 1476. The following year he was appointed *général* in addition. The king's frequent letters ordering him to pay or retrench pensions, pay for troops and fortifications, negotiate with king René over financial inducements and even procure a new style of cape for his master, show him fending off the anger of the latter and that of the officials he was supposed to be paying. Most payments were made by assignations on local receipts; often the money was simply not there, sometimes Genas just procrastinated. Louis became more irritable and dangerous in his last years. In 1479, ordering him to pay a pension he had delayed, Louis wrote that he was 'very amazed … I do not believe you were so ill-advised as to have made such a response … I know if you wish you will content him well and, in doing this you will do me pleasure and, if you do not, I will not be satisfied or have cause to be satisfied with you.' Told that Genas had cut down a pension without his instructions in May 1483, he wrote: 'I can assure you that I am not satisfied with you. So take care, if you do not wish to disobey me, that he be entirely paid so that I hear no more of it. If there is any failure, you will never serve me again. Remember that, were I not the man I am, you would even now be in Monseigneur d'Albi's hands.'[12]

From the war of the Public Weal in 1465 and through the favour of men at court like Jean Bourré and Ymbert de Batarnay, families like the Briçonnet began to make enormous strides in the conquest of the high levels of finance in the generalities and in the accounting posts at court, to the point that they begin to look like a Tours mafia. The founder of the Briçonnet fortunes was Guillaume, son of Jean the elder, receiver of Languedoil 1446–75 and son-in-law of Jean de Beaune. As a money dealer, he left his business and entered royal service in 1480 as *secrétaire des finances* in 1480. In 1483 he acquired the generality of Languedoc, was a member of the council from 1484 and became one of the leading servants of the Beaujeu regime, in the course of which he incurred the hostility of Commynes.[13] He overcame the problem of low birth by taking holy orders and receiving the cardinal's hat in 1495. His brother Pierre Briçonnet had acquired the office of *notaire et secrétaire du roi* by 1478 (its cost in 1511 was 3700 *lt.* and it carried ennoblement ex officio from 1485). While in itself not a powerful post, it was close to the royal council and therefore conveyed influence. Of the college of 120, there were 20 from Tours in 1461–83 and 40 from 1483–1514. The crown of such a career was a *maîtrise* or a *présidence* in the *chambre des comptes* via a generality. Cardinal Guillaume Briçonnet had a brother, two nephews, an uncle and two brothers-in-law who were members of the *collège des finances*. At court, among the finance officials he had one son, four brothers-in-law, a nephew and a cousin. In addition, his brother Robert was cardinal-archbishop of Reims and chancellor in 1495 while his son Guillaume became bishop of Meaux and succeeded Robert as president of the *chambre des comptes* (see p. 379).[14]

As indispensable handlers of the king's credit, these men made enemies and were subjected to charges of corruption. These were easy to exaggerate and indeed Chevalier claims that, when their work can be examined, it shows a high degree of zeal for the defence of the king's interests. Examples are Pierre Briçonnet's instructions for sparing the people from oppression in the collection of the *taille* or Semblançay's attacks on corruption.[15] But the fact that they were indispensable in finance, the council, army administration, and worked largely in the background stoked enmity to them and to some extent dictated that they defend themselves by group solidarity. A spectacular instance came during the trial of marshal Gié in 1506 in which they used contacts with the queen and Louise of Savoy to get the sentence against one of their own, Jean du Bois, reduced and turned the tables on their enemy, admiral de Graville.[16] These dangerous events revealed how dependent they were on the favour of the king and queen.

Some members of the finance oligarchy made fortunes but there was a risk. They were free of *tailles* but had to pay for the costs of administration themselves and were subject to periodic demands from the crown for special loans in emergencies. The fortunes they left were below those of the aristocracy but substantially greater than those of the mass of the petty nobility and were

roughly on the level of the middle ranking nobility of the chevaliers and lesser titled nobles. Jean de Beaune left 13,310 *lt.* in
property. While such families strove to attain respectability in the
late fifteenth and early sixteenth centuries by the acquisition of
estates, castles and titles of chivalry (Pierre Briçonnet became a
chevalier in 1500 and Pierre Le Gendre in 1510; Thomas Bohier
was knighted on the battlefield at Genoa in 1507 and Guillaume
de Beaune at Marignano), the finance families avoided much
intermarriage with the sword nobility and sought to strengthen
their position by the acquisition of high church benefices. The
contrast was even more apparent in the decades around 1500
when the stock of available estates was drying up, with the recovery of the old nobility, and devices of stealth had to be used to
acquire land.[17] The characteristics of the elite were political
rather than social, then. The rise into the true sword nobility of a
family like the Neufvilles is instructive in its slowness. Beginning
in the fish trade in late fourteenth-century Paris, passing through
lesser finance office, they reached the level of *secrétaire des finances*
(1514) and chevalier (1518) with Nicolas I (d.1549), secretary of
state with Nicolas II (d.1598) and Nicolas III de Villeroy and
finally the highest nobility with a dukedom in 1651.

The transfer of high policy and supervision after 1523 to a new
combination of a *trésorier de l'Epargne* working with the royal council
dealing with finance, and the attack on the financiers that culmin-
ated in Semblançay's execution, drastically altered the role of the
financial oligarchy, though it retained some of its offices. In fact
the proliferation of *généralités* after 1542 enlarged the number of
offices available and opened access to more families and the
financial administration thus became slightly less oligarchical. It
should, however, be remembered that the leading government
figure of the 1520s remained chancellor cardinal Antoine Duprat.
Duprat, promoted to high office in 1515 through the favour of
Louise of Savoy, owed his initial fortunes to the fact that he was first
cousin to the *généraux des finances*, Thomas and Henri Bohier.[18]

The Management of State Finance and Tax Levels

Messieurs des finances were in effect responsible for the yearly
budget, though that word was unknown in France until the mid-

eighteenth century. In the sixteenth century, they referred instead to 'les revenues et dépenses du roi'.[19] The term 'finances' was applied to the management of the king's revenues and expenditure. Such financial planning as there was – and it should be pointed out that the fifteenth–sixteenth-century concept of 'finances' did not strictly allow for much strategic planning[20] – consisted in the establishment of the following year's envisaged expenses and then the fixing of revenues to defray them. The few surviving *états par estimation* (or *de prévoyance*) *des finances* typical of such procedures were largely matters of accounting formalities, in that their main point was to balance revenue and expenditure.[21] They did, in effect, constitute a form of rudimentary budget. By the fifteenth century, the exercise began in the July of the year preceding the account with an *état de prévoyance* and was completed at the end of the period with an *état au vrai*, which in turn served as the basis for the *état de prévoyance* for the following year.[22] It was from this accounting procedure that the idea of the budget was gradually to take shape.

One further point is crucial. Despite the creation of the office of *trésorier de l'Epargne* and the subordinate *receveur des parties casuelles* (for irregular revenue) in 1522–3, in an attempt to centralise revenues and keep track of them, expenditure in practice continued to be effected by 'assignations' on specific 'receipts'. The accounts of the *Epargne* thus remained partly notional. The fact was that the operation was too great for one official and a small staff. However, the changes did have one of their planned effects, which was to begin the destruction of the exclusive control over state finance by the ring of tightly related Tours families already discussed. The execution of Semblançay in 1527 was meant to seal this.[23]

The finances locally, however, continued to be in effect managed by *officiers*, who received 'gages' (not 'salaires') and who, confounding the king's revenues with their own, were deemed 'accountable' for them. The vast ramifications of the financial edifice of the state were, in effect, in the hands of a *corps* of *grands commis*, financiers who submitted their own accounts for verification in the *chambre des comptes*. Only after the 1520s was the preponderance of the Tours financiers in this domain challenged.[24]

The methods of planning the finances of the crown in the sixteenth century explain Francis I's celebrated reply to a Venetian ambassador's enquiry as to how much he could raise from his sub-jects: 'everything I need, according to my will.'[25] Study of the financial resources of the French state is severely hampered by the fragmentary nature of the sources. There is no usable general *état* before 1523. Estimates of the global revenues based on computa-tions of the *taille* and other revenues vary considerably.[26] The classic work of Clamageran on the history of taxes used the con-ventional distinction between the ordinary (domain) and extra-ordinary (taxation, direct and indirect) revenues, though in fact the latter are much more significant. Confusion easily arises since the *taille* and other impositions were destined, after the changes of 1523, for classification under ordinary revenues, whereas the army for which they in effect existed – notably the infantry – was in peacetime still classified as extraordinary expenditure.[27] Whereas domain revenues stood at 39 per cent of the total under Philippe le Bel, by the reign of Louis XI the stage of virtual com-plete effacement of the importance of domain revenues had been reached (2.85 per cent in 1461; 2.17 per cent in 1483; though rising to 7.25 per cent in 1514, this still remains a minor source of revenue).[28] While the state in late fifteenth-century England was revived by the reorganisation of the crown's domain revenues, in France these were relatively feeble. However, despite this, in the late fifteenth century the French monarchy was already the most fiscally well-endowed in Europe. Contamine has drawn our atten-tion to the severe fiscal pressure applied by Louis XI towards the end of his reign. In 1482, total revenues amounted to 5.4 million *lt.* – largely direct taxes at 3.9 to 4.4 million – at a time when the economy was not generating high revenues in indirect form. The second half of the reign represents an apogee of direct taxation. Commynes analysed revenues in one year thus: domain 100,000 *lt.*, 'extraordinary' at 4,565,000 (including 665,000 *aides*); the royal domain was virtually insignificant. The increase of 1461–79 was 105.71 per cent in terms of *livres tournois*, though only 57.71 per cent when expressed in terms of gold and 71.42 per cent in terms of silver.[29] In fact, the reign of Louis XI marked an important turning-point in the taxation capacity of the French state, step-ping well beyond the bounds of what had been possible during the previous century and a half.

The sharp reductions that resulted from the political conces-sions made by the Regency government of Charles VIII were broadly maintained during the Italian wars so that even in 1500 the total stood at 3.5 million *lt.* By 1523, the figure had risen to 5.6 million (though this was achieved mainly by rises in indirect levies). The overall figure in 1543 was much the same but had risen to 7.4 million in 1547 and attained an average of 13.54 million during the reign of Henri II, the second peak of financial demands in this period.

None of the surviving *états de prévision* gives a very realistic picture of receipt and expenditure. The most detailed, the celebrated account of 1523 analysed by Roger Doucet, reveals a staggering scale of inaccuracy and plain 'massaging' of the figures. Nevertheless, it is still clear that the state's finances were nearly 2.8 million *lt.* in deficit even before the start of the exercise, a feature which could only be handled by prodigious anticipations of the following year's direct taxes.[30] From the *état* of 1549, it is clear that, should the king's debts to his creditors (2.4 million) be repaid on term, there was a deficit of 3.1 million *lt.*[31] In all these *états*, the absence of full payments for the infantry and the navy is a severe limitation to the picture. In 1523, they do not appear at all. In 1549, there are some infantry payments but, when compared with the records of the *extraordinaire des guerres* these are clearly not complete. From 1 October 1520 to 25 June 1525, the *trésoriers de l'extraordinaire* received assignations for 9,290,556 *lt.*, or nearly 2 million a year.[32] In the *état de prévision*, the overwhelming amounts were assigned to the payment of the gendarmerie, the royal household and guards and pensions, either to French *pensionnaires* or to the Swiss and English for their alliance.

Of course, figures like these are not much use without reference to population figures, bullion values and purchasing power. We have already seen that the population was going through a period of dynamic growth in the second half of the fifteenth century.[33] This century had experienced a worsening shortage of precious metals reflected in state currency manipulation and the declining value of the money of account, the *livre tournois*. That measure of value continued to decline slowly in the sixteenth century from 22 g of silver in 1475 to 14 g in 1560, partly because of population increase and partly as a result of silver importation from the new world after 1540. In France, it was the prerogative of the crown to declare the value of the money of account and it did this by promulgating increases in the nominal value of coins, usually with the immediate effect of hyperinflation in commodity prices. Since the real form of money was bullion, the crown could actually do little to offset the effects of bullion shortage. Louis XI at first refrained from following his predecessors' policies of debasement but, faced with increased costs like war and the payments to Edward IV in the 1470s, he returned to that road.[34] However, 1475 saw the establishment of a gold coin of lasting solidity, the *écu d'or*. Although the crown issued ever-increasing sums of coin, rising from 2.5 million *livres* in 1500 to 6 million around 1550, an average yearly inflation rate of 2.6 per cent between 1510 and 1580 meant that the value of coins issued in terms of grain at market prices dropped from 2,164,000 *sétiers* of wheat in 1500, to 1,544,000 in 1550 and then 822,000 around 1575.[35]

In terms of fine silver, the crown's revenues in the last years of Louis XI attained 110–140 tonnes p.a. In 1484, this was drastically reduced to 60 tonnes and had only slightly risen to 63 tonnes by 1515 (though the rise from 2.35 million to 3.5 million *livres tournois* is explained by the slight fall in the rate of the *livre* against silver). The stabilisation of revenues during 1484–1515 is thus starkly apparent at a time of falling prices (expressed in silver) and the increase in the purchasing power of silver characteristic of the period 1470–1520.

Revenues had risen to 93 tonnes in 1523, at which they were maintained until the later years of Francis I, when they attained 115.5 tonnes. The average for 1547–59 was 209 tonnes.[36] Such figures must also be checked by examination of purchasing power. It is undeniable that the global fiscal burden grew heavier under Francis I in order to sustain the military and diplomatic policies of the crown, but how much heavier? For the period of Francis I's reign when taxes were rising by 183 per cent in terms of silver, the purchasing power of silver was declining, so that prices in terms of silver rose by 160 per cent.˙ In local terms, whereas direct taxes on the towns of Auvergne increased three times during 1450–1550, the price index of wheat was 233 on a base of 100 over the same period.[37] In these terms, the increase in taxation looks far less formidable. This did not mean that there was not the customary opposition to the paper increases in taxation figures (for instance in the well-known case of Dauphiné) but it does explain the ability of French society to sustain what look like heavy increases.[38]

How were the increases in Francis I's reign implemented? The level of the *taille* was fixed at 2.4 million *lt.* in 1515 and remained the same until 1541; increases were effected by regular supplements or *crues* of never less than 600,000 after 1522. The real level of the *taille* was around 3 million early in Francis I's reign. The massive deficit in royal finances recognised in 1523 forced the implementation of an exceptional *crue* of 2.7 million. With regular *crues* this brought real levels of demand nearer to 5.5 million in the 1520s, although there was a decline in the 1530s which brought the average for 1524–41 to 4,269,000 *lt.* From 1542, reality was accepted and the ordinary *taille* raised to 4 million and full levels to 4.5 million.

Later in the reign of Francis I new fiscal instruments were used to tap the resources of the kingdom, notably the *soldes des gens de pied* levied in the walled cities, many of which had been protected from direct taxation by special privileges. This had raised 1.8 million *lt.* in 1543. The large increase in the global fiscal burden under Henri II took place in the context of relative price stability and only minor modifications in the value of the *livre tournois*. As has been seen, in the last year of Francis I the global burden had been 115.5 tonnes of silver. For the reign of Henri II it was 209 tonnes on average. It hardly needs to be stressed that the increased costs of war lay behind this push forward, but how did society sustain it? The formal limitation of the *taille* to 4 million was retained but increases were levied in the form of a new supplement called the *taillon*, raised to defray the increased costs of the gendarmerie from 1549 onwards. Even so, the average in *tailles* moves from 3,803,666 *lt.* under Francis I to 5,818,000 under Henri II, an increase of 53 per cent and, including the *taillon*, 83 per cent. The most significant rise was in indirect taxes, some 160 per cent, and levies in the form of *dons gratuits* and *décimes* on the clergy as well as in levies on offices and forced loans.[39]

This massive increase in the fiscal burden under Henri II is comparable to, though slightly weaker than, that pushed through by Louis XI in the late 1470s and early 1480s, the latter at least the result of a return to coinage debasement, and must be seen as a major source of political instability. It was in that period, with increased war levies on the towns, that urban autonomy first came seriously into question. However, there was a greater proportionate increase in indirect taxes that affected all strata of society (very

much in contrast to the reign of Louis XI). If we examine the proportion of real wealth taken in taxes over this century, represented by the rising grain production in a time of population
growth, we discover that the percentage of total grain production
taken in taxes in 1453 was 18.5, in 1482, 26.5, in 1515, 13, in 1523,
9.1, in 1547, 8.4, rising again to 14.8 in 1559. In terms of the
number of days' work needed to pay taxes by each head of household, we see the figure rise from 5.3 in 1453 to 10.4 in 1482,
falling to 7.2 in 1523 and rising to 8.8 in 1559 (in 1683, the figure
was to be 34.2). Even at the height of Louis XI's fiscal pressure in
the 1480s, the rise in productivity was sufficient to render it
absorbable.[40]

The higher bureaucracy itself, although oligarchical and partly
venal, operated under a system of rules which ostensibly sought to
maintain justice and fairness in the apportionment of taxation.
Pierre Briçonnet's celebrated instructions, c.1500, repeatedly
stressed the necessity for the *élus* and local assessors and collectors
to act with fairness and probity, 'the strong supporting the weak',
without favours to friends or for money, while village apportionment was not supposed to be carried out by the rich at the
expense of the poor. In practice, the frequent complaints about
the *élus* over assessment make it abundantly clear that an *impôt de
répartition* like the *taille personelle* or a variant of land tax like the
taille réelle could not hope to be fair in such a society.[41]

The general failure of royal revenues to cope with increased
demands of military expenditure forced a resort to borrowing, initially in the form of *rentes* guaranteed on the credit of the Paris
municipality.[42] This was the main way in which the wealth of the
bourgeoisie contributed (to its profit) to the state. Already at the
start of Henri II's reign, loans contracted through the international banking system were well established. In the budget estimate of January 1549, the deficit was 3,131,183 *lt.*, largely resulting from accumulated loans at Lyon of 2,421,846 and interest of
387,764. Without the loans, the deficit was only 709,337.[43] The
increasing importance of credit is symbolised by the creation, for
the Italian Albisse del Bene in January 1550, of an office of *surintendant*, linked to banking facilities, for purposes of contracting
loans and making payments in Italy and Germany. Del Bene was
contracting loans on the authority of the royal council in financial
matters, headed by Montmorency, who had to issue personal

guarantees for which they were discharged by the crown in turn.[44] Interest rates were as high as 16 per cent in 1549 and remained at this level into the 1550s, though the rates paid by the emperor were generally much higher. During the war years of 1552 and 1553, moderate sums of 1.1 and 1.7 million were borrowed but the middle of the 1550s clearly saw a growing problem of a general shortage of credit on the international markets. Between March and October 1555, in the *Grand Parti* of Lyon, the crown converted its short-term high interest loans into long-term debt at uniform interest of 16 per cent in order to secure a new loan of 500,000 *écus* and instal a system for discharging the debt in ten years. Interest was to be secured on yearly revenues of 1.3 million *lt.* specifically set aside for this purpose.[45] In fact, however, payments of the *Grand Parti* rapidly fell into arrears and were superseded by the need to contract more loans; the revenues set aside for interest topped 2 million *lt.* [46] During the 1550s, the loans contracted by del Bene for which records survive amount to just over 8 million *lt.* and may have risen to over 13 million by 1559. By 1559, the total royal debt may have stood at 43 million livres, three times the annual 'budget'.[47] That the international financial disturbances at the end of the 1550s made the contracting of loans more difficult is obvious but should not obscure the fact that the French monarchy was able to construct and use financial instruments of extraordinary complexity and sophistication in the 1550s.

Consultation

All these features help to explain why the apparent expansion of the fiscal demands of the state during the first half of the sixteenth century could be sustained. This did not mean, however, that the direct financial demands of the crown on its subjects were not resented or felt to be onerous. In part this resulted from the obvious inequalities of burden between the different regions of France, mostly stemming from custom. The existence of provincial estates was not the only determinant of this. Instead of the usual dichotomy of *pays d'états* and *pays d'élections* it is important to remember that there were at least four basic types of tax-raising mode: *pays d'élections, pays d'états, pays d'états à élus, pays à commissaires.* M. Wolfe has argued that absolute taxation powers were seized by Charles VII so that after 1453 even provinces with estates lost the right to refuse to grant the king subsidies,[48] although in some areas, such as Dauphiné, it was probably the activity of Louis XI that proved decisive.[49] The presence or absence of estates does not explain the disparities. Normandy, for instance, a *pays d'états* with *élus* as a result of the takeover by the crown in the mid-fifteenth century of the effective English taxation system, paid around 25 per cent of the total *taille*

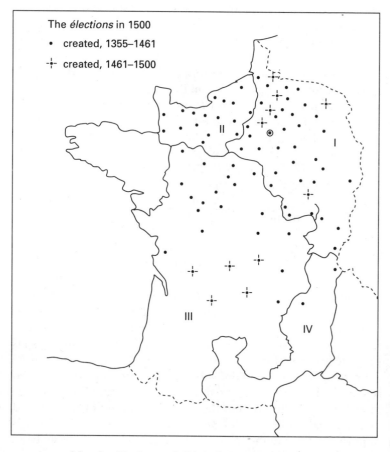

The *élections* in 1500

• created, 1355–1461

-+- created, 1461–1500

Map 6   *Elections* and *Généralités* around 1500–20

of the kingdom in the later fifteenth century. Languedoc, a *pays d'états* pure and simple where the estates received the royal mandate to raise the taxes, paid around one-third of this sum (roughly 9 per cent in the later fifteenth century). The disparity was to remain well into the seventeenth century.[50] Among the provinces acquired in 1477, both Burgundy, with estates, and Picardy, without very regular meetings of estates and considered *pays d'élections*, were relatively under-assessed. The provinces of the centre – Ile-de-France, Orléanais, Loire – also largely without estates, were relatively heavily burdened but on the other hand benefited substantially from the largesse of the monarchy. Demands made by the estates of Normandy in 1491 for a new *recherche générale des feux*, leading to a revision of its proportion from a quarter to a fifth, were wrecked on the rocks of opposition from other provinces to a disturbance of the existing balance. This indicates the limitations of change. Additional trouble had also stemmed from the fact that the *crues de tailles* were being levied automatically only on the four old generalities of the kingdom (in other words the kingdom before its expansion under Louis XI). These therefore tended to be overcharged and the negotiations of 1491–3 did indeed lead to a reduction of the *taille* of Languedoc by 20,000 *lt*, though the provincial estates had to fight to retain it. In fact, between 1484 and 1511 an important shift did take place. Although the overall level of the *taille* was similar in both years, the burden was noticeably shifted to the generality of Languedoil, where the tax rate per head had been estimated in 1491 at 19s., in comparison with 27s. for Outre-Seine, 60s.8d. for Normandy and 68s. for Languedoc.[51] However, the latter, as *pays de taille réelle*, was not strictly comparable.

Where estates existed, it might be thought that they were able to resist the demands of the crown for increased revenue. The customary composition of the taxes voted by the Estates of Languedoc, for instance, made up of the *equivalent* (a fixed sum of 73,000 *lt.* voted under Charles VII to account for the former *aides* and the variable *aide*, both amalgamated by 1474 in the fixed sum known as the *aide*, of 187,975) had always been supplemented by demands for further flexible sums in accordance with the variation of the principal of the *taille* (called in Languedoc the *octroi*) to which were added the province's portion of the *crues de taille*, also, of course, variable. From 1516, this arcane system was under pressure from royal representatives who no longer recognised the origins of the initial fixed sums and sought to introduce a principal levy more in line with the assessment of other provinces. In these circumstances the 20,000 *lt.* reduction dating from 1491 was virtually lost sight of, despite the determination of the estates to defend their rights.[52]

In fact, estates often proved too divided internally to present a united front. Dauphiné was a province ruled by the *dauphin* or the king as Vicar of the Empire and under its own constitution or *statut* of 1349 that exempted it from regular taxation. Despite this, Louis XI had squeezed very heavy taxes from the province and the agreement of 1484, whereby the crown agreed to limit its demands to 20,000 *lt.* a year (1.34 per cent of the total for the kingdom), while it set a limit, in fact created a precedent for fairly automatic taxation under the guise of a *don et octroi gracieux.* Levies were computed on the basis of a property valuation of 1457–61 that estimated the province at 4800 *feux,* reduced to 4600 in the 1490s and remaining throughout the sixteenth century the essential taxable unit, despite disputes as to its meaning.[53] In October 1536, though, the estates met to levy an 'extraordinary' grant of 100,000 *lt.* (35,000 above Louis XI's greatest demand), followed by a supplementary 180,000 in February 1537 and 382,000 in October 1538. Clearly, something extraordinary was happening here since, even with special levies like the king's ransom (1529–30), royal demands had not greatly exceeded the customary 20,000 under Francis I. Taxes did not return to normal until 1540. The main explanation seems to have been the role of Dauphiné in military activity during the campaigns of 1536–7 in Piedmont. Dauphiné was excused from the *solde des gens de pied* levied in 1538 but the towns were called upon to pay 45,000 for this levy in 1543 and subsequent levies of *soldes* continued.[54]

In Dauphiné, the estates had few common interests. By the 1540s, deep resentments in the rural communities at the acquisition of property by exempted townsmen, thus taking that property off the tax list and increasing the burden in this territory of mixed *taille réelle* and *taille personelle,* created long-running discord within the estates. The crown in 1548 issued an *arrêt* in the interests of the rural communities that called for a new assessment of *feux* and ruled that townsmen were to pay taxes on all rural property acquired in the previous 30 years. In future, the provincial governor was to rule on whether changes to the tax assessment were disproportionately levied on one estate. These changes served to push town and rural representatives together in the third estate for the first time, since they were now more likely to be treated on the same terms. One consequence was the disintegration of the harmonious working of the provincial estates.[55] It is clear, therefore, that the increasing fiscal demands of the 1540s and 1550s found the local estates in Dauphiné deeply divided in terms of their fundamental interests. The refusal of the clergy and nobility to contemplate changes in the traditional tax structures allowed the crown increasingly to respond to demands for intervention on the part of both the towns and the rural communities after 1548.

In another area, it was tension between the estates of different provinces over the levels of taxation that opened the way for royal intervention. It was the tradition that the crown fixed the global sum demanded on the four provinces of Rouergue, Quercy, Agenais and Périgord, part of the *recette-générale* of Guyenne, created in 1523. These were *pays d'états* where the estates continued to meet but where royal *commissaires* shared out the obligations of the parishes. In 1532, the largest of the provinces, Rouergue, tried to obtain diminution of its proportion on the argument that it was less productive than the others. The other three provinces registered opposition and the case remained undecided until royal letters brought it before the Parlement of Paris in 1549. In this year, the *taille* of Quercy alone was raised by 2000 *lt.* and the case should be placed in the context of rising taxes. The judicial proceedings gathered by the estates of Agenais throw the case into relief. In 1551, the *conseil privé* ordered that Rouergue should pay one-quarter of the *taille* while a thorough enquiry in the *commodités* of the provinces was carried out by a Parisian jurist, Nicolas Compaing. This in effect registered the greater land surface of Rouergue while trying to evaluate the productive capacity of the whole region in a complex set of calculations producing an *allivrement* for each province (Rouergue, 2459 *lt.*, Agenais, 2083, Quercy, 1121 and Périgord, 1077). The outcome was something of a compromise. In December 1553 the crown ordered the division of the global *taille* into 12 parts; Rouergue would pay 3.5, Quercy and Agenais 3 each and Périgord 2.5. Only Périgord, therefore, benefited from the whole process. The main aim of the crown was to obtain its revenue rather than to establish exact justice and at the same time it was alienating the domain in Quercy (the royal domain in Rouergue and Agenais was the dower of queen Léonore).[56]

The general picture needs also to be compared with the fiscal burden on a province without estates that played a part in raising taxes. Among those provinces acquired by Louis XI in the 1470s, Picardy falls into this category (Artois, Burgundy and Franche-Comté all having estates). The proportion envisaged for the generality of Picardy in the assessment proposed in 1484 was 3.6 per cent (though the generality did not then include all of the province of Picardy). However, the proportion for the whole province was even lower by 1549–50 at 2.7 per cent (as it happens exactly the likely proportion of the population of Picardy in the kingdom: 500,000 out of 18 m). Even this is an overestimate since the province was then enjoying extensive tax remissions as a result of war damage.[57]

Without estates, the natural resentments between town and country over the apportionment of taxation had no forum for expression, although, when tax exemptions for the towns were extracted from the king, the *généraux des finances* sometimes opposed them on the grounds that they would be to the detriment of the *plat pays*. It is clear, however, that the privileges conceded by Louis XI in the 1470s were of great value to the towns and that the story of royal encroachments on them in the course of the sixteenth century is a chequered one, somewhat different from what has been seen in Dauphiné. Besides exemption from the *tailles* conceded to most of the walled towns of Picardy in the 1470s, Louis XI issued separate privileges concerning the use of *octrois*, technically royal sales taxes which the municipalities were allowed to raise in order to defray their defence costs.[58] In the case of Amiens, the *échevinage* was allowed to raise *aides* without special royal *lettres d'octroi* (bringing in 8000–11,000 *lt.* in the sixteenth century) and the royal *aides* were abolished. An important turning point came in 1518. Up to that time, the town had informally exempted tavern-keepers from the *aides* on drink during the *francs-fêtes* in order to encourage business but in that year the increasing costs of fortifications led the *échevinage* to insist on payment and raised a case which eventually went before the Parlement of Paris. The latter had always raised doubts over the original privilege accorded by Louis XI and, by dragging out the case, eventually, in 1536, forced the town to solicit annual renewal of the privilege before it would rule against the tavern-keepers. This effective defeat reopened the need to obtain *lettres d'octroi* which were now, in accordance with general royal policy, much more strict on the audit of the *octrois* and their restriction to fortification expenses. However, having given way on the principle of self-imposition of dues, the *échevinage* received considerable benefits as the costs of fortification rose through the sixteenth century, notably when new *aides royales* were conceded to the town in 1557.[59]

Octrois were, however, only one aspect of the impact of royal fiscality in the sixteenth century. There was general resistance in Picard towns to any tax that would involve general levies based on surveys of property. Louis XI usually refrained from them in his anxiety to win support but there were repeated demands for special levies from 1486 onwards either in the form of the 'free gift' or, more usually, a loan to the king or the provincial governor for war expenses. The principle of loans goes back to the four-teenth century, but it was one of Louis XI's most characteristic financial devices. Moreover, his successors continued the practice with avidity. There was much bargaining over demands, with a compromise figure usually emerging. Even Louis XII did this, though less frequently. In 1513 he demanded 3000 *lt.* of Poitiers and Tours, 2000 of Angers. Francis I was more insistent in his demands. From Amiens he demanded: 6000 *lt.* in 1519, 2000 in 1521, 4000 in 1524, 12,000 in 1527 for the ransom, 6000 in 1537.[60]

Even more than this, the crown in this reign used the device of confiscating the *deniers communs* from the *octrois* to its own use on the argument that they were technically royal taxes anyway. This happened in 1527, 1539, 1542 and 1544. Finally, the *soldes des gens de pied* levied periodically from 1538 and more or less annually from 1547 effectively breached the exemption of the towns from what was in effect a supplement to the *taille*. While the Habsburg–Valois wars continued, Amiens was only lightly bur-dened (at 1200 *lt.* p.a. out of 2400 for the *bailliage*) but by the 1570s it was more usually paying 8000 p.a.[61]

More than anything else, the gradual imposition of special sup-plementary levies on the towns in this region encouraged them to raise loans and contract long-term debts, rather than make general levies on the population, which were always divisive. The taxes thus

turned into a form of public credit. Bernard Chevalier has recently
examined the relations between the crown and the cities of France
by analysing the letters and acts of the chancellery that concerned
the towns. He has concluded that the autonomy of the towns of
France was not seriously in question, even under Louis XI, until the
increased demands for special war levies in the 1550s.[62]

Resistance to Taxation

Resistance, sometimes ferocious, to the levying of taxes by the
crown is a leitmotif of Ancien Regime history. Behind it lay the
deep rooted ideas that permanent taxes were profoundly unnecessary as well as levied under unfair conditions which always
favoured the rich. This was the case despite the formal principle
that the 'strong should support the weak' in tax assessment. The
realities of politics demanded exemption not only for the nobility
but for a wide range of office-holders and whole towns. Whenever
unusually heavy demands for taxes coincided with difficult economic conditions and particularly with the oppression of uncontrolled soldiery, an explosion of popular anger became likely.[63]
In fact, the revolts of the late Middle Ages are often difficult to
analyse in terms of motivation, the Jacquerie of 1358 being the
outstanding example.[64] This has variously been interpreted as a
major class confrontation, as the response of an exasperated peasantry to military chaos or to the 'hidden hand' of bourgeois and
aristocratic provocation. Indeed, in the late Middle Ages cities
and towns were increasingly the focus of such upheavals when
they concerned the impact of taxes. Purely rural revolts had one
main feature in common: the destructive presence of French or
foreign soldiers or that of *routiers*. Given the natural confusion in
the minds of the peasantry between nobles and soldiers, these
movements often take on what seem to be the aspects of confrontation between the social orders. Moreover, the most severe
revolts, Jacquerie and Tuchins, for example, took place in territories which in the late Middle Ages constituted great apanages.[65]
    Henry Heller has argued that Calvinism in the sixteenth
century became a mass movement partly at any rate by mobilising
a wide range of social and economic resentments, the evidence for
which is apparent from the *émeutes* of the earlier sixteenth century

stemming from the unfavourable trend of wages in relation to prices.[66] In this context of economic distress, the late medieval revolt sparked by the intolerable presence of uncontrolled soldiery tends, from the late fifteenth century, to give way to some extent to a mixture of resentments surrounding the apportionment and administration of taxes. Such movements, though, are evident from the start of Louis XI's reign, the king's inept handling of his father's advisers, and disappointment when expected tax remissions failed to materialise, provoking a reaction. The years 1458–62 were times of depression throughout western Europe. It may be from this period that François Bourdin, *receveur* at Paris, wrote to Louis XI's secretary Bourré:

> There is not a single denier left ... I assure you, Monsieur, that it is a great pity to gather money, that the people have nothing left and whatever efforts I make or have made I can get nothing. It is impossible to gather the first quarter until the end of next May, for money is still due from last year.[67]

The consequence was a series of uprisings like the *Tricotins* of Angers and the *Micquemaque* of Rheims.[68] Such rebellions took the form of attacks on the property of royal *officiers* and rich bourgeois, according to contemporary chronicle accounts. In Normandy, as Thomas Basin recounted, expectations of lighter taxes were swiftly disappointed: 'The first years of the new king's reign, who had been expected to be so benevolent and merciful, were more difficult to bear than the previous years, both because of the levies themselves and for the abuses which are the usual consequence.'[69] A letter, unfortunately not dated, from the governor, Louis d'Estouteville, to Bourré may be dated at this time. Five hundred peasants around the Seine estuary, led by a priest as their *grand conducteur*, had risen:

> yesterday we had a great storm from these villagers and in the end part of them said they would not pay this quarter unless they knew they would be reduced and equalised. However, we hope they will obey.[70]

They said they had been levied at 20s. per hearth and demanded to see the royal warrant for it.[71] Similarly, the rebels at Rheims refused to believe the new taxes to be the work of a king who had so recently indulged in benevolent promises.[72] At any rate, the consequence there was severe repression, the respectable bourgeois shifting responsibility onto the shoulders of 'a small group of men of low extraction' a myth subsequently encapsulated in royal letters of remission. The first years of Louis XI saw similar upheavals at Alençon and Aurillac.

Revolts naturally followed the rhythms of royal taxation. The period from 1462 to 1474 was quiet on this front though wracked by aristocratic conspiracy. When taxation began to rise again in the mid-1470s, generated by the renewal of the Burgundian wars and Louis's need to lay hands on Charles the Bold's inheritance, they began again, with the sedition at Bourges in April–May 1474. There, the levy of a due at the gates for the reconstruction of the fortifications, not by local officials but by royal officers, provoked a rebellion among the tradesmen most heavily hit. As was often the case, the local officials were slow to repress the movement and Louis XI chose to believe this was the work of a party which had been long hostile to him as a result of its loyalty to his late brother, Charles duke of Berry. The king was savage in his demands for punishment and took the opportunity to remodel the city government to his liking. Only after the initial shock was the severity moderated.[73]

The acceleration of tax demands in the king's last years provoked rebellions of a different kind, involving a resistance of communities who saw their autonomy threatened, particularly in the south-west. In 1480, the tradesmen of Limoges rose up against Louis's bizarre proposal to transfer individuals from all over France to repopulate Arras.[74] In 1477–8, the demands of the king for military support taxes in the territories of the sire d'Albret provoked a rural uprising in five parishes.[75] Elsewhere, at Le Puy in 1477 and Agen in 1481, it was the inequality of tax assessment that detonated the explosion. Le Puy, a turbulent town throughout the late Middle Ages, had evolved an oligarchical regime controlled by the rich bourgeois, who by the 1470s were under sharp pressure to share power. The consuls were accused of lining their own pockets by levying more *octrois* than they needed and pocketing the difference, as well as by exaggerating the town's part in the *aide royale.* Crisis was precipitated by the king's spontaneous remission of 10 years' taxes on a visit to the shrine in 1476. The consuls claimed this could not apply to arrears, the tax payers that it involved taxes already owed. The result was a riot and an attack on the consuls and the tax commissioners.[76] Despite Louis's irritated reaction, the discontent continued to simmer for two decades. At Agen, the consolidation in the wealth and power of a local oligarchy linked to the wine trade had established between 1450 and 1470 a powerful group of interlinked families that manipulated local finance. The imposition of new dues on wine and a supplementary due on butchers provoked a lawsuit in the Parlement of Bordeaux.[77] The events at Agen under Louis XI took place also in a town where the exemptions of the nobles, clergy and consuls were resented, the latter also having failed to avoid the levy of victuals for a turbulent garrison under the count of Comminges. The result was a struggle for power between the consular oligarchy and the *gens de métier*, ultimately resolved in favour of the former.[78]

The most striking features of these disturbances are the salient part played by the towns, the leading role played by those outside the oligarchies in opposition, and the resentment directed against the exempt rich and against magistrates who failed to defend their communities against the imposition of unfamiliar or oppressive dues. That French society was able to sustain the enormous increases in direct as well as indirect taxes and forced loans levied in the later years of Louis XI is a remarkable fact, to be explained by the increase in productive resources. When the trend turned against the producer, roughly after the 1520s, the impact of taxes was more problematic. The generation from 1483 was able to benefit from the decisive moderation of the tax regime that lasted down to about 1520 and gave the reign of Louis XII its benevolent reputation. We have seen already that taxes under Francis I scarcely outstripped inflation and that the significant increases came in the 1550s. Nevertheless, as Heller has pointed out, any increase in taxes in the context of declining standards of living would prove disruptive.[79]

Revolts against taxation formed only the minority of disruptive social movements in the first half of the sixteenth century and nearly always coincided with the effects of undisciplined billeting of soldiers. Of the 47 movements listed by Heller between 1504 and 1554 (representing only a proportion of the whole) no more than eight involved reactions against taxation.[80] Examples of these are the revolt of 1514 at Agen against a new tax levied by the oligarchical consulate for the upkeep of a bridge. The subsequent explosion of anger revealed festering resentment of the *menu peuple* against the consuls 'who for thirty years now have been linked by blood or affinity ... and the most rich, strong and powerful have been elected'. Moreover, they enjoyed exemption from the *taille* and other taxes. The *taille royale*, stable in the years around 1500, had risen sharply in 1512–13 in anticipation of the renewal of war in Italy and the north.[81] The Russian historian who discovered the programme of the insurgents in the municipal archives argued that royal taxes were an unimportant issue in comparison with local taxes. However, such local levies were *octrois* collected by the consulate formally for defence works on the authority of the crown. It is true that they allowed a greater degree of local autonomy but ultimately provided the crown with justification for interference. The main point is that military levies in the form of local taxes had become intolerable to all except a very narrow local elite by 1514.[82] The 1536 upheaval at Le Puy, which continued to be a divided and turbulent community through the sixteenth century, occurred over contributions for military provisions.[83]

A distinctive feature of the reign of Francis I is the growing antagonism between the country dwellers who paid the bulk of the *tailles* and the assemblies of estates dominated by the privileged orders who apportioned them. In Dauphiné, where the global tax burden increased significantly, as has been seen, this generated quarrels between the towns and the country bourgs.[84] During the 1540s, a dispute arose within the communities of Velay over the apportionment of the *taille* between the countryside and the town of Le Puy and those areas under its control. The latter was advantaged, the former disgruntled. The estates of Velay were controlled by the clergy and nobility and the notables of Le Puy itself. The bulk of the taxpayers had no say. Although the *Grands Jours* in 1548 ordered the estates to call representatives from the bourgs and villages, it refused to do so. The same resentments surfaced over the levy of the *taillon* in Basse-Auvergne by the estates at Clermont in 1554; here again the countryside had little role.[85] In many cases the late 1540s saw the emergence of peasant leagues, for instance in Comminges, Velay, Agenais and Dauphiné, precisely those areas which had already seen contestation over the control of tax apportionment by provincial estates that traditionally took no account of the interests of the *plat pays*. In Comminges, the peasant leagues or *syndicats* were formed in 1546 in response to the increase in taxes for 143 communities in the low country of the county to the profit of the mountain areas, resulting from the survey carried out by the estates. The outcry that resulted revealed deep divisions in local society. One of the *syndicats* covered 108 villages which mandated their *syndics* through village assemblies. The revised *assiette* had to be cancelled as a result of the syndicates' appeal to the *cour des aides* at Montpellier and replaced by a modified one carried out in 1552–3.[86]

The feature most apparent under Louis XI, divisions between wealthy oligarchies and the *gens de métier*, surfaced even more notably at La Rochelle, where the crown, in the person of the governor, Chabot de Jarnac, was able to exploit divisions. Until 1540, the provinces of the south-west, land of the kingdom's most productive salt marshes, lived under their own regime of the *quart du sel* instead of the *grandes et petites gabelles* which applied in the rest of the kingdom outside Brittany. There, in a network of *greniers*, the merchants had to sell their salt to be resold to the public on the basis of a minimum consumption per hearth. In the territory of the *quart*, the merchants brought their produce to a regional office where an official levied a tax for the crown at a quarter of its agreed sale price. The merchant could then sell it to the public on the market.[87] When the crown tried to introduce a more rigorous form of the *gabelle* in 1541, abolishing existing arrangements and introducing a uniform administration by which the same levy of 44 *lt.* per *muid* was levied on the salt from the marshes, all parties came together to oppose it. Jarnac's introduction of troops in August 1542 was met by full-scale opposition and his men were cut to pieces. Even after the subsequent reduction of the uniform levy to 24 *lt.*, the effects of the new system were ruinous for the salt trade in the south-west. Francis I restored the privileges of a chastised La Rochelle in 1543 and even restored the old system of the salt tax in May 1543.[88]

However, the idea of creating a uniform system was not abandoned. In 1544 two edicts introduced the system of *greniers à sel* throughout the kingdom and set in train resentment that was to culminate in the Guyenne rebellion of 1548, the most formidable mass movement to confront the crown in the first half of the sixteenth century.[89] The machinery for the control of the explosion of contraband was feeble: no more than a captain and 12 archers. The easiest way was to introduce private enterprise and farm out the tax; the consequence was a large increase in personnel to be paid and in the unfairness of controls.[90] Heller's determination to see class confrontation throughout is at its most strained at this point.[91] The revolt involved all sectors of society: hence the punishment later meted out to those magistrates who had done nothing to control it. The attacks directed against castles involved seigneurs who had taken part in the *gabelle* administration; those against individuals at Bordeaux itself in the violence of August 1548 involved financiers and office-holders. Among the leaders of the revolt, Bois-Menier was a bourgeois of Blansac, and Puymoreau, so-called colonel of the communes of Guyenne, was an obscure, possibly bastard, member of the minor nobility of Saintonge, much like those who participated in revolts under Richelieu.[92]

There was a strong element involving the defence of the local community against outside interference but the movement took the name of 'communes' and came to consist in effect of peasant armies. Their demands were drawn up in the form of the *Articles des habitants et communes de Guyenne*. These testify on the one hand to a conservative opposition to 'innovations', especially in the system of taxes, but also to a radical critique of the creation of new offices for sale in state and church. The king, it was claimed, had at his accession announced his desire to manage with the ordinary taxes 'and nevertheless has constrained his people to the said levies'. The *Articles* amount, in fact, to a full-scale critique of the tax system as it had developed since the beginning of the century.[93]

Meanwhile, the magistrates of Bordeaux itself, notably the councillors of the Parlement, had become increasingly vocal during the 1540s in the deployment of claims to defend those privileges in return for which the region had placed itself once more under the king of France's sceptre in the mid-fifteenth century. The problem for them was that their interests diverged from those of the rural communes whose grievances, as elsewhere, also involved the unfair administration of the royal taxation system by local notables of the estates. It has therefore been argued that the supposed complicity of the Parlement of Bordeaux in the rising was more apparent than real and certainly the Parlement was reinstated after investigation of its role in the rising in 1550.[94]

An extraordinary phenomenon not easily to be explained is the fact that the summit of state tax demands in the 1550s saw if anything a relaxation of popular anti-tax agitation in comparison with the movements of the 1540s. Whether this was connected with the channelling of energies into the creation of Calvinist churches, as Heller suggests, or the subsequent relaxation of the *gabelle* regime after the savage suppression of 1548–9 has yet to be decided. However, amnesty was proclaimed in 1549 and in December 1553 the *gabelle* was suppressed in Guyenne and its offices repurchased by the estates. Until the end of the Ancien Regime, Guyenne was to be free of the oppressive salt-tax regime that prevailed elsewhere.[95]

Conclusion

The taxation system in this century remained a complex and unsystematised one. At its highest level, reform and innovation touched principally the relatively small oligarchy that controlled the financial organisation of the monarchy until the early sixteenth century. The basic principles remained untouched. The tax burden undoubtedly grew, sharply in the early 1480s and 1550s, but not by an insupportable increase in the basic taxes levied on the peasantry. Taxes moved on in rhythm with the rise in population. Controversy raged essentially over innovations in military and salt taxes that more clearly seemed to infringe immemorial privileges of provinces, or else generated divisions and rancour between social groups within them. Faced by such innovations, the estates in those provinces endowed with them were able to make no systematic or united attempts at opposition. Rebellions, when they broke out, emerged overwhelmingly from local conditions and resentments. The curious absence of large-scale rebellions in the 1550s, when they might have been expected, may partly be the result of timely concessions. At any rate, the sharpest burdens fell on the clergy in that decade. However, this was an ominous lull before a storm. There is every reason to suppose that excessive state expenditure and taxation in that period, made necessary by the demands of war and foreign policy, could not be indefinitely sustained. It left the crown with a crippling burden of debt and seriously undermined the natural loyalty upon which the crown had come to rely.

6. The French Nobility in the Renaissance

Status and Wealth

The relationship between the nobility and the crown, in an Ancien Regime society still largely dominated by landed wealth, has naturally played a part in attempts to explain the construction of Absolutism. Augustin Thierry argued in 1850 that the alliance of the crown and the bourgeoisie from the thirteenth century onwards created the modern state and started the destruction of the 'powers and privileges of the feudal order ... to the profit of the king and the people'. For Maulde-la-Clavière, the years around 1500 saw the disappearance of an 'aristocracy' and its replacement by a 'nobility' endowed with anachronistic privileges, to act as the crown's satellite and people its antechambers.[1] The idea that the history of France can be explained in simple terms of class alliances or deliberate subordination is no longer easily sustainable.[2] Allied to such arguments is the view that the upheavals of the later sixteenth century were a noble reaction to indebtedness incurred during the period of the Renaissance.[3] This is a view certainly expressed at the time both by Venetian ambassadors in trying to explain the troubles and by military memoirist La Noue. To some extent it underlies the description of the later sixteenth century as a 'crisis' of the nobility, in terms both of wealth and of self-esteem, which generated a substantial literature on the theme of what it was to be noble.[4]

Pierre de Vaissière, accepting completely the view that the nobility faced an alliance between the crown and the urban communes, argued, from a selection of private writings, accounts and letters of remission, that the mass of the nobility remained firmly attached to its provincial estates throughout the sixteenth century, suspicious of the court and fiercely loyal to its region. This can stand only in very general terms.[5] The continuing predominance of land as a source of wealth is certainly reflected in the attention of landowners to the profitable administration of their property and this in itself generated a natural desire to remain close to estates. But even in the sixteenth century, the

French nobility was formidably numerous and virtually impossible to analyse in terms of a single social group with uniform attitudes and problems.

An earlier 'crisis', the severe collapse of revenues brought about by the calamitous years of 1350–1450, has often been seen as pivotal in the development of the nobility. At the end of the Middle Ages, it has been argued, it lost the principal pillars upon which its power and authority had rested: the right to make war, to administer justice and to tax its subjects, at the time when the crown was monopolising these powers.[6] The weakening of landowners' economic bargaining-power in the fourteenth and fifteenth centuries was once thought to have enabled other classes to emancipate themselves from control and allowed the crown to build up a political system based on permanent taxation and a bureaucracy. It seems evident that some decisive steps towards the *Etat de finance* were taken in the late thirteenth and early fourteenth centuries; after this there was a retreat of royal fiscalism until the mid-fifteenth century. Another perspective would view the nobility as a central component in the reconstruction of the monarchical state; their economic problems in the fifteenth century actually led them to accept a more authoritarian political system in order to restore their fortunes at the expense of an increasingly emancipated peasantry.[7]

That there was a crisis in seigneurial revenues during the epoch of the Black Death is not in doubt. Boutruche in his study of the Bordelais was convinced of the distressed state of the nobility there by 1450, a point made by Perroy generally for the same period.[8] What is debatable is the nature of the response to that crisis and whether the nobility responded as a whole. Guy Bois has argued that 'the impoverishment of the nobility was the phenomenon that pushed the growing crisis of feudalism beyond the sphere of economic life into generating the crisis of the whole society.'[9] The nobility was unable to accept a slow decline in its revenues because of its consciousness of its rank and needs. It was this that proved the 'explosive element' in the problems of the social order, provoking both military destruction and the re-establishment of royal fiscalism as well as confrontation with a more organised peasantry.

Nothing could be more misleading than to regard the nobility in the period from 1460 to 1560 from the perspective of the eighteenth century, as a closed caste. If we consider the nobility as a whole, it is striking that, in comparison with the period 1250–1350, in the century up to 1460 there was a startling and accelerating expansion in the avenues of promotion into the nobility as the crown sought to widen its support. Indeed, Raymond Cazelles argued that, in the fourteenth century, the distinction between nobles and non-nobles should not be over-emphasised, especially when considering nobles without high justice.[10] In many ways access to the nobility was surprisingly open but one feature of the fourteenth and fifteenth centuries was the increased emphasis on precise definition. Many of the arguments concerning the medieval French nobility stem essentially from haziness in the definition of and access to the noble order (e.g. the concept of 'living nobly' or of access to noble status through bearing arms) and the fifteenth century saw increasing emphasis on the idea of 'derogation' by nobles who engaged in trade.[11] It is possible that Louis XI envisaged a removal of the stain of trade from the concept of derogation and, indeed, he issued letters in 1463 enabling the nobility of Languedoc to engage in trade without dishonour. As with several of that king's ideas, there was no continuation of the policy under his successors.[12] It is true that Louis XII conceded letters of nobility to Pierre Briçonnet of Angers specifically declaring that his engaging in trade was 'honest and very useful for the public weal'. The nobility of Marseilles was able to trade by the late fifteenth century and this was specifically recognised by law in 1566. It is obvious, though, that there was great hostility to this view.[13]

With the increasing emphasis on fiscal 'privilege' as a mark of noble status from the mid-fifteenth century, it becomes somewhat simpler to define who is noble but the lines of distinction between nobility and 'trade' were never as clear cut as is often supposed. Although the *échevins* of Poitiers and their posterity were ennobled in 1372 and even though Louis XI could confer nobility widely on town councillors, as well as ennobling en masse in Normandy in 1470, there remained a rooted objection to the continuation of trade if the individual was freed from taxes.[14] By convention a noble could cultivate no more than four *charrues* of land himself if he wished to retain exemption from the *taille*, though this remained vague in practice and much more could be involved. Nobles often took a hand in the management of their woodland and frequently undertook enterprises in glass-making, metallurgy and mining, all thought compatible with nobility because they were appurtenances of seigneuries. Glass-making was even considered a preserve of 'gentlemen glassmakers'. Even forges were run by nobles and in the county of Comminges most of the industries connected with building materials were noble-owned. Forges enjoyed royal privileges renewed by Francis I in 1516 and in 1548 Henri II conceded to the sieur de Roberval a monopoly of mining exploration.[15] The notion of a completely disdainful attitude to 'mechanical' skills among the nobility is an exaggeration.

Other privileges included the right to armorial bearings and the ability to hold fiefs without paying the *droit de franc fief* owed by *roturiers* in possession of noble fiefs.[16] When investigations into noble status took place they also asked whether family property had enjoyed *partage noble*, the right to advantage the eldest. The custom of Poitou, for instance, decreed that acquirers of fiefs would enjoy this privilege after four successive homages. The revision of 1514 appreciably strengthened the *droit d'ainesse* involved. They asked, too, whether the individual and his forebears had borne arms and were known as nobles. From the thirteenth century, holding a noble fief was no longer enough automatically to ennoble its holder; it was still necessary to 'live nobly'. The life of a nobleman involved war, hunting and honest pastimes and it is unsurprising that, with the expansion of the latter in the late Middle Ages, some attention was paid to what 'games' nobles should play. Chess was certainly regarded as a noble game; among the physical sports, the *jeu de paume* was widely played. Curiously, a law of 1495 confined the right to play dice and cards in the precincts of the Châtelet to men of 'estat et honneur'. The continuing importance attached to military activity is also revealing. When the claims of the Norman sire de Gouberville were examined in 1555, he was only declared to be 'reputed' noble (his documents went back no further than 1473) but, as for bearing arms, this was not his calling.[17] The absence of a generally understood rule about military service, other than for the feudal levy, even the impossibility for most nobles to participate in the king's military service themselves, naturally rendered this criterion a difficult one to sustain.

Passage into the nobility 'par prescription' was to some extent founded on 'forgetting' origins and a degree of complicity in the crown. Louis XI's act of ennoblement of Norman fief-holders in 1470, however, served to underline the fact that holding such fiefs

did not automatically confer ennoblement and also stressed the
role of the crown in defining nobility.[18] The problem became
more urgent in the sixteenth century with the increasing acquisition of noble fiefs by non-nobles; hence, the act of 15 October
1539 for declaration of all alienations of fiefs, the edict of 3
January 1543 on the feudal levy, and the various acts concerning
franc-fiefs promulgated at the start of Henri II's reign.[19] Hence
also the fact that the crown periodically – 1486, 1487, 1490, 1521
– instituted enquiries even concerning Louis XI's ennoblements
in Normandy and threatened the estates of Languedoc with periodic enquiries into the holders of fiefs, which they were allowed
to buy off in 1494. Francis I agreed to cessations of enquiries for
40 years in return for payment. The concept of the ennobling
power of holding a fief survived longest in the *pays de taille réelle*
but even there it was on the retreat in the early sixteenth century
(surviving mainly in Béarn) and suppressed in 1579.[20] Until that
time, it had been in the interests of the nobility, bourgeoisie and
the crown to allow the situation to continue.

The crisis of noble revenues was therefore accompanied by the
very process that came to define the nobility during the Ancien
Regime: fiscal privilege and the continuation of the nobility's military ethos. The second half of the sixteenth century saw the
codification of dictums on the matter of the origin of noble
status, which varied but shared certain common assumptions.
Thus, Charles Loyseau (1610): 'It is wrong to think that nobility is
founded on descent from the Franks. Rather, it comes from three
other sources: that is, lesser lordships, ennobling offices continued
for two generations and immemorial possession'; or Bacquet
(1582): 'there are two sorts of ennoblement, either by the king's
letters-patent duly verified or through estates or offices held.'[21]

From the sixteenth century, the principal distinction within the
nobility was, firstly, between the *nobles de race* entitled to seats in
assemblies of estates, and the *anoblis* and *noblesse de dignité*,
counted among the third estate. This was a fairly recent phenomenon. It is clear that the acceleration of ennoblement through
offices aggravated the touchiness of nobles of ancient lineage confronted by the arrogant judges and councillors so vividly
described by Vaissière.[22] Within the *noblesse de race* the main
distinction was between *chevaliers* and *écuyers*. *Chevaliers*, broadly
speaking the higher nobility, could be called such by royal act

(and even *annoblis* could be knighted by the king), by holding certain posts or a *fief de dignité* (at the least a *baronnie*). The century from 1450 to 1550 saw a development of titles within the nobility. For instance, the number of Auvergnat nobles not claiming to be 'seigneurs' in 1488 was 166, whereas by 1551, there were only 11 'non-seigneurs' among the 140 claiming the status of nobles of 'ancienne race'. Among those of middle rank in the same period, there was a tendency to differentiate themselves by the acquisition, either by royal grant or usurpation, of *fiefs de dignité* as baron, count or viscount.[23] Technically a *comte* had to hold at least 2 *baronnies* and 3 *châtellenies* with powers of justice. The frequent creation of new counties and duchies by the crown was justified by the proximity of a family to the royal *lignage* and, as in Louis XII's creation of the duchy of Longueville in 1505, 'so that those called to assist the king in great affairs should be raised in dignity and surround him with splendour'.[24]

We need, of course, to understand how many nobles there were and how they can be categorised, a task made immensely difficult by the nature of the various attempts to list nobles in the late medieval and early modern periods. It has been estimated that around 1328 there were 200,000 nobles in 40,000–50,000 families, well above 1 per cent of the population and more than one noble family per parish. In the 1470s, another estimate gives 30,000–40,000 families in a population reduced to 10–12 million, a proportion not significantly reduced. Within these figures, we should envisage significant regional variations, with a high density of nobles in the western regions of Brittany, Anjou and Maine, average in Poitou and Saintonge and low in Burgundy and Champagne.[25]

How many nobles were there in the sixteenth century? Later in the century writers attempted estimates which ranged from 20,000 to 100,000. Manfred Orléa's computations based on rolls of fiefs drawn up for the feudal levy in the various *bailliages* between 1544 and 1607 lead us to envisage a figure of 25,000 gentlemen (plus their families) after 1560, 2000 of them constituting the *haute noblesse* of *chevaliers*, including just over 600 titled.[26] If this is the case, there had clearly been a significant contraction in the number of those enjoying noble status since the early fourteenth and mid-fifteenth centuries. In fact the number of the higher nobility was probably slightly smaller than this. Contamine has estimated the number of *chevaliers* in the late fifteenth century as about 1000. By the middle of the sixteenth century, the number of posts and fiefs conferring *chevalerie* did not exceed 1300. At any rate, there was a clear transformation in the position of the *chevaliers* in the fourteenth and fifteenth centuries. Around 1300 there had been between 5000 and 10,000 of them, while the number of the higher nobility of 'princes, dukes, counts, viscounts, barons and knights banneret' may have been 400–800 families only, c.1340.[27] In part, the decline seems to have resulted from the contraction of the number of chevaliers within the active armed forces during the fourteenth century.[28] On the other hand, the number of titled nobles above the level of baron certainly increased in the late Middle Ages as a result of royal acts and the fact that the princes as well as kings could create counts, viscounts and barons (though only kings ever conferred dukedoms),[29] and the conferment of *chevalerie* by the king came increasingly to be regarded as a reward for service and a sign of fidelity. Louis XII conferred chivalry, with the customary chaplet, on a legal official 'in order to give him the heart to perservere in our service'.[30] Throughout the first half of the sixteenth century, even kings continued to address those who had knighted them as 'mon père'. However, the general trend tended to make the title of *chevalier* rarer and therefore more sought-after so that the simple *chevaliers* by the sixteenth century can be considered the middle rank of the nobility.

The royal order of Saint-Michel, created by Louis XI, at first contributed to the prestige of *chevalerie*. The king had decided to create it in 1469 on the model of the Golden Fleece but, contrary to the statutes, seems never to have held a chapter, certainly not the one often ascribed to his visit to Mont Saint-Michel in 1470. His motives are uncertain but the composition of the order certainly indicates that it was supposed to include the king's most powerful supporters as well as the leading magnates of the realm and that the king was aiming to break up the *clientèles* of the princes by attaching men of lower rank to him. There were supposed to be 36 *chevaliers*; in 1484 there were actually 30 of them (10 had died since the creation of the order). Unlike the Toison d'or, the Saint-Michel never developed spectacular ceremonies or indeed held chapters with any regularity. On the other hand, it was a mark of high honour always given prominent place in a nobleman's titulary and the selection of *chevaliers* showed great attentiveness to gaining fidelity or rewarding signal services.[31] The king addressed members as 'mon cousin' and the role of the *chevaliers de l'ordre* in the royal councils was prominent. In fact, the dignity of the order and its socio-political significance remained high until the end of Henri II's reign. Only under Francis II did the excessive number of creations destroy its value.[32]

Within the nobility, there was constant replenishment to make up for the natural extinction of lineages. E. Perroy demonstrated how, in the county of Forez, of the 215 lineages in the thirteenth century, 66 had gone by 1300, of the remainder 80 had disappeared by 1400 and 38 by 1500. By 1789, only 5 lineages went back to the thirteenth century.[33] There were several means by which the losses could be made good. In 1470, for instance, at the height of the political crisis in his resumption of power in Normandy, Louis XI conferred collective ennoblement on all existing non-noble fief-holders in the duchy, 'provided they lived nobly' and on all future acquirers of fiefs who held them for 40 years. For Louis, money was partly the goal since the mass ennoblement was designed to circumvent Norman opposition to the duty of paying *droit de franc fief* by commoners. His ennoblement act netted in principle over 47,000 *lt*.[34] Louis XI, who conferred at least 180 individual letters of ennoblement in 22 years of his reign, used the device widely to confer collective ennoblement on town councils he wished to win over or control. There was, however, a sting in the tail: taxes would continue to be paid unless the ennobled councillors 'lived nobly'.[35] This probably put a limit to the extent to which Louis XI was prepared to promote trade by allowing the newly ennobled to continue in business, for instance in his ennoblements at Arras in 1481: 'anyone who wishes to trade can do so ... without impugning his nobility', since evidently there was an incentive to abandon trade to live nobly if taxpaying were at stake.[36] Francis I issued at least 183 individual letters, probably a few more, over 32 years, a large proportion in 1522 and 1543–4.[37] Ellery Schalk, in an analysis of some 3000 royal ennoblements between 1345 and 1660, has argued that no particular pattern emerges, though it is plain that there were great concentrations in the later fourteenth century and, to a lesser extent, under Louis XI and during the Wars of Religion. His overall interpretation of the nobility's transformation from a warrior force to an hereditary caste in the later sixteenth century leads him to the view that the status of nobility was not so important as wealth or office in the definition of the elite.[38]

Not until the end of the fifteenth century was access to the nobility through the holding of office at all significant in numbers, although the principle of exemption from taxes for royal servants, even domestics, was established by the mid-fifteenth century. Exemptions from practically all dues of commoner status were conferred on the company of royal *notaires et secrétaires* by Louis XI and extended into full hereditary nobility with the right to attain knighthood by the Regency in 1484. Between then and 1515 the principle was accepted that councillors of the Parlements should be regarded as hereditary nobles once their offices had been in the family for three generations.[39] Thereafter, and particularly with the generalisation of venality under Francis I, ennoblement through the holding of various categories of office becomes much more significant in terms of numbers than simple letters of ennoblement, which were issued for money certainly, but with a degree of restraint under Francis I.[40]

One further source for the replenishment of the nobility must be considered. It is now clear that the fifteenth century was the golden age of aristocratic bastards. The very fact that the word *bâtard* had honourable connotations in old French should alert us to its significance among the nobility but it seems that the late Middle Ages was a particularly favourable period for the illegitimate offspring of nobles for, although they could not inherit *apanages* or the *propres* of a family, no stigma attached to the bastard in higher noble circles. A survey of the higher civil and ecclesiastical offices held by bastards between 1345 and 1523 indicates an acceleration of the conquest of such positions in the first half of the fifteenth century and a great concentration in the second half, with 39 such posts held. There are a number of quite clear reasons for all this. Bastards actually bolstered the numbers within a noble family and were used to strengthen its influence either through marriage alliances or by the acquisition of administrative functions. They could be used to protect the influence of the legitimate members of the family without actually threatening their inheritance and, indeed, could be viewed as more trustworthy by their fathers since they posed no direct threat. As love children, they were often viewed as more handsome and personable than their legitimate siblings (the bastard of Dunois is the great case). Thus, as Harsgor reasonably argues, the expansion of their influence represented 'an aggrandisement of the sphere of influence of the nobility in general'.[41] Although Contamine has observed a restriction of bastards' access to higher military commands at the end of the fifteenth century,[42] aristocratic bastards played a significant part in the group of dominant figures, the 'masters of the kingdom', well into the sixteenth. Charles, last count of Armagnac, liberated from prison after the death of Louis XI, left a bastard, Pierre, who had a brilliant career at court under Charles VIII and Louis XII, was invested with the barony of Caussade, and whose legitimised son Georges, cardinal d'Armagnac, in turn became one of the great ecclesiastical statesmen of the sixteenth century. Georges in turn had a bastard daughter to whom La Caussade descended, while he made his nephew his vicar-general.[43]

As far as the royal family itself was concerned, the kings of the fifteenth century tended to recognise only female bastards, using them for careful marriage alliances designed to assemble an affinity around the throne. Other great princely houses produced many more. The family of the Valois dukes of Burgundy produced not less than 68 bastards, many of whom filled important administrative posts and came to be 'a sort of bastardocracy'. Philip the Good alone sired 26 natural children, while there are spectacular cases like Jean II de Cleves with 63 bastards. One further explanation of their rise is the vast increase in military employment offered by the Hundred Years War. Roughly 4 per cent of the commands in the royal armies of the fifteenth century were held by aristocratic bastards.

While Harsgor argued that it was mainly the higher nobility that used bastards in this way, Charbonnier's study of Auvergne indicates the same pattern existed at the level of the middle and lower lordship. Among families like the Vernines and d'Estaing they were fully accepted and frequently found military employment and wielded their swords in the private feuds of their fathers. Well into the sixteenth century, we find bastards continuing their attachment to the *lignage* and fighting the feuds of their legitimate brothers. They replaced the earlier phenomenon of the younger sons who served their family but renounced a family of their own; few of them founded their own *lignages*, contrary to the pattern found among the higher nobility. However, they were 'mobilised in the service of the *lignage*, compensating the relative diminution of legitimate offspring, with the advantage of not dismantling the patrimony.' However, from the middle of the sixteenth century, although there was no decline in the number of bastards at this level, there are signs that noble bastards were beginning to draw away from simple attachment to the service of their legitimate family and found *lignages* of their own.[44]

The decline in recognised bastards took place after the first quarter of the sixteenth century, one of the signs being Francis I's reluctance to recognise illegitimate offspring. The Italian wars possibly provided less employment than the internal wars of the fifteenth century, but it seems just as likely that the main reason was the demographic expansion of the legitimate nobility and the squeeze on offices available for them generally. Added to that, both the Protestant and Catholic reforms took a dim view of sexual irregularity and sought to control it, while the higher robe and wealthy commoners had long viewed bastardy as an aristocratic foible to be avoided. For its part, the crown saw the expansion in the number of families exempt from taxes by the foundation of bastard noble lines as a danger. In 1600 and 1629, noble bastards lost their right to inherit nobility (this privilege was henceforth confined to the royal family).[45]

Contamine has argued, following Perroy, that the concentration of provincial power in the hands of the magnates in the course of the fourteenth and fifteenth centuries transformed the political role of the nobles from one in which, in the years around 1300, a relatively large number of middle rank nobles had been pressing for a limitation of royal power, to one around 1500 in which the higher nobility sought essentially to maintain their position by the control of the council.[46] This may exaggerate the importance of the magnates by the 1480s. Harsgor's work on the *maîtres du royaume* by that period indicates the predominance of the middle ranking nobility, essentially the *chevaliers*, in the staffing of the great administrative corps. Nevertheless it is possible that the sixteenth century saw a widening of the gap between the great aristocrats and princes on the one hand and the provincial nobility on the other.

If at the start of the sixteenth century the *rhétoriquer* Jean Bouchet could praise the independence and liberty of the country gentlemen of France, at the end Brantôme acerbically asked what great princes would be without the nobles to fill 'their armies, their halls and their chambers with our presence' and yet 'it is we who pay court to the great'.[47] Recalling his efforts to make his way in the world as a young man, he reflected ruefully that, despite claims of kinship with great houses like Savoy and Nemours, he would not press his case: 'I do not put a bigger pot in the fire or raise my banner higher', as he put it, for 'princes are so glorious that they disdain everybody and they think they all issue from one great line, God knows', or elsewhere 'when they are in their greatness, they become so glorious that they scorn their relatives, friends and servants'. Brantôme was, after all, a provincial nobleman of a not unimportant family and yet looked back at an earlier time when it seemed normal for royal personages to act as godparents to his family or address them as 'mon cousin'.[48]

The mass of the *noblesse de race* was constituted by the *écuyers* holding one or more fiefs, usually in a small *pays*. In later years, they were to be described as *hobereaux*, a sort of noble plebs, pathetically keeping up appearances in the face of hostile economic forces. However, the mass of the nobility cannot be viewed as a single economic group; to do so leads to all sorts of sterile arguments. J.-M. Constant has argued that there was no single French nobility. The differences between dukes and presidents of Parlements, princes and squires were enormous.[49] There was a chasm between a gentleman with a small fief, a younger son, a gambler and a careful manager such as the archetypal Norman squire, the sire de Gouberville in the mid-sixteenth century. What they shared was the practice of, or the aspiration to, a complex set of values summed up by the simple term 'living nobly'.

If we consider the background of the economic catastrophe of the fourteenth and fifteenth centuries, Guy Bois proposes that the contrast between the fortunes of the small country gentlemen of the epoch of Louis XI and the *hobereaux* of the sixteenth and seventeenth century was enormous.[50] In Normandy, the yield of the *cens* in this milieu was reduced by two-thirds from the mid-fourteenth to the mid-fifteenth century. Those lands bearing the highest fixed rents were most affected while the effective end of serfdom, except for a few isolated pockets, further reduced customary dues. Only dues paid in kind, for instance for the mill, or *lods et ventes* linked to sale prices of land, held up. Neither was a retreat to domain farming on the small scale of 15–30 hectares easy. The adjuncts of the domain – farms, mills and forests – were peculiarly vulnerable to war damage but even more than this, the fall in the prices of agricultural produce and the rise in those of labour and manufactures were bound to affect the profitability of domain farming in the fourteenth and fifteenth centuries. Moreover, the recourse to *fermage* at variable leases was practically universal. The landowner exploiting his own domain by *corvée* labour was rare by the fifteenth century. Faced by these problems, the higher nobility, with their vast forest domains and complexes of estates, were best placed to take advantage of the recovery which came in the later fifteenth century. Others who had retained some control of the domain were also in a position to benefit. The most difficult problem was faced by a seigneur who had a few fiefs held in tenures with fixed rents. In Béarn, there was a little damage to the seigneuries whereas in the Bordelais there was repeated devastation. But in general terms we can assert that by the time reconstruction was under way in 1500 the revenues of the seigneuries had still not regained their levels of 1300 while the daily wage of a labourer had tripled in the same period. We can suggest that the economic circumstances of the fourteenth and fifteenth centuries devastated the revenues above all of the petty nobility, and opened the way to systematic royal fiscalism as the alternative to the seigneurial system as a means of extracting the surplus of the peasantry. However, it is essential to tie all this to specific details.

Of course, different areas responded to problems in different ways. The great cereal regions of the north suffered badly during the Hundred Years War but were also able to take advantage of the restoration. In the Ile-de-France, the desertion of the countryside from 1400 to 1450 devastated the revenues of all landlords but reconstruction of the seigneurial system along traditional lines from the late fifteenth century ensured that, except in the land immediately around Paris, the middle–high ranking noble families retained their lordships intact and only sold them when they were aiming to consolidate elsewhere. This was particularly the case with families also successful in court politics such as the Montmorency, Levis and Malet de Graville (transferred to the Balsac d'Entragues in 1526). In all, Guy Fourquin insisted that, despite the success of great *parlementaire* families like the Budé and Jouvenal des Ursins there was no great 'invasion' of the seigneuries around Paris by the bourgeois of the capital.[51] This view must be modified slightly in the light of Jean Jacquart's research on the Hurepoix region south of the capital from the mid-sixteenth century. In the vicinity of the city, he observed, through an analysis of seven representative land surveys in the area amounting to 6069 ha, that the two most dominant landowning groups were the court nobility (like the cardinal of Lorraine for instance), with 1050 ha, and the Parisian administrative families of the robe like the Neufvilles, with 1400 ha. The clergy held 1162 ha and the rest were held by the country people. Further south-west, away from the city, the country squires remained less disturbed by new neighbours and were mostly holders of a few fiefs. This region shaded gradually into the Beauce region around Chartres, with its proverbially indigent nobles ('Beggars like the gentlemen of Beauce, who stay in bed while their shoes are repaired'). Here, service in the army was an important supplement to nobles' income, but is must be stressed that J.-M. Constant's important study of the nobility of this area has made it clear that the minor landowners effectively expanded their incomes in defiance of the rules of *dérogeance* and actively exploited their resources. Clearly, the average country squire in this district with 84 ha of land could not cut a great figure but the mockery is largely the result of metropolitan disdain for absence of conspicuous consumption rather than of absolute poverty.[52]

Every major city witnessed the phenomenon of investment in land by judicial or financial office-holders. The patterns of this were varied. At Rouen, the magistrates of the Parlement in the course of the sixteenth century invested their wealth significantly in this way and emerged as the leaders of local society. The merchants of Lyon, while effecting a conquest of the surrounding countryside between 1470 and 1520, did so largely at the expense of the peasantry. Investment in vineyards was the main attraction. Until the early sixteenth century, acquisition of large seigneuries was very difficult for merchants but the sale of portions of the royal domain in Dauphiné, Forez and elsewhere from the 1530s gave the *entrée* for merchant capital into the seigneurial system. At Poitiers, the town oligarchy was patiently building up small estates from the fourteenth century onwards but much more effectively from the 1450s and largely at the expense of indebted small landowners. Again, it was the profitability of grazing and vineyards that was attractive, though the prospect of becoming a *seigneur* was also important.[53]

The preservation from the middle of the fifteenth century of continuous series of seigneurial accounts gives reason to suppose that receipts were pushing upwards generally for all sorts of landowners in the last quarter of the century, despite the often burdensome charges (litigation in particular, as will be seen). It is particularly the case that, among the higher nobility able to take advantage of royal patronage, the opportunities for exploitation of resources were particularly strong towards the end of the fifteenth century. Contamine has drawn attention to one vivid example in the county of Dammartin, held by Antoine de Chabannes (d.1488), *grand maître* under Louis XI, and then by his son Jean. An enquiry of 1499 gives the revenues for 1439 as 115 *lt.* and 1499 as 900 *lt.* For Saint-Fargeau, acquired by Antoine in the mid-fifteenth century with a revenue of 115 *lt,* 552 *lt.* was registered in 1488 and 1996 *lt.* in 1499. Five other seigneuries yielding together 1225 *lt.* in 1488 had risen to 2968 *lt.* in 1499.[54] Numerous other examples could be given. Among the revenues of Marie de Luxembourg, countess of Saint-Pol, for instance, the long series of seigneurial accounts of Lucheux, starting in the 1440s, and Vendeuil in the 1470s indicate a steady rise in revenues during the last quarter of the fifteenth century and first of the sixteenth, in this case partly as a result of the systematic exploitation of forest revenues. This involved the development of a sophisticated estate administration with a council at La Fère-sur-Oise inherited by the Bourbon-Vendôme family. The latter also inherited the bulk of the Foix-Albret lands with the kingdom of Navarre, in which revenues easily outstripped inflation during the course of the sixteenth century.[55]

All this should be borne in mind when considering Pierre de Vaissière's point that the French nobility as a whole in the sixteenth century remained attached to residence on its estates and that the period from 1480 to 1560 was 'an era of exceptional prosperity' for them.[56] It was a mode of life best fitted to the careful management of resources revealed not only in the celebrated *Journal* of Gilles de Gouberville for Normandy (1549–62) but also in lesser known cases like the *livres de raison* of Jean Jacques de Monteynard (1530–40) and François de Terraules (1585–90) in Auvergne.[57] The nobility generally tended to continue to live in the castles adapted for the military purposes of the Hundred Years War, only gradually adapted to modern tastes by the opening of larger windows, *lucarnes* and richer furnishings. Most could still be defended, as was the case with the sumptuous Bourbon castle of La Fère-sur-Oise in the 1590s. Above all, the idea that the early modern nobility was a class of idle rentiers uninterested in estate management should be abandoned. In fact they have been called one of the essential motors of the economy in the management of small and large-scale agricultural enterprises. The small landlords of Poitou patiently assembled land by lending money to peasants in trouble through bad harvests and put together estates of around 60 ha for cattle-rearing.[58]

To some extent royal patronage was a key to the prosperity of great domains. Its importance is shown by the case of the well-documented La Trémoïlle revenues. At first sight, it looks as though the fortunes of the family were weak around 1480. Although seigneurial revenues had grown slightly in comparison with 1400, loss of royal patronage had led to an overall decline in income in terms of money of account. In addition, debts to the tune of five years' revenues had built up. Neither Charles VII nor Louis XI had favoured the heads of the family, though the latter had done much for the younger brother, Craon. However, this difficult situation was deceptive, for the La Trémoïlle were on the verge of a period, 1460–1540, of great advances in their fortunes. In part this was accomplished by the concentration, by the time of François de La Trémoïlle's death in 1542, of their holdings in the west and especially in Poitou (80 per cent), whereas in the fourteenth century the family's lands had been very widely scattered throughout France. The holdings in Burgundy were abandoned to a junior branch and those in Poitou much augmented by the Amboise inheritance acquired through royal favour in 1488 (Thouars, duchy 1563, Talmont, etc.) and that of the Coëtivy in 1517 (Taillebourg, Royan). The accounts and correspondence surviving from the time of Louis I at the end of the fifteenth century show close attention to estate management and high revenues from sales of grain and wood. The great expansion of litigation under Louis II in the sixteenth century shows clear interest in the maintenance of seigneurial rights. The correspondence of François reveals a high degree of energy and ability in management – the word 'profit' was one of his favourites. Like Marie de Luxembourg in the north, he spoke of 'mes gens de conseil' and worked with a network of local officials, rather like a government in miniature.[59]

In crude revenue terms, the total yield of the La Trémoïlle properties in 1396 was 40, 355 *lt.* By 1484, it had fallen to 15,000 (only 7000 to the head of the family) largely as result of the loss of royal emoluments. In the subsequent generations, however, it was seigneurial revenues that were the great success. The average revenue for 1486–96 was 8200 *lt.* and for 1497–1509, 11,200. In 1517–23 it was 17,500 *lt.* and under François de La Trémoïlle (1526–42) 26,200 *lt.* (an increase of 220 per cent, 135 per cent taking account of inflation). If we add to this the emoluments received from the crown, we see an increase from 15,000 *lt.* in 1484 to 39,200 *lt.* in 1542. This meant that the bulk of the growth in revenue came from efficient estate management but royal patronage was still valuable. Louis II received in all 375,000 *lt.* from his emoluments. The picture that emerges from the La Trémoïlle archives, therefore, is one of a great success in the period from 1480 to the middle of the next century and the foundation of a solid landed fortune concentrated in western France and ultimately crowned by a duchy and a peerage in the second half of the sixteenth century.

An interesting phenomenon of the first half of the sixteenth century is the construction of a vast fortune by a member of the ancient nobility of the Ile-de-France, Anne de Montmorency. The Constable built up one of the greatest fortunes in France but his estate was, to use M. Greengrass's term, 'grafted on' to an old fortune. Royal patronage was crucial not so much in the form of grants and alienations of the domain (though of course the Constable's emoluments were important) as the effects of powerful royal favour in furthering the steady pressure of litigation used by Montmorency to extend his holdings. Between 1522–3 and 1561–4 the Constable had multiplied the income inherited from his father from roughly 11,000 *lt.* to 125,000– 150,000 *lt.* p.a., probably outstripping the duke of Guise and the duke of Nevers (usually regarded as the wealthiest of the dukes of 'foreign' origin – Cleves). With all other sources of income, Montmorency cannot have been receiving less than 180,000 *lt.* p.a. under Henri II, probably the largest lay aristocratic income outside the royal family, although outstripped by the prodigious 300,000 *lt.* enjoyed by the cardinal de Lorraine in 1550.[60]

Despite the clear evidence that the French nobility as a whole were not ruined by the economic and social trends of the sixteenth century, the great mass of them remained solvent only by avoiding extravagance. This is probably the reason why only a minority became regular courtiers or why Gouberville on his 200 *lt.* of revenue could make only one brief journey to court during the 14-year period of his journal. Moreover, despite the increasing yields of revenue and access to royal patronage in the first half of the century, it seems that indebtedness was an endemic problem for the higher aristocracy by the mid-sixteenth century. The house of Bourbon-Vendôme built up a store of debts (in the form of *rentes* encumbering the estate) that it was able to discharge in 1549 only by the cashing in of a lucrative due on the port of Bruges, which had become somewhat unreliable because of warfare with the Netherlands.[61] The second duke of Guise, with an income of around 200,000 *lt.* left debts of 200,000 *écus* in 1563. D. Crouzet has argued that debts, from being the norm, attained the level of crisis in the second half of the century. The ducal dynasty of Nevers (Cleves), which passed to the Gonzaga family after 1564, is to be classed in financial resources alongside the Montmorency and Guise, with a large collection of estates across northern France and sovereign lordships in the Empire. Duke François made no mention of debts in his will of 1554 but by 1561 had added a codicil to make arrangements for the settlement of debts amounting to repayments of 32,000 *lt.* p.a. (representing a total debt of 340,000 *lt.*), when the revenue of the house in 1551 had been 115,085 *lt.*). Crouzet's analysis of this debt also makes plain the fact that by far the largest reason for this indebtedness was expenditure on jewellery and clothes.[62] This at least makes comprehensible the Venetian envoy's point that when nobles lived at court 'where everything is expensive, they ruin themselves by the excessive cost of servants, horses, clothes and food'.[63] The other major source of debt was the contraction of loans to cover running expenditure. The debts of the duke of Nevers grew more serious during the Wars of Religion, with the implications one might expect in factional politics. Yet Crouzet has pointed out the positive side for the aristocratic family, for the circle of creditors built up a network of clients whose fate was closely linked to the fortunes of the family. Thus: 'aristocratic indebtedness is far from being negative for the family in debt. On the contrary, it creates *fidélités* for it and links its fortunes with men who, knowing their fortune associated with the family of Nevers, devote themselves to its service ... it establishes powerful links of interest with the many creditors whose annual revenues depend on the destiny of the Nevers.'[64]

It is tempting to concentrate on the fortunes of the higher aristocracy if only because their papers are relatively well preserved. The contrast between the sort of revenues just discussed and the annual income of a sire de Gouberville fluctuating around 200 *lt.* is obvious. In the *bailliage* of Caen in 1551, the average revenue declared for the feudal levy was 85 *lt.*, which should probably be doubled for the real figure, and 20 per cent of nobles had no fief. In Beauce, a landowner in 1559 was regarded as rich with an annual income of 500 *lt.* and the average landed estate was 84 hectares.[65] It is useful to view the problem through regional studies of property relations, some of which throw light on the fortunes of the middle and lesser nobility. In upland Quercy, for instance, the total depopulation produced collective agreements over *cens* between villages and lords eager to attract labour around 1440–50. It is clear, though, that lords like the Thémines and Saint-Sulpice were capable of using litigation in order to raise the fixed *cens* appreciably on the argument that the lands were worth much more in 1470 than they had been a generation before. In addition they altered the proportion of pasture to arable as population growth ensued. In Poitou, especially the Gâtine poitevine, the lesser nobility was involved in a patient construction of estates by the 'rounding out' of its properties at peasant expense from the 1460s onwards and the formation of *métairies.*[66]

In Anjou around 1470, the vast disparities of wealth within the nobility are revealed by the fact that, of the 842 nobles convoked to the feudal levy, 85.2 per cent were unable to serve on horseback with a lance (this in a levy in which equipment was viewed as an index of the value of a fief). Only one-sixth or one-seventh of the nobility had an income above 300 *lt.* a year. These were the holders of the main seigneuries, the *grandes châtellenies.* Below that level of income were the middle *châtellenies* and rural seigneuries yielding 200–300 a year and small rights to dues. The top of the pyramid was occupied by great lords holding properties in several provinces such as the La Trémoïlle family. These included the county of Beaufort and the *châtellenie* of Champtoceaux. The rigorous rules of primogeniture in Anjou ensured that the *baronnies* and *châtellenies* were not divided and this helped the heads of families. Thus, among the landowners whose interests were confined to Anjou itself, we find the increasing concentration of holdings in fewer hands.[67] By the time of the survey of noble holdings of 1539, there was a strong concentration of wealth in the middle ranks of 300–1000 *lt.*

Where revenues depended largely on money rents, we find, as in the accounts for the seigneurie of la Basse-Guerche in the 1490s, a certain stability, but the accounts of the properties of the chapter of Saint-Maurice, which had important farmed domains of woods, meadows and pastures, show a significant rise in farm revenues between 1450 and 1475, which continued more slowly into the middle of the sixteenth century. There, the landowner was an ecclesiastical institution, which was often in a better position to exploit the trend. Church temporalities by 1500 were in a fairly strong position.[68]

In Anjou, the great *châtellenies* depended for their most lucrative revenues not on farms or rents in kind but on dues. In the 1480s, at Champtoceaux, river and land tolls brought in 47 per cent of revenues as against 23 per cent for the mills. At Rochefort, the figure for dues was 45 per cent while purely agricultural revenues account for only 10 per cent. Not until the 1520s did the great *châtellenies* begin to benefit from the rise of cereal prices. How much did these *grandes châtellenies* bring in? At the top of the list come Champtocé and Ingrandes, which belonged to the dukes of Brittany in the fifteenth century and which were deemed to be worth 4000 and then 4500 *lt.* in the 1450s. They had been sold by Gilles de Rais for 100,000 *écus* in 1439, indicating a 4 per cent p.a. return on capital. Next comes Beaufort, farmed for 2700 *lt.* in 1546–7 and 2900 in 1560. Below that comes the barony of Craon held by Georges de La Trémoïlle, yielding 1000 *lt.* in 1396 but 1650 in 1458, and 1780 in 1490–1500.[69]

Among the middle ranking *châtellenies*, La Poissonière moved from an average net revenue of 525 *lt.* in 1488–94 to 774 *lt.* in 1518–24. Doué was yielding 700 *lt.* in 1471 but still only 700 in 1527–33. Candé and Chateauneuf actually declined in revenue in that period. Below the level of seigneuries bringing in 300 *lt.*, there were few rents in kind or dues and with a vineyard or a couple of *métairies*, perhaps yielding no more than 100 *lt.* the seigneur was no better off than a prosperous peasant. Only after 1450 did confidence return to the land market and transactions increase in volume but indebtedness continued among some families.

Sometimes advantageous marriage alliances were a way out of this, as with the marriage of Louis de Montjean to Jeanne du Châtel in 1485 and their son René's lucrative marriage in 1526. Otherwise noble indebtedness continued into the sixteenth century. One consequence was that, in Anjou, debt opened the way in the period of the revival of the land market for successful royal officials like Bourré, Bernard and Pincé to move in and buy up land and, as elsewhere, the search for royal pensions and military posts was lively.[70]

In Auvergne, as elsewhere, the late fifteenth century saw a restoration after a period of calamities in which seigneurial revenues had in any case stood up. The main seigneurs did not return to domain farming but sought to maximise their profits. Where remaining parcels of domain were granted out after 1450, this was usually in return for the *percière* or rent in kind. However, in the sixteenth century it became more usual to lease out parcels of domain on the short term. As for the other lucrative adjunct of domain, forests, these were not granted out but leased for relatively high money rents after 1450. In the village of Barmontet, for instance, where there were 8 families in a *terrier* of 1552 'the village has been reduced to domain'. In the course of the sixteenth century, out of 127 seigneuries, 37 new domains were constituted. Between 1450 and 1590 there was a multiplication of 10 in the price of grain in the region and, though the money *cens* remained fixed, part of it was paid 'en nature' so that, whereas elsewhere the *cens* had become derisory, it retained its significance in Auvergne. On the other hand, the *banal* revenues on properties such as mills had been fixed in silver and were not so flexible. At any rate, around 1550 the last grants of seigneurial domains for the *cens* or the *percière* take place and thereafter it was more common to practise *métayage*, receiving one-half of the grain yield of the property.[71]

In the richly documented Murol domain until the 1480s, Guillaume de Murol had continued direct exploitation of his estates but their division on his death meant that certain parcels necessary for the integral functioning of the estate were detached and renting out appears, for instance of the Chagourdeir hills. The d'Estaing successors towards the end of the sixteenth century had abandoned direct management. As late as 1540 the seigneur of Beaulieu retained his direct cultivation but this was becoming unusual. Only among the smaller proprietors of the western hills was there much retention of direct farming, in their case of hill pasture.[72] By the end of the century, most Auvergnat seigneurs had become 'rentiers'.

The declaration for the feudal levy in Auvergne of 1551, when compared with that of 1488, indicates a small shift of wealth from the lowest stratum of the nobility to the middle ranks. In 1551 the largest category was of revenues in the 50–100 *lt.* range, though 15 per cent still had less than 15 *lt.* p.a.; in 1488 the largest group had been in the 15–29 *lt.* range. There was a doubling in the revenues of the middle nobility, based on the declared values of 30 seigneuries (in a period when the rise in prices was less than 100 per cent), not as a result of seigneurial reaction, since in Auvergne the seigneurs chose not to press down on their subjects so much as consolidate their revenues. It was largely a consequence of *rentes en nature* and rising prices. The Murol properties rose from 780 *lt.* around 1440 to 6275 *lt.* in 1595. Even over the short term, we find Vernines moving from 686 *lt.* in 1533 to 1540 *lt.* in 1566. Charbonnier makes it quite clear that the revenues of the Auvergnat nobility certainly retained their purchasing power over the period 1450 to 1600.[73] Expenditure, of course, has to be balanced against this. In Auvergne, pious foundations contracted; the owners of Allagnat for instance maintained a constant level of expenditure in money terms in this form through the sixteenth century, which represents a real contraction. At the church of Orcival there was a sharp decline in endowments by nobles in the sixteenth century when compared with the previous one. This is perhaps significant when one remembers the point made by Boutruche on Bordelais seigneurs of the fifteenth century that the average pious legacy there was 1500–3000 *lt.* among families of the annual income of 400 *lt.*[74] The cost of food changed little; bread rose in price but consumption contracted relative to other foodstuffs. The main increase in costs was in the salaries of employees. The Murol domain indisputably employed far more people in the late sixteenth than in the late fifteenth century. Extraordinary expenses also burdened this estate. The seigneur had to borrow 320 *lt.* to equip his son for the army in 1525 (whereas 100 years before the same had cost 200). Litigation (a dozen cases in progess in 1525) was a rising cost, as were dowries. By the end of the sixteenth century, the seigneur of Murol was paying 40,000 *lt.* for a dowry (a comparable family paid 20,000 in mid-century). If we compare overall estate budgets for the Murol domain in 1525–30 and in the 1620s, we find a certain level of indebtedness in the earlier period transformed into a healthy balance in the second, when the domain had been expanded by acquisitions and then divided between heirs.[75]

Conversely, notarial records from the period 1526–33 indicate a high level of indebtedness among the lower nobility, particularly in the high country of western Auvergne where the opportunities for profitable grain farming were naturally limited. One creditor acquired 54 parcels from petty nobles eager to borrow on their estates to finance lawsuits or pay dowries. These transactions often sought to retain the noble's residuary right to the property and any mortgage revenue and did not rule out reacquisition.[76]

In the small Pyreneean county of Comminges, the enquiries into taxable land carried out first by the estates and then by royal commissioners in the 1540s reveal that, of the 423 properties listed as noble for tax purposes, 343 (80.85 per cent) were in noble hands, held by 163 heads of families. Of these, 152 were held by 86 seigneurs with powers of justice, though it is clear that the latter were less common in the mountain region of the county. The king was direct lord of 20 per cent of the rural communities. The upper ranks of the local nobility were characterised by estates of 200–300 hectares concentrated in one *châtellenie*, mainly in the *Bas-pays*, or scattered throughout the county and mainly held by lords with properties in other provinces of the kingdom. Beneath them came the mass of the *hobereaux* with 80–100 hectares. From the data available it seems that, with rising grain yields and inflation only moderately felt by the middle of the sixteenth century, the general economic conditions for landowners in Comminges were still favourable on the eve of the Wars of Religion but masked underlying problems.[77]

All this evidence, taken from many different provinces of France and in some ways contradictory, fails to permit the continued use of the assertion that the French nobility as a whole was affected by a serious economic crisis in the sixteenth century.

The Nobility and Clientage

The links between patrons and clients are now seen as an essential cement of the governing order in early modern French society, both in terms of the relationships between the crown and the nobility and those within the nobility. It is tempting to see in clientage a form of political and social framework which provided the transition between feudalism and the modern world and, indeed, it fits very closely ideas on the conditionality of obligations that were developed among the French nobility in the second half of the sixteenth century. In fact, 'clientage' cannot be periodised simply; it has existed in different forms at many different epochs. There has always been a certain haziness about its definition which stems from the nature of the relationship itself. The depth of loyalty and its exclusiveness varied in what was usually an·unwritten mutual obligation and it is this largely unwritten quality that separates the world of clientage from that of feudalism. J.-P. Genet has suggested that the English term 'bastard feudalism' describes the phase of transition between feudalism and the modern state in France. The crisis of the fifteenth century had obliged the aristocracy to enter the 'market' of bastard feudalism 'of which the crown is, in the final analysis, the master'.[78] Even this, though, is too categorical.

The terminology is sometimes confusing, with *clientèle* overlapping *fidélité*, *amitié* and *familiarité* and all to some extent covered by the English term 'patronage'. The subject is further confused by the disparity between the usages of modern historians and their divergence from early modern assumptions. Roland Mousnier, for instance, has stressed the distinction from *clientèle* of the relationship of *fidélité*, an intensely personal bond that was supposed to last until death, and which he saw as characteristic of the early modern period.[79] The essence of *fidélité* has been outlined for the entourage of the prince of Condé in the seventeenth century at a period when *clientèle* was becoming subsumed in domestic service. One of the terms in use for dependents in the period was clearly *serviteur*, but the degree of service this entailed is not always clear.[80] Sharon Kettering's important work on early modern patronage has tended to stress the 'obligatory reciprocity' of the contract between patron and client, although she is fully aware of the pitfalls of terminology.[81] However, *clientèle* could also consist of a much looser bond, of a more or less temporary nature, and in the fifteenth and early sixteenth centuries the terms are used so interchangeably that they are impossible to disentangle. To them should perhaps be added the term *amour*, used widely to indicate a level of obligation. When Brantôme entered the *suite* of the duke of Guise in the 1550s, for instance, he recalls that the great man 'did me the honour (though I was very young) to love me for the love of my late uncle La Chataigneraie'. The prior of Capua (François de Lorraine), whom he followed to Italy, 'loved me greatly and did me more honour than I merited'.[82] One term emerged only later in the sixteenth century: *créature* was first recorded by Henri Estienne in 1578 as a recent coinage among the court nobility denoting a dependent of a *seigneur*.[83]

Robert Harding's study of provincial governors has drawn attention to the centrality of material considerations in patronage and to its uses in high politics during the sixteenth century, though his argument that the patronage available to provincial governors seriously declined during the Wars of Religion is not universally accepted.[84] His idea that governors had to supplement the amount of patronage at their disposal by embarkation in religious conflict has a superficial attraction but is not entirely satisfactory. In any case, there is reasonable evidence that the military patronage available to governors through their gendarmerie companies continued to be significant.[85] Kettering has added the point that clientage connections could cut across religious affiliations and survived fully into the seventeenth century. In her view, the case of the *fidèle* faithful to death was relatively rare by then, though there was a much larger number of clients in any connection, a point also made by Madeleine Foisil.[86]

Very broadly speaking, then, we can divide interpretations of these networks into those, like Kettering's and Robert Harding's, which stress the material reciprocity and those like Mousnier's which stress the emotional bonds. In addition, Kristen Neuschel, in her study of the prince of Condé's following in Picardy during the Wars of Religion, has tended to play down the centrality of clientage as a clearly organised system, and has stressed the multiplicity of noble relationships, including the emotional ones. However, her argument that the attitude and motives of the nobility can be located 'in a warrior culture which was materially and psychologically independent of the state' leads to serious difficulties.[87] When Jacques d'Armagnac, duke of Nemours, was brought to trial in 1477 as part of Louis XI's vendetta against his family, he was reported to have said of the king 'The very devil makes him live. Will we always be troubled by him ?' but added 'in the end, though, if the king leaves me with what is mine, I will find the means to avoid him'.[88] This was an attitude increasingly impossible for the highest aristocracy in the sixteenth century. Service to the crown and the benefits of its patronage came to be regarded as central to the lifeblood of the nobility from the fifteenth century onwards. The crown and the nobility were profoundly interdependent. The very region upon which Neuschel based her study yields different conclusions for other historians. The argument that verbal courtesies conveyed complex implications about relationships is difficult to sustain.[89] Moreover, in some regions service to the crown stood at the heart of the aristocratic self-image. The lawyer of the bâtard d'Harcourt in 1483 advanced a case in the Parlement of Paris that 'the house of Harcourt is a great house and has done great services to the kingdom'.[90] At the heart of Brantôme's thinking on the subject a century later lay the idea of a just reward for service to a beneficent king. The two interpretations may, however, be complementary once we bear in mind the continuing regionalisation of France, intensified in certain periods such as the Wars of Religion. This, along with the growing propensity to change patrons and the continuing mentality which led the nobility to think in terms of its direct access to the king, may well have made the civil wars a particularly confused period in terms of clientage.[91]

It is therefore essential to understand how clientage, patronage and *fidélité* worked from the late medieval period onwards if we are to understand its further development during and after the Wars of Religion, the period upon which most historians have concentrated. At the lower reaches of the hierarchy, clientage was a response to the dissolution of the feudo-vassalistic framework, precipitated by the economic and social crisis of the fourteenth century at a time when the crown was unable to provide a system of general security. The creation of chivalric orders like those of the Golden Fleece (Burgundy), Saint Michael (by Louis XI) and the Crescent (by René of Anjou) is a sign of a quest for more secure relationships. It is certainly the case that feudal relationships were maintained in the legal sense and that, in the aftermath of the great crisis, lords began to seek to re-establish at least the formal requirement of homage from their vassals for landed fiefs. In general, homage brought little by way of revenue but did permit in theory the *retrait féodal* for lack of heirs.[92] By the mid-sixteenth century, however, recourse to the *retrait féodal* was very rare. In general, the role of homage was a matter of prestige rather than real power by the sixteenth century; there are examples of noblemen purchasing fiefs from suzerains and seigneurial administration certainly aimed to maintain their *mouvance*, but the suzerain–vassal relationship cannot be counted on to provide any significant loyalty.[93] In Auvergne, personal service by vassals had ceased while the aim of the crown to demand declarations from all vassals in 1540 and 1610 established the principle of the crown's immediate link with all vassals.[94]

By contrast the fourteenth and fifteenth centuries also witnessed a change in attitudes towards a ritual of homage that involved a kiss on the mouth and kneeling. The association of kissing between men and illicit sexuality, as well as dislike among nobles of kneeling before anyone but the king, wrought changes in the ritual of homage so that, in the course of the sixteenth century redaction of customs, the kiss on the mouth disappeared. Distaste for ritual homage of any kind made either land or money fiefs (*fief-rente*) less attractive than the indenture (*lettre de retenue, alliance*) for purposes of rewarding and retaining servants. In the fourteenth and fifteenth centuries, formal indentures, sworn on the Gospels and of varying degrees of specificity, became widespread. However, Louis XI placed no faith either in vassalage or in indentures and instead had recourse to elaborate oaths to bind men to him. The count of Armagnac was made to swear loyalty 'on my honour, the Baptism by which I have been brought from the depths, on the peril and damnation of my soul'. Written indentures passed out of use and were not revived until the outbreak of the Wars of Religion and then with very partial success. John Russell Major has integrated this indenture system into that of the whole clientage network.[95] Clearly, though, the ties of clientage that prevailed in the sixteenth century were normally more informal and these, too, have their origins in an earlier period.

Nobles in the mid-fifteenth century certainly recognised the force of the bonds of the master–servant relationship. Harsgor has drawn attention to the case of a *serviteur* of Jacques de Brézé, arrested for trying to rescue his master from prison for murdering his wife, and pardoned for his position as servant 'through which nature prompted him to seek to aid his master's escape'. The late fifteenth century saw still the employment of 'lacquays, baillis, serviteurs et familiers' to prosecute the feuds of great families.[96] If we judge by research on Auvergnat domains like those of the Murol family studied by Charbonnier, around the seigneurs there were to be found *serviteurs*, not a new phenomenon, and a more recent development, the *clients*. The two were sometimes the same but in the fifteenth century individuals seem to have moved into the role of *client* through the intermediate stage of *serviteur*. Clients, in this view, formed a 'corps d'élite' of the seigneurial class differentiated fundamentally from the feudal vassals by the absence of any specific contract between lord and client or any connection with a fief that implied heredity. Links were in no sense automatic.[97] The terms of relations were informal and only expressed by chance, as when Guiot de Chassa declared to the bâtard de Bourgogne in the 1470s 'he had no master but him and wherever he would go, he would follow him', or Jean Gaudit, *valet de chambre* to the count of Maine, swearing 'he would never serve anyone but our said cousin'.[98] Harsgor has pointed out, also, the use of noble bastards as both 'centres of groups of *serviteurs* and *fidèles*' in the fifteenth century and also the 'fanatisme farouche' with which some landless bastards enlisted in the service of protectors.[99]

In fifteenth century Auvergne, seigneurs necessarily had around them domestic servants like valets, who saw to their personal needs, transport and escort. They had, too, the technical service of administrators: *receveurs* for the collection of revenues and *maîtres d'hôtel* for the supervision of procurement and expenditure; *procureurs* for the administration of justice; *capitaines* for defence of the seigneurial domains; manual servants; clerics. Such people were drawn from the local tenantry of a domain and in the fifteenth century it is clear that the numbers of such servants rose significantly, seigneurs aiming to build up their prestige and their subjects eager to seek employment at the château. In a survey of 250 letters of remission for the Auvergne during the century, there were only three which concerned *serviteurs* discontented with their masters. The relationship was a firm one. Between the early fourteenth and the late sixteenth century, there was a doubling of the employed personnel on the Murol-d'Estaing domain in Auvergne.[100] In the early fifteenth century, each member of the Murol family had one personal servant; by the end of the sixteenth century, two were the norm. In all, the estate employed 68 persons in 1590, most of the additions to the strength coming from technical or legal experts and, not surprisingly in view of the disturbed times, military guards. Only 22 of them had no specific function and serving in the vicomte's *train* can be regarded as the top level of servants.[101]

Beyond the realm of personal service, the fifteenth century saw the development of the *clientèle*. These were men who, by the gratifications they received and the service they performed, cannot simply be called 'servants'. The term used was *familiers*, though that was a term which could also be used of a certain level of lower servant. Harsgor has suggested that ties of *fidélité* linked the great noble families to the mass of more modest nobles called their *familiers*, as well as to the administrative officers such as *baillis* and to *serviteurs domestiques* or *lacquays*. Charbonnier suggests a pyramid of *clientèles*, with this sort of connection existing on different social levels. Guillaume de Murol made specific bequests in his will to two clients in the early fifteenth century. Guillaume Martin, whom his master called 'Guamet', is mentioned frequently in the *journaux* of Murol, was a tenant of the seigneur and an administrative agent; Bernard Renoux of Clermont was an unofficial sort of agent without holding any specific post. In their turn, the lords of Murol were *clients* of the counts of Auvergne and, in return for providing unspecified support, they received substantial benefits in the form of property and money.[102] When the counts declined in power through mismanagement, the Murols turned first to the Avignon Popes (Guillaume de Murol's uncle Jean was a cardinal) and then to the dukes of Berry (Jean de Murol, son of Guillaume, was *chambellan* to Berry in 1416) and then finally to the sires de Latour.

One feature that is worth remembering in this period is that, though *clients* of lesser lords usually had only one patron and moved from one to another rather than having several patrons at the same time,[103] Harsgor has argued that the phenomenon of 'double fidelity' is a distinguishing feature of the fifteenth-century struggles between the great princes and the crown. At that time, exclusive loyalty to one master could lead to catastrophe and poverty. Louis de Culant, a *fidèle* of duke Jean II of Bourbon, found himself cast out of the council and in poverty when the play of faction forced the duke to reduce the number of his men in royal government. Thus families like the Pot of Burgundy were to be both *fidèles* of their dukes and royal servants; or witness the slippery Odet d'Aydie, who constantly 'shopped around' for a master between Louis XI, his brother Charles and the duke of Brittany, testament to the political uncertainties of the time.[104] Clientage was therefore a supple enough framework to be adapted to different social levels and different political circumstances.

At this stage, the functions of clientage as they develop later are clearly visible: the duty to form the entourage of the lord and advise him, to provide a fitting escort during his travels; in the fifteenth century armed service as part of the lord's 'compaignie' in battle is still apparent in the obligations.[105] A study of feudal service in Anjou in the late Middle Ages makes clear that the term *clientèle* gradually supplants that of *vassalité* in the entourage of the dukes of Anjou.[106] The client could also be relied on to carry out confidential missions and, on occasion, to lend money to the lord. In return, the lord provided protection and his intervention with public authorities in the legal interests of his clients (such as in obtaining royal letters of remission), negotiated marriages on their behalf and was present at family occasions. The seigneurs of Vernines in Auvergne, for instance, in the 1470s made payments for masses for the souls of individuals who had been in some sense their clients. Although clients did not receive regular payments, they often ate at the lord's table and received sumptuous presents of clothes as well as occasional gifts and grants. These clientage links often expressed a long-term relationship over several generations between the patron and client. In the case of the Murol family, the Bedos were clients from the late fourteenth century into the 1460s, among the 'compères' of the seigneurs.[107] The pattern continued into the sixteenth century with only minor changes.

By the end of that century, the *clientèle* of the Murols is still important but has undergone some changes. The clients serve long and sometimes fight and die for their master, while looser ties of *clientèle* continue to link the lower nobility to the middle ranking d'Estaing. In their turn, the middle ranks were linked to the great princes. In the 1551 list for the feudal levy in Basse Auvergne, all those in the western mountains serving in the army formed part of the *gendarmerie* company of the marshal Saint-André, who held several important lordships there. The private feuds which accompanied the wars of the League in Auvergne show that military clientage continued to play a central part in the life of the lesser nobility.[108]

The pattern is close to that displayed in the administration of the sixteenth-century Luxembourg–Bourbon domain of the dukes of Vendôme in northern France: a network of *receveurs* for each property (as well as associated legal and administrative agents); captaincies of castles held by lesser gentry of the region long associated with the great family; and a central core formed firstly by the household and its staff of *maîtres d'hôtel* and gentlemen and then by the administrative directorate of the *chambre des comptes*, formed first by the Constable of Saint-Pol in the mid-fifteenth century and refounded by his grand-daughter, Marie de Luxembourg, around 1500. The servants of this domain, like those of the Murol family in Auvergne, remained in its service over several generations: among the gentry the Coucy-Vervins, Stavaye and Longueval families as captains and (later in the century) *intendants*; among the financial experts the Laumosnier, Dennet and Flavigny families. In the ducal household inventoried in 1549, the posts of *chambellan*, *maître d'hôtel* and *gentilhomme* provided a means of drawing in the allegiance of a score of militarily active Picard gentlemen (Lavardin, Hames, Chépoy, Brichanteau, etc.) who are the nearest we come here to a real *clientèle*. The domain centred on the castle of La Fère was like a miniature royal administration. The wages of the 118 household members cost 4941 *lt.* a year and their feeding 32,400. Antoine de Bourbon's great rival, François, duke of Guise, had, with his wife, a household of 130 in 1552 costing 15,905 *lt.* in wages. Here again, the top posts were held by gentlemen who were also active in the duke's gendarmerie company (La Brosse, Potrincourt).[109]

One major point, however, should be borne in mind about clientage from the fifteenth century onwards. As a loose and informal connection, it could not guarantee the disposition of a totally reliable following. At a higher level of society and politics, the ties of clientage were decidedly flexible in the fifteenth century. The following of the Constable of Saint-Pol in the 1460s and 1470s was rooted in the petty nobility of northern France and the Low Countries in the vicinity of his estates around La Fère (Aisne), Ham (Somme) and a number of lands in Flanders and Hainault. One interesting feature shared with the Auvergnat nobility is the importance of the role played by the 'gens de son lignage' in the maintenance of an 'affinity'; in this case the brother, sons, uncles, and cousins of the Constable. However, after 1470 the Constable was seriously weakened by his isolation from many members of his *lignage* when his lands in the Low Countries were confiscated and 'who are in the service of and subject to my lord Burgundy'.[110] He wrote to the duke of Burgundy to ask if he might 'make use of the men of his *lignage*, seeing the matter concerned was a private one' but the most useful of them, Richebourg, was prevented. In fact, in the aftermath of the catastrophe of 1475, the Luxembourg family became deeply divided over the eventual succession to various properties and the extent to which they can still be considered a *lignage* by the middle of the sixteenth century is very limited.[111]

Saint-Pol had at his disposal the patronage afforded by a formation of 400 *hommes d'armes* commanded by him and paid for by the crown. However, in the event this availed him little since his two principal lieutenants, Moy and Genlis, quite clearly to be defined as *clients*, Picard lords with their property close to the Constable's, were prepared to abandon him in favour of serving Louis XI. Genlis came of a family long in royal service, most notably under Charles VII, and he had only taken service with Saint-Pol in the reaction after Louis XI's accession.[112] Even Saint-Pol's secretary and *fidèle*, Jean Richier, had earlier been Louis XI's secretary. On the other hand, his *écuyer* Louis de Sainville only left the king's service for the Constable 13 months before his fall and he remained faithful, while Commynes expressed the view that, had Saint-Pol been more prepared to trust some of his company of gendarmerie, he would have found more faithful service.[113]

A comparison with the fall of a later Constable of France, Bourbon, in 1523 would be instructive. Here, compared with the situation of chronic suspicion and fear engendered by the policy of Louis XI, Bourbon's relations with Francis I were open in the early years of the reign and the vast emoluments and revenues he enjoyed testified to his grandeur. On the other hand, the potential blow to his income threatened by the move of Louise of Savoy to lay hands on the patrimony of his wife, Suzanne de Bourbon, in 1521 was not just a cause of discontent since it threatened both his income and his prestige; to accept it without a struggle was unthinkable. It was the measure of Louise's rapacity that she was prepared to drive him into treason over the matter. Hence the words he spoke to a king who could have set all right at Moulins: 'mains ce procès ... la misère qui m'attend', recalled in 1527.[114]

Unlike Saint-Pol, Bourbon was an apanage prince with the power to raise taxes in his territory. His household was enormous and his military retinue impressive, including captains of gendarmerie Jean de Poitiers, sr. de Saint-Vallier and Aymar de Prie. Yet when it came to the point of either defying the crown or flight in 1523, the constable's *clientèle* proved decidedly feeble. Two leading *fidèles* of the house, Antoine de Chabannes, bishop of Le Puy and Jacques Hurault, bishop of Autun, were opposed to each other, the former asking the Constable when he boasted of his following of 1000 gentlemen of France: 'Will you be followed, Monseigneur?' Among the lesser followers were household men like the *écuyers* Pelloux, Livry, Lollières, all intimately involved in the plot, as well as Jean de l'Hospital, ducal *bailli* of Haute-Auvergne, and Joachim de Pompéranc, a gentleman who had entered Bourbon's service at the age of twenty and in fact owed his life to him. In all, 10,000 men were supposed to be at the call of the Constable, to be led by men like Lollières and Toussanes.[115]

At the crucial gathering at Montbrison on 18 July 1523, the list of participants was drawn up and those involved sworn on a fragment of the true cross by the bishop of Autun. One gentleman, Saint-Bonnet, was so sworn and given a mission to the emperor, ostensibly to seek the latter's guarantee of his sister's hand, but he became suspicious and turned back. Two others, Argouges and Matignon, decided to betray their master's confidence to the king. On the other hand, a devoted servant of the Constable at court, Espinac, rode in haste to warn him of the plan to arrest him. In the event, Bourbon fled from Chantelle on 8 September with only a small following: Lollières, Pelloux, La Chuse, L'Hospital, Godinière, Pompéranc, Buzançonais the *pannetier* and Bartholomé and Guinot his *valets de chambre*, most of them his household servants. At first there was a suite of 240 horsemen as escorts but they were given leave to make their own way to Carlat the next day. A plan to assemble the gentlemen of Auvergne there was, in any case, abandoned. It is perhaps significant that, received with honour by Antoine de La Fayette at Monteil-Gelat on the first day of the flight, the Constable saw fit not to inform him of what he was doing.[116] In his final escape, Bourbon seems to have had only Pompéranc as escort.

An aspect of clientage is the resource provided by the *gendarmerie* companies in the army, commanded by the high aristocracy and paid (though not always promptly) by the crown. Most of these companies placed 40 posts as *hommes d'armes* and 60 as archers at the disposal of the nobleman commanding them and there was keen competition for places, especially as officers. Many such appointees should be regarded as *fidèles* in the full sense of the word. In 1550, for instance, on the unexpected death of the first duke of Guise, the lieutenant of his company wrote to the duke's son: 'Alas, my lord, I have lost my master and my hope unless it please you to take pity on me and my poor children'.[117]

Patronage was not an exclusively aristocratic phenomenon. The more loose form of *clientèle* or *fidélité* proved a powerful force in the mobilisation of ambitious and wealthy commoners in the service of the monarchy. The great Briçonnet family of Tours owed their ascent in royal service during the fifteenth century in part to their ties with Louis XI's secretary, Jean Bourré, whose own interests were served by the establishment of men who owed their promotion to him.[118]

What emerges from all this is the way in which an apparently powerful *clientèle*, deeply rooted in the particularism of a region, was incapable of sustaining a movement against the crown. Bourbon's secretary, Marillac, had written that 'all that country bore such great love to my said lord and held him in such great esteem that they felt they could not give him too much'.[119] In the event, of course, the Constable chose not to put this loyalty to the test. The earlier signs of this were the way in which Louis XI had been able to undermine the foundations of Saint-Pol's following in the 1470s or, slightly earlier, that of his brother, Charles de France, by placing his own *fidèles* in the entourage of the latter. When Bourbon in 1523 tried to, as it were, change the rules under which clientage had come to operate since the middle of the fifteenth century, setting himself up as an alternative 'pole of attraction', he courted disaster.[120]

The Crown and the Nobility

With slow communications and a relatively small bureaucracy, the crown was bound to seek to maintain order through the prevailing ties of clientage; in fact, it had to be a supreme patron in order to reinforce the vertical ties which bound the provinces together. Provinces like those of the west and and north, which from the mid-fourteenth century had been well established bases of royal power, continued to the end of the sixteenth century to produce a disproportionate number of politically active nobles, to judge by the ranks of the chevaliers of Saint-Michel.[121] Distant provinces more recently absorbed, like Provence, or too distant to control directly, like Languedoc, produce a different profile. It was from the mid-fifteenth century that the latter regions were incorporated into the vertical clientage networks of the kingdom as a whole. All this in essence demanded the binding of the nobility's interests to the crown by inducements and rewards.

Nothing confirms the interdependence of the crown and the nobility so much as the examination of the relationship between landed income and income derived from royal favour. The latter is to be envisaged as income in the form of pensions, grants of the royal domain and perquisites. Pierre de Vaissière argued that the modest provision for pensions and court offices in the earlier sixteenth century explained the continued attachment of the nobility as a whole to their estates. Jean Bouchet, however, in one of the most personal passages of his *Epistres*, addressed a long denunciation to 'Messieurs de la court', asking how they could have acquired their wealth. The common people ask: how can a man who has but 1000 *écus* in pension or salary spend each year 1000 livres and acquire an estate worth 100,000? 'It must be, then, that beneath the fine array of governor, he either robs the king or the people.' Admiral Louis de Graville was so touched by conscience on his deathbed in May 1513 over the 'large pensions and posts' he had received, that is his will he left 'to the public weal', as he put it, the 80,000 *lt.* he had lent the king in 1512.[122] Pensions already played a crucial role in the life of the nobility in the fifteenth century. P. S. Lewis has drawn attention to the way in which the royal pension acted as a form of reward for faithful service to the crown and was concentrated into the hands of a fortunate few during the reign of Louis XI. Indeed it would not be unfair to see in this one of the principal instruments of Louis's policy. Royal pensions amounted to 326,123 *lt.* in 1470. In the pensions lists of 1480–1, the crown paid out 950,000 *lt.* to 760 people, with 50 per cent of the money going to 8 per cent of the recipients and 75 per cent of the money going to 27 per cent of recipients.[123]

In Louis XI's last years, the demands on his resources for military expenditure and political manoeuvres alike increased to breaking point. Thus, he was forced to concede a promise of 60,000 *lt.* to king René to secure the eventual succession to the Anjou domains in 1478; in the event, it was largely unpaid because of René's death in 1480. [124] René in any case was already listed for a pension of 10,000 *lt.* and although half had been retrenched in 1478, the king ordered payment in full the following years. On that occasion, however, the *général des finances* of Languedoc proved very obstructive, claiming to have no authorisation. Louis was angered: 'You can well understand the great affairs I have at the moment over the war ... and also that I must sustain (*entretenir*) the said king of Sicily and various other lords.'[125] On the other hand, he chose to divert pensions for other purposes when money was short and he felt able to do so. On other occasions, the local finance officials could retain pensions on their own initiative and force individuals to petition the king directly. In the case of the bâtard d'Aveluy (near Ancre, Somme), the reduction of his pension from 1200 to 600 *lt.* at the end of Louis's reign laid him open to pressure from the local receiver of *tailles* to engage an act of revenge for the latter in order to fraudulently obtain the full amount.[126]

Not surprisingly, the numbers on the pensions lists increased in the 1480s and 1490s with the need of the Beaujeu regime and its successors to attract support, although the overall amount spent did not increase much.[127] After that, greater care was exercised and under Louis XII expenditure on pensions, as the Venetian envoy noted, was got under control: 498,000 *lt.* in 1498, 529,000 in 1502, 647,000 in 1503, but 202,000 in 1505 and 105,000 in 1511 – back to 383,000 in 1514. In addition, royal servants could be required to forgo their pensions as a form of temporary advance to the crown.[128] Such figures perhaps explain Vaissière's point of view. Sums paid fluctuated startlingly according to the other, usually military, needs of the crown.

The royal budget of 1523 provided for the payment of 500,000 *lt.* to 250 persons with a further list of 465 (supposed to receive 234,833 *lt.*) unpaid for lack of funds.[129] This list in itself indicates how the lion's share of royal pensions was increasingly concentrated in the hands of the most powerful. A provisional list for 1525 (provisional presumably because of the upheavals of that year) allocated 571,574 *lt.* for about 640 persons and another (incomplete) dated c.1526–8 allocated 518,000 *lt.* to around 150 names.[130] Clearly, a very large proportion of names on the pensions lists received very modest sums while the major share went to a favoured few of around 150–200 individuals. In 1532, the royal pensions list envisaged the payment of 419,560 *lt.* to 133 persons, though no less than 200,000 *lt.* went to the first 13 on the list, princes, officers of state and governors. Significantly, the list 'will be paid or appointed according to the quittances the king will expedite'. In other words, the list itself did not guarantee payment.[131] In the general *état par estimation* of 1549, 800,000 *lt.* was assigned for pensions of princes, *chevaliers* of the order, captains and others.[132] The general pattern of payments in pensions, therefore, indicates that the overall sum followed quite closely the pattern of the crown's income from taxation and other sources, with the peaks coming in the later part of Louis XI's reign and under Henri II (and with adjustment for purchasing power, the higher sum in the reign of Louis XI).

Louis XI had made grants of pensions to individual servants in return for service and, for example in the appointment of a *premier échanson* in 1461, 'so he may henceforth more honourably undertake our service'. A *conseiller et chambellan* appointed in 1484 received a small pension 'by which to honestly undertake our service and bear the costs and expenses'.[133] By the reign of Francis I, a pension was increasingly regarded as an essential supplement to the relatively feeble level of the stipends paid to a wide range of royal servants at court, in the army and in the command of fortresses. Of the half-million *livres* allocated in 1526, for instance, 116,000 went to just five men: the king of Navarre, the duke of Vendôme, Lorraine, the Admiral Chabot and *Grand Maître* de Montmorency.[134] It was a supple instrument in that it made rewards for service uncertain enough to force the recipients to lobby in order to assure their payment.[135] Oudart du Biez had to appeal to his patron Montmorency's 'toute puissance' in 1528 to get his pension paid when he was short of money. Jean d'Humières, who was close to the royal household though often absent on military command, having been told by Montmorency in 1530 to remind him about his pension, also got a promise from Louise of Savoy, while refraining from touching on the matter in an interview with the king; next he asked the chancellor to expedite his pension and was put off until the next meeting of the council at Saint-Germain. He then sent again 'fearing that he would fob me off with excuses'. He too asked Montmorency 'to have a word with him, for I am in great need'. This was the normal stuff of lobbying.[136]

It is clear, therefore, that access to royal patronage formed a crucial part of the income of a significant portion of the high aristocracy and their dependents. The highest pensions under Louis XI were the 20,000 *lt.* to Pierre de Beaujeu, or the 12,000 *lt.* to the marshal d'Esquerdes. Under Louis XII, the duke of Bourbon received 24,000 *lt.* and the duke of Savoy 25,000 *lt.*[137] The apanage house of Vendôme rose from 2000 in 1482 to 14,000 *lt.* in 1525 and 24,000 in 1532. By 1555–7, the then duke (as king of Navarre) was receiving 33,000 *lt.* in pensions and *états* for offices.[138] How did such sums compare with other sources of income? For an apanage prince in the making like Francis I's youngest son, Charles duke of Orléans, total revenues of 168,782 *lt.* in 1541–2 included no less than 66,650 *lt.* in pensions and royal gifts.[139] This was a spectacular example of the continued use of the royal domain as a resource for endowing princes alongside the pension system. At a less exalted level, one of Louis XI's trusted agents in Burgundy, Georges de La Trémoïlle, sr. de Craon, received for his services in all 140,000 *lt.* in the years 1468–77. When his personal budget for 1473 is broken down, we find the yield for his seigneuries was 7510 *lt.* (including 400 for seigneuries granted by the king) as against 15,787 *lt.* for his pensions, gifts and emoluments. Royal favour was therefore responsible for 69.48 per cent of his income.[140] His brother Louis I and nephew Louis II were not so favoured by Louis XI, but the latter began to recover royal favour from the time the crown allowed him to take up the Amboise inheritance in 1488. Over the period 1486–1523, in fact, he received in all 375,000 *lt.* as his emoluments from various offices, gifts and pensions.[141] Other figures of political importance received gifts of land and pensions: Commynes received 65,000 *lt.* and lands over 11 years. Of the income of Charles d'Anjou, count of Maine, in 1462, 77.2 per cent (54,157 *lt.*) was provided by royal grant. In 1493–4, Louis de La Trémoïlle was receiving only 7664 *lt.* from his 16 seigneuries but 25,700 from royal pensions and gifts, with 10,000 specially transferred because of his rights to the principality of Talmont then held by Commynes.[142]

Precise figures are not available for another great royal servant of the late fifteenth century, Ymbert de Batarnay, who was able to found a family influential in royal service throughout the sixteenth century. However, his extensive surviving papers make abundantly clear the role of royal influence in the construction of his fortune; Louis XI jokingly called him 'le riche comte'. Early in his career, the minor Dauphiné squire was able to use his favour with Louis to secure not only the estates of Montchenu but also the hand of the daughter, with whom fortunately he lived a long and amicable life. In 1472, part of the Armagnac inheritance and the title, in the event little used, of count of Fésenzac came his way. In 1476, there followed lands confiscated from the duke of Nemours in Auvergne and Picardy and others, less easy to defend against the heirs, from the house of Luxembourg. The years 1474–8 saw his first acquisitions of land in Touraine at Bridoré, which under Charles VIII he was able to round out by the acquisition, at a knock-down price, of Montrésor, effected against its heirs' protests by royal order. There he started to build a comfortable new *château*. With his captaincies of castles and his post in the royal household it is clear that he was able to build up a substantial fortune, including 13,175 *écus* in cash held with the Medici bank at Florence down to 1494. His biographer insists on his attention to business and his unwillingness to let servants take decisions for him. Moreover, as a beneficiary of royal grants he needed, as did many others, to be an able litigant in order to defend his claims against the horde of suitors for royal favour.[143]

In the sixteenth century, rewards for royal service could take many different forms: not only pensions but grants out of the royal domain, profits and offices. The Chabannes family received two hefty subventions from the crown. When Joachim de Chabannes was captured at Saint-Quentin in 1557 and ransomed, dying just before his liberation, Henri II granted his widow 20,000 *lt*. In 1588, Henri III granted François de Chabannes 8000 *écus*.[144]

The greatest rewards accrued, of course, to the supreme royal confidant Anne de Montmorency: captain of 100 lances, marshal (1522) and Constable (1538) in the military sphere; *gentilhomme de la chambre* (1515), *premier gentilhomme de la chambre* (1520) and *grand maître de France* (1526) at court; governor of Languedoc in 1526 and governor of Nantes, Saint-Malo etc. While his father had received 5500 *lt*. in pensions and emoluments, in the period

1526–38 Anne was receiving a maximum of 44,450 *lt.*, roughly four times his income from his estates in that period. From 1538 as Constable, his income from the crown rose to 56,450 *lt.* Even though he was in disgrace between 1541 and 1546, his very unusual return to favour under Henri II brought him a hefty compensation for losses in pensions during that period. In the mid-1550s, his pension and *gaiges* as Constable brought him 24,000 *lt.* while his pensions and emoluments as governor of Languedoc and other posts brought in 51,500 *lt.* Even in his second period of relative disfavour after 1559, he was still receiving 45,500 *lt.* in 1567 under a reduced pension regime.[145] In the reign of Henri II, Antoine de Bourbon, duke of Vendôme, was receiving a pension of 24,000 *lt.* (the same as the Constable) plus 9000 *lt.* as governor and admiral of Guyenne. The duke of Guise received a pension of 18,000 *lt.* and marshal Saint-André 20,000 *lt.*[146]

The king's household played a crucial role in the revenues of many nobles from the mid-fifteenth century onwards. A gentleman of the Ile-de-France, Charles de Villac, sr. de Moncel, would have found his two houses and 150 *arpents* of land, 20 of meadows and 34 of woods (with another estate entirely waste) a poor living without the post of *panetier du roi* he acquired in 1479. The office of *chambellan du roi* would have been essential to the living of Louis de Bouhaut, whose *châtellenie* of Bruyères-le-Châtel was in ruins around 1460. Vaissière argued forcefully that the mass of the nobility kept aloof from court but the evidence simply from the nobility of the Ile-de-France makes this impossible to accept for the late fifteenth century.[147]

In fact, though the accounts of the royal household are fairly precisely known for this period, it is impossible to be categorical about how many of the nobility had repeated recourse to court. There were a few hundred paid posts available there but the penumbra of courtiers was much larger. Service at court brought a salary of 1200 *lt.* for a gentleman of the chamber in 1559, though of course such service entailed expenses. There were the salaries of provincial governors or deputy governors.[148] In Auvergne, for instance, the seigneur of Saint-Nectaire received as deputy governor the sum of 2250 *lt.* from the Estates in 1548.[149] Montmorency received an *ex gratia* payment from the Estates of Languedoc of 12,000 *lt.* in 1526 and 20,000 in 1533. In Auvergne, the most important landowners of the western region, like Saint-

André and Saint-Nectaire, had major posts at court, such as *gentil-homme de la chambre*, in the mid-sixteenth century but, in propor-tion to the nobility as whole, they were few. Here, there were definite geographical differences since among the nobility of Picardy, court offices and administrative posts, as well, of course, as military posts, were very important. So, although it is usually supposed that the nobility were pushed aside in the scramble for offices in the sixteenth century this was not uniformly the case.[150] Sometimes, nobles who were essentially warriors also had skills as courtiers, even though they may never have held posts in the royal household. Thus, Gaspard de Saulx-Tavannes, marshal of France, proved agreeable enough a companion to please Montmorency, Tournon, the duke of Orléans, Henri II and Catherine de Medici. His high spirits – as one of the *bande enragée des enfants de France* he once distinguished himself by riding his horse in a leap from one rock to another in the forest of Fontainebleau – made him an ideal courtier. Nevertheless, he clearly understood his interests. On hearing at court in later life that his son was dangerously ill, he exclaimed: 'if I lose him, saddle my horses. I'm only here in the interest of my (family)'.[151]

The ideal of nobility remained, of course, military service but how many actually followed the standards? That there was a strong taste for adventure and feats of arms in the Italian and Habsburg–Valois wars is undeniable. According to the account in the Vieilleville memoirs of a meeting of the *conseil privé* to plan the campaign against the Emperor in 1552, Henri II was counting on not only 4500 *gens d'armes* but also 6000 light horse, 8000–10,000 men of the feudal levy and 8000 gentleman volun-teers, 26,000–28,500 men in all.[152] This would have represented the entire adult male nobility of the time, as has already been shown. In practice, opportunities for military employment were usually very much more restricted and the trauma of pay-off at the end of a war an ever present threat. There was wide variation between the 40 per cent of the Picard nobility involved in royal service of some kind according to the feudal levy of 1557 [153] and the 13.8 per cent of the Auvergnat nobility who served in Francis I's Italian expedition of 1523–4. In the Auvergne feudal levy, there were only 4.3 per cent in royal service. There, residence on and administration of estates was still more important. Yet in neighbouring Périgord, 35 per cent were in royal service in 1557.

In the *bailliage* of Caen the number was as low as 3 per cent in 1552.[154] Among the nobility of Beauce it has been computed that about a quarter of those families who participated in military campaigns during the sixteenth and seventeenth centuries did so in the Habsburg–Valois wars and that the military vocation was higher at that time than in subsequent generations.[155] However, it seems that by the 1570s opportunities for military employment directly by the crown were distinctly limited. In practice, on average perhaps no more than 20–30 per cent of the nobility were militarily active.[156]

Conclusion

The century from the accession of Louis XI to the Wars of Religion undoubtedly saw some remarkable developments for the French nobility. From having been an order under severe economic pressure, it had, with many variations, surmounted the greatest problems. Notions of a nobility in economic decline are crude and wide of the mark. At the same time it was entering into a new and more complex relationship with the state. There can be little doubt that the self-image of the nobility, ranging from its military functions to the ideal of the country squire, was undergoing long-term changes as the nobility gradually adapted to new political conditions that precluded the automatic control of provincial power by great magnates and their retinues. The rise of the office-holding bureaucracy opened a field of competition for power with men of different social origins. However, involvement in royal service became more significant and the nobility as a whole ceased to regard the crown with suspicion and sought rather to profit from it. Over the same period, the inherited ties of social and personal relationships developed into the immensely fluid and subtle world of clientage and fidelity, with the establishment of a vast range of possibilities in the relations between individuals and groups within the nobility. Until the 1560s, the crown was able effectively to use its patronage to keep that still turbulent world in order.

7. The French Church in the Age of Reform

Traditions of Reform

The late fifteenth and early sixteenth centuries saw a series of profound upheavals in the religious sensibilities of Frenchmen that have no simple explanations. The period from 1530 to 1560 saw the development of a clandestine and, to the majority, an increasingly threatening and divisive element within the community. The divisions that became open and violent after 1560 are not the main consideration here, however; rather, the aim is to examine the break-up of unity and the attempts to re-establish it. Of course, in order to understand that we need to examine the state of religious belief in the period before the impact of Protestantism during the late fifteenth and early sixteenth century. If anything certain can be said about this, it is that religion was certainly alive. That it was well remains a much debated assertion stemming from the model traditionally offered for the explanation of the Protestant Reformation: that the church was decadent, steeped in 'abuses' and woefully inadequate for the demands placed upon it; that anti-clerical opinions were rife and the church generally unpopular. Upon this scene, the humanist 'pre-reform' movement led in France by Lefevre d'Etaples and reforming bishops like Briçonnet of Meaux laid the groundwork for the essential critique of the church that led part of its followers to break definitively with the church in the 1530s as part of a 'great divide' in the humanist world.[1]

Since Lucien Febvre, in his seminal study of the French Reformation, shifted the perspective away from the old argument about how 'French' the French Reformation actually was, an approach that underlay Imbart de la Tour's magisterial and still indispensable *Origines de la réforme*, it has become usual to dismiss the idea of seeing the Protestant Reformation as a reaction against abuses.[2] Imbart argued that the equilibrium of the late medieval church had been fatally undermined by individualism, class interests and the rivalries between crown, popes and feudataries. The response of the best men of the late fifteenth century was to say that institutional reform was not enough; like Jean Standonck, they called for a return to the lives of the holy fathers.[3] The work of modern scholars such as John Bossy and Jean Delumeau has taken up Febvre's suggestion that reform ideas of the sixteenth century stemmed from a common origin in the years around 1500 out of which emerged not only Protestantism but also a revitalised Catholic Church.[4] The pre-reform movement in this light appears as part of a long-term organic regenerative movement within the church, a view with which Imbart de la Tour would not have disagreed. This is not to underestimate the significance of the shattering break in the unity of the church; such issues are of paramount importance for the history of France if only because of the obvious point that France was ultimately to remain an overwhelmingly Catholic country. In the sixteenth century it became a bitterly divided one partly because of the failure of Protestantism, for a complex range of reasons, to establish its supremacy in the first surge of its popularity.

That the ultimate destiny of France was to remain a Catholic country has tended to puzzle outside observers more than the French themselves. French nationalism in the nineteenth century, despite the prevailing anti-clericalism, easily took on a Catholic cultural tone and it was natural to see in the triumph of French Catholicism the affirmation of a national tradition. Yet the reason for the ultimate failure of Protestantism to be any more than a fragile minority, in a society which shared many of the characteristics of those which became fully Protestant, remains an awkward problem. This persists despite the most radical recent re-evaluation of the matter by Denis Crouzet.[5] His emphasis on the overwhelming fear of damnation and of the end of the world as possibly the most significant nourishment of Catholicism in the first half of the sixteenth century perhaps underestimates the fact that such fears do not seem to have seriously impeded the development of Protestantism elsewhere and particularly in areas like the Low Countries where the political context and the chronology are comparable. We must, then, continue to look for a specifically French religious history in the period of the Protestant Reform.

A word about terminology is in order at this point. It has been pointed out that the word *réforme* applies to the whole current moving towards the transformation of the church for centuries before Luther and was thus common to both Catholics and

Protestants. In the sixteenth century, *réformation* signified the effective implementation of a set of ideas in the institutional sense.[6] That there was a quickening in the discussion of reforms in the late fifteenth century is certain. Michel Bureau wrote in the 1490s that 'in our time the word reform has so well resounded in the ears of the people that when you speak to any man the subject frequently arises.' The discussions at the time of the General Council of the French church (1493), with the debates over gradual or radical reform, also testify to this. Naturally, all participants, whether conventuals, mendicants or secular clergy, were prone to offer responses to the problems which differed in immediate objectives while sharing the consciousness of the need for reform. Jean de Cirey, abbot of Cîteaux, was speaking of the monastic orders when he declared that 'reformation is the reduction of deformation or deviation from the first form of religion'.[7] It is increasingly evident in the most recent work on the history of the late medieval church, that the shift in religious sensibility in the fifteenth century that made the Protestant Reformation possible formed part of a continuous process of renewal within the church. This in turn went back at least until the fourth Lateran Council (1215) and was immensely boosted by the concilar movement of the fourteenth and fifteenth centuries, with its vocation to *reform* the church in head and members, when faced by the manifest failure of the Papacy.[8]

Unless these points are clearly understood, it is impossible to evaluate the ferment of clerical reform that became so widespead in the fifteenth century and we too easily return to the facile assumption that the clergy were overwhelmingly steeped in corruption on the eve of the Protestant Reformation and ignore too much the inner regeneration of French Catholicism before the middle of the sixteenth century. The picture offered by Lucien Febvre is now well known: that the rhetoric of critique directed against abuses at the end of the fifteenth century was largely conventional and that at that time traditional piety, far from being moribund, was intact and vital. It was expressed in the soaring *flamboyant* churches built in the period throughout France, including extraordinary creations like Saint-Etienne du Mont in Paris, the facade of the Sainte-Chapelle of Vincennes, or Saint-Wulfran of Abbeville. Gothic cathedrals like Beauvais or Rodez were actually being built after 1500, while a church like transitional Saint-Eustache at Paris was not begun until 1532, besides the many parish churches embellished in the surrounding countryside. In an area like the Somme nearly 300 churches were rebuilt after 1480.[9] Febvre actually argued that the approach to reform offered by the church was inadequate, failing to respond to this heightened religiosity and, crucially, unprepared for the religious demands of a bourgeoisie eager to reconcile its faith and life. It now looks as though Febvre seriously underestimated the power of Catholic reform. He also tended to dismiss the popular religiosity of the late medieval period as essentially a response to economic problems, quick to spring into life and quick to die down again.[10] This view, pursued by Jean Delumeau in his picture of medieval Christendom as barely Christianised, has been sharply criticised by John Bossy and Euan Cameron as underestimating the extent to which the medieval church conveyed both a moral and a liturgical message.[11]

As early as the first quarter of the fifteenth century, the sermons of Vincent Ferrier, notorious for his organisation in the Midi and Auvergne of flagellant processions and eschatological preaching, in reality had more to do with the transformation of the moral life of the sinner. Canonised in 1455, he became the inspiration of a wide range of confraternities.[12] In Brittany around 1450, friar Pierre Morin began a campaign against depravity and luxury. Their work presaged a great expansion of preaching crusades by the Mendicant orders and others, especially in the Midi, around the turn of the sixteenth century. The Cordelier Antoine Fradin scored a great intitial success in his 1478 sermons against immorality at Paris, leading crowds of loose women to the portals of convents. His efforts were abruptly terminated, however, when he started to inveigh against the government and declared that 'the king is ill-served and has about him servants who are traitors'.[13]

Such preachers bordered not only on political scandal but also on heterodoxy and the range of heresies for which they were attacked reveals a great deal about the contemporary critique of the church. This could include the well-established defence of the Mendicants against the Seculars and non-Observants, denial of the validity of sacraments administered by sinful priests, a critique of the excesses of the cult of saints and, among the Dominicans, denial of the Immaculate Conception promulgated by the Council of Basle in 1439 and made by the University of Paris in

1497 a condition of entry under oath. While it would be mistaken to see these as essentially 'precursors of the reformation', the agenda for popular critique of the church that they reveal is important.[14] The greatest preachers of the years around 1500, drawn from the Mendicant orders or close to them, sometimes influenced by the *devotio moderna* of the Low Countries, also offered in their Lenten sermons a certain vision of what the church ought to and might be. The Francisan Olivier Maillard denounced clerical abuses in violent language; the Cordelier Michel Menot in his sermons of 1508–18 declared that 'every abuse of our time takes place in the Temple. If anyone wants to deal in trade, luxury, pomp, let him come to church.' Indeed, in the sermons of Jean Vitrier, Jean Clérée, Jean Raulin and others, an extraordinarily powerful image of the church corrupt and in need of reform emerges. The limits of that reform will be discussed later but at this point the denunciations of the preachers in the years around 1500 should perhaps caution us against accepting Febvre's notion that late-medieval anti-clericalism in France was largely formalistic.[15]

On the other hand, signs of inner devotionalism are seen in the cult of the Rosary, encouraged by the evangelism in Germany and the Low Countries of the Dominican Alain de La Roche from the 1470s and the appearance of a new devotion to the stations of the cross. For Febvre, the fact that the images of the Christ of the Passion and of the Virgin of Mercy were gripping the imagination of the masses was sign enough of spiritual turmoil rather than of decadence.[16] In this context, even the obsessive personal devotions of such a worldly figure as Louis XI take on a different meaning. The attachment of high princely families closely related to the royal family, like the houses of Anjou and Savoy, to the members of the Observant orders as their spiritual counsellors, as well of the Valois-Angoulême to the ideas of Francis of Paola, testifies to the significance of intense personal piety, especially for high-born aristocratic women, before the Reformation. Saint Francis, founder of the Minims (Hermits of Saint Francis) came to France in 1482 and exercised a strong influence on Louis XI in his last year, going on to play a crucial public role under Charles VIII. The Minims were fostered by the protection of great conciliar clans like the Briçonnets and the Beaunes. Along with that of the *devotio moderna*, Saint Francis's influence on French mysticism in the late fifteenth century was paramount. The story of Louise of Savoy's request for his successful prayers to remedy her childlessness no doubt explains the role of the French crown in obtaining his canonisation in 1519. The continuity between such piety and the religiosity of the first generation of evangelical aristocratic women like Louise de Montmorency is striking.[17]

The role of the mystic and scholar, Jean Standonck, friend of Saint Francis de Paule, ornament of the *collège* de Montaigu and the University of Paris, abbot of Citeaux, claimant to the archbishopric of Rheims (1497) and yet stern castigator of the immorality of kings and clergy, was gradually to promote the formation of groups of scholars and clergy devoted to the idea of reform.[18] Standonck enjoyed the protection of another high court politician of the 1490s, admiral de Graville. Indeed, Chevalier has argued that the role of what might be called a 'dévot' party *avant la lettre*, including Olivier Maillard, vicar-general of the Observant Franciscans (1493) and favourite of Charles VIII, was significant enough to constitute a powerful political pressure group for reform.[19]

The Sorbonne's imposition in 1497 of the oath to the Immaculate Conception was further testimony to the liveliness of a cult of the Virgin actually promoted by the Councils. Images, too, retained their power over popular imagination. The late fifteenth and early sixteenth centuries were a golden age for confraternities and associations, such as the *Puy d'Amiens* devoted to the poetic and mystic celebration of the Virgin.[20] The special devotion of the French to images is seen in the crowds pressing to see the frescos of the Mysteries of the Passion, newly painted by a Fleming in a little chapel at Montélimar in 1517 and visible still at Paris when, in 1542, a sceptical German youth mocked the French for their veneration of images: 'they come running from all parts to adore them.' Febvre was inclined to explain Protestantism both in terms of this religiosity and in terms of a reaction, invoking Heimpel's dictum that 'the image makers were the image breakers'.[21]

Febvre estimated that the period of the worst clerical abuses was well and truly over by the early sixteenth century, certainly in the case of the royal abbeys, and used this point to argue that anti-clericalism was somewhat routine. This is something of an exaggeration, as is the argument advanced both by Imbart de la Tour and Renaudet that the great ecclesiastical statesmen and pluralists who monopolised the abbeys throughout the period had had a disastrous financial effect on the viability of these institutions. The abbey of Saint-Denis had suffered a series of 'scandalous' abbots in the fifteenth century, usually drawn from the regional nobility of royal service, appointed largely by royal favour and to provide them with revenue. Some, like Jean de Villiers (1473–99) and Antoine de La Haye (1499–1505) had actively dilapidated the abbey. The nadir came with Pierre Gouffier (1505–17), closely related to a powerful court family, an absentee whose main interest in the abbey was his own profit. However, his brother Aimar (1517–28) resided as abbot and was very much more solicitous about the properties in his charge. Saint-Germain-des-Près, in the hands of a worldly Auvergnat prelate, Robert de Lespinasse, from 1467 and impervious to the desire for reform on the part of its abbot Geoffroy Floreau (d. 1503), fell in 1504 to archbishop-chancellor Guillaume (IV) Briçonnet who resigned it, much to the disgust of the unregenerate monks, to his son Guillaume (V), later bishop of Meaux, in 1507. Both Briçonnet and his successor cardinal de Tournon (1528) were effective reformers and administrators. Indeed, it has been reasonably argued that the foibles of individual abbots made little difference to the effective wealth of these abbeys, which was capably handled throughout the period of reconstruction by a succession of permanent treasurers and receivers. As the sixteenth century went on, the drive to institute reforms, even when abbeys were held *in commendam* by secular clergy or by pluralists was still strong. In such cases, religious reform and the regularisation of revenues and administration were seen as inseparable. Thus Arnoul Ruzé, member of a family of high state servants, undertook the reform of Notre Dame de la Victoire (Senlis) from 1524.[22]

That humanists like Josse Clichtove could both recognise these achievements and sense the continuation of a malaise was reason enough for Febvre to consider that the problems of the church lay elsewhere and, indeed, it is the case that competent management of funds and estates could not guarantee the spiritual vitality of the church.[23]

Since Febvre's time, archival work has begun to deepen our knowledge of the late medieval church in France. Imbart de la Tour's emphasis on the importance of episcopal activity in the pre-Reformation period is to some extent borne out by this. The issue is crucial since episcopal reform aimed first of all at order and was often at odds with the preaching movements and with elements of society which resented increased episcopal authority (after all, a feature of the Counter-Reformation). The failure of bishops to be good pastors or to be chosen for their vocations was an established theme of the preaching movement.[24] This may be because the bishops and the preachers envisaged reform in different ways. The remarkably full visitation conducted by Jean Mouchard for the archdeaconry of Josas south of Paris (1458–70) reveals an extraordinary attention to parish detail. Jacques Jouvenal, bishop of Poitiers, issued diocesan constitutions requiring the parish clergy to preach on the sacraments, works of charity and mortal sin.[25] The rich visitation records for the diocese of Rodez reveal the crucial role of a succession of bishops, most importantly Guillaume de La Tour (from the 1440s) and François d'Estaing in the early sixteenth century, in the reform of all aspects of religious life. The effect was a major restoration of the fabric of parish churches, of the ornaments for the eucharist, of the benefice system and, above all, of the moral and intellectual life of the clergy. By the early sixteenth century, only 2 per cent of the churches in Rodez were ruinous, church ornaments were well kept and there was a large increase in printed liturgical books available.[26] The concubinage of the clergy remained a problem, although in Rodez the proportion was better than the average of one-fifth living with concubines in France as a whole.[27] It is, in any case, likely that anti-clericalism was stimulated not so much by the unacceptability of concubinage (this depended on the general attitude to it in any area) but by the extent to which the laity considered that the clergy was or was not carrying out its professional duties. In Rodez, there was an astonishingly high number of clergy, perhaps one per 40 inhabitants in the survey of hearths and communicants of 1524–5.[28] In some, though not all, areas this meant that the clergy was far more able to carry out its duties than before.

The reform of the clergy was undoubtedly accompanied by significant changes in the routines of lay religious life. The characteristic devotionalism of the late Middle Ages is reflected in the spread of dedications of new lay confraternities under the aegis of the Passion, the Cross, the Virgin and Corpus Christi in the years around 1500. Most of these continued to stress collective devotion, though some saw the appearance of routines of individual piety. At Vaison and Carpentras in the early sixteenth century, there was a drive to emphasise the devotion of the laity to the eucharist and the Virgin. In the visitations conducted south of Paris in the 1460s, rigorous attendance at Sunday Vespers, yearly confession and communion and observance of the Sabbath were considered priorities. In Rodez during the episcopacy of François d'Estaing, though some resistance was met with from the parish clergy to his pet projects of the Angelus bell and the cult of guardian angels, the theatricality of the eucharist was substantially increased for the laity. As Nicole Lemaître has put it: 'It was really at the end of the Middle Ages that the eucharistic cult developed in parish reality'.[29]

The break which eventually came within the church should clearly, then, be seen in the context of the general movement towards religious reform that was already well established but what other implications did that reform movement have for the tenor of French Catholicism? Perhaps the most obvious point is that the strength of the Catholic Church in any particular area to some extent depended on the vigorous activity in promoting reform linked to traditional piety in the generation before the impact of Protestantism. The contrast between the rigour of François d'Estaing and the relatively easy-going defence of Catholicism by his princely successor in office, Georges d'Armagnac, illustrates this. This alone could not, of course, have determined the outcome but it explains some regional variations. In Brittany, where in any case the local cult of saints and of the dead was extremely strong, bishop Mayeuc of Rennes was so as-siduous in his maintenance of orthodoxy that heresy made little headway outside the town of Nantes or in the domains of noble families like the Rohans.[30] The failure of the officials of the diocese of Rouen to take the threat seriously or to tighten up their response allowed the initiative to pass to the Protestants in Normandy during the 1550s.[31] At Meaux, the late fifteenth-century reforming bishop, Jean l'Huillier (1483–1500), had pro-mulgated statutes in the Synod of 1493 that emphasised obser-vance of the sacraments and pastoral responsibility and which were not changed until Briçonnet's Synod of 1526. The work of Briçonnet and Lefèvre as his vicar-general in promoting evangelical reform at Meaux in the 1520s turned it, unintention-ally, into a Protestant stronghold until the 1560s.[32]

The significance of a reform imperative is clear in Marc Venard's study of the diocese of Avignon. While insisting on the achievement of fabric restoration very similar to that of Rodez in the late fifteenth century, he hints at a rather routine approach to reform, confined to the clergy alone. The repetitions of synodal statutes during the late fifteenth and early sixteenth century are only interrupted by the unusually careful statutes issued by vicar-general François de Gentilly in 1512–14; here, the goal is defined as 'the reform of all the clergy and people'. The earliest preserved visitation is of Carpentras in 1496–7 but it was not until the 1530s that visitations became effective in Avignon as a whole.[33] To some extent this must be explained by the general predominance of absentee bishops there. In Venard's analysis of the statistics of six-teenth-century clerical ordinations in the dioceses of Avignon, Carpentras, Cavaillon, Orange and Vaison, only Carpentras stands out as an exception to the general picture by which these dioceses look like priest-making machines in the first half of the century, turning out hundreds of subdeacons a year with scant regard for qualifications. The main explanation was not so much the non-residence of the bishops as a combination of the attractive presence of the Papal Legate at Avignon, with his powers of dis-pensation and clerical patronage, and the fact that dioceses, like Avignon and Cavaillon, were administrated by suffragans who treated the ordination of new priests as a lucrative source of revenue. At Carpentras, especially in the episcopate of Sadoleto (1518–47), participant in the *Consilium de emendanda Ecclesia*, there were few ordinations or *dimissoires* and none of the latter during his period of residence after 1527. Thus, the fact that so many aspirant priests from all over southern France came to dio-ceses like Avignon, rather than to others like Aix, Vienne and Embrun where the bishops were resident or careful to conduct visitations, is largely to be explained by the favourable conditions offered by the clerical authorities there in ordaining the margin-ally qualified.[34] There was a vast disparity between dioceses like Rodez, where in most areas the clergy was intensely local and embedded in the social fabric of the region and those like Avignon where not only *bénéficiers* but also *curés* were overwhelm-ingly strangers to the region.[35]

It now remains to judge how effective internal church reform had been by the middle of the sixteenth century. Here, Venard's analysis of the visitations carried out throughout France in 1551 for the projected Council of the French Church provides crucial evidence. *Procès-verbaux* survive in one form or another for 14 dioceses spread through every region of the kingdom. Some were evidently more attentive than others, probably as a result of local traditions. As far as the clergy are concerned, there was a disparity in the density of their distribution, varying from the diocese of Lombez, where there were only 154 priests to serve 91 parishes, to the diocese of Léon in Brittany with exceptionally dense concentrations of clergy. As for the residence of the clergy, in the 392 parishes of Beauvais, there were only 80 resident *curés* (20.4 per cent), distributed rather unevenly, the rest replaced by *vicaires*. Numbers and residence seem not to have made much difference to the attitudes of the parishioners. At Lombez and Autun, the people, in local solidarity, professed themselves satisfied. In Brittany, the complaints about the drunkenness and luxury of the clergy were rife. Contradictions emerge, for instance, in the parish of La Fare (Gap) where the people declared that 'their *curé* is a man of good life but they add, however, that he is inadequate to have charge of souls, that he does not shrive them or exhort them as he should'. In general, the responses are not dissimilar from those of the country people south of Paris in the 1460s, where there were obviously problems (36 resident *curés*, 36 absentees replaced by *vicaires*) but the parishioners only denounced their priests five or six times to the archdeacon for immorality.[36] If there was a motif of the laity's responses, especially in the southeast, it was a vast appetite for religious observance, sometimes not satisfied by the clergy. Even where the parishioners may have been satisfied, the bishops often were not convinced that their clergy read the Bible and knew how to administer the sacraments. As for the monasteries, there were quite evidently vast disparities between well-governed and dilapidated establishments; being held *in commendam* did not seem to determine this, though there is a suspicion that certain orders such as the Cistercians were less respectable than the Mendicants.[37]

What emerges from these visitations is not a strictly quantifiable view of the state of the French church but it does testify to the various approaches to reform. First, there was the traditional kind that we have seen already vividly effective at Rodez, with its concern for the re-establishment of decent services, the church fabric and the basic learning of the clergy. In some areas, the preoccupation was natural: the visitations conducted in the area south of Paris in the 1450s and 1460s had revealed a catastrophic state in the fabric of the churches and religious houses, repeatedly blamed on 'wars and divisions'.[38] Episcopal visitation was a model of reform perhaps more concerned with outward decency. The improvement of administration in the dioceses of Normandy in the late fifteenth century contributed to revenues and expansion in the number of the clergy but might have neglected other vital needs.[39] In contrast, the approach of the vicar-general of Beauvais, Louis Le Bouteiller, in his visitation of 1551 was evidently shaped by humanist assumptions and an instinctual anti-Roman Gallicanism inherited from Briçonnet of Meaux. His critique of clerical ignorance in his diocese was severe. He expressed a desire for a liturgy and breviary more suitable 'for a religion purified of all superstition', by which he meant the rejection, canvassed for more than a century in the Gallican tradition, of pious legends and confraternity celebrations outside the control of the bishops.[40] Finally, the provincial Council of Narbonne reveals the approach to reformation more characteristic of the Council of Trent: the strict restatement of traditional doctrine (along the lines of the Declaration of the doctors of the Sorbonne, 10 March 1542, enacted into law by Francis I in 1543) hand in hand with the rejection of Lutheran heresy. What is more, its assumptions were Roman rather than Gallican.[41]

One further point should be made about the visitations of 1551. The 'humanist Gallicanism' of the vicar-general of Beauvais had much to say on the state of the clergy but little on the relations between the latter and society. At Beauvais, in fact, relations between the bishop, cathedral clergy and the city were, especially after the accession of Odet de Coligny as bishop-count in 1536, endemically rancorous, as a result of the property held by the clergy and the extensive ecclesiastical jurisdictions in conflict with that of the city.[42] These problems could be replicated widely throughout France. At Albi in the 1490s, the jurisdictional conflicts between town and bishop undermined Louis d'Amboise's attempts to reform the Franciscan friary, prompted by the bishop's contacts with the reformist but anti-Mendicant Cluniac monk Jean Raulin, and leading to a siege of the bishop's palace.[43] The concentration of some episcopal reform on the 'reform' of the monasteries by the implantation of the Observant Franciscans in them was frequently a highly disruptive move. As Chevalier has pointed out, the scope for new foundations was limited; the only course was to 'purge' existing houses, both regular and Mendicant, and yet the latter particularly had powerful protectors in local communities. All this was despite the fact that the preaching of the Observants was welcomed. Thus, Standonck, while failing completely in 1495 to reform the Cordeliers of Amiens, with the help of his patron Graville, then governor of Picardy, was eagerly welcomed as Lenten preacher at Abbeville.[44] When preachers took it upon themselves, however, to attack the tyranny of town councils, the story was very different. Amiens seems to have been particularly sensitive: the *échevinage* reprimanded a local Augustinian in 1485 for preaching against the divisions between the town council and the church and causing 'murmurings' in the crowd; in January 1499 they called in a Minim who had been reported for preaching against excessive municipal taxes levied by the 15 or 16 men 'who governed everything' and wasted money on the gilding of the arms over the town gates. Some towns, like Tours after 1461, refused to go on paying for preachers. One that continued to do so, Poitiers, nevertheless saw opposition by magistrates to critical preaching.[45]

The Church and the Crown

France at the close of the Middle Ages was a kingdom like many others in which the relationship between church and state was so intimate that developments in one could not fail to affect the other. The failure of the French crown to take the path of fostering a Protestant state reformation has obvious consequences for any judgements about the nature of religious reform in France. There can be little doubt about the uncertain and disputed institutional state of the French church in the pre-Reformation period, although the implications of this for its spiritual vitality are not straightforward. The crown, while it did not break with Rome, took the view both before and after the Concordat of 1516, that it had a responsibility to promote the reform of the church. The regency convoked a Council of the clergy at Sens in 1485 and Charles VIII another at Tours in 1493 to reform the church in France.[46] The legatine powers held by the chief minister of Louis

XII, cardinal d'Amboise from April 1501 until his death in 1510, conferred on him a virtual dictatorship for reform of the French church which was regarded with great suspicion by the Parlement of Paris.[47] Another series of assemblies, in fact provincial rather than national councils, met in 1528 at Sens, Lyon, Bourges and possibly Rouen, to restate the doctrine of the church, and at Vienne in 1533. In 1551, Henri II prepared a Council of the Gallican church to proceed to reform from above 'for the good of the Gallican church and the entire conservation of our religion'. [48] The fundamental contradiction involved here is revealed by the fact that the Council was summoned in order to out-manoeuvre the Papacy and avoid the return of the Council of Trent, judged too favourable to the emperor. Religious policy could never be viewed independently from the demands of power and diplomacy.

The struggles over the institutional government of the church were shaped by the formation of two main strands of thinking about the church in France which can be classified as 'Gallican': the theological, which sought to make of the universal church a limited monarchy and to undertake a profound 'reformation' of its structure; and the political, the doctrine above all of the Parlement of Paris, which invoked the king's supreme jurisdiction in its refusal to allow the free exercise of papal jurisdiction in France.[49] These two strands of thought came together in the idea of hostility to Rome and found their formulae, during the Great Schism and the Conciliar movement, in the royal *ordonnances* of 1407 and 1418 and the Pragmatic Sanction of Bourges (drawn up by the clergy in July 1438 and registered July 1439). Specifically, the regime established by the Pragmatic had been formed in the period of the conciliar movement and was in turn profoundly shaped by a 'Gallican' idea of the church which was intimately linked to the development of a French national identity. The mid-sixteenth-century theorists of Gallicanism, Jean du Tillet and Charles Dumoulin, regarded fifteenth-century developments in the French church as a valuable source of their precedents.[50] The Pragmatic sought effectively to remove all papal power over the French church by confining the role of the Pope to simply confirming episcopal and abbatial elections and abolishing various papal dues on benefices. However, it had a reforming aspect in that it followed the Council of Basle in providing, through a complex rota system, for the promotion of university graduates to one-third of the benefices as they came vacant.[51]

It would, however, be highly misguided to suppose that the ideology of Gallicanism and the interests of the crown coincided. The crown may have sought to impede the flow of specie in the form of Annates to Rome in the fourteenth and early fifteenth centuries [52] but several important and permanent interests linked the crown and the Papacy; despite the clash between Philip IV and Boniface VIII in the early fourteenth century they had historically buttressed each other against their enemies, diplomacy had frequently dictated alliance and the Papacy had in practice conceded to the crown much patronage over the appointments to benefices.[53] Furthermore, the Pragmatic's aim to re-establish free elections and restore ecclesiastical jurisdictions was at least as damaging to royal power as to papal.

Negotiations between Charles VII and Rome to arrive at a compromise failed but the accession in 1461 of Louis XI, who had already abolished the Pragmatic in the Dauphiné, brought a more devious policy. Louis had no interest in defending the liberties of the Gallican church but used the bargaining power that the existence of the Pragmatic gave him to extract support for his Italian diplomacy. The support of leading bishops for the aristocratic opposition movement of the *Bien public* was an even greater incentive for him to extend his control over episcopal appointments. His policy, therefore, of alternate abolition and then of resuscitation of the Pragmatic was useful for royal policy vis-à-vis the church but ultimately a source of confusion.[54] In 1472, the Concordat of Amboise promulgated a compromise which anticipated that of Bologna in 1516, whereby Annates and the jurisdictional authority of the Papacy over the French church were restored, cases over benefices were to be judged in royal courts and then on appeal to Rome, collations were to be shared between the Pope and the ordinaries on a six-monthly basis but the Pope was bound to reserve a certain number during his term for clergy designated by the king. However, Louis still regarded himself as not bound by this, thought it conceded too much and delayed ratification. In 1475, a French church assembly reaffirmed the Pragmatic Sanction. There is doubt as to whether Louis thought the Concordat should continue during his last years and he may genuinely have sought to cooperate with the

Papacy over episcopal appointments. However, there is no doubt about the extent to which he sought to maintain an iron grip on them.[55] Meanwhile, continuing to use the negotiations in order to further his Italian diplomacy, by 1480–1 the king had obtained most of his objectives, including effective control of all the important benefices of France.

Louis XI's death saw an 'explosion of Gallicanism' that ultimately posed a threat to both the Regency and the Papacy. The Estates-General of Tours had seen common cause between the clergy and the nobility in protesting against the abuse of commendators, papal provisions, payments to Rome and the abandonment of the conciliar decrees. In effect, however, once the estates were dispersed the crown and the Papacy reverted in each specific case to the method of appointment to benefices already in practice: royal nomination followed by papal provision. The Papacy was in need of French support and usually did the bidding of the crown, while Charles VIII had no scruples in using the usual methods of pressure when necessary: the prohibition of payments to Rome and appeals to the Council. One of Louis d'Orléans's populist claims, in the manifesto he issued to the *bonnes villes* in January 1485, was that the Beaujeu government, after the Estates-General, 'seeks to break the Pragmatic Sanction and the liberties of the Church of France, so that all the kingdom's money can be taken to the court of Rome'.[56]

Louis's accession as king, when he declared his approval of the Pragmatic in 1499, and the pontificates of Alexander VI and Julius II, ironically ushered in a period of cooperation that in effect anticipated the Concordat regime: strengthening royal control over the church and papal primacy at the same time. In the first years of the sixteenth century, the Pope regularly intervened to forbid chapters from proceeding to elections while the king's will was awaited.[57] Although the quarrel between the king and the Pope in 1511 led to the king's appeal to a council of the church, the interruption in royal–papal relations was relatively brief.

There is no doubt that the involvement of the high church hierarchy in royal government and local society rendered most prelates highly worldly in their comportment. This is itself did not preclude reforming activity on the part of bishops; François d'Estaing of Rodez lived an aristocratic life with a household of 80. But it did contribute to the impression that reform from within was not enough. In addition, competition for benefices became fiercer and the period from 1484 to 1515 saw a decided rise in the number of disputed episcopal elections (sometimes violent as at Poitiers, Sarlat, Pamiers, Alès and Tarbes; just disputed as at Rodez, Arras, Soissons, Vienne, Angoulême, and Comminges). The regime of the Pragmatic Sanction had already become unworkable and the rules were no longer clear. To some extent this resulted from a high degree of uncertainty over whether the Pragmatic was in fact in force. But in addition to this, there is no doubt that all the powerful members of the royal council were constantly on the lookout for vacancies and determined to take advantage of their influence while repressing local attempts to elect.[58] The great abbeys were in no better case, their elections being subjected to inordinate pressures by the local nobilities. In 1484, the lords of Créquy, Mailly and Rubempré invaded the abbey of Corbie in order to compel the monks to accept the authority of François de Mailly, who had received papal provision some years earlier. Injuring some, they drove the rest to take refuge in the bell-tower without food or drink, though Jean de Mailly claimed later that he had been attempting to enforce his kinsman's wish to reform the abbey against the resistance of a faction of corrupt monks. Mailly, he said, was the king's man in a crucial region of still dubious loyalty.[59]

A contemporary memorandum on the 'Abuses of the Church' concentrated on the insecurity and lack of order stemming from constant litigation over benefices. It was a picture of chaos that could still at the end of the sixteenth century provide the basis for Brantôme's forceful attack on the corruption of elections under the Pragmatic.[60] The quarrels arose not so much because of the election of rival candidates as from the election by a local faction of a candidate unacceptable both to the crown and to the papacy. There is no doubt that the benefice system was crucial, or that suggestions for its overhaul in order to appoint more qualified men, along the lines of Jean Marre, bishop of Condom's *Instruction au Roy Louis XII* (1509), were bound to affront vested interests.[61]

The fifteenth-century French church was deeply divided and could not be expected to sustain the defence of a principle such as free election, even if it had not been incompatible with all the assumptions of a society like France which was suffused by the idea of patronage.[62] In such a society, the existence of elections to such posts of power and influence was bound to become enmeshed in energetic and violent struggles both within the church and within the provincial nobility. If we look at specific examples we can see how things worked. At Rodez, the see had been dominated by a clan, that of the La Tour and Polignac families, through much of the fifteenth century and the bishops they produced had been in the main effective pastors. In 1501, the chapter quickly decided to invoke its rights and the principles of Gallicanism in order to elect in François d'Estaing a prominent member of a rival local family supported by a powerful range of local nobles. In doing so, it must have been aware of the difficulties since no speedy election had been made good in recent times against the will of the crown or of the Papacy, simply because rival candidates were bound to appeal. The Polignacs eventually found their rival candidate in the form of Charles de Tournon and appealed to the archbishop, while d'Estaing appealed to the Parlement. In the event, it was Tournon who received both royal and papal approval and it was only his death in 1504 that left d'Estaing the only candidate, accepted with ill grace by the crown and thus one of the few bishops in the period to make good a claim through capitular election.[63] In the same period, the archbishopric of Rheims became vacant on the death in June 1497 of Robert Briçonnet, a member of a clan powerful among the 'masters of the kingdom'. His brother Guillaume, already bishop of Saint-Malo and a cardinal, exerted all his family's influence through corruption, the influence of the crown and friends among the regional nobility, and finally the provocation of street demonstrations, to gain his election in the chapter by 67 votes out of 68. The one recalcitrant fled to Paris and was persuaded to offer his vote to Standonck, who then laid claim to the archbishopric. The case became a political one when Standonck's candidacy became a symbol for the struggle against pluralism and simony. Charles VIII's support was enlisted through his confessor Jean de Rély but he died before he could annul Briçonnet's election. Louis XII, crowned by Briçonnet and offended by Standonck's criticism of his divorce in 1499, was indifferent to his claims at first but took the reformer into his favour just before his death in 1504.[64]

Such confusion did not reign only in the realm of episcopal and abbatial elections. The collational practice for all benefices was in a shambles since the inevitable consequence of the existing system was for battles to persist between rival patrons and for multiple claims to benefices to be made. The rota system, 'la tour', for those with *lettres de scolarité* to be listed for one-third of available benefices in all categories, was open to extensive fraud, especially since, despite royal *ordonnances* of 1497, there was no national list of declared vacancies and complexities of the list system gave easy opportunites for collators to benefices to escape the rules.[65]

Such was the background to the conclusion of the Concordat of Bologna between Francis I and Leo X in December 1515 which was promulgated at Rome in August 1516. Regarded too easily as the main explanation for the French crown's failure to follow the path of Henry VIII in breaking with Rome, conveying as it did effective power of patronage to more than 600 benefices within France, it was in reality the confirmation of trends in church–state relations that had been long established.[66] The agreement should be seen as part of a well-established tradition for the French monarchy to bring pressure to bear on the Papacy by alternately rescinding and reviving the Pragmatic. The concession in 1515 of the principle of papal primacy by Francis I in return for the cooperation of Rome with his Italian ambitions was a small price, from his point of view, especially since the practical control of appointments to benefices remained much the same. The abolition of the Pragmatic and of capitular elections was portrayed by Duprat, chief negotiator of the deal, as an effective preservation of the liberties of the French church, while he was able to tell the assembly of the towns called at Paris in March 1517 that it was hoped eventually to restore elections in a purer form. The opposition to the revocation of the Pragmatic from the Parlement was grounded on the conviction that appeals to Rome should be restricted and that Annates were likely to be restored. The University of Paris for its part feared that the privileged access of its graduates to one-third of the benefices would be lost. Duprat declared in 1518 that the promotion system for graduates 'had come to such a pass, that persons of great learning, respectability and conscience no longer sought to compete in that way and as a result of all that horsetrading the only ones to come forward were canvassers, intriguers, stirrers-up of trouble, people who had nothing else to do to occupy their time.'[67] All this formed part of the crown's aim to convey the impression that little had changed in practice and that the Concordat held out hope of a better regime.

The registration under duress of the Concordat by the Parlement, with secret protestations indicating its continued loyalty to the Pragmatic Sanction in March 1518, has been amply discussed by Professor Knecht. His view of the Concordat is that its objectives were primarily diplomatic and that it only added marginally to the power of the crown over the church, certainly not enough to provide the incentive in itself for Francis I's continued support of the Papacy. When invited by Henry VIII to follow his example in breaking with Rome in 1534, Francis was categorical: 'in view of the fact that he does not have the same reason and it would give him disturbance and travail, considering that he is at his ease, it seems to him that he should not do it.'[68]

It should not be assumed from this that, in confirming the effective power of royal patronage over the church, the Concordat accelerated the process by which the episcopacy was discredited by worldly prelates. This will hardly bear serious scrutiny. While the Concordat itself provided for papal monitoring of unsuitable nominees, this was in practice allowed to sleep. The provision for elections in certain special cases where it could be proved that they had been long authorised by Rome apart from the Pragmatic Sanction was in practice manipulated. Any move away from a 'reforming' episcopacy of the late fifteenth century to a more 'worldly' one of the sixteenth would need to be explained in other ways since the patterns of patronage were broadly comparable.

The Concordat undoubtedly strengthened the practical control of the crown over appointments to the abbacies and dioceses of France, if only in removing the moral obstacle of having to override the Pragmatic Sanction in order to annul elections. The registration of the Concordat was by no means the end of the story since litigation over benefices continued to be viewed by the Parlement and the withdrawal of cases by *évocation* to the *Grand Conseil* continued to be a major irritant until the confrontation between Francis I and the court in 1527.[69] How extensive were the exceptions to the Concordat? In the 101 dioceses and 12 archdioceses under the authority of the king of France between 1516 and 1531, there were 125 provisions in 75 of them. Of these, 21 were made after capitular elections and a further 10 attempted elections that were subsequently quashed, and for 18 there is no evidence. Most of these dioceses were in the centre and south-west of the country. In June 1531, however, the Pope agreed to annul by indult all surviving electoral privileges for the king's lifetime except in the case of houses governed by the heads of religious orders.[70] Even so, of the 243 bishops appointed between 1516 and 1559, 86 were elected by their chapters. These bodies sometimes managed to maintain their claims, in fact, by electing bishops whom it would be impossible for the king to reject (as did Bourges in electing du Bueil in 1520 and Tournon in 1525) or king's councillors, where the interest of the king was clear. Nevertheless, as Paul Ourliac pointed out in 1943, the line from 1472 to 1516 is clear: 'in 1472 the pope and the king had sealed their joint hegemony over the church in France. They did not do anything else in 1516.'[71] At the height of the crisis between France and the Papacy in 1551, with the kingdom on the point of schism because of the Pope's diplomatic policy, Julius III wrote an emollient letter to Henri II in which he observed: 'in the end, you are more than Pope in your kingdoms ... I know no reason why you should wish to become schismatic.'[72] Although the Gallican lawyer Charles Dumoulin might have hoped that the king would swing behind reform, schism in 1551 was out of the question for a monarchy already deeply anxious about the spread of Protestantism. In that context, an independent French church would have looked like a one-way ticket to Geneva.

Julius III, though, was being somewhat disingenuous. The institutional system was not fixed and had continued to evolve as the Papacy sought to make use of those parts of the Concordat which allowed it to fill sees of its own volition. Thus, while the Concordat applied perpetually to the kingdom, Dauphiné and the county of Die and Valence (confirmed by the 5th Lateran Council, December 1516), it only applied in Provence, Brittany and lands acquired thereafter by special indult renewed at the start of each papal and royal reign (on the argument that these had never been subject to the Pragmatic Sanction). In addition, the *Apud sedem Apostolicam* clause confirmed by the Concordat allowed the Pope to fill the sees of bishops who died in Rome and, since there was always a number of episcopal ambassadors and French cardinals at Rome, this gave some scope for horse-trading, as over the succession to the four sees held by the cardinal Jean de Lorraine when he died at Rome in 1550, or those of cardinal du Bellay in 1560. In these cases, the bulls of *non vacando*, that had suspended the papal prerogative of appointments to sees vacant *apud sedem apostolicam*, were themselves in doubt because of a change of papal reign.[73] As F. J. Baumgartner has made clear, it was this, as much as any preference for Italian *fuorusciti* on the part of Henri II, that allowed the Papacy to insert so many Italian bishops into the French episcopacy during the middle years of the sixteenth century. In the period 1516 to 1560, 20 per cent of the French bishoprics were filled by Italians and in 1557 roughly one-quarter, an anomaly in the history of the French church but in the years before the Wars of Religion an aggravation. Not all those prelates inserted by the Papacy were unwelcome to the crown but the uncertain nature of remaining papal prerogatives in France was the cause of frequent acrimonious bargaining in the Curia.[74]

How far, then, did all this lead to an effective decline in the calibre of the episcopacy? Not all the Italians were careless absentees, as the work of Jacopo Sadoleto at Carpentras shows. However, many of the Italian appointees under Francis I and Henri II were absentees and most seem to have used their promotions in order to resign them for pensions after a decent period. Some were causers of great scandal, like Antonio Caracciolo, bishop of Troyes, who became a Protestant and yet wanted to retain his see. Caracciolo, though, was a startling and perhaps disconcerting exception as an Italian bishop who actually came to his diocese and sought to preach there.[75] In fact, most of them were titularies of southern sees and it was in the Midi that the real problems arose (only Quimper, Treguier and Troyes were held by Italians in the north). Although most of the sees in that area were poor, some were important. The archbishopric of Narbonne had no resident incumbent between 1524 and 1574.[76]

The canonical requirement of a minimum age of 30 for a bishop was, as before, overridden by special dispensations when necessary under Francis I. As for education, there were under Francis I only six known commoners promoted as bishops who in fact owed their positions to their scholarship and close relationship to the royal household. The Concordat in its final form also dispensed princes of the blood and members of great families from the requirement of a University degree, although the king had the phrase: 'the king will name a qualified person, that is to say a graduate or a noble' modified by deleting the last three words in order to minimise lobbying.[77] However, the overwhelming noble status of the bishops appointed after 1516 is clear. According to M. Edelstein, 182 men were appointed bishops under Francis I; of the 144 Frenchmen, 129 have identifiable social origins and of these 123 were noble, including 7 per cent princes of the blood and 76 per cent of the sword nobility. The pattern seems comparable to that of the late Ancien Regime analysed by Ravitch, though in between those two periods, the late sixteenth century saw the start of something of a challenge to the old nobility.[78]

Edelstein argues that the trend of appointments under Francis I was away from those members of the robe or nobles of royal service (the Briçonnets and Robertets, for example) who had been prominent in the fifteenth-century episcopate. She adds that the great robe families were spurned in terms of the episcopacy after the period of cardinal Duprat.[79] However, what we know about the composition of the bench in the fifteenth century indicates that there was hardly any change in the social profile of the episcopate before and after 1516. Of the 102 bishops in place in 1516, 58.8 per cent were nobles of old family, 15.6 per cent foreign nobles, 12.8 per cent recently ennobled, and 3.9 per cent commoners. Of the 243 bishops appointed between 1516 and 1559, 54.6 per cent were old nobles, 19.7 per cent foreigners, and 14.8 per cent recently ennobled. Curiously, in view of the opposition of the Parlement to the Concordat, one of the notable changes was that, whereas there were only 2.7 per cent of the 1516 bishops drawn from the sovereign courts, of those appointed between 1516 and 1559 there were 10.2 per cent.[80] The late fifteenth century and the years from 1516 to 1560 shared a tendency for the bishoprics to be dominated by a composite elite of families whose principal point in common was control of the state rather than social status. Many of them were indeed successful 'robe' families, like the Briçonnets (holding nine bishoprics in the period 1483–1515 whereas the Bourbons held five).[81] In the late fifteenth century, the Amboise, a middle ranking sword noble family from the Loire, were among the most successful ecclesiastical dynasts. Relatively poor though high in favour from the 1470s, Charles I d'Amboise, looking for income for his 17 siblings, procured the abbey of Jumièges (1474) and that of Cluny (1481) for Jacques, the bishopric of Albi (1474) for Louis, that of Poitiers (1481) for Pierre and the *grand-prieuré* in France of the

Hospitalers of Rhodes for Ayméri (1482). Another brother, Georges, became an abbot at the age of 15 in 1475, went on to become *grand aumônier*, archbishop of Rouen, protonotary apostolic, cardinal and papal legate. This was a classic 'episcopal dynasty'.[82]

In reality, the largest proportion of the bishops both before and after 1516 came from the nobility of the provinces in which their sees were situated, overwhelmingly so in the south-west, Provence, Dauphiné, Brittany and Normandy. Thus, 38 bishops in 1516 were born in their sees, a further 80 sees were occupied by 72 members of episcopal dynasties (Tournon, Hangest, Levis, Armagnac, Albret, etc.). Those bishops who were non-provincials were overwhelmingly either ennobled or noble members of the royal entourage, like the Tours families, Briçonnet and Beaune. The presence of the small number of commoners is to be explained by their service to the king as almoners or, like Guillaume II Pellicier, by their service as diplomats. The avenues of promotion were the same before and after 1516: roughly 27 per cent of bishops obtained their posts by family connection, 36 per cent by local influence and 25 per cent by their service to the king at court. In Michel Peronnet's memorable phrase, 'the episcopate remained a cousinage, though it was the king who chose the cousins'.[83]

Specific examples reveal something of the effect of all this on the calibre of the episcopate. Within the same episcopal family approaches could differ: in an important archdiocese like Rouen, Georges I d'Amboise (1494–1510) promoted reform, actually resigning his other benefices when he obtained Rouen, while his nephew Georges II (1511–50) neglected his duties there. In the see of Rodez discussed earlier, the first bishop appointed under the regime of the Concordat, Georges d'Armagnac in 1530, might seem at first sight a classic example of a worldly and political prelate given the post in order to sustain his role as diplomat and royal councillor. Son of a bastard son of the last count of Armagnac, brought up from the age of 10 by Marguerite of Navarre, ordained priest by Guillaume Briçonnet, he was aged 29 on his appointment, and thus technically needed a papal dispensation. However, despite his lengthy service as ambassador, he sought to acquit his canonical obligation to visit his diocese at Easter and remained attached to the ideas of humanist reform generated by the Briçonnet circle. Although Marguerite seems to have regarded him as too worldly by the 1540s, she nevertheless pushed for his elevation as cardinal. He was represented by his nephew, Jacques de Corneilhan, as vicar-general and on his return from Rome in 1550 he did begin to take a serious interest in the reform of the diocesan statutes. Thus, though it is clear that the main work of reform had been accomplished by François d'Estaing and that Armagnac took a more easy-going role, any caricature of him as a purely worldly absentee bishop would be wide of the mark. He seems to have avoided an episcopal visitation during the general movement of 1551 but took instead the course of issuing new statutes for his diocese in the context of the provincial council held at Narbonne in December of that year.[84]

The Social Context of Reform

The humanist Josse Clichtove, observing the great attempts made in his own time to reform the religious orders and the efforts of the bishops to bring order into their dioceses, was puzzled by what seemed to be a continuing malaise in the church.[85] In the late fifteenth century, the discourse of criticism of abuses was apparent within the church itself: Jean Standonck, in the commission set up by the national council of 1493, had sonorously denounced 'ignorant preachers of ill repute', the traffic in benefices and ecclesiastical judges who 'only pillage and vex the poor people'.[86] In the mid-sixteenth century it was commonplace to attack the abuses of the church, even for persons of unimpeachable orthodoxy. When Henri II addressed his circular letter to the bishops in 1551 on the general visitation, he blamed the peril of the church on 'enormous faults, errors, abuses and scandals which nowadays pullulate throughout Christendom'.[87] As we have seen, the extent of this criticism, viewed in the light of genuine attempts at reform, may demonstrate the vitality of religious faith.

However, it is plain that by the early sixteenth century there was no consensus as to how radical and how fast internal reform should be. This was apparent during the 1490s in the critique offered by some moderate reformers of the idea that the religious orders could instantly be brought back to their pristine purity.[88] The limits of reform from above were perhaps revealed by the effective failure, in the first decade of the sixteenth century, of the cardinal d'Amboise, with his legatine powers to create or suppress benefices, to achieve very much of significance. Indeed, given the investment of his own family in the existing benefice system, it is difficult to see how much could have been achieved. It was easier to pursue the controversial campaign of reforming the monasteries along Observant lines. Even where a regional public institution like the Parlement of Toulouse, on dubious legal grounds, supported the plans of superiors for the reform of the regular orders and actively attacked clerical immorality, the combined hostility of local clergy and of Rome itself effectively checked it.[89]

Lucien Febvre noted that 'the benefice system, endowing each ecclesiastical function with property, naturally ended up in the eyes of its holders as more important than the function itself'. For reformers in the early sixteenth century, it has been pointed out, 'all effort was paralysed by the benefice system'.[90] The institutions, especially relating to the relations between church and state examined above, probably go far to explain why, despite the reforming zeal that we have seen from the late fifteenth century onwards, some people found it ultimately impossible to remain within the church, despite the great dangers involved in breaking from it. Those dangers – the enormity of contemplating life outside the community of the one universal church – should never be underestimated. The reasons why some chose to run such risks and others did not are beset by problems of evidence and may never be possible to resolve definitely, certainly not in terms of a single theory.

Historians have increasingly come to view the Reformation in relation to social change and in particular have placed the emphasis on the reasons for the growth of Protestantism. The great social historian Henri Hauser advanced the view at the end of the nineteenth century that Protestantism in France drew its strength from the discontent of the working people faced by the fall in manufacturing prices. Put this way, the theory no longer finds general favour, though attempts have been made to adapt it to new research by stressing the antagonism between artisans and 'notables' and the adverse economic conditions of the 1540s.[91] Hauser argued, from the writings of the contemporary publicist Symphorien Champier, that the urban upheaval in Lyon known as the *Grande Rebeyne* in 1529 was in part a religious revolt, a view that has since been effectively dismissed by the historian of the city, Richard Gascon, who argued convincingly that it was in essence a classic grain riot.[92] Yet the notion that people chose their religious faith because of their job or their social resentments, what may be called the 'social geography' of Protestantism, continues to inform both Marxist interpretations (most recently, of course, by Henry Heller) and non-Marxist empiricism. Heller's assertion that France in the sixteenth century was profoundly polarised in class terms between rich and poor provides a point of departure for an interpretation which sees the adoption of Calvinism, for instance, in the years of depression and dearth in the mid-1540s, as a radical religious response to extreme suffering. The appearance of embryonic reformed churches at places like Senlis, Orléans, Soissons, Rouen, Tours and Agen in this period is seen as directly connected with these conditions.[93] However, such conditions can be interpreted differently. The 1540s were undoubtedly a decade of adverse economic conditions but in some respects these might have made matters more difficult for reformers. In the Vaucluse region, for instance, Venard has insisted that the economic circumstances precipitated repression rather than stimulated Protestantism. He certainly disposes effectively with the notion that the complex and varied Protestantism of Provence was born of class conflict between peasants and lords.[94]

The identification of early Protestantism with the aspirations of the skilled workers, especially artisans in the textile industries, has become a seductive explanatory framework also linked, as has been pointed out, to the adverse economic conditions of the 1540s. The prominent role of artisans in many Protestant communities, for instance reflected in the records of French exiles in Geneva, has become a banal feature of modern historiography. Although the criticism that artisans were the effectively mobile class, able to take their skills anywhere, is a powerful one, there seems no reason to suppose that the lack of a rural contingent in the *Livre des habitants de Genève* gives us a falsified picture. It is confirmed by the distinct absence of peasants from the ranks of those prosecuted for heresy before the Parlements in the generation before 1560.[95] However, we are left with the difficulty that, in the most careful analyses of reformed communities by Natalie Davis, Janine Garrisson or Philip

Benedict all social groups, artisans included, look profoundly divided.[96] At Lyon, the Protestant printers studied by Davis were perhaps the most *déraciné* members of the community but there is no doubt that the ideas of the Reformation found recruits in all social strata. There is never any clear-cut correlation between social occupation and religious loyalty. Lyon proved to be the city in which Protestants made their greatest gains in the early period, though the turbulence of a city that sucked in large numbers of immigrants and was developing new industries led to significant divisions within the community of the reformed.[97]

At Paris, we find that although the clandestine Protestant community recently explored through the entry registers of the *Conciergerie* by Barbara Diefendorf drew its strength from the middle and upper classes, the most significant fact is that families were deeply divided by religious choices: wives defied their husbands, children their fathers.[98] Janine Garrisson's survey of the Protestant community in 1559 relies perhaps too much on the evidence of how the community developed later on but there seems little reason to challenge the importance she detects for the petty nobility, legal intelligentsia, financiers and certain specific artisanal trades or the feeble role of the peasantry.[99]

In towns like Paris, Bordeaux and Toulouse, all of them seats of *parlements*, the *gens mécaniques* remained overwhelmingly Catholic and it was a minority of royal officials and clergy who constituted the Protestant community. Bordeaux had been shocked, of course, by the royal campaign of repression in 1548 and the numbers of Protestants there remained small even though there were many converts in the neighbouring Agenais and Saintonge region, focus of the gabelle revolt in 1548.[100] At Toulouse, the deep divisions in local society that came out in 1562 showed the isolation of the Protestants against a background of the collapse of the town's staple industry, pastel manufacture. At Grenoble, lawyers and merchants took the lead in the Protestant community. For Le Roy Ladurie, the material and cultural poverty of the *laboureurs* around Montpellier led them to remain Catholic while the equally poor artisans of the textile trades became Protestant.[101] Analysis of the important Protestant community in the city of Amiens in the mid-sixteenth century has revealed the predominance of the poorer textile workers, supposedly at odds with the big merchants and increasingly subjected to the policing of their trade by guilds controlled by the rich. There, the most literate parishes had fewer reformers.[102]

Such an approach suffers from the disadvantage that it can only provide a series of answers; every town and region seems to have had different determinants for its religious destiny. Indeed, David Nicholls, in his subtle analysis of early Protestantism in Normandy, plainly with a view to setting religious choices in a social and economic context, reveals that the only pattern that seems to emerge is one of profound diversity even within this one province. Once thought to be a major example of Protestantism in the north of France built up from a position of economic expansion and vitality, in Normandy the picture of the economic life of the lower classes in the sixteenth century was fundamentally adverse. This in itself did not condition religious loyalty and there seems no evidence for the contention that economic misery led people to seek a new religion. The idea is also dismissed by Davis on the basis of her study of Lyon.[103]

One fruitful insight has been to correlate the degree of literacy with Protestantism in the analysis of the extent to which the religious differences were related to a cultural divide. Reformers obviously attached centrality to the words of God in the Bible. The initiative for the Olivétan Bible (Neuchâtel, 1535) came first from the leaders of the Luberon Vaudois, whose language was not even French. A high correlation has indeed emerged between Protestantism and the literacy rates in studies as diverse as those of Davis on Lyon, Venard on Avignon and Farr on Dijon, although in the latter case neighbourhood solidarities were judged as at least as significant as literacy. As has been pointed out, Amiens does not follow the same pattern. There Protestantism was successful among the poorer and less literate and in areas of probable low literacy such as the Norman *bocage*, there were also converts. Moreover, as Nicholls has pointed out, the argument is a circular one: Protestantism presupposes high levels of literacy; therefore it must have recruited among the most literate. In a period when it is very difficult to establish literacy rates, this is dangerous.[104]

Most of such studies are limited by the fact that they concentrate on the towns and tend to reinforce the stereotype of Protestantism as the religion of urban man. In such conditions, the particular social and economic structure of each town is bound to break up the general picture. It has become commonplace to assume that the countryside remained largely impervious to Protestantism. The existence in the Cévennes of a long-lasting and formidable redoubt of rural Protestantism always posed an awkward problem for the sociological approach; Hauser got round this by arguing that the reformed faith was in some way 'implanted' by 'rural artisans' such as blacksmiths, clearly a highly contrived view. More recently, Molinier has shown that Protestantism in the Cévennes could prosper without the usual paraphernalia of literacy and artisan consciousness and has gone on to suggest a close correlation between it and a long period of hostility to outsiders and especially tax collectors from the lowlands of Languedoc.[105]

If the 'social geography' of Protestantism is unable fully to provide an overarching explanatory framework for the religious changes of the sixteenth century, in fact in the words of Denis Crouzet has reached 'a certain impasse',[106] one of the consequences of concentrating on it has also been to draw attention away from the crucial problem of explaining the depth of Catholic enthusiasm in France, arguably a phenomenon that outstripped Calvinism in its vitality.

Crouzet's model seeks to provide a completely different approach, the avowedly 'naïve' idea of suggesting that 'religious impulses lie behind the religious crisis', 'a matter of individual sensibility'.[107] It is not suggested that the social framework is ignored, that there were no collective sensibilities, simply that it will not explain all the inconsistencies of behaviour. Concerned above all with the wellsprings of religious violence, Crouzet allows his narrative to emerge from the details contained in the vast number of contemporary pamphlets describing newsworthy events in order to attain the 'discourse' of violence. He thus adds significantly to what N. Z. Davis and Janine Garrisson had already revealed about the symbolic or 'gestural' forms of violence.[108] The importance of all this is as a testimony not to the decadence of pre-Reformation Catholicism but rather to enthusiasm for it; mysticism, rather than a sign of decay, was a sign of the offensive dynamic of Catholicism even before the advent of Luther. The violent nature of popular Catholicism, therefore, on the margins of the institutional church, emerges as an indicator of the 'prophetic tendency' of Catholic Christianity, a tendency that Calvinists sought to distance themselves from by returning to a lost 'truth' which in fact permitted a 'liberating radicalism', moving away from the mystical world of Catholic piety towards a world in which God was, though all powerful, less immanent. This choice was therefore psychological rather than social in its fundamentals. 'What counts, for the individual, in his adherence to a religious system, is the psychic function that underlies belief.'[109]

As Professor Knecht has pointed out, the truth about the French Reformation probably lies somewhere in between the extreme social determinism proposed by Henry Heller and the haunted psychodrama adumbrated by Crouzet.[110] It would be foolish to ignore the tribal connotations of any religion and M.P. Holt's examination of the dynamics of popular Catholicism in Burgundy, in terms of a 'socio-cultural' relationship between the wine-growing community (some 20 per cent of the population of Dijon itself) and the Catholic Church should be remembered. The *vignerons*, in fact, in conjunction with the city council of Dijon, posed an irreducible bastion against the progress of Protestantism in Burgundy.[111] Moreover, Crouzet's notion that revived Catholicism does not have much to do with the signs of Catholic pre-reform that have already been examined here seems wide of the mark and unnecessarily dogmatic.[112]

However, in the context of a universal religion in the course of fracture, there is no doubt that the psychological picture of eschatological anxiety in the early sixteenth century is extremely suggestive for the explanation of many attitudes. By looking at almanachs and *Kalendriers* published to predict weather and the future by the conjunction of the stars, vectors for myth-makers in Crouzet's view, we learn that predictions of an imminent deluge are to be found in the work of 56 writers in 131 books during the period 1500–20. The *Practica* of Lucas Reyman, in predicting the end of the world in 1524–5, was part of a widespread wave of eschatological anxiety that came to a climax with the belief, announced by Henry de Fines, that the earth would definitively end at 10.18 a.m. on 2 February 1524.[113] As ever, the failure of specific predictions of doom did not extinguish the appetite for them; quite the reverse. The rapid spread of heresy in Germany, its occasional revelation within France and the anxieties consequent on the obsession with the end of the world, led Catholicism in France to draw its strength from astrologers who claimed that adverse planets were in the ascendant and that it was necessary to repent. Individuals took bizarre measures, like the president of the Parlement of Toulouse who, Bodin later recalled, built an ark on a nearby hill.[114]

Signs and portents were important because of the tendency of people to understand the significance of events in terms of whether they fulfilled prophecies. In doing so, they could at least situate them in an intelligible scheme of things. The chronicler known as the *bourgeois* of Paris noted them for the first time in 1522 as a portent of evil and his pages become suffused by signs of the evil times.[115] So also the Provins chronicler Claude Haton understood the events of the civil wars by recalling Nostradamus's prognostications for 1555 and noted that the prosperity and appetite for novelty in 1555 'predicted a future unhappiness for France'.[116] Blaise de Monluc, with his famous propensity for prophetic dreams in which he claimed, for instance, to have seen the death of Henri II before it happened, was engaged in the same discourse.[117] The proliferating reports of monstrosities, such as Gabriel Symeoni's *Les prodiges merveilleux* of 1556 or Pierre Boaistuau's *Histoires prodigieuses* of 1560, were seen as indicators of God's anger: the message was rammed home by the words supposedly reported from the monster's mouth at Cracow, 1543: 'repent, for the coming of God is at hand'.[118] However, it should also be remembered that Badeto, the Dominican inquisitor charged with heresy at Toulouse in 1534, was evidently an astrological determinist, while the Sorbonne had pronounced against occultism in 1494 and obstructed Lefevre d'Etaples's plans to write on the subject.[119]

All this anxiety may serve to explain why it was Lutheranism which broke up the church while the long current of reform in the late Middle Ages did not. France was as affected by it as Germany, although the opposition of the crown to Lutheranism impeded its triumph. Of course, the direct appeal of Calvin as a French humanist scholar to his own community, as well as the formative power of his theology, go far to explain the fact that he rather than Luther or Melanchton shaped French Protestantism. Thus Venard, in his study of reformed loyalties in the Vaucluse, came to the conclusion that the principal force behind conversion to Protestantism lay in 'the attraction of a simple and clear word ... a liberating word vis-à-vis the quantity of rites and gestures of the traditional religion'.[120]

By going too far towards the mystical obsession with the precariousness of human existence, the church of the early sixteenth century may well have provoked an opposite reaction.[121] Calvinists for their part were told by Calvin in the *Traité ... contre l'astrologie*

(1549) that the idea that it was a gift from God was false and contrary to the doctrine of *sola fide*. Beza in 1563 rejected almanachs as incitors of Catholic violence. Instead, Calvinism sought to exorcise anguish about salvation, the fear of God and of the end of the world by offering certainty, a 'theology of calm and serenity' in the rejection of the idea that God could be appeased, in the embrace of salvation through faith and a predestination memorably described in the English church as of 'unspeakable comfort'. Not for nothing did the Calvinist address God with the familiar *tu*; for him the deity, though unimaginably immense, engendered no fear.[122] The anguish of fear of death is removed and the true follower of Christ assured that he can be saved. Calvinists were taught that they were not to know the mind of God and, though they lost the immanence of God and the magic of Catholicism they gained an end to their fear about coming face-to-face with God as sinners.[123] The Calvinists in the France of the mid-sixteenth century did not break with the church, then, largely in the desire to return to primitive purity but rather as a way of breaking out of the circle of prophetic anguish. As Calvin put it: 'Since then this life serves us to understand the goodness of God, should we then think it has nothing good in it?' It is in the full living of life on earth without fear 'that we begin here to taste the sweetness of His benignity and His blessings, so that our hope and desire should be incited to understand the full revelation'.[124]

On the Catholic side, addiction to prophecies served the purpose of buttressing the faith. The author of the *Signes prodigieux* of 1560 declared that false prophets in the form of 'false preachers, disseminators of false doctrine... enemies of our holy mother church' were the sign of the last days.[125] Prophecy was for Catholics partly an outpouring of Old Testament panic about the imminence of divine punishment, expressed also in the proliferation of late medieval paintings of the Last Judgement. Hence the fervour of crowds at Le Puy in 1549 praying for God's mercy when the crucifix was mutilated. The press was brought to work for the Catholic Church as for the reformers. In the period 1545–62 in France, there were 71 pamphlets (at 800–1000 per edition) published in which heresy and the Devil were associated. The crude but effective verse denunciations of the Catholic priest Artus Desiré, for instance *Les combatz du fidèle papiste* (1550), served to deepen the image of the heretic as harbinger of the end of the world and from the late

1550s increased in the tone of vituperation: 'every filthy Lutheran should be burned over a slow flame'. On the more respectable level, clerics like Antoine de Mouchy of the Sorbonne sought to provide intellectual legitimacy for anti-Protestant violence.[126]

Other than pamphlets, preachers were a key to Catholic mobilisation. Pierre Le Picart, Parisian preacher between 1530 and 1550, predicted the day of judgement and announced that Henry VIII's capture of Boulogne in 1544 was a sign of God's anger.[127] Preachers spread out throughout France with the same message. Other signs were the exorcism at Bourges in 1546, the miracles reported near Tonnerre in 1557 worked by a spine from the Crown of Thorns, the increased use of processions with relics, and pilgrimages to ward off natural calamities and manifestations of heresy. The climax was reached near the end of 1561 with the miracle of the Belle-croix of Troyes that was seen to change colour and proceeded to start working miracles for the crowds of sick that flocked to it.[128] By 1560, therefore, the ground was ready for the explosion of mass hysteria that accompanied the slide into civil war.

In examining the fears of Catholics in the period from 1520 to 1560, it is easy to assume that they felt threatened by a coherent Protestant doctrine. In fact, the term 'Lutheran' was for a long time simply one of abuse that conveyed very little doctrinal accuracy. How much continuity was there between the religious revival of the late fifteenth century and the Protestantism of the mid-sixteenth? The problem may be viewed in terms both of the popular revivalism of the late fifteenth century and of more ordered structured approaches to reform from above on the part of bishops and of humanists (who of course were sometimes the same people). Firstly, as far as popular revivalism is concerned, there is some possibility that the preaching crusades of the Mendicants filled the same role in the lives of the people as the Protestant *prêches* in the open air outside the walls of towns in the 1560s.[129] As David Nicholls has argued, there is some similarity, despite doctrinal differences, between the Franciscans and the more unorthodox wandering Protestant preachers of the 1550s and 1560s. Hervé Martin has shown that there was in any case a very fluid dividing line between orthodoxy and heresy in the critique of clerical vice and abuse offered by the preachers of the years around 1500, while it seems to be the case that some of the

more virulent castigators of clerical inadequacies passed into the
ranks of the Protestants, to be in turn denounced by Calvin as
demagogues: 'These horrible beasts ... having rejected their
habits, retain the stains, hypocrisy and malice of their order. They
are credulous, lazy, superficial, gossiping, curious and vain.'[130] We
could add that the Mendicant orders of the late Middle Ages were
sometimes viewed with suspicion by the church hierarchy as a
source of disorder. However, it is clear that despite the great
enthusiasm for Observant preaching crusades from the late
fifteenth century, there was then no great enthusiasm locally for
attempts to purge or reform the existing religious houses,
Mendicant or otherwise. An interesting point of connection
between the reform movement of the early sixteenth century and
the later Protestantism is revealed by the arrest of a preacher at
Nîmes in 1532. An Augustinian friar had been invited by the
consuls, who were concerned about the failure of pastoral care, for
the Lenten sermons. He preached to their satisfaction but was
arrested by the Parlement of Toulouse and the bishop because he
had dared to preach in the cathedral. There is reason to suppose
that heresy had already appeared at Nîmes but the consuls were
more concerned about the pretensions of the bishop (a feature we
have already noted elsewhere).[131]

It is worthwhile repeating at this point the observation that late
medieval France experienced no major heretical movement
which might have provided the 'critical springboard', to use A.G.
Dickens's phrase, for Lutheranism in its early stages.[132] It is certainly the case that the Vaudois of the Alps and of the mountains of
Provence constituted a tenacious and self-contained heretical community. The implantation of the peasant Vaudois of Provence
seems to have taken place from the late fifteenth century onwards
as a result of pressure put upon them in their Alpine refuges. Their
beliefs were not fossilised but subject to considerable evolution and
complexity in the sixteenth century. The denunciations of the
Inquisitor Jean de Roma in 1533 should be compared with the
profession of faith of the people of Cabrières in 1533: 'We believe
in the Holy Spirit, the Catholic church ... we have not believed in
Pierre de Valde or in Luther except where they have declared the
word of God.' However, their influence on the rest of France was
small even in the period when they were beginning to come to
terms with Protestantism in the 1530s and 1540s (for instance in

their Confession of Chanforan, 1532) and when, in 1545, having been mobilised by the devastation of their land by Montmorency in 1536 and increasingly out of control, they were subjected to savage persecutions by the secular authorities. However, the Vaudois were an overwhelmingly peasant community, whereas all we know about early Provençal Protestants indicates that there were few peasants among them. In fact, the existence of the Vaudois masks the virtually complete failure of Protestantism to make any headway in Provence otherwise. This in turn is a powerful further argument for the vitality of popular Catholicism in the generation before 1560.[133]

It may well be that the absence of a major heretical challenge in the rest of France predisposed the episcopal visitations of the earlier sixteenth century to ignore the question of heresy in the main, with the predictable exception of the diocese of Grenoble in 1506 and of the Provençal dioceses in 1546–7.[134] Even when the presence of Protestantism was obvious by the middle of the century and episcopal visitors asked specific questions about it, the responses were overwhelmingly negative. The parish priests seem to have been highly reluctant to denounce their people, for whatever reason, and the community on the whole closed ranks against outsiders. The conclusion must be that the visitation was in effect useless for the detection of heresy.

The world of the early Protestants in France as revealed in Nicholls' important work is disordered and anarchical and provides a valuable illustration of Lucien Febvre's view of the period as one of a 'long period of magnificent religious anarchy'. Even after 1560, in Nicholls' view, Protestantism was riven with 'schisms based ultimately on an ambiguous attitude to authority' between the very different social groups that made up the Calvinist community.[135]

As Henri Lemonnier aptly put it, 'early Protestantism in France was so wide and open that you could enter it without believing you had left Catholicism'.[136] There is little doubt that, well into the 1540s, and at least until the appearance of the first French edition of Calvin's *Institutes* in 1542, the doctrinal profile of Protestantism was undefined. Although the Sorbonne used the term 'Lutheran' systematically after the condemnation of Luther in 1521, it plainly became one of abuse. Florimond de Raemond called Lefèvre d'Etaples, Farel and Roussel 'Lutheran Zwinglians', Arnauld Fabrice wrote in 1535 of the 'sects of Zwinglians and

Oecolampadians that they call commonly Lutherans'. An order of 1538 issued by the Parlement of Toulouse talked of 'certain heresies and errors called commonly the Lutheran error and heresy because one called Martin Luther gave commencement to them and with or after him there have adhered to them other men of diabolical spirit'.[137]

Nicholls has argued that the attempted imposition of Calvinist orthodoxy from the 1540s onwards actually damaged the popular vitality of the proto-Protestant communities. This probably introduced serious divisions to the extent that the Calvinist community by 1562 was an uneasy coalition of nobles, urban leaders and artisans of all kinds whose interests did not necessarily coincide and, as Koenigsberger suggested, this ultimately led to a break-up.[138]

Early heresy had taken the form, at popular level, of an anarchical critique or mockery of the church very much within the traditions of medieval anti-clericalism. The first arrest for Protestantism in the diocese of Rodez was that of Jean Junius, first master of the school at Villefranche, accused in 1554 before the *présidial* court of 'having introduced the new religion' because he laughed while listening to the irreverent remarks of his pupils. Mocking laughter like that of Jean Regnault of Sancerre in 1540, 'Come and see God at the mass!' was evidently an important ingredient at this early stage.[139]

Added to this, the impetus given by the availability of Scripture, actively promoted at Meaux by Briçonnet and Lefèvre from the 1520s, gave much new scope for individual ideas, from the sublime to the lunatic, on theological questions. This is one of the reasons why the municipal schools and colleges became such sources of disquiet to the authorities. The consuls of Nîmes prohibited the use of Scripture by schoolmasters in 1538 'to avoid the errors which it is said have hitherto been spread because of the reading of Holy Scripture' and the statutes the *Collège* created in 1539 excluded matters of faith from the curriculum.[140] The range of the ideas that could be spread by this means was very wide: the hermit Jean Vallière burned at Paris in 1523 for denying the Immaculate Conception; Jean Guibert was banished for denial of the value of attending mass or of prayers for the dead; André Berthelin of Annonay burned in 1539 for not kneeling to an image.[141] Prosecutions for 'blasphemy', increasingly categorised as simple or heretical, also reveal a degree of anarchical attitudes.

Charges of 'sacramentarian' attacks on the mass were present in the 1520s, grew during 1538–41, and emerged as charges of attacks on the 'holy Catholic faith' and all the other sacraments of the church from 1542 as the authorities began to realise heretical propositions of individuals were beginning to take on a doctrinal thrust. Thus, one Jean Bourssault was charged before the Parlement in 1540 with 'heretical and scandalous blasphemies, false erroneous and scandalous propositions against the honour of God, of the holy sacrament of the altar, and of the saints in paradise, and of the holy Catholic faith and church.' With the beginnings of mockery and then physical attacks on images as 'idols', bizarre personal fads like those of Pierre Rivière, who denied that Judas was damned to hell, or Pierre Vallier of La Rochelle who refused to answer charges on the grounds that he was the son of God, created an explosive mixture without much sign of doctrinal definition.[142]

Plainly these ideas could not go much farther; they represented an anarchical critique of the existing order but provided little positive alternative. The interesting group of dissidents revealed by the prosecution of the circle around Jean de Caturce and Arnauld de Badeto at Toulouse in 1532–4 shows that some Lutheran ideas on free will were present, though the evidence is inconclusive.[143] As for theological consistency, that was the role of Calvinism in its vision of salvation. Whether, as Nicholls argues, the chasm between Calvin's doctrinal formulations and the distance which most critical Frenchmen wished to travel was unbridgeable; whether the vision of the future offered by Geneva was so at odds with a peasantry 'stuck in a cyclical view of time, an eternal present' is, of course, debatable.[144]

One of the enduring myths about the genesis of the Wars of Religion is that the nobility were latecomers, eager to jump on the bandwagon of Protestantism in 1555–61 in order to prosecute their secular interests or in the pursuit of their clientage obligations. The date 1555 is repeated largely because the evidence is much clearer from that date. When we find isolated scraps of evidence in visitation records, the nobles are present. For instance, during the visitation of the diocese of Nantes in 1554, it was reported that the seigneur of Plessis de Lagaine never went to church and had in his company 'an old man with a grey beard claiming to be a servant of the house of Belleville. This man, it is said, has about him a little book which he reads from every morning and before meals, while all those present are on their knees, and they go to no other mass.'[145] In any surveys of the incidence of early Protestantism, including the registers of exiles in Geneva, nobles are always present.

There seems to be a willingness to ascribe a baser sort of motive to the nobility than to any other social class. Thus the so-called 'economic crisis' of the nobility was invoked by Hauser to explain their rush to convert. We have seen already that this economic crisis is largely a myth and may have affected only atypical individuals. The nobility certainly converted in large numbers: in the *élection* of Bayeux 40 per cent were Protestants by the end of the 1560s, in Beauce around 19 per cent in 1560, in the *bailliage* of Blois 48 per cent in the 1570s, in Péronne (1577), 16 per cent. Constant ascribes their conversion to an act of conscience when in contact with new religious ideas but reinforced by the ties of kinship solidarity which in fact created interrelated Calvinist clans, 40–75 per cent of which were in existence even before the spread of Calvinism in Beauce.[146]

The connection between genuine conversion and the role of kinship and friendship among the nobility is perhaps most strikingly illustrated by studies of aristocratic women in the early period of the Reformation by Nancy L. Roelker.[147] The combination of the effects of Renaissance scholarship on the traditional *querelle des femmes* and the vastly increased scope offered for women of the highest birth in public life, firstly from the period of Anne of Britanny and then at the court of Francis I, proved to be an extraordinary moment for the opportunities of women such as the duchess of Etampes, a royal mistress but later a stalwart of the Protestant cause.[148] The piety of the late fifteenth century led on through the learning of Lefèvre d'Etaples to produce a small but highly-placed group of women in the royal family like Marguerite of Navarre and Renée de France, crucial in the cultivation of a much larger group of women who were to play a central role in the organisation of Calvinism. Marguerite of Navarre's circle included figures like Louise de Montmorency, the Constable's sister and mother of the Coligny brothers, as well as Madeleine de Mailly, Jacqueline de Longwy, duchess of Montpensier, Michelle de Saubonne (ancestress of the Rohan-Soubise as well as governess of Louis XII's daughter Renée de France, duchess of

Ferrara) and Isabelle de Rohan. These women carefully nurtured an evangelical faith that in many cases turned to Calvinism and produced the military and political leadership of the cause in the 1560s. Condé and La Rochefoucauld were married to daughters of Madeleine de Mailly.[149] In the case of Renée de France, the daughter of a king of France, if not openly Calvinist, she corresponded regularly with Calvin and returned to France for the last years of her life as an open, if unaggressive, sympathiser with the Huguenot cause.

Many of these women were in personal contact with Calvin by letter and the genuine converts seem sincerely to have embraced a doctrine, perhaps indirectly through Calvin's guidance rather than theological study. This in many ways offered a secular 'calling' to women in their own sphere, partly in its appeal for man to glorify God by work in the world and partly by Calvin's emphasis on the dignity of conjugal love and the reciprocal rights of husbands and wives. For instance, Calvin's draft *ordonnances* at Geneva offered women the right to initiate divorce for adultery that was largely absent under traditional marriage laws: 'in that the wife is no more subject to the husband than the husband to the wife.'[150]

The Repression of Dissent

The reason for the relative circumspection of the aristocracy as a whole in the period from the 1520s to the 1550s is to be sought principally in the risks run by personal declarations of heretical views for a class whose interests were so closely interrelated with those of the crown. The extreme disfavour into which Coligny's brother Andelot had fallen at the end of Henri II's reign is clear testimony of this. The fate that attended Louis de Berquin, a Picard nobleman whose case before the Parlement of Paris became a test of Francis I's attitudes to evangelical reform in the 1520s, remained an ominous warning.

It is certainly the case that the king's initial sympathies for humanist reform in the 1520s softened the effects of some attempts to make examples of prominent reformers, but this could not last, especially as major cases of heresy were dealt with by the Parlements. In France, the primacy of royal justice decreed that the secular courts have cognisance of heresy. Lay and church courts were supposed to collaborate but the latter were in fact confined to cases of individuals in higher clerical orders. In all cases of open preaching of heresy by a churchman, the Parlement was the competent judge. The prosecution of heresy, it has been suggested, stemmed essentially from a set of attitudes and institutions in all medieval European societies that were shaped in order to promote uniformity and consensus.[151] This, as much as anything else, dictated the rhythms of attacks made against Protestants.

The famous *Affaire des placards* (1534) was obviously a turning-point. It used to be thought that the king's sharp change of direction was an indication of his basically capricious views on religion; that his conception of personal affront at the fact that a *placard* had been affixed to the door of his chamber at Amboise shaped his religious policy. In fact, the tracts written by Antoine Marcourt were so luridly sacramentarian in their attack on the mass that a monarchy fundamentally linked to the Catholic Church could not ignore them.[152] The Parlement of Paris issued orders in January 1535 offering rewards for those who denounced heretics and punishments for concealment. In February, the printing industry was controlled by the suspension of royal licences for several months. The edict issued at Coucy in July 1535 extended the death penalty to the propagation of heresy by any means. An uneasy situation resulted in the first period of exile for many Protestants. As was to be the case again, however, the need of the crown for the establishment of alliances with German princes, many of them now openly Lutheran, decreed the easing of conditions.[153]

The truce of Nice in 1538 and a brief rapprochement with the emperor brought further developments. The edict of Paris, 24 June 1539, those of Fontainebleau, 31 May 1540, and of Paris, 23 July 1543, ordered a renewal of prosecutions of heretics and clarified the nature of the procedures. These restricted the function of ecclesiastical courts to the establishment of cases against the clergy and 'common crimes' (*délits communs*) among the laity. All the rest involving public 'scandal' (in practice, most of them) were *cas privilégiés* and went to royal courts.[154] A special tribunal of the Parlement for enforcing royal edicts and decisions of the Paris Theology Faculty was set up. Its working was suspended during the period 1541–4 when France again needed the alliance of the German Protestants but the secret article of the Peace of Crépy in

September 1544 provided for the renewal of heresy trials in France.[155] 1544 saw the burning in public of the works of Etienne Dolet and of Calvin, while in April 1545 the atrocious massacres of the Vaudois villages in Provence began. The Parlement of Aix had condemned the people of Mérindol specifically in November 1540 but this had been suspended by the king in March 1541 on the advice of Guillaume du Bellay. The decision had been taken at court to activate repression by Christmas 1544: 4000 people were killed or transported to the galleys, partly as a result of the isolation of the Vaudois as scapegoats at a time when all the local authorities – papal legate, Parlement of Aix and local lords – were anxious about increasing social discontent and able to influence the king.[156]

The accession of Henri II seems to have given some impetus to anti-Protestant moves. The special tribunal of Parlement judges, popularly called the *Chambre ardente*, was revived, though the Parlement itself was suspicious of such extraordinary bodies. The Parlement, when handling cases through its criminal court, was not indiscriminate: in 1546, out of 122 judgements in cases of heresy, there were 6 acquittals, 64 cases of insufficient evidence leading to release, 7 recantations and 45 condemnations. There was a rise in the proportion of condemnations between 1547 and 1549 but with little effect. Of the 557 cases examined, only 39 led to burning at the stake.[157] The modification of the heresy laws in November 1549, restoring a role to church courts in heresy cases, and June 1551 (the edict of Chateaubriant), giving jurisdiction over heresy cases without appeal to the *présidial* courts, added further categories of actions, such as flight to Geneva, for prosecution. However, all the surviving evidence from the archives of the nine Parlements in France shows that, although there was a massive increase in prosecutions in the 1540s and 1550s, the effects in controlling heresy were very limited.[158]

One of the main problems was the innate suspicion of secular royal courts about church jurisdiction. When Henri II, possibly under the influence of cardinal de Lorraine, proposed the creation of a formal Inquisition in order to circumvent judges in the Parlements deemed to be too soft on heresy, the opposition of the Parlements made it impossible. Except in the papal territories around Avignon, the royal courts had long overshadowed the inquisitions created to combat heresy in the fourteenth century. Indeed, one reason for the survival of Jean de Roma's 1533 inquisition dossier about the Vaudois was the enquiry by the Parlement of Aix into his having conducted such a process without royal permission.[159] A draft regulation for the relations between Parlements and the proposed Inquisition drawn up in 1552, makes it clear that the intention was to remove heresy cases from the effective cognisance of the Parlements even in cases of *appel comme d'abus* (the normal procedure for overturning judgements in church courts), except in limited cases. The order appealed in a curious way to French opinion in that 'the Inquisition in France is the first in any Christian kingdom, exercised in this kingdom by Saint Dominic against the Albigensian error'. But it could not possibly have been accepted by the Parlements.[160] When Henri II submitted an edit for the establishment of the Inquisition in 1554, President Séguier argued that it would damage the king's rights and infringe secular jurisdiction. Laymen were apparently to be brought before church jurisdictions without appeal. When in 1557 the king returned to the idea, he was evidently considering the formation of an Inquisition along the lines of those in Italy, 'in the accustomed form and manner of law under the authority of the Holy Apostolic See'. The Pope in fact appointed cardinals Lorraine, Bourbon and Châtillon in April 1557 and in July 1557 the edict of Compiègne extended the death penalty in heresy cases. The Parlement resisted registration for six months and it is clear that the Inquisition never became effective before the death of Henri II changed the agenda.[161]

It seems obvious that the salient point about the persecution of heresy before 1560 was that it was patchy, inconsistent and scarcely effective in controlling the spread of ideas. Conversely, it served well enough to contribute to the mythology of the Protestants that they were being subjected to a time of tribulation in order to test their worth.

Conclusion

The spread of Protestantism in France was plainly impeded by institutions and by politics but the constraints were breaking down by the time of Henri II's death in 1559. Confrontation of some sort was therefore likely but took on alarming political connotations only with the political factionalism of 1559–62. The underlying predicament of Protestantism in any society in which it had to remain a minority was a struggle for survival. However, there are other and perhaps more important reasons for the minority appeal of Protestantism in France. The most important is that the very ferment that gave birth to the Protestant Reformation also reinvigorated the Catholic Church in the long run. The latter, in any case, was gradually being reformed from within before the sixteenth century began, despite the problems posed by the institutional church–state relations and the dead weight of the benefice system. There was corruption in the late medieval church but also much will to reform and the inception of a more intense devotional life for individuals. This, coupled with the impetus of eschatological fear that turned heretics into demons for many Frenchmen by the middle of the sixteenth century, produced a Catholic community determined to fight to the end the spread of Protestantism by 1560. The result was the confrontation of two activist forces and two cultures unwilling, perhaps unable to compromise over toleration until the end of the century.

8. French Foreign Policy, 1460–1560

For Pierre Choisnet, writing the *Rosier des guerres* under the direction of his master Louis XI around 1481–2, 'the noble kings of France have always aimed and worked to expand and enlarge their kingdom'. Given the perpetuation of the ideology of the princely warrior and chevalier, arguably at least down to the reign of Henri IV, war was an inescapable reality for those in control of state policy and for the whole population. There was no choice because, in a sense, war was the raison d'être both of the state and of the social order.[1]

The reign of Louis XI had seen a decisive expansion of the king's power and domain. Louis for the first half of his reign was preoccupied essentially by survival. The combined threat of Burgundian power and aristocratic disaffection at home, not least that of his brother Charles de France, came to a head in the War of the Public Weal (1465). This strained to the limit his famed capacity to escape from a tight corner.[2] Fortunately for him, the power of England was to some extent neutralised by dynastic struggles and Louis's ability to use his Lancastrian allies against Edward IV. Not until 1475 did England again intervene actively in France and then to little effect in view of the inability of Charles the Bold of Burgundy and Edward IV to cooperate.[3]

Louis simply managed to survive the setbacks of the Treaty of Conflans (1465) that ended the War of the Public Weal and the Treaty of Péronne (1468), which was extracted from him by Charles the Bold. The tide only really began to turn between 1470 and 1472. That was the period in which Louis went onto the offensive against Burgundian power in Picardy by detaching the Constable de Saint-Pol from his alliance with Burgundy. The death of Charles de France (1472) removed a major source of his insecurity and the crushing of Armagnac power in the capture of Lectoure presaged the downfall of major aristocratic opposition. The executions of Saint-Pol (1475) and Nemours (1477) added to the aura of intimidation at home.[4] All this laid the groundwork for the rapidity with which Louis was able to seize the initiative in January 1477, when Charles the Bold's power was crushed at the battle of Nancy. Commynes thought the king was too greedy in seeking to lay hands not only on the Burgundian territories that could rightly be said to revert to the crown (the duchy of Burgundy and Picardy) but also on those like Artois and the Franche-Comté of Burgundy in which Mary of Burgundy had a powerful succession right. Louis even moved on territory of the Empire such as Hainault.[5] The ultimate result was that, though Louis managed to gain fairly firm control in the two Burgundies, Picardy and Artois, he generated enough hostility in Flanders to land himself with a debilitating war against the consort of Mary, Maximilian of Habsburg, who arrived later in 1477 to rescue her inheritance.

The inconclusive nature of the wars between 1477 and 1482, a period which saw Louis's war expenditure at its height and included one severe military reversal for France at the battle of Guinegatte (1479), finally convinced the king of the need for an agreement. This was eventually reached in the Treaty of Arras of 1482, by which the marriage between Margaret of Austria, daughter of Mary and Maximilian, and the dauphin Charles was pledged as the guarantee of a settlement between the two dynasties with the ultimate return of Artois and Franche-Comté to the couple as its objective. As was usually the case with such settlements, it was probably seen as a breathing space by both sides. Louis's military expenditure had reached disruptive proportions, while his ability to stir up trouble for Maximilian in Flanders was unabated. The death of the French king in the following year initiated something of a change of direction.

Although the basic administrative personnel remained in place after 1483 and there were still figures in power in France like marshal d'Esquerdes who were determined to push for an aggressive policy in Flanders, the drift of the Regency government was at first away from ambitious schemes that involved high taxes. This was because it was preoccupied by a renewal of internal dissension, led by Louis of Orléans in alliance with Brittany. The overthrow of Richard III by Henry Tudor in 1485, with a modicum of help from France, was a short-term gain but could not solve the fundamental problem. The great debate in French government circles in the 1480s was whether to resume the offensive in Flanders or to turn attention to a Brittany that was seen more and more as the key weakness in the position of the French crown.[6] In the 1480s, however, France was also on the threshold of a new phase in her external policies, the age of the Italian wars that were to lead on to the generalised conflict with the Habsburg dynasty on all fronts.

Historians have naturally been led to ask why France became embroiled in the Italian wars. One answer was to point out that, centuries before, kings of France had mounted crusades to the Levant in 1270 and to Aragon in 1285, their kinsman Charles d'Anjou had led an army to Sicily in 1266 and French interests had been established in Naples. The expedition mounted by Charles VIII in pursuit of his claims to Naples in 1494 may be seen as a return to a highly traditional orientation of French policy towards Italy and possibly the Levant. Neither was the idea of a crusade against the Ottoman threat, with revived claims to the kingdom of Jerusalem or the Empire of Constantinople, viewed as entirely absurd, certainly by some royal propagandists. These important points were overstressed, however, by François Delaborde in his study of the 1494 expedition, the thesis of which was that for two centuries Naples had been a 'fatal attraction' for the French.[7]

Henri Lemonnier pointed out the fallacy of viewing French policy as determined by two centuries of interest in Italy: the period was too long for any consistent policy to be maintained throughout, while earlier expeditions to southern Italy had been the result of individual enterprises within a feudal monarchy rather than policies of the monarchical state. To this we may add that the two centuries between the age of Saint Louis and that of Charles VIII had wrought fundamental transformations. The combined economic and demographic crisis and the English invasions led first to a decomposition of the kingdom and then to its reconstruction around the principles of monarchical legitimacy. The disasters of the Hundred Years War had shaped some fundamental reorganisations of French military power supported by permanent taxation. Yet it was essentially the social and economic revival of the late fifteenth century as well as the effectiveness of the state that returned France to the quasi-hegemonic role in Europe that it had held in the thirteenth century. By the end of the fifteenth century, the king of France was the ruler of the most populous and effectively taxed kingdom of western Europe, a view firmly held by the Venetian ambassadors in France.[8]

What, then, were to be the objectives of those who controlled the policies of the French state during the Renaissance? Were they to follow traditional patterns and how far were they conditioned by the fundamentally aristocratic nature of French political society?

Choisnet's idea that kings naturally strove for conquest was in fact modified by his warnings against the perilous and adventurous nature of war and the higher duty of the king to defend his subjects and strive for peace. Yet the role of crusading ideals, the accumulation of notions of chivalry and honour as well as dynastic title, all conspired to give a centrality to the personal decision taken by Charles VIII, under the influence of his friends and of Italian exiles, to invade Italy. Pierre d'Urfé, *grand écuyer*, wrote to the king in June 1494: 'You alone, sire, took the decision, did the deed and conducted the matter to this advanced stage.'[9]

At the end of the fifteenth century, there remained some common customary distinctions between wars waged for gain and those waged for glory. *The Débat des herauts d'armes de France et d'Angleterre* (c.1453–61) put it thus: 'I make great distinction between common war and the war of magnificence. For I say that the common war is for itself against neighbours or members of the *lignage* and the war of magnificence is when princes at the head of their armies march to the conquest of distant and foreign countries and fight for the Catholic faith.'[10] There seems little doubt that contemporaries would have regarded the Italian wars of the 1490s as 'wars of magnificence', especially with their overtones of a crusade in the making. The contrast with Louis XI's dogged wars with the house of Burgundy was plain to see.

The most consistent tradition of the Capetian and Valois kings, however, was that of the expansion of their French-speaking territories. For this reason, the path of the Italian wars, what Brantôme later in the sixteenth century was to call the 'smoke and glory of Italy', was severely judged by the classic French diplomatic historians, who saw it as a course which wasted French energies and in the end produced no profit. As Henri Lemonnier put it, given the need of France to digest and consolidate its recent gains 'in such a situation, it obviously needed a morbid imagination, with the survival of medieval ideas and chimeras, to revive Angevin rights to Naples and dream of the conquest of Constantinople.'[11] The turning away of France from the further acquisition of land in the Low Countries by the treaty of Senlis in 1493 was seen to be a fundamental error.

In fact, the contrast between the policies of Louis XI and those of his successors was not as great as this would suggest. Certainly the conquest of Roussillon in 1462 and then of the Burgundian lands and Picardy-Artois in 1477, followed by the effective annexation of Provence, look like a hard-headed extension of French border territories but Louis was no less interested in Italy and in fact managed by the end of his reign to attain something of a position of arbiter there.[12] Similarly, although Charles VIII's Italian expedition might appear quixotic, the abandonment of interests in the north-east (Artois, Franche-Comté) and south (Cerdagne and Roussillon) by the treaties of Senlis (May 1493), Etaples (November, 1492) and Barcelona (January, 1493), so long criticised by French historians, liquidated problems and in some ways was unavoidable. The treaty of Etaples was a good bargain with Henry VII and in effect dictated that a treaty be signed with the Catholic kings. The treaty of Senlis was not a total abandonment of Artois and France retained important legal claims and outposts both in Artois and Flanders that could be reactivated at another time.[13]

It is certainly the case that there were sharp debates within the council over the wisdom of the Italian expedition but these took shape as part of a general struggle for power between the king's favourites, de Vesc and Miolans, on the one hand and, on the other, the Beaujeus and old servants of Louis XI who preferred to concentrate French energies on their northern domains. The Milanese ambassador in May 1493 described the efforts of admiral de Graville and his allies, marshals de Gié and Esquerdes, to oppose the signature of the treaty of Senlis. Ludovico Il Moro's envoy in France was under orders to liaise with this 'opposition' group in order to keep the French out of Italy. However, the Florentine ambassador wrote in 1493 that 'Monsieur and Madame no longer oppose the torrent' leading to involvement in Italy.[14]

One of the preconditions for French intervention in Italy was the decisive defeat of Breton and allied forces at the battle of Saint-Aubin-du-Cormier on 28 July 1488. The consequence was the effective end of Breton independence, sealed by the treaty of Sablé in August and the death of duke Francis II in September. This, and a further round of campaigning, by 1491 gave France the control of the young duchess Anne and with her of the whole Channel and Atlantic seaboard for the first time.[15] It led directly to the formation, in effect, of a triple alliance between the rulers of England, the Low Countries and the Iberian kingdoms in the defence of Breton independence, still regarded as a crucial feature of the international scene. Although the alliance fell apart quite rapidly, it prefigured the linkage of marriage alliances between the ruling houses of Habsburg, Tudor and Trastamara that were to lead indirectly to the inheritance of the emperor Charles V. The Habsburg dynastic empire of the sixteenth century may be seen, therefore, as a direct outcome of fears engendered by the revival of French power. The claims made by French royal publicists for the imperial rights of Charles VIII and prophecies that the king would be 'monarch of all Europe' should alert us to the fears about French power at the end of the fifteenth century.[16] Whereas around 1450 the principal enemy and problem for France had been England and its dependencies in France, by the 1490s England, while retaining Calais as its outpost on the Continent, was but one among a number of possible enemies or diplomatic partners for France in a game which placed France at the centre of strategy and negotiations. Its relative weakness was revealed by the Boulogne campaign of 1492.

This was the period which saw the effective implantation of a permanent diplomatic system on the Italian model north of the Alps, with the first permanent ambassadors appointed to reside in foreign courts. The first quarter of the sixteenth century saw the generalisation of this pattern and the formation of the French diplomatic service based upon the activities of royal servants drawn from the ranks of much the same middle nobility, royal clerics and robe technocrats who formed the basis of most other organs of royal government. Francis I commissioned 615 known embassies or negotiating teams during his reign, carried out by around 315 individuals. The real 'diplomatic service', though, consisted of the 114 envoys sent out on more than three missions or holding resident posts (72 of these). Surprisingly, there were only 21 clerics among this group, the vast majority being members of the court and council, royal secretaries and councillors or presidents of the Parlements. There were some high ministers like Bonnivet, Duprat and Tournon but the high aristocracy was largely absent. By the 1520s and 1530s, the phenomenon of the career spent largely in diplomatic service to the crown was beginning to appear. This applied not only to individuals who spent most of their lives abroad in resident posts but also to figures such as the brothers Guillaume and Jean du Bellay. The two latter were, with the royal favourites Chabot, Montmorency and

Morette, an Italian diplomat in French service, Jean-Joachim de Passano and Christophe de Siresmes, *élu* of Avranches, the most frequently commissioned envoys. Of the 22 men in receipt of more than seven commissions, there were 7 officers of the court and chamber, 2 lesser royal servants (valets/secretaries), 4 bishops, 1 other theologian, 3 lawyers, 2 members of the higher administration, and 3 other nobles.[17]

There can be little doubt that the profile of the French diplomatic service was formed largely by royal trust and favour. There has been much discussion about the fundamental springs of foreign policy during the Renaisance. Its formation was a quintessential royal prerogative in any monarchical state and especially so in one like France. Kings like Charles VIII, Louis XII and Francis I no doubt viewed the world around them in terms of a princely sporting event in which they engaged in personal combat with their royal competitors to vindicate of their 'honour' and 'glory'. As Blaise de Monluc wrote, honour was 'to be purchased at whatever price'. Brantôme's view of all this was that war was inevitable given the resentment of Francis I at seeing 'his vassal greater than him'. 'What other king would have endured it?', he asked. Charles V remarked to Wolsey in 1521 that 'the law of God byndeth every man to claim and ask his right'. In 1547 some French nobles visited the emperor in Vienna in hope of employment. Charles had just made peace with the Turks but Brantôme reports that he told them that he liked peace no less than they; however, they were not to worry since the 'ambitions' of their master would soon provide work for them: 'never can two such powerful and covetous neighbours live in peace'. Robert Thorne reminded Henry VIII that all princes had a natural urge to extend their lands. There was also pure personal rivalry to be accounted for, both between the French and English kings and also between Francis I and Charles V. By 1521, it had been brought to the emperor's attention that Francis thought him an 'idiot, ill-intentioned, ignorant and lacking in courage'. When they later met in person, such slights would be momentarily forgotten.[18]

The game of marriage negotiations and alliances seemed to make the international system a vast family concern. The entire intellectual formation of princes gave reality and meaning to claims of inheritance. In such a framework, the vindication of dynastic rights was bound to occupy a high rhetorical profile, especially in manifestos and declarations that accompanied the opening of wars. French ancestral rights to the kingdom of Naples occupied by the Habsburgs, Habsburg claims to the duchy of Burgundy, the claims of the descendants of the French Albret family, related to the royal family, to the kingdom of Navarre annexed by Ferdinand of Aragon in 1512, provided extensive reasons or pretexts for war. Margaret of Austria warned her father the emperor Maximilian that the French king would always try to make good his suzerainty over Flanders. When it is remembered that, despite the abandonment of that suzerainty in 1525 and 1529, Louis XIV 150 years later reflected that it had been a fixed objective of French rulers ever since to regain it, the power of such claims is revealed.[19] The inability of conquest to nullify dynastic right is revealed by the failure of France to maintain its control of Piedmont after 1559, while the continuing use of claims to Navarre in the seventeenth century shows how long the memory of monarchs for their rights could be.

Whether such rights and preoccupations should be regarded as the fundamental cause of war is another matter. When we consider the non-existence of the option of doing without war for more than brief intervals, it becomes more apparent that, in some senses, there was no choice for the rulers of late medieval and early modern Europe. War was so probable that precautions and preparations for it had constantly to be in hand. Whether there was any conception of the necessity of war for social equilibrium is more difficult to assess, since opinions were divided. Certainly Jean Bodin thought in the 1560s, looking back on the generation of war up to his time, that 'the foreign wars we had until the religious troubles were only the purgation of the evil humours necessary to the body of a Commonwealth'. On the other hand, Jean du Tillet in the 1570s thought that 'the length and continuation of the wars under the late kings of happy memory Francis I and Henri II have accumulated a great excess of evil humours which little by little accustomed the body of this state to undergo change and alteration.'[20] When, as in the early sixteenth-century Europe, the dynastic claims and personal rivalries of monarchs like Francis I, Charles V and Henry VIII coincided with very significant geopolitical clashes, war and diplomatic rivalry were unavoidable.

Despite all these arguments, it might still seem strange that the French crown and a significant portion of the nobility were prepared to engage down to the 1550s so obstinately in a struggle for power in Italy, leaving France itself effectively at risk. Either the objectives were regarded as too compelling to ignore or the risks at home as not serious. It is in fact the case that France was repeatedly invaded: in 1524 by an imperial force under Bourbon, in 1536 in the north (the siege of Péronne), by the emperor himself in 1536 (via Provence) and 1544 (the siege of Saint-Dizier), by the English in 1513, 1522–3 (Suffolk's march to Montdidier) and 1544 (siege of Boulogne), and finally by Emmanuel-Philibert of Savoy in 1557 (the siege of Saint-Quentin). What stands out from these campaigns is the impossibility of wars of rapid movement into the body of the kingdom itself. Every campaign was held up by debilitating, if sometimes successful, sieges. Neither could set-piece battles determine the outcome. The battle of Pavia in 1525 was as near a complete disaster as could strike any state in the sixteenth century, with the capture of the king and the loss of many leading military noblemen, yet within 18 months Francis I, restored to liberty, was planning to overthrow the treaty that had been extorted from him at Madrid and which he had never in any case intended to observe.[21] It is perhaps also the case that, until 1521 the main cost of the Italian wars had been borne by Italy itself rather than France. It is certainly a fact that the burden of the direct taxes remained at the low levels set after the death of Louis XI throughout the first stage of the Italian wars.[22]

Why was it that Italy in particular became the battleground in the late fifteenth and early sixteenth centuries? The differences of view in 1494 were sharp but this did not prevent those who opposed war in Italy for such a wide range of reasons from joining the Italian expeditions when they were formed. Indeed, it may be asked how a society led socially by the class of *gentilshommes* could fail to wage war abroad once the opportunity was presented. The northern and eastern frontiers were important but the terrain in the Low Countries and the Rhineland was difficult, as Charles the Bold and after him the duke of Alva found. In Italy, the terrain was ideal and the power vacuum created by the failure of the Italian states to achieve stability too inviting to be ignored.[23] Modern attempts to analyse French policy in terms of economic motives, particularly regarding the strategic position of places like Genoa, Pisa and Livorno, have not really been successful. The kingdom of Naples was widely thought to be a rich prize but those who were well-informed knew that it would cost more to defend than, in the long run, it would yield in revenue. If such ideas were there in the background they were not formulated by politicians.[24] What was blindingly obvious was that possession of the duchy of Milan was, for economic and geopolitical reasons, the key to general dynastic politics. When all these forces are joined with the dynastic claims of Charles VIII to the kingdom of Naples as inheritor of the first and second houses of France–Anjou, claims which were only operative after 1482 and were, of course, absent in the formulation of earlier policies towards Italy by the French crown; and when we remember the claims of Louis XII as descendant of the Visconti dukes of Milan, then the fatal convergence between opportunity and rights stands revealed.[25]

In fact, despite some brilliant successes which had the effect of permanently dislocating the relations between the Italian states, French policy in Italy after 1494 produced very mixed results that convey an air of ultimate futility. On his return from Naples in 1494, Charles VIII only narrowly escaped defeat at Fornovo (July 1495). An agreement with Spain to divide Naples at the treaty of Alcalà (November 1497) was a short-term solution. Louis XII successfully conquered Milan in 1499 but French forces in Naples were defeated on the Garigliano in December 1503 and Louis was pushed out of the kingdom by Ferdinand. The French successfully suppressed the revolt of Genoa in 1508 but their engagement in the War of the League of Cambrai against Venice did not produce the desired result for Louis, despite his personal victory at Agnadello in May 1509. Pope Julius II's Holy Alliance for driving the French out of Italy next brought the Swiss in against France. The French defeated the Spaniards and their allies in the hard-fought and bloody battle of Ravenna in April 1512 but their general, Gaston de Foix, was killed and they had to withdraw from the Romagna. By now Louis XII was himself faced by a coalition of the Pope, Maximilian, Ferdinand of Aragon, England and the Swiss and was forced to seek the alliance of the Venetians he had attacked in 1508. The defeat of the French army at Novara in June 1513 by the Swiss allies of the Pope swept French power out of Lombardy, established Swiss power there and gave Henry VIII of England the opportunity to come in against France to capture Thérouanne and Tournai, isolated French outposts in the Artois and Flanders.[26]

Despite its great reputation, the French army in the sixteenth century was to experience mixed fortunes, especially in the 1520s. This was despite the fact that the greater part of the state's energies was channelled into its organisation. In part this resulted from the conflict of conservative and innovative tendencies. The reputation of French power stemmed from the reorganisation of the military carried out under Charles VII between 1445 and 1448 that proved so effective against the English in the campaigns of 1449–53. This had formed the nucleus of a powerful artillery train and placed the heavy cavalry, the *gendarmerie*, on a firm basis supported by permanent taxation. The *gendarmerie* was a largely noble formation and from the late 1470s provided employment for around 3000–4000 'lances' (depending on the requirements of the crown), that is 9000–12,000 men. Although their reputation and prestige were high, the key to success in warfare lay increasingly in the organisation of an effective infantry and here France was at a disadvantage. Attempts at creating a 'national' infantry from Louis XI in 1479–81 to the 'legions' created by Francis I in 1534 proved unsatisfactory and France had to rely increasingly on foreign mercenaries, Swiss pikes and German lansquenets, for its crack formations down to 1559. Needless to say, periodic payment problems meant that they were not entirely reliable. France also adapted to the new arm of infantry equipped with firepower relatively slowly and learned a severe lesson in the defeat of Pavia in 1525.[27]

Warfare was to remain largely static in the sixteenth century and, despite some spectacular battles, revolved around siege operations. Here France was much better placed to maintain its position so that, while campaigns in Italy proved ultimately sterile, the defence of the kingdom could be sustained. The first half of the century saw the increasing elaboration of an effective war commissariat that was capable of paying, feeding and moving armies over limited distances and also of providing the crucial artillery support for siege warfare. All around the frontiers of France, new fortresses or refortified cities, often designed by Italian engineers, rendered invasion of the kingdom increasingly difficult.

In the late fifteenth century, commissioning and moving armies of 20,000 for the invasion of Italy were major operations. Francis I had 70,000 men on all fronts in 1542 (nearly 50,000 of them foreign). By the 1550s, Henri II was commanding armies of 50,000 on the northern front, though this could not be sustained

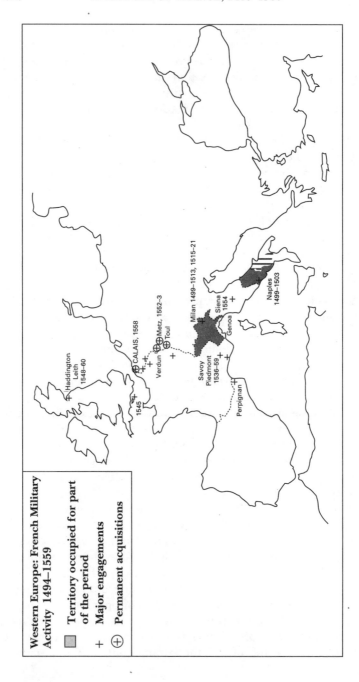

Western Europe: French Military Activity 1494–1559

Territory occupied for part of the period

+ Major engagements

⊕ Permanent acquisitions

Haddington
Leith
1548–60

1545

CALAIS, 1558

Verdun   Metz, 1552–3
         Toul

Milan 1499–1513, 1515–21

Siena
1554

Genoa

Savoy
Piedmont
1536–59

Naples
1499–1503

Perpignan

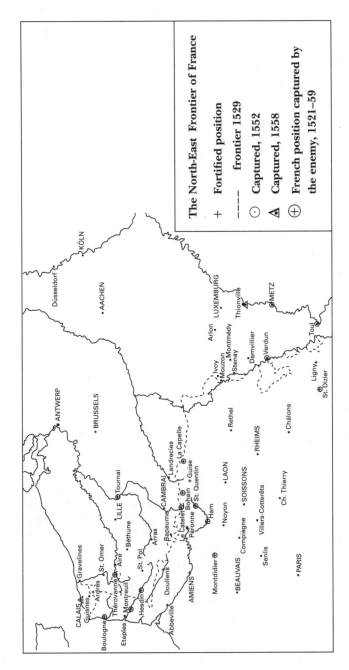

The North-East Frontier of France

+   Fortified position

----   frontier 1529

⊙   Captured, 1552

▲   Captured, 1558

⊕   French position captured by
       the enemy, 1521–59

Map 7   Battles and Sieges Involving French Forces, 1490–1560

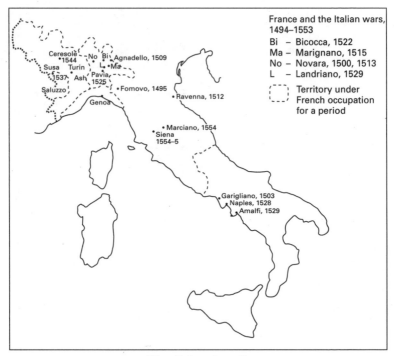

France and the Italian wars,
1494–1553

Bi – Bicocca, 1522
Ma – Marignano, 1515
No – Novara, 1500, 1513
L – Landriano, 1529

[⌐ ¬]   Territory under
[⌐ _]   French occupation
          for a period

Ceresole
1544
Susa   Turin
1537   Ash
Saluzzo
Genoa
No Bi Agnadello, 1509
L Ma
Pavia,
1525
Fomovo, 1495
Ravenna, 1512
Marciano, 1554
Siena
1554–5
Garigliano, 1503
Naples, 1528
Amalfi, 1529

Map 7 (continued)

for more than two or three years. The costs of the military were a
major problem and shortage of money undermined French campaigns in Italy during the 1520s. It was, however, only really in the
1550s that expenditure on warfare became an impossible
burden.[28] (For the figures, see Appendix IV.)

The immediate preoccupation of Francis I on his accession was
the vindication of his rights in Italy. He needed to re-establish the
honour of the French crown and satisfy the thirst of the French
military nobility for revenge by mounting a new expedition to
Milan. His victory against the Swiss at Marignano (13–14
September 1515), which so redounded to his credit, was won by
good fortune, by old-fashioned tactics of hard slog and the
belated arrival of the Venetians, against technically superior
infantry.[29] The consequence, paradoxically, was to establish the
need for a permanent alliance with the Swiss cantons in French
diplomacy in order to ensure the services of the Swiss pikes and

also, of course, to establish the French administration in northern Italy just at the time that the Habsburg dynastic empire was about to take full shape. Conflict over the dominance of the plains of Lombardy was probably inevitable given these ingredients and once the French king had failed in his bid to get himself elected Holy Roman Emperor in 1519.

The emerging threat of the Habsburg dynastic empire was registered perhaps only slowly. The marriage treaty that had arranged the alliance between Louis XII's oldest daughter, Claude, and the young Charles of Habsburg (1503) had been designed to reach a settlement over Naples. However, it was viewed widely as a threat to the kingdom's ultimate integrity and rejected by the specially convoked Assembly of Estates in 1506 in favour of her marriage to Francis of Angoulême, the future Francis I. Yet Francis was able to agree a favourable treaty with Charles in March 1515 in order to free his hand for the invasion of Italy in that year. Treaties between France and the Habsburgs at Noyon in 1516 and Cambrai in 1517 give the impression that French policy could work much along the lines prevalent under Louis XII, with France in periodic alliance with the Habsburgs for the sake of its manoeuvres in Italy. These treaties were probably themselves no more than delaying tactics. The Treaty negotiated at London by cardinal Wolsey, the so-called treaty of Universal Peace, has been much discussed as a possible framework for international arbitration that was derailed by events. It should perhaps be better viewed as one more short-term expedient. The deaths of king Ferdinand in Spain (1516) and of the emperor Maximilian (1519) brought the imminent prospect of a vast accumulation of territories under the sceptre of a ruler with ancestral claims to Burgundy, and French policy seems to have become preoccupied by a major confrontation.

The candidature put forward by Francis for the imperial throne was not such a wild throw as it has sometimes appeared, the kings of France having from time to time put their claims forward over previous centuries. Although French envoys shrewdly denied their master's ambition claiming that the Empire would be more of a burden than an asset to the French crown, in the context of 1519 the plan registered the awareness of the French government that a new sort of threat was emerging. The strategy misfired because the French (who spent 400,000 *écus* in bribes) failed to understand that the Electors were simply using their bargaining power. Even though

Francis affected to take it 'in good part', his agents were not slow to underline the 'incredible treasons' of French allies.[30]

The threat of a Habsburg emperor was much more evident from the 1520s. Soon after his accession, an English envoy had reported that Francis I's aim was 'that the monarchy of Christendom shall rest under the banner of France as it was wont to do'. From 1519, it was the emperor who was pictured thus. At first this was done in terms of the emperor's dynastic claims but soon French diplomats began to spread the idea that Charles V was aiming at universal domination, what they called the *monarchie* of all Christendom. This became a theme of French diplomacy for the next generation. At first there was some restraint. In his letters for the forced loan of August 1527, Francis I declared that, had it not been for the League of Cognac, the emperor 'would by now have been *monarque* of all Italy'. Until the very end of his reign and after several agreements and projects to cooperate, Francis I was still telling his ambassadors that Charles's policy 'continues to be to make himself *monarque*', while d'Urfé, ambassador at Rome, could inform Henri II in 1551 of the emperor's continued will to be 'seul Dominateur' of Italy. For the Gallican lawyer Charles Dumoulin, Charles V was a tyrant emperor who had subverted the Empire by turning against the princes and allying with the Pope. Jean de Fraisse, a subtle and experienced diplomat of the 1540s and 1550s, wrote of the emperor that he 'does nothing except by artifice', of 'his extreme ambition', and that 'never did prince work to carry off the states of others more than did the Emperor'. He had corrupted the princes and 'debauched' the king of England into his alliance. This remained a theme of French diplomatic propaganda until the end of Charles V's reign.[31]

The experience of Fraisse in negotiations with the princes and cities of Germany is useful in that it alerts us to one of the major themes of French foreign policy after 1520. There seems no reason to doubt that Francis willingly precipitated war with the emperor in 1521 with a number of pretexts. The loss first of Tournai (1521) and then of Milan with the battle of Bicocca (1522), made the stakes much higher. Given the French commitment to Italy as well as the looming power of an emperor with so many states and the dominion of the Indies, how was France to respond? The answer was to increase her military strength but also to construct a network of alliances which might 'restrain' the 'monarchical' ambitions of the emperor. This network took shape only slowly and with much trial and error.

One of the most difficult aspects of this was the relationship with the England of Henry VIII. England had played a cautious diplomatic game until 1512 but its interests linked it inevitably to those of the rulers of the Low Countries. The rapprochement of 1518 that led to the return to France of Thérouanne and Tournai presaged what was obviously an attempt to line up England on the French side.[32] The culmination of this was the greatest piece of diplomatic theatre in the sixteenth century, the Field of the Cloth of Gold staged near Calais in 1520. The reasons for the failure of this negotiation have been much debated and are linked not only to the adverse effects of personal relations but also to the fact that English interests were more naturally led at the time into alliance with the Habsburgs and war with France. The machinery of international mediation set up in 1518 became, at Calais in 1521, a means of maintaining English 'face' while allowing Henry VIII to come in on the emperor's side.[33] Anglo-French war began in 1522. However, the failure of Henry VIII to press home the advantage presented by the emperor's capture of Francis I at Pavia in 1525 is also revealing. It did not take much of Louise of Savoy's astute diplomacy to convince Henry that his interests would not be served by the complete triumph of the emperor.[34] The following negotiations conducted by Wolsey, including the treaties of More and Amiens, ushered in a remarkable period of Anglo-French understanding (to the point of tentative military cooperation against the Habsburgs in 1528–9) that came to fruition in the second meeting between the two kings at Boulogne in 1532 and the attempt by Henry VIII to enlist the French king in support for negotiations over his divorce.[35] France had briefly detached England, during a period rendered unusual because of the English king's matrimonial problems, from its normal alignment with the Netherlands and thus shifted the overall balance of diplomacy. England, largely neutralised by internal problems, would not return to the path of war with France again until 1543.

Elsewhere, the aim of French foreign policy was to open up as many avenues for counterbalancing the emperor as possible. There was in any case a long tradition of protective or friendly relations between France and the princes of the Rhineland. When, by the end of the 1520s, the promulgation of state

Reformations placed those princes – notably Philip of Hesse and the Elector Palatine – in opposition to the emperor (for instance over the restoration of the duke of Württemberg to his estates in 1534), the way was open for French diplomats such as the able and experienced brothers Jean and Guillaume du Bellay to establish the links that were to come to fruition in the 1550s. The formation of the Schmalkaldic League formed a basis on which to build and in 1534, Francis met Philip of Hesse at Bar-le-duc. From 1536, the 'pension' that had been paid to the king of England and had been reactivated in 1525 was diverted to the German princes. Germany was vital for reasons other than diplomatic; it constituted the most important source of mercenaries for the French crown, troops without whom it would have been impossible to have a credible military strategy. On the other hand, the emergence of a much more hostile policy towards heresy in France in 1534 certainly rendered negotiation with the German princes more difficult, though not impossible. One of the main themes to be observed is the balancing of religious and diplomatic policies to the needs of the moment. This did not always work successfully, as was to be seen in the middle of the 1540s, but matters were handled with greater care after 1550.[36]

French diplomats were ranging far afield by the 1530s. In Scandinavia they cultivated Christian III of Denmark and Gustavus Vasa of Sweden. In Italy, it was necessary to rebuild some sort of diplomatic base from scratch. Francis I had entered the Holy League of Cognac with the Italian states and Papacy in 1526, only seriously to misjudge and mismanage the affair. Venice was by now warily neutral in the European struggle, anxious to avoid the repetition of the catastrophes of 1508–12, fully aware of the near power of the Habsburgs and determined to maintain correct relations. The destruction of the Florentine Republic in 1530 and the restoration of the Medici family removed the last important ally of France in the peninsula. A start was made by the conclusion of the negotiations with Pope Clement VII at Marseilles with a marriage alliance between the house of France and the non-ruling Medici in 1533. From there, we see the beginning of a policy which was to guide French interests in Italy over the next century, the bolstering of the 'stati liberi' wherever possible. It was for this reason that the struggle over the succession to the small duchies of Parma and Piacenza from 1547 was to usher in a new phase of warlike and active French policy in Italy in the 1550s.[37]

Finally, the French crown had no scruples in establishing a working relationship with Ottoman power from the 1530s onwards. Its agreement in 1534 with the Ottoman ally and corsair Barbarossa helped the latter to overthrow Muley Hassan of Tunis, the emperor's ally. In 1536, Jean de La Forêt was in Constantinople holding talks with the Grand Vizir which seem to have produced an informal agreement to cooperate. This in effect came to fruition with the joint French and Turkish naval attack on Nice in 1543 and the subsequent wintering of Barbarossa's fleet at Toulon. Even Francis I was to find this too embarrassing.[38]

Given the slow and sometimes unsuccessful practice of diplomacy along these lines, can any broad continuities be observed in French objectives throughout the period? It has often been argued by French diplomatic historians that the period after 1540 saw a welcome move away from the wasteful wars of magnificence to the pursuit of a more hard-headed strategy of the attainment of natural frontiers, away from Italy to the security of the north and north-east borders of the kingdom. This should be treated with some caution.[39] The most obvious element of continuity in French policy throughout the period was the obsession with Italy and, though there are undoubted signs that other problems were being taken more seriously by the mid-sixteenth century, there is not much diminution in the fascination with Italy. What changed were the possibilities and limitations of policy.

The renewal of French interest in Italy with the League of Cognac and the declaration of a new war with the emperor in 1528 had been premature, though understandable given the king's need to recover possession of his two sons exchanged in return for his release from captivity in 1526. The disintegration of Lautrec's army at Naples and the loss of the count of Saint-Pol's army at Landriano seemed to destroy French hopes in Italy. The treaty negotiated at Cambrai by Louise of Savoy and Margaret of Austria (3 August 1529) was more important than that of Madrid in that it provided a more realistic framework for settling the dynastic disputes.[40] While it confirmed French abandonment of suzerainty over Artois and Flanders (rights not to be underestimated) it set aside the Habsburg claim to Burgundy.

The diplomatic offensives of the early and mid-1530s were plainly designed to permit the renewal of prosecution of war in Italy. This was duly precipitated by the death of Francesco Sforza of Milan (a duchy already under Habsburg military control) and claims to the duchy made by Francis on behalf of his second son. The emperor was unwilling to contemplate this and eventually invested his son Philip with the duchy. The invasion of Savoy by the French in January 1536 was designed as a bargaining counter and could only lead to full-scale war once the emperor had returned from Tunis.[41] Although he had the opportunity of sweeping the French out of Piedmont, he opted for a fruitless summer invasion of Provence that ruined his army and added to Montmorency's reputation for prudent command. The *grand maître* added to this in the spring 1537 campaign in Artois, designed as a reply to the Habsburg invasion of Picardy in the summer of 1536. In the north, honours were more or less even when the truce of Bomy was concluded with the Netherlands government in July 1537. This released Montmorency's troops for an attack in Piedmont through the pass of Susa that relieved French garrisons and earned the king's gratitude in the form of the Constable's sword in February 1538.

For the next two years, Montmorency's control of foreign policy led to a serious attempt, with papal prompting, at reconciliation with the emperor. It is significant that the rival dynastic claims were so difficult to settle that the outcome was the truce (rather than a treaty) at Nice (June 1538) but the subsequent meeting of the sovereigns at Aigues-Mortes gave substance to the policy. The emperor's passage through France in 1539 gave Francis I reason to think the Constable's idea of regaining Milan through a marriage deal with the Habsburgs might work. In fact, there was never very much hope of this once Charles V was confronted with the real possibility of having to evacuate Lombardy. The French king's sense of betrayal was perhaps rather synthetic but it had a disastrous effect on his confidence in Montmorency, whose star began to sink in the middle of 1540. By the summer of 1541 he was excluded from influence and new policies were the order of the day, especially when the French diplomat-spies Rincon and Fregoso were murdered by imperial agents in Italy.[42]

The fighting of 1536–8 had seen some important developments on the northern frontiers. When war began again in July 1542, after the emperor's failure at Algiers, campaigns were planned on two fronts: in the north in Luxemburg and in the south at Perpignan. Both were unsuccessful and in the meantime France effectively lost the diplomatic and military neutrality of England. After the coolness of the years 1538–40 (when France could afford to spurn English interests) a serious effort was made to win back the alliance of Henry VIII. This was in vain since Henry by May 1542 had probably opted for the Habsburg alliance but was keeping his options open in order to increase his bargaining power. French intrigues in Scotland added to Henry's grievances against France, which included the non-payment of his pension since 1536, while his aggressive moves in Scotland during 1542 threatened the independence of an important small ally of France. The Anglo-imperial agreement was struck in February 1543 and war was declared between France and England in June 1543.[43]

A notable French victory at Ceresole in Piedmont, won by the Bourbon count of Enghien in February 1544, was much celebrated in France but could not lead anywhere. France was now on the defensive and faced by a double offensive in the summer. That the invasions led in person by Charles V and Henry VIII were not more disastrous is to be explained by the capacity of France to conduct defence in depth. The holding up of the two invading armies at Saint-Dizier and Boulogne seriously weakened them, while French troops were kept in reserve.[44] The fact that Boulogne was lost and could not be recaptured immediately immensely complicated relations with England for the rest of the decade. The peace agreed between the two sovereigns at Crépy in September had advantages for both sides. Charles was in an awkward situation and was able to disentangle himself. Francis was able to clear his territory of the enemy with little loss. The treaty was a more solid agreement than the truce of Nice in that it contained provisions for settling dynastic claims and frontier disputes. Moreover, the religious dimension of foreign policy was secretly dealt with by an agreement to cooperate against heresy. Charles was considering the option of asserting himself in Germany at last. Francis was surrounded by advisers who were warning of the spread of heresy.

Except for unfinished business with the English and in Scotland, this was Francis I's last war. That was not, however, his intention since it is more than likely that the emperor's successes in Germany during 1546 and 1547 would have led to new conflicts. The death of the king's youngest son Charles in September 1545 removed the prince for whom the treaty of Crépy had stipulated a negotiated return of Milan. France was deeply involved in negotiations with the Schmalkaldic princes, its policy to some extent checked by divisions at home over a Protestant alliance and uncertainty about what to do. Francis I instructed his envoy Bassefont Taine in November 1546: 'proceed carefully without committing yourself except when it might serve to prolong their war.'[45]

The foreign policy of Henri II was at first, under the restored influence of Montmorency, cautious. Nevertheless, there is good reason to suppose that the new king intended some notable feat in order to establish his reputation in the approved way. Diplomatically, this was prepared by the stimulation of conflict in Italy over the succession to Parma, the frustration as far as possible of English designs in Scotland by the despatch of significant military aid, and the extension of French contacts in Germany. Henri's accession coincided with a rupture between Pope Paul III and the emperor and he took the opportunity to seal a Franco-Farnese alliance by agreeing the marriage of his natural daughter Diane with Orazio Farnese, the Pope's grandson (June 1547; the marriage was celebrated in 1551). The murder by imperial agents of Paul III's son, Pier Luigi duke of Parma (September 1547), initiated a struggle for control of the strategic duchy of Parma and Piacenza, a revival of French interests throughout the peninsula, stirrings of discontent at Siena and, in August 1548, a full-scale French military display of force in Piedmont. The unusually well preserved correspondence between the king and the Constable in September–November 1548 gives us an insight into their thinking. The emperor, Montmorency said, had only one main objective: to weaken the king by cutting off his allies in Germany, breaking his alliance with the Pope, supporting the English, reinforcing his troops in Italy and preventing the Swiss from renewing their alliance with France. Montmorency's main advice was to stir the pot in Germany: 'the Emperor can be more damaged in Germany by our spending 100,000 *écus* there than he could be by our making war elsewhere for a million.' French policy was never to be so sharply focused. Deceptive offers by the emperor were seen by the king as giving him space to deal more aggressively with the English in Scotland and Boulogne.[46]

   Lucien Romier viewed French foreign policy in these years in terms of the tension between the Constable's cautious and rational approach, supported by career diplomats like Jean de Morvillier, and the adventurism of the Guise. The king himself was diffident and inclined towards the north. French policy in Italy was therefore an anomaly in the circumstances, driven by Guise family ambition.[47] This polarises the issue excessively and does not take account enough of the king himself. It is more than likely that the king's bellicosity was encouraged firstly by the Neapolitan and Tuscan exiles in France who were anxious to draw French attentions back to Italy. Catherine de Medici herself was resentful at what she considered the usurpation of her rights in Florence by the junior branch of her family led by Grand Duke Cosimo. It is certainly the case that the king's Guise favourites had interests both in Scotland and in Italy. Their alliance with the Estes of Ferrara by the marriage of François, the second duke, to Anne, daughter of Ercole II and Renée de France, gave them an incentive to work for the transfer of the duchy of Parma to Ercole, who already held the nearby county of La Mirandola. In May 1551, however, the French crown formally became 'protector' of duke Ottavio of Parma (Orazio's brother) and the way was open for French forces to intervene against the papal and imperial troops. The election of a new pro-imperial Pope, Julius III, in November 1549 had not interrupted the French policy of support for the Farnese. In July 1552 a meeting of French allies in Italy at Chioggia decided on intervention in Siena against the Medici allies of the emperor.[48]

   French policy in Italy should not be seen in isolation but as part of a wider view of supporting states which could damage the emperor. The device of 'protection' was a theme of French foreign policy everywhere in these years. The removal of Mary Stuart from Scotland prepared the way for Henri to make claims to a 'protectorate' of sorts over that kingdom.[49] In July 1548, he told his ambassador in London to declare that he was obliged 'to the protection, defence and conservation of the said kingdom of Scotland as of my own'. It was the collapse of English military power in Scotland and the effect of Henri II's brief campaign to Boulogne in August–September 1549 that eventually produced the treaty of Boulogne in March 1550. This initiated a period of unusually close relations between the Northumberland regime in

England and the French court. In 1550, Henri II declared that, having pacified Scotland and obeyed in France, 'I have joined another to them, in England, so that the three kingdoms together may now be regarded as one monarchy.'[50]

'Protection' was taken to its full extent in the complex and subtle negotiations with the German Protestant princes handled by Sébastien de L'Aubespine and Jean de Fraisse in these years. As dauphin, Henri II had been proposed in 1546 as an alternative to the emperor in a new imperial election and French envoys began to raise the idea of the king of France as 'protector of German liberties'. In the context of imperial dominance after the battle of Mühlberg, such ideas could readily be used to play on the fears and cupidity of rulers like Maurice of Saxony. The German Protestants were eager to settle the outstanding dispute between the French and English as a prelude to a new French intervention in Germany and made strenuous efforts in 1549. Serious talks began between the German princes and French agents in 1550. The treaty of Torgau in May 1551 created a new union of princes dedicated to the 're-establishment of German liberties'. On the table was the proposal for Henri II to take over Metz, Toul and Verdun as 'imperial vicar' and even to be elected emperor himself. In the event, it was the former proposal that was pursued, though the king made it clear that he intended to protect the princes, not the Reformed religion. These terms, with guarantees of French military backing for the princes and German promises to join an attack on the Low Countries, were agreed by the king at Blois in July 1551 and eventually formulated in the treaty of Lochau (October 1551) and ratified at Chambord in January 1552.[51]

By this time, general war between France and the emperor had already begun. The reason was the suspicion of French military preparations against the Netherlands. In May 1551, Henri II had come to an agreement with the Turks for naval cooperation against the Pope and the emperor in the western Mediterranean. Even though Julius was ultimately intimidated, the threat of the descent of French troops into Italy stood. For all these reasons, diplomatic relations were broken off in July 1551. War began in the autumn and was accompanied by another of the emperor's now traditional manifestos against the perfidy of the French king.[52] So opened the last, and most destructive, phase of the Habsburg–Valois wars. Campaigns were to extend along the entire northern and eastern frontiers of France (and well into the Low Countries), Lorraine and Italy.

Although the campaign that assured the control of Metz in the spring of 1552 was a great success and the holding of the city against the emperor's counter-attack in the autumn even more so, that was about the limit of solid French successes. The campaigns of 1553 and 1554 in the southern Low Countries were inconclusive except for the definitive loss by the French of Thérouanne and Hesdin (where Orazio Farnese was killed) in June–July 1553. The victory of Renty in the Boulonnais (August 1554) was without consequence and the large-scale royal armies ranging along the Low Countries frontier and into the Ardennes achieved little except massive devastation. In Italy, a war of attrition was being waged between Piedmont and Lombardy and French troops were used to bolster up Parma against the imperial siege. Above all, in July 1552 the people of Siena revolted against Florence in the name of a French king who declared himself their 'protector' and the 'war of Siena' had begun, with more and more French aid being channelled into the defence of the city. Despite French successes against the Genoese in Corsica (where French allies were led by Sampiero Corso), the outcome was yet another disaster for French arms, the complete defeat of marshal Piero Strozzi at Marciano (August 1554), following closely the death of his admiral brother Leone, the prior of Capua. This enabled the imperial forces to close the siege of Siena, which was, however, well stocked and capable of holding out until its capitulation in April 1555.[53]

A sense of exhaustion led first to tentative peace talks at Marck near Calais in May 1555 and then to further serious discussions at Vaucelles in the winter, leading to a general truce signed there in February 1556. The stage of European politics was already beginning to change. In 1553, with the accession of Mary I, England had passed into the Habsburg orbit. Between October 1555 and January 1556, Charles V abdicated all his titles except that of emperor to his son Philip. But the truce was never more than a pause for the great powers. Pope Paul IV (a Neapolitan) was an irreconcilable enemy of the Habsburgs and provoked an invasion of the papal states by the Spanish viceroy in September 1556. The despatch of a powerful French army to his aid under the duke of Guise was already under way when the truce of Vaucelles broke down as a result of a raid led by Coligny, governor of Picardy, on

Lens in January 1557. In June 1557 England declared war on France. The final phase had begun.[54]

The outcome was decided, not by events in Italy but by the invasion of France commanded by duke Emmanuel-Philibert of Savoy in the summer of 1557. The attempt by Montmorency to relieve the besieged town of Saint-Quentin with a small army was smashed and the Constable was captured on 10 August. With the duke of Guise in Italy, northern France was in a perilous position, although the besieged towns held out long enough (until the end of August) for the government to begin the assembly of a new army and recall the duke of Guise from Italy. He made the journey rapidly, leaving most of his army behind. Guise received his orders at Rome on 14 September and was back at court by the first days of October. There, he was given the post of *Lieutenant-général* of the kingdom and took command of a new army, which he moved north to besiege Calais. The English fortress surrendered on 7 January 1558.[55]

The duke of Guise added immeasurably to his reputation by this coup as well as by his subsequent successes against Thionville and Arlon in the Ardennes (June). The effects of the triumph were muted by the severe defeat that the French army suffered at the hands of the Habsburg and English forces when, under Paul de Termes, it crossed the frontier towards Dunkirk and Gravelines (13 July). Although the king assembled one of the largest French armies yet seen at Pierrepont in Picardy at the end of July it did no more than manoeuvre along the Somme. Henri II was already tired of the duke of Guise's dominance. The captured Constable was working hard at peace negotiations in order to recover his liberty and power at court. Having established the agenda, Montmorency visited his master at the camp of Amiens on 10 October and proceeded to lay all the problems that had built up since the breaking of the truce of Vaucelles at the door of the Guise. Talks opened at Cercamp on 12 October.

The accumulated problems of 60 years were too difficult to sort out in this first session. A truce was concluded and the talks ajourned on 30 November. In the recess, the implications of Elizabeth I's accession in England and the return of Montmorency to full power in France could be digested. The peace conference reopened in neutral territory at Le Cateau-en-Cambrésis at the start of February 1559 with both major participants (if not the

crown had always sought in its public pronouncements to gal-
vanise support. In the orders to stage public celebrations of victories, Te Deums or processions to intercede with God at times of
disaster, there was a rudimentary attempt to incorporate the
enthusiasm of the urban establishment. In the towns of northern
France, we note processions and bonfires to mark the victory of
Marignano, processions on the news of Pavia, and Te Deums for
the alliance with the Pope the same year, processions for peace in
1529, processions for the truce of Nice in 1538 and sermons to
explain it, thanksgivings for the peace of Crépy in 1544, bonfires
and prayers at news of peace with England in 1546 and, for the
treaty of Cateau-Cambrésis, great bonfires and sermons.[60]

Francis I occasionally appeared at Paris in order to drum up
support for war loans or special taxes. In October 1522, he came to
support such a loan and a tax for the infantry. In July 1523, he
spoke to the notables at the town hall about the need to send an
army to Italy to recover his duchy of Milan and in March 1524 to
the same assembly expounded the 'great envies' of other princes
against the kingdom and the treachery of Bourbon. Francis also
used assemblies of local estates to vocalise support, as for instance
in the rejection of the Treaty of Madrid.[61] Henri II resumed these
declarations in the 1550s. In January 1552, he spoke to the
Parlement of Paris to justify the campaign shortly to be launched
into the Empire on the basis of a just response to the wrongs done
by Charles V and the need to restore 'Germanic liberty'. Most striking was his long speech to the Assembly of the Three Estates called
at Paris for 5 January 1558. Firstly defending the renewal of war as
caused by the need to succour allies who could not honourably be
abandoned, he outlined the course of war since 1557 and the
'deep wounds' sustained. The expenses of replacing the forces lost
in August 1557 had been so great 'he had been astonished' and
the enemy's preparations for war in the coming year and the sufferings of his subjects at the hands of 'barbarians' required the formation of a greater army than had ever been seen before. This
could not be done 'without the aid of his good and loyal subjects'
to whose honour and that of their wives and children he finally
appealed. Secretary Fresne, who recorded this speech, thought he
spoke 'so discretely and with such gravity and softness that it would
be difficult to describe his grace'. The conclusion of the assembly
to vote a forced loan was helped by news of the victory of Calais. As

English) determined on peace. The interlocking treaties between France and England and those between France and Spain and Savoy were signed on 2 and 3 April 1559. The conditions were controversial. England agreed to leave Calais in French hands for eight years only (a face-saving formula). Navarre was left to Spain (a conclusion highly unwelcome to Antoine de Bourbon and fuel to his discontent). It is probably the case that old dynastic claims to Italy that had started the wars off had by now sunk into the background in the calculations of policy-makers. What was needed was an acceptance of the reality that the costs of war had got out of hand. The marriage alliances included in the treaty were entirely traditional devices for the assurance of peace. Most other conquests were restored: Saint-Quentin and the other Picard towns were to be restored and French conquests in Italy and Luxemburg handed back. Mechanisms were set up for the definitive settlement of the disputed frontier between France and Artois. Above all, Savoy and Piedmont were to be evacuated in stages. In effect, French Italian ambitions were liquidated. There was much huffing and puffing from the military nobility, who took the view that all this was a humiliation for France and a liquidation of its hard-won gains. However, we should distinguish between the remarks of aristocrats and military memoirists and the sentiments of the population as a whole, which was desperate for peace.[56]

It may reasonably be doubted how definitive the Treaty of Cateau-Cambrésis was meant to be. There had been other comprehensive settlements (Madrid, Cambrai, Crépy). None had held. The difference was that France in the spring of 1559 was on the eve of a political crisis that was to neutralise its foreign policy for a generation.

During the period 1494 to 1559, two years out of three were years of war, yet by the treaty of Cateau-Cambrésis all France had to show for her military prowess were the towns of Metz, Toul and Verdun in the Empire, occupied in 1552, and Calais, reconquered in January 1558. Of the whole Italian enterprise, virtually nothing was left. On the other hand, France maintained its territorial integrity despite the power of the Habsburgs and some great military disasters. The explanations for this must be sought firstly in the nature of a diplomatic system that enabled France ultimately to balance the power of the Habsburgs and secondly in the military organisation that, while failing in terms of aggression, assured the defence of the kingdom.

War and Public Opinion

In all departments, the burden of war contributions rose sharply in the 1550s as the culmination of a lengthy process at work since the earlier years of the century when, as has been seen, the cost had been to some extent exported. The balancing of French and Habsburg power led to a period of obstinate attrition on both sides. How, finally, did the people of France respond to the burden? As has been seen, the right of the crown to control foreign policy went unchallenged and public discourse was monopolised by those who glorified war. Their rhetoric of honour and their preoccupations were assumed by kings to be shared by their subjects.[57]

The nobles, above all, were assumed to share such ideas. When Brantôme praised the truce of Vaucelles in 1556 as 'so advantageous for all France' and argued that its breaking was 'so unhappy', he was referring to the disasters that followed rather than praising peace in itself. Jean Bouchet's panegyric of La Trémoïlle saw his hero as fighting for 'honour', 'loyalty' and 'fidelity' to 'the kings of the house of France'. The lawyer Jean du Tillet put it differently: the role of the nobles was 'to fight for the country and for the extension of the frontiers (*limites*) or to prevent the least of our villages from being overrun and pillaged by foreigners'. Military memoirists naturally thought of war positively. Blaise de Monluc, recalling his youth and entry into a military life, said he had to 'make known the name of Monluc' as the eldest of six children sired by a father who had sold most of his patrimony. For him, 'the days of peace were like years'. The attitude has been called that of a 'military Utopia'.[58]

How far was there a 'public opinion' about war beyond the nobility? Under Louis XII, the theatrical guild of the Parlement clerks, the *Basoche*, much given to irreverent entertainments, was coopted to stage satires of the king's Italian enemies: Sforza, the Venetians, the Pope, the Swiss and Maximilian were all pilloried. However, such entertainments were increasingly frowned on under Francis I, when other methods had to be relied on.[59] The

Fresne pointed out, 'when the people see their money well employed and affairs prosperous, they are much more ready to hand over their money than when fortune is against us'.[62]

Such occasions and public declarations of war were highly dramatic manifestations of the relations between the king and his subjects. Normally, it was in the routine *brevets de taille* that most people heard an enunciation of royal policy and a justification for taxes. Year after year, communities were informed that their taxes were needed for the 'guard and defence' of the kingdom or to 'resist the damnable attempts' of the king's enemies to invade. An unusually detailed demand of 1492 listed the need to resist Henry VII and Maximilian, repair fortresses, equip the artillery, supply victuals, to outfit ships to help Perkin Warbeck ('the duke of York') in Ireland, and meet the expenses of the hearth survey demanded by Normandy. In the odd years when there was no war, the 'costs' of negotiating treaties and marriage alliances were invoked. In 1532, the tax demands mentioned the need to resist the enterprises of the Turks, the Moors and other enemies of Christendom as well as the cost of negotiating a 'universal peace'.[63]

How successful the propaganda was is difficult to judge. Although the king might be called upon to keep his troops in order and spare the 'poor people', there was as yet no theoretical framework for envisaging an alternative to the king's personal prerogatives in war and foreign policy. There seems little doubt where the sympathies of town councils lay. The most elaborate theatrical entry of the age staged at Abbeville was the pageant of 1527 for cardinal Wolsey, consisting of four vast allegories of peace as the supreme gift of God.There was also a conventional view that the 'sad and miserable state of war', as it was described at Compiègne in 1552, was in some sense a punishment visited by God on a sinful people. When war opened in 1536, the consul Etienne de Médicis at Le Puy could only comment that 'all the country of Languedoc, Provence and Dauphiné suffered greatly'. Of the tribulations of war in 1542–4 he wrote: 'I think that, of all the sufferings and adversities that fell on the shoulders of the poor people, sin is the cause.'[64]

This, however, does not mean there was no discontent. Nicolas Versoris of Paris recorded profound hostility to the king's foreign adventures in the early 1520s. The people were 'not content' at repeated demands for special war levies and the bourgeois were anxious that the king was leaving his realm undefended because of his obsession with Milan. A contemporary anonymous chronicler claims that the people were 'very oppressed and molested' by all this. By the 1550s, it was possible for individuals privately to express systematic criticism of the obsession with Italy. Etienne Pasquier in 1557 expressed what he thought were the Constable's own sceptical views on the duke of Guise's expedition to Italy: 'I do not see that Italy has served as anything but a grave for us', and, in a summary of the duke's career written in 1563 he added that, although Guise had achieved the signal triumph of actually bringing back his army in one piece, for the most part Italy had been a country that 'allured the French to its conquest only to serve as their cemetery'.[65]

In the 1540s, there were a number of cases where riots broke out as a result of the economic effects of war on business. In 1542, there was an attack at Rouen on a ship being loaded with grain for export at a time when the renewal of war with Charles V had caused shortages and unemployment. At Tours, artisans rioted because of damage to the silk industry. In Languedoc, the outbreak of war in 1541 was thought by the authorities to have aggravated their subsistence crisis. In April 1552, with the king on campaign in alliance with the German Protestant princes, preachers at Paris started to declaim on 'affairs of state to raise the people to rebellion' about the impropriety of an alliance with heretics and the taxation of the church. What alarmed the queen was their presumption in putting their own judgement above that of the king and his council, especially as people were 'easy to provoke to tumult under the guise of zeal and devotion'. She consequently sent orders for a reliable preacher to be commissioned to make out the government's case and stage a procession. What was the case? Essentially, that the enemy was a worse threat than church taxes and, as for the German alliance, the benefits would appear in due course. The seditious preachers were forced to recant so that, afterwards, the cardinal de Bourbon improbably reported that 'all the people returned well edified and disposed to obedience and service to the king'. The link between discussion of policy and the demands of religion is an indicator of the tendency, growing in the later sixteenth century, for debate on foreign policy to widen as its religious implications were worked out.[66]

Added to this was the endemic tension between urban communities and the garrisons quartered on them, manifested in events like the 'day of the lansquenets' at Caen in 1513. The widespread fear of 'mauvais garçons, adventuriers', essentially soldiers out of control, in the early 1520s is another sign of this. Robert Muchembled has called the relations between soldiers and rural communities 'constantly and systematically conflictual' in this period. The way of life of the soldier set him apart and the dividing line between the military and brigandage was fine. Border country, like Artois and Picardy, was territory for recruitment and those who enlisted, often unstable and brutal, were not unnaturally regarded with hostility. The case of the soldier Jean Yver, who in 1488 killed a man he had previously threatened in the forest of Aumale, is fairly typical. The other man had got some friends together and waylaid him but Yver was more used to weapons and killed his enemy. He had to flee the country and did not seek pardon until ten years later. There are many such examples from Artois.[67]

How far were war and foreign policy thought to be for the general good? Gaston Zeller thought that a divergence of interest between the crown and the bourgeoisie over war policy was reflected by the fact that trade continued during hostilities. Louis XI allowed the Rochellais to trade with England in 1472 and an enquiry of 1503 revealed that the merchants of Guyenne carried on trade during war by means of false safe-conducts. The custom of arresting foreigners at the start of war was established by the reign of Francis I but when this was done at Lyon in 1524, the merchants protested that they had always had the privilege of commerce during war except with the English. In response, the king confirmed this and even extended it to the English. In the war of 1528, local 'merchant' truces allowed merchants of Guyenne and the north of France to trade across frontiers. In 1558, Henri II formally issued permission to trade with enemy countries. The conclusion that Zeller reached was that war was the king's business; merchants sought to carry on their trade regardless. The very fact that merchants in Normandy were exporting grain contrary to royal orders in 1543 stimulated riots on the part of the poor, whose interests were different from those of the merchants. War and its impact therefore provoked divergent public responses.[68]

By 1559, although Blaise de Monluc might have castigated the abandonment of strongholds and claims in Italy and it might have seemed that the efforts of two generations had been thrown away, although the allies of France in Italy and Germany felt abandoned, there is no mistaking the sense of relief in the celebrations staged by the *bonnes villes* as, most of all, in Paris, where wine flowed, bread was distributed and bonfires blazed on every hand.

Conclusion

It was in the period from the mid-fifteenth to the mid-sixteenth century that the idea of the state built upon monarchical legitimacy, linked to the capacity of the crown effectively to draw upon the wealth of its subjects as well as to regulate their affairs, was for the first time fully established. Norbert Elias denied, in his classic analysis of the 'civilising process', that the Absolute State was an instrument of class power. Instead, he saw it as a balancing act; no king could face down a whole society but, vis-à-vis individuals or groups, his power would outclass them. If we take Elias's definition of the core of the modern state as the monopoly of violence and of the power to tax, then very significant moves towards this were made in the generations between Louis XI and Henri II. As has been emphasised, the 'rise of the modern state' is a process which should not be artificially allocated to any short period. There are elements of it present from the late thirteenth century and the process continued into the nineteenth. As Colette Beaune showed, the building-blocks for the idea of a French identity were being assembled in the early Middle Ages. However, the emergence of France from the great crisis of the Hundred Years War gave a new impetus to the formation of a French kingdom that would not again fall apart. By 1560, the stage had not yet been reached when governmental collapse was out of the question but the nucleus of a stable system had been established.

France remained, of course, socially and economically a highly diverse country in which communications could be laborious and it was still very much a kingdom of provinces with varied institutions. Some provinces had been incorporated into France very recently; others were governed as apanages into the sixteenth century. A wide array of representative bodies, assemblies of estates and provincial Parlements continued to express regional loyalty as well as representing their interests to the crown. Although French was increasingly the dominant language of the provincial elites, Breton, Basque, Occitan and Provençal continued to be spoken widely. The era of the 'kingdom of Bourges' in the early reign of Charles VII had, however, by locating the centre of the monarchy in the Loire, inaugurated a lengthy process by which parts of the French kingdom which had always been isolated from the nucleus of France, particularly in the south, were more closely integrated into it. This continued in the reigns from Louis XI to Louis XII, when the kings of France still spent the greater part of their time in the Loire region. Not until 1514, for instance, did Louis XII spend nearly half the year in the area of Paris. This changed notably from the start of Francis I's reign since both he and Henri II passed much of their time in the *châteaux* of the Paris region circumscribed by their routine progresses between Saint-Germain-en-Laye, bois de Vincennes, Fontainebleau, Villers-Cotterêts and Compiègne (see Appendix III). Louis XI set a pattern for incessant journeys around his kingdom that his successors maintained. They certainly remained monarchs on the move and undertook lengthy progresses around their kingdom, making the monarchy visible to its subjects. In this they were very different from Henry VIII in England. But there is a certain sense in which the French crown became more focused in a central region around Paris just as the great institutions of administration such as the Parlement of Paris and the Chambre des Comptes were already centred there.

In some ways, the emergence of a sort of 'royal religion' offset the continuing centrifugal forces in French society. The great developments in public ceremonial during the Renaissance, building on earlier traditions but adding both simple and complex messages derived from classical learning, served to bolster the mystique of monarchy. The Most Christian King of the Middle Ages becomes also visibly a conquering Roman Emperor and, for some theorists, the image of God on earth. The sombre and imposing ceremony of the king's funeral, the spectacular arrangements for royal interment, the elevation of the king at his coronation and the inauguration of his mystical healing powers were there to inspire awe. During his reign, the festivities of the court surrounded the monarch in his new palaces with magnificence and the grandeur of the *entrée* saw his subjects parading before him in extravagant devotion. All this reinforced the power of the state without, in France at least, being meant to create a slavish subordination. Legitimate monarchy had to remain highly visible and the king accessible to his subjects. What this meant in practice was that the king had to cultivate the image of 'first gentleman' of the kingdom and treat the nobility with informal familiarity.

Thought about the nature of and the limits to royal power was remarkably diverse in this period. Some theorists placed few practical limits on the exercise of royal power but this was by no means the exclusive or even predominant view. Until the middle of the sixteenth century, plainly anti-monarchical ideas were rare and most thinkers and officials operated within the framework of legitimate monarchy. It is, however, significant that the reign of Henri II with its intense fiscal burden, should have seen the stirrings of a reasoned critique of the monarchical state itself. The Parlement lawyer Etienne de La Boetie may have drafted the first version of his *De la servitude volontaire* in the mid-1550s but he sharpened his attack on the monarchy in the uncertain days of 1561. La Boetie significantly scoffed at symbols such as the *fleur de lys*, the *sainte ampoulle* and the *oriflamme* that he likened to the small devices used by past tyrannies to anchor their power. He professed scepticism about dynastic history and said he would prefer to leave tales of king Clovis to poets like Ronsard. In fact, La Boetie advanced a precociously sophisticated programme of opposition. There was no need to combat tyanny; the answer to it, he argued, was 'that the country should not consent to servitude'. In other words, the people should no longer pay taxes to tyrants: 'if they are given nothing, if they are not obeyed then without a blow they are left naked and defeated and are nothing. Be but resolved to serve no longer and there you are, free'.[1]

Such ideas have been seen as the expression of the determination of a disgruntled *Parlementaire* elite to make its power felt. There is no doubt that relations between the crown and one of the chief organs of authority, the Parlement of Paris, were extremely acrimonious in the 1520s. Despite the actions of Francis I in 1527, those relations began to sour again in the 1550s. However, La Boetie was working within an old anti-tyrant topos in the fraught circumstances of the 1550s that combined fiscal pressure, military failure and growing religious dissension. As for the supposed pressure for more authority from the legal elite, there is no reason to think that the government of France in the Renaissance was an exclusive class preserve. It functioned through the broad participation of the financial oligarchy, the Parlement lawyers, middle ranking nobility and members of the royal affinity. The royal court served as a focus for activity and a generator of loyalty. Its growing magnificence provided, too, a cultural focus that was increasingly to mesmerise the nobility of France.

It was in this period that the nobility first fully realised that the state, rather than being a distant and hostile competitor, had potential as a source of power and profit for itself and could be integrated into its deeply laid patterns of alliance and clientage. Louis XI, beleaguered by conspiracies and threats, was regarded with fear and suspicion by many of the grandees of his time. The contrast with the relationship under rulers like Louis XII and Francis I could not be greater. The main reason why the state retained its stability during the Renaissance was that clientage and monarchy worked together. The king was the supreme patron; through his intimates and favourites, mostly noblemen, the ties of fidelity and loyalty of the rest of the nobility could be integrated into those of the king and his entourage. Louis XI began the grandiose distribution of pensions that was to be a mainstay of the political system of the sixteenth century. Kings, as Jean de Saulx-Tavannes was later to point out, were 'made of the same wood' as their nobles.[2] There was no systematic conflict between crown and nobility.

The stable relationship between the crown and the nobility was, however, a notably fragile one. It depended not only on royal bonhomie and accessibility but also upon the availability of funds to pay salaries, pensions and army pay. For much of the period between the 1490s and the 1550s, the imminent prospect of employment in war for those who needed and wanted it (a large minority of the nobility) was an important source of stability. This was the case despite the periodic conclusions of peace treaties since those treaties were widely understood not to have solved the fundamental dynastic and strategic conflicts until 1559. The fragile nature of the crown's financial resources, revealed in part by the upheavals of the 1520s, was also masked at least in part by the transfer of some of the costs of war to Italy. By the 1550s, this was no longer possible and the financial resources of the state were plainly overstretched.

Etienne Pasquier remarked in 1562 that 'there are three things that should be infinitely feared in any state ... largeness of debts, the minority of a king and disturbance in religion. None of these can fail to bring change to a state.[3] The disturbing burden of high taxes and royal loans was all too apparent by that time. Much of the energy of the state during the Renaissance period was channelled into the raising of taxes and the management of the army. 'Reform' in government, both of justice and finance, was as much an issue as reformation in religion. There is no doubt that there was constant evolution in the governmental organs during this period as well as concentrated changes in some periods. The 1520s saw the great overhaul in the central financial offices associated with the destruction of Semblançay and the rest of 'Messieurs des finances'. The 1530s saw energy concentrated on great *ordonnances* for the reform of the processes of justice and the law courts that should remind us that the French state was still an *état de justice*. The consciousness that access to justice was slow, inequitable and obscure informed many of these changes. Henri II's brief but important reign saw further significant development of the finance administration (the role of the *intendants des finances*, for instance), major attention to the way in which provincial governors worked and, in justice, the creation in 1552 of the new level of the higher courts, the *présidiaux*, with the aim of speeding up justice. Through all this, there is a certain continuity of approach to government from Louis XI to the Wars of Religion: the concentration of real power in a smaller council surrounding the person of the monarch, the maintenance of close and permanent contact of the royal entourage with provincial governors and towns through a vast and complex correspondence, the extension of the council's judgements to the provinces and striking augmentation in the sheer volume of legislation prepared in it.

In religion, it was not within the power of the crown to act decisively. Religious disturbances accelerated between 1559 and 1562. It is worth asking whether it was ever in the power of the crown to head off this trouble. The Gallican traditions of France and of many prominent royal servants naturally gave the crown an interest in the reform of the church both in the late fifteenth century and during the reign of Francis I. On the other hand, the ecclesiastical underpinning of legitimate authority and the crown's foreign policy eventually limited its options to the defence of religious orthodoxy tempered by partial toleration when necessary. The configurations of French society gave to Protestantism a skewed profile, heavily concentrated in the towns and, ultimately, in the southern and western provinces. The revival of an aggressive Catholicism by the 1550s rendered compromise impossible.

The burdens and dislocations of war were obvious for all to see by the end of the 1550s. A preacher at Limoges was arrested in the spring of 1559 for declaring that 'as long as the house of Valois reigns the people will never be free from oppressions since it is too given to tyranny'.[4] This startling anticipation of the Catholic and Protestant invective of the Wars of Religion corresponds closely with the ideas of La Boetie already in circulation. Criticism was also built on the traditions of the critique of secular society by Mendicant preachers whom we have seen at work from the late fifteenth century and was given added impetus by the heavy increase in the tax burden during the reign of Henri II. The end of the wars in 1559 and the partial dismantling of the military machine built up during the 1550s should have eased the stress. In fact, however, problems were accumulating beneath the surface which may not have been fully apparent to contemporaries.

The threats of heresy and schism were, of course, blatant as were the pathological fears they generated of divine wrath. The discovery of the Protestant community in Paris at worship in the rue Saint-Jacques on 4 September 1557, following so quickly upon the alarms of the fall of Saint-Quentin and threats of Spanish invasion, provoked riots that were to set the pattern for religious violence. Beneath the surface, as we have seen, the conditions of life for the mass of the people had taken a distinct turn for the worse in France since the 1530s and 1540s, with the deterioration of purchasing power and consequent growth of poverty and social disorder. These may not in themselves have caused religious violence or civil war but they provide the essential context for them.

Within eighteen months of Henri II's death in July 1559, France had travelled rapidly down the road to civil conflict which was fuelled initially by the factional hatreds within the court nobility that had grown up since the 1540s. These were vastly augmented by what seemed to be the exclusive control of royal power by one clan and its adherents in the house of Lorraine. In May 1561, the diplomat Jean de Morvilliers could write from Lyon that 'for the last year news from court has been on the same theme: of risings, troubles, seditions everywhere in this kingdom. Where the people are incited by malignant spirits, the fire bursts out then dies down in one place after another. Where there is more corruption and licence, so the outcome is most tragic. In many towns the people usurp the office of the magistrate'.[5] This rapid slide towards civil war and communal violence between 1559 and 1561 can only be understood in terms of the social, economic and cultural context. The first full session of the Estates-General since 1484, summoned in 1560 to bolster the factional regime of the Guise, expressed, when it met, not only the accumulated grievances of a generation but also many radical ideas on the conduct of political power, with even the king's control of foreign policy coming into question.

War and religion therefore ultimately destabilised the society of Renaissance France and the workings of noble clientage without an effective crown to control it allowed the formation of rival armies. That France did not disintegrate entirely during nearly 40 years of sometimes savage civil war; that the monarchical state could be so rapidly reconstituted by the entourage of Henri IV at the end of the century, is largely the consequence of the patterns of governance and thought about public power established in the century before 1560. It has been the argument behind this book that the century between Louis XI and the outbreak of the Wars of Religion established a broad enough basis for the identity of France as an aristocratic and royal state for it to survive the next 40 years.

Abbreviations

AD	Archives départementales
AM	Archives municipales
AM	*Annales du Midi*
Amer.H.R.	*American Historical Review*
ANG	*Acta Nuntiaturae Gallicae*
AN	Archives Nationales, Paris
AS	Archivio di Stato
BL	British Library
BM	Bibliothèque municipale
BN	Bibliothèque Nationale, Paris
BEC	*Bibliothèque de l'Ecole des Chartes*
BIHR	*Bulletin of the Institute of Historical Research*
BSHPF	*Bulletin de la Société de l'histoire du Protestantisme français*
Bull.hist.phil.	*Bulletin historique et philologique du comité des travaux historiques*
CAF	*Catalogue des actes de François Ier*
CAH	*Catalogue des actes de Henri II*
CDI	Collection des documents inédits sur l'histoire de France
CNRS	Centre National des Recherches Scientifiques
EHQ	*European History Quarterly*
EHR	*English Historical Review*
ESR	*European Studies Review*
FH	*French History*
FHS	*French Historical Studies*
HHSA	*Haus-, Hof- und Staatsarchiv (Vienna)*
HJ	*Historical Journal*
JMH	*Journal of Modern History*
L&P	*Letters and Papers … of the reign of Henry VIII*
MC	Musée Condé, Chantilly
MSAP	*Mémoires de la Société des Antiquaires de Picardie*
Ordonnances	*Ordonnances des rois de France de la troisième race*
Ordonnances, François Ier	*Ordonnances des rois de France: règne de François Ier*
P&P	*Past and Present*
PWSFH	*Proceedings of the Western Society for French History*
RH	*Revue historique*
RHMC	*Revue d'histoire moderne et contemporaine*
SCJ	*Sixteenth-Century Journal*
SHF	Société de l'histoire de France
St.P.	*State Papers of the Reign of Henry VIII*
TRHS	*Transactions of the Royal Historical Society*

Notes

1. J. du Bellay, *The Defence and Illustration of the French Language* (1549) trans. G.M. Turquet (London, 1939), pp.29–30; Fr. Rabelais, *Oeuvres*, ed. A. Lefranc, III, pp.102–3, *Pantagruel*, bk II, ch. 8; M. Françon, *Autour de la lettre de Gargantua à son fils* (Rochecorbon, 1957), p.68. F. Simone, *Il Rinascimento francese: studi et ricerche* (Turin, 1965), II, ch.5, pp.381–439. J. Burckhardt, *The Civilisation of the Renaissance in Italy*, trans. S.G.C. Middlemore (New York, 1960); G. Voigt, *Die Wiederbelebung des classischen Altertums, oder der erste Jahrhunderts des Humanismus*, 2 vols (Berlin, 1881–2). Certain preconceptions are shared by A. Renaudet, *Préréforme et humanisme à Paris pendant les premières guerres d'Italie (1494–1517)*, 2 vols (Paris, 1953).

2. F. Simone, *Il Rinascimento francese* (Turin, 1964), trans. as *The French Renaissance* (London, 1969); Simone, *La coscienza della Rinascita negli umanisti francesi* (Rome, 1949). For a useful review of the literature on this subject, cf. E. Beltran, 'L'humanisme français au temps de Charles VII et Louis XI', in C. Bozzolo and E. Ornato (eds), *Préludes à la renaissance. Aspects de la vie intellectuelle en France au XVe siècle* (Paris, CNRS, 1992), pp.123–62.

3. B. Guenée, 'L'Histoire de l'état en France à la fin du moyen âge vue par les historiens depuis cent ans', *RH*, 472 (1964), 346 and in his *Politique et histoire au moyen âge* (Paris, 1981).

4. B. Guenée, 'Histoire de l'état', *RH*, 472 (1964), 346.

5. R. Mousnier, *Les institutions de la France sous la monarchie absolue, 1598–1789*, 2 vols (Paris, 1974), I, p.496.

6. R. de Maulde-la-Clavière, *Les origines de la révolution française au commencement du XVIe siècle* (Paris, 1889), pp.278–85. This oddly titled book is in effect a survey of French society under Louis XII.

7. P. Anderson, *Lineages of the Absolute State* (London, 1974, pbk edn, 1979), *passim.*

8. J.P. Genet (ed.), *Genèse de l'état moderne, bilans et perspectives* (Paris, CNRS, 1990), esp. pp.261–81.

9. R. Mousnier, *Les hiérarchies sociales de 1450 à nos jours* (Paris, 1969), p.19. On this see below chapter 6, on the nobility.

10. E. Le Roy Ladurie, *L'Etat royal de Louis XI à Henri IV* (Paris, 1987), pp.17, 23.

11. Ibid., p.78.

12. P. Contamine, 'De la puissance aux privilèges: doléances de la noblesse française envers la monarchie aux XIVe et XVe siècles', in

his *La France aux XIVe et XVe siècles. Hommes mentalités, guerre et paix* (Paris, 1981), p.255.

13. Ladurie, *L'Etat royal*, p.73.

14. J. Garrisson, *Royaume, Renaissance et Réforme, 1483–1559, Nouvelle hist. de la France moderne* (Paris, 1991), p.11; P.–R. Gaussin, *Louis XI, un roi entre deux mondes* (Paris, 1976); T. Basin, *Histoire de Louis XI* (ed. trans. C. Samaran, Paris, 1963–72) I, p.42. Brantôme, *Oeuvres complètes*, ed. J.A. Buchon, Panthéon Littéraire, 2 vols (Paris, 1838), I, p.194; Ronsard, *Poésies choisies*, ed. P. de Nolhac (Paris, 1963), p.259.

15. G. Zeller, 'Procès à reviser? Louis XI, la noblesse et la marchandise', *Aspects de la politique française sous l'Ancien Régime* (Paris, 1964), p.253.

16. R.J. Knecht, *Francis I and Absolute Monarchy* (London, Hist. Assoc., 1969); *Francis I* (Cambridge, 1982; 2nd edn under new title, *Renaissance Warrior and Patron: the reign of Francis I* (1994)), passim.

17. C. Beaune, *La naissance de la nation France* (Paris, 1985), p.309. On Venice, cf. G. Cozzi and M. Knapton, *La Reppublica di Venezia nell'età moderna* (Turin, 1986), part 2.

18. R. Mousnier, *Les institutions*, I, p.57.

19. Ladurie, *L'état royal*, pp.3–31.

20. J. Jacquart, *François Ier* (Paris, 1981), p.298.

21. R. Bonney, 'Bodin and the development of the French monarchy', *TRHS* (1990).

22. M. Antoine, 'L'administration centrale des finances en France du XVIe au XVIIe siècle', in *Le dur métier de Roi* (Paris, 1986) pp.31–60.

23. P.S. Lewis, *Later Medieval France: The Polity* (London, 1968); A. Demurger, *Temps de crises, temps d'espoirs, XIVe–XVe siècle* (Paris, 1990).

24. J.H. Salmon, *Society in Crisis* (London, 1973); H.A. Lloyd, *The State, France and the Sixteenth Century* (London, 1983); Ladurie, *L'état royal*.

25. H. Lemonnier, *Les guerres d'Italie: la France sous Charles VIII, Louis XII et François Ier* (1494–1547), vol.V of E. Lavisse (ed.), *Histoire de France* (Paris, 1903); J.S.C. Bridge, *A History of France from the Death of Louis XI*, 5 vols (Oxford, 1921–36). Garrisson, *Royaume, Renaissance et Réforme*. Roland Mousnier's Sorbonne lectures covered the period and were published in typescript as *La France de 1492–1559* (Paris, Cours de Sorbonne, 1971).

26. Y. Labande-Mailfert, *Charles VIII et son milieu (1470–1498). La jeunesse au pouvoir* (Paris, 1975); B. Quilliet, *Louis XII, Père du Peuple* (Paris, 1986); Knecht, *Francis I;* Jacquart, *François Ier*; I. Cloulas, *Henri II* (Paris, 1985); F.J. Baumgartner, *Henry II* (Durham, 1987).

27. In particular, J. Russell Major, *Representative Institutions in Renaissance France, 1421–1559* (Madison, 1960); Russell Major, *Deputies to the Estates General in Renaisance France* (Madison, 1960); Russell Major, *Representative Government in Early Modern France* (New Haven, London, 1980).

INTRODUCTION: FRENCH SOCIETY AND ITS IDENTITY

1. See letters of remission in J. Quicherat, 'Rodrigue de Villandrando', *BEC*, 6 (1844), p.163 etc.; (1880), pp.294–301; Jean du Port, 'La vie de Jean d'Orléans dit le bon, comte d'Angoulême', ed. J.F.E. Castaigne, *Bull. Soc. Archéologique de la Charente*, ser.3, 3 (1862), 32.

2. H. Denifle, *La désolation des églises, monastères et hopitaux en France pendant la Guerre de Cent Ans*, 2 vols (Paris, 1897–9). See the classic study of R. Boutruche, 'The devastation of rural areas during the Hundred Years War and the agricultural recovery of France', in P.S. Lewis (ed.), *The Recovery of France in the Fifteenth Century* (London, 1971) pp.23–51. On the Paris region: Y. Bézard, *La vie rurale dans le sud de la région parisienne de 1450 à 1560* (Paris, 1929), pp.45–54, p.49 on Magny; G. Fourquin, *Les campagnes de la région parisienne à la fin du Moyen Age* (Paris, 1964), pp.389–97, 430–43 for a corrective to this picture. R. de Maulde-la-Clavière, *Étude sur la condition forestière de l'Orléanais au Moyen Age et à la Renaissance* (Orléans, 1871) pp.245–8.

3. Thomas Basin, *Histoire de Charles VII et de Louis XI*, ed. J. Quicherat (Paris, 1856), p.13; J. Fortescue, *The Governance of England*, ed. Plummer (London, 1885), p.114; P. de Commynes, *Mémoires*, ed. J. Calmette (Paris, 1924) I, p.26.

4. G. Fourquin, *Les campagnes de la région parisienne*, p.404.

5. R. Gandilhon, *La politique économique de Louis XI* (Paris, 1941), which argues that Louis had a conscious economic policy, but cf. the critique of L. Febvre, 'Activité politique ou histoire économique. A propos de Louis XI', *Ann. d'Hist. sociale*, 3 (1941), 35–40.

6. Claude de Seyssel, *Histoire du roy Louys XII*, ed. T. Godefroy (Paris, 1615), p.128. See also Jean Bodin: 'In the last hundred years an infinite country of forest and heathland has been brought under the plough'. in H. Hauser (ed.), *La vie chère au XVIe siècle. La Response de Jean Bodin à M. de Malestroit, 1568* (Paris, 1932), pp.13–14.

8. J. Masselin, *Journal des Etats Généraux, de France tenus à Tours en 1484*, ed. A. Bernier (Paris, 1835), p.504; P. Contamine, 'The French nobility and the War' in his *La France au XIV et XVe siècles* (X), p.136.

9. Guenée, 'L'histoire de l'état', *RH*, 472 (1964), 352.

10. P. de Mézières, *Le Songe du Vieil Pélerin*, ed. G.W. Coopland (Cambridge, 1969), I, 38–9, 446–623.

11. C. de Seyssel, *La monarchie de France*, ed. J. Poujol (Paris, 1961).

12. Zeller, 'Procès à reviser?', *Aspects*, p.246.

13. *Rosier des guerres*, fo.59r; section *du Monde*, cf. A. Stegman, 'Le Rosier des Guerres', in B. Chevalier and P. Contamine (eds), *La France de la fin du XVe siècle – Renouveau et apogée* (Paris, 1985), p.317.

14. Mousnier, *Les hiérarchies sociales*, ch.VI.

15. E.g. A. Ariazza, 'Mousnier and Barber: the theoretical underpinning of the "Society of Orders" in early modern Europe', *P&P*, 89 (1980), 39–57, esp. 42, 45–7, 49–50; H. Heller, *Iron and Blood: Civil Wars in Sixteenth-Century France* (Montreal, London, 1991).

16. B. Guenée, 'Espace et état en la France au Moyen Age', *Annales*, 23 (1968), 744–58 and his *Politique et histoire au Moyen Age*.

17. J. Yver, *Egalité entre héritiers* (Paris, 1966).

18. P. Chaunu, 'L'état', in F. Braudel and E. Labrousse (eds), *Histoire économique et sociale de la France* (Paris, 1977), I, i, pp.96–8.

19. R. Giesey, 'Rules of inheritance and strategies of mobility in pre-revolutionary France', *Amer.H.R.*, 82 (1977), 276.

20. On the link between language and nationhood cf. above all C. Beaune, *La naissance de la nation France* (Paris, 1985), pp.291–308 and p.296: in 1444, Jean d'Armagnac had had to negotiate with the English in Latin since he knew little French. Clément Marot, *Oeuvres poétiques*, ed. Y. Giraud (Paris, 1973), p.222.

21. J. Nouaillac, *Histoire du Limousin* (Tulle, 1981), p.253; J.C. Dawson, *Toulouse in the Renaissance. The Floral Games; University and Student Life; Etienne Dolet* (New York, 1923), p.11.

22. S. Lusignan, 'Le latin était la langue maternelle des Romains: la fortune d'un argument à la fin du Moyen Age', in C. Bozzolo and E. Ornato, *Préludes à la Renaissance* (Paris, 1992), p.264–82.

23. A. Leguai, 'Emeutes et troubles d'origine fiscale pendant le règne de Louis XI', *Le moyen âge* (1967), 448.; J. Heers, *L'occident aux XIVe et XVe siècles. Aspects économiques et sociaux* (Paris, 1966), pp. 296–7.

24. *Ordonnances, François Ier IX, p563*, art.50; A. Croix, *Nantes et le pays nantais au XVIe siècle. Étude démographique* (Paris, 1974), pp.18–19.

25. BN Dupuy 519 fo.232v–233; P. Contamine, 'Contribution à l'histoire d'un mythe: les 1,700,000 clochers au royaume de France (XVe–XVIe siècles)', in his *La France au XIVe et XVe siècles*, pp.425–6; A. Spont, 'Une recherche générale des feux à la fin du XVe siècle', *Ann.-bull.SHF* (1892), pp.222–36.

26. F. Lot, 'L'Etat des paroisses et des feux de 1328', *BEC*, 90 (1929), 51–107, 256–316.

27. J. Dupâquier (ed.), *Histoire de la population française*, I & II (Paris, 1988), I, pp.259–63.

28. C. de Seyssel, *Louenges du roy Louys XII* (Paris, Verard, 1508); Spont, 'Une recherche générale des feux'.

29. R. Mousnier, *Le conseil du roi de Louis XII à la Revolution* (Paris, 1970), p.19; Braudel and Labrousse, *Histoire économique et sociale*, I, ii, p.904.

30. Dupâquier (ed.), *Histoire de la population*, II, pp.52–3, 76–7.

31. W. Prévenier, 'La démographie des villes de Flandre aux XIVe et XVe siècles', *Revue du Nord*, 65 (1983), 255–75.; W.P. Blockmans

et al., 'Tussen crisis en welvaert: sociale veranderingen 1300–1500', *Algemene Geschiedenis der Nederlanden*, IV (1980), pp.42–7.

32. Dupâquier (ed.), *Histoire de la population*, I, p.394.

33. Ibid., I, p.371.

34. On Quercy, see J. Lartigaut, 'Seigneurs et paysans du Quercy vers la fin du XVe siècle', *Annales du Midi*, 86 (1974), 237–52, and numerous other works by him. On Normandy, G. Bois, *Crise du féodalisme* (Paris, 1976), p.66.

35. Dupâquier (ed.), *Histoire de la population*, I, p.372. Numerous local catalogues of epidemics have been made. We can cite, for instance, C. de Marsy, 'La peste à Compiègne (XVe, XVIe et XVIIe siècles)', *La Picardie* (1878–84), pp.281–301; G. Le Borgne, *Recherches historiques sur les grandes épidémies qui ont regné à Nantes* (Nantes, 1852), pp.40–5.

36. E. Le Roy Ladurie, *L'Etat Royal*, pp.49–50; P. Chaunu, R. Gascon in Braudel etc., *Histoire économique et sociale de la France*, I, i, pp.40–64; J. Jacquart, 'Le poids démographique de Paris et de l'Ile-de-France au XVIe siècle', in his *Paris et l'Ile-de-France au temps des paysans* (Paris, 1990), pp.227–35, esp. 233–5. The document used for the evaluation of the influence of Paris is the *solde des gens de pied* of 1538, *Ordonnances, François Ier*, IX, pp.80–1. Fourquin, *Les campagnes*, pp.516–27. R. Gascon, *Grand commerce et vie urbaine au XVIe siècle: Lyon et ses marchands*, 2 vols (Paris, 1971), II, pp.341–50; Gascon, 'L'immigration et croissance au XVIe siècle: l'exemple de Lyon (1529–1563)', *Annales*, 25, iv (1970) 988–1001.

37. E. Baratier, *La démographie provençale du XIve au XVIe siècle* (Paris, 1961); E. Bautier, 'Feux, population et structure sociale au milieu du XVe siècle. L'exemple de Carpentras', *Annales*, 14 (1959), 255–68.

38. E. Le Roy Ladurie, *The Peasants of Languedoc* (Urbana, 1974), pp.54–5, 56–66, 73–6.

39. P. Charbonnier, *Une autre France. La seigneurie rurale en Basse Auvergne du XIVe au XVI siècle*, 2 vols (Clermont–Ferrand, 1980), II, pp.843–7, 850–5.

40. A. Bocquet, *Recherches sur la population rurale en Artois à la fin du Moyen Age* (Arras, 1969).

41. M. Belotte, *La région de Bar-sur-Seine à la fin du Moyen Age* (Lille, 1973) cit. in P. Contamine, introduction to Chevalier and Contamine, *La France de la fin du XVe siècle* (Paris, 1985), p.3.

42. H. Neveux, *Vie et déclin d'une structure économique. Les grains du Cambrésis, fin du XIVe – debut du XVIIe siècle* (Paris, The Hague, 1980), pp.167–78, 186–93; Neveux, 'L'expansion démographique du Cambrésis: Saint–Hilaire (1450–1575)', *Annales de démographie historique* (1971), 265–98. D.L. Potter, *War and Government in the French Provinces: Picardy 1470–1560* (Cambridge, 1993), pp.22–4.

43. Dupâquier (ed.), *Histoire de la population*, I, p.384.

44. Croix, *Nantes et le pays nantais au XVIe siècle*, pp.161–70, 221–4.
45. Fourquin, *Les campagnes de la région parisienne*, p.443 ; J. Jacquart, *La crise rurale en Ile-de-France, 1550–1670* (Paris, 1974), p.44.
46. Y. Bézard, *La vie rurale dans le sud de la région parisienne*, pp.48–9, 201–10; Fourquin, *Les campagnes de la région parisienne*, pp.430–62, evidence on *censives*; Jacquart, *La crise rurale en Ile-de-France*; Jacquart, 'Le poids démographique de Paris et Ile-de-France au XVIe siècle' in his *Paris et l'Ile-de-France au temps des paysans*, pp.227–30.
47. Fourquin, *Les campagnes*, pp.453–5; M. Bloch, *Les caractères originaux de l'histoire rurale française*, 2 vols (Paris, 1960–1), I, p.120. Jacquart, *La crise rurale*, p.139. R. Boutruche, *Crise d'une société. Seigneurs et paysans du Bordelais pendant la Guerre de Cent Ans* (Strasbourg, 1947) and summary (same title) in *Annales*, 2 (1947) 336–45.
48. Bloch, *Les caractères originaux*, p.111–; Bloch, *Rois et serfs. Un chapitre d'histoire capetienne* (Paris, 1920); J. Garnier, *Chartes de communes et d'affranchissements en Bourgogne*, 2 vols (Dijon, 1867–8), II, intr. p.207–.
49. G. Fourquin, *Les campagnes*, pp.514–15.
50. J. Goy and E. Le Roy Ladurie, *Les fluctuations du produit de la dîme* (Paris, 1973), pp.21–30, 334–.
51. M. Baulant and J. Meuvret, *Prix des céréales extraits de la mercuriale de Paris (1520–1698)*, 2 vols (Paris, 1960–2); Gascon, *Grand commerce et vie urbaine*, II, pp.538–49. H. Hauser, *Recherches et documents sur l'histoire des prix en France de 1500 à 1800* (Paris, 1936), eg. pp.307–464 on Dauphiné. Hauser based his work on two to four base figures for a mean per civil year (cf. M. Venard, *L'eglise d'Avignon au XVIe siècle*, 5 vols (Lille, 1980), I, pp.459–60); Fourquin, *Les campagnes*, p.445.
52. Ladurie, *The Peasants of Languedoc*, pp.98–9.
53. Ibid., pp.102–3.
54. Ibid., pp.107–8.
55. H. Hauser, *La réponse de Jean Bodin à M. de Malestroit*, pp.xvii–xviii, p.14, on export of labour to Spain.
56. Neveux, *Vie et déclin*, pp.308–11: index of 100 in 1460–9 to 19.6 in 1540–49.
57. Neveux, *Vie et déclin*, p.311; M. Baulant, 'Le salaire des ouvriers du bâtiment à Paris de 1400 à 1726', *Annales*, 26 (1971), 463–83; Bézard, *La vie rurale dans le sud de la région parisienne*, pp.233–43 (unfortunately, the figures given, converted into money of 1914, are not easily usable and Bézard seems determined to place an optimistic interpretation on them). R. Gascon in Braudel (ed.), *Histoire économique et sociale*, I, i, pp.424–5.
58. B. Geremek, 'Criminalité, vagabondage, paupérisme: la marginalité à l'aube des temps modernes', *RHMC*, 21 (1974), 350; Geremek, *The Margins of Society in Late Medieval Paris* (Cambridge, 1987), pp.29–43; B. Chevalier, *Les bonnes villes de France du XIVe au XVIe siècle* (Paris, 1982), pp.291–9, Nicolas Versoris, *Livre de raison*, pub. by P. Joutard

as *Journal d'un bourgeois de Paris sous François Ier* (Paris, 1963), pp.52, 54–5, 60–2, 63, 128, 133. L. Lalanne (ed.), *Journal d'un bourgeois de Paris sous le règne de François Ier (1515–36)* (Paris, 1854), pp.36, 119, 152, 197–201.

59. B.B. Davis, 'Poverty and poor relief in 16th century Toulouse', *Historical Reflections*, 17 (1991), 267–96; Gascon, *Grand commerce et vie urbaine*, II, pp.794–801. For the text of Jean de Vauzelles's *Police subsidiaire* cf. H. Baudrier (ed.), J. de Vauzelles, *Assistance publique donnée à la multitude des pauvres accourus à Lyon en 1531* (Lyon, 1875) and *Police de l'Aumône de Lyon* (Lyon, Gryphius, 1539). On wages at Lyon, cf. Gascon, *Grand Commerce*, II, pp.752–9. *Le livre de Podio ou Chroniques d'Etienne de Medicis, bourgeois du Puy*, ed. A. Chassaing (Le Puy, Recueil des Chroniqueurs du Puy-en-Velay, I, 1869), p.305.

60. Croix, *Nantes et le pays nantais*, pp.141–3.

61. H. Hauser, 'Une grève d'imprimeurs parisiens au XVIe siècle', *Rev. internat. de Sociologie* (1917).

62. J.-P. Gutton, *La société et les pauvres en Europe (XVIe–XVIIIe siècle)* (Paris, 1974), pp.105–10; Ladurie, *The Peasants of Languedoc*, pp.135–7.

63. On this cf. P.S. Lewis, *Later Mediaeval France*, pp.59–77; 'War Propaganda and historiography in fifteenth-century France and England', *TRHS*, ser.5, 15 (1965); B. Guenée, 'Etat et nation', *RH* (1967), 17–30; G. Dupont-Ferrier, 'Le sens des mots "patria" et "patrie" en France au moyen âge et jusqu'au début du XVIIe siècle', *RH*, 188–9 (1940), 89–104. P. Contamine, 'Mourir pour la patrie', in P. Nora, *Lieux de mémoire La Nation*, III, p.19.

64. B. Guenée, 'Etat et nation en France au Moyen Age' in his *Politique et histoire au Moyen-Age*, pp. 151–64. P. Arabeyre, 'La France et son gouvernement au milieu du XVe siècle d'après Bernard de Rosier', *BEC*, 150 (1992), 245–85, esp.255–7.

65. On the idea of the Christian kingdom, cf. C. Beaune, *Naissance de la nation France*, pp.207–29 and on the imagery of France, ibid., pp.310–23; Beaune, 'Saint Clovis: histoire, religion royale et sentiment national en France à la fin du Moyen Age', in B. Guenée (ed.), *Le métier d'historien au Moyen Age* (Paris, 1977). Other refs to Claude de Seyssel, *La Monarchie de France*, ed. J. Poujol, p.115; J. Poujol, 'Jean Ferrault on the king's privileges', *Studies in the Renaissance*, 5 (1958), 15–26.

66. Contamine, 'Mourir pour la patrie', p.25; J. d'Auton, *Chroniques de Louis XII* (Paris, 1885), I, p.88; P. de Commynes, *The Memoirs of Philip de Commines*, 2 vols, trans. A. Scoble, Bohn Libr. (London, 1855–6), p.257.

67. Pierre de Bourdeille de Brantôme, *Oeuvres complètes*, ed. L. Lalanne, 12 vols (1864–96) VII, pp.232–3.

68. On this see R.C. Christie, *Etienne Dolet* (London, 1899), pp.100–15; J.C. Dawson, *Toulouse in the Renaissance*, pp.154–62 and 106–10 (on student 'nations').

69. G.R. Elton, review of O. Ranum, *History and Political Culture in Early Modern Europe*, in *HJ*, 18, iv (1975).

70. A. Jouanna, 'La quête des origines dans l'historiographie française', in Chevalier and Contamine (eds), *La France de la fin du XVe siècle*, pp.302–3; R.E. Asher, 'Mythes légendaires et nationalisme dans le poésie du XVIe siècle français', in F. Simone (ed.), *Culture et politique en France à l'époque de l'humanisme et de la Renaissance* (Turin, 1974), pp.235–48, esp. 235–6.

71. N. Gilles, *Compendium de origine et gestis francorum* (1492), fo.l.

72. Jouanna, 'La quête des origines', p.301–.

73. M. Schmidt-Chazan, 'Histoire et sentiment national chez Robert Gaguin', in B. Guenée, *Le métier d'historien au Moyen Age* (Sorbonne, 1977); Jouanna, 'La quête des origines', p.311.

74. G. Huppert, *The Idea of Perfect History: Historical Erudition and Historical Philosophy in Renaissance France* (Urbana, Ill., 1970), pp.14–15; K. Davies, 'Late fifteenth-century French historiography as exemplified in the Compendium of Robert Gaguin and the De Rebus gestis of Paulus Aemilius' (Edinburgh Univ. Thesis, 1954).

75. J. du Bellay, *Le Deffence et illustration de la langue françoyse* (1549), ed. Chamard (Paris, 1948), pp.18–20; trans. G.M. Turquet, *The Defence and Illustration of the French Language* (London, 1939), p.24.

76. A. Jouanna, *L'idée de race en France au XVIe siècle et au début du XVIIe*, 2 vols (Montpellier, 1981), II, pp.410–15; M. Bloch, *Les rois thaumaturges. Etudes sur le caractère surnaturel attribué à la puissance royale particulièrement en France et en Angleterre* (Paris, 1961), pp.346–7.

77. F. Simone, 'Historiographie et mythographie dans la culture française du XVIe siècle: analyse d'un texte oublié', in *Actes du colloque sur l'humanisme lyonnais au XVIe siècle: mai 1972* (Grenoble, 1974), pp.125–48. R.E. Asher, 'Myth, legend and history in Renaissance France', *Studi francesi*, 39 (1969), 409–19.

78. D. Maskell, *The Historical Epic in France 1500–1700* (Oxford, 1973), p.37; Jouanna, 'La quête des origines', p.310. A. Jaquet, 'Le sentiment national au XVIe siècle: Claude de Seyssel', *Rev. quest. hist.*, 13 (1895), 400–40, esp. 408–15.

79. G. Huppert, *The Idea of Perfect History*, pp.76–8.

80. Asher, 'Myth, legend and history', pp.410–11; C. Visconti, 'Les *Recherches de France* d'Estienne Pasquier', in P. Nora, *Lieux de mémoire*; G. Huppert, 'Les "Recherches" d'Estienne Pasquier', *Annales*, 23 (1968), 69–105; Jouanna, 'La quête des origines', p.311; E.E. Ehmke, 'Gauls and Franks in 16th-century French historical writing: the theory of François Connan', *PWSFH*, 6 (1978), 78–87; D.R. Kelley, '"Fides historiae": Charles Dumoulin and the Gallican View of History', *Traditio*, 22 (1966), 347–402, esp. 389–91.

81. E. Pasquier, *Recherches de France* (Amsterdam 1723), I, ch.ix. Dumoulin, *Opera omnia* (Paris, 1681), II, v, viii, cf. Kelley, 'Fides historiae', p.392.

82. J. Garnier, *Chartes de communes et d'affranchissements*, III, p.101.
83. M. Fogel, *Les cérémonies d'information dans la France du XVIe au XVIIe siècle* (Paris, 1989), pp.133–88.
84. H. Stein and L. Le Grand, *La frontière d'Argonne* (843–1659). *Procès de Claude de La Vallée* (1535–61) (Paris, 1905), p.28.
85. L. Febvre, 'Frontier, the Word and the Concept', in *A New Kind of History from the Writings of Febvre*, ed. P. Burke (London, 1973); B. Guenée, 'Les limites de la France' in his *Politique et histoire au moyen-âge* (Paris, 1981), pp.73–93 esp. p.84; Guenée, 'Des limites féodales aux frontières politiques' and D. Nordman, 'Des limites d'état aux frontières nationales' in P. Nora, *Lieux de Mémoire, II La Nation*, pp.11–33 and 35–61; D. Nordman, 'Frontiere e confini in Francia', in C. Ossola and C. Raffestin (eds), *La frontiera da stato a nazione. Il caso Piemonte* (Rome, 1987), pp.39–55. For a specific example cf. letters of June 1496 for the privileges of Comminges: 'which is situated on the *lizière frontière* of the kingdom of Aragon' and the *cahier de doléances* of the same county in 1560 'mostly situated in the Pyrenees mountains, *pays limitrophe* of the kingdom of Aragon' (R. Souriac, *Le comté de Comminges au milieu du XVIe siècle* (Paris, 1977), pp.303, 321).
86. P. Sahlins, *Boundaries: The Making of France and Spain in the Pyrenees* (Berkeley, 1989), p.6.
87. Stein and Le Grand, *La frontière d'Argonne*.
88. On the northern frontier, cf. Potter, *War and Government in the French provinces*, ch.8.
89. BN fr.2900 fo.18: memorandum on the treatment of German troops in French service.
90. *Acta Nuntiaturae Gallicae* VI, no.38; G. Zeller, 'Les Rois de France candidats à l'Empire', in *Aspects;* Zeller, *La réunion de Metz à la France;* J.-D. Pariset, 'La France et les princes allemands. Documents et commentaires (1545–57)', *Francia*, 10, (1982), doc. 27, p.259.
91. C. Beaune, *La naissance de la nation France*, pp.338, 347–51.
92. G. Procacci, 'La Provence à la veille des guerres de religion. Une periode décisive: 1535–45', *RHMC*, 5 (1958), 245–51, citing Z.V. Mosina, 'Iz istorii borby francuzkovo naroda za nacionalnoe gosudarstvo', *Srednie Veka* (Moscow, 1953), IV, p.225.
93. Commynes, trans. Scoble, p.257. B. Guenée, 'Etat et nation en France au Moyen Age', in his *Politique et histoire au moyen-âge*, p.152.
94. Cf. above all R. Fawtier, 'Comment, au début du XIVe siècle, un roi de France pouvait-il se représenter son royaume?', in *Académie des Inscriptions & Belles-Lettres: Comptes rendus des Séances de l'année 1959* (Paris, 1960), pp.117–23. J.P. Genet (ed.), *La genèse de l'état moderne, bilans*, p.261.
95. P. Contamine, 'Contribution à l'histoire d'un mythe', in *La France des XVe et XVe siècles;* J. Krynen, 'Genèse de l'état et histoire des idées

politiques en France à la fin du Moyen Age', in J.P. Genet (ed.), *Culture et idéologie dans la genèse de l'état moderne* (Rome, 1985), p.403.

96. R. Fawtier, 'Comment le roi de France au début du XIVe siècle pouvait-il se représenter son royaume?'; Jean Chartier, *Chronique de Charles VII roi de France*, ed. A. Vallet de Viriville, 3 vols (Paris, 1858), II, p.234.

97. Contamine, 'Contribution à l'histoire d'un mythe', pp.424–5.

98. On Louis XI's information, cf. M.-A. Arnould, 'Les lendemains de Nancy dans les "Pays de par deça" (janvier–avril 1477)', in W.P. Blockmans (ed.), *Le privilège général et les privilèges régionaux de Marie de Bourgogne* (Anciens Pays et Assemblées d'Etats, 1985), pp.2–3. Potter, *War and Government*, p.26.

99. On 'the sense of space' in the early Middle Ages, cf. B. Guenée, *Histoire et culture historique dans l'Occident médiéval* (Paris, 1980), pp.176–7 and J. Tricard, 'La Touraine d'un Tourangeau au XIIe siècle' in Guenée (ed.), *Le métier d'historien au Moyen Age* (Paris, 1977), pp.79–93.

100. On these maps, cf. Potter, *War and Government*, ch.8. On earlier frontier inquests, cf. J. Richard, 'Les débats entre le roi de France et le duc de Bourgogne sur la frontière du royaume à l'ouest de la Saône: l'enquête de 1452', *Bull. hist. phil.*, année 1964 (1967), 113–32.

101. L. Drapeyron, 'L'image de la France sous les derniers Valois (1525–1589) et sous les premiers Bourbons (1589–1682)', *Revue de la Géographie*, 24 (1889), 1–15; N. Broc, 'Quelle est la plus ancienne carte "moderne" de la France?', *Annales de Géographie*, 513 (1983), 513–30. F. Dainville, *Cartes anciennes de l'Eglise de France* (Paris, 1956).

102. D. Nordman, 'La connaissance géographique de l'état (XIVe–XVIIe siècles)', in N. Coulet and J.P. Genet, *L'état moderne: le droit, l'espace et les formes de l'état* (Paris, 1990), pp.175–88, esp.180–2.

1. THE MONARCHY: IDEOLOGY, PRESENTATION AND RITUAL

1. B. Guenée, *Les entrées royales françaises de 1328 à 1515* (Paris, 1968), p.7, repr. in his *Politique et histoire au moyen-âge*, p.127.

2. J. Krynen, 'Genèse de l'état et histoire des idées politiques en France à la fin du moyen âge', p.402.

3. P.S. Lewis, *Later Mediaeval France*, pp.78–101.

4. Ibid.; Guenée, 'L'histoire de l'état en France à la fin du moyen âge', pp.350–1.

5. K. Daly, 'Mixing business with leisure: Some French royal notaries and secretaries and their histories of France, c.1459–1509', in C. Allmand (ed.), *Power, Culture and Religion in France, c.1350–c.1550* (Woodbridge, 1989), pp.99–115.

6. B. Guenée, 'Les généalogies entre l'histoire et politique: la fierté capétienne en France au Moyen Age', *Annales* (1978), 465; C. Beaune, 'Saint Clovis: histoire, religion royale et sentiment national en France à la fin du Moyen Age', p.148.

7. J. Vaesen (ed.), *Lettres de Louis XI*, 12 vols (Paris, 1883–1909), VIII, pp.276–7.

8. N. Grévy-Pons, 'Propagande et sentiment national pendant le règne de Charles VI: l'exemple de Jean de Montreuil', *Francia*, 8 (1980), 127–45; P.S. Lewis (ed.), *Ecrits politiques de Jean Juvenal des Ursins*, 2 vols (Paris, 1978–85), II, pp.201–11; N. Grévy-Pons, 'Une exemple de l'utilisation des écrits politiques de Jean de Montreuil: un mémorandum diplomatique rédigé sous Charles VII', in C. Bozzolo and E. Ornato (eds), *Préludes à la Renaissance*, pp.243–64.

9. B. Guenée, 'Y a-t-il un état des XIVe et XVe siècles?' in *Politique et histoire au moyen-âge*, p.34; B.-A. Pocquet du Haut-Jussé, 'A political concept of Louis XI: subjection instead of vassalage', in Lewis, *The Recovery of France*, pp.196–215; H. Hauser, 'Le traité de Madrid et la cession de la Bourgogne à Charles-Quint', *Revue bourguignonne*, 22 (1912).

10. M. David, *La souveraineté et les limites juridiques du pouvoir monarchique en France du IXe au XVe siècle* (Paris, 1954); J. Quillet, *Les clefs du pouvoir au Moyen Age* (Paris, 1972), p.78. Above all J. Barbey, *Etre roi. Le roi et son gouvernement de Clovis à Louis XVI* (Paris, 1992), pp.165–208 on the 'marks of sovereignty'.

11. E.H. Kantorowicz, *The King's Two Bodies. A Study in Medieval Political Theology* (Princeton, 1957); A. Boureau, *Le simple corps du roi. L'impossible sacralité des souverains français XVe–XVIIIe siècle* (Paris, 1988), pp.16–23, 62–3. Grassailles quoted in E.H. Kantorowicz, 'Mysteries of state. An absolutist concept and its late medieval origins' in his *Selected Studies* (New York, 1965), p.396; Charles Dumoulin, *Les petites dates* (1551) quoted in Kelley, "Fides historiae": Charles Dumoulin and the Gallican view of history', p.392. R. Descimon, 'Les fonctions de la métaphore du mariage politique du roi et de la république en France, XVe–XVIIIe siècles', *Annales*, 47 (1992), 1127–47, esp.1139.

12. R. de Maulde-La-Clavière, *Procédures politiques du règne de Louis XII* (Paris, 1888), p.242–; Ronsard, *Poésies choisies*, ed. P. de Nolhac (Paris, 1963), p.259, ode to Henri II, 1555; A.-M. Lecoq, 'La symbolique de l'Etat. Les images de la monarchie des premiers Valois à Louis XIV', in P. Nora (ed.), *Lieux de Mémoire. La Nation*, II, pp.145–92. N.O. Keohane, *Philosophy and the State in France* (Princeton, 1980), pp.15–16.

13. Guenée, 'Etat et nation en France au Moyen Age', in his *Politique et histoire au moyen-âge*, pp.151–64, esp.152–3. N. Machiavelli's 'Ritratto di cose di Francia' in *Opere di Niccolo Machiavelli*, ed. E. Raimundi (Milan, 1966), p.810. See e.g. *Ordonnances* XVIII, p.315 'l'Etat et seureté de la chose publique' (22 Dec. 1477).

14. H.H. Rowen, *The King's State: Proprietary Dynasticism in Early Modern France* (Rutgers UP, 1980); R. Cazelles, *La société politique sous Jean le bon et Charles V* (Paris, 1982), pp.505–16. Krynen, 'Genèse de l'état et histoire des idées politiques', p.407. Charles Dumoulin, quoted in L. Romier, *Le royaume de Catherine de Médicis* 2 vols (Paris, 1922), II, p.47. E. Chenon, 'De la transformation du domaine royale en domaine de la couronne du XIVe au XVIe siècle', *Rev.hist. Droit français et étranger*, ser.4, 4 (1925).

15. R.W. Scheller, 'Ensigns of authority: French royal symbolism in the age of Louis XII', *Simiolus*, 13 (1982–3), 121–3. D. Haigneré, *Dictionnaire historique et archéologique ... du Pas-de-Calais* (Arras, 1880), I, p.230; N. Weiss, *La chambre ardente: étude sur la liberté de conscience sous François Ier et Henri II (1540–1550)* (Paris, 1889); S. Mochi Onory, *Fonti canonistiche dell'idea moderna dello stato* (Milan, 1951), pp.166, 220, 243: 'unum jus, unum imperium', etc.

16. R. Boussuat, 'La formule "le roi est empereur en son royaume", son emploi au XVe siècle devant le Parlement de Paris', *Revue hist. de Droit français et étranger* (1961), 371–81; G. Zeller, 'Les rois de France candidats à l'Empire', in *Aspects de la politique francaise*, p.62; A. Le Glay, *Négociations diplomatiques entre la France et l'Autriche*, 2 vols (Paris, 1845), II, pp.497, 500; C. Weiss, *Papiers d'état du cardinal de Granvelle*, 9 vols (Paris, 1842–52), I, p.161.

17. Jean Thenaud, *Le voyage d'Outremer*, ed. C. Shefer (Paris, 1884), p.2; Charles de Grassailles, *Regalium Franciae libri duo 1545*, p.159; S. Champier, *De monarchia ac triplici imperio* (Lyon, 1537).

18. R.W. Scheller, 'Ensigns of Authority' pp.75–141, esp. 97–9; H. Hauser, 'Le transport des règnes et empires des Grecs ès Français', *Revue des études rabelaisiennes*, VI (1908).

19. Kelley, 'Fides historiae', pp.387–8.

20. R.W. Scheller, 'Imperial themes in art and literature of the early French Renaissance: the period of Charles VIII', *Simiolus*, 12 (1981–2), 12–15, 66–7; *L&P*, V, 1316. J. du Tillet, *Recueil des Roys de France* (Rouen, 1578), pp.131–2; Kelley, 'Fides historiae', p.388; V. Hoffmann, 'Donec totum impleat orbem: symbolisme impérial au temps de Henri II', *Bull. de la Soc. de l'hist. de l'art française*, 1978 (1980), 29–42.

21. J. Krynen, *L'idéal du prince et pouvoir royal en France à la fin du Moyen Age (1380–1440)* (Paris, 1981), pp.207–40; Krynen, 'Genèse de l'état et histoire des idées', p.411; P.S. Lewis, *Later Mediaeval France*.

22. That Louis XI inaugurated 'le régime du bon plaisir' was argued by C. Petit-Dutaillis, *Charles VII, Louis XI et les premières années de Charles VIII* in Lavisse, *Histoire de France*, IV, ii (Paris, 1902), p.407: the executive phrase of the letter-close was 'car tel est nostre plaisir'. Jean Masselin, *Journal des Etats-Généraux*, pp.140–57, esp.149; Q. Skinner, *The Foundations of Modern Political Thought* (Cambridge, 1978), I, pp.61–5: Marsilius and Bartolus had denied the Thomist argument

that the 'people' alienated rather than delegated sovereign authority. Aquinas had argued that a true sovereign must be *legibus solutus*.

23. J.L. Bourgeon, 'La Fronde parlementaire à la veille de la Saint-Barthélemy', *BEC* (1990), 25, n.19.

24. F. Aubert, *Le Parlement de Paris depuis Philippe le Bel à Charles VII (1314–1422)* (Paris, 1886), p.189; C. de Seyssel, *La monarchie de France*, ed. J. Poujol (Paris, 1961), p.117.

25. AN X/1A 1517 quoted in F. Decrue, *De consilio regis Francisci I* (Paris, 1885), p.45. The text of Guillart's speech, AN X/1A 1530 fos.350–7 is newly edited by R.J. Knecht in *FH* (March 1992), 75–83; 1498: AN X/1A 1504, quoted in B. de Mandrot, *Ymbert de Batarnay, seigneur du Bouchage* (Paris, 1886), p.214.

26. Ordonnance of 25 Sept.1523, *Ordonnances, François Ier*, IV, no.359, pp.299–300.

27. P. Choisnet, *Le Rosier des guerres*, ed. by M. Diamant-Berger, *Enseignements de Louis XI pour le Dauphin* (Paris, 1925); P.R. Gaussin, *Louis XI*, p.44. *Journal de Jean Barrillon, secrétaire du chancelier du Prat, 1515–21*, ed. P. de Vaissière, 2 vols (Paris, 1897–99), I, p.279.

28. J. Poujol, 'L'évolution et l'influence des idées absolutistes en France de 1498 à 1559', *L'information historique*, 18 (1956), 43–4; Poujol, 'Cadre idéologique du dévelopment de l'absolutisme en France à l'avènement de François Ier', *Théorie et pratique politiques à la Renaissance. Colloque internationale de Tours, 1974* (Paris, 1977), pp.259–72, esp. 268, 269–70.

29. Point made by R. Jackson, *Vive le Roi! A History of the French Coronation from Charles V to Charles X* (Chapel Hill, 1984), p.113.

30. R. Mousnier and F. Hartung, 'Quelques problèmes concernant la monarchie absolue', *Relazione de X Congresso Internationale di Scienze Storiche*, IV (Rome, 1955), esp. pp.25–35. R. Doucet, *Les institutions de la France au XVIe siècle*, 2 vols (Paris, 1948), I, p.49.

31. Speech of the count of Rochefort, 1560: L. Lalanne, *Brantôme, sa vie et ses écrits* (Paris, 1896), p.261. C.W. Stocker, 'The politics of the Parlement of Paris in1525', *FHS*, 8 (1973–4), 191–211, esp.199–200, 210–11, J.-L. Bourgeon, 'La Fronde parlementaire à la veille de la Saint-Barthélemy', *BEC* (1990), 17–89.

32. Estienne Pasquier, *Oeuvres* (Amsterdam, 1723) II, col.1557: Pasquier is commenting on the king's agreement in the Edict of Blois (1579) 'with a royal and worthy magnanimity, to put a limit to his absolute power in the matter of evocations'.

33. N. Henshall, *The Myth of Absolutism: Change and Continuity in Early Modern European Monarchy* (London, 1992) is generally suggestive on all this but unfortunately lacks much depth of theoretical analysis. On the legislative power, see J. Barbey, *Etre roi*, pp.173–83. On Bodin, cf. R. Bonney, 'Bodin and the development of the French monarchy', *TRHS* (1990), 40–61. The documents of 1525–7 are discussed in R. Doucet, *Etude sur le gouvernement de François Ier dans ses rapports*

avec le Parlement de Paris, 2 vols (Paris, 1921–6), II, pp.103–10, 251–2 and E. Maugis, *Histoire du Parlement de Paris*, 3 vols (Paris, 1913–16), I, pp.559–66, 580 and most recently by R.J. Knecht, 'Francis I and the "Lit de Justice": a "Legend" defended', *FH* (March 1993), 53–83.

34. R. Giesey, 'The juristic basis of dynastic right to the French throne', *Transactions of the American Philosophical Society*, 51 (1961), 3–47; on the 'seconde personne de France' see Scheller, 'Imperial themes', p.67; Jackson, *Vive le Roi*, pp.155–67. On Loyseau, cf. Mousnier and Hartung, 'Quelques problèmes'.

35. Lecoq, 'La symbolique de l'état', pp.145, 172. On Charles VIII's imperial entries: Brantôme, *Oeuvres*, ed. Buchon I, p.181, after Gaguin, *Compendium*; R.W. Scheller, 'Imperial themes... the period of Charles VIII', pp.33, 56–7 (MS of 1497 showing Charles with an imperial crown and the sun), 66–7; Scheller, 'Ensigns of Authority', pp.108–111. D. Gaborit-Chopin, *Regalia. Les instruments du sacre des rois de France* (Paris, 1987), pp.91–2; Gaborit-Chopin, 'Les couronnes du sacre des rois et des reines au trésor de Saint-Denis', *Bulletin monumental*, 133 (1975), 165–74; G. Bapst, *Histoire des joyaux de la couronne de France* (Paris, 1889), p.39; *Ordonnances, François Ier*, VIII, p.807.

36. G. Zeller, *Les institutions de la France au XVIe siècle* (Paris, 1948), p.100.

37. P.E. Schramm, *Der König von Frankreich. Das Wesen der Monarchie vom 9. zum 16. Jahrhundert*, 2 vols (Weimar, 1939, repr. 1960); J.M. Bak, 'Medieval symbology of the state: Percy E. Schramm's contribution', *Viator*, 4 (1973), 33–63; R. Jackson, *Vive le Roi*.

38. *L'Ordre du Sacre et couronnement du roy Très chrétien notre sire François de Valoys* (1515); T. Godefroy, *Le cérémonial françois*, 2 vols (Paris, 1649), I, pp.245–63; M. Valensise, 'Le sacre du roi: stratégie et doctrine politique de la monarchie française', *Annales*, 41 (1986), 543–77, esp. 547–8 on the idea of the *dignitas* of kingship; J. Krynen, '"Le mort saisit le vif". Genèse médiévale du principe d'instantanéité de la succession royale française', *Journal des savants* (1984).

39. Jackson, *Vive le Roi*, pp.117, 81–5.

40. Ibid., pp.85–6; Godefroy, *Le cérémonial*, I, pp.279–93, p.293 on the *largesse*. H. Stein, 'Le sacre d'Anne de Bretagne et son entrée à Paris en 1504', *Mém. Soc. hist. Paris* (1902), 268–305; C. de Grassailles, *Regalium Franciae*, p.217, quoted in Kantorowicz, 'Mysteries of State', pp.387–90; S. Hanley, *The Lit de Justice of the Kings of France: Constitutional Ideology in Legend, Ritual and Discourse* (Princeton, 1983), pp.83–4, argues that Selve's speech in December 1527 announced an innovative theme. However, the idea of the marriage of king and kingdom was present in the fourteenth century, cf. Kantorowicz, *The King's Two Bodies*, pp.212–19. This has been confirmed by Descimon, 'Les fonctions de la métaphore du mariage politique du Roi et de la République', pp.1132–4. See also a speech of *avocat* Hennequin in the Parlement, 8 April 1525: 'Paris, which is

the example and heart of the kingdom, the king's bride and where he takes possession of his crown' (AN X/1A 1527 fo.318v).

41. J. Le Goff, 'Reims, ville de sacre', in P. Nora, *Lieux de mémoire* I, pp.89–184, esp. p.136. Godefroy, *Le cérémonial*, I, p.486.
42. M. Bloch, *The Royal Touch* (London, 1973), pp.108–76.
43. R. Giesey, *The Royal Funeral Ceremony in Renaissance France* (Geneva, 1960), pp.41–50; A. Boureau, Le *simple corps du roi*, pp.24–34 (pp. 93–114 for text of 1498 funeral).
44. R. Giesey, *The Royal Funeral Ceremony in Renaissance France*, pp.125–44.
45. Jackson, *Vive le Roi*, pp.134–46.
46. C. Beaune, 'Les sanctuaires royaux', in P. Nora, *Lieux de mémoire*, I, p.64–; J.P. Babelon, 'La Renaissance', in *Le Roi, la sculpture et la mort. Gisants et tombeaux de la basilique de Saint-Denis, Bulletin des archives départementales de la Seine-Saint-Denis*, 5 (1976), 31–45. B.S. Hochstetler in a Johns Hopkins PhD thesis (1976), 'The Tomb of Louis XII and Anne of Brittany in Saint-Denis' argued that the innovation of the *priant* figures was a concrete expression of the King's Two Bodies idea. A.M. Lecoq, *François Ier imaginaire* (Paris, 1987) p.357 and n. points out that this could more easily have been done by the traditional *gisant*, while of course the queens of the period were shown in the same way and the theory could not be applied to them.
47. R.A. Schneider, *Public Life in Toulouse, 1463–1789* (Ithaca, 1989), pp.74–81. E. de Médicis, *Le livre de Podio ou Chronique*, pp.338–9, 343.
48. J.E. Brink, 'Royal power through provincial eyes: Languedoc 1510–1560', *PWSFH*, 10 (1982), 52–9.
49. L.M. Bryant, 'The medieval entry ceremony at Paris' in J.M. Bak, *Coronations* (Berkeley, 1990), pp.111–12. E. Konigson, 'La cité et le prince: premières entrées de Charles VIII (1484–1486)' in *Fêtes et cérémonies de la Renaissance*, 3 (Paris, 1975), pp.55–69.
50. The only exception is the group of print makers issuing copies or interpretations of the decorations of Fontainebleau in the 1540s, cf. H. Zerner, The *School of Fontainebleau* (London, 1969), pp.17–38.
51. Etienne de Médicis, *Livre de Podio*, pp.338–58 for the entire text of this entry ceremony. On Béziers, 1533, see L. Domairon (ed.), *Entrée de François Ier dans la ville de Béziers* (Paris, 1866).
52. J. Chartrou, *Les entrées solonelles et triomphales à la renaissance (1484–1551)* (Paris, 1928), I, pp.85–8.
53. P. Richards, 'Rouen and the Golden Age: the Entry of Francis I, 2 August 1517', in C. Allmand (ed.), *Power, Culture and Religion*, pp.117–30.
54. Bryant, 'The medieval entry ceremony', p.107.
55. M. McGowan, *L'entrée de Henri II à Rouen, 1550* (Amsterdam, nd.), pp.19–20.
56. M. McGowan, 'Form and themes in Henri II's Entry into Rouen', *Renaissance Drama*, I (1968), 217–.

57. R.W. Scheller, 'Ensigns of Authority', pp.101–4; R. Giesey, 'Modèles du pouvoir dans les rites royaux en France', *Annales* (1986), 591. G. Sabatier, '*Rappresentare il principe*, figurer l'état. Les programmes iconographiques d'état en France et en Italie du XVe au XVIIe siècle', in Genet, *Genèse de l'état moderne*, p.248.

58. I.D. McFarlane, *The Entry of Henri II into Paris, 16 June 1549* (New York, 1982), pp.28–35, 47–50, 75.

59. L.M. Bryant, *The King and the City in the Parisian Royal Entry Ceremony: Politics, Ritual and Art in the Renaissance* (Geneva, 1986); Bryant, 'The medieval entry ceremony', p.107. C.R. Baskerville (ed.), *Pierre Gringore's Pageants for the Entry of Mary Tudor into Paris. An Unpublished Manuscript* (Chicago, 1934); M. Sherman, 'Pomp and circumstances: pageantry, politics and propaganda in France during the reign of Louis XII, 1498–1515', *SCJ*, 9, iv (1978), 13–32 argues that the message of these ceremonies can be interpreted in terms of the political context.

60. L.M. Bryant, 'The medieval entry ceremony', pp.88–90, 97–100, 104.

61. Ibid., pp.104–5.

62. On the etymology, cf. S. Hanley, *The Lit de Justice*, p.18.

63. Ibid., pp.52–71.

64. R.J. Knecht, 'Francis I and the "lit de justice": a "Legend" Defended', *FH* (March 1992), 53–83, esp. 64–74; M.P. Holt, 'The king in Parlement: the problem of the *lit de justice* in sixteenth-century France; *HJ*, 31 (1988), 507–23.

65. Hanley, *The Lit de Justice*, pp.127–31.

66. Jean du Tillet, *Les mémoires et recherches* (1577), expanded as *Recueil des roys de France* (1580).

67. A. Bonnardot (ed.), *Le livre et forest de messire Bernardin Rince...et le festin de la Bastille* (Paris, 1876); Lecoq, *François Ier imaginaire*, pp.50–1, 116–17.

68. V. Hoffmann, 'Le Louvre de Henri II: un palais impérial', *Bull. de la Soc. de l'hist. de l'art française*, 1982 (1984), 7–15. M. Boudon, M. Châtenet and A.-M. Lecoq, 'La mis en scène de la personne royale en France au XVIe siècle: premières conclusions'; G. Sabatier, '*Rappresentare il principe*, figurer l'Etat', both in Genet, *Genèse de l'état moderne. Bilans*, pp.235–45, 247–60.

69. Lecoq, 'La symbolique de l'état', pp.155–6.

70. Lecoq, *François Ier imaginaire*, pp.18–19. Hoffmann, 'Donec totum impleat Orbem', p.33.

71. Scheller, 'Ensigns of Authority', pp.81–2; J. Lafaurie, *Les monnaies des rois de France* I (Paris, 1951); C. Maumené and L. d'Harcourt, *Iconographie des rois de France*, I (Paris, 1928)

72. Lecoq, *François Ier imaginaire*, pp.38–52.

73. Ibid., pp.484–5, 53–138; Lecoq, 'La symbolique de l'état', p.166.

74. Lecoq, *François Ier imaginaire*, p.142.

75. Scheller, 'Ensigns of Authority', pp.123–8.

76. On the sun imagery, see E.H. Kantorowicz, 'Oriens Augusti-lever du roi', *Dumbarton Oaks Papers*, 17 (1963), 119–77, esp.162; A.-M. Lecoq, 'La symbolique de l'état', pp.176–8. J Barbey, *Etre roi*, pp.189–91; C.R. Baskerville, *Pierre Gringore's Pageants for the Entry of Mary Tudor*, Hanley, *The Lit de Justice*, p.54; de Grassailles, *Regalium Franciae*, p.2; Ronsard, *Oeuvres*, ed. G. Cohen, I, pp.1015–17; 'Epithalmium sur le mariage du Roy', in *Advertisement du sacre, couronnement et mariage du Très chrestien roy de France et de Pologne Henry III* (Lyon, 1575).

77. J.L. Biget et al., 'Expressions iconographiques et monumentales du pouvoir d'état en France et en Espagne à la fin du moyen âge: l'exemple d'Albi et de Grenade', in Genet, *Culture et idéologie dans la genèse de l'état moderne*, pp.245–63.

78. On the Puy d'Amiens, see A.M. Lecoq, 'Le Puy d'Amiens de 1518. La loi du genre et l'art du peintre', in *Revue de l'Art*, no.38 (1977), 63–74; Lecoq, *François Ier imaginaire*, pp.326–36; Lecoq, 'La symbolique de l'état', p.174.

79. Lecoq, 'La symbolique de l'état', pp.152–5; Lecoq, *François Ier imaginaire*, pp.485–92.

2. THE COURT OF FRANCE: FROM LOUIS XI TO HENRI II

1. P. de Vaissière, *Gentilshommes campagnards de l'ancienne France* (repr. Etrepilly, 1986) pp.11–35. P.M. Smith, *The Anti-Courtier Trend in Sixteenth Century French Literature* (Geneva, 1966). F. Decrue, *La cour de France et la société au XVIe siècle* (Paris, 1888), p.68. The most important recent work includes: J. Boucher, *Sociétés et mentalités autour de Henri III*, 4 vols (Lyon thesis, 1977, Lille, 1981); Boucher, *La cour de Henri III* (Rennes, 1986); J.-F. Solnon, *La cour de France* (Paris, 1987); R.J. Knecht, 'The court of Francis I', *Eur.Stud.Rev.*, 8 (1982), 1–22; Knecht, 'Francis I, prince and patron of the northern Renaissance' in A.G. Dickens (ed.), *The Courts of Europe* (London, 1977).

2. Blaise de Monluc, *Commentaires*, ed. P. Courteault, 3 vols (Paris, 1911–25), pp.767–8; Y. Durand (ed.), *Hommage à Roland Mousnier: clientèles et fidélités en Europe à l'epoque moderne* (Paris, 1981) p.280.

3. J. du Tillet, *Recueil des Roys de France* (1580), p.325.

4. Vaesen, *Lettres de Louis XI*, X, pp.267–8.

5. B. de Mandrot, *Ymbert de Batarnay*, pp.23–4 (on Mont-St-Michel, held by the family for 100 years); order by Louis XI 'to write in my hand as you are accustomed to do', pp.323–4, pp.286–91 (on René). Dropped in 1547, Count René was restored to the chamber in 1549.

6. H. de Chabannes, *Histoire de la maison de Chabannes'* 4 vols (Dijon, 1892–1900).

7. R. de Maulde-la-Clavière, *Louise de Savoie et François Ier: trente ans de jeunesse* (Paris, 1895), pp.35–58, 390; C. Sauzé, 'Correspondance de M. de Lansac (Louis de Saint-Gelais)', *Archives historiques de Poitou*, 33 (1904), intro.

8. M. Dassonville, *Ronsard. Etude historique et littéraire*, I (Geneva, 1968), pp.31–5, 45–51; Lecoq, *François Ier imaginaire*, pp.179–86.

9. M. Harsgor, 'Fidélités et infidélités au sommet du pouvoir', in Durand (ed.), *Hommage à Roland Mousnier*, pp.259–77.

10. R. Scheurer (ed.), *Correspondance du cardinal Jean du du Bellay*, 2 vols (Paris, 1969–73), I, pp.1531–3, passim.

11. Potter, *War and Government in the French Provinces*, ch.2.; Potter, 'A treason trial in 16th century France: the fall of marshal du Biez', *EHR*, 105 (1990), 595–623; du Biez to Montmorency, 20 March (1528), BN fr.3004 fos 41–2.

12. Decrue, *La cour de France et la société du XVIe siècle*, p.3; Solnon, *La cour de France*, p.15; E. Schalk, 'The court as "Civiliser" of the nobility: Noble attitudes and the Court of France in the late sixteenth and early seventeenth centuries' in R.G. Asch and A.M. Birke (eds), *Princes, Patronage and the Nobility* (Oxford, 1991), pp.245–63, esp.p. 249.

13. M.L. Douet-d'Arq, *Comptes de l'hôtel des rois de France aux XIVe et XVe siècles* (Paris, 1865), pp.i–xlii; R. Cazelles, *La société politique sous Jean le bon et Charles V*; Zeller, *Les institutions*, p.94.

14. Knecht, 'The court of Francis I'.

15. C. Samaran, 'Cinquante feuillets retrouvés des comptes de l'argenterie de Louis XI (1466–71)', *Bull. hist. phil.* (1928–9). Samaran argues that these papers found at Montélimar were the copies kept by the Chambre des comptes. They seem to me more likely to be the copies kept by the *argentier* Guillaume de Varye, who had long before been an assistant to Jacques Coeur.

16. 'C'est l'ordre que le Roy veult doresnavant gardé au faict de son argenterie', Blois, 26 July 1550, BN fr.18153 fo.251v; order of *conseil privé* 7 Dec.1550, ibid., fos 198v–9v.

17. AN KK 62, account of André Briçonnet as *commis* for the account of 'le fait de nostre chambre', 1469–70. Briçonnet had replaced Pierre Jobert in 1466. For all these changes, see L.L. Borrelli de Serres, *Recherches sur divers services publics du XIIIe au XVIIe siècle*, 3 vols (Paris, 1895–1909), pp.187–206, esp.200–1, 205.

18. AN J 964 no.57, acc. for *trésorerie de l'hostel* Jan–Feb.1527 by Tertreau with commission 'to hold the account and make the payments of the *chambre aux deniers, officiers de l'hostel, argenterie, escuyrie et menuz de la chambre*'; no.58, ibid., Jan.–Dec.1527 and nos 59–61 quarterly accounts April 1526–Nov. 1526.

19. As *trésorier et payeur des officiers domestiques*, Bochetel paid off the last members of Francis I's household: BN fr.26131 no.24, 36 (May–June 1547), A *notaire et secrétaire du roi*, he went on to become a *secrétaire*

des guerres and ambassador. Cf. R. Mousnier (ed.), *Le conseil du roi*, pp.109–10. Berthereau's accounts in BN fr.21450. By 1550, the *trésorier et payeur des officiers domestiques* is known as *trésorier de la maison* (cf. argenterie account, BL Add. 8879 fos.52v–62v.)

20. For Doulcet as *maître de la chambre aux deniers* cf. BN fr.2930 fos.95–9, *rôle* for généralité of Oultre-Seine, 1502–3. Lettres d'office for Pierre Briçonnet as *maître de la chambre aux deniers*, BN fr.5085 fo.92.

21. Examples from A. Lapeyre and R. Scheurer, *Les notaires et secrétaires du roi…1461–1515* (Paris, 1978) nos 51, 74, 97, 99 bis, 478, 479.

22. Example: a royal order to quit the *trésorier de la maison* for 900 *lt.* paid to Estissac as gent. of the chamber from 1 April 1547 because he had been omitted from the *estat* of the household officers, 31 Dec.1547, BN fr.5127 fo.61v.

23. Original accounts: *officiers de l'hôtel*: 1498–9, AN KK 87; 1523–9, KK 98–9; *états des officers de l'hôtel*, 1524–7, AN J 964 nos 54 bis–58; 1550: BN fr.3132; 1551, BN Clair. 813; *menus plaisirs/affaires de la chambre*: 1478–81, KK 64 (pub.Douet d'Arcq, *Comptes de l'hôtel*, pp.348–96); 1490–1, KK 76; 1528–9, KK 101; Jan.–May 1530, KK 100; *argenterie*: 1463–71, AN KK 58–61 bis; 1487–92, KK 70–2; 1536–41, KK 91–2; Jan.–June 1549, BL Add.8879; Jan.–Mar.1552, BL Egerton 884; 1557, AN KK 106; *chambre aux deniers*: 1478–9, KK 63; 1515–20, AN KK 94; 1524–8, AN J 964; 1525, BN fr.10384; 1556–8, AN KK 107–8; *écurie* 1487–8, AN KK 74; 1497–8, KK 74. Extracts from various accounts for the reigns of Louis XI and Francis I were pub. by Cimber et Danjou, 'Extraits des comptes et dépenses de Louis XI' and 'Extraits des comptes et dépenses de François Ier', in L. Cimber and F. Danjou, *Archives curieuses de l'histoire de France*, 13 vols (1834–49) ser.1, vol.II, pp.91–109, III, pp.79–100. For the *payeurs* of the *vénerie et fauconnerie*, Guillaume de Villemontre, 1549–50, BN fr.26133 nos 307, 455, 537. For the *payeurs* of the various companies of household guards: Swiss, Jacques Groyet, 1550, BN fr.26133 no.443; *100 gents. de l'hôtel*, Jean Vyon, 1547, BN fr.26131 no.126; Scots, Jean Thizard, 1549, fr.26133 no.450.

24. *Grand veneur*, pay of 3600 *lt.* p.a. for his pay and the entire expenses of the *vénerie* in 1548, BN fr.26132 no.307. *Grand fauconnier*, pay of 600 *lt.* in 1550, BN fr.26133 no.537.

25. 21 Mar.1527/8, BL Egerton 17 fo.144.

26. La Rochepot to Montmorency, 9 July, MC L XI fo.244.

27. Scheurer, *La correspondance…Jean du Bellay*, I, p.198.

28. The figures for Charles VIII's household are in T. Godefroy, *Histoire de Charles VIII par Guillaume de Jaligny* (Paris, 1684), pp.704–8; Solnon, *La cour de France*, p.46. Figures are not borne out by Table 1, though the latter does not include the stables, hunt and royal guards. For the period from 1560, we have the figures in J. Boucher, 'L'évolution de la maison du roi: des derniers Valois aux premiers Bourbons', in *XVIIe siècle*, 137 (1982), 359–79.

29. 1463: 102 officers, excluding the hunt, BN fr.7853, pp.1489–94.
30. Knecht, 'The court of Francis I', p.2.
31. BN fr.7853; fr.21449, copies and summaries of the *rôles des officiers*.
32. BN fr.3898 fos165–71.
33. Th. Lhuillier (ed.), 'Rôles journaliers de dépenses pour le service de la maison royale et de la maison du dauphin', *Rev. des soc. savantes*, ser.5, IV, p.436–; V. de Beauvillé, *Recueil de documents inédits pour servir à l'histoire de Picardie*, 4 vols (Paris, 1865–90), II, pp. 215–17; IV, pp.291–3, 296–7.
34. Total 356: Th. Lhuillier (ed.), 'La maison des princes, fils de François Ier', *Bull.trav.hist.* (1889), 212–13. For lists of officers of this household, 1526–38, cf. BN fr.7853, pp.1728–43 and accounts of the *trésorier gén.*, 1534, AN KK 230.
35. R. Doucet, *L'état des finances de 1523* (Paris, 1923), p.88.
36. Mandrot, *Ymbert de Batarnay*, pp.273–7.
37. Household of Francis I's children, BN fr.7853, pp.1738–43; of Orléans 1540–5, ibid., pp.1752–9.
38. Lists of queen Claude's household, BN fr.7853, p.1704–; queen Léonore's household, 1530–47, BN fr.7853, pp.1760–79. Castillon continued to act for the queen after 1547, cf. her instructions to him, 1548, in Vienna HHSA, Frankreich, Varia 6, nachtrag 1548. fos 54–5: disputes about the claims of Charles de Roye, appointed by Henri II to be head both of her household and council as the Constable was for the king. 'We declared to the said sr. de Roye that we intended that our household would be a *logis de paix* and that we wished to avoid all divisions and partialities.' Mme de Roye had also told the queen that she would not leave her service except for two reasons: firstly 'if our amity towards her were diminished' and secondly 'if the king our son entered into suspicion of her for being in our service'.
39. *State Papers of Henry VIII*, Record Commissioners (London 1830–52), VIII, p.305.
40. P. de Vaissière, *Charles de Marillac, ambassadeur et homme politique sous les règnes de François Ier, Henri II et François II (1510–60)* (Paris, 1896), p.69.
41. BN fr.17889 fo.146, 164r; J. des Monstiers-Merinville, *Un évêque ambassadeur au XVIe siècle: Jean des Monstiers, seigneur du Fraisse* (Limoges, 1895), p.121; A. Thierry, *Recueil des monuments inédits de l'histoire du Tiers-État*, 4 vols (Paris, CDI, 1856–70), II, p.647.
42. Solnon, *La cour de France*, p.47.
43. Ibid., p.17
44. BN fr.3898 fos131–4, 146–62 (2nd draft), 109–26.
45. Y. Labande-Mailfert, *Charles VIII et son milieu*, p.139. The salaries of the king's domestic officers were 105, 175 *lt.* in 1495 (T. Godefroy, *Histoire de Charles VIII*, pp.704–6).
46. BN fr.20502 fos108–10: the cost of the household was in this quarter roughly 17% of total expenditure.

47. C. Paillard, 'La mort de François Ier et les premiers temps du règne de Henri II, d'après les dépêches de Jean de Saint-Mauris', *RH*, 5 (1877), 115; *état par estimation* of 1549: BN fr.3127 fo.91–3 (Table 4).
48. BN fr.18676 fo.135.
49. BL Add.8879 fos51v–52v.
50. E.g. Solnon, *La cour de France*, pp.38–9. The *gentilshommes* were not formally mentioned in a royal edict until 1525: *Ordonnances, François Ier*, IV, p.74, Pierre de Warty's mission to conclude a truce with Marguerite of Austria, 1525; given a place in the order of precedence by Robertet for processions in the Parlement, ibid., V, p.158.
51. Du Tillet, *Recueil des Roys de France*, 1607, p.418; C. Loyseau, *Cinq livres des offices* (1610), p.430; Knecht, 'The court', p.6.
52. Du Tillet, *Recueil*, 1580, p.303–. N.B the *valets de chambre* in the account of 1527 were demoted in the order to the same section as the menials, BN fr.3898 fos 109–26; P.L. Roederer, *Louis XII et François Ier: III: Conséquences du système de cour établi sous François Ier* (Paris, 1833), correctly saw that the *gentilshommes* were to replace the *chambellans*.
53. Quoted in B. Bedos-Rezak, *Anne de Montmorency, seigneur de la Renaissance* (Paris, 1990), p.113.
54. Account of André Briçonnet for 'le fait de nostre chambre', 1469–70, AN KK 62. Example: 'for a journey starting from Orléans 16 October from Orléans to Gamaches or elsewhere wherever was Joachim Rouault, lord of the said place, carrying letters close … to signify to him the news received by the king of the capture of the earl of Warwick.'
55. BN fr.7853, pp.1592–1605.
56. *Catalogue des actes de François Ier*, Académie des Sciences Morales et Politiques, 10 vols (Paris, 1887–1910), V, 237, 15897.
57. Paget, 20 Jan.1543, *St.P.*, IX, p.267.
58. Octavian Bosso: at Antwerp in Chapuys's service, 1544, *L&P*, XIX, i, 731; in du Biez trial, BN Dupuy, fo.72r; his mission to Picardy, 1555–6, AM St.Quentin 138 no.28. Christophe Richer, missions to Germany 1551–2, J.D. Pariset, 'La France et les princes allemands', *Francia*, 10 (1982); on his Scandinavian missions, cf. N. Camusat, *Mémoires du sieur Richer* (1625) and documents in a sale catalogue, esp. a letter of Francis I, 17 March 1547.
59. BN fr.5127 fo.37v.
60. P. de Commynes, *Mémoires*, ed. J. Calmette, III, p.313; BN fr.7853, pp.1648–52; orig. account, 1514, AN KK 240.
61. Confusion is caused by the continued use of the honorific title *conseiller et chambellan*, e.g. by Jean, sr. de Créquy, cf. quittance of 6 June 1546, BN fr.26131 no.34. His son Canaples was a *gent.de la chambre* who became captain of 100 *gents. de l'hôtel* under Henri II. Same for Crussol, 15 May 1547, fr.26131 no.29. La Rochepot, governor of Picardy, used the title *chambellan ordinaire du roi* in 1548, though no

longer a *gentilhomme de la chambre* and there are no *chambellans* in the household list, cf. BN p.o. 2031, fr.28515, no.98. The sr. de Luce was also called *chambellan du roi* in 1539, though he was then a *gentilhomme de la chambre*, cf. *CAF* IV, 39, 11178.

62. *Ordonnances, François Ier*, VII, no.665.
63. 9 out of 29 in 1526. The 1523 *état des finances* (ed. Doucet), pp.117–18, list of 14 of the 22 *gentilshommes* who received pensions of 1200 *lt*. This may be because up to that time, as an innovation, they were paid as *pensionnaires* rather than as *officiers de la maison*.
64. 1524: BN fr.3898 fos109–26, for 5 *noble pages de chambre*. 1540: fr.21450; 1550: BN Clair. 813, p.52. 1528: AN P 2305 fo.15.
65. C. Marchand, *Charles Ier de Cossé, comte de Brissac et maréchal de France (1507–63)* (Paris, Angers, 1889), p.45, n.1; BN fr.21450; fr.3132.
66. BN fr.26133 no.461, 516.
67. BN fr.21450.
68. BN fr.2997 fos 16–17. NB all depended on the activation of the pension by a specific royal order. There are many of these in *CAF*.
69. V.-L. Bourrilly, *Guillaume du Bellay, seigneur de Langey (1491–1543)* (Paris, 1905).
70. Marchand, *Brissac*.
71. BN fr.21450 fo.26v; on his role in the enquiries about the death of the dauphin François, 1536, cf. Brantôme, *Oeuvres complètes*, ed. Lalanne, III, p.446.
72. *CAF* III, 645, 10647; VII, 525, 26436; III, 346, 9113; IV, 151, 11692; IV, 170, 11779.
73. S.-C. Gigon, *Révolte de la gabelle en Guyenne, 1548–9* (Paris, 1906), no.11; *Archives hist. de Poitou*, 12; BN Clair.346 fo.8.
74. Instruc. to Humières, 30 Oct. 1552, BN fr.3134 fos1–2; AD Midi-Pyrénées, E 580.
75. BN fr.21450 fo.147r; BN Clair.813; A.D. Lublinskaya, *Documents pour servir à l'histoire des guerres d'Italie* (Moscow, 1962), no.144, 146; letter of du Bellay, 10 Nov.1548, BN fr.5150 fo.58r; L. Romier, *Les origines politiques des guerres de religion*, 2 vols (Paris, 1913–14), I, p.64; instructions 18 Aug.1549; BN fr.3099 fos118–20, 1552–2, BL Egerton 2 fo.53v; Prés. Hiver, *Papiers des Pot de Rhodes, 1529–1648* (Paris, 1864); Triqueti, 'Papiers de M. de Pot de Chemault', *BSHPF*, 21 (1872).
76. BN fr.2957 fo.39, fr.2858 fo.101; E. Charrière, *Négociations de la France dans le Levant*, 4 vols (Paris, 1848–60), II, p.18. Described as *gc* in 1547 but not on the list, cf. Corresp. Morvilliers, fr.2957 fo.39, 101, fr.3131 fo.86. Killed 1562, T. de Bèze, *Histoire ecclésiastique des églises réformées du royaume de France*, ed. G. Baum and E. Cunitz, 3 vols (Paris, 1883–9), I, p.887; *P&P*, 59, 75–6. Mission to gov. of Champagne, 1552, Montmorency to Nevers, Nov., BL Egerton 3 fo.205.
77. AN KK 63, chambre aux deniers 1471–2, 1472–3, 1475–6, 1478–9, 1479–80; fo.68 lettres de retenue for Rocques de Poix, Beauvais, 24

March 1471, fo.73 for Richard Macé, N-D de la Victoire, 25 March 1478; fo.74 for Jean Guérin, Puiseaulx, 18 June 1479.
78. BN fr.7853; fr.20449 fo.7853–.
79. J.-Y. Mariotte, 'François Ier et la ligue de Smalkalde', *Schweizeriche Zeitschrift für Geschichte*, 16 (1966) 214; Marburg St.A. 1834 fo.4.
80. Potter, *War and Government*, ch.4. BN fr.26132 no.336.
81. Brantôme, *Oeuvres*, ed. Lalanne, III, p.275.
82. Examples of officers serving by quarters in the 1520s: Lescars, *panetier* to *gent.chambre*, 1541; Laval, *panetier* to *gent.chambre*, A. de LaRochefoucauld, *échanson* to *gent.chambre*, 1522, Clermont de Dauphiné, *échanson* to *gent.chambre*, 1549; Montéjean, *valet tranchant* to *gent.chambre*, 1528–, later marshal.
83. BN fr.3898 fo.109–; fr.21450.
84. Quittances: BN fr.26131 no.28, 430.
85. J. Bouchet, *Epistres morales et familières* (Paris, 1545), Ep.III to the Nobility, ch.8, quoted in R. de Maulde-la-Clavière, *Louise de Savoie et François Ier*, p.258.
86. Wallop to Henry VIII, 17 Nov.1540, *St.P.*, VIII, p.483; Cheyney, 3 July 1546, ibid., XI, p.230; Lisle, 1546, ibid., p.253. H.R. Baillie, 'Etiquette and planning of the state apartments in baroque palaces', *Archaeologia* (1967), 182–3.
87. F. Boudon et al., 'La mise en scène de la personne royale en France au XVIe siècle'; pp.235–43; M. Châtenet, 'Une demeure royale au milieu du XVIe siecle. La distribution des espaces au château de Saint-Germain-en-Laye', *Revue de l'Art*, 81 (1988), 20–30. Nicholas de Neufville-Villeroy to Montmorency, 13 Aug. (1530) BN fr.2976 fos53–4.
88. Châtenet, 'Une demeure royale', p.29; BL Egerton 884 fos2r–v, 33r, etc.
89. Baillie, 'Etiquette'. S. Thurley, *The Royal Palaces of Tudor England* (London, 1993), pp.113–44.
90. D.L. Potter and P.R. Roberts, 'An Englishman's view of the court of Henri III', *FH*, 2 (1988). M. Châtenet, 'Henri III et "l'ordre de la cour". Evolution de l'étiquette à travers les règlements généraux de 1578 et 1585' in R. Sauzet (ed.), *Henri III et son temps* (Paris, 1992) pp.133–9.
91. The letter is published from a sixteenth-century copy in H. de La Ferrière-Percy (ed.), *Lettres de Catherine de Médicis*, 10 vols (Paris, 1889–1909), II, pp.91–5. La Ferrière dates it 1563 and this would be a fair date if the copy's label that it was written to Charles IX were accepted. However, there is some possibility, based on the internal references to the malign untruths being spread abroad that the king does not care for his subjects' well-being, 'to make you hated', that it was written for Henri III and formed part of the consultations leading to his reform of the court in 1578. Cf. Potter and Roberts, 'An Englishman's view of the court of Henri III', pp.317–19.

92. *Relazione* of Capello, 1554, in N. Tommaseo (ed.), *Relations des ambassadeurs vénitiens sur les affaires de France*, 2 vols (Paris, 1888), I, p.370; on the 'circle' of Catherine, cf. Brantôme, *Oeuvres*, ed. Lalanne, III, p.279, J.-M. Mehl, *Les jeux au royaume de France du XIIIe au début du XVIe siècle* (Paris, 1990), pp.205–6.

93. BN fr.7853, p.1428.

94. 'Ancienne mémoire dont l'on vivoit à la cour de France', BN nafr.7857 fo.77; BN fr.18153 fo.292v.

95. La Ferrière, *Lettres de Catherine de Médicis*, II, p.92.

96. Edicts of 1 Nov.1530: *Ordonnances, François Ier*, VI, pp.122–3; Joinville, 31 Oct. 1546: *St.P.*, XI, p.359. Francis I was known to be angry at leaks from the queen's household from 1542: in March he wrote to her: 'I have been warned by men abroad that certain false news has been given to ambassadors at my court by your maids, which displeases me greatly' and ordering certain of them to be dismissed, Vienna HHSA, Frankreich, Varia 5 fos18–19.

97. *Règlement*, St.Germain, March 1549, BN fr.18153 fos 65–6, repeated, Chambord, 20 Dec.1559, BN nafr.7857 fos 41–8. Edict of March 1560, in *Catalogue des actes de François II* (Paris, 1991), fasc.2, pp.721–8. *Règlement* of duke of Guise as *grand maître*, 1561, BL Lansdowne 112, fos39–72.

98. BN fr.18153 fo.292v.

99. Edict of July 1522, *Ordonnances, François Ier*, IV, no.319, pp.186–8.

100. BN fr.18153 fo.282v. In April 1549 the king, on the Constable's advice, had ordered the *prévôt* to hand over two men caught stealing silks to a captain of galleys rather than proceeding with the case, ibid., fo.167r.

101. R.J. Knecht, 'Francis I, Prince and Patron of the Northern Renaissance', pp.99–109. E. Bourciez, *Les moeurs polies et la littérature de cour sous Henri II* (repr.Geneva, 1967), passim, on the multiple influences of medieval romance traditions, humanism and Italian culture at the court.

102. Schalk, 'The court as 'Civiliser' of the nobility', pp.244–51, 263.

3. THE KING, HIS COUNCIL AND THE SECRETARIAT

1. M. Antoine, 'L'administration centrale des finances' in his *Le dur métier de roi*.

2. 1 June 1468, letters for the chancellors to receive the accustomed oath 'et appeller en noz conseilz et affaires', B. de Mandrot, *Ymbert de Batarnay, seigneur de Bouchage* (Paris, 1886), pp.295–6.

3. M. Harsgor, *Recherches sur le personnel du conseil du roi sous Charles VIII et Louis XII*, 4 vols (thesis, Paris IV, Lille, 1980), I, 213.

4. Potter, *War and Government*, pp.254–8; R. Favreau, *La ville de Poitiers à la fin du Moyen Age*, 2 vols (Paris, 1978), pp.363–6.

5. Favreau, ibid.

6. H. Michaud, *La grande chancellerie et les écritures royales* (Paris, 1967).

7. *Le régime d'un jeune prince* (Harsgor, *Recherches*, I, p.220); Vigner, *Histoire des...comtes de Luxembourg*, 1619 (Harsgor, I, p.203); *Le nef des princes* (Harsgor, I, p.220).

8. *Le songe du Vieil pélerin*; *Le corps de policie* (Harsgor, I, p.189).

9. M. Harsgor, *Recherches* I, p.171; N. Valois, 'Le conseil du roi et le grand conseil', *BEC* (1882) (1883), 160f, on disputes between these two bodies.

10. Harsgor, *Recherches*, IV, p.2747.

11. Commynes, *Mémoires*, bk II, ch.2, ed. J. Calmette, I, p.103; Jean d'Auton, *Chronique* (SHF), p.339; C. de Seyssel, *La monarchie de France* (ed. Poujol), pp.133–4.

12. N. Valois, 'Le conseil', *BEC* (1883), 137–68; M. Pelletier, 'Le Grand Conseil de Charles VII à François Ier', *Positions des thèses de L'Ecole nationale des Chartes* (1960), pp.85–90.

13. Valois, 'Le conseil du roi et le Grand Conseil', *BEC* (1882), 600.

14. C. Potvin, *Oeuvres de G. de Lannoy* (Harsgor, I, p.192); Harsgor, IV, pp.2747, 2752. Commynes, *Mémoires*, bk II, ch.2, ed. J. Calmette, I, p.103.

15. A. Bernier (ed.), *Procès-verbaux des séances du Conseil de Régence* (Paris, 1836); N. Valois, 'Le conseil', *BEC* (1882), 618–22.

16. Michaud, *La grande chancellerie*, pp.222, 256, 262, 269–72. The main problem is that, as H. Michaud had made clear, the practices of the chancellery were undergoing considerable development in the six-teenth century (mainly in the substitution of written *rôles* for verbal authorisation as records of the origination of royal acts), one of the consequences being the breakdown in any consistent meaning to be attached to traditional formulae such as *De par le roy*, *De par le roy en son conseil* or *à la relation de son conseil*, which permit for the fourteenth and fifteenth centuries a precise identification of the authorisation and import of such acts. This applies also to the lists of presences, so effectively used by Gaussin and Harsgor in their analysis of the council under Louis XI, Charles VIII and Louis XII. It is clear that, from the early sixteenth century, presence lists on acts *De par le roy en son conseil* become much more sketchy; in fact virtually unusable. However, the disintegration of chancellery consistency also permits us to infer that many of the acts promulgated at the *jussio De par le roy* are in fact emanations of the *conseil* and these do often retain full presence lists, probably to give weight and authority to them.

17. P.-R. Gaussin, 'Les conseillers de Louis XI', in Chevalier and Contamine (eds), *La France de la fin du moyen âge*, pp.105–34.

18. Harsgor, *Recherches*, I, pp.269–70, 298–.

19. Ibid., I, pp.438–42.

20. Ibid., I, pp.438–43. For a convenient summary of some of Harsgor's conclusions, see J.A. Guy, 'The French king's council, 1483–1526', in R.A. Griffiths and J. Sherborne (eds), *Kings and Nobles in the Later Middle Ages* (New York, 1986), pp.274–94.
21. R. Mousnier (ed.), *Le conseil du roi de Louis XII à la Revolution*, p.21.
22. *Journal de Barillon* (SHF), p.17.
23. *Bull. des comités historiques*, 2, p.126.
24. Analysis of lists drawn from *Ordonnances, François Ier*.
25. V.-L. Bourrilly and F. Vindry (eds), *Ambassades de Jean du Bellay en Angleterre* (Paris, 1905), 9 June 1528, pp.282–8: 'my lords of the council remaining at Paris'; ibid., no.106, p.288.
26. BN fr.3082 p.89; *Ambassades de Jean du Bellay*, pp.370–1, n.
27. *L&P*, XV, 574.
28. Jean du Tillet, *Recueil des Roys de France* (1587). J.A.Guy, 'The French king's council' argues that there could have been no clear differentiation before 1526 but accepts the idea of a *conseil des affaires* from 1526, pp.277–8.
29. F. Decrue, *De Consilio Regis Francisci I*, p.67.
30. *Ordonnances, François Ier*. V, no. 486, p.138.
31. N. Valois, *Etude historique sur le conseil du roi. Introduction de inventaire des arrêts du conseil d'état* (Paris, 1886), I, p.xli.
32. Decrue, *De Consilio*, app.II & III; p.58 (29 Dec.1530); *Ambassades de Jean du Bellay*, p.114–. A. Le Glay, *Correspondance de l'empereur Maximilien Ier*, 2 vols (Paris, 1839), II, p.267. *Ambassades de Jean du Bellay*, p.109; Scheurer, *Correspondance de Jean du Bellay*, I, p.195n, p.197; NB Bonvalot, imperial ambassador, described him as a member of the *conseil d'état*. V.-L. Bourrilly and C. Weiss, 'Jean du Bellay, les Protestants et la Sorbonne' *BSHPF*, 52 (1903), 114–. Text of council list, 1543, in Decrue, *De Consilio*, appendix V, 'establytant pour les dictes finances que pour les matières d'estat'.
33. Decrue, appendix V; series of letters of Francis I to Tournon, 1542, in Archives de L'Aubespine, chateau de Villebon, liasse 20.
34. Annebault 'has had the affairs of Piedmont very amply reported to the king's council' in 1537. (BN fr.5155 fo.17, quoted, Decrue, *De Consilio*, p.48, n.) The town of Senlis in Aug.1544 sent a delegation to Tournon, secretary Bayard 'and others of the *conseil privé*', AM Senlis BB 6 fos10r, 17v, 31v.
35. Saint-Vincent to Charles V, 16 Feb.1541, Vienna HHSA, Frankreich, 9.
36. Vienna HHSA, Frankreich, Varia 6, nachtrag, fo.27.
37. Valois, *Inventaire des arrêts*, pp.xlviii–ix. On the *maîtres des requêtes*: M. Etchechoury, *Les maîtres des requêtes de l'hôtel du roi sous les derniers Valois (1550–1589)* (Paris, 1991).
38. Henri II to Montmorency, 24 Aug.1548, AN AB XIX, 3622.
39. *L&P*, XVI, 350; Montmorency to Marillac, 28 Feb.1541, *L&P*, XVII, 1132; BN fr.18153 fo.3.

40. On the customary historical distinctions between these councils, see Doucet, *Les institutions*, I, pp.140–9; Salmon, *Society in Crisis*, pp.66–7. For lists of the council in 1547: G. Ribier, *Lettres et mémoires d'estat* (Paris, 1666), II, pp.1–2; also *ANG*, VI, p.180; BN Dupuy 218 fos165–6. N. Valois, *L'inventaire des arrêts du conseil du conseil d'état...*, pp.xl–xli.

41. BN fr.18153 fo.158.

42. BN fr.18153 fos297r, 318r.

43. G. de L'Homel, *Nouveau recueil de documents...Montreuil-sur-mer* (Compiègne, 1910), p.127. BN fr.18153 fo.115r; *L&P*, XVIII, i, 163. Minute of the council at Blois, 21 March 1551, on the abbey of Saint-Riquier, sr. de Sceaulx, *maître des requêtes, role* dated Chambord, 5 April, BN fr.3154 fo.79v.

44. BN fr.18153 fo.299r.

45. Valois, *Inventaire des arrêts*, pp.xl–xli; BN Dupuy 218 fo.213–(1616).

46. C. Paillard, 'La mort de François Ier', *RH* (1877), 112.

47. Monluc, *Commentaires*, ed. A. de Ruble, I, pp.243–55; BN fr.4742 no.1, fo.20r.

48. Valois, *Inventaire*, pp.xli–ii; BN f.it. 1715 p.62 (14 March 1541).

49. Alvarotti to Ercole II of Ferarra, 9 May 1546, Modena, AS, Francia B 22 fasc.3, pp.155–65.

50. Scheurer, *La correspondance de Jean du Bellay*, I, p.250.

51. Vienna, HHSA, Frankreich, Varia 5 fo.171v.

52. Letters of Symeoni to Nantouillet, BN fr.4052 fos19, 47–8.

53. *L&P*, XVI, 895, 1427; XVII, 9.

54. AN J 794 no.25/34.

55. Lapeyre and Scheurer, *Les notaires et secrétaires du roi*; Michaud, *La grande chancellerie*, pp.90–126.

56. Vaesen, *Lettres de Louis XI*, vol. I, introduction; J. Vaesen, 'Notice biographique sur Jean Bourré', *BEC*, 43 (1882), 433–60. M. François, 'Les signatures de Louis XI', *Bull. hist. phil.* (1959), 221–9.

57. On the appointment of special war secretaries, BN fr.5085 fos 6–7 (1513) and H. Michaud, *La grande chancellerie*, p.131 (1522). Robertet: A. Desjardins (ed.), *Négociations diplomatiques de la France avec la Toscane*, 6 vols (Paris, 1859–86), II, pp.509–15 and passim; G. Robertet and E. Coyecque, *Les Robertet au XVIe siècle*, vol.II, fasc.I *Registre de Florimond Robertet (1524–25)* (Paris, 1888), intro.

58. Michaud, *La grande chancellerie*, pp.145–6.

59. N. Sutherland, *The French Secretaries of State in the Age of Catherine de Medici* (London, 1962).

60. V.N. Malov, 'Les archives d'un secrétaire d'état sous Henri II retrouvées à Moscou', *BEC*, 135 (1978), 313–39. A.D. Lublinskaya had already started the publication of this source before her death.

61. N. Sutherland, *The French Secretaries of State*; V.-I. Comparato, 'Guillaume Bochetel' in R. Mousnier, *Le conseil du roi de Louis XII à la Revolution* (Paris, 1970), pp.105–29.

62. Michaud, *La grande chancellerie*, p.135.

63. Ibid., pp.146–9; BN fr.18153 is a volume of *arrêts* of the *conseil privé* kept by all the secretaries, whereas BN fr.5127 is a register of commands kept by Bochetel which includes council *arrêts*, 1546–9 and fr.5128 is a similar register kept by Clausse for 1551–5. BN fr.3154 is a collection of the original *rôles*, or records, on which such registers were drawn up, probably kept by du Thier. They also contain *arrêts* of the council. For 1520s: G. Robertet, *Les Robertet au XVIe siècle*, pp.xii–xiii. G. Jacqueton, *La politique extérieure de Louise de Savoie* (Paris, 1892), p.13 pointed out that this was a notebook kept by Robertet himself of all the measures decided in council.

64. Du Thier: Malov, 'Les archives d'un secrétaire d'état', p.313. G. Ribier trawled the du Thier papers in *Lettres et mémoires d'estat des roys, princes, ambassadeurs…sous les règnes de François Ier, Henri II et François II*, 2 vols (Paris, 1667). Those for 1538–40 are in: Chantilly, Musée Condé, L XVI and BL; for L'Aubespine: BN fr.6604–21 and the archives of the château de Villebon, Eure-et-Loire; for Bourdin: BN fr.23191–3, nafr.21698; fr.20471 passim and Rés.impr. F 159–230 (copies).

4.   THE CROWN, ADMINISTRATION AND THE PROVINCES

1. P. Saengher, 'Burgundy and the inalienability of Appanages in the Reign of Louis XI', *FHS*, 10 (1977). A. Leguai, *Les ducs de Bourbon pendant la crise monarchique du xve siècle* (Paris, 1962) argues that the principalities were not feudal but weak 'states' modelled on the king's government.

2. On the Armagnac inheritance, cf. C. Samaran, *La maison d'Armagnac au XVe siècle* (Paris, 1907), pp.358–61; Potter, *War and Government*, pp.71–2 on rival Bourbon claims. On the Anjou inheritance, cf. Vaesen, *Lettres de Louis XI*, vols IX and X passim. For a convenient list of fiefs, see H. Montaigu, *La guerre des Dames. La fin des féodaux* (Paris, 1981), app.

3. Potter, *War and Government*, pp.29–64. On the rising of 1484, AN X/2a 49 fos 1987r–96r, esp.190v.

4. R. Souriac, *Le comté de Comminges au milieu du XVIe siècle* (Paris, 1977), pp.1–15, 170.

5. C. Longeon, *Une province française à la Renaissance: la vie intellectuelle en Forez au XVIe siècle* (Saint-Etienne, 1975), p.22. On the Bourbon domain in Auvergne, see Leguai, *Les ducs de Bourbon*, pp.1–11, 34, 99. On the royal takeover, A Bossuat, *Le bailliage royal de Montferrand (1425–1556)* (Paris, 1957), pp.79–102.

6. Scheurer, *Correspondence de Jean du Bellay*, I, pp.125–6, 149, 152. Vaissière, *Charles de Marillac*, p.397 on Jacqueline de Longwy, duchess of Montpensier. For a history of these properties cf. J.M. La

Mure, *Histoire des ducs de Bourbon et des comtes de Forez*, 4 vols (Paris, Lyon, 1860–97), II, 174–.

7. Charbonnier, *Une autre France*, II, pp.895–7.
8. E. Gabory, *L'Union de la Bretagne à la France: Anne de Bretagne, duchesse et reine* (Paris, 1941); *Ordonnances*, XXI, pp.148–53.
9. *Ordonnances, François Ier*, VI, pp.28–34.
10. Knecht, *Francis I*, pp.242–3; J. de La Martinière, 'Les états de 1532 et l'union de la Bretagne à la France', *Bull. Soc. polymathique du Morbihan* (1911), 177–93; *Ordonnances, François Ier*, VI, pp.275–9.
11. *ANG*, I, p.471, 30 Oct. 1539; F. Isambert, *Recueil général des anciennes lois françaises*, 29 vols (Paris, 1822–33), XII, p.298.
12. The method chosen by the king was a promise of a large subsidy, paid slowly in anticipation of king René's early death, cf. Louis XI to François de Genas, 8 Sept.1478, Vaesen, *Lettres de Louis XI*, VII, p.157; same to same, 17 Jan. and 24 June 1480, ibid., VIII, pp.119–21, 221–2; in the event René died on 10 July 1480. On the succession to Provence, cf. A. Lecoy de Marcie, 'Louis XI et la succession de Provence', *Rev. des quest. hist.*, 43 (1888), 121–57. On Guise: L. Germain, *René II duc de Lorraine et le comté de Guise* (Nancy, 1888).
13. Vaesen, *Lettres de Louis XI*, VIII, p.276n; AN K 72 no.62/2. G. Procacci, 'La Provence à la veille des guerres de religion', pp.243–4.
14. Brantôme, *Oeuvres*, ed. Lalanne IV, pp.271–2.
15. Vaesen, *Lettres de Louis XI*, X, p.333; comte de Dienne, 'Une émeute en Albret sous Alain le Grand', *Revue de l'Agenais* (1904), 343–55.
16. D.L. Potter, 'The Luxembourg Inheritance', *FH*, 6 (1992); S.A. Eurich, 'Anatomy of a Fortune: the house of Foix-Navarre-Albret'(Emory Univ. Thesis, 1988); Marguerite of Navarre told Norfolk in 1533 that Vendôme 'hath ben and yet is and ever wolbe fast imperiall, the grettest part of his lyvyng lying in themperours domynions'. (PRO SP1/77 fo.84r). J. Russell Major, 'Noble income, inflation and the wars of religion in France', *Amer.H.R.*, 38 (1981), 21–48.
17. Favreau, *La ville de Poitiers*, II, pp.366–71; Knecht, *Francis I*, pp.368–9.
18. Samaran, *La maison d'Armagnac au XVe siècle*, pp.305–7, 321–6.
19. Charbonnier, *Une autre France*; AN K 73 no.12, letters of Charles VIII, 15 Mar.1484. Zeller, 'Les premiers gouverneurs d'Auvergne', *Rev. d'Auvergne*, 47, 5 (1933).
20. G. Zeller, 'Gouverneurs de provinces au XVIeme siècle', *RH*, 185 (1939), 225–6; Zeller, 'L'administration provinciale avant les intendants. Parlements et gouverneurs', *RH*, 197 (1947), 180–215.
21. Knecht, *Francis I*, p.346 but cf. B. Chevalier, 'Gouverneurs et gouvernements en France entre 1450 et 1520', *Francia*, Beihefte, band 9 (Actes du XIVe colloque historique franco-allemand, Tours ...1977, Munich, 1980), pp.291–307, esp.p.302: 'no doubt is possible...the governors are, formally speaking, officers.' On the hybrid quality of

the post, M. Antoine, 'Genèse de l'institution des intendants', *Journal des savants* (July–Dec. 1982), pp. 283–317, esp. p.286.

22. On the entries of governors, see J.E. Brink, 'Royal power through provincial eyes', pp.55–7.

23. Chevalier, 'Gouverneurs et gouvernements', pp.291–307.

24. Potter, *War and Government*, pp.92–100.

25. R. Harding, *Anatomy of a Power Elite. The Provincial Governors of Early Modern France* (New Haven, London, 1978), pp.28–9.

26. Potter, *War and Government*, pp.103–4.

27. On 1548, cf. G.Zeller, 'L'administration monarchique avant les intendants', in *Aspects de la politique française*, pp.204–6; M. Antoine, 'Institutions françaises en Italie sous le règne de Henri II: gouverneurs et intendants (1547–59)', *Mélanges de l'Ecole française de Rome. Moyen Age, Temps modernes*, 94 (1982), 759–818, esp.764–6 on the instructions of 1550 and de Bellay's letter of 1547.

28. M. Antoine, 'Genèse de l'institution des intendants', pp.283–317. Etchechoury, *Les maîtres des requêtes*, pp.133–58. R. Bonney, *Political Change in France under Richelieu and Mazarin* (Oxford, 1978), p.140 deals with the earliest proper commissions as *intendant de justice*, which he regards as the true precursors of the seventeenth-century intendancy. Many of the commissions found by Antoine deal with finance and other matters. The earliest justice commission is for Pierre de Panisse in Corsica, 1556 (Antoine, 'Institutions françaises en Italie', pp.815–18). R. Bonney, 'Bodin and the development of the French monarchy', *TRHS* (1990), 43–61, esp. 50.

29. Mousnier, *Le conseil du roi*, pp.17–20.

30. P. Chaunu, 'L'état', in Braudel and Labrousse, *Histoire sociale et économique de la France*, I, i, pp.35–9. NB that his percentages are wrong here but right on p.193 and that Mousnier suggests 18 million.

31. Chaunu, 'L'état', pp.114, 197; Mousnier, *Le conseil du roi*, p.46.

32. R. Mousnier, *La vénalité des offices sous Henri IV et Louis XIII* (Paris, 2nd edn, 1971), pp.35–56; C. Stocker, 'Public and private enterprise in the administration of a Renaissance monarchy: the first sales of office in the Parlement of Paris (1512–24)', *SCJ*, 9, ii (1978), 4–29, esp. 21–5.

33. Mousnier, *La vénalité des offices*, pp.44–51.

34. M. Harsgor, 'Maîtres d'un royaume. Le groupe dirigeant français à la fin du XVe siècle', in Chevalier and Contamine, *La France de la fin du XVe siècle*, pp.135–46.

35. Stocker, 'Public and private enterprise', p.19.

36. D. Hervier, *Pierre le Gendre et son inventaire après décès* (Paris, 1977), pp.18–87.The main alliance of the Le Gendre was with the secretarial Neufville-Villeroy family. R.J. Kalas, 'The Selve family of Limousin: members of a new elite in early modern France', *SCJ*, 18 (1987), 147–72.

37. Imbart de la Tour, *Les origines de la réforme*, 4 vols (Paris, 1905–35), I, pp.444–7.

38. B. Chevalier, *Tours, ville royale (1356–1520)* (Paris, 1975), pp.471–2, 475.

39. P. Hamon, 'Culture et vie religieuse dans le monde des offices: les Ruzé dans la première moitié du XVIe siècle', *Bib. Hum. Ren.*, 53 (1991), 49–64.

40. Harsgor, *Recherches sur le personnel du conseil du roi*, III, p.2127; Chevalier, *Tours, ville royale*, pp.484–7, 501. Hamon, 'Culture et vie religieuse', p.52.

41. Harsgor, *Recherches sur le personnel*; Potter, *War and Government*, p.49–50; on Armagnac, cf. C. Samaran; N. Lemaître, *Le Rouergue flamboyant, Le clergé et les fidèles du diocèse de Rodez* (1417–1563) (Paris, 1988), pp.395–447.

42. Constant, *Les Guise*, pp.20–51.

43. B. Guenée, *Tribunaux et gens de justice dans le bailliage de Senlis à la fin du Moyen Age* (Strasbourg, 1963); Chaunu, 'L'état', pp.102–3.

44. Guenée, ibid.; Chaunu, 'L'état', p.111; B. Quilliet, *Le corps d'officiers de la prévôté et vicomté de Paris et de l'Ile-de-France de la fin de la guerre de Cent Ans au début des guerres de religion: étude sociale*, Paris IV thesis, 1977, 2 vols (Lille III, service de reprod. des thèses, 1982).

45. J. Boca, *La justice criminelle...Abbeville, 1184–1516* (Lille, 1930), pp.73–5.

46. Zeller, *Les institutions de la France au XVIe siècle* (1948), pp.196–7.

47. On the earlier sixteenth century, see R. de Maulde-la-Clavière, *Les origines de la révolution française au commencement du XVIe siècle. La veille de la Réforme* (Paris, 1889), pp.97–8,, 311, n.50–1 (examples from AN JJ 232–4). Lalanne (ed.), *Le journal d'un bourgeois de Paris*, p.166. J. Nouaillac, *Histoire du Limousin*, pp.267–8. Royal letters of 14 May, 31 Dec. 1558, 17 Dec. 1559, AD Pas-de-Calais 9B 2 fos 63r–v, 107r–v, 132–3, AD Somme B 1 fos 35r, 38–9. Auvergne and Poitou, 1523: Lalanne (ed.), *Journal d'un bourgeois*, pp.166–8.

48. E. Teall, 'The myth of royal centralization and the reality of the neighbourhood. The journals of the sire de Gouberville 1549–62', in M.U. Chrisman and O. Grundler (eds), *Social Groups and Religious Ideas in the Sixteenth Century* (Kalamazoo, 1978), pp.1–11.

49. Scheurer, *Correspondance de Jean du Bellay*, I, p.160.

50. B. de Mandrot, *Ymbert de Batarnay*, pp.76–8, 307–10.

51. Charbonnier, *Une autre France*, II, p.911.

52. R. Muchembled, *Le temps des supplices. De l'obéissance sous les rois absolus, XVe–XVIIIe siècle* (Paris, 1992), pp.54–60, points out the high degree of insecurity in this region in the 1460s as seen from the evidence of Jacques du Clercq's *Mémoires*.

53. Comte de Marsy, 'L'exécution d'un arrêt de Parlement au XVe siècle', *MSAP*, 26 (1880), 149–64. AN X/2A 49 fos 187r–196r (3 June 1484).

54. A. Ledru, *Histoire de la maison de Mailly*, 3 vols (Paris, 1894), I, pp.378, 383, 387–8; II, pp.248–52, 255–7.

55. Ledru, *La maison de Mailly*, I, pp.179–81, II, pp.270–3.
56. Knecht, *Francis I*, p.351.
57. B. Chevalier, *Les bonnes villes de France du XIVe au XVIe siècle* (Paris, 1982), p.299; Muchembled, *Le temps des supplices*, pp.65–6, 82–103.
58. AM Péronne: (1510): BB 6 fos 226v, 228v, 229v, 230v, 231r–v; (1512): BB 6 fos 303r, 304r, 306r.
59. AM Péronne BB 7 fos 15r, 28r, 33v, 43r, 52r, 53r–v, 61r–v, 77v, 84v, 89r, 92r, 93r, 96r–v, 124v.
60. N.Z. Davis, *Fiction in the Archives* (Stanford, Cal., 1987).
61. R. Muchembled, *La violence au village. Sociabilité et compartements populaires en Artois du XVe au XVIIe siècle* (Paris, 1989), pp.15–23.
62. Ibid., pp.23–46; Muchembled, *Le temps des supplices*, p.92. C. Gauvard, *'De grace espécial': crime, état et société en France à la fin du moyen âge* (Paris, 1991).
63. AN JJ 230 no.289 fo.135, Sept.1498; JJ 236 no.358, fo.337r (Feb. 1524).
64. AN JJ 260/2, fos 109–10, told in Vaissière, *Gentilshommes campagnards*, pp.24–6.

5. THE TAXATION SYSTEM AND ITS BURDENS

1. *Ordonnances,* XVI, p.297, On money and war, see royal edict, 7 Sept. 1551 du Tillet, *Recueil,* III, pp.375–6: 'money is said to be the ornament of peace and the sinews of war'; speech of Henri II at the Estates of Jan.1558, see Rabutin, *Commentaires,* ed. G. de Taurines (Paris, 1932–42); 'Argent, qui pis est, estant le nerf de la guerre', Brantôme, *Oeuvres,* ed. Buchon, I, p.180. See N. Machiavelli, *The Discourses* bk. II, ch.x.
2. Chaunu, 'L'état', in *Histoire économique et sociale de la France,* I, i, pp.40–1.
3. M. Rey, *Les finances royales sous Charles VI: les causes du déficit, 1388–1413* (Paris, 1965); Chevalier, *Tours, ville royale,* p.473.
4. On the usage, 'messieurs de finances', Favreau, *La ville de Poitiers,* pp.373–4 (1473). M. Wolfe, *The Fiscal System of Renaissance France* (New Haven, Conn., 1972), pp.261–3; Antoine, 'L'administration centrale des finances', p.33. Isambert, *Anciennes lois,* XII, no.356, XIII, no.179. For the changes of 1547 see A. Fontanon, *Les édicts et ordonnances des rois de France,* 4 vols (1611), II, pp.631–6; *CAH,* I, no.77.
5. Chevalier, *Tours,* pp.473–4.
6. Mousnier, *La vénalité des offices,* p.9.
7. Chevalier, *Tours,* p.487.
8. G. Caster, *Le commerce du pastel et de l'épicerie à Toulouse de 1450 environ à 1561* (Toulouse, 1962), p.84; A. Viala, *Le Parlement de Toulouse et l'administration royale, 1420–1525* (Albi, 1953).

9. Chevalier, *Tours,* p.495.
10. Ibid., pp.475–6.
11. *Procédures politiques du règne de Louis XII,* ed. R. de Maulde-la-Clavière, p.1047.
12. On Genas, cf. comte de Balincourt, 'Un général sous Louis XI', *Revue du Midi,* I (1887); *Bulletin du comité des monuments écrits de l'histoire de France, histoire, sciences, lettres,* III (1852), about 30 letters (at château of Cabrières) to him, 1476–83 in Vaesen, *Lettres de Louis XI,* vols VI–X, passim. Letters of 1479, ibid., VIII, p.32; of May 1483: ibid., X, pp.109–10.
13. Quoted in Chevalier, *Tours,* p.484: Charles VIII was 'fearful of displeasing those he gave credit to, and especially those who have managed the finances like the said cardinal, his brothers and relatives.'
14. Chevalier, *Tours,* pp.479–80, 483.
15. Ibid., p.487.
16. Ibid., p.490; BN Joly de Fleury 2504 fos 48–68.
17. On Briçonnet, G. Jacqueton, *Documents sur l'administration financière en France de Charles VII à Francois Ier (1443–1523)* (Paris, 1891), p.102; Chevalier, *Tours,* pp.498–505.
18. Knecht, *Francis* I, pp.126–32, 377–9. Cf. also here the next section.
19. A. Guéry, 'Le roi dépensier. Le don, la contrainte et l'origine du systeme financier ... d'Ancien Régime', *Annales,* 39 (1984), 1254.
20. A. Guery, 'Les finances de la monarchie française sous l'ancien régime', *Annales,* 33 (1978), 216, 219.
21. Doucet, *L'état des finances de 1523*; Guéry, 'Les finances', p.221; *relazione* of Contarini, ibid., note 25 on procedures.
22. Doucet, *L'état des finances,* p.10; J. Favier, *Finance et fiscalité au bas Moyen Age* (1971), pp.288–303.
23. Jacqueton, 'Le Trésor de l'Epargne sous Francois Ier'.
24. Guéry, 'Les finances', p.222; Chevalier, *Tours ville royale.* On this see also the section on administration.
25. Tommaseo, *Relations,* I; Guéry, 'Les finances', p.221.
26. Chaunu, 'L'état' in Braudel and Labrousse, *Histoire économique et sociale,* I, i, figures, to be compared with Guéry's figures – figures in terms of silver, etc.
27. Guery, 'Les finances', pp.220, 221; Clamageran, *Histoire de l'impôt en France,* 3 vols (Paris, 1867–76).
28. A. Spont, 'La taille en Languedoc de 1450–1515', *Annales du Midi* (1890), pp.368–70; Ladurie, *L'état royal,* p.38.
29. Clamageran, *Histoire de l'impôt*; Chaunu, 'L'état', p.150; P. Contamine, 'Guerre, fiscalité royale et économie en France (deuxième moitie du XVe siècle)', *7th International Economic History Congress,* ed. M. Flinn, II (Edin. 1978), pp.268–9.
30. Doucet, *L'état des finances,* p.8.
31. BN fr. 3127 fos 91–3.
32. BN fr.4523.

33. Bois, *Crise de la féodalité*, pp.63–9, 329–36.
34. H. Miskimin, *Money and Power in Fifteenth Century France* (London, 1984), pp.54–73.
35. Ladurie, *L'état royal*, pp.58–9. On the *livre tournois* see Miskimin; H. Hauser (ed.), *La response de Jean Bodin à M. de Malestroit* (Paris, 1932), introduction; R. Tortajada, 'M. de Malestroit et la théorie quantitative de la monnaie', *Rev. écon.*, 38 (1987), 853–76.
36. Chaunu, 'L'état', pp.39–42; NB Ladurie gives a rise from 140 to 190 tonnes in this period, cf. *L'état royal*, p.170–; Cf. also Guéry, 'Les finances'.
37. Charbonnier, *Une autre France*, II, p.907.
38. Chaunu, 'L'état', p.160.
39. Ibid., pp.164–5.
40. *Histoire économique et sociale de la France*, I, ii, pp.978–81; Contamine, 'Guerre, fiscalité', p.271.
41. Circular of P. Briçonnet, c.1500: G. Jacqueton, *Documents relatifs à l'administration financière*, pp.102–12.
42. M. François, *Le cardinal François de Tournon* (Paris, 1951).
43. BN fr.3127 fos 91–3.
44. M. François, 'Albisse del Bène, surintendant général des finances françaises en Italie', *BEC*, 94 (1933), 337–60; M.-N. Baudouin-Matuszek and P. Ouvarov, 'Banque et pouvoir au XVIe siècle: la surintendance des finances d'Albisse del Bène', *BEC*, 149 (1991), 248–91.
45. Baudouin-Matuszek and Ouvarov, pp.276–8 and 'Mémoire sur le grand parti de Lyon', pp.290–1; R. Doucet, 'Le grand parti de Lyon au XVIe siècle', *RH*, 171 (1933), 473–513.
46. Cloulas, *Henri II*, pp.512–15.
47. Ladurie, *L'état royal*, p.171; Baudouin-Matuszek, 'Banque et pouvoir', pp.286–7.
48. Wolfe, *The Fiscal System of Renaissance France*, pp.47–51.
49. A. Dussert, 'Les états du Dauphiné de la Guerre de Cent Ans aux Guerres de Religion', *Bull. de l'Acad. delphinal*, ser.5, 8 (1922); L.S. van Doren, 'War taxation, institutional change and social conflict in provincial France', *Proc. Amer. Philo. Soc.*, 121 (1977), 71, n.7.
50. Chaunu, 'L'état', pp.148–9.
51. A. Spont, 'Une recherche générale des feux à la fin du XVe siècle', *Ann. bull. Soc. hist. France* (1892), 222–36; Spont, 'La taille en Languedoc', *AM* (1890), 487–8; P. Dognon, 'La taille en Languedoc de Charles VII à François Ier', *AM* (1891), 340–65, esp. 349. *Doléances* of the estates of Languedoc, c.1501, BN fr.2930 fos 62–7, esp.fo.73v.
52. Dognon, 'La taille en Languedoc'.
53. van Doren, 'War taxation', p.73 n.15. On the legal status of Dauphiné as territory of the Empire, cf. Jean Bodin, *Six livres de la Republique* (1580 edn), p.187.
54. van Doren, 'War taxation', p.81.

55. D. Hickey, *The Coming of French Absolutism. The Struggle for Tax Reform in the Province of Dauphiné, 1540–1640* (Toronto, 1986), pp.23–5.
56. J. Bousquet, *Enquête sur les commodités du Rouergue en 1552. Procès entre l'Agenais, le Quercy et le Périgord* (Toulouse, 1969), pp.15–25.
57. Potter, *War and Government in the French Provinces*, pp.233–64.
58. Ibid.
59. Maugis, *Essai sur le régime financier de la ville d'Amiens* (Mém. Soc. Antiq. de Picardie in-4to), pp.400, 422–32.
60. On forced loans on the towns of the west, see Favreau, *La ville de Poitiers*, pp.356–60, esp.359.
61. Ibid., pp.442–3.
62 Potter, *War and Government*, pp.247–53. B. Chevalier in N. Bulst and J.-P. Genet (eds), *La ville, la bourgeoisie et la genèse de l'état moderne* (1988); Chevalier, *Les bonnes villes de France*.
63. A. Leguai, 'Le révoltes rurales dans le royaume de France du milieu du XIVe à la fin du XVe siècle', *Le moyen age*, 88 (1982), 49–76.
64. Leguai, 'Les révoltes', p.76; R. Cazelles, 'La Jacquerie fut-elle un mouvement paysanne?' *Acad. des Inscript. et Belles-Lettres – comptes-rendus* (1978), pp.654–66; Cazelles, *La société politique sous Jean le bon et Charles V*, pp.318–37.
65. Leguai, 'Les révoltes', p.74: the Jacquerie was centred on the county of Clermont, belonging to duke Louis II of Bourbon, the Tuchins in Forez, belonging to Jean de Berry.
66. H. Heller, *Iron and Blood, Civil Wars in Sixteenth-century France* (Montreal, London, 1991), pp.12–15.
67. Bourdin to Jean Bourré, Paris, 19 March, BN fr.20487 fo.12.
68. A. Leguai, 'Emeutes et troubles d'origine fiscale pendant le règne de Louis XI', pp.452–3.
69. T. Basin, ed. Samaran, I, p.65.
70. Loys d'Estouteville to Bourré, Pont-Audemer, 17 March, BN fr.20487 fo.73.
71. The movement of the Norman *Bocage* in 1466–7 known as the *Galants de la Feuille* (roughly fighters of the woods) was a response of the classic kind to destruction wrought by Breton soldiers (Leguai, 'Les révoltes', p.73).
72. Leguai, 'Emeutes', pp.454–7.
73. Ibid., pp.460–2, 468–9.
74. On this cf. R. Gandilhon, *La politique économique de Louis XI*, ch.III, pp.121–35; H. See, *Louis XI et les villes* (Paris, 1981), p.179.
75. Leguai, 'Emeutes', pp.473–6.
76. Ibid., pp.476–80.
77. V.I. Raytses, 'Le programme d'insurrection d'Agen en 1514', *Annales du Midi*, 93 (1981), 265.
78. Leguai, 'Emeutes', pp.482–3.
79. Heller, *Iron and Blood*, p.23.
80. Ibid., pp.42–4.

81. Raytses, 'Le programme d'insurrection', pp.268–9: levels of the *taille* at Agen: 1511 – L 341; 1512 – L 546; 1513 – L 892.
82. Raytses, 'Le programme d'insurrection', pp.270–1.
83. Heller, *Iron and Blood*, pp.25–6.
84. van Doren, 'War taxation and institutional change', pp.7–96.
85. Heller, *Iron and Blood*, pp.35–8.
86. Ibid., p.37; R. Souriac, 'Mouvements paysans en Comminges au XVIe siècle', in J. Nicolas (ed.), *Mouvements populaires et conscience sociale XVIe–XIXe siècles* (Paris, 1985), pp.266–76, 282–5.
87. S.-C. Gigon, *La révolte de la Gabelle en Guyenne*, pp.20–1.
88. *Voyage du roy Francoys en La Rochelle* in Cimber et Danjou, *Archives curieuses*, ser.1, III (1835), pp.35–64.
89. Gigon, *La révolte de la Gabelle*, p.24: 4 provinces – Brittany, Provence, Languedoc and Dauphiné – retained special arrangements.
90. Gigon, *La révolte de la Gabelle*, pp.26–8.
91. Heller, *Iron and Blood*, pp.39–40.
92. Gigon, *La révolte de la Gabelle*, pp.205–7; story of Puymoreau given by Paradin, *Histoire de nostre temps* (1552); add to this that Puymoreau was arrested at Dieppe and taken to Abbeville in May 1549, when he was called 'Puymoreau, dit le duc de Guyenne', BN fr.26132 no.290, payments by Moreau *trés.de l'extraordinaire des guerres*.
93. Gigon, *La révolte de la Gabelle*, pp.230–2.
94. J. Powis, 'Guyenne 1548: the crown, the province and social order', *Eur. Stud. Rev.*, 12 (1982), 4–5, 10–12.
95. Heller, *Iron and Blood*, p.45.

6. THE FRENCH NOBILITY IN THE RENAISSANCE

1. A. Thierry, *Essai sur l'histoire de la formation et des progrès du Tiers Etat* (1867 edn), p.45; *Considérations sur l'histoire de France* (1846 edn), p.26; R. de Maulde-la-Clavière, *Les origines de la révolution*, p.100; B. Guenée, 'L'Histoire de l'état en France à la fin du Moyen Age', p.333.
2. Guenée, 'L'Histoire de l'état', p.352.
3. L. Romier, *Le royaume de Catherine de Médicis*, I, pp.160–97.
4. N. Tommaseo, *Relations* cited in D. Crouzet, 'Recherches sur la crise de l'aristocratie en France: les dettes de la maison de Nevers', *Histoire, économie, société*, 1 (1982), 7. On the later sixteenth century see D. Bitton, *The French Nobility in Crisis* (Stanford, 1969) and above all the work of A. Jouanna, *L'idée de race en France au XVIe siècle et au début du XVIIe* (thesis, 3 vols, Lille, 1976) and *Le devoir de révolte. La noblesse française et la gestation de l'état* (Paris, 1989).
5. P. de Vaissiére, *Gentilshommes campagnards*, pp.13–21.
6. Guenée, 'L'Histoire de l'état', pp.331–58.

7. P. Anderson, *Lineages of the Absolute State*, pp.19–20.

8. E. Perroy, *La guerre de Cent Ans*, p.292.

9. G. Bois, 'Noblesse et crise de revenues seigneuriaux en France au XIVe et XVe siècles', in P. Contamine, *La noblesse au moyen âge, XIe–XVe siècles* (Paris, 1976), p.228.

10. R. Cazelles, *La société politique et la crise de la royauté sous Philippe de Valois* (Paris, 1958), p.290; R.H. Lucas, 'Ennoblement in late medieval France', *Medieval Stud.*, 39 (1977), 239–60, eps. 239–40.

11. Contamine, 'The French nobility', in *La France au XIVe et XVe siècles*, p.141.

12. Zeller, 'Proces à reviser?' in *Aspects*, pp.244–5.

13. J.-M. Constant, *La vie quotidienne de la noblesse française aux XVIe et XVII siècles* (Paris, 1985), pp.99–103.

14. Favreau, *La ville de Poitiers*, II, p.531; H. Sée, *Louis XI et les villes*, pp.77, 311; J.-R. Bloch, *L'anoblissement en France au temps de François Ier* (Paris, 1934), pp.1–9: e.g. the councillors of Cognac were noble from 1471, of Abbeville from 1477; confirmation in 1561 of the immemorial noble status of those Angoulême, La Rochelle, Poitiers, Niort, etc.

15. Bloch, *L'anoblissement*, pp.43–4; Zeller, 'Procès à reviser?', *Aspects*, p.247; Constant, *La vie quotidienne*, pp.92–9.

16. 'marque indélébile de sa roture', Zeller, *Aspects*, p.247.

17. Guenée, *Tribunaux et gens de justice ... Senlis*, p.201; Favreau, *La ville de Poitiers*, II, pp.531–2; J.-M. Mehl, *Les jeux au royaume de France*, pp.195–9; A. Jouanna, *Le sire de Gouberville. Un gentilhomme normand au XVIe siécle* (Paris, 1981).

18. Contamine, 'The French nobility', pp.143–4; Bloch, *L'anoblissement*, p.44.

19. Bloch, *L'anoblissement*, pp.40–1.

20. Ibid., pp.45–6, 52.

21. Ibid., p.18.

22. Vaissière, *Gentilshommes campagnards*, pp.29–31.

23. Charbonnier, *Une autre France*, II, pp.1074–5.

24. *Ordonnances*, XXI, p.324 (May 1505).

25. Contamine, 'The French nobility', p.138.

26. M. Orléa, *La noblesse et les états généraux de 1576 et 1588* (Paris, 1980), pp.53–4, 54–5, 59. J.-M. Constant, 'Les barons français pendant les guerres de religion', in *Quatrième centenaire de la bataille de Coutras* (Pau, 1989), pp.49–62.

27. Contamine, 'The French nobility', p.145.

28. Contamine, 'Points de vue sur la chevalerie à la fin du moyen âge', *Francia*, 4 (1976) and *La France aux XIVe et XVe siècles*, X, pp.259–60.

29. Contamine, 'The French nobility', p.143, based on A. de la Sale.

30. BN fr.3085 fo.46, *lettres de chevalerie* for the lieutenant of the sénéchal of Quercy.

31. P. Contamine, 'Sur l'ordre de Saint-Michel au temps de Louis XI et de Charles VIII', *La France aux XIVe et XVes siècles*, pp.230, 236.

32. There were 364 creations in 1568, cf. M. Orléa, *La noblesse et les états*, p.62.

33. E. Perroy, 'Social mobility among the French *noblesse* in the later middle ages', *P&P*, 21 (1962), 27.

34. *Ordonnances*, XVII, pp.337–9: in return for a lump sum of 47, 250 *lt*.

35. R. Gandilhon, *La politique économique de Louis XI*, p.112; Contamine, 'The French nobility', p.143; R.H. Lucas, 'Ennoblement in late medieval France', pp.252–3.

36. Zeller, 'Procès à reviser?', pp.247–8: e.g. *congé de marchander à un noble*, BN fr.5727 fo.56.

37. Bloch, *L'anoblissement en France au temps de François Ier*.

38. E. Schalk, 'Ennoblement in France from 1350 to 1660', *Jour. Social Hist.*, 16 (1982), 101–10; Schalk, *From Valor to Pedigree: Ideas of Nobility in France in the Sixteenth and Seventeenth Centuries* (Princeton, 1986).

39. Contamine, 'The French nobility', p.143; Guenée, *Tribunaux et gens de justice*, pp.409–15; Lucas, 'Ennoblement in late medieval France', pp.256–7.

40. Bloch, *L'anoblissement*, pp.73–101, 211.

41. M. Harsgor, 'L'essor des bâtards nobles au XVe siècle', *RH*, 253 (1975), 319–24, 345.

42. P. Contamine, *Guerre, état et société à la fin du moyen âge* (Paris, The Hague, 1972), pp.400–4, 550–1.

43. Samaran, *La maison d'Armagnac*, pp.358–61; Samaran, 'La jeunesse et les études toulousaines du cardinal d'Armagnac', in his *Une longue vie d'érudit*, 2 vols (Paris, 1978), II, pp.735–47.

44. Charbonnier, *Une autre France*, I, pp.559–61, II, pp.1086–7. I, p.561, II, p.1087.

45. Harsgor, 'L'essor des bâtards', pp.351–3.

46. Contamine, 'De la puissance aux privilèges', p.256.

47. J. Bouchet, *Epistres morales et familières* (1545 edn), part 2. esp.III, ch.8; Brantôme, *Oeuvres complètes*, ed. Lalanne, VI, pp.52–3, note the contrast supposed with the Spanish nobleman who says 'Je suis gentilhomme comme le roy; il es est vray que je n'ay pas tant d'écus.'

48. Brantôme, *Oeuvres*, X, p.102; VI, p.51.

49. Constant, *La vie quotidienne*, p.10.

50. Bois, 'Noblesse et crise de revenues' in Contamine (ed.), *La noblesse au moyen âge*.

51. Fourquin, *Les campagnes de la région parisienne*, pp.465–74.

52. Jacquart, *La crise rural en Ile-de-France*, pp.104–8, 161–4; J.-M. Constant, *Nobles et paysans beaucerons aux XVIe et XVIIe siècles* (thesis, Lille, 1981).

53. J. Dewald, *The Formation of a Provincial Nobility. The Magistrates of the Parlement of Rouen (1499–1610)* (Princeton, 1980); R. Gascon, *Grand*

commerce et vie urbaine au XVIe siècle, II, pp.813–19, 826–30; Favreau, *La ville de Poitiers*, II, pp.523–30.

54. Contamine, Introduction to *La France de la fin du XVe siècle*, pp.4–5.
55. D. Potter, 'The Luxembourg inheritance', *FH* (1992); J. Russell Major, 'Noble income, inflation and the Wars of Religion in France', *Amer. Hist. Rev.*, 38 (1981), 21–48.
56. Vaissière, *Gentilshommes campagnards*, p.37.
57. On Gouberville, see Jouanna, *Le sire de Gouberville*; K. Fedden, *Manor Life in Old France from the Journal of the Sire de Gouberville for the Years 1549 to 1562* (New York, 1933); G. Huppert, *Les bourgeois gentils-hommes: an Essay on the Definition of Elites in Renaissance France* (Chicago, 1977). On Monteynard and Terraules, Charbonnier, *Une autre France*, II, pp.1077–8. For other areas, see J. Lartigaut, 'L'image du baron au début du XVIe siècle: Caumont contre Thémines', *Annales du Midi*, 94 (1982), 151–71; Marsy, 'L'adjudication d'un arrêt de Parlement au XVe siècle ...Raincheval', *MSAP*, 26 (1880), 149–64, on self-help and violence. Also, A. Ledru, *Histoire de la maison de Mailly*, I, pp.179–81, II, 250–1, 270–3.
58. Vaissière, *Gentilshommes campagnards*, pp.48–59; Constant, *La vie quotidienne*, pp.71–103; P. Raveau, *L'agriculture et les classes paysannes dans le Haut-Poitou au XVIe siècle* (Paris, 1926).
59. W. Weary, 'La maison de la Trémoïlle', in Chevalier and Contamine, *La France de la fin*, p.197.
60. Greengrass, 'Property and politics', pp.373–7, 382.
61. Potter, 'The Luxembourg inheritance'.
62. Crouzet, 'Recherches', pp.8–9, 17–18.
63. Tommaseo, *Les relations*, I, p.489.
64. Land alienations in the late 1570s, constitutions of rentes, esp.in 1587–9, Crouzet, 'Recherches', p.48; Harding, *Anatomy of Power Elite*.
65. J.B. Wood, *The Nobility of the Election of Bayeux, 1463–1666* (Princeton, 1980); Constant, *Nobles et paysans beaucerons;* Constant, *La vie quotidienne*, pp.83, 85.
66. J. Lartigaut, 'Seigneurs et paysans du Quercy vers la fin du XVe siècle', *Annales du Midi*, 86 (1974), 237–52; Lartigaut, 'L'exploita-tion des herbages du Causse de Gramat au XVe siècle', ibid., 82 (1970), 147–69; Lartigaut, *Les campagnes du Quercy après la Guerre de Cent Ans, vers 1440–vers 1500* (Toulouse, 1978); L. Merle, *La métairie et l'évolution agraire de la Gâtine poitevine de la fin du Moyen Age à la Révolution* (Paris, 1958), p.64–.
67. M. Le Mené, *Les campagnes angevines à la fin du moyen âge (v.1360–v.1530)* (Nantes, 1982), pp.487, 492.
68. Ibid., pp.472, 487.
69. Ibid., pp.474, 489–90.
70. Ibid., pp. 490–1, 497, 489–99.
71. Charbonnier, *Une autre France*, II, pp.946–50, 969nl, 968, 963.
72. Ibid., pp.972–3.

73. Ibid., pp.975, 978.
74. Boutruche, *Seigneurs et paysans du Bordelais*, pp.77, 280–1.
75. Charbonnier, *Une autre France*, II, pp.982–4.
76. Ibid., p.985.
77. Souriac, *Le comté de Comminges au milieu du XVIe siècle*, pp.140–77.
78. Genet (ed.), *Genèse de l'état moderne*, conclusion, p.268; Krynen, 'Genèse de l'état et histoire des idées politiques en France à la fin du moyen âge', in ibid., p.403.
79. R. Mousnier, 'Les concepts d'ordres, d'états, de fidélité', *RH*, 502 (1972), 289–312; Mousnier, 'Les fidélités et les clientèles en France', *Histoire sociale*, 15 (1982), 35–46; Mousnier, *La vénalité*, pp.531–78. See also Y. Durand, 'Clientèles et fidélités dans le temps et dans l'espace', in Durand (ed.), *Hommage à Roland Mousnier*, pp.3–24.
80. P. Lefebvre, 'Aspects de la fidélité en France au XVIIe siècle', *RH*, 507 (1973), 59–106.
81. S. Kettering, *Patrons, Brokers and Clients in Seventeenth-Century France* (New York, 1986), pp.18–22; Kettering, 'Patronage in early modern France', *FHS*, 17 (1992), 839–62, esp. 844.
82. Brantôme, *Oeuvres*, ed. Lalanne, IV, pp.232, 164.
83. Jouanna, *Le devoir de révolte*, p.76.
84. Harding, *Anatomy of a Power Elite*, pp.68–87.
85. M. Greengrass, 'Noble Affinities in early modern France: the case of Henri I de Montmorency', *EHQ*, 16 (1986), 275–311. For a recent reinterpretation of the military patronage available to the dukes of Guise, cf. S. Carroll, '"Ceux de Guise": the Guise family and their affinity in Normandy, 1550–1600' (London PhD, 1993), chs 5 and 6.
86. S. Kettering, 'Clientage during the Wars of Religion', *SCJ*, 20 (1989), 221–39; M. Foisil, 'Parentèles et fidélités', in Durand (ed.), *Hommage à Roland Mousnier*.
87. K. Neuschel, *Word of Honor. Interpreting Noble Culture in Sixteenth-Century France* (Ithaca, London, 1989).
88. B. de Mandrot,'Jacques d'Armagnac, duc de Nemours', *RH*, 43 (1889), 44 (1890), 250.
89. Cf. previous section on noble revenues; Potter, *War and Government in the French Provinces*, pp.92–154; Kettering. 'Patronage in early modern France', pp.854–9 for a detailed critique of Neuschel's interpretation.
90. AN X/1A 4824 fo.104; Harsgor, 'L'essor des bâtards', p.332.
91. A. Jouanna, 'Réflexions sur les relations internobiliaires en France aux XVIe et XVIIe siècles', *FHS*, 17 (1992), 872–41.
92. Charbonnier, *Une autre France*, I, pp.548–9.
93. Neuschel, *Word of Honor*.
94. Charbonnier, *Une autre France*, II, pp.1085–6.
95. J. Russell Major, 'Bastard feudalism and the kiss: changing social mores in late medieval and early modern France', *Jour. Interdisciplinary Hist.*, 17 (1987), 509–35; Russell Major, 'Vertical ties through

time', *FHS,* 17 (1992), 863–71. The few preserved series of indentures (which have a different nomenclature in France than in England), are studied in E. Perroy, 'Feudalism or principalities in 15th century France', *BIHR,* 20 (1943–5), 180–1, and P.S. Lewis, 'Decayed and non-feudalism in later medieval France', *BIHR,* 37 (1964), 157–84.

96. Harsgor, 'Fidélités et infidélités', pp.262–3.
97. Charbonnier, *Une autre France,* I, pp.576–7.
98. W. Paravicini, 'Peur, pratiques, intelligences. Formes d'opposition aristocratique à Louis XI', in Chevalier and Contamine, *La France de la fin du XVe siècle,* p.192.
99. Harsgor, 'L'essor des bâtards', pp.345, 346.
100. Charbonnier, *Une autre France,* I, p.565; II, p.981.
101. Ibid., II, pp.1089–106.
102. Ibid., I, p.567.
103. Ibid., I, p.577. This is something that arguably changed in the sixteenth century.
104. Harsgor, 'Fidélités et infidélités', pp.268–72.
105. Charbonnier, *Une autre France,* I, pp.570–1.
106. Le Mené, *Les campagnes angevines.*
107. Charbonnier, *Une autre France,* I, pp.575, 576, 582.
108. Ibid., II, pp.1106–9.
109. Potter, 'The Luxembourg inheritance', p.49; BN fr.22429, fo.130–.
110. BN fr.3869 fos 23–4.
111. Harsgor, *Recherches sur le personnel;* Potter, 'The Luxembourg inheritance'.
112. Harsgor, *Recherches,* II, p.1523–.
113. Paravicini, 'Peur, pratiques, intelligences', pp.192–3.
114. G. Paul, *Un favori du duc de Bourbon, Joachim de Pompéranc* (Paris, 1923), pp.18, 29, 31.
115. C. Felgeres, 'La trahison du connétable de Bourbon', *Revue d'Auvergne* (1927), 307.
116. Ibid., pp.311–12, 315, 317.
117. 1 June 1550, BL Add.38035 fos 261–2.
118. Harsgor, 'Fidélités', p.267.
119. *La vie du connétable de Bourbon de 1490 à 1521,* ed. Buchon, *Panth. Litt.* (1836).
120. Harsgor, 'Fidélités', pp.261, 273.
121. J.B. Henneman, 'The military class and the French monarchy in the late Middle Ages', *Amer.H.R.,* 83 (1978), 946–65, esp.952–5. Henneman argues that this was the power-base of the crown, in view of the predominance of northern and western nobles among the 180 leading military commanders between 1360 and 1407. The same regions had proved the most oppositional in the previous period, cf. R. Cazelles, *La société politique et la crise de la royauté sous Philippe de Valois* (Paris, 1958), pp.81–4. Winning back the northern nobility

was to be crucial for Louis XI, cf. Potter, *War and Government*, pp.45–51. On the later period, see Constant, 'Les barons français pendant les querres de religion', pp.55–8.

122. Vaissière, *Gentilshommes campagnards*, pp.12–13. Jean Bouchet, *Epistres morales et familières* (1545), fo.9v: it should be added that this passage seems to blame ennobled lawyers more than any others: 'How, from such a writing desk, pen and paper could a poor lawyer so soon, so many goods acquire?' P.M. Smith, *The Anti-Courtier Trend*, pp.91–2, in considering this passage omits a large section. For Graville's will, cf. R. de Maulde-la-Clavière, *Origines*, p.309, n.45 (AN J 406, no.23).

123. P.S. Lewis, 'Les pensionnaires de Louis XI', in Chevalier and Contamine (eds), *La France de la fin du XVe siècle*, pp.167–81; Spont, 'La taille en Languedoc', p.498.

124. Vaesen, *Lettres de Louis XI*, VII, p.157; VIII, pp.112, 142, 221.

125. Ibid., VIII, pp.30, 31, 34.

126. Bp. of Albi's pension, 1481: *Lettres de Louis XI*, IX, pp.37–8; *sénéchal* of Quercy's, 1483; ibid., X, p.109. On Aveluy, AN X/2A fos 187r–188r (3 June 1484).

127. Potter, *War and Government*, pp.92–112.

128. L. Firpo, *Relazioni di ambasciatori Veneti al Senato V* (Turin, 1978), p.38; Spont, 'La taille en Languedoc', p.510.

129. Doucet, *L'état des finances de 1523*.

130. List of 1525 AN J 964 no.55 follows the 1523 list in format; the list dated c.1526–8, AN J 964 no.66 (wrongly allocated by Vaissière, *Gentilshommes campagnards*, pp.12–13 to 1520) is longer and, even then, incomplete.

131. BN fr.2997 fos 16–17. Curiously, the quarterly budget for the *Epargne* in Jan. – March 1532 noted 154,000 *lt.* paid in pensions due in February (77,000 écus) which, as a yearly figure would have yielded a sum of 616,000 *lt.* (BN fr.20502 fos 108–10).

132. BN fr.3127 fos 91–3; for a list of all those receiving pensions from the 1520s to the 1550s, cf. BN fr.4523.

133. Lewis, 'Les pensionnaires de Louis XI', p.180; AN K 73 no.2, lettres de retenue for Antoine de Salignac, 1484.

134. AN J 964 no.66.

135. As under Louis XI, pensions were diverted under Francis I. The count of Brienne was assigned on the *recette-générale* of Picardy for 1528 but it was countermanded by the king and the governor, Vendôme, warned that he would have to 'retire to his house, which would be a great displeasure to me'. In 1531, Vendôme's own pension was delayed. When he did get an assignation on a receipt 'I found it was worthless' (BN fr.3072 fo.13, 21, fr.6637 fo.6).

136. BN fr.20507 fo.60; fr.3038 fo.103; fr.3082 fo.64.

137. BN fr.2900 fo.15v; Louis XII – BN fr.2930 fos 195–9; 2927 fos 48–59.

138. BN fr.2900 fo.12v; AN J 964 no.55; BN fr.2997 fos 16–17; 1555–7: BN fr.4523.

139. Account of G. de Moraynes, *receveur-général* for the duke of Orléans, 1541–2, AN KK 273.

140. AN 1AP 178 no.19; P. Contamine, 'Georges de La Trémoïlle', p.72.

141. W. Weary, 'La maison de La Trémoïlle' in Chevalier and Contamine (eds), *La France de la fin du XVe siècle*, p.209.

142. Ibid., and Contamine, *Guerre, état et société*, p.440.

143. Mandrot, *Ymbert de Batarnay*, pp.9–19, 44–5, 56–7, 71 (Nemours lands), 81(Bridoré), 103 (Luxembourg lands), 187–91.

144. Chabannes, *Histoire de la maison de Chabannes*, II, 54, 82; Charbonnier, *Une autre France*, II, p.978.

145. Greengrass, 'Property and politics', pp.378, 380.

146. BN fr.4523.

147. Fourquin, *Les campagnes de la région parisienne*, pp.467–8. Vaissiére, *Gentilshommes campagnards*, pp.13–14.

148. AN KK 129. In the fifteenth century, there was a distinction between the *estat* and *gaiges* of governors. In 1485, the governor of Picardy was receiving 3000 *lt.* for each (Harsgor, *Recherches*, II, p.1099). By the 1530s, this was paid as a single sum of 6000 *lt.*, though from the late 1530s, some governors were paid 12,000 *lt.* (BN p.o. 2031 no.76, 81). There was also the governor's *plat* or expense account (*CAF*, VIII, 210, 31212).

149. Charbonnier, *Une autre France*, II, p.979.

150. Bitton, *The French Nobility and Crisis*, p.52; Greengrass, 'Property and politics', p.381.

151. L. Pingaud, *Les Saulx-Tavannes, étude sur l'ancienne société française* (Paris, 1876), pp.6, 99, based on the memoirs of his son Jean de Saulx; cf. also L. Pingaud (ed.), *Correspondance des Saulx-Tavannes* (Paris, 1887) on his easy relations with the court in the 1550s; Constant, *La vie quotidienne*, pp.55–7.

152. Vincent Carloix(?), *Mémoires de François de Scepeaux, seigneur de Vielleville* (Michaud et Poujoulat), ser.1, vol.IX, pp.124–5.

153. Potter, *War and Government*, p.302, n.30.

154. Charbonnier, *Une autre France*, II, p.919; Constant, 'Les barons français pendant les guerres de religion', p.54.

155. Constant, *Nobles et paysans beaucerons au XVIe et XVIIe siècles* (Thesis, Lille III, 1981).

156. Orléa, *La noblesse aux états-généraux;* Constant, *La vie quotidienne de la noblesse*, p.72.

7. THE FRENCH CHURCH IN THE AGE OF REFORM

1. Renaudet, *Préréforme et humanisme à Paris*.

2. L. Febvre, 'Une question mal posée. Les origines de la Réforme française', *RH*, 161 (1929), repr. in *Au coeur religieux du XVIe siècle*

(Paris, 1957); trans. in *A New Kind of History* (London, 1973), ed. P. Burke.

3. P. Imbart de la Tour, *Les origines de la réforme*, II, p.496.

4. J. Bossy, 'The Counter-Reformation and the People of Catholic Europe', *P&P*, 47 (1970), 51–70; Bossy, *Christianity in the West, 1400–1700* (Oxford, 1985); J. Delumeau, *Catholicism from Luther to Voltaire: A new View of the Counter-Reformation* (London, 1977); Delumeau, 'Christianisation et déchristianisation, XVe–XVIIIe siècles', in *Etudes européennes offerts à V.-L. Tapié* (Paris, 1973), pp.111–31.

5. D. Crouzet, *Les guerriers de Dieu. La violence au temps des troubles de religion, vers 1525–vers 1610*, 2 vols (Seyssel, 1990).

6. M. Venard, 'Réforme, réformation, préréforme, Contre-réforme ... Etude de vocabulaire chez les historiens récents de la langue française', in *Historiographie de la Réforme* (Paris, 1977), pp.352–65; G. Alberigo, 'Réforme en tant que critère de l'histoire de l'église', *R. Hist. éccl.* (1981), 72–83.

7. 'Tractatus novus super status ecclesiatici', by Michael Bureau, letter of the monk J. Quimon, quoted in Imbart de la Tour, *Origines*, II, p.511; ibid., pp.494–502. M. Godet, 'Consultation de Tours pour la réforme de l'église de France (12 novembre 1493)', *Rev. hist. église de France*, 2 (1911), 175–96, 333–48, esp. 342.

8. E. Cameron, *The European Reformation* (Oxford, 1991).

9. Bézard, *La vie rurale*, pp.274–5. G. Durand, 'Les tailleurs d'images d'Amiens du milieu du XVe siècle au milieu du XVIe siècle', *Bulletin monumental*, 90 (1933), 333.

10. Febvre, *Au coeur religieux*, p.27.

11. Bossy, *Christianity in the West*; Cameron, *The European Reformation*

12. N. Lemaître, *Le Rouergue flamboyant. Le clergé et les fidèles du diocèse de Rodez, 1417–1563* (Paris, 1968), pp. 101–4.

13. Jean de Roye, *Journal connu sous le nom de Chronique scandaleuse*, ed. B. de Mandrot (Paris, 1894–6), II, pp.70–3.

14. H. Martin, 'Les prédicateurs et les masses au XVe siècle', in J. Delumeau (ed.), *Histoire vécue du peuple* (Toulouse, 1979), II, pp.9–41; Delumeau, 'Les prédicateurs déviantes, du début du XVe siècle au début du XVIe siècle, dans les provinces septentrionales de la France', in B. Chevalier and R. Sauzet (eds), *Les réformes. Enracinement socio-culturel*, Colloque de Tours 1982 (Paris, 1985), pp.251–66. Cf. also L.J. Taylor, *Soldiers of Christ. Preaching in Late Mediaeval and Reformation France* (Oxford, 1992).

15. M. Piton, 'L'idéal épiscopal selon les prédicateurs français de la fin du XVe siècle et du début du XVIe', *Rev. hist. eccl.*, 61 (1966), 77–118, 393–423, esp.85–99. On Maillard, cf. A. Mabille de Poncheville, *Etude sur la chaire et la société française au quinzième siècle. Olivier Maillard* (Paris, 1891).

16. Bézard, *La vie rurale*, pp.303–4 pointed out the predominance of the themes of suffering in the many churches restored and embellished in the Hurepoix during the first half of the sixteenth century: 'Perhaps no art better expressed the desires of modest souls than the country churches of Francis I's reign.'

17. Lecoq, *François Ier imaginaire*, pp.436–7.

18. Imbart de la Tour, *Origines*, II, pp.492–3; Renaudet, *Préréforme et humanisme*, pp.160–246; Renaudet, *Humanisme et Renaissance. Dante, Petrarque, Standonck* (Geneva, 1958), pp.114–61; M. Godet, 'Jean Standonck et les frères mineurs', *Archivum franciscanum historicum* (1909), pp.398–406. Piton, 'L'idéal épiscopal', pp.406–11.

19. B. Chevalier, 'Le cardinal d'Amboise et la réforme des réguliers', in Chevalier and Sauzet (eds), *Les réformes*, pp. 111–21, esp.p.115.

20. A. Breuil, 'La confrérie de Notre Dame du Puy d'Amiens', *MSAP*, ser.2, vol.3 (1854), 485–662; A.-M. Lecoq, 'Le Puy d'Amiens de 1518', pp.63–74; Lecoq, *François Ier imaginaire*, pp.325–40. On the Puys in Normandy, cf. E. de Robillard de Beaurepaire, *Les Puys de palinods de Rouen et de Caen* (Caen, 1907).

21. A. de Beatis, *Le voyage du cardinal d'Aragon* (1517–18), trans. M. Harvard de La Montagne (1913), p.219; also trans. by J.R. Hale, *The Travel Journal of Antonio de Beatis* (London, 1979); D. Nicholls, 'The nature of popular heresy in France, 1520–1542', *HJ*, 26 (1983), 273.; B. Moeller, *The Imperial Cities and the Reformation* (Philadelphia, 1972), p.60; H. Heimpel, 'Das Wesen des deutschen Spätmittelalters', in *Der Mensche in seiner Gegenwart* (Göttingen, 1954), p.154.

22. Febvre, 'Une question mal posée'; Imbart de la Tour, *Origines*, II, pp.199–204; Renaudet, *Préréforme*, pp.1–21. Fourquin, *Les campagnes de la région parisienne*, pp.414–17; on Briçonnet at Saint-Germain, cf. M. Veissière, 'Guillaume Briçonnet, abbé réformateur de Saint-Germain-des-Près (1507–34)', *Rev. hist. église de France*, 60 (1974), 65–80. Hamon, 'Culture et vie religieuse...les Ruzé', pp.54–9.

23. On Clichtove's humanist anti-Lutheran critique and emphasis on the eucharist, cf. J.P. Massaut, *Josse Clichtove, l'humanisme et la réforme du clergé* (Paris, 1968); Massaut, 'Thèmes ecclésiologiques dans les controverses anti-lutheriennes de Clichtove: pouvoir, ordre, hiérarchie', in Chevalier and Sauzet (eds), *Les réformes*, pp.327–35.

24. This is the major theme of Piton, 'L'idéal épiscopal', pp.99–118.

25. J.-M. Alliot (ed.), *Visites archidiaconales de Josas* (Paris, 1902); Favreau, *La ville de Poitiers*, II, p.462.

26. Lemaître, *Le Rouergue flamboyant*, pp.185–209.

27. Ibid., pp.180–3.

28. Ibid., p.390.

29. M. Venard, *L'église d'Avignon au XVIe siècle*, 5 vols, Paris IV thesis, 1977 (Lille, 1980), I, pp.13–31, 180–4, 186–91; on devotion to the Virgin, ibid., pp.243–50; Bézard, *La vie rurale*, pp.294–304. Lemaître,

Rouergue flamboyant, p.318. M. Rubin, *Corpus Christi. The Eucharist in Late Medieval Culture* (Cambridge, 1992).

30. Mousnier, *La France de 1492 à 1559*, II, p.172.

31. D. Nicholls, 'Inertia and Reform in the Pre-Tridentine French Church: the Response to Protestantism in the Diocese of Rouen, 1520–1562', *Jour. Eccl. Hist.*, 32 (1981), 185–97.

32. M. Veissière, 'La vie chrétienne dans le diocèse de Meaux entre 1496 et 1526 d'après les synodes diocésains: continuités et innovations', *Rev. hist. église de France*, 77 (1991) p.71–81; Veissière, 'Guillaume Briçonnet, évêque de Meaux et la réforme de son clergé', *Rev. hist. eccl.*, 84 (1989), 657–72; Veissière, *L'évêque Guillaume Briçonnet (1470–1534)* (Provins, 1986); H. Heller, 'Famine, Revolt and Heresy at Meaux: 1521–1525', *Arch. Ref. Gesch.*, 68 (1977), 133–57; Heller, 'The evangelicism of Lefèvre d'Etaples', *Stud. in the Ren.*, 19 (1972), 42–77.

33. Venard, *L'église d'Avignon*, I, pp.132–7. On visitations, cf. pp.127–8, 146–52.

34. M. Venard, 'Pour un sociologie du clergé au XVIe siècle. Recherche sur le recrutement sacerdotal dans le province d'Avignon', *Annales*, 23 (1968), 987–1016, esp.991, 995, 997–8; cf. also Venard, *L'église d'Avignon*, I, pp.138–9, 162–70.

35. Venard, 'Pour une sociologie', pp.1009–16.

36. M. Venard, 'Une réform gallicane? Le projet de concile national de 1551', *Rev. hist. église de France*, 67 (1981), 202–25, esp. 220. Bézard, *La vie rurale*, pp.293–4.

37. Bézard, ibid., pp.215–19.

38. Alliot (ed.), *Visites archidiaconales de Josas*, passim, esp. pp.5, 12, 20, 26–8, 39, 52, 134. Fourquin, *Les campagnes de la région parisienne*, p.394: 11 churches in ruin, 16 or 17 in need of major repairs, no *curé* in 6.

39. Nicholls, 'Inertia and Reform', p.185.

40. Venard, 'Une réforme gallicane?', pp.221–2. NB that Le Boutheiller probably became a Prostestant.

41. Venard, 'Une réforme gallicane?', pp.223–5.

42. BM Beauvais, Coll. Bucquet 57 pp.569, 571, 574 (1539–40); 58 p.91: on demands for the clergy to pay for the upkeep of the poor; p.92 (1560): 'the procurator fiscal of M. le cardinal by-passes the justice of the town by his demands to have cognisance of all personal cases.'

43. A. Vidal, 'Révolte des Albigeois contre l'évêque Louis d'Amboise', *Rev. hist. scient. et litt. du dép. du Tarn*, 8 (1890–91), offprint, 1892; Piton, 'L'idéal épiscopal', pp.116–17; D.Nicholls, 'Looking for the Origins of the French Reformation', in C. Allmand, *Power, Culture and Religion*, p.135.

44. Chevalier, 'Le cardinal d'Amboise', pp.114–15, 118; M. Godet, *La congrégation de Montaigu* (Paris, 1912), p.17. In July 1499, the *échevinage* of Abbeville agreed to Louis XII's proposal for the establishment of an Observant friary with the consent of the priory of Saint-

Pierre, BM Abbeville MS 378 fo.5v, but by 1507 the proposal by the local governor for a house of Poor Claires was turned down, ibid. fo.7r; cf. also A. Ledieu, *Inventaire sommaire des archives de la ville d'Abbeville* (Abbeville, 1902) p.134.

45. AM Amiens BB 14 fo.190v, BB 18 fo.76v (24 Jan.1499); Chevalier, *Tours, ville royale*, Favreau, *La ville de Poitiers*, II, p.469.
46. Imbart de la Tour, *Origines*, II, p.491–. Godet, 'Consultation de Tours pour la réforme de l'Eglise de France', pp.175–8 and passim.
47. Renaudet, *Préréforme*, p.346. Whether he achieved much is in doubt, cf. Chevalier, 'Le cardinal d'Amboise', passim. J.-L. Gazzaniga, 'Le pouvoir des légats pontificaux devant le Parlement' in A. Stegman (ed.), *Pouvoir et institutions en Europe au XVIe siècle* (Paris, 1987), pp.227–35.
48. Mousnier, *La France de 1492 à 1559*; Venard, 'Une réforme gallicane?', pp.215, 201–2.
49. Imbart de la Tour, *Origines*, II, pp.74–85.
50. V. Martin, *Les origines du gallicanisme*, 2 vols (Paris, 1939), II, passim; N. Valois, *Histoire de la Sanction Pragmatique de Bourges sous Charles VII* (Paris, 1906). Kelley, 'Fides historiae', 352.
51. Imbart de la Tour, *Origines*, II, pp.224–7 for this system.
52. Miskimin, *Money and Power in Fifteenth-century France*, pp.73–85.
53. Imbart de la Tour, *Origines*, II, 89.
54. Imbart de la Tour, *Origines*, II, p.228. The Pragmatic was abolished in 1461, revived 1463, theoretically abandoned in 1467.
55. P. Ourliac, 'The Concordat of 1472: an essay on the relations between Louis XI and Sixtus IV', in Lewis (ed.), *The Recovery of France in the Fifteenth Century*, pp.102–84, esp. 161–9.
56. Imbart de la Tour, *Origines*, II, p.101; A. Bernier (ed.), *Journal des Etats Généraux de ... 1484 ... par Jean Masselin*, app., p.662. Text of Louis's letter, 20 Jan. 1485: AM Péronne BB 6 fos 1–2.
57. Imbart de la Tour, *Origines*, II, pp.105–6.
58. Ibid., II, pp.213–42, esp. 218–, 228. Harsgor, 'Maîtres d'un royaume', p.138.
59. Ibid., *Origines*, II, p.220 does not make clear this nuance from AN X/1A 4825 fos 236r–237v.
60. Venice, Bibliotheca Marciana 3625 fo.149, quoted in Ourliac, 'The Concordat of 1472', p.183. Brantôme, *Oeuvres*, ed. Buchon, I, pp.251–2.
61. Chevalier, 'Le cardinal d'Amboise', p.117.
62. Imbart de la Tour, *Origines*, II, pp.215–16.
63. Lemaître, *Rouergue flamboyant*, pp.217–22.
64. Piton, 'L'idéal épiscopal', pp.411–17.
65. Imbart de la Tour, *Origines*, II, pp.223–4, 224 -.
66. R.J. Knecht, 'The Concordat of 1516', in H. Cohn, *Government in Reformation Europe* (London, 1971), pp.91–3.
67. *Le journal de Jean Barrillon*, II, p.57.

68. Knecht, 'The Concordat'; *Francis I*, pp.55–63. BN fr.3005 fo.129, reply to English ambassadors, April 1534.

69. These disputes, for instance over the archbishopric of Sens, have recently been re-examined by Knecht, 'Francis I and the "Lit de Justice"', pp.58–64.

70. M. Boulet, 'Les élections épiscopales en France au lendemain du concordat de Bologne (1516–31)', *Mélanges de l'Ecole française de Rome*, 58 (1940), 190–234, esp.227–34.

71. Knecht, 'The Concordat', p.97; M.C. Péronnet, *Les évêques de l'ancienne France*, 2 vols (Paris IV thesis, 1976, Lille, 1977), I, p.489; P. Ourliac, 'The Concordat of 1472', in Lewis (ed.) *The Recovery of France in the Fifteenth Century*, p.183.

72. *Acta Nuntiaturae Gallicae* VI, pp.521–6; Kelley, 'Fides historiae', p.358; L. Romier, *Les origines politiques*, I, p.258–.

73. H.O. Evennett, 'Pie IV et les bénéfices de Jean du Bellay', *Rev. hist. église de France*, 22 (1936).

74. F. Baumgartner, 'Henri II's Italian bishops: a study in the use and abuse of the Concordat of Bologna', *SCJ*, XI, 2 (1980), 49–58. M.C. Péronnet, *Les évêques de l'ancienne France*, I, p.491.

75. A.N. Galpern, *The Religions of the People in Sixteenth-century Champagne* (Harvard, 1976), pp.117–21.

76. Baumgartner, 'Henri II's Italian Bishops', p.55.

77. M.M. Edelstein, 'The social origins of the episcopacy in the reign of Francis I', *FHS*, 8 (1973–4), 377–92, esp.389. J. Thomas, *Le concordat de 1516, ses origines, son histoire au XVIe siècle*, 3 vols (Paris, 1910), I, pp.334–5, 353.

78. N. Ravitch, *Sword and Mitre: Government and Episcopate in France and England in the Age of Aristocracy* (Paris, The Hague, 1966), pp.69–70.

79. Edelstein, 'Social origins of the episcopacy', pp.383–4.

80. Péronnet, *Les évêques de l'ancienne France*, I, pp.482–94 and tables 59 and 60, II, pp.1441–3.

81. Harsgor, 'Maîtres d'un royaume', pp.137–8: in the 109 dioceses between 1483 and 1515, 44 bishops were members of the council and 88 of their families.

82. Harsgor, *Recherches*, II, pp.918–79.

83. Péronnet, *Les évêques de l'ancienne France*, pp.482–94.

84. Lemaître, *Rouergue flamboyant* pp.395–447, esp.420–1, 427–32.

85. L. Febvre, 'Une question mal posée', *RH*, 161 (1929); Massaut, *Josse Clichtove*.

86. Imbart de la Tour, *Origines*, II, pp.494–5; Godet, 'Consultation de Tours', pp.185, 188–9.

87. J. Roserot de Melin, *Antonio Caracciolo, évêque de Troyes* (Paris, 1923), pp.396–8.

88. Imbart de la Tour, *Origines*, II, p.497.

89. Chevalier, 'Le cardinal d'Amboise', pp.114–16. J.-L. Gazzaniga, 'Le Parlement de Toulouse et la réforme des réguliers (fin du XVe

siècle debut du XVIe siècle)', *Rev. hist. église de France*, 77 (1991), 49–60.

90. Febvre, 'Une question mal posée', p.21; Piton, 'L'idéal episcopal', p.84.
91. H. Hauser, 'The French Reformation and the French people in the sixteenth century', *Amer. H. R.*, 4 (1899), 217–27; Hauser, *Etudes sur la reforme française* (Paris, 1909), pp. 89–103; Hauser, *Ouvriers du temps passé* (Paris, 1913); H. Heller, 'Les artisans au début de la Réforme française: hommage à Henri Hauser', in Chevalier and Sauzet, *Les réformes*, pp.137–50.
92. H. Hauser, 'Etude critique sur le rebeine de Lyon', *RH*, 61 (1896), 265–307; R. Gascon, *Grand commerce et vie urbaine au XVIe siècle: Lyon et ses marchands, 1520–1580*, 2 vols (Paris, 1971), II, pp.767–75.
93. Heller, 'Famine, revolt and heresy at Meaux: 1521–1525', pp.153–57; Heller, *The Conquest of Poverty: the Calvinist Revolt in Sixteenth-century France* (Leiden, 1986); cf. recent discussion in D. Nicholls, 'Looking for the origins of the French Reformation', in Allmand (ed.), *Power, Culture and Religion*, pp.131–44.
94. Venard, *L'église d'Avignon*, I, p.483 (in the context of his discussion of the attack on the Vaudois).
95. At Toulouse, of 424 heretics with known occupations, there were only 2 rural workers, cf. R.A. Mentzer, *Heresy Proceedings in Languedoc, 1550–1560 (Proc. Amer. Philo. Soc.*, Phildelphia, 1984); for a similar picture at Bordeaux, cf. *Les débuts de la réforme protestante en Guyenne, 1527–59: arrêts du Parlement*, ed. H. Patry (Bordeaux, 1912).
96. M. Prestwich, 'Calvinism in France, 1555–1629' in M.Prestwich (ed), *International Calvinism, 1541–1715* (Oxford, 1985); N.Z. Davis, *Society and Culture in Early Modern France* (Stanford, 1976); P. Benedict, *Rouen During the Wars of Religion* (Cambridge, 1980); J. Garrisson, *Les Protestants du Midi, 1559–1598* (Toulouse, 1980).
97. N.Z. Davis, 'Strikes and Salvation in Lyon' in her *Society and Culture*, pp.1–16; Gascon, *Grand commerce et vie urbaine* I, pp.348–50, II, pp.463–536.
98. B. Diefendorf, 'Prologue to a massacre: popular unrest in Paris, 1557–72', in *Amer. H. R.*, 90 (1985), 1067–91; Diefendorf, 'Les divisions religieuses dans les familles parisiennes avant la Saint-Barthèlemy', *Hist. Econ. Soc.*, 7 (1988), 55–77; Diefendorf, *Beneath the Cross: Catholics and Huguenots in Sixteenth-century Paris* (Oxford, 1991), pp.107–44.
99. J. Garrisson, *Les Protestants au XVIe siècle* (Paris, 1988), pp.226–41.
100. R. Boutruche (ed.), *Bordeaux de 1453 à 1715. Sociologie et pastorale* (Paris, 1964); Garrisson, *Les Protestants au XVIe siècle*, pp.231–3.
101. G. Caster, *Le commerce du pastel et de l'épicerie à Toulouse*; J. Davies, 'Persecution and Protestantism: Toulouse, 1562–1575', *HJ*, 22 (1979), 31–51; M. Greengrass, 'The anatomy of a religious riot in Toulouse in May 1562', *Jour. Eccl. Hist.*, 34 (1983), 367–91; R.A.

Mentzer, 'Heresy suspects in Languedoc prior to 1560: Observations on their social and occupational status', *Bib. Hum. Ren.*, 39 (1977), 561–69; Mentzer, 'The legal response to heresy in Languedoc, 1500–1560', *SCJ*, 4 (1973), 19–30, 19–30; J.J. Hémardinquer, 'Les Protestants de Grenoble au XVIe siècle', *BSHPF*, 111 (1965), 15–22; Ladurie, *Les paysans*, I, pp.341–56, esp.348.

102. D. Rosenberg, 'Social Experience and Religious Choice, a Case Study: the Protestant Weavers and Woolcombers of Amiens in the Sixteenth Century' (Yale Ph.D. thesis, 1979); R. Hubscher (ed.), *Histoire d'Amiens*, pp.129–31.

103. D.Nicholls, 'Social change and early Protestantism in France: Normandy, 1520–60', *ESR*, 10 (1980), 288; N.Z. Davis, 'The rites of violence', *P&P*, 59 (1973), 70–1 and in *Society and Culture*, pp.152–87.

104. G. Audisio, *Les vaudois du Luberon: une minorité en Provence* (Mérindol, 1984), pp.183–7. P. Chaunu, 'Niveaux de culture et réforme', *BSHPF*, 118 (1972), 305–25; Davis, 'Rites of violence'; 'Strikes and salvation'; Venard, *L'église d'Avignon*, IV, p.1811–12; J.R. Farr, 'Popular religious solidarity in sixteenth-century Dijon', *FHS*, 14 (1985), 192–214; Nicholls, 'Social change and early Protestantism', p.289.

105. A. Molinier, 'Aux origines de la réforme cévenole', *Annales*, 39 (1984), 240–64.

106. On the term 'social geography of French Protestantism', cf. the effective survey by M. Greengrass, *The French Reformation* (Oxford, 1987), pp.42–62. D. Crouzet, *Les guerriers de Dieu*, I, p.74.

107. Ibid., I, pp.74, 151.

108. Ibid., I, p.81.

109. Ibid., I, p. 145.

110. R.J. Knecht, rev. of Heller, *Iron and Blood* in *FH*, 6 (1992), 222–3.

111. M.P. Holt, 'Wine, community and reformation in sixteenth-century Burgundy', *P&P*, 138 (1993), 58–93, esp.72–90.

112. Crouzet, *Guerriers de Dieu*, I, p.211.

113. Ibid., I, pp.103–10.

114. Ibid., I, pp.112–26.

115. V.-L. Bourrilly (ed.), *Le journal d'un bourgeois de Paris sous le règne de François Ier* (Paris, 1910 edn), p.81.

116. Claude Haton, *Mémoires*, ed. F. Bourdelot, 2 vols (Paris, 1857), I, p.17.

117. Crouzet, *Guerriers de Dieu*, I, p.179.

118. Ibid., I, pp.164–6.

119. D.S. Hempsall, 'The Languedoc, 1520–1540: a study of pre-Calvinist heresy in France', *Arch. Ref. Gesch.*, 62 (1971), 225–44, esp. 242.

120. Venard, *L'église d'Avignon*, IV, p.1809.

121. Crouzet, *Guerriers de Dieu*, I, p. 151.

122. E.C. Dixon, *The Thirty-nine Articles of the Church of England* (London, 1906), p.459; Garrison, *Protestants au XVIe siècle*, pp.29–32.

123. P. Chaunu, 'Le XVIIe siècle religieux. Reflexions préalables', *Annales*, 22 (1971), 296–; Crouzet, *Guerriers de Dieu*, I, pp.144–6.

124. J. Calvin, *Institution de la religion chrestienne*, ed. J. Pannier (Paris, 1936), ch.XVII, pp.282–3.
125. Crouzet, *Guerriers de Dieu*, I, p.168.
126. Ibid., I, pp.191–2, 201.
127. Sermons published by Nicolas Chesneau, 1561–6, in Crouzet, *Guerriers*, I, p.206.
128. Ibid., I, p.212.
129. Chevalier, *Les bonnes villes de France*, p.260.
130. Nicholls, 'Looking for the origins of the French Reformation', p.138; H. Martin, 'Les prédications déviantes', pp.257–9; Imbart de la Tour, *Origines*, IV, p.233.
131. Hempsall, 'The Languedoc, 1520–40', pp.228–30.
132. R.J. Knecht, 'The early Reformation in France and England: a comparison', *History*, 57 (1972), 1–16.
133. E. Cameron, *The Reformation of the Heretics: the Waldenses of the Alps, 1480–1580* (Oxford, 1984). Audisio, *Les vaudois du Luberon*, esp. pp.178–97 and docs. pp.498–9. On the Valdenses of Provence, cf. Venard, *L'église d'Avignon*, I, pp.366–415 (the most important source for beliefs is the register of the Inquisitor Jean de Roma in 1533, AN J 851*); on Protestants, IV, pp.1800–12, on popular Catholicism, p.1814, 1825–. For the text of the Inquisitor's examination of the Vaudois *barbe* Pierre Griot, cf. G. Audisio, *Le barbe et l'inquisiteur: procès du barbe vaudois Pierre Griot par l'inquisiteur Jean de Roma (Apt, 1532)* (Aix-en-Provence, 1979).
134 M. Venard, 'Les "notes" de l'hérésie au début du XVIe siècle, selon les visites pastorales françaises', in Chevalier and Sauzet, *Les réformes*, pp.375–81.
135. L. Febvre, *Au coeur religieux du XVIe siècle* (Paris, 1968 edn), p. 66; Nicholls, 'Looking for the origins', p.141.
136. Molinier, 'Aux origines de la réformation cévenole', p.240.
137. Febvre, *Au coeur religieux*, pp.12–13; Hempsall, 'The Languedoc, 1520–40', p.226.
138. H.G. Koenigsberger, 'The organisation of revolutionary parties in France and the Netherlands during the sixteenth century', *JMH*, 27 (1955), 335–51; Nicholls, 'Social change in early Protestantism, p. 300.
139. Lemaître, *Rouergue flamboyant*, pp.449–50; Nicholls, 'Nature of popular heresy', p.264.
140. Hempsall, 'The Languedoc, 1520–40', p.233; G. Huppert, 'Classes dangereuses: Ecole et Réforme en France, 1530–1560' in Chevalier and Sauzet, *Les reformes*, pp.209–18.
141. Nicholls, 'Nature of popular heresy', pp.268–9.
142. Ibid., pp.271–2, 274.
143. Hempsall, 'The Languedoc, 1520–40', pp.236–43.
144. Nicholls, 'Nature of popular heresy', p.275.

145. E. Catta, 'Essai sur l'état religieux du diocèse de Nantes de 1554 à 1573, d'après les visites pastorales', *Recherches et travaux de l'Université Catholique de l'Ouest* (Angers), 3 (1948), 43–50.

146. Figures from M. Orléa, *La noblesse aux Etats généraux de 1576 et 1558* (Paris, 1980), pp.50–67 and on Beauce from J.M. Constant, 'La pénétration des idées de la réforme protestante dans la noblesse provinciale française à travers quelques exemples', in Chevalier amd Sauzet, *Les réformes*, pp.321–6.

147. N.L. Roelker, 'The role of noblewomen in the French Reformation', *Arch. Ref. Gesch.*, 63 (1972), 168–95; Roelker, 'The appeal of Calvinism to French noblewomen in the sixteenth century', *Jour. Interdisc. Hist.*, 2 (1971–2), 391–413.

148. On Mme d'Etampes, cf. D.Potter, 'Marriage and cruelty among the Protestant nobility in sixteenth-century France', pp.5–38.

149. Cf. esp. the tables in Roelker, 'The Appeal', pp.414–18; also C.J. Blaisdell, 'Renée de France between Reform and Counter-Reform', *Arc. Ref. Gesch.*, 63 (1972), 196–225.

150. A. Bieler, *L'homme et la femme dans la morale calviniste* (Geneva, 1963), p.63; G. Baum and E. Cunitz, *Calvini opera* (Brunswick, Berlin, 1863–1900), Corpus Reformatorum, 29–87, XI, p.41: Calvin's draft *ordonnance* on marriage, 1545.

151. R.I. Moore, *The Formation of a Persecuting Society* (Oxford, 1987).

152. R.J. Knecht, 'Francis I "Defender of the Faith"?' in *Wealth and Power in Tudor England*, ed. E.W. Ives et al. (London, 1978); R. Hari, 'Les Placards de 1534', in *Trav. hum. Ren.*, 28 (1957); L. Febvre, 'L'origine des placards de 1534', *Bib. hum.Ren.*, 7 (1945), 62–75.

153. V.-L. Bourrilly, *Guillaume du Bellay, seigneur de Langey*; Bourrilly, 'François Ier et les Protestants. Les essais de concorde en 1535', *BSHPF*, 49 (1900), 337–65, 477–95; Bourrilly, 'Jean du Bellay, les Protestants et la Sorbonne', ibid., 52 (1903), 53 (1904); 'Lazar de Baif et la landgrave de Hesse', ibid. (1901).

154. N. Sutherland, *The Huguenot Struggle for Recognition* (New Haven, London, 1980), pp.33–5.

155. D.L. Potter, 'Foreign policy in the age of the Reformation: French involvement in the Schmalkaldic War, 1544–47', *HJ*, 20 (1977), 525–44.

156. P. Gaffarel, 'Massacres de Cabrières et de Mérindol en 1545', *RH*, 107 (1911), 241–71; B. Peyre, *Histoire de Mérindol-de-Provence* (Avignon, 1939); G. Procacci, 'La Provence à la veille des guerres de religion', *RHMC*, 5 (1958), 241–64 concentrates on the social and political background. Venard, *L'église d'Avignon*, I, pp.483–512 gives the best recent analysis and G. Audisio, *Procès-verbal d'un massacre. Les Vaudois du Luberon* (Paris, 1992) important new documentation.

157. Weiss, *La chambre ardente*. 366 *arrêts* May 1548–Feb. 1550.

158. Greengrass, *The French Reformation*, p.36–. Isambert, *Recueil général des anciennes lois*, Henri II: Paris, 19 Nov. 1549. pp.134–8; Chateaubriand, 27 June 1551, pp.189–208.
159. G. Audisio, *Le barbe et l'inquisiteur*, pp.12–13, 19–26. Note that in 1532 the governor of Provence, the count of Tende, had ordered all officials to help the Inquisitor.
160. This document is endorsed 'Nouvelles de la court aoust Vc lij' and was probably sent to the *prévôt de Paris* Antoine Duprat. BL Egerton 19 fos 35–9.
161. N. Sutherland, 'Was there an Inquisition in Reformation France?' in her *Princes, Politics and Religion, 1547–1589* (London, 1984), pp.13–29.

8   FRENCH FOREIGN POLICY, 1460–1560

1. P. Choisnet, *Le Rosier des Guerres*, ed. M. Diamant-Berger as *Enseignements de Louis XI pour le Dauphin* (Paris, 1925); Gaussin, *Louis XI*, p.44. Barbey, *Etre roi*, pp.171–2.
2. P. de Commynes, *Mémoires*, ed. B. de Mandrot, I, p.257.
3. J. Calmette and G. Périnelle, *Louis XI et l'Angleterre* (Paris, 1930).
4. B. de Mandrot, 'Jacques d'Armagnac, duc de Nemours, 1433–77', *RH*, 43 (1889); 44 (1890), 241–312; Paravicini, 'Peur, pratiques, intelligences', pp.183–96.
5. Potter, *War and Government*, pp. 32–9; M.-A. Arnould, 'Les lendemains de Nancy dans les "Pays de par deça"', in W.P. Blockmans (ed.), *Le privilège général et les privilèges régionaux de Marie de Bourgogne* (Standen en Landen, 1988).
6. Potter, *War and Government*, p.43.
7. A. Marongiu, 'Carlo VIII e la sua ... crociata (come problema storiografica)', *Byzantine, Norman, Swabian and later Institutions in Southern Italy* (London, 1972), p.20; F. Delaborde, *L'expédition de Charles VIII en Italie*, 2 vols (Paris, 1870).
8. H. Lemonnier, *Les guerres d'Italie: la France sous Charles VIII, Louis XII et François Ier*, pp.15–16. A. Fontana, 'L'échange diplomatique. Les relations des ambassadeurs vénitiens en France pendant la Renaissance', in *La circulation des hommes et des oeuvres entre la France et l'Italie à l'époque de la Renaissance* (Colloque International de la Sorbonne, novembre 1990) (Paris, 1992), pp.19–37, esp.p.27.
9. For the best discussion, see Y. Labande-Mailfert, *Charles VIII*, pp.169–218, esp.196; M. de Bouard, *Les origines des guerres d'Italie* (Paris, 1936).
10. L. Pannier and P. Meyer (eds), *Le débat entre les hérauts d'armes de France et d'Angleterre* (Paris, 1877), p.12. See also Labande-Mailfert, *Charles VIII*, pp.176–85.
11. Lemonnier, *Les guerres d'Italie*, p.16

12. Gaussin, *Louis XI*, pp.333–48.
13. Labande-Mailfert, *Charles VIII*, pp.117–38.
14. P.M. Perret, *Notice biographique sur Louis Malet de Graville, amiral de France* (Paris, 1889), pp. 155–6; Labande-Mailfert, *Charles VIII*, pp. 219–31; C. Petit-Dutaillis, *Charles VII, Louis XI et les premières années de Charles VIII*, p.453.
15. B.A. Pocquet du Haut-Jussé, 'Les débuts du governement de Charles VIII en Bretagne', *BEC*, 115 (1957), 138–55; M. Jones, *The Creation of Brittany. A Late Medieval State* (London, 1988), pp.1–12.
16. R.W. Scheller, 'Imperial themes in art and literature of the early French Renaissance', pp.63–4.
17. G. Mattingly, *Renaissance Diplomacy* (1st edn 1955, 1965), pp.153–210; R. de Maulde-la-Clavière, *La diplomatie au temps de Machiavel*, 3 vols (Paris, 1892–3); J. Russell, *Peacemaking in the Renaissance* (London, 1986). For the late fifteenth and early sixteenth centuries, see the comparison of the French and English diplomats in C. Giry-Deloison, 'La naissance de la diplomatie moderne en France et en Angleterre au début du XVIe siècle (1475–1520)', *Nouvelle revue du seizième siècle*, 5 (1987), 41–58; Giry-Deloison, 'Le personnel diplomatique au début du XVIe siècle. L'exemple des relations franco-anglaises de l'avènement de Henry VII au camp du drap d'or (1485–1520)', *Journal des Savants* (1987), 205–53. Giry-Deloison concludes that the same range of middle ranking nobles and technocrats who dominated the council acted as ambassadors, with a heavy concentration on men who came from three regions: the north, Normandy and the Loire (as may be expected for diplomats dealing with England). In the earlier sixteenth century, he argues, there was no 'diplomatic service'. By the mid-sixteenth century, however, it seems that such a service was emerging in the careers of men like the du Bellays, Fraisse, Bassefontaine, Morvillier, etc. My analysis of the French diplomatic service under Francis I is based on an index compiled from *CAF*, IX, pp.6–87.
18. Monluc: I. Roy (ed.), *The Habsburg–Valois Wars...*, p.37; E. Hall, *The Triumphant Reign of King Henry VIII*, ed. C. Whibley, 2 vols (London, 1904), I, p.228; Brantôme, *Oeuvres complètes*, ed. Buchon, pp.11, 14.; Thorne: M.J. Rodriguez-Salgado, *The Changing Face of Empire: Charles V, Philip II and Habsburg Authority, 1551–59* (Cambridge, 1989), p.25; J. Black (ed.), *The Origins of War in Early Modern Europe*, p.37–8; Le Glay, *Négociations diplomatiques entre la France et l'Autriche*, II, 28 Aug. 1521.
19. Margaret of Austria, Feb. 1514, Le Glay, *Correspondance de l'empereur Maximilien Ier et de Marguerite d'Autriche*, II, pp.222–3.
20. Hauser (ed.), *La response de Jean Bodin*, p.13; J. du Tillet, *Advertissement à la noblesse de France* (Paris, 1574), sig.Aii.
21. H. Hauser, 'Le traité de Madrid et la cession de la Bourgogne à Charles-Quint', *Rev. bourguignonne*, 22 (1912) and repr.

22. Chaunu, 'L'état' in Braudel and Labrousse, *Histoire économique et sociale de la France*, I, i, p.155.

23. Harsgor, *Recherches sur le personnel du conseil*, I, p.223.

24. F. Catalano, 'Il problema dell'equilibrio et la crisi della libertà italiana', *Nuovi questioni di storia medioevale* (Milan, 1964), pp. 357–98, esp.381–5; Labande-Mailfert, *Charles VIII*, p.195.

25. P. van der Haeghen, 'Examen des droits de Charles VIII sur le royaume de Naples', *RH*, 28 (1885), 98–111, thought these claims were largely pretexts. M. Robinson, 'The claim of the house of Orléans to Milan', *EHR*, 3 (1888), 278–91; on cultural incentives, see J.-P. Séguin, 'La découverte de l'Italie par les soldats de Charles VIII', *Gazette des Beaux-Arts*, 50, 127–.

26. J.C.S. Bridge, *A History of France from the Death of Louis XI*, on Louis XII's Italian wars; Quilliet, *Louis XII*, pp.240–94, 374–414; B. Zeller, *La Ligue de Cambrai* (Paris, 1886).

27. For what follows: P. Contamine, *Guerre, état et société*; Contamine (ed.), *Histoire militaire de la France*, 2 vols (Paris, 1992), I, pp.201–301; Contamine, 'Naissance de l'infanterie française', *Avènement d'Henri IV. Quatrième centenaire de la bataille de Coutras* (Pau, 1989), pp.63–88; G. Dickinson (ed.), *Fourquevaux's Instructions sur le faict de la Guerre* (London, 1954); F. Lot, *Recherches sur les effectifs des armées françaises des Guerres d'Italie aux Guerres de Religion, 1494–1562* (Paris, 1962); G. Zeller, *Le siège de Metz par Charles-Quint* (Nancy, 1943), pp.51–86; Potter, *War and Government*, pp. 155–99; Potter, 'Les Allemands et les armées françaises au XVIe siècle', *Francia*, 20, ii (1993), 1–20; 21, ii (1994) 1–62.

28. H. Michaud, 'Les institutions militaires des guerres d'Italie aux guerres de religion', *RH*, 523 (1977), 29–43; J.-E. Iung, 'L'organisation du service des vivres aux armées de 1550 à 1650', *BEC* (1983), 269–306; P.D. Solon, 'War and the *Bonnes Villes*: the Case of Narbonne, c.1450–1550', *PWSFH*, 17 (1990), 65–73; J. Brink, 'The king's army and the people of Languedoc', *PWSFH*, 14 (1986); Contamine, *Histoire militaire*, pp.263–7. On the 1542 figures, *L&P*, XVII nos 517, 528, 554.

29. Knecht, *Francis I*, pp.33–50; H. Harkensee, *Die Schlacht bei Marignano* (Göttingen, 1909); A.Spont, 'Marignan et l'organisation militaire sous François Ier', *Rev. quest. hist.* (1899), 59–77.

30. Francis I's correspondence with his agents in Germany, 1519: in A. Kluckhohn (ed.), *Deutsche Reichstagsakten unter Kaiser Karl V*, I (Göttingen, 1962), passim, esp. p.139 and n.383; F. Mignet, *La rivalité de François Ier et de Charles-Quint*, 2 vols (Paris, 1875), II, pp.188–96. *Journal de Barrillon*, ed. P. de Vaissière, II, pp.120–40; G. Zeller, 'Les rois de France candidats à l'empire', *RH*, 173 (1934), 497–534 and *Aspects de la politique française*.

31. Wingfield, 1516, *L&P*, II, 2536; A. Le Glay, *Négociations diplomatiques entre la France et l'Autriche*, II, pp.665–7; G. Baguenault de Puchesse,

Jean de Morvillier, évêque d'Orléans ... étude sur la politique française au XVIe siècle (Paris, 1870), pp.58–9; G. Ribier, *Lettres et mémoires d'estat*, II, p.315; Kelley, 'Fides historiae', p.388; *Histoire particulière de la cour de Henri II*, ed. Cimber et Danjou, pp. 275–6, 302; 'the *monarchie* that the Emperor wishes to create in Germany and elsewhere', report of 1548 in J.D. Pariset, 'La France et les princes allemands', *Francia*, 10 (1982), 246. Henry VIII played on such fears in trying to detach Francis I from the Emperor in 1540: 'that which hath ben long suspected of thEmperour, that is to saye, that he shuld have in his hedd ones to bring Christendom to a monarchie' (*St.P.*, IX, p.249).

32. C. Cruikshank, *Army Royal* (Oxford, 1969); *English Occupation of Tournai* (Oxford, 1971).

33. J. Russell, *The Field of the Cloth of Gold* (London, 1969); Russell, 'The Search for Universal Peace: the Conferences at Calais and Bruges in 1521', *BIHR*, 44 (1971), 162–93. P. Gwynn, 'Wolsey's foreign policy and the conferences of Calais and Bruges reconsidered', *HJ*, 23 (1980), 755–72; Le Glay, *Négociations*, II, pp.483–586.

34. S. Gunn, 'The Duke of Suffolk's march on Paris in 1523', *EHR* (1986), 496–558. G.W. Bernard, *War, Taxation and Rebellion in early Tudor England. Henry VIII and the Amicable Grant of 1525* (Brighton, 1986), pp.3–75; G. Jacqueton, *La politique extérieure de Louise de Savoie* (Paris, 1892).

35. Père Hamy, *Entrevue de François Ier avec Henry VIII Boulogne-sur-Mer en 1532* (Paris, 1898); V.-L. Bourrilly, 'François Ier et Henry VIII: l'intervention de la France dans l'affaire du divorce', *Rev. d'hist. mod. contemp.*, 1 (1899), 271–84.

36. V.-L. Bourrilly, *Guillaume du Bellay*; Bourrilly, 'François Ier et les Protestants: les essais de concorde en 1535', *BSHPF*, 49 (1900); Bourrilly, 'Jean du Bellay, les Protestants et la Sorbonne', ibid. (1903–4); Bourrilly, 'Lazar de Baif et le landgrave de Hesse', *BSHPF* (1901); J.-Y. Mariotte, 'François Ier et la ligue de Smalkalde', *Zeitschrift für Schweizerische Geschichte* (1966) 206–47; D.L. Potter, 'Foreign policy in the age of the Reformation: French involvement in the Schmalkaldic war, 1544–47', *HJ*, 20 (1977), 525–44. L. Pinvert, *Lazar de Baif* (Paris, 1900).

37. Père Hamy, *Entrevue de François Ier avec Clément VII à Marseille, 1533* (Paris, 1900); V.-L. Bourrilly, 'La cardinal Jean du Bellay en Italie', *Rev. des études rabelaisiennes*, 5 (1907), 246–53, 262–74. L. Romier, *Les origines politiques*, I, pp.132–4.

38. V.-L. Bourrilly, 'Antonio Rincon et la politique orientale de François Ier', *RH*, 13 (1913), 64–83, 268–308; J. Ursu, *La politique orientale de François Ier* (Paris, 1908).

39. G. Zeller, 'Histoire d'une idée fausse', *RHMC* (1933) and in his *Aspects de la politique francaise*, pp. 90–108.

40. G. de Boom, *Correspondance de Marguerite d'Autriche avec ses ambassadeurs à la cour de France...* (1935) for documents on the Cambrai

negotiations. For a recent examination of the diplomacy of the period see R. Scheurer, 'Les relations franco-anglaises pendant la négociation de la paix des Dames', in P.M. Smith and I.D. McFarlane (eds), *Literature and the Arts in the Reign of Francis I* (Lexington, Ken., 1985), pp.142–62.

41. Knecht, *Francis I*, pp.277–88; M. François, *Le cardinal François de Tournon* (Paris, 1951), pp.90–120.

42. L. Cardauns, *Von Nizza bis Crépy, europaische Politik in den jahren 1534 bis 1544* (Rome, 1923); A. Segre, 'Documenti ed osservazioni sul congrezzo di Nizza (1538), *Accademia dei Lincei*, 10 (1901), 72–98; G.E. Bers, *Die Allianz Frankreich-Kleve* (Cologne, 1969); F. Decrue, *Anne de Montmorency, grand maitre et connétable de France* (Paris, 1885); A. de Ruble, *Le mariage de Jeanne d'Albret* (Paris, 1877), pp.53–139; J. Zeller, *La diplomatie française vers le milieu du XVIe siécle* (Paris, 1881) on relations with Venice.

43. On French policy in this period, see D.L. Potter, 'Diplomacy in the mid-16th century: England and France 1536–50) (Cambridge Ph.D. thesis, 1973), pp.43–80.

44. A. Rozet and J. Lembey, *L'invasion de France et le siège de Saint-Dizier par Charles-Quint en 1544 d'après les dépêches italiennes* (Paris, 1910); C. Paillard, *L'invasion allemande de 1544* (Paris, 1884).

45. D.L. Potter, 'Foreign policy in the age of the Reformation', p.529–; A. Hasenclever, 'Die Geheimartikel zum Frieden von Crépy von 19. September 1544', *Zeitschrift für Kirchengeschichte*, 45 (1926), 418–26. Essential documentation: J.D. Pariset, 'La France et les princes Allemands, pp.240–2.

46. On Montmorency's policy: F. Decrue, *Anne de Montmorency, connétable et pair de France* (Paris, 1889); G. Ganier, *La politique du connétable Anne de Montmorency* (Le Havre, 1957), pp.11–40; Montmorency's memoirs, 17 Sept., 9 Oct. 1548, J.D. Pariset, 'La France et les princes allemands', pp.246–7; on Italy: A.D. Lublinskaya, *Documents pour servir à l'histoire des guerres d'Italie, 1547–48*, drawing on the papers of secretary of state Du Thier; L. Romier, *Les origines politiques*, I, pp.181–271.

47. Romier, *Les origines politiques*, I, pp.39–45.

48. Henri II, 18 Oct. 1548, BN fr.6620, fo.7. On Scotland: see M.-N. Baudouin-Matuszek, 'Un ambassadeur en Ecosse au XVIe siècle: Henri Clutin d'Oisel', *RH*, 281 (1988), 77–131 and the thesis of E. Bonner, 'The First Phase of the Politique of Henri II in Scotland' (University of Sydney, Ph.D. thesis, 1993). On Italy: Romier, *Les origines politiques*, I, pp.132–77, on the *fuorusciti*, pp.318–21 on the assembly of Chioggia. C. Sauzé (ed.), 'Correspondance politique de Louis de Saint-Gelais', *Archives hist. de Poitou*, 33 (1904).

49. A. Cremer, 'La "protection" dans le droit international public européen du XVIe siècle', in *Théorie et pratiques politiques à la Renaissance. Colloque international de Tours, 1974* (Paris, 1977) pp.145–58.

50. Henri II to Selve, July 1548, *Amateur d'autographes*, 8 (1869), 22; D.L. Potter, 'The Treaty of Boulogne and European Diplomacy, 1549–50', *BIHR*, 55 (1982), 50–65; Potter, 'Documents concerning the negotiation of the Anglo-French Treaty of March 1550', *Camden Miscellany 28* (London, 1984), pp.58–180. G. Ribier, *Lettres et mémoires*, II, p.288.

51. J.-D. Pariset, *Les relations entre la France et l'Allemagne au milieu du XVIe siècle* (Strasbourg, 1981), pp.102–15.

52. An example in Bourdin's papers: BN Clair. 345 fo.209–. For Henri II's anxiety to counter imperial propaganda on his dealings with the Turks, see G. Ribier, *Lettres et mémoires*, II, pp.358–9.

53. Zeller, *La réunion de Metz à la France*, II; Romier, *Les origines politiques*, I, pp.317–456.

54. Romier, *Les origines*, I, pp.461–528, II, pp.97–187; Baumgartner, *Henri II*, appendix C, on the breaking of the Truce. See Charles de Marillac's *Discours sur la rupture de la trêve* (Paris, 1556), discussed in Vaissière, *Charles de Marillac*, pp.295–.

55. D.L. Potter, 'The duc de Guise and the fall of Calais, 1557–8', *EHR*, 118 (1983), 481–512.

56. On the treaty negotiations, see Romier, *Les origines*, II, pp.297–347; A. de Ruble, *Le traité de Cateau-Cambrésis* (Paris, 1889); more recently, J. Russell, *Peacemaking in the Renaissance*, pp.81–9; M.J. Rodriguez-Salgado, *The Changing Face of Empire*, pp.305–37. On reactions in France, see I. Cloulas, *Henri II*, pp.571–77.

57. Rodriguez-Salgado, *The Changing Face of Empire*, pp.25–7. J.A. Fernandez-Santamaria, *The State, War and Peace: Spanish Political Thought in the Renaissance, 1516–59* (Cambridge, 1977), pp.120–60 on the just war.

58. Brantôme. *Oeuvres complètes*, ed. Buchon, I, p.8; P. Contamine, 'Mourir pour la patrie' in Nora (ed.), *Lieux de mémoire, La Nation*, III, pp.19–28; J. du Tillet, *Advertisement à la noblesse*, sig.b. On Monluc, see A. Jouanna, *L'idée de race en France*, I, pp.327–32.

59. M. Sherman, 'Pomp and circumstances', p.24. C.R. Baskerville, *Pierre Gringore's Pageants for the Entry of Mary Tudor*.

60. J.-P. Séguin, *L'information en France de Louis XII à Henri II* (Geneva, 1961); Séguin, 'L'information à la fin du XVe siècle: pièces d'actualité imprimés sous le règne de Charles VIII', *Arts et traditions populaires*, 4 (1956), 309–30; M. Fogel, *Les cérémonies d'information*, pp.133–88 on the Te Deum. For examples; BM Abbeville MS 378 fo.6 (1501), AM Péronne BB 6 fo.196 (1509), BB 7, fo.6v (1515), AM Amiens AA 12 fo.150v (1525), AA 14 fo.159 (1559), BM Beauvais, Coll. Bucquet 57, pp.475–6 (1525), p.617 (1546), AM Senlis BB 5 fo.268r (1529), AM Compiègne BB 19 fos 2v–3r (1538), BB 20 fo.27v (1544).

61. N. Versoris, *Journal d'un bourgeois de Paris*, pp.40, 46–7, 56–7; *Le journal d'un bourgeois de Paris sous François Ier*, ed. L. Lalanne, pp.120–1, 164–6, 183–4. R.J. Knecht, 'Francis I and Paris', *History* 66 (1981).

62. BN fr.4742 fos 35r–v. G. Ribier, *Lettres et mémoires*, II, pp. 376–8.
63. Examples from the many *brevets de tailles* preserved in AM Chauny (Aisne), BB 1 fo.10r, BB 4 fo.53, EE 1. The letters for the *taille* sent to the estates of Languedoc, pub. in *Ordonnances, François Ier* and in C. Devic and J. Vaisette, *Histoire générale de Languedoc* (Toulouse, 1874–1904), XII, pp.367–71, 378–87 can be compared. A fuller study is needed of the propaganda arguments employed in preambles to edicts, etc. For the declaration of war against England in 1522, Lalanne (ed.), *Le journal d'un bourgeois*, pp. 128–9.
64. A. Ledieu, 'Réception du cardinal de York à Abbeville, 1527', *Cabinet historique* (1889–90) 95–6, 117–25. AM Compiègne BB 21 fo.56v (1552); *Le livre de Podio ... d'Etienne de Médicis*, ed. A. Chassaing, pp.373, 390.
65. Versoris, *Journal d'un bourgeois de Paris*, pp.40, 42, 54, 57. Lalanne (ed.), *Le journal d'un bourgeois*, pp.120–1 and 147, 150 on criticism of the king. E. Pasquier, *Lettres historiques pour les années 1556–1594*, ed. D. Thickett (Geneva, 1966), pp.22, 129.
66. Heller, *Iron and Blood*, pp.27–8; J.E. Brink, 'The king's army and the people of Languedoc', pp.1–9, esp.4–5. 1552 preachers: Ribier, *Lettres et mémoires*, II, pp.389–90; Henri II, 20 April 1552, BM Laon; cardinal de Bourbon, 27 April 1552, BL Egerton 20 fo.63.
67. Lalanne (ed), *Le journal d'un bourgeois*, pp.36, 119, 152. Muchembled, *La violence au village*, pp.107–18. AN JJ 230 no.86 fo.44 (July, 1498). Potter, *War and Government*, pp.200-32.
68. G. Zeller, 'Le commerce international en temps de guerre sous l'Ancien Régime', in his *Aspects de la politique française*, pp.189–9, 195, quoted E. Fabvier.

CONCLUSION

1. E. de La Boetie, *De la servitude volontaire*, discussed in J.L. Bourgeon, 'La Boetie pamphlétaire', in *Bibliothèque d'humanisme et Renaissance*, 51 (1989), 289–300.
2. Jouanna, *L'idée de race en France*, I, pp.373–4.
3. Pasquier, *Lettres historiques*, ed. D. Thickett, p.100.
4. Antoine de Bourbon to Henri II, 26 April 1559, Ribier, *Lettres et mémoires d'estat*, II, p.799.
5. Jean de Morvilliers to B. Bochetel, 26 May 1561, BL Egerton 23, fo.303.

Appendices

1. Military Administration

Connétables de France

Artus III, duc de Bretagne, comte de Richemont	1425–58
Louis de Luxembourg, comte de Saint-Pol	1465–75
Jean II, duc de Bourbon et Auvergne	1483–88
Charles III, comte de Monpensier, d. de Bourbon	1515–23
Anne, baron et duc de Montmorency	1538–67
Henry I duc de Montmorency	1593–1614

Maréchaux de France

André de Laval, sr. de Lohéac	1429–86
Jean, bât. d'Armagnac	1461–73
Joachim Rouault, sr. de Gamaches	1461–76
Pierre de Rohan, sr. de Gié	1475–1504
Philippe de Crèvecoeur, sr. d'Esquerdes	1486–94 (repl. Lohéac)
Jean, sr. de Baudricoourt	1488–99
Jean-Jacques de Trivulce, marq. de Vigève	1500–18 (repl. Baudricourt)
Charles II d'Amboise, sr. de Chaumont	1504–11 (repl. Gié)
Jacques II de Chabannes, sr. de La Palice	1515–25
Robert Stuart d'Aubigny	1515–43
Odet de Foix, sr. de Lautrec	1515–28
Gaspard I de Coligny, sr. de Châtillon	1516–22 (new charge)
Anne de Montmorency	1522–38 (repl. Châtillon)
Thomas de Foix, sr. de Lescun	1521–25
Theodore Trivulce	1526–31 (repl. La Palice)
Robert III de La Marck, sr. de Fleuranges	1526–37 (repl. Lescun)
Rene de Montéjean	1538 (repl. Montmorency)
Claude d'Annebault	1538–47 (repl. La Marck)

Oudart, sr. du Biez	1541–47 (repl. Montéjean)
Antoine de Lettes, sr. de Montpezat	1543–64 (repl. Stuart)
Jean Carracciolo, pr. de Melphe	1544–50
Robert IV de La Marck, duc de	
Bouillon	1547–56
Jacques d'Albon, sr. de Saint–André	1547–62 (repl. Du Biez)
Charles I de Cossé, c. de Brissac	1550–63 (repl. Melphe)
Piero Strozzi, sr. d'Épernay	1554–58
Paul de La Barthe, sr. de Termes	1558–62 (repl. Strozzi)
François de Montmorency	1559–79

Capitaines généraux/Grand-maîtres de l'artillerie

Jean Chollet	c.1477–79
Guillaume Picart, sr. d'Estellan	1479
Jacques Ricard de Genouillac,	
dit Galiot	1479–88
Guy de Lauzières, sr. de Monstreul	1488–1504
Jean de La Grange	
Jacques Galiot de Genouillac	1516–46
Jean de Taix	1546–47
Jean d'Estrées	1547–63

Amiraux de France

Jean, sire de Montauban	1461–65
André de Laval, sr. de Lohéac	1465-
Louis, bâtard de Bourbon. c. de	
Roussillon	1466–86
Louis Malet de Graville	1486–1509
Charles II d'Amboise, sr. de	
Chaumont	1509–12
Louis Malet de Graville	1512–16
Guillaume Gouffier, sr. de Bonnivet	1517–1525
Philippe Chabot, sr. de Brion. c. de	
Charny	1526–43
Claude d'Annebault, bar. de Retz	1544–52
Gaspard de Coligny, sr. de Châtillon	1552–72

2. Chancellery, Council and Secretariat

Chanceliers et Gardes des sceaux

Guillaume Jouvenal des Ursins	1445–61
Pierre de Morvilliers, sr. ce Clary	1461–65
Guillaume Jouvenal des Ursins	1465–72
Pierre d'Oriole, sr. de Loire-en-	
Aunis	1472–83
Guillaume, sr. de Rochefort	1483–92

Adam Fumée, sr. des Roches*	1492–94
Robert Briçonnet, Arch. de Reims	1495–97
Guy de Rochefort, sr. de Pleuvant	1497–1508
Jean de Ganay, sr. de Persan	1508–12
Etienne Poncher, év. de Nantes*	1512–15
Antoine Duprat, sr. de Nantouillet, cardinal	1515–35
Antoine Dubourg, bar. de Saillans	1535–38
Mathieu de Longuejoue, év. de Soissons*	1538
Guillaume Poyet, bar. de Beyne, ab. de Berdoues	1538–45
François de Montholon, sr. de Vivier*	1542–43
François Errault, sr. de Chemans*	1543–44
Mathieu de Longuejoue*	1544–45
François Olivier	1545–60
Jean Bertrand, sr. de Frazin*	1552–59
Michel de L'Hospital, sr. de Vinay	1560–73

*Keepers of the Seals (*Gardes des Sceaux*)

*Secrétaires du roi**

Jean Bourré, sr. de Jarzé & du Plessis-Bourré	1461–83
Nicole Tilhart, sr. du Plessis-aux-Tournelles	1464–76
Antoine Disome (secr. des guerres, 1473)	1465–81
Jean Mesme, greffier au Conseil, 1484	1468–89
Etienne Petit, greffier au Conseil, 1484	1472–96, d.1523
Pierre Parent	1476–82

* the main secretaries for royal missives

Secrétaires des finances/commandments/d'état

Macé Picot, sr. d'Amboile	1475–79
Germain de Marle	1479–81 (d.1504)
Jean de La Primaudaye, sr. de Villemartin	1483–95
François Bochetel (secr. des guerres)	1484–85
Jean Mesme, sr. de Marolles-en-Hurepoix	1485–89

Jean Robineau, sr. de La	
Bretonnière	1485–99 (d.1507)
Florimond Robertet, sr. d'Alluye	1495–1526
Jean Cottereau	1498–1519
Robert Gedoyn	1499 (conf.1515)–28
Nicolas I de Neufville	1515–42
Jean Robertet	c.1521–
Thierry Fouet, dit Dorne	1522–after 1534
François Robertet	1526–32
Gilbert Bayard, sr. de La Font	1528–47
Jean Breton, sr. de Villandry	1528–43
Guillaume Bochetel*	1530–58
Philibert Babou, sr. de La	
Bourdaisière	1531–57
Jean Duval	c.1537–47
Claude Robertet d'Alluye	1538–
Jacques Hurault, sr. de Vibraye	1542–67
Guillaume Prudhomme (for the	
council at Lyon)	1542
Nicolas II de Neufville, sr. de	
Villeroy	1542–
Claude de L'aubespine, sr. de	
Châteauneuf*	1543–67
Claude Burgensis, sr. de Villesavin	c.1545–67
Jean du Thier, sr. de Beauregard*	1547–58
Cosme Clausse, sr. de	
Marchaumont*	1547–58
Jacques Bourdin, sr. de Villaines*	1550(1558)–67
Florimond Robertet, sr. de Fresne*	1554(1558)–67
Jacques Bochetel, sr. de La Forêt	1556–
Florimond Robertet, sr. d'Alluye*	1558–69

* having charge of *affaires d'estat* as *secrétaires des commandements* after 1547, date of promotion from *secrétaire des finances* for those who followed in brackets. From 1559, the two posts of *secrétaire d'état* and *secrétaire des finances* were increasingly divergent.

3.   Main Finance Officers

'Messieurs des finances'

Jean Bourré	*T* Languedoil, 1463–74
Michel Gaillart, sr. de Chilly	*G* Languedoil, 1473–7;
	Languedoc, 1477–8;
	Outre-Seine, 1483–1501
François de Genas	*G* Languedoc, 1478–83

Guillaume Briçonnet, sr. du Plessis-Rideau, cardinal	*G* Languedoc, 1483–93
Pierre Briçonnet, sr. de Cormes	*G* Languedoc, 1493–151-; Languedoil, 1495–1509
Henri Bohier, chev. sr. de La Chesnaye	*G* Languedoc, 1510–22
Jacques Hurault, sr. de Cheverny	*T* Normandy, 1498–1501; *G* Outre-Seine, 1501–15
Thomas Bohier, sr. de Chenonoeaux	*G* Normandy, 1494–1524
Jacques de Beaune, sr. de Semblançay	*G* Languedoïl, 1510–16; overall, 1518–23
Florimond Robertet, sr. d'Alluyes	*T* Normandy, 1501–27
Raoul Hurault, sr. de Cheverny	*G* Oultre-Seine, 1515–23
Morelet du Museau, sr. du Ru	*G* Oultre-Seine, 1523 -
Guillaume Prudhomme, sr. de Fontenay	*G* Normandy, 1524–42
Philibert Babou, sr. de La Bourdaisière	*T* Languedoil, 1520–37

(*G* = *général des finances*; *T* = *trésorier de France*)

Trésoriers de l'Epargne

Philibert Babou	1523–25
Guillaume Prudhomme	1525–40
Jean Duval	1540–47
Andre Blondet	1547–

Contrôleur-général

Jean du Thier	1547–

4. The Court and Royal Household

Grand-maîtres de l'Hôtel

Raoul VI, sr. de Gaucourt	1453–62
Antoine, sr. de Croy	1461–65
Charles de Melun, sr. de Nantouillet	1465–68
Antoine de Chabannes, c. de Dammartin	1468–88
François-Guy XIV, c. de Laval	1498–1500
Charles II d'Amboise, sr. de Chaumont	1502–11
Jacques II de Chabannes, sr. de La Palice	1511–15

Artus Gouffier, sr. de Boisy	1515–19
René, bât. de Savoie, c. de Tende	1519–25
Anne, bar. de Montmorency	1526–58
François de Montmorency	1558–59
François de Lorraine, duc de Guise	1559–63

Grands Ecuyers

Jean de Guarguesalle, sr. de Coulaines	1461–66
Charles, sr. de Bigny	1464–65
Alain Goyon, sr. de Villiers	1470–
Pierre II d'Urfé	1484–1505
Galeas de Saint-Severin	1505–25
Jacques de Genouillac, dit Galiot	1526–46
Claude Gouffier, duc de Rouannais	1546–70

Grands Chambellans

Antoine de Chateauneuf, bar. de Lau	146?–68
François I d'Orléans, c. de Dunois & Longueville	1484–86
René II, duc de Lorraine & Bar	1486–87
Philippe, sr. de Rothelin, marq. de Hochberg	1491–92
Philippe de Crèvecceur, sr. d'Esquerdes	1492
Louis de Luxembourg, c. de Ligny, pr. Altamira	1498–1503
François II d'Orléans, duc de Longueville	1504–12
Louis I d'Orléans, duc de Longueville	1512–16
Claude d'Orléans, duc de Longueville	1519–25
Louis II d'Orléans, duc de Longueville	1525–37
François II d'Orlèans, duc de Longueville	1537–53
François de Lorraine, duc de Guise	1553–63

Grands chambriers

Jean II duc de Bourbon	1456–88
Pierre II duc de Bourbon, sr. de Beaujeu	1488–1503

Charles III de Bourbon-Monpensier, duc 1503–23
Henri de France, duc d'Orléans   1527–36
Charles de France, duc d'Orléans   1536–45

Grands aumôniers
Angelo Catho   –1497
Geoffroy de Pompadour, év.
  d'Angoulême   c.1484
François Le Roy Chavigny,
  protonotaire   1515
Adrien Gouffier, év. de Coutances   1519
François de Moulins, ab. de
  Saint-Mesmin   1519–26
Jean Le Veneur, év. de Lisieux,
  cardinal   1526–43
Antoine Sanguin, cardinal de
  Meudon   1543–47
Philippe de Cossé, év. de Coutances   1547–48
Pierre du Chastel, év. de Mâcon et
  Orléans   1548–52
Bernard de Ruthye, ab. de
  Pontlevoy   1552–56
Louis de Brézé. év. de Meaux   1556–59
Charles d'Humières, év. de Bayeux   1559–60
Jacques d'Amyot, év. d'Auxerre   1560–89

Premier gentilhomme de la chambre
Guillaume Gouffier, sr. de Bonnivet   1515–17
René de Puyguyon, sr. de Boisrené   1517–19
Anne de Montmorency   1520–22
Jean de La Barre   1523
Anne de Montmorency   1524–43
Claude d'Annebault   1544–47
Jacques d'Albon, sr. de Saint-André   1547–59

II. PRINCIPAL PROVINCIAL GOVERNORS, 1461–1560

Normandy

Louis d'Estouteville	1461–63
Louis de Luxembourg, c. de Saint-Pol	1466–75
Louis, bâtard de Bourbon	1466–71
Louis Malet de Graville	1490–91
Louis, duc d'Orléans	1491–98
Georges I d'Amboise	1498–1510
Louis de La Trémoille	1512
Louis de Brézé. c. de Maulevrier	1512–15
Charles, duc d'Alençon	1515–25
Louis de Brézé, c. de Maulevrier	1526–31
François de Valois, dauphin	1531–36
Henri de Valois, dauphin	1536–47
Claude d'Annebault	1547–52
Robert de la Marck, duc de Bouillon	1552–56
Henri-Robert de La Marck, duc de Bouillon	1556–74

Picardy

Antoine de Chabannes, c. de Dammartin	1470–73 (frontier)
André de Laval, sr. de Lohéac	1471–73 (Amiens only)
Jean d'Estouteville, sr. de Torcy	1473–77 (Amiens only)
Louis de Luxembourg, c. de Saint-Pol	1473–
Philippe de Crèvecoeur, sr. d'Esquerdes	1477–94
Louis de Luxembourg, c. de Ligny	1494–1504
Jean de Bruges, sr. de la Gruthuse	1504–12
Louis de Hallewin, sr. de Piennes	1512–19
Charles de Bourbon, duc de Vendôme	1519–37
François de Montmorency, sr. de La Rochepot	1537–38
Antoine de Bourbon, duc de Vendôme	1538–55
Gaspard II de Coligny, sr. de Châtillon	1555–60

Ile-de-France

Jacques de Villiers, sr. de l'Isle-

Adam	1461
Bertrand de Beauvau	1463–64
Charles de Melun, sr. de La Borde	1465–
Charles d'Artois, c. d'Eu	1465
Joachim Rouault, sr. de Gamaches	1465
André de Laval, sr. de Lohéac	1466
Charles, sr. de Gaucourt	1472–79
Charles I d'Amboise, sr. de Chaumont	c.1480
Jean Allardeau, ev. de Marseille	1480–83
Louis duc d'Orléans	1483–85
Antoine de Chabannes, c. de Dammartin	1485
Charles II d'Amboise	1493–
Louis duc d'Orléans	1491–93
Gilbert de Bourbon, c. de Montpensier	1493–96
Charles II d'Amboise	1496
Guillaume de Poitiers	1496–1513
Charles de Bourbon, duc de Vendôme	1515–19
François de Bourbon, c. de Saint-Pol	1519–23
Charles de Bourbon, duc de Vendôme	1523–26
Michel-Antoine, marq. de Saluces	1526–28
François de La Tour, vic. de Turenne	1529–32
Antoine de La Rochefoucauld, sr. de Barbezieux	1532–37
François de Montmorency, sr. de La Rochepot	1538–42
Antoine de Bourbon, duc de Vendôme	1542–47
François de Montmorency, sr. de La Rochepot	1547–51
Gaspard de Coligny	1551–56
François de Montmorency	1556–79

Champagne

Jean d'Estouteville, sr. de Thorcy	1463–65
Louis de Luxembourg, c. de Saint-Pol	1464
Louis de Laval, sr. de Châtillon	1465–72
Charles d'Amboise, sr. de	

Chaumont	1473–81
Jean de Baudricourt	1481–83
Louis, duc d'Orléans	1483–85
Jean d'Albret, sr. d'Orval	1488–1524
Claude de Lorraine, c. de Guise	1524–43
Charles de Valois, duc d'Orléans	1543–45
François I de Cleves, duc de Nevers	1545–61

Burgundy

Georges II de La Trémoille	1477
Charles I d'Amboise, sr. de Chaumont	1477–81
Jean, sr. de Baudricourt	1481–89
Englibert de Cleves, c. de Nevers et d'Eu	1499–1506
Louis II de La Trémoille	1506–25
Philippe Chabot, sr. de Brion	1526–43
Claude de Lorraine, duc de Guise	1543–50
Claude de Lorraine, duc d'Aumale	1550–73

Brittany

Charles duc d'Alençon	1515–25
Guy XVI, c. de Laval	1526–31
Jean de Laval, sr. de Chateaubriant	1531–43
Jean de Brosse-Bretagne, duc d'Etampes	1543–65

Guyenne

Jean bâtard d'Armagnac	1461–73
Charles III d'Anjou, c. du Maine	1461–65
Gaston, c. de Foix	1465–66
Philippe de Savoie, sr. de Bresse	1466–68
Jean de Foix, vic. de Narbonne	1468–69
Jean, bât. d'Armagnac	1469
Antoine de Chabannes, c. de Dammartin	1469
Pierre II de Bourbon-Beaujeu	1472–83
Odet d'Aydie, c. de Comminges, sr. de Lescun	1484–87
Pierre de Bourbon	1487–88
Charles d'Orléans, c. d'Angoulême	1488–92
Mahieu, grand bâtard de Bourbon	1496–1502
Alain, sire d'Albret	1503
François II d'Orléans, duc de Longueville	1505–12
François de Valois, duc d'Angoulême	1512

Odet de Foix, sr. de Lautrec	1515–28
Henri d'Albret, roi de Navarre	1528–55
Antoine de Bourbon, roi de Navarre	1555–62

Languedoc

Charles III d'Anjou, c. du Maine	1439–65
Jean II duc de Bourbon	1466–88
Pierre II de Bourbon-Beaujeu	1488–1503
Charles duc de Bourbon	1503–23
Anne de Montmorency	1524–42
François de Bourbon, c. d'Enghien	1544–46
Jacques de Genouillac, bar. de Capdenac	1546
François de Valois (François II)	1546–47
Anne de Montmorency	1547–63

Provence

Palamède de Forbin, sr. de Solies	1481–83
Office suppressed	1483–91
François de Luxembourg, vic. de Martigues	1491–93
Gouverneurs et Sénéchaux:	
Philippe, marg. de Hochberg	1493–1503
Louis I d'Orléans, marq. de Rothelin	1504–14
Jean de Poitiers, sr. de saint-Vallier	1514–15
René, bâtard de Savoie	1515–23
Claude de Savoie, c. de Tende	1525–66

Lyonnais

Tanneguy III du Chatel	1462–63
Galeazzo Maria Sforza	1465–68
Jean bâtard d'Armagnac	1468–73
Jean II duc de Bourbon	1475
Philippe II de Savoie	1486
Cesare Borgia, c. de Valentinois	1498–99
Jean-Jacques de Trivulce	1507–18
Jacques de Chabannes, sr. de La Palice	1518–25
Charles de Chabannes, sr. de la Palice	1526
Théodore Trivulce	1526–32
Pomponio Trivulce	1532–39
Jean d'Albon, sr. de Saint-André	1539–49
Jacques d'Albon, sr. de Saint-André	1550–62

Dauphiné

Jean, bâtard d'Armagnac	1461–73
Louis, sr. de Crussol & Beaudisner	1473
Louis Richard, sr. de Saint–Priest	1473–4
Jean de Daillon, sr. du Lude	1474–81
Palamède de Forbin, sr. de Soliès	1481–82
Jacques de Miolans, sr. d'Anjou	1482–83
François d'Orléans, duc de	
Longueville	1483–85
Philippe de Savoie, c. de Bugey,	
sr. de Bresse	1485–91
Jacques de Miolans	1491–96
Jean, c. de Foix, & Etampes	1496–1501
Antoine de Grolée	1501–03
Gaston de Foix, duc de Nemours	1503–12
Jean de Poitiers	1512–14
Louis d'Orléans, duc de	
Longueville	1514–16
Artus Gouffier, sr. de Boisy	1516–19
Guillaume Gouffier, sr. de Bonnivet	1519–25
Michel-Antoine, marq. de Saluces	1525–26
François I de Bourbon, c. de	
Saint-Pol	1526–45
François II de Bourbon, c. de	
Saint-Pol	1545
François de Lorraine, c. d'Aumale,	
duc de Guise	1547–63

Auvergne

Jean de Doyat	1478–83
Claude de Montfaucon	1483–87
Jean Stuart, duke of Albany	1526–
Jean de Brosse-Bretagne,	
d. d'Etampes	1538/9
Jean d'Albon, sr. de Saint-André	1547–49
Jacques d'Albon, sr. de Saint–André	1549–62

Italian Provinces

Duchy of Milan

Gian Giacomo Trivulzio	1499–1500
Charles d'Amboise, sr. de	
Chaumont	1500–11
Gian Giacomo Trivulzio	1511–13
Charles, duc de Bourbon	1516, Jan.–May

Odet de Foix, sr. de Lautrec	1516–21
Michele-Antonio, marq. of Saluzzo	1524–5

Savoy-Piedmont

Jean d'Humières	1537, March–Nov.
René de Montéjean	1537–39
Claude d'Annebault	1539–43
François de Bourbon. c. d'Enghien	1543–45
Jean Caracciolo, prince of Melphi	1545–50
Charles de Cossé, c. de Brissac	1550–59

III   MOVEMENTS OF THE COURT, 1461–1560

Percentage of each year spent by the king and court in Ile-de-France:

1461 (July–)	8.8	1502	8.2
1462	0	1503	0
1463	71.1	1504	16.9
1464	6.3	1505	16.7
1465	29.9	1506	0
1466	0	1507	0
1467	17	1508	0
1468	10.7	1509	0
1469	0	1510	5.5
1470	3	1511	0
1471	8.5	1512	0
1472	0	1513	16.7
1473	0	1514	44.4
1474	21.4	1515	35.1
1475	34	1516	4.7
1476	0	1517	71.8
1477	2.7	1518	12.3
1478	2.7	1519	62.3
1479	0	1520	33.7
1480	3	1521	9.9
1481	0	1522	57.3
1482	0	1523	53.2
1483	0	1524	10.4
1484	39.9	1525	0
1485	41.1	1526	17
1486	58.4	1527	91.2
1487	2.7	1528	100
1488	24.3	1529	57.3
1489	11.2	1530	7.1
1490	0	1531	85.2
1491	0	1532	20.5
1492	62.6	1533	21.6
1493	51	1534	50.4
1494	0	1535	21.9
1495	0	1536	7.1
1496	0	1537	47.1
1497	0	1538	29.6
1498	43.8	1539	75.3
1499	5.5	1540	40.7
1500	4.6	1541	23.3
1501	0	1542	19.5

1543	46.6	1552	26
1544	77	1553	86.3
1545	22.7	1554	76.2
1546	59.5	1555	89.6
1547	94	1556	47.3
1548	47.8	1557	90.7
1549	89.6	1558	54.5
1550	64.1	1559 (to July)	100
1551	32.9		

The area defined as the Ile-de-France is encompassed by the main royal residences around Paris: Saint-Germain-en-Laye, Fontainebleau, Melun, Vincennes, Villers-Cotterêts, Compiègne.

Sources: the itineraries of all the monarchs from Louis XI to Francis II are now established and can be found in:

(1) J. Vaesen, *Lettres de Louis XI*, XI, pp.3–236.
(2) E. Petit, 'Séjours de Charles VIII', *Bull. hist. phil.* (1896), 629–90.
(3) F. Maillard, 'Itinéraire de Louis XII', Ibid. (1972), 171–201.
(4) 'Itinéraire de François Ier', in *Catalogue des actes de Francois Ier*, VIII, pp.411–548.
(5) M.-N. Baudouin-Matuszek, 'Itinéraire de Henri II', in *Catalogue des actes de Henri II*, III, pp.1–72.
(6) M.-J. Martel, *Catalogue des actes de Francois II* allows the general establishment of an itinerary but this has not been included here.

IV.   TOTAL MILITARY EXPENDITURE, 1484–1555
(figures in *livres tournois*, based on BN fr.4523 fos43–51, text pub. in Lot,
Recherches, pp.241–53)

Year	Ordinary[a]	Extraord[b]	Artillery	Total
1484	899,124			
1485	774,132		51,389	
1486	935,208	177,455	9,506	1,122,169
1487	865,272		98,434	
1488	?	296,171	149,159	
1489		324,306	111,734	
1490		319,908	47,568	
1491		774,238	?	
1492		371,092	43,559	
1493	1,066,152	172,713		
1494	901,356	593,865[c]	72,208	1,567,429
1495	1,004,772	223,944	90,529	
1496	771,156	?	50,640	
1497	?	?		
1498	767,808	?	39,578[@]	
1499	966,456	649,519	?	
1500	827,328	792,914	?	
1501	808,356	?	?	
1502	615,288	?	?	
1503	611,940	?	?	
1504	567,300	?	?	
1505	560,372	?	?	
1506	608,220	?	?	
1507	673,320	?	?	
1508	673,320	?	?	
1509	673,320	?	?	
1510	673,320	?		
1511	796,080	?	133,772	
1512	885,360	?	189,657	
1513	1,328,040	?	237,024	
1514	1,229,460	?		
1515	1,119,720	2,673,051		
1516	924,048	2,484,626	214,556	
1517	872,340	605,130		
1518	833,280	728,953[*]	?	
1519	876,060	1,351,230[*]		
1520	906,936	571,833[*]	15,791[@]	
1521	498,852	5,009,272[@]	212,716	
1522	872,340	?	90,382	
1523	1,362,636	?	101,319	

Year				
1524	876,432			
1525	588,132	4,281,285d	178,200	
1526	805,380	?	?	
1527	848,160	?	83,000	
1528	532,332	731,486	95,323	
1529	550,024	1,367,248		
1530	810,960			
1531	379,812	688,807		
1532	759,624			
1533				
1534		363,506		
1535	?	?	166,830	
1536		4,339,891	213,277*	
1537		5,274,655		
1538		2,113,618		
1539	?	?		
1540		410,389@	207,106	
1541	?	?	?	
1542		4,725,019	?	
1543	1,300,320	5,937,940	332,070	7,570,330
1544	1,343,520	6,249,927	358,001	7,951,448
1545	1,304,640	2,894,638	429,948	4,629,226
1546	1,321,920	1,581,091	166,330	3,069,341
1547	1,032,840	374,589	131,000	1,538,069
1548	1,023,480	2,357,364	196,628	3,577,832
1549	1,041,120	2,677,460	217,245	3,718,580
1550	1,687,000	1,900,049	?	
1551	1,687,000	3,489,472	130,239	5,306,711
1552	1,687,000	7,553,792	440,238	9,681,030
1553	1,925,000	10,580,633	461,189	12,505,633
1554	1,932,000	11,055,078	?	
1555	1,932,000	10,102,165	?	

a From 1484 to 1496 the receipt and expense of the *tréscriers de l'ordinaire* is given, thereafter only the number of lances in each year. The numbers recorded do not evidently include those paid out of Italian revenues during the early sixteenth century. Thus, the figure for 1502 is 1654 lances, whereas the total was then 2175, the residue paid by the kingdom of Naples (BN fr.2930 fo.95). In years when the number of lances changed from quarter to quarter, the average is given and part lances rounded up. In order to standardise, the money figure has been computed for the whole series as a multiple of the lance. Thus from 1484 to 1533, the pay per lance was 372 *lt.* In 1534, it was raised to 432 (despite the reduction in number of archers) by the augmentation of part of the pay, the *grande paye.* In 1551, the whole pay of the *gendarmerie* was raised through the *taillon* giving an equivalent of 700 *lt.* per lance (though by then the lance was fictional figure). It must also be remembered that the cost of officers' pay is not included here. In order for this to have been done, the number of companies in each year was needed. This is not known in enough detail. Judging from the expense figures of 1484 to 1496, around 100,000 *lt.* should be added for the pay of the officers and the expenses of the officials of the *ordinaire des guerres*, rising to 200,000 after 1550.

b The accounts of the *extraordinaire des guerres* are not easy to compare in the earlier period, since they sometimes cover a period longer than one year or are based on a different accounting that ending in December. Only those roughly comparable have been included.

* indicates a figure covering an accounting year ending at the end of September in the year in question.

@ a roughly 18-month period ending in the year in question.

c In the year of the expedition to Italy, the receipt of the *extraordinaire* was 1,211,657 *lt.* but the expense only as shown. The surplus was probably diverted to another special account for the war.

Genealogical Tables

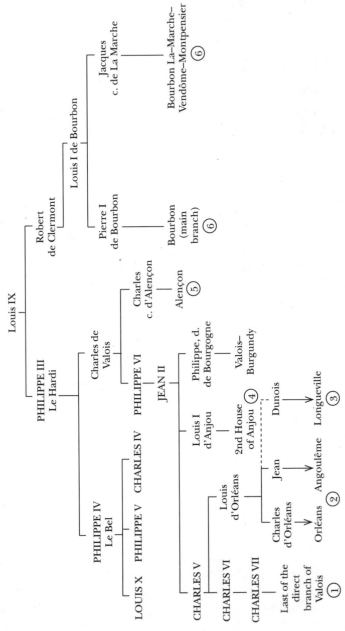

I Key to the Main Branches of the Capetian Dynasty

371

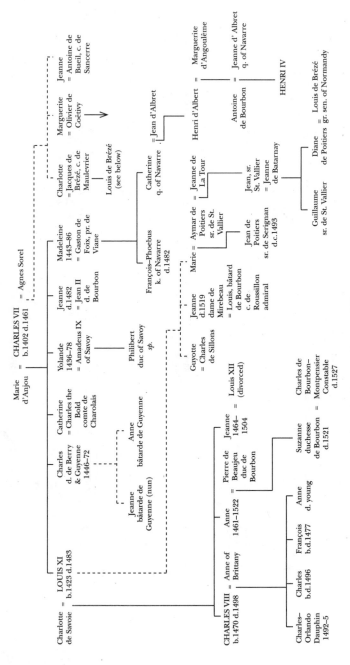

1 Descendants of Charles VII

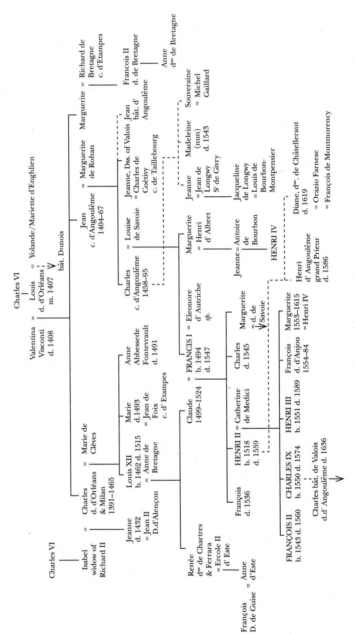

2 Orléans–Angoulême

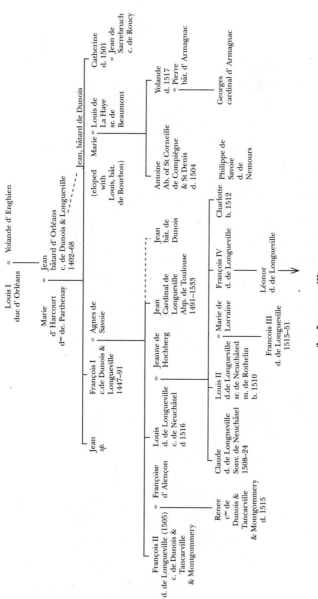

3 Longueville

374

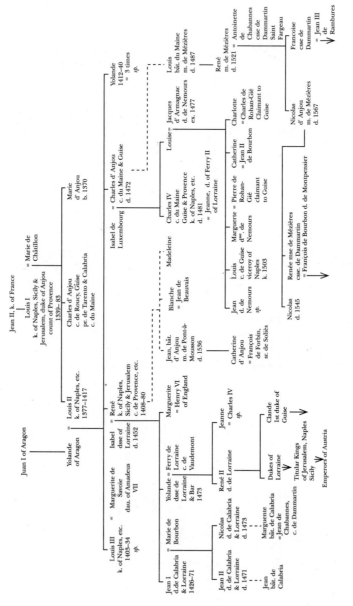

4 France–Anjou

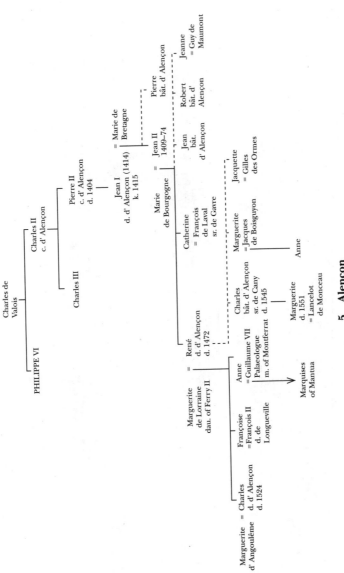

5 **Alençon**

376

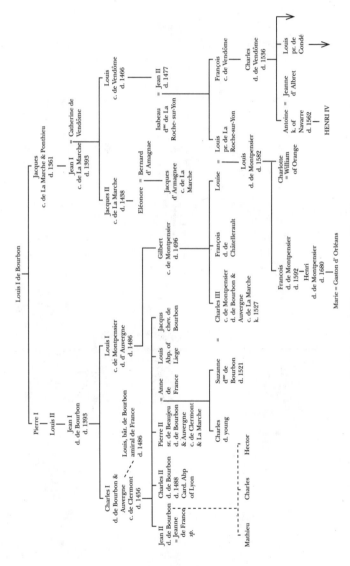

6 Bourbon–Montpensier–Vendôme

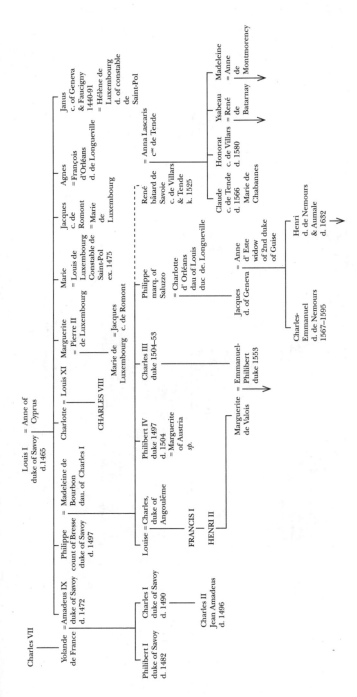

II The House of Savoy and France

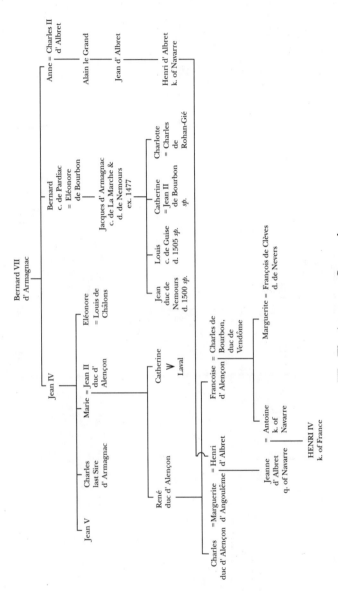

III The Armagnac Succession

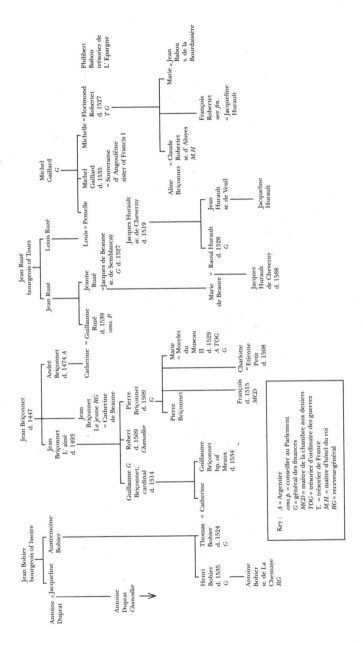

IV   The Financial Oligarchy

380

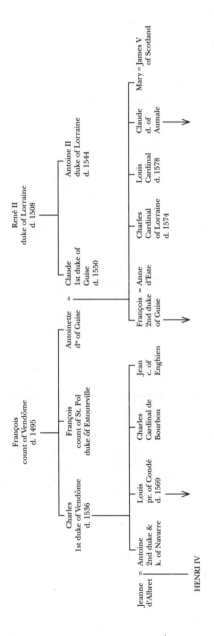

V Bourbon and Lorraine

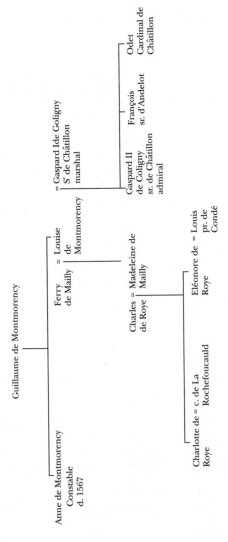

VI Protestant Families

BIBLIOGRAPHY

PRIMARY SOURCES AND CONTEMPORARY WORKS

Acta Nuntiaturae Gallicae; Correspondance des nonces en France (Univ. Pontificale and Ecole française de Rome), 14 vols (1961–).

Advertissement du sacre, couronnement et mariage du très Chrestien roy de France et de Pologne, Henry III (Lyon, 1575).

Auton, Jean d', *Chroniques de Louis XII*, ed. R. de Maulde-la-Clavière (Paris, 1885).

Basin, T., *Histoire de Charles VII et de Louis XI*, ed. J. Quicherat (Paris, 1856).

—— *Histoire de Louis XI*, ed. C. Samaran, 2 vols (Paris, 1963–72).

Baskerville, C.R. (ed.), *Pierre Gringore's Pageants for the Entry of Mary Tudor into Paris. An Unpublished Manuscript* (Chicago, 1934).

Barrillon, J., *Journal de Jean Barrillon, secrétaire du chancelier du Prat, 1515–21*, ed. P. de Vaissière, 2 vols (Paris, 1897–9).

Beatis, A. de, *Le voyage du cardinal d'Aragon (1517–18)*, trans. M. Harvard de la Montagne (Paris, 1913); ed. J.R. Hale, *The Travel Journals of Antonio de Beatis* (London, 1979).

Beauvillé, V. de, *Recueil de documents inédits pour servir à l'histoire de Picardie*, 4 vols (Paris, 1865–90).

Bernier, A., *Procès-verbaux des séances du Conseil de Régence du roi Charles VIII* (Paris, 1836).

Bèze, T. de, *Histoire ecclésiastique des églises réformées du royaume de France*, ed. G. Baum and E. Cunitz, 3 vol (Paris, 1883–9).

Bodin, J., *Six livres de la République* (1580 edn).

Bonnardot, A. de (ed.), *Le livre et forest de messire Bernardin Rince ... et le festin de la Bastille* (Paris, 1876).

Bouchet, J., *Epistres morales et familières* (Paris, 1545).

Bourrilly, V.-L. and P. de Vaissière (eds), *Ambassades de Jean du Bellay en Angleterre* (Paris, 1905).

Boom, G. de, *Correspondance de Marguerite d'Autriche et de ses ambassadeurs à la cour de France, concernant l'exécution du Traité de Cambrai* (Brussels, 1935).

Brantôme, P. de Bourdeille de, *Oeuvres complètes*, ed. J. Buchon, 2 vols (Paris, 1838); ed. L. Lalanne, 12 vols (Paris, 1864–96).

Bueil, J. de, *Le Jouvencel*, ed. C. Favre and L. Lecestre, 2 vols (Paris, 1857–9).

Calendar of State Papers, Spanish, ed. G. Bergenroth, P. de Gayangos, M. Hume, R. Tyler, G. Mattingly, 13 vols (London, 1862–1954).

Calvin, J., *Institution de la religion chrestienne*, ed. J. Pannier (Paris, 1936).

—— *Calvini quae supersunt opera*, ed. G. Baum and E. Cunitz (Brunswick, Berlin, 1863–1900, Corpus reformatorum, vols 29–87).

Camusat, N., *Mémoires du sieur Richer* (Paris, 1625).

Catalogue des actes de François Ier, ed. P. Marichal et al., 10 vols (Paris, 1887–1910).

Catalogue des actes de Francois II, ed. M.-J. Martel (Paris, 1991).

Catalogue des actes de Henri II, ed. M.-N. Baudouin-Matuszek et al., 3 vols so far (Paris, 1979–90).

Champier, S., *De Monarchia ac triplici imperio* (Lyon, 1537).

Charrière, E. de (ed.), *Négociations de la France dans le Levant,* 4 vols (Paris, 1848–60).

Chartier, J., *Chronique de Charles VII roi de Fance,* ed. A. Vallet de Viriville, 3 vols (Paris, 1858).

Choisnet, P., *Le Rosier des guerres,* ed. M. Diamant-Berger as *Enseignements de Louis XI pour le Dauphin* (Paris, 1925).

Cimber, L. and F. Danjou, *Archives curieuses de l'histoire de France,* 30 vols (Paris, 1834–49).

Commynes, P. de, *Mémoires,* ed. J. Calmette, 3 vols (Paris, 1924); trans. A. Scoble, 2 vols (London, 1855–6).

Desjardins, A. (ed.), *Négociations diplomatiques de la France avec la Toscane,* 6 vols (Paris, 1859–86).

Dickinson, G. (ed.), *Fourquevaux's Instructions sur le faict de la guerre* (London, 1954).

Domairon, L. (ed.), *Entrée de François Ier dans la ville de Béziers* (Paris, 1866).

Douet d'Arcq, M.L., *Comptes de l'hôtel des rois de France aux XIVe et XVe siècles* (Paris, 1865).

Du Bellay, M. and G., *Mémoires,* ed. J.F. Michaud and J. Poujoulat, ser.1, vol 5 (Paris, 1836); ed. V.-L. Bourrilly and F. Vindry, 4 vols (Paris, 1908–19).

Du Bellay, Joachim, *La Deffence et Illustration de la langue françoyse,* ed. Chamard (Paris, 1948); trans. G.M. Turquet (London, 1949).

Dumoulin, C., *Opera omnia* (Paris, 1681).

Du Port, J., 'La vie de Jean d'Orléans dit le bon, comte d'Angoulême', ed. J.F.E. Castaigne, *Bull. de la Soc. Archéologique de la Charente,* ser.3, vol. 3 (1862).

Du Tillet, J., *Advertissment à la noblesse de France* (Paris, 1574).

—— *Recueil des roys de France* (Rouen, 1578; Paris, 1580, 1610).

Firpo, L. (ed.), *Relazioni di ambasciatori veneti al Senato,* vol. V, *Francia* (Turin, 1978).

Fontanon, A., *Les édicts et ordonnances des roys de France,* 4 vols (Paris, 1585, 1611).

Fortescue, J., *The Governance of England,* ed. Plummer (London, 1885).

Gail, J.B., *Lettres inédites de Henri II, Diane de Poitiers, Marie Stuart, François II, roi dauphin etc.* (Paris, 1818).

Gilles, N., *Compendium de origine et gestis francorum* (1492).

Godefroy, T., *Le cérémonial françois,* 2 vols (Paris, 1649).

—— *Histoire de Charles VIII par Guillaume de Jaligny* (Paris, 1684).

Grassailles, C. de, *Regalium Franciae libri duo* (Paris, 1545).

384   BIBLIOGRAPHY

Guevara, A., *Le favory de cour* (Paris, 1555).

Guise, François de Lorraine, duc de, *Mémoires-journaux*, ed. Michaud and Poujoulat, ser.1, vol.6 (1850).

Hall, E. *The Triumphant Reign of Henry VIII*, ed. C. Whibley as *Henry VIII*, 2 vols (London, 1904).

Haton, C., *Mémoires*, ed. F. Bourdelot, 2 vols (Paris, 1857).

'Histoire particulière de la court du Roy Henry II', in Cimber and Danjou, *Archives curieuses*, q.v.

Hiver, président, *Papiers des Pot de Rhodes, 1529–1648* (Paris, 1864).

Isambert, F.-A., *Recueil général des anciennes lois françaises*, 29 vols (Paris, 1822–33).

Journal d'un bourgeois de Paris sous le règne de François Ier (1515–36), ed. L. Lalanne (Paris, 1854); ed. V.-L. Bourrilly (Paris, SHF, 1910).

Juvenal des Ursins, J., *Ecrits politiques*, ed. P.S. Lewis, 2 vols (Paris, 1978–85).

Kluckhohn, A. (ed.), *Deutsche Reichstagsakten unter Kaiser Karl V*, I (Göttingen, 1962).

La Ferrière-Percy, H. de, *Lettres de Catherine de Médicis*, 10 vols (Paris, 1889–1909).

Ledieu, A., *Inventaire sommaire des archives de la ville d'Abbeville* (Abbeville, 1902).

Le Glay, A., *Correspondance de l'empereur Maximilien Ier et de Marguerite d'Autriche ... 1507–1519*, 2 vols (Paris, 1839–45).

—— *Négociations diplomatiques entre la France et l'Autriche*, 2 vols (Paris, 1845).

Letters and Papers, Foreign and Domestic, of the Reign of Henry VIII, ed J. Brewer, J. Gairdner and R. Brodie, 21 vols (London, 1862–1932).

L'Homel, G. de, *Nouveau recueil de documents pour servir à l'histoire de Montreuil-sur-Mer* (Compiègne, 1910).

Lhuillier, T. (ed.), 'Rôles journaliers de dépenses pour le service de la maison royale et de la maison du Dauphin (François II)', *Rev. des Sociétés Savantes*, ser.5, vol.IV, pp.436–41.

—— 'La maison des princes, fils de François Ier', *Bull. du comité des travaux hist. et philologiques* (1889), pp. 212–23.

L'ordre du sacre et couronnement du roy Très Chretien notre sire François de Valoys (1515).

Loyseau, C., *Cinq livres des offices* (Paris, 1610).

Lublinskaya, A.D., *Documents pour servir à l'histoire des guerres d'Italie, 1547–48* (Moscow, 1962).

Machiavelli, N., *Opere*, ed. E. Raimundi (Milan, 1966).

Marot, C., *Oeuvres poétiques*, ed. Y. Giraud (Paris, 1973).

Masselin, J., *Journal des états généraux de France tenus à Tours en 1484*, ed. A. Bernier (Paris, 1835).

Maulde-la-Clavière, R. de, *Procédures politiques du règne de Louis XII* (Paris, 1888).

McFarlane, I.D., *The Entry of Henri II into Paris, 16 June 1549* (New York, 1982).

Médicis, E. de, *Le livre de Podio ou Chronique d'Etienne de Médicis, bourgeois du Puy*, ed. A. Chassaing (Le Puy-en-Velay, 1869).

Mézières, P. de, *Le Songe du Vieil Pelerin*, ed. G.W. Coopland, 2 vols (Cambridge, 1969).

Monluc, B. de, *Commentaires*, ed. P. Courteault, 3 vols (Paris, 1911–25; ed. A. de Ruble, 5 vols (Paris, 1864–72); ed. I. Roy, *The Habsburg–Valois Wars and the French Wars of Religion* (London, 1971).

Paillard, C., 'Documents relatifs aux projets d'évasion de François Ier ainsi qu'à la situation intérieure de la France', *RH*, 8 (1878), 297–367.

—— 'La mort de François Ier et les premiers temps du règne de Henri II d'après les dépêches de Jean Saint-Mauris', *RH*, 5 (1877), 84–120.

Pannier, L. and P. Meyer (eds), *Le débat entre les hérauts d'armes de France et d'Angleterre* (Paris, 1977).

Paradin, G., *Histoire de nostre temps* (1552).

Pariset, J.-D., 'La France et les princes allemands. Documents et commentaires (1545–57)', *Francia*, 10 (1982), 229–301.

Pasquier, E., *Oeuvres*, 2 vols (Amsterdam, 1723).

Pasquier, E., *Lettres historiques* (Geneva, 1966).

Pingaud, L. (ed.), *Correspondance des Saulx-Tavannes* (Paris, 1887).

Police de l'Aumône de Lyon (Lyon, Gryphius, 1539).

Potter, D.L. (ed.), 'Documents concerning the negotiation of the Anglo-French Treaty of March 1550', *Camden Miscellany 28* (London, 1984), pp.58–150.

Rabelais, F., *Oeuvres*, ed. A. Lefranc, 6 vols (Paris, 1913–22).

Rabutin, F. de, *Commentaires des guerres de la Gaule Belgique*, ed. G. de Taurines, 2 vols (Paris, 1932–42).

Ribier, G., *Lettres et mémoires d'estat*, 2 vols (Paris, 1666).

Robertet, G. and E. Coyecque, *Les Robertet au XVIe siècle* vol.II, fasc.1, *Registre de Florimond Robertet* (1524–25) (Paris, 1888).

Ronsard, P. de, *Oeuvres complètes*, ed. G. Cohen, 2 vols (Paris, 1950); *Poésies choisies*, ed. P. de Nolhac (Paris, 1963).

Roye, J. de, *Journal connu sous le nom de Chronique scandaleuse*, ed. B. de Mandrot, 2 vols (Paris, 1894–6).

Rozet, A. and J. Lembey, *L'invasion de France et le siège de Saint-Dizier par Charles-Quint en 1544* (Paris, 1910).

Sauzé, C. (ed.), 'Correspondance de M. de Lansac (Louis de Saint-Gelais)', *Archives hist. de Poitou*, 33 (1904).

Scheurer, R. (ed.), *Correspondance du cardinal Jean du Bellay*, 2 vols (Paris, 1969–73).

Seyssel, C. de, *Histoire du roy Louys XII*, ed. T. Godefroy (Paris, 1615).

—— *Louenges du roy Louys XII* (Paris, Véard, 1508).

—— *La monarchie de France*, ed. J. Poujol (Paris, 1961).

State Papers, published under the Authority of His Majesty's Commission: King Henry the Eighth, 10 vols (London, 1830–52).

Thenaud, J., *Le voyage d'Outremer,* ed. C. Shefer (Paris, 1884).

Thierry, A. (ed.), *Recueil des monuments inédits sur l'histoire du Tiers Etat,* 4 vols (Paris, 1856–70).

Tommaseo, N. (ed.), *Relations des ambassadeurs vénitiens sur les affaires de France,* 2 vols (Paris, 1838).

Triqueti, M., 'Papiers de M. de Pot de Chemault', *BSHPF,* 21 (1872).

Vaesen, J. and E. Charavay (eds), *Lettres de Louis XI,* 12 vols (Paris, 1883–1909).

Versoris, N., *Journal d'un bourgeois de Paris sous François Ier,* ed. P. Joutard (Paris, 1963).

—— *La vie du connétable de Bourbon de 1490 à 1521,* cont. by A. de Laval, ed. J. Buchon (Paris, 1836).

Vieilleville, F. de Scépeaux de, *Mémoires,* ed. Michaud and Poujoulat, ser.1, vol. IX.

Voyage du Roy Françoys en la ville de La Rochelle, ed. Cimber and Danjou, *Archives curieuses,* q.v. ser.1, iii (1835).

Weiss, C., *Papiers d'état du cardinal de Granvelle,* 9 vols (Paris, 1842–52).

MODERN SECONDARY WORKS

Alberigo, G., 'Réforme en tant que critère de l'histoire de l'église', *Rev. hist. eccl.* (1981), 72–83.

Alliot, J.-M., *Visites archidiaconales de Josas* (Paris, 1902).

Allmand, C. (ed.), *Power, Culture and Religion in France, c.1350–c.1550* (Cambridge, 1989).

Anderson, P., *Lineages of the Absolute State* (London, 1974, pbk 1979).

Antoine, M., 'Genèse de l'institution des intendants', *Journal des Savants,* (1982), 283–317.

—— 'Institutions françaises en Italie sous le règne de Henri II: gouverneurs et intendants (1547–59)', *Mélanges de l'Ecole française de Rome. Moyen âge, temps modernes,* 94 (1982) 759–818.

—— *Le dur métier de Roi. Etudes sur la civilisation politique de la France de l'Ancien Régime* (Paris, 1986).

—— 'L'administration centrale des finances en France du XVe au XVIIe siècle', *Francia,* 9 (1980), 511–33 and *Le dur metier,* q.v.

Arabeyre, P., 'La France et son gouvernement du milieu du XVe siècle d'après Bernard de Rosier', *BEC,* 150 (1972), 245–55.

Ariazza, A., 'Mousnier and Barber: the theoretical underpinning of the "society of orders" in early modern Europe', *P&P,* 89 (1980), 39–57.

Arnould, M.-A., 'Les lendemains de Nancy dans le "Pays de par deçà" (janvier–avril 1477)', in W.P. Blockmans (ed.), *Le privilège général et les privilèges régionaux de Marie de Bourgogne* (Anciens Pays et Assemblées d'Etats, 1985).

Asher, R.E., 'Mythes légendaires et nationalisme dans la poésie du XVIe siècle français', in F. Simone (ed.), *Culture politique en France* q.v.

—— 'Myth, legend and history in Renaissance France', *Studi francesi*, 39 (1969), 409–19.

Aubert, F., *Le Parlement de Paris depuis Philippe le Bel à Charles VII (1314–1422)* (Paris, 1886).

Audisio, G., *Le barbe et l'inquisiteur: procès du barbe vaudois Pierre Griot par l'inquisiteur Jean de Roma (Apt, 1532)* (Aix-en-Provence, 1979).

—— *Les Vaudois du Luberon: une minorité en Provence* (Mérindol, 1984).

—— *Procès-verbal d'un massacre. Les Vaudois du Luberon* (Paris, 1992).

Babelon, J.-P., 'La Renaissance', in *Le Roi, la sculpture et la mort. Gisants et tombeaux de la basilique de Saint-Denis*, Bull. arch. department de la Seine-Saint-Denis, 5 (1976), pp.31–45.

Baguenault de Puchesse, G., *Jean de Morvillier, évêque d'Orleans ... étude sur la politique française au XVIe siècle* (Paris, 1870).

Baillie, H.R., 'Etiquette and planning of the state apartments in baroque palaces', *Archaeologia* (1967), 169–99.

Bak, J.M., 'Medieval symbology of the state: Percy E. Schramm's contribution', *Viator*, 4 (1973), 33–63.

—— *Coronations* (Berkeley, Cal., 1990).

Balincourt, comte de, 'Un général sous Louis XI', *Revue du Midi*, 1 (1887).

Bapst, G., *Histoire des joyaux de la couronne de France* (Paris, 1889).

Baratier, E., *La démographie provençale du XIIIe au XVIe siècle* (Paris, 1961).

Barbey, J., *Etre Roi. Le Roi et son gouvernement de Clovis à Louis XVI* (Paris, 1992).

Baudouin-Matuszek, M.-N., 'Henri II et les expéditions françaises en Ecosse', *BEC*, 145 (1987), 339–82.

—— 'Un ambassadeur en Ecosse au XVIe siècle. Henri Clutin d'Oisel', *RH*, 281 (1988), 77–131.

—— and P. Ouvarov, 'Banque et pouvoir au XVIe siècle: la surintendance des finances d'Albisse del Bène', *BEC*, 149 (1991), 248–91.

Baudrier, H. (ed.) (Jean de Vauzelles), *Assistance publique donnée à la multitude des pauvres accourus à Lyon en 1531* (Lyon, 1875).

Baulant, M., 'Le salaire des ouvriers du bâtiment à Paris de 1400 à 1726', *Annales*, 26 (1971), 463–83.

Baulant, M. and J. Meuvret, *Prix des céréales de la mercuriale de Paris (1520–1698)* 2 vols (Paris, 1960–2).

Baumgartner, F.J., 'Henri II's Italian bishops: a study in the use and abuse of the Concordat of Bologna', *SCJ*, 11, ii (1980), 49–58.

—— *Henry II* (Durham, 1987).

Bautier, R.H., 'Feux, population et structure sociale du milieu du XVe siècle. L'exemple de Carpentras', *Annales*, 14 (1959), 255–68.

Beaune, C., 'Saint-Clovis: histoire, religion royale et sentiment national en France à la fin du Moyen Age', in B. Guenée (ed.), *Le métier d'historien au Moyen Age*, q.v.

—— *La naissance de la nation France* (Paris, 1985).

—— 'Les sanctuaires royaux', in P. Nora (ed.), *Lieux de mémoire. La Nation*, I, q.v., p.64–.

Bedos-Rezak, B., *Anne de Montmorency, seigneur de la Renaissance* (Paris, 1990).

Belotte, M., *La région de Bar-sur-Seine à la fin du Moyen Age: du début du XIIe siècle au milieu du XVIe siècle. Etude Economique et sociale.* Dijon thesis (Lille, 1973).

Beltran, E., 'L'humanisme français au temps de Charles VII et Louis XI', in C. Bozzolo and E. Ornato, *Preludes à la Renaissance*, q.v.

Benedict, P., *Rouen During the Wars of Religion* (Cambridge, 1980).

Bergin, J., 'The Guises and their benefices, 1588–1641', *EHR*, 99 (1984).

Bernard, G.W., *War, Taxation and Rebellion in Early Tudor England. Henry VIII and the Amicable Grant of 1525* (Brighton, 1986).

Bers, G.E., *Die Allianz Frankreich-Kleve ... 1539–43* (Cologne, 1969).

Bézard, Y., *La vie rurale dans le sud de la région parisienne de 1450 à 1560* (Paris, 1929).

Bieler, A., *L'homme et la femme dans la morale calviniste* (Geneva, 1963).

Biget, J.L. et al., 'Expressions iconographiques et monumentales du pouvoir d'état en France et en Espagne à la fin du moyen âge: l'exemple d'Albi et de Grenade', in J.-P. Genet (ed.), *Culture et idéologie* q.v.

Bitton, D., *The French Nobility in Crisis* (Stanford, Cal., 1969).

Black, J. (ed.), *The Origins of War in Early Modern Europe* (Edinburgh, 1987).

Blaisdell, J., 'Renée de France between Reform and Counter-Reform', *Arch. für Reformationsgeschichte*, 63 (1972), 196–225.

Bloch, J.-R., *L'anoblissement en France au temps de François Ier* (Paris, 1934).

Bloch, M., *Rois et serfs. Un chapitre d'histoire capétienne (Paris, 1920)*.

—— *La caractères originaux de l'histoire rurale française*, new edn, 2 vols (Paris, 1960–1).

—— *Les rois thaumaturges. Etudes sur la caractère surnaturel attribué à la puissance royale, particulièrement en France et Angleterre* (Paris, 1961), trans. as *The Royal Touch. Sacred Monarchy and Scrofula in France and England* (London, 1973).

Blockmans, W.P., 'Tussen crisis en welwaert: sociale veranderingen 1300–1500', in *Alegemene Geschiedenis der Nederlanden*, IV (1980).

Boca, J., *La justice criminelle de l'échevinage d'Abbeville au moyen-âge (1183–1516)* (Lille, 1930).

Bocquet, A., *Recherches sur la population rurale en Artois à la fin du Moyen Age* (Arras, 1969).

Bodin, J., *Les Suisses au service de France. De Louis XI à la Légion étrangère* (Paris, 1988).

Bois, G., *Crise du féodalisme* (Paris, 1976).

—— 'Noblesse et crise de revenues seigneuriaux en France au XIVe et XVe siècles: essai d'interprétation', in P. Contamine (ed.), *Le noblesse au moyen âge* q.v., pp.219–34.

Bonner, E., 'The First Phase of the *Politique* of Henri II in Scotland' (Univ. of Sydney, Ph.D., 1993).

Bonney, R., *Political Change in France Under Richelieu and Mazarin, 1624–1661* (Oxford, 1978).

—— 'Bodin and the development of the French monarchy', *TRHS* (1990), 40–61.

Borrelli de Serres, L.L., *Recherches sur divers services publics du XIIIe au XVII siècle*, 3 vols (Paris, 1895–1909).

Bossuat, A., *Le bailliage royal de Montferrand (1425–1556)* (Paris, 1957).

Bossuat, R., 'La formule "le roi est empereur en son royaume", son emploi au XVe siècle devant le Parlement de Paris', *Rev. d'hist. du droit français et étranger* (1961).

Bossy, J., 'The Counter-Reformation and the people of Catholic Europe', *P&P*, 47 (1970), 51–70.

—— *Christianity in the West, 1400–1700* (Oxford, 1985).

Bouard, M., *Les origines des guerres d'Italie* (Paris, 1936).

Boucher, J., *Sociétés et mentalités autour de Henri III*, Lyon thesis, 4 vols (Lille, 1981).

—— 'L'évolution de la maison du roi: des derniers Valois aux premiers Bourbons', *XVIIe siècle*, 137 (1982), 359–79.

—— *La cour de Henri III* (Rennes, 1986).

Boudet, J.-P., 'Genèse et efficacité du mythe d'Olivier le Daim', *Médiévales*, 10 (1986), 5–16.

Boudon, M., M. Châtenet and A.-M. Lecoq, 'La mise-en-scène de la personne royale en France au XVIe siècle: premières conclusions', in J.-P. Genet (ed.), *L'état moderne, bilans...*, q.v.

Boulet, M., 'Les élections épiscopales en France au lendemain du concordat de Bologne (1516–31)', *Mélanges de l'Ecole française de Rome*, 58 (1940), 190–234.

Bourciez, E., *Les moeurs polies et la littérature de cour sous Henri II* (repr. Geneva, 1967).

Boureau, A., *Le simple corps du roi. L'impossible sacralité des souverains français, XVe–XVIIIe siècle* (Paris, 1988).

Bourgeon, J.-L., 'La Fronde parlementaire à la veille de la Saint-Barthélemy', *BEC* (1990), 17–89.

Bourrilly, V.-L., 'François Ier et Henry VIII: l'intervention de la France dans l'affaire du divorce', *RHMC*, 1 (1889), 271–84.

—— 'François Ier et les Protestants. Les essais de concorde en 1535', *BSHPF*, 49 (1900), 337–65, 477–95.

—— 'Lazar de Baïf et le landgrave de Hesse', *BSHPF* (1901).

—— *Guillaume du Bellay, seigneur de Langey, 1491–1543* (Paris, 1905).

—— 'Le cardinal Jean du Bellay en Italie', *Rev. des études rabelaisiennes*, 5 (1907), 246–53, 262–74.

—— 'Antonio Rincon et la politique orientale de François Ier', *RH*, 113 (1913), 64–83, 268–308.

Bourrilly, V.-L. and N. Weiss, 'Jean du Bellay, les Protestants et la Sorbonne', *BSHPF*, 52 (1903), 97–127, 193–231; 53 (1904), 97–143.

Bousquet, J., *Enquête sur les commodités du Rouergue en 1552: procès entre l'Agenais, le Quercy et le Périgord* (Toulouse, 1969).

Boutruche, R., 'La crise d'une société', *Annales*, 2 (1947), 336–48.

—— *La crise d'une société. Seigneurs et paysans du Bordelais pendant la Guerre de Cent Ans* (1947, new edn, Strasbourg, 1963).

—— 'The devastation of rural areas during the Hundred Years War and the agricultural recovery of France', in P.S. Lewis (ed.), *The Recovery of France in the Fifteenth Century*, q.v.

—— *Bordeaux de 1453 à 1715. Sociologie et pastorale* (Paris, 1964).

Bozzolo, C. and E. Ornato (eds), *Préludes à la Renaissance. Aspects de la vie intellectuelle en France au XVe siècle* (Paris, 1992).

Braudel, F. and E. Labrousse (eds), *Histoire économique et sociale de la France*, I, 2 vols (Paris, 1977).

Bridge, J.S.C., *A History of France from the Death of Louis XI*, 5 vols (Oxford, 1921–36).

Brink, J.E., 'Royal power through provincial eyes: Languedoc 1510–1560', *PWSFH*, 10 (1982), 52–9.

—— 'The King's army and the people of Languedoc, 1500–1560', *PWSFH*, 15 (1986), 1–9.

Broc, N., 'Quelle est la plus ancienne carte "moderne" de la France?' *Annales de géographie*, 513 (1983), 513-30.

Brueil, A., 'La confrérie de Notre Dame du Puy d'Amiens', *Mém. Soc. Antiq. de Picardie*, ser.2, 3 (1854), pp.485–662.

Bryant, L.M., *The King and the City in the Parisian Royal Entry Ceremony: Politics, Ritual and Art in the Renaissance* (Geneva, 1986).

—— 'The medieval entry ceremony at Paris', in J.M. Bak (ed.), *Coronations*, q.v.

Bulst, N. and J.-P. Genet (eds), *La ville, la bourgeoisie et la genèse de l'état moderne, XIIe–XVIIIe siècles*, Colloque de Bielefeld, 1985 (Paris, 1988).

Burckhardt, J., *The Civilisation of the Renaissance in Italy*, trans. S.G.C. Middlemore (New York, 1960).

Burke, P. (ed.), *A New Kind of History from the Writings of Lucien Febvre* (London, 1973).

Calmette, J. and G. Périnelle, *Louis XI et l'Angleterre* (Paris, 1930).

Cameron, E., *The Reformation of the Heretics: the Waldenses of the Alps, 1480–1580* (Oxford, 1984).

—— *The European Reformation* (Oxford, 1991).

Cardauns, L., *Von Nizza bis Crépy. Europaische Politik en den jahren 1534 bis 1544* (Rome, 1923).

Carroll, S.M., '"Ceux de Guise": the Guise family and their affinity in Normandy, 1550–1600' (London, Ph.D. thesis, 1993).

Caster, G., *Le commerce du pastel et de l'épicerie à Toulouse de 1450 environ à 1561* (Toulouse, 1962).

Catalano, F., 'Il problema dell'equilibrio et la crisi della libertà italiana', *Nuovi questioni di storia medioevale* (Milan, 1964), pp.357–98.

Catta, E., 'Essai sur l'état religieux du diocèse de Nantes de 1554 à 1573, d'après les visites pastorales', *Recherches et travaux de l'Univ. catholique de l'Ouest* (Angers), 3 (1948), 43–50.

Cazelles, R., *La société politique et la crise de la royauté sous Philippe de Valois* (Paris, 1958).

—— 'La Jacquerie, fut-elle un mouvement paysan?' *Acad. des Inscriptions et Belles-Lettres – comptes-rendus* (1978), pp.654–66.

—— *La société politique sous Jean le Bon et Charles V* (Paris, 1982).

Chabannes, H. de, *Histoire de la maison de Chabannes*, 4 vols (Dijon, 1892–1900).

Champion, P., 'Henri III: la légende des mignons', *Trav. d'humanisme et Renaissance*, 6 (1939).

Charbonnier, P., *Une autre France. La seigneurie rurale en Basse-Auvergne du XIVe au XVIe siècle*, 2 vols (Clermont-Ferrand, 1980).

Chartrou, J., *Les entrées solonelles et triumphales à la Renaissance (1484–1551)* (Paris, 1928).

Châtenet, M., 'Une demeure royale au milieu du XVIe siécle. La distribution des espaces au château de Saint-Germain-en-laye', *Revue de L'art*, 81 (1988), 20–30.

—— 'Henri III et "l'ordre de la cour". Evolution de l'étiquette à travers les règlements generaux de 1578 à 1585', in R. Sauzet (ed.), *Henri III et son temps* (Paris, 1992).

Chaunu, P., 'Le XVIIe siècle religieux. Réflexions préalables', *Annales*, 22 (1971), 296–.

—— 'Niveaux de culture et réforme', *BSHPF*, 118 (1972), 305–25.

—— 'L'état' in Braudel and Labrousse, *Histoire économique et sociale*, I, q.v.

Chenon, E., 'De la transformation du domaine royale en domaine de la couronne du XIVe siècle', *Rev. d'hist. du droit français et étranger*, ser.4, 4 (1925).

Chevalier, B., *Tours, ville royale (1356–1520)* (Paris, Louvain, 1975).

—— 'Gouverneurs et gouvernements en France entre 1450 et 1520', in *Francia*, 9 (1980), 291–307.

—— *Les bonnes villes de France du XIVe au XVIe siècle* (Paris, 1982).

—— 'Le cardinal d'Amboise et la réforme des réguliers', in Chevalier and Sauzet, *Les réformes*, q.v., pp.111–21.

Chevalier, B. and P. Contamine (eds), *La France de la fin du XVe siècle – Renouveau et apogée* (Paris, 1985).

Chevalier, B. and R. Sauzet (eds), *Les réformes. Enracinement socio-culturel* (Colloque de Tours, 1982) (Paris, 1985).

Chevallier, P., *Henri III, roi shakespearien* (Paris, 1985).

Christie, R.C., *Etienne Dolet* (London, 1899).

Clamageran, J.-J., *Histoire de l'impôt en France*, 3 vols (Paris, 1867–76).

Cloulas, I., *Henri II* (Paris, 1985).

Comparato, V.-I., 'Guillaume Bochetel', in R. Mousnier (ed.), *Le conseil du roi*, q.v.

Constant, J.-M., *Nobles et paysans beaucerons aux XVIe et XVIIe siècles* (thesis, Lille, 1981).

—— *Les Guise* (Paris, 1984).

—— *La vie quotidienne de la noblesse francaise aux XVIe–XVIIe siècles* (Paris, 1985).

—— 'La pénétration des idées de la réforme dans la noblesse provinciale française à travers quelques exemples', in Chevalier and Sauzet, *Les réformes*, q.v., pp. 321–6.

—— 'Les barons français pendant les guerres de religion', in *Quatrième centenaire de la bataille de Coutras* (Pau, 1989), pp. 49–62.

Contamine, P., *Guerre, état et société à la fin du Moyen Age. Etudes sur les armées des rois de France, 1337–1494* (Paris, the Hague, 1972).

—— 'Points de vue sur la chevalerie à la fin du moyen âge', *Francia*, 4 (1976) and in his *La France aux XIVe et XVe siècles*, q.v., XI, pp.255–85.

—— 'The French nobility and the war', in his *La France aux XIVe et XVe siècles*, q.v.

—— (ed.), *La noblesse au moyen âge, IXe–XVe siècles. Essais à la mémoire de Robert Boutruche* (Paris, 1976).

—— 'Sur l'ordre de Saint-Michel aux temps de Louis XI et de Charles VIII', in his *La France aux XIV et XVe siècles*, XII, pp.212–36.

—— 'Contribution à l'histoire d'un mythe: les 1,700,000 clochers au royaume de France (XVe–XVIe siècles)', in his *La France aux XVe et XVe siècles*, q.v.

—— 'Georges de La Trémoïlle', in his *La France aux XIVe et XVe siècles*, q.v.

—— 'Guerre, fiscalité royale et économie en France (deuxième moitié du XVe siècle)', *7th International Economic History Congress*, ed. M. Flinn, II (Edinburgh, 1978), pp.266–72.

—— 'De la puissance aux privilèges: doléances de la noblesse française envers la monarchie aux XIVe et XVe siècles' in his *La France aux XIVe et XVe siècles*, q.v.

—— *La France aux XIV et XVe siècles. Hommes, mentalités, guerres et paix* (Paris, 1981).

—— 'Mourir pour la patrie, Xe–XXe siècle', in P. Nora (ed.), *Lieux de mémoire. La Nation*, III, pp.11–43.

—— 'Naissance de l'infanterie française (milieu XVe siècle–milieu XVIe siècle)', *Quatrième centenaire de la bataille de Coutras* (Pau, 1989).

—— (ed.), *Histoire militaire de la France*, 2 vols (Paris, 1992).

Coulet, N, and J.-P. Genet (eds), *L'état moderne: le droit, l'espace et les formes de l'état* (Paris, 1990).

Cozzi, G. and M. Knapton, *La reppublica di Venezia nell'età moderna* (Turin, 1986).

Cremer, A., 'La "protection" dans le droit international public européen du XVIe siècle', in *Théorie et pratiques politiques à la Renaissance. Colloque international de Tours, 1974* (Paris, 1977), pp.145–58.

Croix, A., *Nantes et le pays nantais au XVIe siècle. Etude démographique* (Paris, 1974).

Crouzet, D., 'Recherches sur la crise de l'aristocratie en France: les dettes de la maison de Nevers', *Histoire, économie, société,* 1 (1982), 7–49.

—— *Les guerriers de Dieu. La violence au temps des troubles de religion vers 1525–vers 1610,* 2 vols (Seyssel, 1990).

Cruickshank, C., *Army Royal* (Oxford, 1969).

—— *The English Occupation of Tournai* (Oxford, 1971).

Dainville, F., *Cartes anciennes de l'église de France* (Paris, 1956).

Daly, K., 'Mixing business with leisure: some French royal notaries and secretaries and their histories of France, c.1459–1509', in C. Allmand, *Power, Culture and Religion,* q.v.

Dassonville, M., *Ronsard. Etude historique et littéraire,* I (Geneva, 1968).

David, M., *La souveraineté et les limites juridiques du pouvoir monarchique en France du IXe au XVe siècle* (Paris, 1954).

Davies, J., 'Persecution and Protestantism: Toulouse, 1562–1575', *HJ,* 22 (1979), 31–51.

Davies, K.L., 'Late fifteenth-century historiography as exemplified in the Compendium of Robert Gaguin and the De Rebus Gestis of Paulus Aemilius' (Univ. of Edinburgh, Ph.D. thesis, 1954).

Davis, B.B., 'Poverty and poor relief in sixteenth-century Toulouse', *Historical Reflections,* 17 (1981), 267–96.

Davis, N.Z., 'Strikes and salvation at Lyon', *Arch. für Reformationsgesch.,* 56 (1965) and her *Society and Culture,* q.v. pp.1–16.

—— 'The rites of violence', *P&P,* 59 (1973), 51–91 and her *Society and Culture,* q.v., pp. 152–87.

—— *Society and Culture in Early Modern France* (Stanford, Cal., 1976).

—— *Fiction in the Archives. Pardon Tales and Their Tellers in Sixteenth-Century France* (Stanford, Cal., 1987).

Dawson, J., *Toulouse in the Renaissance. The Floral Games; University and Student Life; Etienne Dolet* (New York, 1923).

Decrue, F., *De consilio regis Francisci I.* (Paris, 1885).

—— *Anne de Montmorency, grand maître et connétable de France à la cour, aux armées et au conseil du roi François Ier* (Paris, 1885).

—— *L cour de France et la société au XVIe siècle* (Paris, 1888).

—— *Anne de Montmorency, connétable et pair de France sous les rois Henri II, François II et Charles IX* (Paris, 1889).

Delaborde, F., *L'expédition de Charles VIII en Italie,* 2 vols (Paris, 1870).

Delumeau, J., 'Christianisation et déchristianisation, XVe–XVIIIe siècles', in *Etudes européennes. Melanges offerts à Victor-Lucien Tapié* (Paris, 1973).

—— *Catholicism from Luther to Voltaire: a New View of the Counter-Reformation* (London, 1977).

Demurger, A., *Temps de crises, temps d'espoirs, XIVe–XVe siècle* (Paris, 1990).

Denifle, H., *La désolation des églises, monastères et hopitaux en France pendant la Guerre de Cent Ans,* 2 vols (Paris, 1897–8).

Dermenghem, E., 'Un ministre de François Ier: la grandeur et disgrace de l'amiral Claude d'Annebault', *Rev. du XVIe siècle,* 9 (1922), 34–50.

Descimon, R., 'Les fonctions de la métaphore du mariage politique du roi et de la république en France, XVe–XVIIIe siècle', *Annales*, 47 (1992), 1127–47.

Des Forts, P., *Le château de Villebon* (Paris, 1914).

Des Monstiers-Mérinville, J., *Un évêque ambassadeur au XVIe siècle: Jean des Monstiers, seigneur du Fraisse* (Limoges, 1895).

Devic, C. and J. Vaisette, *Histoire générale de Languedoc* (Toulouse, 1872–1904).

Dewald, J., *The Formation of a Provincial Nobility. The Magistrates of the Parlement of Rouen (1499–1610)* (Princeton, NJ, 1980).

Diefendorf, B., 'Prologue to a massacre: popular unrest in Paris, 1557–72', *Amer.H.R.*, 90 (1985), 1067–91.

—— 'Les divisions religieuses dans les familles parisiennes avant la Saint-Barthélemy', *Histoire, économie, société*, 7 (1988), 55–77.

—— *Paris City Councillors in the Sixteenth Century* (Princeton, 1983).

—— *Beneath the Cross: Catholics and Huguenots in Sixteenth-century Paris* (Oxford, 1991).

Dienne, comte de, 'Une émeute en Albret sous Alain le Grand', *Rev. de l'Agenais* (1904), 343–55.

Dognon, P., 'La taille en Languedoc de Charles VII à Francois Ier (à propos d'un article récent de M. Spont)', *AM* (1891), 340–65.

Doucet, R., *Etude sur le gouvernement de François Ier dans ses rapports avec la Parlement de Paris*, 2 vols (Paris, 1921–6).

—— *L'état des finances de 1523* (Paris, 1923).

—— 'Le grand parti de Lyon au XVIe siècle', *RH*, 171 (1933), 473–513.

—— *Les institutions de la France au XVIe siècle*, 2 vols (Paris, 1948).

Drapeyron, L., 'L'image de France sous les derniers Valois (1525–89) et sous les premiers Bourbons (1589–1682)', *Rev. de la géographie*, 24 (1889), 1–15.

Duffy, C., *Siege Warfare: the Fortress in Early Modern Europe, 1494–1660* (London, 1979).

Dupâquier, J. (ed.), *Histoire de la population française*, I & II (Paris, 1988).

Dupont-Ferrier, G., 'Le sens des mots "patria" et "patrie" en France au Moyen Age et jusqu'au début du XVIIe siècle', *RH*, 188–9 (1940), 89–104.

Durand, G., 'Les tailleurs d'images d'Amiens du milieu du XVe siècle au milieu du VIe siècle', *Bulletin monumental*, 30 (1933).

Durand, Y., 'Clientèles et fidélités dans le temps et dans l'espace', in Durand (ed.), *Hommage à Roland Mousnier*, q.v., pp.3–24.

—— (ed.) *Hommage à Roland Mousnier: clientèles et fidélités en Europe à l'époque moderne* (Paris, 1981).

Dussert, A., 'Les états en Dauphiné de la Guerre de Cent Ans aux Guerres de Religion', *Bull. de l'Académie delphinal*, ser.5, 8 (1922).

Edelstein, M.M., 'The social origins of the episcopacy in the reign of Francis I', *FHS*, 8 (1973–4), 377–92.

Ehmke, E.E., 'Gauls and Franks in sixteenth-century French historical writing: the theory of François Connan', *PWSFH*, 6 (1978), 78–87.

Etchechoury, M., *Les maîtres des requêtes de l'hôtel du roi sous les derniers Valois (1550–1589)* (Paris, 1991).

Eurich, S.A., 'Anatomy of a fortune: the house of Foix-Albret-Navarre' (Emory Univ. Ph.D. thesis, 1988).

Evenett, H.O., 'Pie IV et les bénéfices de Jean du Bellay', *Rev. d'histoire de l'église de France*, 22 (1936).

Farr, J.R., 'Popular religious solidarity in sixteenth-century Dijon', *FHS*, 14 (1985–6), 192–214.

Favier, J., *Finances et fiscalité au bas Moyen Age* (Paris, 1971).

Favreau, R., *La ville de Poitiers à la fin du Moyen Age. Une capitale régionale*, 2 vols (Poitiers, 1978).

Fawtier, R., 'Comment, au début du XIVe siècle, un roi de France pouvait-il se représenter son royaume?', *Acad. des Inscriptions et Belles-Lettres – comptes-rendus*, 1959 (Paris, 1960).

Febvre, L., 'Une question mal posée. Les origines de la Réforme française', *RH*, 161 (1929), repr. in his *Au coeur religieux du XVIe siècle*, q.v. and trans. in P. Burke, *A New Kind of History*, q.v.

——— 'Activité politique ou histoire économique. A propos de Louis XI', *Annales d'histoire sociale*, 3 (1941), 35–40.

——— 'L'origine des Placards de 1534', *Bibliothèque d'humanisme et Renaissance*, 7 (1945), 62–72.

——— *Au coeur religieux du XVIe siècle* (Paris, 1957, repr. 1968).

——— 'Frontier, the word and the concept' in Burke, *A New Kind of History*, q.v.

Fedden, K., *Manor Life in Old France from the Journals of the Sire de Gouberville for the Years 1549 to 1562* (New York, 1933).

Felgeres, C., 'La trahison du connétable de Bourbon et sa fuite à travers d'Auvergne', *Revue d'Auvergne* (1927), 305–28.

Fernandez-Santamaria, J.A., *The State, War and Peace: Spanish Political Thought in the Renaissance, 1516–59* (Cambridge, 1977).

Fogel, M., *Les cérémonies d'information dans la France du XVIe au XVIIe siècle* (Paris, 1989).

Foisil, M., 'Parentèles et fidélités', in Durand (ed.), *Hommage à Roland Mousnier*, q.v.

Fontana, A., 'L'échange diplomatique. Les relations des ambassadeurs vénitiens en France pendant la Renaissance', in *La circulation des hommes et des oeuvres entre la France et l'Italie à l'époque de la Renaissance* (Colloque International de la Sorbonne, novembre 1990) (Paris, 1992).

Fourquin, G., *Les campagnes de la région parisienne à la fin du Moyen Age* (Paris, 1964).

François, M., 'Albisse del Bène, surintendant des finances en Italie', *BEC*, 94 (1933), 337–60.

—— 'Les signatures de Louis XI', *Bull. hist. phil.* (1959), 221–9.

—— *Le cardinal François de Tournon. Homme d'état, diplomate, mécène, humaniste (1489–1562)* (Paris, 1951).

Françon, M., *Autour de la lettre de Gargantua à Pantagruel* (Rochecorbon, 1957).

Gaborit-Chopin, D., 'Les couronnes du sacre des rois et des reines au trésor de Saint-Denis', *Bulletin monumental*, 133 (1975), 165–74.

—— *Regalia. Les instruments du sacre des rois de France* (Paris, 1987).

Gabory, E., *L'union de la Bretagne à la France: Anne de Bretagne, duchesse et reine* (Paris, 1941).

Gaffarel, P., 'Massacres de Cabrières et de Mérindol en 1545', *RH*, 107 (1911), 241–71.

Galpern, A.N., *The Religions of the People in Sixteenth-Century Champagne* (Harvard, 1976).

Gandilhon, R., *La politique économique de Louis XI* (Paris, 1941).

Ganier, G., *La politique du connétable Anne de Montmorency* (Le Havre, 1957).

Garnier, J., *Chartes de communes et d'affranchissements en Bourgogne*, 2 vols (Dijon, 1867–8).

Garrisson, J., *Les Protestants du Midi, 1559–1598* (Toulouse, 1980).

—— *Les Protestants au XVIe siècle* (Paris, 1988).

—— *Royaume, Renaissance et Réforme, 1483–1559* (Paris, 1991).

Gascon, R., 'L'immigration et croissance au XVIe siècle. L'exemple de Lyon (1529–1563)', *Annales*, 25 (1970), 988–1001.

—— *Grand commerce et vie urbaine au XVIe siècle: Lyon et ses marchands*, 2 vols (Paris, 1971).

Gaussin, P.-R., *Louis XI, un roi entre deux mondes* (Paris, 1976).

—— 'Les conseillers de Louis XI', in Chevalier and Contamine, *La France de la fin du XVe siècle*, q.v.

Gauvard, C., *'De grace especial': crime, état et société en France à la fin du moyen âge* (Paris, 1991).

Gazzaniga, J.-L. 'Le pouvoir des légats pontificaux devant le Parlement' in A. Stegman (ed.), *Pouvoir et institutions en Europe*, q.v.

—— 'Le Parlement de Toulouse et la réforme des réguliers (fin du XVe siècle, début du XVIe siècle)', *Rev. d'hist. de l'église de France*, 77 (1991), 49–60.

Genet, J.-P. (ed.), *Culture et idéologie dans la genèse de l'état moderne* (Rome, 1985).

Genet, J.P. (ed.), *Genèse de l'état moderne, bilans et perspectives* (Paris, 1990).

Geremek, B., 'Criminalité, vagabondage et paupérisme: la marginalité à l'aube des temps modernes', *RHMC*, 21 (1974), 337–75.

—— *The Margins of Society in Late Medieval Paris* (Cambridge, 1987).

Germain, L., *René II duc de Lorraine et le comté de Guise* (Nancy, 1988).

Giesey, R., *The Royal Funeral Ceremony in Renaissance France* (Geneva, 1960).

—— 'The juristic basis of dynastic right to the French throne', *Trans. American Philosophical Soc.* 51 (1961), 3–47.

—— 'Rules of inheritance and strategies of mobility in prerevolutionary France', *Amer.H.R.*, 82 (1977), 271–89.

—— 'Modèles du pouvoir dans les rites royaux en France', *Annales* (1986), 579–99.

Gigon, J.-C., *Révolte de la Gabelle en Guyenne, 1548–49* (Paris, 1906).

Giry-Deloison, C., 'La naissance de la diplomatie moderne en France et en Angleterre au début du XVIe siècle (1475–1520)', *Nouvelle revue du seizieme siècle,* 5 (1987), 41–58.

Giry-Deloison, C., 'Le personnel diplomatique au debut du XVIe siècle. L'exemple des relations franco-anglaises de l'avènement de Henry VII au camp du drap d'or (1485–1520)', *Journal des Savants* (1987), 205–53.

Godet, M., 'Jean Standonck et les frères mineurs', *Archivium franciscanum historicum* (1909), pp. 398–406.

—— 'Capitulation de Tours pour la réforme de l'église de France (12 Novembre 1493)', *Rev. hist. de l'église de France,* 9 (1911), 175–96, 336–48.

—— *Le collège de Montaigue* (Paris, 1912).

Goy, J. and E. Le Roy Ladurie, *Les fluctuations du produit de la dîme* (Paris, 1973).

Greengrass, M., 'The anatomy of a religious riot in Toulouse in May 1562', *Jour. Ecclesiastical Hist.,* 34 (1983), 367–91.

—— 'Noble affinities in early modern France: the case of Henri I de Montmorency', *European Hist. Quar.,* 16 (1986), 275–311.

—— *The French Reformation* (Oxford, 1987).

—— 'Property and politics in the sixteenth-century: the landed fortune of the Constable Anne de Montmorency', *FH,* 2 (1988), 371–98.

Grévy-Pons, N., 'Propagande et sentiment national pendant le règne de Charles VI: l'exemple de Jean de Montreuil', *Francia,* 8 (1980), 129–45.

—— 'Une exemple de l'utilisation des écrits politiques de Jean de Montreuil: un mémorandum diplomatique rédigé sous Charles VII', in Bozzolo and Ornato, *Préludes à la Renaissance,* q.v.

Guenée, B., *Tribunaux et gens de justice dans le bailliage de Senlis à la fin du Moyen Age* (Strasbourg, 1963).

—— 'L'histoire de l'état en France à la fin du Moyen Age vue par les historiens français depuis cent ans', *RH,* 472 (1964), 331–60 and his, *Politique et histoire au Moyen Age,* q.v.

—— 'Espace et état en France au Moyen Age', *Annales,* 23 (1968) 744–88 and in *Politique et histoire au Moyen Age,* q.v.

—— *Les entrées royales françaises de 1328 à 1515* (Paris, 1968).

—— 'Y-a-t-il un état des XIVe et XVe siècles', *Annales* (1971), 399–406 and in *Politique et histoire au Moyen Age,* q.v.

—— (ed.) *Le métier d'historien au Moyen Age* (Paris, 1977).

—— 'Les généalogies entre l'histoire et politique: la fierté capétienne au Moyen Age', *Annales* (1978) and in *Politique et histoire au Moyen Age*, q.v.

—— *Histoire et culture historique dans l'occident médiéval* (Paris, 1980).

—— *Politique et histoire au Moyen Age. Recueil d'études sur l'histoire politique et historiographie médiévale* (1956–1981) (Paris, 1981).

Guery, A., 'Les finances de la monarchie française sous l'ancien régime', *Annales*, 33 (1978), 216–39.

—— 'Le roi dépensier. Le don, la contrainte et l'origine du système financier de la monarchie française d'ancien régime', *Annales*, 39 (1984), 1241–69.

Gunn, S., 'The duke of Suffolk's march on Paris in 1523', *EHR* (1986), 496–558.

Gutton, J.-P., *La société et les pauvres en Europe (XVIe–XVIIIe siècle)* (Paris, 1974).

Guy, J.A., 'The French king's council, 1483–1526', in R.A. Griffiths and J. Sherborne (eds), *Kings and Nobles in the Later Middle Ages* (New York, 1986).

Gwynn, P., 'Wolsey's foreign policy: the conferences of Calais and Bruges reconsidered', *HJ*, 23 (1989), 735–72.

Haigneré, D., *Dictionnaire historique et archéologique ... du Pas-de-Calais*, 15 vols (Arras, 1875–84).

Hamon, P., 'Culture et vie religieuse dans le monde des offices: les Ruzé dans la première moitié du XVIe siècle', *Bib. d'humanisme et Renaissance*, 53 (1991), 49–64.

—— 'Un après guerre financier: le rançon de François premier', *Etudes Champenois* (1990).

Hamy, père, *Entrevue de François Ier avec Henry VIII, Boulogne-sur-Mer en 1532* (Paris, 1898).

—— *Entrevue de François Ier avec Clément VII vu à Marseille*, 1533 (Paris, 1900).

Hanley, S.M., *The Lit de Justice of the Kings of France: Constitutional Ideology in Legend, Ritual and Discourse* (Princeton, 1983).

—— 'Constitutional discourse in France, 1527–1549', in P. Mack and M.C. Jacobs (eds), *Politics and Culture in early Modern France* (Cambridge, 1987).

Harding, R., *Anatomy of a Power Elite. The Provincial Governors of Early Modern France* (New Haven, London, 1978).

Hari, R., 'Les Placards de 1534', *Travaux d'humanisme et Renaissance*, 28 (1957).

Harkensee, H., *Die Schlacht bei Marignano* (Göttingen, 1909).

Harsgor, M., 'L'essor des bâtards nobles au XVe siècle', *RH*, 253 (1975), 319–53.

—— *Recherches sur le personnel du conseil du roi sous Charles VIII et Louis XII*, Paris IV thesis, 4 vols (Lille, 1980).

—— 'Fidélités et infidélités au sommet du pouvoir', in Y. Durand (ed.), *Hommage à Roland Mousnier*, q.v., pp.259–77.

—— 'Maîtres d'un royaume. Le groupe dirigeant français à la fin du XVe siècle', in Chevalier and Contamine, *La France de la fin du XVe siècle*, q.v., pp.135–46.

Hasenclever, A., 'Die Geheimartikel zum Frieden von Crépy von 19. September 1544', *Zeitschrift für Kirchengeschichte*, 45 (1926), 418–26.

Hauser, H., 'Etude critique sur la rebeine de Lyon', *RH*, 61 (1896), 265–307.

—— 'The French Reformation and the French people in the sixteenth century', *Amer.H.R.*, 4 (1899), 217–27 and as 'La réforme et les classes populaires en France au XVIe siècle', in his *Etudes sur la réforme française*, q.v., pp.83–103.

—— *Les sources de l'histoire de France*, part 2 (Paris, 1901–).

—— 'Le transport des règnes et empires des Grecs es Français', *Rev. des études rabelaisiennes*, 6 (1908).

—— *Etudes sur la réforme française* (Paris, 1909).

—— 'Le traité de Madrid et la cession de la Bourgogne à Charles-Quint', *Rev. bourguignonne*, 22 (1912).

—— *Ouvriers du temps passé* (Paris, 1913).

—— 'Une grève d'imprimeurs parisiennes au XVIe siècle, 1539–42', *Rev. internationale de Sociologie* (1917) and in *Travailleurs et marchands*, q.v.

—— *Travailleurs et marchands dans l'ancienne France* (Paris, 1920).

—— *La vie chère au XVIe siècle. La response de Jean Bodin à M. de Malestroit, 1568* (Paris, 1932).

—— *Recherches et documents sur l'histoire des prix en France de 1500 à 1800* (Paris, 1936).

Heers, J., *L'occident aux XIVe et XVe siècles. Aspects économiques et sociaux* (Paris, 1966).

Heimpel, H., 'Das Wesen des deutschen Spätmittelalters', in *Der mensche in seiner Gegenwart* (Göttingen, 1954).

Heller, H., 'The evangelicism of Lefèvre d'Etaples', *Stud. in the Renaissance*, 19 (1972), 42–77.

—— 'Famine, revolt and heresy at Meaux, 1521–25', *Arch. für Reformationsgesch.*, 68 (1977), 133–57.

—— 'Les artisans au début de la réforme française: hommage à Henri Hauser', in Chevalier and Sauzet, *Les réformes*, q.v., pp.137–50.

—— *The Conquest of Poverty: the Calvinist revolt in Sixteenth-Century France* (Leiden, 1986).

—— *Iron and Blood. Civil Wars in Sixteenth-Century France* (Montreal, London, 1991).

Hémardinquer, J.J., 'Les Protestants de Grenoble au XVIe siècle', *BSHPF*, 111 (1965), 15–22.

Hempsall, D.S., 'The Languedoc, 1520–1540: a study of pre-Calvinist heresy in France', *Arch. für Reformationsgesch.*, 62 (1971), 225–46.

Henneman, J.B., 'The military class and the French monarchy in the late Middle Ages', *Amer. H.R.*, 83 (1978), 946–65.

Henshall, N., *The Myth of Absolutism: Change and Continuity in Early Modern European Monarchy* (London, 1992).

Hervier, D., *Pierre Le Gendre et son inventaire après décès* (Paris, 1977).

Hickey, D., *The Coming of French Absolutism. The Struggle for Tax Reform in the Province of Dauphiné, 1540–1640* (Toronto, 1986).

Hochstetler, B.S., 'The tomb of Louis XII and Anne of Brittany in Saint-Denis' (Johns Hopkins Univ. Ph.D. thesis, 1976).

Hoffmann, V., 'Donec totum impleat orbem': symbolisme impérial au temps de Henri II', *Bulletin de la Société de l'histoire de l'art française*, 1978 (1980), 29–42.

—— 'Le Louvre de Henri II: un palais impérial', ibid., 1982 (1984) 7–15.

Holt, M.P., 'The king in Parlement: the *lit de justice* in sixteenth-century France', *HJ*, 31 (1988), 507–23.

—— 'Wine, community and reformation in sixteenth-century Burgundy', *P&P*, 138 (1993), 58–93.

Hubscher, R. (ed.), *Histoire d'Amiens* (Paris, 1976).

Huppert, G., *The Idea of Perfect History: Historical Erudition in Historical Philosophy in Renaissance France* (Urbana, Ill., 1970).

—— *Les bourgeois gentilshommes: an Essay on the Definition of Elites in Renaissance France* (Chicago, 1977).

—— 'Classes dangereuses: école et réforme en France, 1530–1560', in Chevalier and Sauzet, *Les réformes*, q.v., pp.209–18.

Imbart de la Tour, P., *Les origines de la reforme*, 4 vols (Paris, 1905–35).

Iung, J.-E., 'L'organisation du service des vivres aux armées de 1550 à 1650', *BEC* (1983), 269–306.

Jackson, R., *Vive le Roi! A History of the French Coronation from Charles V to Charles X* (Chapel Hill, 1984).

Jacquart, J., *La crise rurale en Ile-de-France, 1550–1670* (Paris, 1974).

—— *François Ier* (Paris, 1981).

—— 'Le poids démographique de Paris et de l'Ile-de-France au XVIe siècle', in *Paris et l'Ile-de-France au temps des paysans* (Paris, 1990), pp.227–35.

Jacquet, A., 'Le sentiment national au XVIe siécle: Claude de Seyssel', *Rev. des questions historiques*, 13 (1895), 400–40.

Jacqueton, G., *Documents relatifs à l'administration financière en France de Charles VII à François Ier (1443–1523)* (Paris, 1891).

—— *La politique extérieure de Louise de Savoie* (Paris, 1892).

—— 'Le Trésor de l'Epargne sous François Ier, 1523–47', *RH*, 55 (1894), 1–43; 56 (1894), 1–38.

Jones, M., *The Creation of Brittany. A Late Medieval State* (London, 1988).

Jouanna, A., *L'idée de race en France au XVIe et au début du XVIIe siécle*, 3 vols, Thesis (Lille, 1976).

—— *Le sire de Gouberville. Un gentilhomme normand au XVIe siécle* (Paris, 1981).

—— 'La quête des origines dans l'historiographie française', in Chevalier and Contamine, *La France de la fin du XVe siècle*, q.v.

—— *Le devoir de révolte. La noblesse française et la gestation de l'état* (Paris, 1989).

—— 'Réflexions sur les relations internobiliaires en France aux XVIe et XVIIe siècles', *FHS*, 17 (1992), 872–41.

—— 'Faveur et favoris: l'exemple des mignons de Henri III', in R. Sauzet (ed.), *Henri III et son temps* (Paris, 1992).

Kalas, R.J., 'The Selve family of Limousin: members of a new elite in early modern France', *SCJ*, 18 (1987), 147–72.

Kantorowicz, E.H., *The King's Two Bodies. A Study in Medieval Political Theology* (Princeton, NJ, 1957).

—— 'Oriens Augusti – lever du roi', *Dumbarton Oaks Papers*, 17 (1963), 119–77.

—— 'Mysteries of state. An absolutist concept and its late medieval origins', *Selected Studies* (New York, 1965).

Kelley, D.R., '"Fides historiae": Charles Dumoulin and the Gallican view of history', *Traditio*, 22 (1966), 347–402.

Keohane, N.O., *Philosophy and the State in France* (Princeton, NJ, 1980).

Kettering, S., *Patrons, Brokers and Clients in Seventeenth-Century France* (New York, 1986).

—— 'Clientage during the Wars of Religion', *SCJ*, 20 (1989), 221–39.

—— 'Patronage in early modern France', *FHS*, 17 (1992), 839–62.

Kiernan, V.G., 'Foreign mercenaries and absolute monarchy', in T.H. Aston (ed.), *Crisis in Europe* (London, 1965), pp.117–40.

Knecht, R.J., 'The Concordat of 1516: a re-assessment', *Birmingham Hist. Jour.*, 9 (1963), 16–32 and in H. Cohn (ed.), *Government in Reformation Europe* (London, 1971), pp.91–112.

—— *Francis I and Absolute Monarchy* (London, 1969).

—— 'Francis I, prince and patron of the northern Renaissance', in A.G. Dickens (ed.), *The Courts of Europe* (London, 1971).

—— 'The early Reformation in France and England: a comparison', *History*, 57 (1972), 1–16.

—— 'Francis I "Defender of the Faith"?' in E.W. Ives (ed.), *Wealth and Power in Tudor England* (London, 1978).

—— 'Francis I and Paris', *History*, 66 (1981).

—— 'The court of Francis I', *European Stud. Rev.*, 8 (1982), 1–22.

—— *Francis I* (Cambridge, 1982); 2nd. edn under new title, *Renaissance Warrior and Patron: the reign of Francis I* (1994).

—— 'Francis I and the "Lit de Justice": a legend defended', *FH* (1993) 52–83.

Koenigsberger, H.G., 'The organisation of revolutionary parties in France and the Netherlands during the sixteenth century', *Jour. Modern Hist.*, 27 (1955), 335–51.

Konigson, E., 'La cité et le prince: premières entrées de Charles VIII (1484–86)', *Fêtes et cérémonies de la Renaissance*, 3 (Paris, 1975), pp. 55–69.

Krynen, J., *L'idéal du prince et pouvoir royal en France à la fin du Moyen Age (1380–1440)* (Paris, 1981).

—— '"La mort saisit le vif". Genèse médiévale du principe d'instantanéité de la succession royale française', *Journal des savants* (1984).

—— 'Genèse de l'état et histoire des idées politiques en France à la fin du Moyen Age', in J.-P. Genet (ed.), *Culture et idéologie dans la genèse de l'état moderne*, q.v.

Labande-Mailfert, Y., *Charles VIII et son milieu (1470–1498). La jeunesse au pouvoir* (Paris, 1975).

Lafaurie, J., *Les monnaies des rois de France* I (Paris, 1951).

Lalanne, L., *Brantôme, sa vie et ses écrits* (Paris, 1896).

La Martinière, J. de, 'Les états de Bretagne et l'union de la Bretagne à la France', *Bull. de la Soc. polymathique du Morbihan* (1911), 177–93.

La Mure, J.M., *Histoire des ducs de Bourbon et des comtes de Forez*, 4 vols (Paris, Lyon, 1860–97).

Lapeyre, A. and R. Scheurer, *Les notaires et secrétaires du roi … 1461–1515* (Paris, 1978).

Lartigaut, J., 'Seigneurs et paysans du Quercy vers la fin du XVe siècle', *AM*, 86 (1974), 237–52.

—— *Les campagnes du Quercy après la Guerre de Cent Ans, vers 1440–vers 1500* (Toulouse, 1978).

—— 'L' image du baron au début du XVIe siècle: Caumont contre Thémines', *AM*, 94 (1982), 151–71.

Le Borgne, G., *Recherches historiques sur les grandes épidémies qui ont régné à Nantes* (Nantes, 1852).

Lefebvre, P., 'Aspects de la fidélité en France au XVIIe siècle', *RH*, 507 (1973), 59–106.

Lecoq, A.-M., 'Le Puy d'Amiens de 1518. La loi du genre et l'art du peintre', *Revue de l'art*, 38 (1977), 63–74.

—— *François Ier imaginaire. Symbolique et politique à l'aube de la Renaissance française* (Paris, 1987).

—— 'La symbolique de l'état. Images de la monarchie des premiers Valois à Louis XIV', in P. Nora (ed.), *Lieux de mémoire. La Nation*, II, q.v.

Lecoy de Marcie, A., 'Louis XI et la succession de Provence', *Rev. des questions historiques*, 43 (1888), 121–57.

Ledieu, A., 'Réception du cardinal de York à Abbeville, 1527', *Cabinet historique* (1889–90), 95–6, 117–26.

Ledru, A., *Histoire de la maison de Mailly*, 3 vols (Paris, 1894).

Le Goff, J., 'Reims, ville de sacre', in P. Nora (ed.), *Lieux de mémoire. La Nation*, I, q.v., pp.89–104.

Leguai, A., *Les ducs de Bourbon pendant la crise monarchique au XVe siècle. Contribution à l'étude des apanages* (Paris, 1962).

—— 'Emeutes et troubles d'origine fiscale pendant le règne de Louis XI', *Lemoyen âge* (1967), 447–87.

—— 'Les révoltes rurales dans le royaume de France du milieu du XIVe siècle à la fin du XVe siècle', *Le moyen âge*, 88 (1982), 49–76.

Lemaître, N., *Le Rouergue flamboyant. Le clergé et les fidèles du diocèse de Rodez, 1417–1563* (Paris, 1988).

Le Mené, M., *Les campagnes angevines à la fin du moyen âge (v. 1360–v. 1530)* (Nantes, 1982).

Lemonnier, H., *Les guerres d'Italie: la France sous Charles VIII, Louis XII et François Ier (1494–1547)*, vol. 5 of E. Lavisse (ed.), *Histoire de France* (Paris, 1903).

Le Roy Ladurie, E., *The Peasants of Languedoc*, trans. J. Day (Urbana, Ill., 1974) of *Les Paysans de Languedoc*, 2 vols (Paris, The Hague, 1966).

—— *L'état royal de Louis XI à Henri IV* (Paris, 1987).

Lewis, P.S., 'Decayed and non-feudalism in later medieval France', *BIHR*, 37 (1964), 157–84.

—— 'War propaganda and historiography in fifteenth-century France and England', *TRHS*, ser.5, 15 (1965).

—— *Later Mediaeval France: the Polity* (London, 1968).

—— (ed.), *The Recovery of France in the Fifteenth Century* (London, 1971).

—— 'Les pensionnaires de Louis XI', in Chevalier and Contamine, *La France de la fin du XVe siècle*, q.v., pp.167–81.

Lloyd, H.A., *The State, France and the Sixteenth Century* (London, 1983).

Longeon, C., *Une province française à la Renaissance: la vie intellectuelle en Forez au XVIe siècle* (Saint-Etienne, 1975).

Lot, F., 'L'état des paroisses et des feux de 1328', *BEC*, 90 (1929), 51–10, 256–316.

—— *Recherches sur les effectifs des armées françaises des Guerres d'Italie aux Guerres de Religion, 1494–1562* (Paris, 1962).

Lucas, R.H., 'Ennoblement in late medieval France', *Medieval Studies*, 39 (1977), 239–60.

Lusignan, S., 'Le latin était la langue maternelle des Romains: la fortune d'un argument à la fin du moyen âge', in Bozzolo and Ornato (eds), *Préludes à la Renaissance*, q.v.

Mabille de Poncheville, A., *Etude sur la chaire et la société française au quinzieme siècle. Olivier Maillard* (Paris, 1891).

Malov, V.N., 'Les archives d'un secrétaire d'etat sous Henri II retrouvées à Moscou', *BEC*, 135 (1878), 313–39.

Mandrot, B. de, *Ymbert de Batarnay, seigneur du Bouchage, conseiller des rois Louis XI, Charles VIII, Louis XII et François Ier (1438–1523)* (Paris, 1886).

—— 'Jacques d'Armagnac, duc de Nemours', *RH*, 43 (1889), 274–316; 44 (1890), 241–312.

Marchand, C., *Charles de Cossé, comte de Brissac et maréchal de France (1507–63)* (Paris, Angers, 1889).

Mariotte, J.Y., 'François Ier et la ligue de Smalkalde', *Schweizersiche Zeitschrift für Geschichte*, 16 (1966), 206–42.

Marongiu, A., 'Carlo VIII e la sua ... crocciata (come problema storiografica)', *Byzantine, Norman, Swabian and Later Institutions in Southern Italy* (London, 1972).

Marsy, comte de, 'La peste à Compiègne (XVe, XVIe et XVIIe siècles)', *La Picardie* (1878–84), 281–301.

—— 'L'exécution d'un arrêt de Parlement au XVe siècle', *MSAP*, 26 (1880), 149–64.

Martin, H., 'Les prédicateurs et les masses au XVIe siècle', in J. Delumeau (ed.), *Histoire vécu du peuple* (Toulouse, 1979).

—— 'Les prédicateurs déviantes, du début du XVe siècle au début du XVIe siècle, dans les provinces septentrionales de la France', in Chevalier and Sauzet (eds), *Les réformes*, q.v., pp.251–66.

Martin, V., *Les origines du Gallicanisme*, 2 vols (Paris, 1939).

Maskell, D., *The Historical Epic in France, 1500–1700* (Oxford, 1973).

Massault, J.-P., *Josse Clichtove, l'humanisme et le réforme du clergé* (Paris, 1968).

—— 'Thèmes ecclésiologues dans les controverses anti-luthériens de Clichtove: pouvoir, ordre, hiérarchie', in B. Chevalier and R. Sauzet (eds), *Les réformes*, pp.327–35.

Mattingly, G., *Renaissance Diplomacy* (1st edn, 1955, 2nd, 1965).

Maugis, E., *Essai sur le régime financier de la ville d'Amiens* (Mém. Soc. des Antiquaires de Picardie, in-4to, no.33).

—— *Histoire du Parlement de Paris*, 3 vols (Paris, 1913–16).

Maulde-la-Clavière, R. de, *Etude sur la condition forestière de l'Orléanais au Moyen Age et à la Renaissance* (Orléans, 1871).

—— *Les origines de la Révolution française au commencement du XVIe siècle. La veille de la Réforme* (Paris, 1889).

—— *La diplomatie au temps de Machiavel*, 3 vols (Paris, 1892–3).

—— *Louise de Savoie et François Ier: trente ans de jeunesse* (Paris, 1895).

Maumené, C. and L. d'Harcourt, *Iconographie des rois de France* I (Paris, 1928).

McGowan, M., 'Form and themes in Henri II's entry into Rouen', *Renaissance Drama* I (1968), 217–.

Mehl, J.-M., *Les jeux au royaume de France du XIIIe au début du XVIe siècle* (Paris, 1990).

Mentzer, R.A., 'The legal response to heresy in Languedoc, 1500–1560', *SCJ*, 4 (1973), 19–30.

—— 'Heresy suspects in Languedoc prior to 1560: observations on their social and occupational status', *Bib. d'humanisme et Renaissance*, 39 (1977), 561–9.

—— 'Heresy proceedings in Languedoc, 1550–1560', *Proc. Amer. Philosophical Soc.* (1984).

Merle, L., *La métairie et l'évolution agraire de la Gâtine poitevine de la fin du Moyen Age à la Révolution* (Paris, 1978).

Michaud, H., *La grande chancellerie et les écritures royales au XVIe siècle* (Paris, 1967).

—— 'Les institutions militaires des guerres d'Italie aux guerres de religion', *RH*, 523 (1977), 29–43.

Mignet, F., *La rivalité de François Ier et de Charles-Quint*, 2 vols (Paris, 1875).

Mirot, L., *Dom Bévy et les comptes des trésoriers des guerres* (Paris, 1925).

Miskimin, H., *Money and Power in Fifteenth-Century France* (1984).

Mochi Onory, J., *Fonti canonistiche dell'idea moderna dello stato* (Milan, 1951).

Moeller, B., *The Imperial Cities and the Reformation* (Philadelphia, 1972).

Molinier, A., 'Aux origines de la réforme cévenole', *Annales*, 39 (1984), 240–64.

Möller, H.M., *Das Regiment der Landsknechte* (Wiesbaden, 1976).

Moore, R.I., *The Formation of a Persecuting Society* (Oxford, 1987).

Montaigu, H., *La guerre des dames. La fin des féodaux* (Paris, 1981).

Mousnier, R., *Les hiérarchies sociales de 1400 à nos jours* (Paris, 1969); trans. P. Evans, *Social Hierarchies, 1450 to the Present* (London, 1971).

—— *Le conseil du roi de Louis XII à la Révolution* (Paris, 1970).

—— *La vénalité des offices sous Henri IV et Louis XIII* (Paris, 2nd edn, 1971).

—— *La France de 1492 à 1559* (Les cours de Sorbonne, 1971).

—— 'Les concepts d'ordres, d'états, de fidélité', *RH*, 502 (1972), 289–312.

—— *Les institutions de la France sous la monarchie absolue, 1598–1789*, 2 vols (Paris, 1974).

—— 'Les fidélités et les clientèles en France', *Histoire sociale*, 15 (1982), 35–46.

Mousnier, R. and F. Hartung, 'Quelques problemes concernant la monarchie absolue', *Relazione de X Congresso Internationale di Scienze Storiche*, IV (Rome, 1955).

Muchembled, R., *La violence au village. Sociabilité et comportements populaires en Artois du XVe au XVIIe siècle* (Paris, 1989).

—— *Le temps des supplices. De l'obéissance sous les rois absolus, XVe–XVIIIe siècle* (Paris, 1992).

Neuschel, K., *Word of Honor. Interpreting Noble Culture in Sixteenth-Century France* (Ithaca, London, 1989).

Neveux, H., 'L'expansion démographique du Cambrésis: Saint-Hilaire (1450–1575)', *Annales de démographie hist.* (1971), 265–98.

—— *Vie et déclin d'une structure économique. Les grains du Cambrésis, fin du XIVe – début du XVIIe siècle* (Paris, The Hague, 1980).

Nicholls, D., 'Social change and early Protestantism in France: Normandy, 1520–1560', *Eur. Stud. Rev.*, 10 (1980), 279–308.

—— 'Inertia and reform in the pre-Tridentine French church: the response to Protestanism in the diocese of Rouen, 1520–1562', *Jour. Ecclesiastical Hist.*, 32 (1981), 185–97.

—— 'The nature of popular heresy in France, 1502–42', *HJ*, 26 (1983), 261–75.

—— 'Looking for the origins of the French Reformation', in C. Allmand (ed.), *Power, Culture and Religion*, q.v.

—— 'France' in A. Pettegree (ed.), *The Early Reformation in Europe* (Cambridge, 1992), pp. 120–41.

Nora, P. (ed.), *Lieux de mémoire. II La Nation*, 3 vols (Paris, 1986); *III La France*, 3 vols (Paris, 1992)

Nordman, D., 'Des limites d'état aux frontières nationales' in P. Nora (ed.), *Lieux de mémoire. II La Nation*, q.v. ii, pp.36–41.

—— 'Frontiere e confini in Francia', in C. Ossola and C. Raffestin (eds), *La Frontiera da stato a nazione. Il caso Piemonte* (Rome, 1987).

—— 'La connaissance géographique de l'état (XIVe–XVIIe siècle) in N. Coulet and J.-P. Genet (eds), *L'état moderne, le droit, l'espace*, q.v.

Nouaillac, J., *Histoire du Limousin* (Tulle, 1981).

Orléa, M., *La noblesse aux états généraux de 1576 et 1588* (Paris, 1980).

Ourliac, P., 'The Concordat of 1472: an essay on the relations between Louis XI and Sixtus IV', in P.S. Lewis (ed.), *The Recovery of France*, q.v., pp.102–84.

Paillard, C., *L'invasion allemande de 1544* (Paris, 1884).

Paravicini, W., 'Peur, pratiques, intelligences. Formes d'opposition aristocratique à Louis XI d'après les interrogatoires du conétable de Saint-Pol', in B. Chevalier and P. Contamine (eds), *La France de la fin du XVe siècle*, q.v., pp.183–90.

Paris, P., *Etudes sur François Ier*, 2 vols (Paris, 1885).

Pariset, J.-D., *Les relations entre la France et l'Allemagne au milieu du XVIe siècle* (Strasbourg, 1981).

Patry, H. (ed.), *Les débuts de la réforme protestante en Guyenne, 1527–29: arrêts du Parlement* (Bordeaux, 1912).

Paul, G., *Un favori du duc de Bourbon. Joachim de Pompéranc* (Paris, 1923).

Pelicier, P., *Essai sur le gouvernement de la dame de Beaujeu (1483–1491)* (Paris, 1882).

Pelletier, M., 'Le Grand Conseil de Charles VIII à François Ier', *Positions des thèses de l'Ecole nationale des Chartes*, 1960, pp.85–90.

Perjes, L., 'Army provisioning, logistics and strategy in the second half of the seventeenth century', *Acta Historica*, 16 (1970), 1–51.

Peronnet, M.C., *Les évêques de l'ancienne France*, Paris IV thesis, 2 vols (Lille, 1977).

Perret, P.M., *Notice biographique sur Louis Malet de Graville, amiral de France* (Paris, 1889).

Perroy, E., *La Guerre de Cent Ans* (Paris, 1945) trans. D.C. Douglas (London, 1951).

—— 'Feudalism or principalities in fifteenth-century France', *BIHR*, 20 (1943–5).

—— 'Social mobility among the French *noblesse* in the later Middle Ages', *P&P*, 21 (1962), 25–38.

Petit-Dutaillis, C., *Charles VII, Louis XI et les premières années de Charles VIII*, vol. IV, ii of Lavisse (ed.). *Histoire de France* (Paris, 1902).

Peyre, B., *Histoire de Mérindol-en-Provence* (Avignon, 1939).

Pimodan, G., *La mère de Guises. Antoinette de Bourbon* (Paris, 1925).

Pingaud, L., *Les Saulx-Tavannes. Etude sur l'ancienne société française* (Paris, 1876).

Pinvert, L., *Lazar de Baïf* (Paris, 1900).

Piton, M., 'L'idéal épiscopal selon les prédicateurs français de la fin du XVe siècle et du début du XVe', *Rev. d'histoire ecclésiastique*, 61 (1966), 77–118, 393–423.

Pocquet du Haut-Jussé, B.-A., 'Les débuts du gouvernement de Charles VIII en Bretagne', *BEC*, 115 (1957), 138–55.

—— 'A political concept of Louis XI: subjection and vassalage', in P.S. Lewis (ed.), *The Recovery of France*, q.v.

Porée, C., *Un parlementaire sous François Ier; Guillaume Poyet, 1473–1548* (Angers, 1898).

Potter, D.L., 'Diplomacy in the mid-sixteenth century: England and France, 1536–1550' (Univ. of Cambridge, Ph.D. thesis, 1973).

—— 'Foreign policy in the age of the Reformation: French involvement in the Schmalkaldic War, 1544–47', *HJ*, 20 (1977), 525–44.

—— 'The treaty of Boulogne and European diplomacy, 1549–50', *BIHR*, 55 (1982), 50–65.

—— 'The duc de Guise and the fall of Calais, 1557–58', *EHR*, 118 (1983), 481–512.

—— 'A treason trial in sixteenth-century France: the fall of marshal du Biez, 1549–51', *EHR*, 105 (1990), 595–623.

—— 'Marriage and cruelty among the Protestant nobility in sixteenth-century France: Diane de Barbançon and Jean de Rohan, 1561–67', *Eur. Hist. Quar.*, 20 (1990), 5–38.

—— 'The Luxembourg inheritance: the house of Bourbon and its lands in northern France during the sixteenth century', *FH*, 6 (1992), 24–62.

—— *War and Government in the French Provinces: Picardy, 1470–1560* (Cambridge, 1993).

—— 'Les Allemands et les armées françaises au XVIe siècle. Jean Philippe Rhingrave, chef de lansquenets: étude suivie de sa correspondence en France, 1548–1566', *Francia*, 20, ii (1993); 21, ii (1994).

Potter, D.L. and P.R. Roberts, 'An Englishmen's view of the court of Henri III, 1584–5: Richard Cook's "Description of the Court of France"', *FH*, 2 (1988), 312–44.

Poujol, J., 'L'évolution et l'influence des idées absolutistes en France de 1498 à 1559', *L'information historique*, 18 (1956).

—— 'Jean Ferrault on the king's privileges', *Stud. in the Renaissance*, 5 (1958), 15–26.

—— 'Cadre idéologique du développement de l'absolutisme en France à l'avènement de François Ier', in *Theorie et pratiques politiques à la Renaissance*. Colloque international de Tours, 1974 (Paris, 1977), pp.259–72.

Powis, J., 'Guyenne 1548: the crown, the province and social order', *Eur. Stud. Rev.*, 12 (1982), 1–15.

Prestwich, M., 'Calvinism in France, 1555–1629', in Prestwich (ed.), *International Calvinism, 1541–1715* (Oxford, 1988).

Prévenier, W., 'La démographie des villes de Flandre aux XIVe et XVe siècles', *Rev. du Nord*, 65 (1983), 255–75.

Procacci, G., 'Le Provence à la veille des guerres de religion. Une période décisive, 1535–45', *RHMC*, 5 (1958).

Quicherat, J., 'Rodrigue de Villandrando', *BEC*, 6 (1864); (1880).

Quillet, J., *Les clefs du pouvoir au Moyen Age* (Paris, 1972).

Quilliet, B., *Le corps d'officiers de la prévôte et vicomté de Paris et l'Ile-de-France de la fin de la Guerre de Cent Ans au début des Guerres de Religion*, Paris IV thesis, 1977, 2 vols (Lille, 1982).

—— *Louis XII, père du peuple* (Paris, 1986).

Raveau, P., *L'agriculture et les classes paysannes dans le Haut-Poitou au XVIe siècle* (Paris, 1926).

Ravitch, N., *Sword and Mitre: Government and Episcopate in France and England in the Age of Aristocracy* (Paris, The Hague, 1966).

Raytses, V.I., 'Le programme d'insurrection d'Agen en 1514', *AM*, 93 (1981), 255–77.

Renaudet, A., *Préréforme et humanisme à Paris pendant les premières guerres d'Italie (1494–1517)*, 2 vols (Paris, 1953).

—— *Humanisme et Renaissance. Dante, Petrarque, Standonck* (Geneva, 1958).

Rey, M., *Les finances royales sous Charles VI: les causes du déficit, 1388–1413* (Paris, 1965).

Richard, J., 'Les débats entre le roi de France et le duc de Bourgoigne l'enquête de 1452', *Bull. philol. et hist.*, *année* 1963 (1967), 113–32.

Richards, P., 'Rouen and the golden age: the entry of Francis I, 2 August 1517', in C. Allmand (ed.), *Power, Culture and Religion*, q.v.

Robillard de Beaurepaire, E. de, *Les Puys de palinods de Rouen et de Caen* (Caen, 1907).

Robinson, A.M.F., 'The claims of the house of Orléans to Milan', *EHR*, 3 (1880), 34–62, 270–91.

Rodriguez-Salgado, M.J., *The Changing Face of Empire: Charles V, Philip II and Habsburg Authority, 1551–59* (Cambridge, 1989).

Roederer, P.L., *Louis XII et François Ier, ou mémoire pour servir a une nouvelle histoire de leur règne. III Conséquences du systéme de cour établi sous François Ier* (Paris, 1833).

Roelker, N.L., 'The appeal of Calvinism to French noblewomen in the sixteenth century', *Jour. of Interdisciplinary Hist.*, 2 (1971–2), 391–413.

—— 'The role of noblewomen in the French Reformation', *Arch. für Reformationsgesch.*, 63 (1972), 168–95.

Romier, L., *La carrière d'un favori. Jacques d'Albon de Saint-André* (Paris, 1909).

—— *Les origines politiques des guerres de religion*, 2 vols (Paris, 1913–14).

—— *Le royaume de Catherine de Médicis* (Paris, 1922).

Rosenberg, D., 'Social experience and religious choice, a case study: the Protestant weavers and woolcombers of Amiens in the sixteenth century' (Yale Univ. Ph.D. thesis, 1979).

Roserat de Melin, J., *Antonio Caracciolo, évêque de Troyes* (Paris, 1923).

Rott, E., *Histoire de la représentation diplomatique de la France auprès les cantons Suisses* I (Paris, 1900).

Rowen, H.H., *The King's State: Proprietary Dynasticism in Early Modern France* (Rutgers U.P., 1980).

Rubin, M., *Corpus Christi. The Eucharist in Late Medieval Culture* (Cambridge, 1992).

Ruble, A. de, *Le Mariage de Jeanne d'Albret* (Paris, 1877).

—— *Le traité de Cateau-Cambrésis* (Paris, 1889).

Russell, J., *The Field of the Cloth of Gold* (London, 1969).

—— 'The search for universal peace: the conferences of Calais and Bruges in 1521', *BIHR*, 44 (1971), 162–93.

—— *Peacemaking in the Renaissance* (London, 1976).

Russell Major, J., *Representative Institutions in Renaissance France, 1421–1559* (Madison, Wisc., 1960).

—— *Deputies to the Estates General in Renaissance France* (Madison, 1960).

—— *Representative Government in early Modern France* (New Haven, Conn., 1980).

—— 'Noble income, inflation and the Wars of Religion in France', *Amer. H.R.*, 86 (1981), 21–48.

—— 'Bastard feudalism and the kiss: changing social mores in late medieval and early modern France', *Jour. Interdisciplinary Hist.*, 17 (1987), 509–35.

—— 'Vertical ties through time', *FHS*, 17 (1992), 863–71.

Sabatier, G., '*Rappresentare il principe*, figurer l'état. Les programmes iconographiques d'état en France et en Italie du XVe au XVIIe siècle', in J.-P. Genet (ed.), *Genèse de l'état moderne, bilans*, q.v., pp.247–58.

Saengher, P., 'Burgundy and the inalienability of appanages in the reign of Louis XI', *FHS*, 10 (1977).

Sahlins, P., *Boundaries. The Making of France and Spain in the Pyrenees* (Berkeley, Cal., 1989).

Salmon, J.H., *Society in Crisis. France in the Sixteenth Century* (London, 1973).

Samaran, C., *La maison d'Armagnac au XVe siècle* (Paris, 1907).

—— 'Cinquante feuillets retrouvées des comptes de l'argenterie de Louis XI (1466–71)', *Bull. hist. Phil.* (1928–9).

—— *Une longue vie d'érudit. Recueil d'études de Charles Samaran*, 2 vols (Paris, 1978).

Schalk, E., 'Ennoblement in France from 1350 to 1660', *Jour. Social Hist.*, 16 (1982), 101–10.

—— *From Valor to Pedigree: Ideas of Nobility in France in the Sixteenth and Seventeenth Centuries* (Princeton, 1986).

—— 'The court as "civiliser" of the nobility: noble attitudes and the court of France in the late sixteenth and early seventeenth centuries', in R.E. Asch and A.M. Birke (eds), *Princes, Patronage and the Nobility* (Oxford, 1991).

Scheller, R.W., 'Imperial themes in art and literature of the early French Renaissance: the period of Charles VIII', *Simiolus*, 12 (1981–2), 5–69.

—— 'Ensigns of authority: French royal symbolism in the age of Louis XII', *Simiolus*, 13 (1982–3), 74–141.

Scheurer, R., 'Les relations franco-anglaises pendant la négociation de la paix des Dames (juillet–aout 1529)', in P.M. Smith and I.D. McFarlane, *Literature and the Arts in the reign of Francis I* (Lexington, Ken., 1985), pp.142–62.

Schmidt-Chazan, M., 'Histoire et sentiment national chez Robert Gaguin', in B. Guenée, *Le métier d'historien*, q.v.

Schneider, R.A., *Public Life in Toulouse, 1463–1789* (Ithaca, 1989).

Schramm, P.E., *Der König von Frankreich. Das Wesen der Monarchie vom 9. zum 16. Jahrhundert*, 2 vols (Weimar, 1939, repr. 1960).

Sée, H., *Louis XI et les villes* (Paris, 1891).

Segre, A., 'Documenti ed osservazioni sul congresso di Nizza (1538)', *Accademia dei Lincei*, 10 (1901), 72–98.

Séguin, J.-P., *L'information en France de Louis XII à Henri II* (Geneva, 1961).

—— 'La découverte de l'Italie par les soldats de Charles VIII', *Gazette des Beaux-Arts*, 50, 127–.

Sherman, M., 'Pomp and circumstances: pageantry and propaganda in France during the reign of Louix XII, 1498–1515', *SCJ*, 9, iv (1978), 13–32.

Simone, F., *La coscienza della Rinascità negli umanisti francesi* (Paris, 1949).

—— *Il Rinascimento francese* (Turin, 1964) trans. as *The French Renaissance* (London, 1969).

—— *Il Rinascimento francese: studi e ricerche* (Turin, 1965).

—— *Culture et politique en France à l'époque de l'humanisme et de la Renaissance* (Turin, 1974).

—— 'Historiographie et mythographie dans la culture française du XVIe siècle: analyse d'un texte oublié', in *Actes du colloque sur l'humanisme lyonnais au XVIe siècle, mai 1972* (Grenoble, 1974).

Skinner, Q., *The Foundations of Modern Political Thought*, 2 vols (Cambridge, 1976).

Smith, P.M., *The Anti-Courtier Trend in Sixteenth-Century French Literature* (Geneva, 1966).

Solnon, J.-F., *La cour de France* (Paris, 1987).

Solon, P.D., 'War and the bonnes villes: the case of Narbonne, c. 1450–1550', *PWSFH*, 17 (1990), 65–73.

—— 'Le rôle des forces armées en Comminges avant les guerres de religion (1500–62)', *AM*, 103 (1991), 19–40.

Souriac, R., *Le comté de Comminges au XVIe siècle* (Paris, 1977).

—— 'Mouvements paysans en Comminges au XVIe siècle', in J. Nicolas (ed.), *Mouvements populaires et conscience sociale XVIe–XIXe siècles* (Paris, 1985).

Spont, A., 'La taille en Languedoc de 1450 à 1515', *AM* (1890) 365–84, 478–513.

—— 'Une recherche générale des feux à la fin du XVe siècle', *Ann-bull. de la Société de l'hist. de France* (1892), 222–36.

—— Semblançay (?–1527): la bourgeoisie financière au début du XVIe siécle (Paris, 1895).

—— 'La milice des francs-archers', *Rev. des questions hist.* (1897).

—— 'Marignan et l'organisation militaire de la France sous François Ier', *Rev. des questions hist.* (1899), 59–77.

Starkey, D. (ed), *The English Court from the Wars of the Roses to the Civil War* (London, 1987).

Stegman, A. (ed.), *Pouvoir et institutions en Europe au XVIe siècle* (Paris, 1987).

―― 'Le Rosier des guerres', in B. Chevalier and P. Contamine (eds), *La France de la fin du XVe siècle*, q.v.

Stein, H., 'Le sacre d'Anne de Bretagne et son entrée à Paris en 1504', *Mém. de la Société de l'histoire de Paris* (1902), 268–305.

Stein, H. and L. Le Grand, *La frontière d'Argonne (843–1659): procès de Claude de La Vallée (1535–61)* (Paris, 1905).

Stocker, C.W., 'The politics of the Parlement of Paris in 1525', *FHS*, 8 (1973–4), 191–211.

―― 'Public and private enterprise in the administration of a Renaissance monarchy: the first sales of office in the Parlement of Paris (1512–24)', *SCJ*, 9, ii (1978), 4–29.

Sutherland, N., *The French Secretaries of State in the Age of Catherine de Medici* (London, 1962).

―― 'Was there an Inquisition in Reformation France?', in *Princes, Politics and Religion, 1547–1589* (London 1984).

Taylor, L.J., *Soldiers of Christ. Preaching in Late Mediaeval and Reformation France* (Oxford, 1992).

Teall, E., 'The myth of royal centralisation and the reality of the neighbourhood. The journals of the sire de Gouberville, 1549–62', in M.U. Chrisman and O. Grundler (eds), *Social Groups and Religious Ideas in the Sixteenth Century* (Kalamazoo, 1978), pp.1–11.

Thierry, A., *Considérations sur l'histoire de France* (1846 edn).

―― *Essai sur l'histoire de la formation et du progrès du Tiers Etat* (1867 edn)

Thomas, J., *Le concordat de 1516, ses origines, son histoire au XVIe siècle*, 3, vols (Paris, 1910).

Thurley, S., *The Royal Palaces of Tudor England* (London, 1993).

Tortajada, R., 'M. de Malestroit et la théorie quantitative de la monnaie', *Rev. écon.*, 38 (1987), 853–76.

Tricard, J., 'Touraine d'un tourangeau au XIIe siècle', in B. Guenée, *Le métier d'historien*, q.v.

Ursu, J., *La politique orientale de François Ier* (Paris, 1908).

Vaesen, J., 'Notice biographique sur Jean Bourré', *BEC*, 43 (1882), 433–60.

Vaissière, J., *Charles de Marillac, ambassadeur et homme politique sous les règnes de François Ier, Henri II et François II (1510–1560)* (Paris, 1896).

―― *Gentilshommes campagnards de l'ancienne France* (Paris, 1903, repr. Etrepilly, 1986).

Valensise, M., 'Le sacre du roi: stratégie et doctrine politique de la monarchie française', *Annales*, 41 (1986), 543–77.

Valois, N., 'Le conseil du roi et le grand conseil', *BEC* (1882), 594–625; (1883), 137–68, 419–44.

—— *Etude historique sur le conseil du roi. Introduction d'inventaire des arrêts du conseil d'état* (Paris, 1886).

Van der Haeghen, P., 'Examen des droits de Charles VIII sur le royaume de Naples', *RH*, 28 (1885), 98–111.

Van Doren, L.S., 'War taxation, institutional change and social conflict in provincial France – the royal *taille* in Dauphiné, 1494–1559', *Proc. of the Amer. Philosoph. Soc.*, 121 (1977), 7–96.

Veissière, M., 'Guillaume Briçonnet, abbé réformateur de Saint-Germain-des-près', *Rev. d'hist. de l'église de france*, 60 (1976), 65–80.

—— *L'évêque Guillaume Briçonnet (1470–1534)* (Provins, 1986).

—— 'Guillaume Briçonnet, évêque de Meaux et la réforme de son clergé', *Rev. d'hist. ecclésiastique*, 84 (1989), 659–72.

—— 'La vie chrétienne dans le diocèse de Meaux entre 1496 et 1526 d'après les synodes diocésains: continuités et innovations', *Rev. d'hist. de l'église de France*, 77 (1991), 71–81.

Venard, M., 'Pour une sociologie du clergé au XVIe siècle. Recherche sur le recrutement sacerdotal dans la province d'Avignon', *Annales*, 23 (1968), 987–1016.

—— 'Réforme, réformation, préréforme, contre-réforme ... Etude de vocabulaire chez les historiens de la langue française', in *Historiographie de la Réforme* (Paris, 1977), pp.352–65.

—— *L'église d'Avignon au XVIe siècle*, Paris IV thesis, 5 vols (Lille, 1980).

—— 'Une réforme gallicane? le projet de concile national en 1551', *Rev. d'hist. de l'église de France*, 67 (1981), 202–25.

—— 'Les "notes" de l'hérésie au début du XVe siècle, selon les visites pastorales françaises', in Chevalier and Sauzet (eds), *Les réformes*, q.v., pp.375–81.

Vidal, A., 'Révolte des Albigeois contre l'évêque Louis d'Amboise', *Rev. hist. scientifique et littéraire du département du Tarn*, 8 (1890–91).

Visconti, C., 'Les *Recherches de France* d'Estienne Pasquier', in P. Nora (ed.), *Lieux de mémoire*, q.v.

Voigt, G., *Die Wiederbelebung des classischen Altertums, oder der erste Jahrhunderts des Humanismus*, 2 vols (Berlin, 1881–2).

Weary, W., 'La maison de La Trémoïlle', in Chevalier and Contamine (eds), *La France de la fin du XVe siècle*, q.v.

Weiss, N., *La chambre ardente: étude sur la liberté de conscience sous François Ier et Henri II (1540–1550)* (Paris, 1888).

Wolfe, M., *The Fiscal System of Renaissance France* (New Haven, Conn., 1972).

Wood, J.B., *The Nobility of the Election of Bayeux, 1463–1666* (Princeton, 1980).

Yver, J., *Egalité entre héritiers* (Paris, 1966).

Zeller, B., *La ligue de Cambrai* (Paris, 1886).

Zeller, G., *La réunion de Metz à la France*, 2 vols (Strasbourg, 1926).

—— 'Histoire d'une idée fausse', *RHMC* (1933) and Zeller, *Aspects*, q.v., pp.90–108.

—— 'Les premiers gouverneurs d'Auvergne', *Rev. d'Auvergne*, 47, v (1933).

—— 'Les rois de France candidats à l'empire', *RH*, 173 (1934), 497–534 and Zeller, *Aspects*, q.v.

—— 'Gouverneurs de provinces au XVIe siècle', *RH*, 15 (1939) and Zeller, *Aspects*, q.v.

—— 'L'administration monarchique avant les intendants', in *Aspects*, q.v.

—— *Le siège de Metz par Charles–Quint* (Nancy, 1943).

—— 'De quelques institutions mal connues au XVIe siècle', *RH* (1944), 193–418.

—— 'Proces à reviser? Louis XI, la noblesse et la marchandise', *Annales*, 4 (1946) and Zeller, *Aspects*, q.v., pp.240–53.

—— *Les institutions de la France au XVIe siècle* (Paris, 1948).

—— 'Le commerce international en temps de guerre sous l'Ancien Régime', *RHMC* (1957) and Zeller, *Aspects*, q.v., pp.185–96.

—— *Aspects de la politique française sous l'Ancien Régime* (Paris, 1964).

Zeller, J., *La diplomatie française vers le milieu du XVIe siècle d'après la correspondence de Guillaume Pellicier (1539–42)* (Paris, 1881).

Zerner, H., *The School of Fontainebleau* (London, 1969).

Index